Listening In

ALSO BY SUSAN J. DOUGLAS

Where the Girls Are:

Growing Up Female with the Mass Media

Inventing American Broadcasting, 1899–1922

Listening In

Radio and the
American Imagination

Susan J. Douglas

University of Minnesota Press

Minneapolis · London

Originally published in 1999 by Times Books, a division of Random House, Inc.
Reprinted by agreement with Sterling Lord Literistic, Inc.

First University of Minnesota Press edition, 2004

Published by the University of Minnesota Press
111 Third Avenue South, Suite 290
Minneapolis, MN 55401-2520
http://www.upress.umn.edu

ISBN 0-8166-4423-3

A Cataloging-in-Publication record for this book is available from the Library of Congress.

Printed in the United States of America on acid-free paper

The University of Minnesota is an equal-opportunity educator and employer.

12 11 10 09 08 07 06 05 04   10 9 8 7 6 5 4 3 2 1

for the salmon king

Preface

Between 1966 and 1970, Erik Barnouw published his now-classic *History of Broadcasting in the United States.* It was the first and best overview history of American broadcasting ever published; everyone relied on it, and it was three volumes, each of them about 350 pages.

This book is the first attempt at an overview of radio's nearly hundred-year history since then. It is only one volume. To say that it is incomplete would be a monumental understatement; there are enormous chasms here waiting to be filled by other historians. Each chapter could have been a book in its own right. And there are chapters not included here that could be, like one on children's radio, one on radio drama, another on late-night radio or classical music stations and their listeners or pirate radio or the history of country and western radio. The importance of regional radio to ethnic groups or recent migrants to an area such as Los Angeles should be a book. So should an exploration of how Latino populations have used radio to build and sustain communities in the United States. WDIA, the pioneering Memphis station that was the first in the country to feature an all-black on-air staff, deserves more scholarly attention. I could go on and on. The hard thing for all of us who regard radio as a crucially important area of study—one that still remains neglected, although talented young people around the country are starting to rectify that—is the dearth of archival tapes of what went on the air. Nonetheless, we must excavate, reconstruct, and preserve what we can.

There is still so much history here waiting to be written, so much work to be done examining the act of listening to the radio and its relationship to personal identity and cultural values and practices. Such work is centrally important to our ongoing understanding of who we are as individuals, members of groups, and members of a culture known as "America." And so much more research needs to be done on how the various media engage us cognitively in ways that have major social and political consequences.

I hope that other scholars will fill in these holes and that they will continue to think about and remind us what it has meant to have radio listening help form us and the cultures to which we belong. Because listening, as much as seeing, has made us who we are. So here, gaps and all, I want to put radio listening on the table as an overlooked and crucially important cultural practice that has a history and, I hope, a future.

Acknowledgments

It was August of 1991, and I really was minding my own business, trying to write, when the phone rang. A man who identified himself as Arthur Singer from the Sloan Foundation said he wanted to talk about a new book series Sloan was sponsoring on technology and American culture, and did I have a minute. Instantly I identified this as one of those good-citizenship moments: I assumed he wanted to knock around ideas for the series and get some recommendations for possible writers, while I'd lose forty-five minutes of writing time. So we talked for a while. Gradually it became clear that maybe he wanted *me* to write one of these books. More to the point, the grant Sloan would provide would enable me to take time off from teaching so I actually could get it done.

On that day, Arthur Singer and the Sloan Foundation changed my life, because they did agree to fund my proposal, launching me into an exploration of radio and American culture that has been a challenge and a pleasure. My largest debt of gratitude is to Art Singer, and not just for supporting the proposal, but also for his patience during a writing process that proved to be much more protracted than either of us expected or desired. I also wish especially to thank Victor McIlheny, whom I suspect was the generous colleague who brought me to Singer's attention in the first place.

When my agent, Lizzie Grossman, who had been a wonderful sounding board and constant source of support, decided to change careers, I feared I wouldn't find an agent as simpatico. Happily, Chris Calhoun at Sterling Lord has proved me wrong, and I am indebted to him for his astute advice and warm friendship. Betsy Rapoport, my editor, kept me going when I thought I'd never finish the thing, and did a first-rate job of editing out repetitions and inconsistencies while also boosting my spirits.

Various people agreed to be interviewed, and I would especially like to thank Frank Stanton, Marie Jahoda, Herta Herzog, and Peter Rossi for their insights into the work of Paul Lazarsfeld; and special thanks go to Jahoda and Herzog for their warmth and hospitality when I visited their homes. Tony Pigg and Pete Fornatale were particularly helpful about the FM era, and Michael Harrison, Jim Casale, and Mark Williams took time out to talk to me about the rise of talk radio. Steve Mansfield, David Sumner, and Perry Williams of the ARRL provided invaluable information on ham radio, and I especially want to thank Steve Mansfield for all the time he took out of his hectic schedule to help me. Dr. David Rosenbaum at Penn State and Dr. Mark Tramo at the Harvard Medical School provided crucial information on cognition, perception, and hearing.

I did much of the research for this book by listening to surviving recordings of old broadcasts, and here I was grateful to find so many people who went out of their way to help me track down possible sources. I would like to thank the knowledgeable staff at the Museum of Television and Radio, especially David Hirsch and Rob Scott. Holly Pinkerton and Matt Sohn at Chicago's Museum of Broadcast Communications welcomed me into their collection and expedited my research there. The staff at the Sound Division of the National Archives quickly provided me with stacks of World War II broadcasts to listen to. Tom Conner, Chuck Howell, and Michael Henry at the Library of American Broadcasting went out of their way to provide me with a host of essential resources on very short notice, and researchers will be impressed with how user-friendly their facility is. Rick Ducey at the National Association of Broadcasters generously helped with technical information, and Mark Fratrik of the NAB talked with me about recent economic developments in the field. Various people in the Ann Arbor area agreed to participate in focus groups on talk radio, and I wish to thank Clifford Slay, Ed Sprague, Cheryl Januszka, Richard Straub, Ben Gardner, Storm Farrell, Catherine Powers, Lea Montgomery, Lawrence Palmer, Dirk Brandt, Jerry Klein, and Deanna Allman for their help understanding talk radio's appeal. My research assistants Lisa Davis, Jen Gallant, Alex Russo, Colin Loggins, Ariana Wolf, Tim Stewart-Winter, Nhi Lieu, and Holly McGuire tracked down all kinds of materials and offered suggestions and ideas as well.

My wonderful colleagues at the University of Michigan have provided invaluable support. Mike Traugott brought me into his research group on talk radio; shared books, articles, and survey data; and conducted focus groups with me on why people listen to the talk format. I am deeply grateful to him for his friendship, and for introducing me to work I would not have otherwise known about. His students Kathy Cramer and Margaret Young generously alerted me to relevant material. Rowell Huesmann kept challenging my thinking about listening and cognition, and gave me crucial advice on sources. Vince Price also provided advice and sources, including his own work on associational memory, group identity, and the media. But more important, as our chair, he created an environment in the department that enthusiastically sustained multiple approaches to the study of the mass media, past and present. His personal support during my first years at Michigan will matter more than he'll ever know. Geoff Eley, Gina Marantz-Sanchez, Sid Smith, Greg Grieco, Abby Stewart, David Winter, Gaylyn Studlar, Sonya and Guenter Rose, Peggy Somers, Kris Harrison, Nick Valentino, and Julie Skurski provided essential moral and intellectual sustenance.

Others who gave me very helpful reactions to portions of the book include Pat Aufderheide, Nolan Bowie, Pippa Norris, Victor McIlheny, Sut Jhally, Victor Navasky, Ev Dennis, Rob Snyder, Monroe Price, Eleanor Singer, Sasha Torres, Nick King, Conovery Bolton, Kristen Haring, Susan Smulyan, Gary Frost; my dear, lost mentor, Hugh G. J. Aitken; and the late and terribly missed Roland Marchand. George Lipsitz provided a crucial and typically astute reading of my work on AM radio in the 1950s. Robert K. Merton wrote extensive comments on the chapter dealing with his lifelong collaborator Paul Lazarsfeld. Everett Rogers generously shared with me portions of his book *A History of Communication Study: A Biographical Approach* while it was still in manuscript form. Bill Kenney likewise shared segments of his forthcoming book on the history of the phonograph, and steered me toward work he thought would be most helpful.

Joan Braderman, Mary Russo, Dan Warner, Dan Czitrom, Frank Couvares, and Bruce Laurie helped me through the early stages of the book. Meredith Michaels and Lee Bowie provided essential retreats away from the mainland of stress and insecurity. And my friends Holmes and Mary Ellen Brown, members of the radio generation themselves, talked eagerly with me about the project from its beginning, and also provided much needed escape and solace in the Blue Hills of Virginia. My mother-in-law, Frances Durham, also offered essential insights into what it meant to listen. My daughter, Ella, who has learned the pleasures of writing herself, often had to put up with a distracted mother, or one who was glued to a computer screen, or one who was away doing research, so that this book could be finished. Her love and her zest for life have sustained me through all too predictable maternal guilt.

At so many moments, I lost faith in this project, because it seemed too large and diffuse and thus, to me, too irresponsible. At all these points, there is no substitute for someone who knows you all too well, thinks your work is better than you do yourself, and is willing to put up with your doubts, your questions, your hopes, and your whining. I had this, and more. My husband, T. R. Durham, read the manuscript several times, talked through ideas with me, offered numerous comments and suggestions, prodded, enthused, and cajoled, and made it possible for me, in so many ways, to research and write to complete this project. His unflagging support and belief in the project boosted me up when I needed it the most. As all writers know, there is simply no substitute for such faith. I dedicate the book to him, with all my love.

Contents

Preface ix

Acknowledgments xi

Introduction 3

  1. The Zen of Listening 22

  2. The Ethereal World 40

  3. Exploratory Listening in the 1920s 55

  4. Tuning In to Jazz 83

  5. Radio Comedy and Linguistic Slapstick 100

  6. The Invention of the Audience 124

  7. World War II and the Invention of Broadcast Journalism 161

  8. Playing Fields of the Mind 199

  9. The Kids Take Over: Transistors, DJs, and Rock 'n' Roll 219

10. The FM Revolution 256

11. Talk Talk 284

12. Why Ham Radio Matters 328

Conclusion: Is Listening Dead? 347

Notes 359

Index 391

Listening In

Introduction

A sigh seems such a corny way to start. But that's how so many people, of different ages, begin their musings about the thing. "Ah, radio," they say, and then off they go, into reveries about *Jack Armstrong, the All-American Boy,* or Jean Shepherd, or Wolfman Jack. Few inventions evoke such nostalgia, such deeply personal and vivid memories, such a sense of loss and regret. And there are few devices with which people from different generations and backgrounds have had such an intimate relationship. Ask anyone born before World War II about the role of radio in his or her life, and in the life of the country, and you will see that person begin to time-travel, with an almost euphoric pleasure, to other eras and places, when words and music filled their heads and their hearts. It is a lost world now, a place once overflowing with the music of Duke Ellington, Benny Goodman, and Arturo Toscanini, the jokes of Jack Benny, Burns and Allen, and Fred Allen, and the more sobering words of Franklin Roosevelt, H. V. Kaltenborn, and Edward R. Murrow.

Much of this world is gone forever, having lived only briefly before evaporating in the ether. Only portions of it are preserved on tape. But it's not just Americans who grew up in the 1930s and '40s who get romantic about radio. Millions of us born after World War II remember lying there in the darkness of our bedrooms, or driving around at night in our parents' cars, listening to Sam Cooke, or the Beatles, or the Doors, and feeling illicit pleasures. The music transported us out of the house, out of our dull neighborhoods, and off to someplace where life seemed more intense, more heartfelt, less fettered. Even very hip pop and rock stars of the 1970s—Elvis Costello, Donna Summer, Queen—sang about radio with a sense of longing. As the fabulous Freddie Mercury put it on Queen's classic "Radio Ga-Ga,"

I'd sit alone and watch your light/ My only friend through teenage night/
And everything I had to know/ I heard it on my radio.

The refrain then summed up the sadness, even a hint of betrayal, that radio
had been displaced:

You had your time/ you had the power/ you've yet to have your finest hour/
Radio.

People who grew up with radio still pine for the old radio days, for their intimate relationship with the box in their living room or bedroom, for a culture
without television. They miss what now seems like the simplicity of those
times, the innocent optimism (even during the Depression and the War), the
directness of the medium itself. But what they yearn for most is the way that
radio invited them to participate actively in the production of the show at
hand. A listener could ornament any radio broadcast, whether it was a political speech, *Inner Sanctum, Fibber McGee and Molly,* or the New York Philharmonic Orchestra, with appropriate visuals. This meant more than imagining
the people and their expressions, the setting and its architecture and decor. It
also meant that with words and tone of voice as your only clues (often reinforced by sound effects and music), you conjured up people's emotional states,
their motivations, the tenor of their interactions with others. You envisioned
Mary Livingstone rolling her eyes at Jack Benny's unfounded vanity; you
winced as the entire contents of a closet cascaded out into a hallway; you even
glimpsed the elusive, invisible Shadow. You had to fill in the other senses—
taste, touch, and smell—also. Even though you might be lying on the living
room floor, or lounging in a chair, you were anything but passive.

Listening to radio was like being a child again, having stories read to you
and being expected to have—and use—a vivid imagination. And what radio
listeners miss most are these, their supple, agile, bygone imaginations. They
miss their role in completing the picture, in giving individual meaning to
something that went out to a mass audience. They miss the mental activity, the
engagement, the do-it-yourself nature of radio listening. They miss having
such a free-ranging role in giving mass culture its private and public meanings.
They miss the kinds of conversations radio provoked, in which friends or family or co-workers talked together to fill in the blanks. They miss radio's invisibility. When people sigh about radio, they are yearning for a mass medium that
stimulated the imagination instead of stunting it. They are also acknowledging
how deeply radio burrowed into people's autobiographies, marking, shaping,
and responding to who people were at different points in their lives.

Not that this relationship to radio ended with the advent of television. On the contrary, that generation born after World War II, the baby boom, also had a very special and intense relationship with radio, although the terms were necessarily different. People certainly listened to radio by themselves in the 1930s and '40s, but, especially during the early evening hours, radio listening was largely a family affair. Thirty years later radio listening was often more private. By the mid-1950s most American homes had television, which, dominated as it was by shows like *Zorro, The Real McCoys,* and *The Adventures of Ozzie and Harriet,* was filled with kid shows and family programming. Baby boomers, certainly those born in the 1940s and '50s, went to radio for something else. We turned to radio for rebellion. And we turned to it for an affirmation of our sense that, as a generation, we were indeed different. Young people in the 1990s, searching for the increasingly rare "alternative" stations, or tuning in to what's come to be called modern rock, still use radio to locate others like themselves, to inhabit a world not meant for those over thirty.

One primal experience those born before *and* after the Second World War share is lying in bed, sometimes with the covers just barely over our heads, listening intently to the box next to us. Maybe it was the darkness, the solitude, or being in bed, but the intimacy of this experience remains vivid; listeners had a deeply private, personal bond with radio. One group listened to *The Shadow* or *The Lone Ranger,* another to DJs like Alan Freed, Cousin Brucie, Wolfman Jack, or Tom "Big Daddy" Donahue. Both groups listened to music, to the tunes that would become the theme songs for different moments and eras of their lives. Baseball bridged this generational divide, as tuning in to ball games became a national passion, especially from the late 1930s to the late 1960s.

We also started listening when we were young, even before we became teenagers, and we often listened alone. Radio kneaded our psyches early on and helped shape our desires, our fantasies, our images of the outside world, our very imaginations. Unlike other major technologies—automobiles, airplanes, or trains—that move us from one place to another, radio has worked most powerfully inside our heads, helping us create internal maps of the world and our place in it, urging us to construct imagined communities to which we do, or do not, belong. While radio brought America together as a nation in the 1930s and '40s, it also highlighted the country's ethnic, racial, geographic, and gendered divisions. And radio hastened the shift away from identifying oneself—and one's social solidarity with others—on the basis of location and family ties, to identifying oneself on the basis of consumer and taste preferences.[1] Certainly it has played a central role, over the last nine decades, in constructing us as a new entity: the mass-mediated human, whose sense of space and time, whose emotional repertoires and deepest motivations cannot be extricated from what has emanated through the airwaves.

But while radio listening has been a constant fact of twentieth-century life, the *way* people listened to radio was profoundly shaped by the era in which they began to listen. In the 1920s people had to tinker constantly with their sets to pull in different stations, discovering through their headphones a host of unearthly sounds—static, blasting, feedback—they'd never heard before. By the mid-1930s the noise had cleared enough to allow Americans to concentrate on stories on the radio. By the late 1950s the stories had largely disappeared. In other words, different generations learned to listen to and use the radio differently. So it's not only *what* people listened to—Benny Goodman or the Rolling Stones—that defined generations. It's *how* they listened as well that shaped people's memories, associations with others, their sense of who they were and their place in history.

This book is about those times—whether curled up in our beds, sitting in the living room with our families, or blasting around in our cars—when Americans listened to the radio, often with a passion. It asks what it meant for a culture glutted with visual stimuli to turn, dramatically and avidly, to listening. The book argues that radio's invisibility—the fact that it denies sight to its audience—has been absolutely central to its effects on American culture. It considers what people listened to in different eras as the device and the programming evolved; and it examines how this technology, and the programming on it, introduced us to, and cultivated in many of us, different modes of listening that helped constitute us as individuals, and as Americans. While the impact on radio of inventors, corporate leaders, and certain self-satisfied DJs and talk show hosts has been duly recorded in books both pop and academic, the relationship of us, the listeners, to this invention remains unexplored. This book takes on that exploration.

I confess that this is, at times, a romantic book, in the way that Woody Allen's *Radio Days* is a romantic movie. Allen's valentine to radio acknowledges that its commercials were often sappy and moronic, its stars sometimes pretentious and talentless hypocrites, and many of its shows utterly mindless and politically retrograde. Ever since the 1920s critics have rightly complained about the commercial bastardization of radio. In fact, listening to old programs today—even famous, highly rated ones like *The Edgar Bergen and Charlie McCarthy Show*—one is struck by how bad they often were. From its start radio perpetuated ethnic, racial, and gender stereotypes, and it played a defining role in making consumerism our national religion. By the 1930s radio was under oligopoly control, managed almost exclusively by two networks, CBS and NBC, who in turn had their content tightly regulated by advertising agencies and their corporate clients and, to a lesser extent, the FCC. Radio was hardly an unfettered vehicle for the democratic expression of diverse American voices.

Yet there is something about the medium itself that makes listeners willing to forgive—even forget—much of this. I want to understand why this is so. Radio historians, myself included, have most often had a political and economic emphasis to our work as we have traced how radio fell under, and advanced, corporate fortunes. Indeed, given radio's history, it would be impossible to abandon this emphasis, and I don't intend to do so here. But radio as a tool of corporate agendas is not the only or at times even the most important historical story, although at other times, of course, it is. The sighing about radio should interest us too, the silky nostalgia that swirls around it, and radio's role in constructing and activating the collective memories of so many Americans.

I want to suggest that this nostalgia is especially powerful because it is rooted in the act of listening. In other words, you can't appreciate the importance of radio until you understand the importance of hearing. This may seem baldly obvious. But existing histories of radio—with the exception of Marshall McLuhan's 1964 best-seller *Understanding Media*—do not pause, even for a minute, to meditate on the particular qualities and power of sound, and how these have shaped the power of radio. Yet it is clear that with the introduction of the telephone, the phonograph, and then radio, there was a revolution in our aural environment that prompted a major perceptual and cognitive shift in the country, with a new emphasis on hearing. Because sound is dynamic and fleeting, radio conveyed a powerful sense of "liveness"—it was, from the beginning, "an account of what *is* happening, rather than a record of what *has* happened." Radio was a perceptual technology that extended, deepened, and magnified hearing to completely unprecedented levels. It provided "a flood of aural experience" and a changing relationship to sound.[2]

What I have attempted to do, then, is conduct an archaeology of radio listening from the 1920s to the present, and to lay out what I see as the different modes of listening that radio cultivated in Americans in different eras. I do so because I have become convinced that the modes of listening radio cultivated in us in our formative years powerfully shaped our individual and collective identities and also shaped the contours of American cultural and political history. Listening to the radio has become such an embedded, taken-for-granted feature of everyday life that we are oblivious to how we have come to listen to specific broadcasts differently, and we have forgotten that this was something we all had to learn. It is high time that we stopped, cocked our ears for a bit, and considered the fact that *how* we learned to listen to radio shaped our subjective, inner selves and the generations of which we are part. No, generations are hardly monolithic; they are riven with all sorts of divisions that radio—or any mass medium—could hardly smooth over. But radio surrounded different generations with common and evolving aural soundscapes that their members tuned in, entered, imbibed, or turned off, and understood to be theirs.

It is also time to scrutinize that old bromide "Radio stimulates the imagination," and think about exactly what radio encouraged Americans to imagine during different historical eras and how it did so—through music, sound effects, ambient sound, and the invention of a new form of discourse, radio announcing. With a few exceptions I have identified these modes of listening with particular broadcasting genres: for example, news listening, story listening, baseball listening, and music listening (which has its own subcategories, as people listen to music in multiple ways). But within and across these genres—and certainly modes of listening overlap with one another—listening ranges from flat and informational, as when people take in the weather or the latest headlines, to deeply layered and multidimensional, as when fans envision the geometry of a ballpark and feel they actually see the arcing trajectory of a home run. Americans chose to enter these modes of listening, often with great anticipation, and they learned how to switch modes, often instantly, as *The Chase and Sanborn Hour*, for example, moved them from a solo by Gordon MacRae to a commercial to a skit in which they imagined Mae West as Eve in the Garden of Eden. Individuals developed their own repertoires of listening styles out of these modes and moved fluidly between different cognitive and emotional levels, and all this through hearing alone.

Even today, in the age of TV and the Internet, Americans have learned to turn to radio to alter or sustain particular emotional states: to elevate their moods (classic rock, oldies), to soothe themselves (classical, soft rock, smooth jazz), to become outraged (talk and shock). Some modes of listening have helped constitute generational identities, others a sense of nationhood, still others, subcultural opposition to and rebellion against that construction of nationhood. Most modes of listening generate a strong feeling of belonging. Even as mere background noise, radio provides people with a sense of security that silence does not, which is why they actively turn to it, even if they aren't actively listening.[3]

How has radio listening made Americans who they are? Of course, this is a ridiculous question: there's no "typical American," and it is impossible to speak of some collective "we." People of different generations, regions, sexes, races, and ethnic groups have listened to and used radio very differently. And there have been and remain massive individual differences in how people listen and what they attend to on the air. Most of these differences I am unable to explore here. But my goal is also different, and goes against the grain of much work in media studies that has rightly emphasized the specificity of media impact and the often highly individualized ways in which people interact with and draw meanings from the mass media. While acknowledging these differences as crucial to our understanding of the wide-ranging effects of the mass media, I want to reflect on some of the commonalities of radio listening, on how radio might have shaped very different listeners in sometimes similar ways.

Laying out such a schema is risky business. Radio historians struggle with one of the spottiest, most ephemeral historical records in all of the mass media. So many of the shows weren't recorded; so many of the listeners, who were asked by ratings services which shows they liked (and whether they remembered who the sponsors were), were never asked *how* they listened or why they liked listening to certain kinds of shows. We have less to go on than we would like. And there has been virtually no collaborative work between media historians and cognitive scientists that explores how particular media—in this case one that addresses only the ears—affected the life of the mind. But we must start somewhere. With all the academic attention on the power of "the gaze," the power of hearing to shape individual and collective subjectivity has gotten short shrift.[4] It's time to rectify this.

Radio is arguably the most important electronic invention of the century. Cognitively, it revolutionized the perceptual habits of the nation. Technically, culturally, and economically, it set the stage for television. It forever blurred the boundaries between the private domestic sphere and public, commercial, and political life. It made listening to music a daily requirement for millions of Americans. For the entire span of the twentieth century, listening to radio—first introduced to America as "wireless telegraphy" in 1899—has been a major cultural pastime. Even with the advent of television, which was supposed to make radio obsolete, radio has remained a thriving cultural and political force. Today we have twice as many radios in America as we do people.[5] And they listen in, on average, about three and a half hours a day.

Yet radio as an invention, and a cultural force, is regarded as mattering very little now in the grand scheme of things, especially in the face of cable TV, blockbuster movies, and the Internet. It is low-tech, unglamorous, and taken for granted. There are only a handful of books about radio after World War II, even if we include the recent self-promotional offerings by Howard Stern and Rush Limbaugh.[6] The press and most cultural observers ignore radio, except when Stern pushes his own rather relaxed limits of tastefulness too far, or when conservative talk show hosts instruct their listeners on the best method for gunning down federal officials. It's as if radio fell off the planet after television, when, in fact, the reverse is true.

But radio is also hard for our culture to remember properly. We enshrine and relive our history through images—TV documentaries, movies, museum exhibits, and magazines—or through books. Except for the rare radio documentary, there is simply no form in which the medium's enormous impact on American life can be properly conveyed. Radio, therefore, drops out of all too many of the stories told about our past. So we see World War II through newsreels and think of it as a visual war, when this was, first and foremost, a radio war that millions listened to and imagined. Or we read books about the 1930s and the word *radio* isn't even in the index, even though 40 million people might have listened simultaneously to the same show on a given night. The industrial, commercial forms in which our collective memories are preserved and re-presented are, simply put, biased against what was the dominant mass medium in the country for thirty-five years.

What follows is a thematic history and, of course, a highly selective one—covering one hundred years of this technology's history properly in one volume is impossible. I will not tackle the institutional histories of the networks, the ad agencies, or the Federal Communications Commission. Nor is this a celebration of radio's "golden age," a fond review of all the hit shows and their stars; that has been done, many times. Entire, critically important genres of radio programming, such as dramas, children's shows, soap operas, and many of the comedies, won't appear here. Rather, I have chosen examples of certain kinds of programming, from Duke Ellington to Rush Limbaugh, that exemplify the particular ways in which Americans turned to listening. Beginning in the 1920s, when the "radio boom" swept the nation, and ending with NPR and talk radio in the 1990s, the following chapters will focus on those topics—radio comedy of the 1930s, the invention of broadcast journalism, listening to baseball and boxing on radio, the rise of the DJ and the Top 40 format, the FM revolution of the 1960s and '70s—that capture key moments in the evolution of radio listening in America. In the 1930s we also see the beginning of radio research, the start of turning you and me into a commodity—an audience—to be bought and sold, delivered to advertisers for a price. This, too, has shaped our sense of who we are and why we matter. When you have researchers working in collaboration with advertisers and networks, seeking to unlock the black box of individual motivation and somehow rewire its innards, you have a major recasting of a society's psyche.

The rise of the computer has been accompanied by elegant analyses of its impact on our identities and our models of society, and Sherry Turkle's *The Second Self* suggests how we need to rethink the impact and significance of radio. Turkle explores the profoundly intimate relationships people forge with their computers until the machines become "second selves" that alleviate loneliness but make no unreasonable or threatening demands for intimacy. The computer fulfills the "desire for fusion" with something outside of and bigger than oneself. Turkle suggests that, while providing a sense of community and of technical mastery, the computer undermines our confidence in the distinctiveness and importance of human intelligence. In her follow-up study, *Life on the Screen: Identity in the Age of the Internet*, Turkle found that as people play games and talk with others in cyberspace, the invisibility and anonymity of the medium allow users to assume all sorts of identities. Many come to think of themselves as consisting of multiple personas that are in constant tension with one another, and they often enjoy the ability to create new selves on-line.[7] Turkle's work prompts us to ask how radio, which brought so many diverse personalities into the home, set the stage for this new twentieth-century relationship between the self and unseen others, and between the local and the distant. Radio, by cultivating different modes of listening, also fostered people's tendency to feel fragmented into many selves, which were called forth in rapid succession, or sometimes all at the same time.

Radio played a pivotal role, especially in the first half of the century, in helping us imagine ourselves and our relationships to other Americans differently. It constructed imagined communities—of sports fans, Fred Allen devotees, rock 'n' rollers, ham operators, Dittoheads—and thus cultivated both a sense of nationhood and a validation of subcultures, often simultaneously. Radio did indeed, as the cliché goes, bring the country together, and we need to explore more precisely the linguistic and musical mechanisms through which this occurred. In bringing this about, the radio networks cemented New York City's role as the cultural capital of the nation.

But radio, because it was never totally centralized in America, also did the opposite—provided niches and outposts for different people of different tastes, attitudes, and desires. Even during radio's "golden era," that heyday of network programming and a vast, national audience, certain listeners identified themselves as Fred Allen fans who would never be caught dead listening to Eddie Cantor or *Major Bowes' [Original] Amateur Hour*. Radio, much more than movies, sped up the process whereby people identified themselves, and their relations to others, through the consumerist mirror of taste preferences—in humor, in music, in detergent—a form of identification now rampant today. In part because of radio, such identifications began to destabilize, however imperceptibly over time, those based on ethnicity, locale, political affiliation, and class.

Radio also transformed Americans' relationship to music. Indeed, after radio Americans didn't just have access to music, we *needed* it, often on a daily basis. It is easy to forget that, ever since the 1920s, it has been music that has predominated the broadcast day, even during the height of radio comedy and drama. And this, too, may help explain the powerful nostalgia that radio evokes. Music so effectively taps our emotions—brain mapping by cognitive scientists shows that the brain's musical networks extend into its emotional circuits[8]—that we develop deep, associative memories between particular songs and our own personal narratives. People often remember when they first heard certain songs: where they were driving in their cars, how they felt, what their hopes were.

Radio introduced a new orality to American culture, in which ancient ways of conveying myths, heroic stories, or morality tales intermixed with more modern ways of conveying information, through text and images. And so accustomed are we to turning on the radio and hearing Linda Wertheimer reporting the news, the DJ introducing a new song, a sportscaster giving the play-by-play, that we forget that all these modes of radio talk, just like radio technology itself, had to be invented. How exactly would you do a vaudeville skit on the air so people knew who entered the room when, or what had just happened that was funny? How would you help people rendered blind by this medium see a man hit a line drive? What accents and patterns of speech were acceptable? How could you get people to remember that Kent cigarettes were better because they had "micronite filters"?

Broadcasters on the air had to calibrate how they would speak so that they appealed to as wide a range of socioeconomic classes and geographic regions as possible. They had to figure out how people would remember specific information and particular personalities. In the process radio voices—from comedians and newscasters to DJs—introduced Americans, over the years, to the concept of audio signatures—from "Holy Mackerel" or "This . . . is London" to the howl of a wolfman. Radio talk relied often heavily on repetition, on rhythmic cadences, on alliteration and mnemonic devices to facilitate ready recall and retention.[9] People learned an "acoustic shorthand" that evolved from one era to the next. The constant reinvention of radio talk, and the way its signatures and cadences got grooved into our inner lives, also powerfully shaped generational identity.

These changes have affected nearly all of us, whether we realize it or not. But having said that, I want to suggest that radio has been a critically important and often redefining invention for men. While I don't want to diminish, for a minute, the importance of radio to women and girls, for men and boys there has been something especially liberating about this device.[10] Whether claiming the technology as their own, as legions of crystal set tinkerers and ham operators did, or reclaiming musical virtuosity and music appreciation as distinctly masculine, as jazz musicians did in the 1920s and as millions of male rock 'n' roll fans have done since the 1950s, boys and men have found in radio not only a hobby but also a medium that validates their aesthetic and emotional needs. That radio talk show hosts like Howard Stern, Don Imus, and

Rush Limbaugh brandish distinct yet insistent brands of masculinity and speak to a largely male audience further identifies radio as a medium in which boys really feel they can be boys without apology.

But radio—by making musical pleasure acceptable for men; by producing a fraternal subculture of hams eager to feel a sense of connectedness to each other; and by letting male hysterics like Limbaugh vent their emotions about politics, culture, and women invisibly over the airwaves—has also given men access to those "stigmatized parts of themselves" that have been deemed feminine and therefore inadmissible.[11] In other words, through radio men have also been able to become more like women without appearing to do so.

Of course, masculinity has hardly been an unchanging construct in the twentieth century. Like femininity, it has been both a surprisingly durable concept and one that has been challenged, threatened, and rejuvenated throughout the century. Manhood is not some fixed, wired-in essence: it is a mantle boys and then men must learn how to put on and wear. Masculinity, like femininity, is a fluid, dynamic, and contradictory set of attributes that men must choose from, and during certain eras some attributes are more in favor than others. The self-restrained, honorable, good provider of high moral character—to pick just one archetype—was, at the beginning of the century, at odds with the more uninhibited, physically tough, and pugnacious ladies' man—another archetype, and the latter came to see the former as an overcivilized sissy.[12] John Wayne and Edward R. Murrow, for example, were both icons of resolute manhood in the 1940s and '50s, but their methods of achieving and demonstrating their manliness were quite different indeed.

The historian Gail Bederman cautions us, in her wonderful book *Manliness and Civilization*, against identifying certain eras as constituting "crises" in masculinity, lest we imply that in other eras notions of manhood were somehow set. Bederman is right: warring conceptions of manhood have always vied for supremacy. But in the twentieth century we see four eras in particular when anxieties about manhood became pronounced, and when radio played a central role in enacting and mediating between models of masculinity. These eras were the beginning of the Great Depression—certainly one of the most profound crises in capitalism and patriarchy in this century; the late 1940s and early 1950s, when overcivilized "organization men" seemed to beget their opposite, juvenile delinquents; the late 1960s and early 1970s, when many young men saw in the Vietnam war masculinity run amok; and the late 1980s and 1990s, when a backlash against feminism solidified into various versions of a "men's movement." Radio comedy in the 1930s, the rise of the DJ in the late 1940s, the birth of the "progressive" or "underground" FM format in the late

1960s, and the rise of talk radio and shock jocks were all expressions of these periods of heightened gender anxiety.

Radio, in fact, played a central role in tuning and retuning certain versions of manhood, foregrounding sometimes more "feminine" traits, at other times more "masculine" ones, most frequently negotiating a new hybrid between the two. So I want to encourage a new take on how we think about men and machines. In the 1970s scholars influenced by feminism began to study how scientists, engineers, factory owners, and corporate leaders used a range of technologies to "master" nature (conceived of as female) and to buttress male privilege. These scholars turned their attention to the long-neglected topics of female factory workers, the marginalization of female scientists, and how domestic technologies, like vacuum cleaners and washing machines, often created "more work for mother." Studies of gender and technology, then, focused most frequently on women. When they focused on men, what emerged was an often scathing critique of how technological problem solving, when fused with male arrogance, led to the rape of the environment and the subjugation of women and minorities.[13]

But certainly this is not the whole story, although it is a powerfully important one. Many men have also used technology—and this is especially true of communications technologies and the automobile—to rebel against dominant definitions of masculinity that have insisted they act like ruthless conquerors or corporate cogs. They developed technologies that extended sensory experience, like seeing and hearing, and that allowed for artistic expression. They used technology to reaffirm that they had feelings, and souls. Certainly male privilege remained: technical skill certifies that you are still a man. But such skill could also be a fig leaf, veiling the censored desire to be a nurturing, sensitive, emotionally expressive human being. It is time to take these impulses into account as well when thinking about how and why men use machines.

The radio boom of the 1920s occurred when the ideal of masculinity advanced by Theodore Roosevelt and Tarzan books—men as strenuously living, vigorous, even primitive he-men afraid of nothing, especially wild animals—began to seem rather preposterous in the face of the bureaucratization engulfing male work life. More to the point, being aggressive, overly competitive, and individualistic was actually dysfunctional—contraindicated—in many of the urbanized, industrialized, and corporate workplaces of the twentieth century. Possibilities for individual public distinction, not to mention rugged independence, seemed to shrink year by year. White-collar workers, whose numbers had increased eightfold between 1870 and 1910, found their work increasingly routinized and anonymous. "When changes in the workplace caused men to feel uncertain of their manhood," writes the historian Anthony Rotundo, "their primary response was to seek new forms of reassurance about it."[14]

Radio, often in very different ways, was a perfect vehicle for such reassurances. When tinkering with machines like radios, men affirmed that they had distinctly specialized—and masculine—skills that required control and discipline to achieve. As ham operators they could join a fraternity that, until the 1980s, was almost exclusively male. And they could escape into the air, away from home and work into a place where men like them, who knew a secret code, congregated in comfort.

The content of male entertainments, from spectator sports to swashbuckler films, also addressed anxieties about threatened masculinity. And radio comedy of the 1930s—which has been persistently cast as something that "cheered America up" during the Depression (as if Depression with a capital *D* is the same as depression with a little *d*)—becomes much more interesting and revealing if we look at it from the perspective of gender. Here, the linguistic slapstick—the puns, wordplay, insults, and malapropisms—that so characterized the form enacted the crisis in masculinity that the Great Depression precipitated. Moving from Burns and Allen to Edward R. Murrow and Lowell Thomas, and then to Red Barber and Harry Caray, we see newly reimagined terrain for men and for America, a region of risk and rivalry, of conquest and victory, yet of comradeship and mutual support.

Radio today seems so trapped in the amber of corporate control that it is easy to forget how much of radio technology and programming came from the bottom up, pioneered by outsiders or rebels who wanted something more, or something different, from the box than corporate America was providing. And what they wanted from radio was more direct, less top-down communication between Americans. Whether they were the ham operators who in 1920 pushed a phonograph in front of a microphone and introduced "wireless concerts" at a time when RCA thought radio would be best used to send Morse code messages between corporate clients, or the guys in their bell-bottoms and tie-dyed T-shirts who took a technology barely in use—FM—and transformed it into the dominant form of radio broadcasting, men have used radio to rebel against the technological and programming status quo in the industry. At times they turned tinkering, listening, and programming into a subversive activity. This rebellion is not just interesting culturally; it has had a profound impact on the business and technical history of the industry.

Radio is an especially rich example of such technological insurgency, in which the design and use of inventions is fought over, contested, and reimagined by a host of actors, including consumers, despite the power of corporate control.[15] Technological insurgency has traditionally come from young men. It has been especially robust after wars, when the availability of devices developed for military use interacts with a retreat from the rigid codes of masculinity that battle imposes, and we see hobbyists using technology in more life-affirming ways. It flourishes when industries are in flux and corporate attention is elsewhere. Burgeoning youth cultures sustain and expand such insurgencies.

How radio would be used, and its impact on American culture, was never inevitable, and these dynamics were actually devised and redevised throughout the century, as the industry responded to—and eventually co-opted—insurgencies coming from the grass roots. The radio audience, it turns out, has always been filled with rebels: amateur operators, or "hams" as they were commonly known, who proved that shortwaves weren't worthless, as the experts thought; teenagers in the 1950s who used their transistors to forge a separate, rambunctious, generational identity in a way Bell Labs never anticipated; the hi-fi enthusiasts of the late 1940s and '50s who pushed first the phonograph and then the radio industry to develop receiving equipment that offered genuine fidelity listening. Pushing radio to signal farther and to sound more lifelike—or even better than life—has been the ongoing quest of radio tinkerers. It was the amateurs who pioneered using radio for broadcasting, not Marconi, its inventor, and certainly not David Sarnoff, the president of RCA, who rewrote history to make it seem like broadcasting had been his brainchild. And it was often young people, whether jazz enthusiasts of the 1920s or rock 'n' rollers of the 1950s, who pushed radio beyond the confines of suffocating respectability and into more exciting territory. Changing technologies, from shortwave to satellites, interacted with newly invented programming genres and formats, sometimes with the technology pushing forward cultural innovation and sometimes the other way around.

More than the movies, mass magazines, or television (and up until the Internet), radio has been the mass medium through which the struggles between rampant commercialism and a loathing of that commercialism have been fought out over and over again. There has always been a dialectical relationship between oligopoly control of radio programming and technology on the one hand and technological insurgencies defying this control on the other. Listeners both acquiesced to and rebelled against how radio was deployed by the networks.

It is this contradictory stance toward mainstream culture, the absolute centrality of ambivalence to the American consciousness, that radio, with its hodgepodge of daily delights and outrages, spoke to and heightened. One moment you were elevated, the next, insulted. Whether we consider the debate about network versus local programming in the 1920s or the intense battles over radio and rock 'n' roll in the 1950s, we see in this sweep of history a series of ongoing cultural wars, between the wish for a national culture and the desire for cultural diversity, between the urge to conform and the need to rebel, and between a longing for collectivism and the seductions of narcissistic individualism.

Radio has given full expression to these distinctly American tensions while necessarily exacerbating them. This stems, in part, from a fundamental contradiction that characterizes radio. There is a rift between the inherent technical properties of radio and the economic system in which it was—and is—embedded. The deeply personal nature of radio communication—the way its sole reliance on sound produces individualized images and reactions; its extension of a precommercial, oral tradition; its cultivation of the imagination— all work in stark contrast to the needs of its managers, who seek homogenized responses, and need a like-minded audience instead of idiosyncratic individuals. With television, which is less personal and much less reliant on the imagination, this tension barely exists. With radio, the audience has been continually pulled between the liberating technical properties of the device and the confining properties of how it has been financed and managed. As a result, there has been a cyclical, twenty-year pattern in radio's history, beginning in the mid-1920s, when rebellion and anarchy were ultimately tamed and co-opted on the air, only to reappear through different technologies, formats, and subgroups of listeners.

If radio histories were one's only guide, one would believe that television did "kill" radio in the postwar years. But anyone who lay in bed at night listening to Elvis Presley, the Chiffons, the Chambers Brothers, or Elvis Costello knows otherwise. With the advent of television and the collapse of network programming on radio, the medium turned to more local and more specialized audiences. And one of the fastest growing and most loyal audiences was teenagers. This marriage between radio and the young was cemented first by the invention of the transistor and second by the proliferation, thirty years after its invention, of FM radio in the late 1960s. As radio became more portable—and between 1949 and 1960 the number of portable sets made by U.S. companies quadrupled, while the number of imported Japanese transistor sets increased sevenfold—it accompanied people everywhere, to the beach, to work, in the backyard, and on buses, cars, and subways. *Life* magazine in 1961 proclaimed teenagers especially to be "hooked on sound." For young people, listening first to fast-talking, hip DJs and later to their more somnolent FM counterparts on "free form," radio meant walking that line between conforming with the most defiant examplars of your own generation and rebelling against the homogenized conformity of middle-class adult culture.

What outraged or troubled certain members of the establishment about the teenagers' love affair with radio was that white teenagers—millions of them—were listening to and falling in love with African American music and performers. What used to be safely sequestered as "race music" was now sneaking in through the bedroom windows of suburban households, threatening a cultural miscegenation that made self-appointed moral guardians apoplectic. And here we see another critically important thread in the history of radio: its central role in providing a passageway between white and black culture. Radio—more than any other mass medium—simultaneously reinforced and profoundly destabilized white supremacy and racial segregation in the United States throughout the century.

From *Amos 'n' Andy* and jazz to rap music, radio has supplied white people that private place, that trapdoor into a culture many whites imagine to be more authentic, more vibrant, and richer than their own. Through radio whites could partake of the spirit of black culture without being forced to witness or experience its deprivations and injustices. Whether what they heard was itself an imagining, a simulation—as with *Amos 'n' Andy*—or an accommodation to white norms—as with the Supremes—many whites felt they gained access to something previously hidden, forbidden, and much more genuine than the calculated homogenizations of the culture industry. Since radio simultaneously reinforced and perpetuated racial stereotypes while also making African American music enormously popular, we need to contemplate the consequences of this auditory voyeurism, for black and white listeners, and for black performers.

It is easy to castigate the industry for its long history of intransigent racism: the record of exclusion speaks for itself. But the record isn't this simple. Here I disagree with the media historian Michele Hilmes, whose emphasis in *Radio Voices* is on radio's role in "constructing a national norm of 'whiteness.' "[16] Yes, this was one of the things radio did. But on the radio (as elsewhere in popular culture), white ridicule of black culture and of African Americans mixed with envy, desire, and imitation: with what the University of Virginia scholar Eric Lott has called "Love and Theft." By the time Norman Mailer wrote his famous (and infamous) piece "The White Negro" in 1957, there were already dozens of white DJs trying to pass for black on the air and plenty of white listeners who adored what *New York Times* editor Mel Watkins has labeled "racial ventriloquism." And white Americans didn't make *Amos 'n' Andy* radio's first major hit series only because they were all racists and wanted their prejudices reinforced. Radio may have been used throughout its history to reaffirm the supposed superiority of whiteness. But it has also been used, since the 1920s, to challenge, laugh at, and undermine this flimsy conceit. Borrowing from Toni Morrison,

Hilmes argues that African Americans on the radio served as "our nation's primary 'projection of the not-me.' "[17] This was true. But not always, and not for everyone. For often at the very same time, African Americans, especially through their music and slang, also served for whites as projections of "wish-it-was-me."

With the increasing privatization of American society, where we watch political speeches, take in concerts, shop, attend sporting events, and go to the movies all from the sequestered, solitary comfort of our living room sofas or computer monitors, there remains the powerful, atavistic desire to be part of a larger group, lose ourselves in a crowd, exchange ideas with strangers, and get a more immediate sense of ourselves as part of a nation. While radio can never substitute for what once was, it does, in a small and indeed atrophied way, speak to this desire. The yearning for some form of public discourse, for a place where less slick and less mainstream opinions could be articulated, the desire to be heard: all these shaped the success of talk and call-in radio. National Public Radio, with its more liberal listeners and agenda, and certain (but not all) call-in shows that are more conservative are mirror images of each other in a way, speaking to the desires of people who see themselves as outside of and often at odds with the hypercommercialized, hypercynical mainstream and who want public articulation of a different kind of truth.

Finally, contemplating the ongoing relationship between radio and American consciousness, we have to consider how the rise of television, at the expense of radio, has stunted the American imagination. It is easy to romanticize the glory days of radio and to idealize radio listeners over television viewers. So let's be clear that over the past seventy years radio has had more than its share of political demagoguery, crass, relentless commercialism, and superficial public programming that helped reinforce racism, sexism, and elitism. The shameless radio coverage of the Lindbergh trial in 1935 was every bit as revolting as what we had to witness with the O. J. Simpson case.[18] Having acknowledged this, however, and without falling into a glazed-eye nostalgia about Burns and Allen, Lowell Thomas, or Alan Freed, it is important to reflect on the relative cognitive impact of the different mass media. And the conclusion I believe one will come to is that while radio, banalities and all, expanded the imagination, its successor, television, constricted it, and we are the worse for it as individuals and as a culture.

We don't usually think of having visuals as being a greater constraint than not having them. After all, there is a hunger of the eyes, a desire to see for yourself, the notion that seeing a person or witnessing an event is more complete than just listening. And in many ways this is true. But the small screen requires visual economy, and because of both its technical constraints and the nature of its economic support, it relies on easily conveyed visual stereotypes that reduce uncertainty and confusion. We see the same "types," the same scenes over and over. And the play our own minds are allowed, the room our own imaginings are given, necessarily shrinks. In fact, our imaginings become irrelevant. The musician and writer Ben Sidran has astutely noted, "The advantages of orality have rarely been recognized by Western tradition." It's time for this to change.[19]

In all too many popular accounts of the history of technology, we get an overly simplified "before-and-after" story, in which some machine—the cotton gin, the car, the computer—revolutionizes everyday life. Advertisers past and present have, in selling their clients' products, actively promoted the notion that it is technological change that causes social change (and, in this case, always for the better).[20] The mirror opposite of this also empowers technology—let's say, the nuclear reactor—to transform America, but for the worse. In the mid-1990s we've been witness to all sorts of overheated and contradictory predictions about the Internet: it will re-create political and cultural communities in cyberspace; it will bring pornographers, stalkers, and credit-card scammers into our homes, corrupting our kids and ransacking our privacy. Utopian and dystopian visions, each stark and unrealistic, collide.

But machines can and do accelerate certain trends, magnify cultural weaknesses, and fortify certain social structures while eroding others. Americans— torn as we are between our passion for "progress" and our desperate desire for tradition—love and hate what machines do to and for us, often at the same time. We in America have an embarrassing history of naïvely embracing new technologies as if they could solve all our problems, and produce world peace in the bargain, then excoriating them when they fail to do so. This inclination to invest certain machines, especially communications technologies, with extravagant hopes about their potential to extend democracy, reasserts itself repeatedly in America.[21]

And few technologies have been more freighted, time and again, with such dreams and disillusionment than radio. With all the breathless predictions today about how the Internet will democratize communication and flatten hierarchies among Americans, to bring about a new republic in cyberspace, we should remember that radio—at least as it was envisioned around 1924—was going to provide culture and education to the masses, eliminate politicians' ability to incite passions in a mob, bring people closer to government proceedings, and produce a national culture that would transcend regional and local jealousies. Because radio has taken so many forms over the century and is such a flexible, adaptable, and relatively inexpensive technology, it has been used both to buttress and to challenge the economic, political, and cultural status quo in America. It has been neither the particular technical qualities of the device nor people's goals and ambitions but rather the often unstable, unpredictable marriage between the two that has determined radio's relationship to social change in this country.

What is also critically important to remember about machines and American history—and this is certainly true of radio—is that no technology's consequences are singular or pat: they are messy, contradictory, and not easy to document. As Claude Fischer has pointed out in his prize-winning social history of the telephone, *America Calling*, the telephone simultaneously eased and stimulated people's anxieties.[22] The phone made it possible to know much sooner whether someone has arrived safely after a journey, or is doing well after surgery, or is stranded someplace and needs a ride. But the phone also invaded people's once well-protected privacy, eliminated control over whom one spoke to when (until the advent of the answering machine), and accelerated the arrival of bad news. It is here—in the fluid, barely charted flow between technology and its users—we can explore how people continued to reinvent radio and how it, in turn, sculpted and resculpted the people—the culture—that turned it on.

Machines, of course, do not make history by themselves. But some kinds of machines help make different kinds of histories and different kinds of people than others. That is what we should weigh as we review the role listening in has had in making our society what it is—and what it isn't—today. Radio made history as corporations and individuals used it, sometimes in harmony and sometimes in opposition. Technological change is an ongoing, often unpredictable struggle, and the most noteworthy changes often happen when the industry is in transition and users are feeling rebellious. Radio is currently experiencing a breathtaking corporate consolidation as fewer and fewer companies own more and more stations; many DJs and announcers feel their autonomy suffocated. But history teaches us that as final as this may feel, the struggle over radio listening will continue; too many of us are restless once again.

The year 1999 marks radio's anniversary in the United States—one hundred years since Guglielmo Marconi came from England and demonstrated, during the highly popular America's Cup races, that Morse code signals could be sent "through the air" without any wires. In that one hundred years Americans have embraced the invention in a variety of ways, redesigning how it looked, where it could be taken, and what it conveyed to its listeners. In turn, the invention reshaped America. It is time to reassess the importance of this device, and to reflect on how we have changed radio and how it, in turn, has changed us.

The Zen of Listening

Most of us know that feeling, driving alone at night on a road or highway, surrounded by darkness, listening to the radio. Before so many of us installed tape decks and CD players in our cars or trucks, it was the voices and music on the radio that provided that lifeline we needed, pulling us out of the solitary night and toward our destination. We clung to it to stay afloat, sometimes letting our thoughts drift off, sometimes belting out some song at the top of our lungs (and even adding, in the supposed privacy of our cars, dramatic facial expressions and gestures we would never display before others), sometimes talking back to DJs or newscasters. Relief and pleasure came, too, from not having to work at making conversation, from not being obliged to talk back, and even from not having to pay complete attention.[1] We were taken out of ourselves through radio, yet paradoxically hurled into our innermost thoughts. (Television, by contrast, just doesn't do this.) We felt, simultaneously, an affirmation of the self—so wonderfully narcissistic—and a loss of self—such a joyful escape from scrutiny of the self—and the mixing of the two was often euphoric. Especially thrilling, back before the rise of FM, when 50,000-watt AM stations like WSBK or WABC could be heard for hundreds of miles, was cruising through Ohio or Connecticut or Texas and hearing stations several states away.

There we were alone, yet through this device we were tied by the most gossamer connections to an imagined community of people we sensed loved the same music we did, and to a DJ who often spoke to us in the most intimate, confidential, and inclusive tones. (Cousin Brucie of WABC in New York addressed us as "cousins"; we were all part of the same cool family.)

Our relationship was with the DJ and with our fellow listeners as we imagined them, not as they were. "At an emotional level," writes the Oxford psychiatrist Anthony Storr in *Music and the Mind,* "there is something 'deeper' about hearing than seeing; and something about hearing other people which fosters human relationships even more than seeing them."[2]

Before starting this book at the usual place, with the radio boom of the 1920s, I'd like to explore why the act of listening might be so pleasurable and how it cultivates both a sense of national unity and, at the same time, a conspiratorial sense of subcultural difference, of distance from, even superiority to that national ethos. Then I'd like to link these thoughts about listening to a brief explanation of how radio works—and especially how AM radio works, since that was the first method of broadcasting and the one that defined radio for nearly sixty years.

It has become impossible to use the perfectly innocent term "imagined communities" without citing the Cornell scholar Benedict Anderson, whose highly influential book of the same title gave him a copyright on the term, at least in academic circles. Anderson asked how nationalism—the notion of a country with a distinct identity, interests, and borders to which one belonged—came to emerge so concretely by the end of the eighteenth century. And he insisted that while political states have borders, leaders, and populations, nationality and nationhood are *imagined,* because most of a nation's members will never actually meet one another, "yet in the mind of each lives the image of their communion." Furthermore, divisions based on class, race, and gender aside, people still manage, and still need to conceive of the nation "as a deep, horizontal comradeship."[3] In addition, the nation became imbued with a sense of destiny, and historical upheavals and discontinuities became part of a national story of historical continuity guided by and directed toward some larger, grander purpose.

The most pivotal development, Anderson argued, that transformed hunks of populated territories into imagined communities of nations was the newspaper. Every morning, at roughly the same time, people read the same stories about the nation, its leaders, and some of their fellow citizens in the newspaper. It was this daily ritual of taking in the same stories, the same knowledge, at the same time as you knew those who shared your country were, that forged this sense of comradeship with unseen others. And the paper, through its stories and, later, its images, was a concrete representation—one you held in your hands every day—that such a nation *did* exist and *did* have particular, distinctive characteristics.

Reading the newspaper may have been a crucial first step in cultivating this sense of national communion. But radio broadcasting did this on entirely new geographic, temporal, and cognitive levels, inflating people's desire to seek out, build on, and make more concrete the notion of the nation. For it wasn't just that this technology made imagined communities more tangible because people now listened to a common voice and a shared event at truly the exact moment as others around the region, or the country. Listeners themselves insisted that this technology enhance their ability to imagine their fellow citizens, as well as their ability to be transported to "national" events and to other parts of the country. Certainly advertisers and the networks, seeking to maximize profits by having as big an audience as possible, pushed radio to be "national" and promoted it ideologically as a nation-building technology. The sheer geographic scope that these new, simultaneous experiences now encompassed—when 40 million people, for example, tuned in to exactly the same thing—outstripped anything the newspaper had been able to do in terms of nation building on a psychic, imaginative level.

But before we get too carried away by this vision of one nation under the microphone, we must remember that people also used radio to tune in on difference, and to use that difference to imagine a pecking order within the nation, where they were often—but not always—on top. What survives as radio's historical record—the personal papers, press accounts, recorded shows—favors network history, often erasing the fact that radio was also always a local medium with independent stations. In other words, while it has become a commonplace to assert that radio built national unity in the 1930s and beyond, we must remember that what radio really did (and still does today) was allow listeners to experience at the same time multiple identities—national, regional, local—some of them completely allied with the country's prevailing cultural and political ideologies, others of them suspicious of or at odds with official culture.

There was also a new cognitive dimension to these imaginings that make radio's role in constructing imagined communities—including those that are oppositional to or uneasy with "the nation"—much more powerful than what print can do. This has to do in part with the act of listening itself, with the knowledge that you and other listeners are experiencing that very moment of your lives in exactly the same way. Hearing the president address you and others as "my fellow Americans," or Walter Winchell call out to "Mr. and Mrs. America and all the ships at sea," tied utterly diverse and unknown people together as an audience, even as subgroups of this audience resisted and cast themselves against such nationalist hailings.

In the very early years of radio, characterized by "DXing" (ham radio code for distance signaling), when listeners tried to tune in stations from as far away as possible, people didn't have to imagine their compatriots several states away—they heard them, with all their differences and similarities, on the air. The networks, which brought together a national audience for political conventions, presidential addresses, comedy, and drama, allowed people to hear and participate in the acts of communion—applause, laughter—that annealed them to the concept of nation, and of history "in the making." And there is no doubt that hearing excerpts from old radio shows, and the songs that used to be broadcast, activates a powerful nostalgia old newspapers just don't. Why is this?

Despite the anti-Semitic ravings of Father Coughlin, the "radio priest"; the incessant and irritating jingles for Swan soap, Jell-O, and Rheingold beer; the consignment of black people to roles as servants and buffoons; and despite the numbing repetition of Top 40 radio that made songs like "You and Me and a Dog Named Boo" national hits—we are inclined to remember the medium at its best. Perhaps that's because the music, the shows, the sports, and the news—even from the 1960s—seem so innocent and optimistic by today's standards, so free from the cynicism that now curdles public discourse. And let's not forget that broadcasters themselves consciously wedded radio to nostalgia early on, primarily by playing old favorites that reminded people of their youth. This was true in the 1920s, when old standards were listeners' favorite music to hear, and it was true of foreign-language stations in the 1920s and '30s, when songs from "the old country" transported immigrants back to their motherland and their youth.[4] There are few major radio markets today without an "oldies" station. Radio exploited and nurtured nostalgia, so that many listeners hearing in, say, 1945 a song they had first heard on the radio in 1930 were in fact nostalgic for their old nostalgia.

But I think there's more to radio nostalgia than simply longing for lost youth. Of course people become nostalgic when they see old television shows or movies that remind them of when they were growing up. But there is something very primal about hearing itself, about listening, that makes this medium so prone to being wrapped up in the gauze of nostalgia. "Radio stimulates the imagination"—this is a truly hackneyed platitude that we would do well to unpack, and to do so we have to focus on what happens when we listen. And we have to analyze *how* radio taught us to listen, and to what. Thirty years ago, in his best-selling book *Understanding Media*, Marshall McLuhan called radio "the tribal drum" because the medium promoted a real sense of collectivism among people that harkened back to "the ancient experience of kinship webs." He added that radio was "a subliminal echo chamber of magical power to touch remote and forgotten chords."[5] Although McLuhan had a tendency to get a bit carried away like this—and to cast technology as *the* most powerful and revolutionary force in history—his insistence that radio evoked the responses, desires, and imaginings of preliterate cultures deserves reconsideration.

Most of us probably think as much about all the different ways we've come to listen to radio as we do about how and when we breathe. Radio listening is such a mundane, effortless act that we have become oblivious to its complexities. Yet radio has taught us, socialized us how to listen to different things, and how to feel during different modes of listening. From the interactions between who we are and how—and during what eras—we learn these modes, we develop our own repertoires of listening. Think of the different listening modes we might inhabit in one day alone, and how we often actively seek out those modes, with the pleasurable anticipation of the way they will make us feel and where they might take us, cognitively and emotionally. When people tune in to NPR or Rush Limbaugh, to talk radio or the news, whatever the ideological thrust, they expect to concentrate, to follow histories, biographies, stories, and debates. This is different from listening to Jack Benny or Burns and Allen, and certainly different from channeling into a Top 40 station in the 1960s to hear "Dock of the Bay" or "Will You Love Me Tomorrow?"

In trying to conduct an archaeology of listening in the twentieth century, the radio historian finds herself without much to lean on. Those of us who do media studies, and those who study perception and the brain, have done almost no collaborative work to understand how watching television, or going on-line, might be different from listening to the radio. And surviving broadcasts are not autonomous "texts" that can be analyzed independently: people listened to them under a variety of circumstances. Nonetheless, there is exciting work to draw from, especially more recent research on music and emotions, that helps us understand people's powerful and intimate ties to radio.

It turns out that there probably are compelling physiological reasons people are so nostalgic for radio. People loved radio—and still do—because, as cognitive psychologists have shown, humans find it useful—in fact, highly pleasurable—to use our brains to create our own images. What we call our imagination is something the brain likes to feed by generating images almost constantly: that's what imagination is, the internal production of pictures, of images. Autobiographical accounts from great conceptual scientists like Michael Faraday, James Clerk Maxwell, or Albert Einstein describe a process in which they did their most creative work using visual imagery, which was later translated into equations and theorems.[6]

But even those of us who aren't geniuses often find the visual and spatial imaging that we do quite powerful. In fact, studies show that people tend to remember word sequences they have generated much better than those that have been spoon-fed to them, because such "active engagement" dramatically improves memory.[7] And this holds true for images and ideas as well. (We all know how disappointing it is to go to a movie made from a book we've read and find that the lead characters look nothing like the vivid portraits we had painted in our mind's eye.)

Obviously, people's visual imaging is richest when they aren't being bombarded by interference from externally produced images (as they are, for example, when they watch TV). And the more we work on making our own images, the more powerfully attached we become to them, arising as they do from deep within us. Processing external visual imagery is a very different—and more passive—cognitive mode from imagining one's own and, in fact, can often temporarily shut down, or at least overrun, the brain's own visual imaging apparatus. When two groups of children were given the beginning of a story—one group via radio, the other via TV—the children who had heard the story created much more imaginative conclusions than those who had seen the television version. It is interesting that children who see a story on TV remember the action better; those who hear it on the radio remember the dialogue better. Children also draw more imaginative pictures when they hear a story on the radio.[8] Imaginativeness is a skill that you develop and get better at, a skill that radio enhances.

Here we need to distinguish between hearing and listening. We can passively hear, but we must actively listen.[9] While much radio listening involves conscious attention to the program at hand, listeners can also shift cognitive gears and zone out into a more automatic, effortless mode. Right now, as you read this, you are hearing things you may not be paying much attention to—the light buzz of a computer, the hum of the fridge, birds chirping. Listening is active, and we usually notice when we change modes. You're in the supermarket with the usual Muzak playing—it's like the fluorescent lights, you don't even notice it—until a song you really hate (for me, that would be "Volare") or one you really like comes on and breaks through your concentration on the shopping list. Now you are listening, although certainly not with the same level of concentration as you would be at a lecture or during a news broadcast. Passive hearing, which is a kind of automatic processing, rarely becomes intertwined with what the "I" is thinking or doing; active listening almost always does.[10] And with radio listening, however automatic it may seem to flick the radio on (most come on automatically when we start our cars), we are still making a choice to enter a particular auditory realm. In fact, one of the pleasures of radio may come from the ability to move between such dramatically different states of awareness.

Certainly the listening process is not the same for all of us. And as we see how radio listening has changed over the years, it becomes crucial that we try somehow to historicize what listening "meant" in different eras. Sitting in the garage with headphones on while pulling voices out of a sea of static is related to, but different from, listening to a ball game while mowing the lawn. Listeners learn to respond to certain forms of address, to grow weary of some and embrace others. So while cognitive psychology offers exciting new insights as to why radio listening might be an especially rich pastime for many people, we must also proceed with caution. For learning how we listen and what moves us emotionally when we hear it is culturally determined as well, which is why sitar music might move an Indian to joy or sorrow and leave an American cold. Each culture, in different eras, trains its members' perceptual apparatus in particular ways, so that what might seem "hardwired" is often actually learned.[11] What researchers seem to be discovering is that there are basic structures for and internal sequences of communication within the brain that are then inflected by the culture within which one grows up.

When the radio boom first swept through America in the 1920s, the word *miracle* was used repeatedly to try to convey the revolutionary, and mystical, properties of the device. Radio really was miraculous then, but today the word *miracle* rings hollow and flat. It has been devalued and gutted as it has been used to describe the most banal things, from mayonnaise to laundry detergent. Yet there was a time when radio was pure magic, as hokey, naïve, and inflated as that may sound today. This wasn't simply because of its novelty. The magic was—and is—in the act of listening itself, in relying on and trusting your ears alone to produce ideas and emotions. The magic comes from entering a world of sound, and from using that sound to make your own vision, your own dream, your own world.

It is this absence of imagery that is radio's greatest strength, that allows people to bind themselves so powerfully to this device. It is this feature of radio—its extension and magnification of the ear, of hearing—that defines its meaning to the imaginative transformations of American life in this century. There is a cognitive basis for this. Dr. Mark Tramo, a neurobiologist at Harvard Medical School, emphasizes that when information comes solely through our auditory system, our mental imaging systems have freewheeling authority to generate whatever visuals they want. Many people seek out such sensory purity. Anyone who has camped in the woods at night, associating different night noises with all kinds of soothing and dangerous possibilities, knows the power of sound. And anyone who has darkened a room, closed his or her eyes, and lay down between giant stereo speakers turned up full blast knows the cognitive and emotional pleasure of focusing entirely on the purely auditory.[12] When sound is our only source of information, our imaginations milk it for all it's worth, creating detailed tableaux that images, of course, preempt. No wonder listening in—especially at night, with almost no visual interference—remains a primal experience fusing pleasure, activity, and desire.

I don't mean to suggest that we never use our imaginations when we watch a film or TV: often we are imagining how we would handle the situation we are watching, or we project ourselves into the film or TV show as the hero, the villain, the love object. We can imagine how the place we are seeing smells, or how the wind or sun feels on our skin—we imagine the senses that can't be addressed. But creating our own mental images of how things look is a much more pleasurable and powerful cognitive activity.

When radio listening as a craze, and then as a daily pastime, swept through America in the 1920s and '30s, it disrupted the cognitive and cultural practices of a visual culture and a literate culture in a way that neither the telephone nor the phonograph did. By the 1920s Americans, especially those in cities, took in a kaleidoscope of newspapers, magazines, billboards, advertising posters, vaudeville shows, electric lights, and movies. Illustrations and photographs had transformed nearly all printed material. Everywhere there were more and more pictures to help one reimagine the world and one's place in it. Seeing was regarded as the most important sense, the visual privileged over everything else. Seeing more, seeing farther, seeing better: this was what so much of the new technology in entertainment and in science strove for.

And then came radio. Certainly the device was hailed as the next logical step in some inevitable march toward progress and modernity. Here was a giant auditory prosthesis that extended people's range of hearing to distances previously unimaginable.[13]

But radio also carried people back into the realms of preliteracy, into orality, to a mode of communication reliant on storytelling, listening, and group memory. America became an odd hybrid in the 1920s and after, a modern, literate society grafted together with a traditional, preliterate, oral culture. It was an atavism Americans clearly loved. For orality generates a powerful participatory mystique. Because the act of listening simultaneously to spoken words forms hearers into a group (while reading turns people in on themselves), orality fosters a strong collective sensibility. People listening to a common voice, or to the same music, act and react at the same time. They become an aggregate entity—an audience—and whether or not they all agree with or like what they hear, they are unified around that common experience. So even though the visual system of the brain is larger and much more extensive than its auditory system, it seems that hearing's immediate and transitory quality is what gives it such power. The fact that we hear not only with our ears but also with our entire bodies—our bones, our innards vibrate, too, to sounds, and certainly to music—means that we are actually

feeling similar sensations in our bodies at exactly the same time when we listen as a group.[14]

In part because of this physical response, listening often imparts a sense of
emotion stronger than that imparted by looking. "Listening," argues one researcher on perception, "is centripetal; it pulls you into the world. Looking is
centrifugal; it separates you from the world." While sight allows us some distance and power—the power to gaze, study, dissect, to be removed, apart from
our surroundings—sound envelops us, pouring into us whether we want it to
or not, including us, involving us. Even before we are born, we can hear others.
As infants, when our eyes are still struggling to focus, we are much more
soothed, startled, or scared by sounds than by sights. As we grow up, "hearing
is the precondition for the integration of people into their environment";
through listening, we learn proper social behavior and speech.[15]

Our ears have always been part of humans' early warning system about
danger. We can close our eyes but not our ears; darkness curtails seeing, and
thus accentuates hearing all the more. And sound—a glass shattering, a ball
hitting a bat, a door slamming—usually telegraphs change and often triggers
an emotional response to that change. Listening, without being able to see
what or who goes with the sounds, takes us back to a way of being in the world
nearly obliterated by modern society. And since the auditory world is a fleeting world, an immediate world—words, unlike images, are perishable, gone as
soon as they are uttered—listening encourages a concentration on the present.
"What is heard on the air is transitory, as fleeting as time itself, and it therefore
seems *real*," noted researchers in the 1930s. When the listener turns his dial,
they added, "he wants to enter the stream of life as it is actually lived."[16] It is especially this evanescent nature of what we hear, this absolute simultaneity of
experience, that drives us to bond together.

And let's not forget that radio performers and producers turned the use of
sound into an art. Hadley Cantril and Gordon Allport, two pioneers in radio
research, noted how radio produced "close-ups" of sound, extracting the last
ounce of emotional quality from even the "sound of silence." "When it comes
to producing eerie and uncanny effects," they added, "the radio has no rival."
They noted that even in the early 1930s, listeners would "enhance this distinctive quality of radio" by sitting in the dark and closing their eyes so that "their
fantasies are free." In no time the listener could jump from ancient Rome to a
Los Angeles police precinct, then to a haunted house, and, even better, the
image she conjured up could be three-dimensional, wasn't confined to a movie
screen or a proscenium, didn't have a curtain framing it, and wasn't subject to
any theatrical artificiality. It was, in many ways, *better* than seeing. Celebrating
this new emphasis on "the listener's visual imagery, a relatively neglected func-

tion of the adult human mind," Cantril and Allport offered a prophetic prediction, and this in 1935: "The advent of television will change the situation and will destroy one of the most distinctive benefits that radio has brought to a too literal-minded mankind."[17]

Listening to radio also forged powerful connections between people's inner, thinking selves and other selves, other voices, from quite faraway places. Inner speech is, of course, an almost continuous aspect of our selves, as we think and talk silently to ourselves throughout the day.[18] It accompanies all the rest of our experiences and is the inner thread of continuity to our sense of being in the world. With radio, this interior "I" began oscillating with the voices of those never met, never even seen. Some of these were the voices of the politically powerful and the rich, others were of ministers, educators, or labor leaders, and still others of comedians, singers, and actors. By the mid-1930s, with the highly commercialized network system in place, a great majority of these voices—which sought to sound familiar, intimate, even folksy—represented a centralized consumer culture.

How one's inner voice resonated with these was now part of a new national dynamic. So was the process of imagining who was speaking, of visualizing what was happening and comparing your highly personal yet mediated imaginings with those of others. Obviously, people imagined what was being described on the air. But they could also picture what was not described, adding their own details and flourishes. And they had to imagine the fantastical, things they had never actually seen, like the Martians in *The War of the Worlds*.[19] There were pleasures, then, in belonging to the group while standing above it. There was a reaffirming sense of synthesis, of harmony, in knowing that your vision of Jack Benny's vault, where he hid all his money, was in sync with everybody else's. But at the same time, hearing something rather than seeing it allowed you to hold something in reserve that was just yours, your own distinctive image and vision. Your image of Benny's vault was simultaneously your creation and part of a collective vision. I am not a McLuhanite—I do believe that the actual content of radio programs matters and plays a great role in the device's influence. But we can't really understand radio unless we also focus on its distinctive address to the ears and our own interiority.

At the same time that radio activated people's imaginations in powerful and freeing ways, the medium could be less demanding, especially if you were listening to music. You could do something else while listening, you didn't have to watch and you didn't have to concentrate, depending on what was on. Radio could adjust much more to physical circumstances—cooking dinner, driving to work—than any of the other media. We could "continue with our lives" while listening.[20] This meant that radio listening also became interwoven with the ritualized routines of everyday life—reading the paper, eating meals. So even when radio was little more than an auditory escort through the day, it became enmeshed in people's memories of the stages of their days and their lives.

There is another reason people's associations with the songs on the radio are so intimate and fond: people's relationship to music is so emotionally intense. There is a physiological reason for this too: the brain's musical networks and emotional circuits are connected. According to Mark Tramo, the auditory system of the brain feeds into the limbic system, the part of the brain from which we derive emotions and memory. The limbic system then generates a host of associations and emotional states. Once activated in a pleasurable way, the limbic system may want to sustain that level of arousal. When a DJ seeks to create the perfect segue from one favorite song to another, he is responding to his limbic system's signal back to the auditory system, asking for more of the same.[21]

Cognitive psychologists suspect that there is a physiological explanation for why people like hearing the same piece of music, whether it's *Eine kleine Nachtmusik* or "My Girl," over and over. The brain apparently becomes accustomed to patterns of music based on exposure to different musical traditions and stores knowledge of certain kinds of musical sequences in groups of cells. Based on these stored connections, the brain will predict which notes will come next in a sequence. When this prediction is right, the connections between the brain cells where these sequences have been stored become even stronger. The more we listen to certain kinds of music, then, the more we learn to like it. While the brain seems to like the surprise that comes when musical expectations are violated—such as through syncopation, dissonance, or unusual melodies—evidence suggests that predictability produces more pleasure. Successful music in a range of styles handles this paradox by setting up our musical expectations and then toying with them before providing a familiar resolution.[22]

So the inevitability in music that the brain seems to like is both physiological and cultural, for our culture teaches us what is inevitable and what isn't. As the science writer Robert Jourdain notes in *Music, the Brain, and Ecstasy,* "For every musical style, there is a style of musical expectation." He reminds us, too, of what we already know from everyday life: different people listen differently at different times, some looking for a stimulant, some for a tranquilizer, some for distraction, some for intensity and clamor.[23] It also seems clear that most people's musical tastes get established during adolescence. While people seek out more complex music as they grow up, many reach a point, sometime in adulthood, when their established mental groovings prevent them from enjoying new music, like punk or rap. Hence the success of "oldies" and "swing" stations.

Most people listen to music to enhance, or travel to, a particular mood. Researchers have found that many people, often unconsciously, use various media to alter bad moods or sustain good ones, and men especially choose very involving media to blot out anxieties.[24] This is one reason why the development of "formats" in radio became so successful—when people turn to the "country and western" or "modern rock" or "sports" station, they know exactly what moods and feelings will be evoked and stroked.

Radio in the 1920s and beyond, then, reasserted the importance of listening in a visual culture, and it required—or at least allowed—people to develop a repertoire of listening styles and emotional responses depending on the programming and site of listening. Radio cultivated two broad categories of listening, linguistic and musical. Listening ranged from highly concentrated and serious, as when people tuned in H. V. Kaltenborn during the Munich crisis, to barely attentive, as when radio provided "beautiful" background music. And certainly some music listening, like following an opera or singing along at the top of your lungs with Aretha Franklin, is deeply engrossing and transporting. There are pleasures in listening with others and pleasures in listening alone.

People indeed developed an ear for radio and over the years acquired multiple and overlapping listening competencies. There seem to be three major ways that listening to the radio activates us cognitively. First, of course, is that we listen for information: What did Congress do today? Who won the ball game? Where did the Germans bomb? Why was the Grateful Dead concert canceled? What was the name of that last song? This is a relatively flat kind of listening: we are taking in dates, names, times, concepts, and the like but are not asked to imagine much.

Dimensional listening is another matter and is activated by a range of genres. Here, whether we were listening to *Fibber McGee and Molly,* Edward R. Murrow on a London rooftop during the blitz, Jean Shepherd, or the Chicago Cubs, we created in our mind's eye three-dimensional locales; saw living rooms, cityscapes, battlefields, ballparks; watched the cascading contents of a closet, or distant flares, or a bat cracking a ball. This listening is work—you have to keep track of people and locations—but it is also highly gratifying because it is your own invention.

Concentrated music listening is dimensional as well, for here you enter the layers of the music. Music is dynamic, has patterns of harmonies and sequences, backgrounds and foregrounds that one can move between. A Beethoven symphony and "Purple Haze" both have this dimensional quality, and with popular music listeners often move between memorizing the lyrics and focusing on the instrumentation. Of course, not everyone listens to music this way, or at least not all the time: often, people also let it simply wash over them.

The third way in which radio listening seems to bring forth certain cognitive and emotional modes is through associational listening. Here I'm drawing from recent models of the memory as an "associative network" in which concepts and images are linked together in our brains not according to some grand, chronological scheme but rather according to the often haphazard sensory relations that characterized an event or period in our lives. When one node in the memory is activated, it activates the other nodes with which it was associated at the time.[25] Whatever I might think of the song "Incense and Peppermints" by the Strawberry Alarm Clock (!), I can't help but have the first few bars hurl me immediately back to 1967. Repeated constantly on the radio as I drove around with my boyfriend, went to work, or sunbathed at the beach, the song evokes a host of associations with past people and places. It was this ongoing auditory repetition that allowed radio to forge especially strong links in our memories between our personal lives and the broader sweep of popular culture.

The different modes of listening that radio cultivated drew from and intermixed informational, dimensional, and associational listening to varying degrees. The earliest mode, pioneered by "ham" operators but pursued by millions of others during the 1920s, was exploratory listening, in which people—mostly men—put on headphones to see how far they could listen and what they could pick up. Ham operators today are the remaining devotees of such listening. As radio programming became more routinized, Americans developed both concentrated and distracted musical listening, the former especially promoted by "musical appreciation" programs, the broadcast of opera and symphonies, and later by DJs and by "free-form" programming on FM stations in the late 1960s and early 1970s. The "beautiful music" format, so favored in dentists' offices and elevators, insists on distracted listening, which is why so many music lovers loathe it.

Dramas, plays, soap operas, and many radio comedies tapped into and reshaped story listening, a pleasurable mode of listening that requires concentration on language, wordplay, verbal imagery, and sound effects. While story listening was all but unavailable on radio by the 1960s, people like Jean Shepherd on WOR in New York kept it alive, as does NPR today. News listening called for similar concentration but, especially with the outbreak of World War II, was much more serious and, as cultivated by Edward R. Murrow, H. V. Kaltenborn, and others, required the imagining of national and international maps, a focusing on the fateful relationships between the individual, the family, and the world. Sometimes news listening was strictly informational, but especially when an eyewitness report came on and reporters turned to the first person, listeners were asked to shift quickly into a dimensional mode.

Various rock and pop DJs from the 1950s to the 1970s, on AM and then FM, cultivated breakout listening, a combination of music and patter listening that asked for concentration on the music, especially its beat and lyrics, and encouraged a sense of transport to a rebellious auditory outpost hipper than the rest of the mainstream media. In the 1980s, with the reining in of the music DJ by program directors and syndicators, Don Imus and Howard Stern became the exemplars of a new, even more transgressive version of breakout listening. FM stations—the pioneering classical music stations of the 1950s and then the underground or free-form stations of the late 1960s and early 1970s—cultivated fidelity listening, in which listeners immersed themselves in the lush, layered, stereophonic soundscapes that the new technology made possible.

Governing and encasing much of this was the voice of authority—the ads—which asked for obedient, uncritical listening, although it was not always forthcoming. Ad listening insisted that people concentrate on sales pitches and adopt a worldview in which there is no problem that can't be solved by consumer goods. Since sales pitches are an affront to our autonomy and freedom of choice, while the notion that you can just buy something to solve thorny personal dilemmas is quite seductive, ad listening was and remains a mode of deep ambivalence, in which resentment often predominates but the welcome mat is not entirely hidden.

People's repertoires of listening, of course, varied, depending on their individual traits and their level of education, their race, their gender, their age, and so forth. But radio foregrounded and promoted certain modes of listening that dominated particular eras, and this played a powerful role in forging generational identity. People developed special affinities for the modes of listening that they grew up with and that dominated their lives as young adults. So when people are nostalgic about radio, whether it's for Jack Benny or Wolfman Jack, it is a nostalgia for a distinct, bedrock way of perceiving one's place in the world, through modes of listening, that is tied to one's youth.

In other words, people are nostalgic not just for *what* they listened to but for *how* they listened to it. Researchers know that music helps produce social cohesion among groups, and throughout history music in various forms has been an intrinsic, essential part of cultural rituals. By the early twentieth century in America, music began to take on more of a generational identity, as ragtime, and especially jazz, swing, rock 'n' roll, and rap were generally embraced by the young and shunned by their elders. Because most Americans develop their musical preferences when they are teenagers, they choose certain music to express their solidarity with their peers.[26] And since the 1920s radio has been the key distributor of popular music. When the pleasure of recognition is tied to memory—to songs from one's youth, from the past—the powerful delights of repetition, nostalgia, sense of membership in a generation, and a defined historical moment fuse to further cement people's romantic attachments to the radio of their youth.

The zen of listening comes not only from the transporting qualities of auditory processing. It stems also from the unfathomable and magical nature of radio propagation. The fact that most people didn't really understand how radio worked added to its allure. Here we should turn briefly to technology. That realm out there—first called the ether, then, less romantically, the electromagnetic spectrum—is invisible, but it isn't "the air," even though it became common to refer to radio waves going through the air. People are also nostalgic for the vagaries of radio transmission, for the vexing but romantic unpredictability of shortwave broadcasts from Europe during the war, for the ability to pull in an AM station several states away. What gave AM its particular properties?

For decades scientists and engineers sought to help people understand radio by using the analogy of the pond and the stone. You throw a stone into a pond—that's the radio signal—and ripples flow out in all directions—those are the radio waves—until they hit the shore—your radio receiver. The crests of the waves radiate in a pattern, and the distance between each crest is the wavelength. The longer the wavelength, the lower its frequency: fewer of them hit the shore. And the shorter the wavelength, the higher the frequency. The height of each wave is its amplitude, the number of waves hitting the shore per second is its frequency. Transmitters at AM stations superimpose sound on these waves by altering, or modulating, the waves' amplitude; at FM stations they modulate the frequency. As these signals travel farther and farther from their transmitter, they become attentuated, weaker.

It is about at this point in the explanation that most people's attention begins to wander. This water analogy, which has at least helped most of us understand the rudiments of radio signaling, has also perpetuated the sense that radio waves need a physical medium, like the air, in which to move: if they're going to make ripples, they have to make them out of *something*. Hence the notion of "the ether," that turn-of-the-century phantasm that served as such a crucial bridging concept for everyday people (and many scientists and inventors as well) as they sought to grasp how messages could travel without wires from one place to another.

James Clerk Maxwell, the scientist who predicted the existence of electromagnetic waves in 1865, advanced the notion of this invisible medium, which included light and heat as well as radio waves. Referred to also, even more mystically, as the "luminiferous ether," it was "imponderable"; it filled all unoccupied space, it was invisible and elastic, it was odorless, and while it was everywhere, it did not interfere with the motion of bodies through space.[27] But radio waves were thought to disturb it and produce waves in it, just like the stone in the pond. This was, in other words, a mechanical model, not an electronic one, which is why "the ether" was helpful to people's imaginings about radio but not to their comprehension of how it worked. Efforts to prove the existence of the ether failed, and by the 1920s the notion had been abandoned except by the popular press.

Rick Ducey, of the National Association of Broadcasters, suggests that it's more helpful if we think about radio waves as energy, especially since the radio frequency portion of the electromagnetic spectrum, which we can't see or touch, goes beyond the limits of human perception.[28] But we are familiar with sound as energy, having seen the clichéd demonstration of the singer whose tones shatter glass or watched (and felt) our stereo speakers vibrate when we turn the music up too high. The part of the spectrum that most of us hear as sound is roughly between 1,000 and 12,000 to 15,000 hertz (cycles per second). To put it another way, the energy in that frequency range we experience as sound. (The human ear can detect sounds in the range of 20 to 20,000 hertz, but normal conversation, for example, is usually around 1,000 hertz.) But our personal audio apparatus is not capable of detecting more rapid frequencies, and as you move up the spectrum, you move out of the audio frequency range and, eventually, into the radio frequency range of energy. To detect that energy, at that speed, you need electronic circuitry. Energy way up the spectrum—vibrating at one billion megahertz—our eyes respond to; we perceive this as light.

Most people don't want to know about radio circuitry, or, for that matter, about the electromagnetic spectrum. But people do remain curious about precisely those features of radio that enable or prevent their hearing farther, more clearly, or with more fidelity. Why was it, for example, that in the 1950s and '60s, people could hear far-off AM stations at night but they can't with FM? Why does FM sound better?

Depending on their frequency, radio waves travel around the earth differently. FM, which today is the standard, relies on "direct" waves, which travel only to the horizon and then off into space, which is why FM's range is limited to approximately 50 miles. AM, by contrast, benefits from both ground-wave and sky-wave propagation. Ground waves follow the curvature of the earth before dissipating and thus go farther than direct waves, sometimes up to 75 miles during the day. Sky waves travel away from the earth but can be reflected back to it by the ionosphere. When sky waves are bent back to earth, they can "land" hundreds, even thousands of miles away from the transmitting station.

AM frequencies are not bent as dramatically by the ionosphere as shortwaves are and thus can't achieve the distances that shortwaves can. But at night they can often go much farther than during the day, anywhere from 100 to 1,500 miles from the transmitter. This is because the lower layers of the ionosphere (called the D and E layers by radio technicians), which are approximately 45 to 75 miles above the earth's surface, act like a huge sponge during the day, absorbing the signals that pass through them. But after the sun sets these layers disappear, and the ones above them—anywhere from 90 to 250 miles above the earth—combine to form a dense layer that acts like a mirror to sky waves. The reason that DXing was such an adventure, and so unpredictable, in the 1920s was that the ionosphere itself is constantly moving and billowing, both horizontally and vertically, making the reception of some frequencies, from some locations, crystal clear one night and silent the next.[29]

In other words, the special characteristics of AM propagation made radio listening ideal for building etheric communities, because people could skip over distances and hear so much farther than they can with FM. In the early 1920s some local stations around the country instituted "silent nights," when they went off the air so listeners could try to pick up faraway stations. As transmitters increased in power—from 500 to 5,000 to 25,000 and then 50,000 watts on some stations by the late 1920s—obviously their more powerful signals could travel farther. But stations at the lower end of the AM band, near 550 kilohertz, could cover a much broader area with less power than those higher up the band, between 1,200 and 1,500 kilohertz, which might need ten times the power to cover the same distance.[30] Other factors, like whether the signal travels over water, especially salt water, or whether the soil around a radio station is especially conductive electrically, can also extend a station's reach.

FM—frequency modulation—sounds better than AM in part because it's in a portion of the spectrum less prone to natural interference, and because its channel width is 200 kilohertz—twenty times the 10-kilohertz channel width that AM has. In fact, the discrepancy is even worse, because the AM channel has only a 5-kilohertz information capacity. With so much more frequency space, there's more room in which to encode more information, so FM has a rich sound resolution AM simply can't achieve. FM, because it operates on higher frequencies than AM, is also slightly better at penetrating solids, like buildings, which is why you hear FM slightly longer when you drive through a tunnel, while AM dissolves into static as soon as you enter.[31]

Regulation also ensured network radio's ability to expand its scope. In 1928 the Federal Radio Commission, the predecessor to the FCC and the first government agency empowered to assign radio frequencies and issue licenses, came up with the designation "cleared stations." The FRC divided the United States into five listening zones, with each zone granted eight cleared stations, which broadcast at a maximum of 25,000 and, later, 50,000 watts. The FRC bequeathed these clear-channel allocations to the more expensive, high-powered stations owned by or affiliated with NBC or CBS, like KYW in Chicago, KDKA in Pittsburgh, or WBZA in Boston. Each of these stations got an allocation, like 760 on the AM dial for WJZ, New York, or 650 for WSM in Nashville, that it didn't have to share with anyone else in the country, not even on an opposite coast, unless that station broadcast only during the day.[32] In 1928 only a few stations—KDKA, WGY in Schenectady, WEAF in New York—were broadcasting with 50,000 watts, and this became the upper limit of power that the U.S. government would allow.

The rationale for such "clear-channel" stations was that listeners in rural areas with inexpensive or even homemade sets who were not within range of a radio station, or a station with adequate power (most rural stations in the 1920s were 50- or 100-watt stations; some even as low as 25), could now be served, especially at night. By the 1950s it was these clear-channel, or Class I stations, like WDIA out of Memphis, that listeners at night delighted in reeling in.

As radio programming evolved in the 1920s and '30s, it built on modes of listening that were centuries old. It brought forth new ways of thinking about who was your friend and neighbor, who you were connected to and on what basis, and whether machines destroyed communities and traditions or simply reconfigured them. But most of all the turn to listening reactivated, extended, and intensified particular cognitive modes that encouraged, simultaneously, a sense of belonging to a community, an audience, and a confidence that your imaginings, your radio visions, were the best and truest ones of all.

The Ethereal World

Driving alone at night, in the darkened car, reassured by the night-light of the dashboard, or lying in bed tuned to a disembodied voice or music, evokes a spiritual, almost telepathic contact across space and time, a reassurance that we aren't alone in the void: we have kindred spirits. You engage with a phantom whose voice and presence you welcomed, needed. The feeling isn't some naïve, bathetic sense of universal "brotherly love" (although under certain circumstances, and especially with various mind-altering substances, such an illusion is possible), but there is a sense of camaraderie and mutuality coming from the sky itself. And since there are—unlike on television—so many different musical communities to tie in to by turning the radio dial—rock and pop, religious, country and western, classical music—most listeners find a tribal outpost in the air. Yes, there are commercials too, often plenty of them, and they usually disrupt the sense of rapport we have with that glowing portion of our dashboard. There is reason to believe that people hate radio commercials even more than those on television because of our more intimate relationship with radio, and the greater sense of violation the commercials bring.

Emphasizing radio's connection throughout the twentieth century to a persistent sense of spiritual longing and loss is essential to any understanding of what radio has done to us and for us. This, too, stems from hearing without seeing. For aurality—hearing, listening for voices, to music, to "the word"—is the driving force in cosmologies of many cultures around the world. I don't mean to suggest that listening to Rudy Vallee or Casey Kasem was like a religious experience (although perhaps, for some, it was). I am talking more about the medium itself and the way that receivers reel in distant voices out of that incomprehensible dimension called the spectrum and effortlessly bring them straight to us, inking us, through the air, to unseen others. The fact that radio waves are invisible, emanate from "the sky," carry disembodied voices, and can send signals deep into the cosmos links us to a much larger, more mysterious order.

It is customary for us to regard science and technology as two of the major factors in cutting us off from one another, in undermining our faith that we are part of some grand scheme. Science and technology often have been cast as deeply antagonistic to the soul, to any sense of spirituality. Radio first proliferated in America in the 1920s, when the competition between science and religion over ultimate cultural authority reached a new intensity. (It is noteworthy that the first major trial avidly followed over the radio was the Scopes trial of 1925.) But radio, when it made its debut in America, was different. The way radio was first written about, as a magical, supernatural phenomenon, suggests that "the ether" and its disembodied voices from around the country somehow bridged the widening gap between machines and spirituality, and helped create an imaginative space where these two were reconciled. Radio burrowed into this unspoken longing for a contact with the heavens, for a more perfect community, for a spiritual transcendence not at odds with, but made possible by, machines.

Ever since the 1840s, after the telegraph was introduced, various inventors and crackpots had sought to send signals through water or air without connecting wires. But it was Guglielmo Marconi who exploited Heinrich Hertz's discovery of electromagnetic radiation and showed that radio waves could be used to transmit Morse code over hundreds, and then thousands, of miles. He did so at a time when naval ships still communicated with semaphores, homing pigeons, or flags, and when all ships were on their own, incommunicado, once they lost sight of the shore. The transatlantic cable service was slow, expensive, and under monopoly control. Marconi's invention promised an end to shipboard isolation—and danger—and a new competition for the complacent cable companies. When he introduced his "wireless telegraph" to America in 1899, he was hailed in the press as a hero and a wizard.

Wireless fanned long-standing fantasies and, from its earliest introduction, evoked psychic metaphors. It worked, wrote the *New York Herald* simply, "like magic." Being able to speak to others through the air in an electromagnetic voice "would be almost like dreamland and ghostland," concluded one writer in 1902. It seemed the technical equivalent of telepathy. *Popular Science Monthly* observed that, through wireless, "the nerves of the whole world [were], so to speak, being bound together." *Century Magazine* envisioned friends and relatives calling each other across the world, "from pole to pole," in electronic voices.[2] While we are much less smitten by the wonders of radio today, somewhere in each of us, in each of our lives, is this memory of listening to the radio and feeling something akin to spiritual transcendence. When radio was new, millions felt this way.

The man who most explicitly made this connection between radio and spirituality was Sir Oliver Lodge. And when he did, in 1920, at the start of the radio boom in America, intellectuals, scientists, and newspaper editors posed the same question: Had Sir Oliver become addled? Or, worse, had he turned into a quack? Today this question rings no bells at all—few people have even heard of Oliver Lodge or know that debates about his mental state were a major controversy. But back in the 1910s and early '20s, at the end of the Great War, this question raged through the popular press of England and America.

This was when certain scientists, inventors, and explorers were international celebrities, lionized in the press and admired by millions. As the 1920s historian Frederick Lewis Allen put it, "The prestige of science was colossal." So when Sir Oliver, one of the preeminent physicists in the Western world, spoke to sellout crowds in places like Carnegie Hall not about atoms or electromagnetism but about séances, mediums, and communicating with the dead, it was big news. In the first two months of 1920 alone, *The New York Times* published five editorials, plus a range of articles and book reviews, all critical of Lodge, all wondering "how such a man can believe what he does."[3] Lodge's conversion from science to séances was a minor scandal.

Lodge had become preeminent by experimenting with the transmission of radio waves, and in 1897 he patented his method of "syntonized telegraphy," which embodied the fundamental principles of radio tuning. He also developed theories about the ether—that invisible, mysterious, all-pervading medium through which radio waves allegedly moved—and conducted experiments to establish its properties. He served as president of the Physical Society of London and was one of the leaders of the British Association for the Advancement of Science. King Edward VII knighted him in 1902 in recognition of his contributions to the advancement of physics in general and wireless telegraphy in particular. And now, here he was on the American lecture circuit, praising mediums, insisting the dead don't really die, and describing contacts with the spirit world. Between January and May of 1920, Lodge spoke in fifty

American cities and towns, giving nearly one hundred lectures to tens of thousands of people, the two favorites being "Reality of the Unseen" and "Evidence of Survival."[4]

Lodge was one of the foremost advocates of a huge fad in the immediate postwar years, the stunning rise in spiritualism in both England and America. His prestige as a scientist lent him great credibility, and he became a media celebrity in the late 1910s and early '20s, sought after to give speeches, grant interviews, and write magazine articles. He was often swarmed by autograph seekers, and thousands wrote to him for advice. Denounced by other scientists as a "social menace," and attacked by intellectuals and writers for purveying "nauseating drivel," promoting "the recrudescence of superstition," and exerting a "maleficent influence" on the overly credulous, Lodge responded with articles titled "Between Two Worlds," "The Etherial World," and "How I Know the Dead Exist."[5]

Not since the 1850s had there been such a fascination in America with the occult and such a yearning to believe in psychic phenomena. Throughout the country séances, mediums, photographs of ghosts, and accounts of levitations and intercourse with the dead proliferated, with the help of considerable media sensationalism. As one of Lodge's critics complained, "As usual, the press magnified the phenomenon and our semi-hysterical generation hastened to see and hear the latest novelty." Sales of Ouija boards were enormous—educators denounced them as "an alarming factor in college life"—and they were used by some to speculate on Wall Street or predict the weather as well as to communicate with "the other side."[6]

Sir Arthur Conan Doyle, probably Britain's most popular novelist at the time, was also a believer and toured and wrote widely about communing with the dead and watching what he called ectoplasm emanate from a medium's nose and mouth. Thomas Edison, never one to be left out of the media spotlight, gave an exclusive interview to the *American Magazine* announcing that he was developing "an apparatus designed to enable those who have left this earth to communicate with those of us who are still on the earth." The device would be based, he assured readers, on solid "scientific methods."[7] By the mid-1920s the rage had abated, but while it lasted it was intense and extremely controversial, and few were more controversial than Lodge.

Observers at the time cited the same obvious reason for the fervor: the hideous, senseless carnage of the Great War. The losses still stupefy us: 10–13 million soldiers killed; at least 20 million wounded; half a generation of young men annihilated. And for what? Millions of bereaved parents, siblings, wives, and sweethearts asked this question, and could barely stand their loss. With a growing sense that life might indeed be meaningless—especially with the spread of mechanization—that living for today was all there was, affirmation of an afterlife, especially by men of science, was, at least for some, reassuring, even exhilarating. "It is simply impossible," wrote Frank Ballard in *Living Age,* "that Europe should have gone through these four years of horror amid war's sickening slaughter, without raising to a pathetic pitch the age-long human wonder as to what happens after death—anything or nothing? And if something—what?"[8]

As for millions of others, the war made this question a personal one for Sir Oliver Lodge. In September 1915 his youngest son, Raymond, was killed by a shell fragment while fighting in the trenches of Ypres. Lodge was devastated by the loss. In his son's memory Lodge wrote his most controversial, most vilified, and most profitable book, published in 1916. It was titled, simply enough, *Raymond.* And it was a sensation. Six reprints had to be published in one month to meet the demand, and by 1922 twelve editions has been issued.[9] In the book Lodge asserted that Raymond was still alive in a spirit world and contacted his father regularly. Lodge described the various séances he attended in which "automatists" claiming to write "automatic" messages from the dead, transmitted reassuring messages to him from his son. References to people and events only Raymond or Sir Oliver knew about cemented Lodge's faith in the communications. And the messages comforted Lodge that the boys who had lost their lives so prematurely were content and peaceful "on the other side."

To give these accounts legitimacy, Lodge used the language of science, describing himself as an "experimenter" who collected evidence through careful procedures to develop a "theory of his observations." He argued that direct sensory impressions—the ability to see or hear or touch a natural phenomenon—were simply inadequate to the demands of modern science. And he kept likening radio experimentation to explorations of the supernatural. After all, sending signals, and then the human voice, through "the air," without any connecting wire, was once thought to be a fantastic impossibility; now it was a fact of life. In an invisible region like the spectrum, one had to rely on "the imaginary." Why wouldn't this be true for investigations into the afterlife? You couldn't see electromagnetic waves, or hear them or touch them, yet their existence was now a proven fact. Lodge reminded his readers that the ether is "only strange to us because we have no sense-organ for its direct apprehension." But on the heels of carefully building this argument, Lodge included in *Raymond* reports from mediums that the recently departed men smoked cigars and "call[ed] for whiskey sodas," prompting hoots of ridicule in the press.

It was in writings like this, charged his critics, that "the mingling of physics and psychics is most amazing."[10]

Lodge's mingling of science and the occult helps us understand, in some small way, why the spiritual notion of "the miracle" was used so frequently to characterize the collection of coils, condensers, transformers, and tubes that became the radio. His very phrase "the ethereal world" suggested a magical, psychically intense dimension that could be truly appreciated only by those with imagination *and* intellect. Despite Darwin—in fact, because of science and technology—people could reaffirm their ties to a deity. Lodge, a seminal figure in the development of radio, himself embodied the connections between mysticism and machines. More to the point, he suggested that there were untold connections between radio and spiritualism, and that radio waves and the spirits of the undead inhabited the same dimension, the wavy, murky, howling ether. Here he was backed up by Sir Arthur Conan Doyle, who asserted that messages from the other side would come via radio. "They have transmitters in the line of ether," he announced, "and all we have to have is the receiver."[11]

Lodge argued, in fact, that the inhabitants of the other side were themselves made of ether. As his biographer noted, Lodge "hoped to show that the ether could in some way be the instrument of uniting the material and the spirit worlds." Thus, according to Lodge, the ether "is the connecting link between the worlds and blends them all into a cosmos." Lodge evoked parallel universes, invisible realms, disembodied voices crying out to be heard. He moved back and forth between the language of physics—and especially of wireless telegraphy—and the language of spiritualism, so that the ether was a medium of transmission but so was a person who "allows his or her hand or arm or voice to be actuated by an intelligence not their own." A medium functions like a radio, because he or she "receives impressions or ideas and merely converts them into the ordinary code of language."[12] In either psychical or physical transmission, a medium was required, but the properties of the medium, what allowed it to send and receive, remained mysterious, romantic, thrilling, forbidden.

It is not customary to point to the spiritualism craze as setting the stage for the radio boom that began in 1920. After all, spiritualism was just a fad and had fizzled by the end of the decade. Nor can we document that any of the millions of men and boys who would shortly take to the ether ever heard or read Lodge's dissertations on the afterlife, even though they were widely circulated. Other factors—the rise of mass entertainments like the movies, the spread of consumer technologies from the auto to the washing machine, the increased importance of corporations like AT&T and GE in managing the economy—these seem to have been more closely related to the birth of broadcasting, and of course they were. Indeed, ethereal, otherworldly, renditions of radio's meaning to America stood in stark contrast to the economic and technical facts. By the early 1910s all of the important components of radio were controlled by major corporations like GE and AT&T, and by the mid-1920s the communications company it helped form in 1919—the Radio Corporation of America—were known derisively in the press as "the radio trust."

To those who controlled it, the device had nothing to do with yearnings about immortality or the desire to tap cosmic riddles: it was a business and one they determined to make profitable. The real direction the device was moving in had little to do with setting people and their imaginings free. It would, instead, often tether them to much more materialistic and earthbound discourses.

But overlooking the spiritualism craze, and Lodge's role in it, would be a mistake, for it gives us important clues about the imaginative terrain that radio would initially encounter, interact with, and reshape, a terrain that remains very much a part of the invention's legacy. The special relationship that many listeners had with their phonographs in the late nineteenth and early twentieth centuries suggests why they were willing audiences for Lodge. Edison himself, in promoting the phonograph, emphasized how it brought, for the performer, a form of immortality. "Centuries after you have crumbled to dust," his phonograph "will repeat again and again to a generation that will never know you, every idle thought, every fond fancy, every vain word that you choose to whisper against this thin iron diaphragm." For listeners, as Evan Eisenberg has noted in *The Recording Angel*, "record listening is a séance where we get to choose our ghosts."[13]

But it is the historian William Kenney's fine work on the cultural history of the phonograph that has uncovered listeners' own accounts in the early 1920s of using the device to simulate a kind of temporary resurrection. Many deliberately used their phonograph records of old family favorites to make them feel closer to a dead parent or sibling who had loved the same songs. To achieve this sort of psychic séance, listeners played records that "take us back to Grandfather days" or played the songs sung at a parent's funeral. The invisible voice of the record helped conjure up the loved one's spirit, and the listener simultaneously mourned and felt in contact with the beloved spirit he or she had used music to summon. As Kenney puts it, the phonograph served, in part, as a "mass-produced 'private' shrine at which to summon forth spirits that allowed listeners momentarily to escape from the ravages of time into a domain in which dead loved ones seem to live once again."[14]

Radio listening, while not permitting someone to evoke these feelings on command exactly when he or she wanted to, nonetheless built on these associations between listening to music and summoning the dead. And it added communion with and access to otherworldly sounds. The spiritualism craze reflected many Americans' desire for more psychic intensity, for more contact across the voids of space and time, for participating in communication that was truly meaningful. So did the radio boom.

Lodge's conflation of radio and spiritualism in 1920, at the very moment Frank Conrad at KDKA was inaugurating his pioneering broadcasts, linked exploration in the ether with explorations into the supernatural. And Lodge was not alone: this motif suffused early writing about radio in the 1920s. Phrases like "telepathic impact," "communication on the other side of the veil," and "we ourselves are acting as the medium" evoked as much the romance of early radio as they did the intrigue of spiritualism. For early enthusiasts did feel like they had entered some previously unknown and quite mysterious dimension. One listener recalled that "it was unusual how the people felt about radios; some thought they were a hoax, and others felt they were supernatural." Another remembered when his uncle showed a neighbor that the radio was not connected to any wires, then turned the set on: the neighbor "ran as if black magic would get him."[15]

Many cultural critics in the 1920s suggested that the country had deserted religion and a sense of community and been seduced by machines and the cult of individualism, that America was no longer a spiritual civilization. But Lodge suggested that, in their explorations of the ether, Americans could have it both ways. Radio didn't divide people from their souls or blind them to their spiritual needs: this machine forged a reconciliation.

Newspapers, magazines, and books referred to the electromagnetic spectrum and radio waves themselves in all sorts of romantic ways: the ether was "the trackless deep," the "empyrean"; voices were "borne in on the moonbeams," and so forth. The concept of the ether was extremely convenient for journalists dedicated to inflating their prose, but it also helped people imagine electromagnetic propagation: if waves moved invisibly around the earth, then they had to have a medium; they had to move through *something*. And the way the device transmitted intelligence from one unseen place to another without visible connections made it inherently magical. Remember that radio listening before 1924 was a very personal experience; the listener put on headphones and entered another world, the world of sound. And what he heard—an eerie mix of voices, wails, high-pitched dots and dashes, and static—constituted a new sonic dimension, filled with sounds never heard by humans before. It was like something thought to be dead was coming to life. "You look at the cold stars overhead, at the infinite void around you," observed one writer. "It is almost incredible that all this emptiness is vibrant with human thought and emotion."[16]

As you can see, the melodramatic rhetoric that surrounded radio in the 1920s enhanced that sense of magic. The boom in radio sales was accompanied by a boom in radio commentary. Articles and essays appeared everywhere, new magazines devoted entirely to radio flourished, and within a few years most publications had their own radio columns. And these writers felt perfectly comfortable gushing about the transcendental significance of the invention. Noting that "we are playing on the shores of the infinite," Joseph K. Hart wrote in the *Survey*, "The most occult goings-on are about us. Man has his fingers on the triggers of the universe." "You are fascinated, though a trifle awestruck," added A. Leonard Smith in *The New York Times*, "to realize that you are listening to sounds that, surely, were never intended to be heard by a human being." "Sounds born of earth and those born of the spirit found each other," wrote Rudolf Arnheim.[17] The air had been cracked open, revealing a realm in which the human voice and the sounds of the cosmos commingled.

Lodge, then, had plenty of company among those eager to see in radio access to some supernatural, psychic force. But he occupied a unique position at this intersection between science and the occult, for he had in the 1890s used his scientific expertise to make radio more usable and was now using his not inconsiderable literary skills to make it more seductive and mystical. Throughout his career Lodge had been determined to build bridges between the life of the spirit and the life of the intellect, between religion and science, and radio was the device—and the metaphor—he relied on most frequently.

Of course, radio did not burst on the scene in 1920. It already had a twenty-five-year history. It was known first as wireless telegraphy, because it transmitted the Morse code, and then as wireless telephony, when it transmitted the human voice. The term *radio* began circulating in the 1910s and didn't really take over until the 1920s. During this twenty-five-year period, wireless telegraphy created a sensation, in part because it was so magical—communication with no connecting wires; because inventors like Guglielmo Marconi and Lee De Forest had a flair for publicity and staged dramatic public displays of the device, complete with semidarkened rooms and flashing blue sparks; and because of gripping events, both staged and spontaneous. Marconi got front-page headlines when he announced, in December of 1901, that he had sent the letter *S* across the Atlantic via wireless. He became a media darling, profiled in leading magazines like *Scribner's* and *McClure's*, and praised as on a par with Edison. The press was equally enthusiastic when he equipped ocean liners with the device and offered a transatlantic wireless service to compete with the cable companies, whose prices the press repeatedly condemned as extortionate. But when wireless played a role in saving lives during shipwrecks—and no wreck was bigger news than the 1912 *Titanic* disaster—the importance and power of the invention became indisputable. When Marconi went to the pier in New York to meet Harold Bride, the *Titanic* wireless operator who had helped save so many lives, he was swarmed by relatives of the survivors. "Everyone seems so grateful to wireless," he wrote to his life, "I can't go about New York without being mobbed and cheered."[18] More people, of course, had heard of Marconi than of Lodge, but Lodge had played a key role in making wireless telegraphy a commercially viable technology.

Lodge had always been more elegant, and much more romantic, in his thinking about radio than Marconi, the device's inventor. Simply put, Marconi could never have put together a marketable system of wireless telegraphy without Lodge. Marconi first, in his earliest demonstrations, used a receiver developed by Lodge and then, in violation of Lodge's patent, used his system of tuning. (Lodge was only narrowly beaten out by Heinrich Hertz in 1888 in demonstrating the existence of electromagnetic waves.) Marconi was an entrepreneur, determined to take wireless transmission out of the lab and, most important, to make it pay.

The device Marconi demonstrated, to the Italian government in 1895 and to the British Post Office in 1896, was both miraculous and crude. Today it evokes nothing so much as the apparatus in the labs of Frankenstein movies. Wireless was based on the principle that rapid changes in electric and magnetic forces send waves spreading through space. An electric spark could provide such a necessary change in current, and a spark is exactly what Hertz and Marconi first used. When Marconi closed a Morse key to send a dot or a dash, a current passed from the batteries through an induction coil, then flashed bluish sparks from the transmitter, a "spark gap" consisting of four brass spheres. High-voltage alternating current surged back and forth between the spheres, radiating electromagnetic waves that carried the dot or dash. The signal went through space and was detected by a small glass tube called a coherer, which was in turn connected to a Morse inker. The inker duly recorded the dots and dashes on a thin strip of paper. The coherer was extremely erratic, causing the inker to print static almost as frequently as it printed signals, but it was a critical first step, and it was based almost entirely on a device Lodge had developed in 1894. (Within a few years the inker was replaced by headphones, since the human ear was much more capable of distinguishing real signals from static, and the signals of one station from those of another.)

But it was Lodge's subsequent contribution that was to prove essential. The device Marconi demonstrated in 1896 was indeed amazing, and by 1899 he was sending signals across the English Channel, a distance of thirty-two miles. But all of Marconi's apparatus sent and received on the same general frequency: in fact, spark gaps were so crude and inefficient that they activated a range of frequencies at the same time: they were spectrum hogs. As a result only one transmitter could signal in a given area at a time. And at this time, remember, there was no tuning. This was where Lodge revolutionized the art.

Lodge thought in terms of harmonies in the physical world and dubbed his method of tuning "syntonic" wireless telegraphy, meaning the transmitter and receiver were "in syntony."[19] Lodge studied selective resonance, a phenomenon in which sound waves produce a sympathetic reaction in similar circuits. For example, a tuning fork when struck will generate vibrations in an identical tuning fork nearby. Scientists had discovered that similar electrical circuits could also be resonant, having the same natural frequency of oscillation, and this property provided the basis for Lodge's work. He reasoned that if he could match certain aspects of the circuits in wireless transmitters and receivers and make them electrically resonant, they would respond "sympathetically," as he put it, to each other but not to apparatus not similarly adjusted.

Lodge achieved this sympathy by adding matched induction coils to the aerial connections of both transmitter and receiver and dramatically increased the selectivity of his apparatus. Now he could tune it to a specific frequency. Marconi borrowed this work, extended it, and added what we know today as the tuning dial. Why Lodge did not immediately sue for patent infringement remains unclear. Fourteen years later, in 1911, Marconi's company bought out the small and unsuccessful wireless company Lodge had begun; only then did Marconi have a clear legal right to the basic patents in tuning.

By the time Lodge was lecturing about the "Etherial World" to packed auditoriums, the device that he and Marconi had done such pioneering work in—the wireless telegraph—had become radio. A variety of inventors, particularly Lee De Forest and Reginald Fessenden, had pushed the invention away from sending Morse code and made it capable of sending and receiving voice and music.[20] Fessenden—an extremely difficult but brilliant inventor—and Ernst Alexanderson, an engineer at General Electric who refined Fessenden's work, developed continuous wave transmission. Marconi's apparatus sent out electromagnetic waves in bursts, and these intermittent waves could carry dots and dashes. But carrying the human voice and music would require continuous waves. This was Fessenden's insight, and though hardly anyone has heard of him today, he completely reconceptualized the art of radio.

Receiving the human voice was another matter. Again, Marconi's receivers could pick up Morse code signals but not the continuous oscillations of the human voice. Lee De Forest—never shy about borrowing from the work of others—modified a tube developed by Marconi's assistant, John Ambrose Fleming. Christening his device "the audion" in 1907, De Forest had invented the prototype of the three-element vacuum tube, which was able to receive and amplify music and the human voice. By the 1910s, engineers discovered that the vacuum tube could generate radio waves as well, giving them a compact and relatively inexpensive oscillator.

As early as 1914 De Forest broadcast music and voice—including shameless sales pitches for his audion—from his lab just north of Manhattan. The transformation of wireless telegraphy from a tool for navies and shipping companies into a method of communicating with fellow Americans had begun. Here De Forest received considerable help from the radio enthusiasts known as the amateurs (later to be called hams), who, as early as 1906, took up radio as a hobby, building their owns sets, eavesdropping on military and commercial messages as well as sending their own. They were the hackers of the early twentieth century, pushing the technology to new levels, forming their own fraternity, and thumbing their noses at authority figures who tried to curtail their activities. By the early 1910s the amateurs had established in America a grassroots radio network that filled the air with coded messages, and they responded eagerly to the experimental voice transmissions of De Forest and others. After 1919, with the help of vacuum tubes developed during the war, they started sending voice and music transmissions of their own.

Neither this kind of semianarchic communication nor broadcasting itself had ever been part of Marconi's entrepreneurial scheme. He thought of radio in strictly analogous terms, as a telegraph without wires that transmitted messages from point A to point B and would compete with the underwater cable companies as well as provide ships with a way to remain in touch with the shore. But as Lodge discovered, the invention tapped into a host of emotional and spiritual desires that transcended—and sometimes rebelled against—such confined commercial calculations. Marconi developed wireless telegraphy and successfully shepherded it from the lab to the marketplace. He made the invention an indispensable part of shipping and competed convincingly with the cable companies. But his vision for the device involved a real failure of imagination, a failure more than made up for by the imaginings, and actions, of the listeners, especially in the United States.

That people were hungering for otherworldly contact, for communion with disembodied spirits, for imaginative escapades that affirmed there was still wonder in the world was confirmed by the response to radio in the early 1920s. The rapidity with which the radio craze swept the country between 1920 and 1924 prompted analogies to tidal waves and highly contagious fevers. By 1922 sales of radio sets and parts totaled $60 million (Westinghouse was manufacturing 25,000 sets a month and couldn't keep up with orders); in 1923, $136 million; by 1924, $358 million. "The rapidity with which the thing has spread has possibly not been equaled in all the centuries of human progress," gushed the *Review of Reviews*. "Never in the history of electricity has an invention so gripped the popular fancy." In the record-breaking time of twelve months, reported *The New York Times* in 1922, "radio phoning has become the most popular amusement in America." Listening-in, as it was called, was hailed as the new national pastime. People flocked to radio, wrote the *Times*, because it "brought to the ears of us earth dwellers the noises that roar in the space between the worlds."[21]

This "space between the worlds" was still widely referred to in the 1920s as the ether. (Although *The New York Times* described the concept in 1920 as a "polite fiction," the term didn't really go out of use until the mid- to late 1930s.)[22] Lodge had a role in this as well. He had been determined to document the ether's existence since the 1890s. He wrote two popular books on the subject, *The Ether of Space* (1909) and *Ether and Reality* (1925), and while the existence of the ether was well discredited in scientific circles by the 1920s, it remained a popular—and helpful—notion to a public that did indeed feel as if it were entering another dimension.

Thousands of tinkerers, since the first decade of the century, had fashioned their own wireless and then radio receiving sets, and many young men gained a solid grasp of electricity and electronics through the radio hobby. For them the invention demystified science and engineering. At the same time the very concept of the spectrum—invisible but not the air; a territory with unknown boundaries; an arena defined by wavelengths and kilocycles; someplace, somewhere, in which disembodied voices traveled—was, and is still, extremely difficult to comprehend. The ether was, in these early years, a realm at once inviting and forbidding, accessible yet incomprehensible. Radio was an invention that simultaneously encouraged some to master it and unlock its technical mysteries and others to resign themselves to increased intellectual passivity in the face of technological progress, a duality toward mechanization that dominated 1920s America.

While Lodge lectured around the country, young men and boys in mushrooming numbers were taking to the ether with their crystal sets. And what they heard, unlike the dots and dashes of the prewar years, was a cacophony of screeches, howls, static, phonograph music, and the human voice. Some refused to believe that radio was possible. Others—and not all of them children—kept looking for, or imagining, "the real little people I just *knew* lived in that radio."[23] In this early stage of the boom, between 1920 and 1924, radio was altering the daily habits of only a comparatively small group of Americans. By the end of the decade millions would find the pace of their day-to-day existence, its auditory background, and the mental images inside their heads all quite transformed.

Picking up on the connection between radio and spiritualism, several mediums claimed that radio was a special agent of telepathy. NBC, in 1929, offered a show called the *Ghost Hour,* which featured an advocate of "electro-telepathy" using the stage name Dunniger. Dunniger—with his index finger pointed firmly to his forehead—attempted to "project through the ether" the name of an American president, the second number of three digits, and a drawing of a geometric figure. He then invited listeners to report what they received. He claimed that 55 percent of the respondents had accurately received at least one of the three mental images. "No one is positive by exactly what means Radio waves reach the listener," Dunniger argued, "and perhaps in its rays will be found a clue to the understanding of what telepathy really is."[24]

Today, with much of the fresh wonder of radio long gone, and the airwaves choking with anesthetizing Muzak on the one hand and vituperative talk radio on the other, it may be difficult to appreciate the intimate interconnections between spiritualism and the radio boom. And I am certainly not suggesting that young men, as they donned their headphones and adjusted their crystal sets, were consciously thinking they were going to hear God, or make contact with the recently departed, or even achieve a higher level of consciousness. If asked, most of them would have said they took to the air for fun, or out of curiosity, or to test their technical mettle. But realizing there was a new, invisible dimension out there—the electromagnetic spectrum—that could provide contact with others far away and that opened up a dark yet crackling part of the universe to the human imagination—put people, however temporarily, in further awe of the cosmos of which they were part. One woman recalled the first time her father put earphones on her head so that she could hear the radio. "I can remember the wonder of the moment even today! . . . The thrill of hearing that disembodied voice must have been something like what deaf people feel when a device allows them to hear sound for the very first time. I remember Dad saying, 'Look at her grin!' "[25] And this wonder, this joy of discovery before the commercial forces came in, even the now ridiculous and naïve projections of spiritual longing onto radio and the spectrum—all this we can, and should, remember and even envy.

Exploratory Listening in the 1920s

I t was the early 1920s, nighttime, and around the country, especially in the Northeast and Upper Midwest, American boys and men (and, to a much lesser extent, women and girls) connected themselves umbilically by headphones to small black boxes powered by sets of batteries. They led the way in a cultural revolution: the turn to listening in the 1920s. Painstakingly moving a thin wire known as the cat whisker around a hunk of crystal, they heard a blend of talk, music, and static as their heads became filled with the voices and sounds of nearby and far-off places. Others, usually those with more money, had sets with tuning dials—five of them—all of which had to be perfectly calibrated to reel in particular stations. This was an exploration, and as such it was thrilling and often maddeningly frustrating.

As with the spread of home computing in the late 1980s and 1990s, often it was boys who embraced this device and introduced the rest of the family to it.[1] This was an exploratory listening, predicated on technical expertise and patience, in which people listened not for continuity but for change; not for one message or program from New York but for many messages from all over the place; to see how far they could get, not which celebrity they could hear; and to hear the eerie, supernatural mixture of natural static and man-made voices. They listened to get a more immediate sense of their nation as it was living, breathing, and talking right then and there. They were lured by the prospect of witnessing entirely new auditory spectacles, the aural equivalents of lightning and fireworks. Turning to listening, entering the realm of listening for so many hours each night, was an entirely new cognitive, emotional, and cultural experience and one we still have an only rudimentary understanding of today.

These were the frothy "boom" years of radio, when virtually nothing was fixed—not the frequencies of stations (although at first everyone was supposed to broadcast on the same wavelength), not the method of financial support, not government regulations, and not the design or domestic location of the radio itself. There were no networks—known in the late 1920s as the chains—and there was very little advertising on the air. With a few exceptions, like the Sunday broadcasts of church services, there was not a predictable program schedule. Instead, stories geared for children might be followed by a lecture on "hygiene of the mouth" or "how to make a house a home," which would in turn be followed by phonograph music or "Madame Burumowska, formerly of the Moscow Opera" singing Rimsky-Korsakov's "Hymn to the Sun."[2] Department stores, newspapers, the manufacturers of radio equipment, colleges and universities, labor unions, socialists, and ham operators all joined the rush to start stations.

Today we take it for granted, often wearily, that broadcasting is supported by advertising, that its mission is to promote compulsive consumerism, that most broadcast stations are affiliated with national networks or owned by broadcasting chains, and that broadcasting is regulated by the Federal Communications Commission, all too often in ways that benefit corporate consolidation and greed at the expense of real diversity on, and access to, the airwaves. It seems fixed, as if this system was and is the only one imaginable. It seems so hopelessly and relentlessly top-down.

Many of these precedents got set in the mid- and late 1920s—some of them even earlier—when none of this was taken for granted. In fact, we have had advertising-supported broadcasting for so long—seventy years—that it is easy to forget that this was extremely controversial and hotly debated in the 1920s, condemned as a crass invasion of people's private lives. (We can thank AT&T for pioneering the use of radio advertising in 1922 on its station WEAF.) Susan Smulyan and Bob McChesney, in their excellent books on early radio, remind us that there was nothing inevitable about the way radio came to be financed and regulated.[3] This was a contested process, with educators and labor organizers, corporate interests, amateur operators, and the government all advancing their very different visions for the future.

Because this decade was so formative, radio historians have especially focused on the 1920s and done a fine job chronicling the rise of radio advertising, the emergence of the networks, the establishment of radio regulation, and the evolution of programming from impromptu speeches and soprano solos to regularly scheduled shows like *Amos 'n' Andy*.[4]

I want to explore something else here: what did it mean, amidst the visual onslaught of billboards, magazines, movies, spectator sports, and newspapers, to retreat to your home and turn to listening? I want to get back into the garage, the attic, and the living room—despite the fragmentary nature of the historical record here—to speculate on this new phenomenology of listening and to lay out what was involved in bringing radio into everyday life. People didn't just walk into a shop in 1922, buy a radio, bring it home, plug it in, and hear orchestral music. That wouldn't be possible until the late 1920s at the earliest. Everyday people had to assemble the device (which included stringing up an antenna), had to learn how to listen, how they wanted to listen, and what they wanted to listen to at the same time that stations, and then networks, were deciding what was best to broadcast. So I want to explore how the terms of radio listening itself were constructed, contested, and thus invented in the 1920s, by programmers and by listeners.

I also want to consider how this major perceptual shift in our culture, a concentrated and dedicated turn to listening, inflected evolving and uncertain notions of manhood and nationhood in the early 1920s. It was men and boys who brought this device into the home, and tinkering with it allowed them to assert new forms of masculine mastery while entering a realm of invisibility where certain pressures about manhood could be avoided. At the same time a quest for nationhood and a reversion to its opposite, tribalism—most of which was white tribalism—characterized the 1920s.

This technologically produced aurality allowed listeners to reformulate their identities as individuals and as members of a nation by listening in to signs of unity and signs of difference. By the late 1920s "chain broadcasting" was centralizing radio programming in New York and standardizing the broadcast day so that listeners tuning between stations at night often heard the same chain program. Meanwhile, independent stations featured locally produced programs with local talent. Listeners could tune in to either or both, and tie in, imaginatively, with shows that sought to capture and represent a "national" culture and those that sought to defend regional and local cultural authority. And in the debate about what kinds of shows and stations were better, which often dominated the letters-to-the-editor pages of the popular *Radio Digest*, we see enormous tensions surrounding network radio's role as a culturally nationalizing force.

It is important to emphasize here that what quickly got coined as listening in went through three distinct but overlapping stages in the 1920s, and that shifts in modes of listening were tied to technical changes in radio apparatus. The first stage, roughly between 1920 (although with the hams this had started much earlier) and 1924, was characterized by the phenomenon called DXing: trying to tune in as many faraway stations as possible. Most DXers started with crystal sets, often moved on to tube sets, and listened at first on headphones, the surrounding sounds of home shut out by the black disks on their ears. And while we don't have the kind of detailed surveys of listeners that historians long for, the journalistic record contains various romantic accounts by middle-class "distance fiends" who gushed about the pleasures of DXing. What is especially striking about these accounts is the way they describe using radio listening to imagine America as a nation more harmonious than it was yet simultaneously reveling in and embracing its differences—what divided it, what rebelled against "America" as a homogenizing notion.

The second stage was music listening, which began, of course, at the same time as DXing, since most of what stations played was music, but became more possible and popular with the introduction in 1925 of improved loudspeakers. The third stage, which crystallized with the extraordinary success of *Amos 'n' Andy* in 1929 as a network program, was story listening, in which people sat down at the same time each day or each week to listen to the same characters enact comedic or dramatic performances.

The rapid explosion of exploratory listening would not have occurred without that fraternity called the amateur operators and later known as ham operators.[5] They constituted the very first radio audience in the first decade of the century, and through their technical innovations as well as their social uses of wireless telegraphy, they paved the way for radio broadcasting in the 1920s. But they also extended the nature of such listening. In the 1920s, while most listeners were trying to tune in broadcast stations, the amateurs—who had not only received but also broadcast wherever and whenever they wanted before 1912—were forbidden from transmitting in the broadcast band and were relegated to an etheric reservation then thought of as pretty worthless: waves 200 meters and down, or shortwaves. Shortwaves, it was thought at the time, wouldn't travel any distance at all; longer waves did that. If the amateurs were going to continue as active agents in the spectrum, they had no choice but to figure out whether they could get anything out of the shortwaves. And figure it out they did, long before Marconi or any corporation.

The amateur fraternity in America began to take shape between 1906 and 1907, after the discovery that certain crystals, like silicon or Carborundum, were excellent detectors of radio waves. More to the point, unlike the prototype vacuum tubes new to the market in 1907, crystals were cheap, durable, and reliable. The events at a receiving station were the same as those at the transmitting end but in reverse sequence. At the transmitting end, inventors had to devise the most efficient method of generating very-high-frequency alternating current from a direct current source. At the receiving end, the problem was "rectifying" these oscillations: translating high-frequency alternating current back to a unidirectional pulsating current that could flow through a telephone receiver. Radio waves are of such a high frequency that the telephone diaphragm alone could not handle their speed or rapid reversal. By 1906 the Fleming "valve" and De Forest "audion"—precursors to the vacuum tube—had been developed, and while they allowed the current to run in one direction only, they were very expensive, highly temperamental, and short-lived. Crystals rectified radio signals in the same way, but no one at the time knew how or why.

The discovery of the crystal detector opened up radio—then still called wireless telegraphy and still quite in its infancy—to legions of boys and men who were, basically, hobbyists. They were primarily white and middle-class, located predominantly in urban areas, especially ports, and they built their own stations in their bedrooms, attics, or garages. They became known for their ingenuity in assembling a motley array of electrical and metal castoffs—from curtain rods and bedposts to Model T ignition coils—into highly effective homemade sets. The one component that was often too complicated for most amateurs to duplicate, and too expensive to buy, was the headphone set. Coincidentally, telephones began vanishing from public booths across America as amateurs lifted them for their own stations. By 1910 the amateurs outnumbered everyone else—private wireless companies and the military—on the air.

Popular culture at this time—from the Boy Scout manual and *Tom Swift and His Wireless Message* to articles in *The New York Times*—celebrated amateur radio as an example of "the ambition and really great inventive genius of American boys." These accounts gained force as real-life dramas made heroes of professional operators. On January 23, 1909, two ships, the *Republic* and the *Florida,* collided twenty-six miles southeast of Nantucket in a heavy fog. The *Republic's* wireless operator, Jack Binns, sent distress signals for both ships, and because of his work nearly all of the twelve hundred passengers of both ships were saved. The story was front-page news for four straight days. By the time he got back to New York, Binns was a celebrity, sought after by reporters and autograph hounds, and offered one thousand dollars a week for ten weeks to appear on the vaudeville stage. Amateurs who listened in on Binns's distress calls became heroes by association and brought more converts to the hobby.

At the same time it was becoming clear that not all amateurs were such upstanding Boy Scout types. There were some who deliberately sent false or obscene messages, and their favorite target was the U.S. Navy, the major military user of wireless. The temptation to indulge in such practical joking was enhanced by the fact that detection was virtually impossible. Fights ensued on the air when hams, posing as admirals, sent ships on wild goose chases, and when naval operators couldn't get a message through because local amateurs were comparing the answers to their arithmetic homework and refused to pipe down.[6]

The navy sought, unsuccessfully at first, to get the amateurs banished from the airwaves. The *Titanic* disaster, however, moved public and congressional opinion against the amateurs' unrestricted access to transmitting. The loss of so many lives, when there were ships near enough to rescue the survivors had they only had wireless onboard, drove home the need to require wireless equipment and at least two operators on all ships.

But few aspects of the tragedy outraged people more than the ceaseless interference, cruel rumors, and utter misinformation that dominated the airwaves in the aftermath of the disaster. Immediately after the *Titanic*'s wireless operator, Harold Bride, notified stations that the ship had hit an iceberg, wireless stations all along the northeast coast of North America clogged the airwaves with inquiries and messages. Out of this cacophony emerged a message picked up by both sides of the Atlantic and reprinted in the major papers: "All Titanic passengers safe; towing to Halifax." Editors of the London *Times* and *The New York Times* were appalled to learn the next day that the message was false, and they blamed the amateurs for manufacturing such a cruel hoax.

The etheric congestion that persisted as the survivors made their way to New York further cemented the amateurs' fate. Passed just four months later, the Radio Act of 1912 required that all amateurs be licensed, and it forbade them from transmitting on the main commercial and military wavelengths. They could listen in, but for transmitting they were banished to an area of the spectrum regarded as useless: the shortwaves of 200 meters and less. The power of their sets was restricted to 1,000 watts.

Despite this, the number of amateurs increased in the 1910s, and they improved their image by providing impromptu communications networks when windstorms or other disasters crippled telephone and telegraph lines. In 1914 Hiram Percy Maxim, the inventor and radio enthusiast, organized the American Radio Relay League to establish a formal relay system or network among amateurs that could step in on a regular basis during natural disasters. Now there was a grassroots, coast-to-coast communications network that made it possible, according to *Popular Mechanics*, "for the private citizen to communicate across great distances without the aid of either the government or a corporation."[7]

During World War I the federal government banned all amateur activity and closed all amateur stations to prevent any interference with government transmissions. But by June of 1920 there were already fifteen times as many amateur stations in America as there were other types of stations combined, and the next year there were 10,809 licensed amateurs (many more, with smaller receiving sets, were unlicensed).[8] This was the incipient broadcast audience who would form the core of DXers, whose excited talk about listening in would bring converts to the pastime, and who helped their friends and neighbors set up their own receiving sets.

As these boys and men clamped on their headphones in the early 1920s, they were working their way through various cultural changes that required everyone to navigate between the powerful tides of tradition and modernity. The 1920s seemed, both then and now, a time of cultural extremes, of opposites. And one thing is clear: most Americans were deeply ambivalent about being poised between these poles. The proliferation of new technologies, the shortening of hemlines and bobbing of hair, the spread of modernism in art, literature, and music, and the census report which claimed that, for the first time in history, half of Americans lived in cities (although a city was preposterously defined as 2,500 people or more), all insisted that modernity had arrived, that Victorian culture had been overthrown. In many of those cities, like New York, Chicago, and San Francisco, the combined population of those born in foreign countries and those born here of foreign parents was sometimes double or triple the population of native-born Americans with native-born parents.

Speed and difference seemed to define the culture that radio entered. Although wireless telegraphy had been around, and widely praised in the popular press, since the 1890s, people perceived the rapidity with which radio listening redefined everyday life as unprecedented. "Never in the history of electricity has an invention so gripped the popular fancy," claimed the *Review of Reviews*. "Its rapid growth has no parallel in industrial history," echoed *The Nation's Business*.[9] This perception that Americans were feverishly overthrowing the past—its pace and its substance—was embodied in the radio boom.

Not surprisingly, many Americans wanted to cling to, even restore, life as it had been in the allegedly "Gay Nineties," before cars, movies, the second wave of immigration, women's suffrage, and the Harlem Renaissance. So the 1920s were also characterized by reaction, some of it vicious. Violent race riots in East St. Louis, Chicago, and Washington, D.C., between 1917 and 1919, and the subsequent epidemic of lynchings and rise of the Ku Klux Klan, revealed pathological racial fissures in the culture. The spread of religious fundamentalism, especially in the South, seemed a direct repudiation of the speakeasies and secularism of the ever-growing big cities. Prohibition was "an ethnic conflict . . . an attempt to promote Protestant middle-class culture as a means of imposing order on a disorderly world." The National Origins Act of 1924 severely restricted immigration, especially from southern and eastern European countries. What the Berkeley historian Lawrence Levine has called "Anglo-conformity"—the nativist insistence that immigrants abandon their past and embrace Anglo-American appearances and behaviors—clashed with a refusal by many to assimilate, become homogenized, disappear.[10]

So radio, which historians agree played a central role in delivering and forging a national culture in the 1930s and '40s, did not do so the instant the radio boom started. It couldn't. Rather, in this environment people used radio both to celebrate and strengthen local, ethnic, religious, and class-based communities and to participate in national spectacles, like election returns, the Dempsey-Carpentier boxing match in July 1921, or the World Series.

In 1920s radio, as in 1920s culture, there were strong pulls between opposites: between corporate control and anticonsumerism, between the desire for order and the desire for freedom, between the safety of cultural uniformity and the titillation of subcultural rebellion and insolence. These contradictions and conflicts can sometimes get plastered over in a history that sees a progression from etheric chaos to etheric order. There was such a progression, technically and bureaucratically, but it was one that favored rich and powerful broadcasters—the networks—over smaller, community-based stations with deeply loyal listenerships but inadequate resources or clout.

The institutional history of radio that historians have already covered quite well is an account, in part, of the efforts to impose order and conformity on the airwaves and to extract profits from them as well. The battles that raged in the 1920s over what radio should be produced in 1927 the Federal Radio Commission—the predecessor to the FCC—whose primary job was to decide which stations got allocated which frequencies. Between 1920 and 1922 all stations used the same frequency, 833 kilocycles; by 1922 just two more had been added. (*Kilocycles* was the term used in the 1920s to designate a station's frequency; today the term is *kilohertz*.) By 1926 the airwaves were completely clogged in many areas: New York had 38 stations, Chicago had 40, and nationwide there were 620. What made this intolerable was that no government agency was empowered to assign wavelengths to these stations, although Herbert Hoover, as secretary of commerce (and presidential hopeful) in 1923, began to classify stations by power and to assign wavelengths.[11] Some had high-powered, state-of-the-art transmitters; others were Rube Goldberg jobs broadcasting with just 25 watts.

A series of widely publicized national radio conferences that Hoover staged between 1922 and 1925 did little to resolve the intense competition over access to the few available broadcast frequencies, although his efforts to allocate wavelengths according to a station's power set the stage for who would win and who would lose in the scramble for broadcasting slots. Meanwhile, Eugene McDonald, the president of Zenith and owner of WJAZ in Chicago, which had been pirating unoccupied wavelengths, challenged Hoover's authority to allocate wavelengths at all. In 1926 the U.S. District Court of Northern Illinois found that no law gave Hoover authorization to assign wavelengths to stations.[12]

Etheric hell broke loose. Over seven hundred stations, many of which boosted their power, jumped frequencies, and broadcast when they weren't supposed to, battling over ninety-six channels. Forty-one stations pirated the six wavelengths that had been reserved for Canadian use. Over one hundred stations violated the Department of Commerce's directive that there be a 10-kilohertz division between stations, and in some cities there were only 2 kilohertz separating one station from another. Portable stations multiplied. Interference, often in the form of cross talk, overlapping voices and music, or noise, became so bad that in many areas listeners couldn't receive a consistent broadcast signal and sales began to falter.[13]

Early in 1927 the FRC set the broadcast band at 500 to 1,500 kilocycles (today AM goes from 535 to 1,604 kilohertz) and assigned fixed frequencies to stations, mandating that people refer to these assignments by frequency and not by wavelength, as had been done in the past. Precedent number one: Those stations with the most sophisticated and expensive transmitters (backed by the most money) got the best slots on the AM dial. Others were forced to share frequencies or given daytime-only licenses. The number of educational stations—usually poorly funded and low-powered—dropped from ninety-eight in 1927 to forty-three in 1933, or only 7 percent of all stations on the air. Listeners were quite divided about the reallocations; some could no longer get their favorite stations. And interference, while lessened, did persist, as high-powered stations, or stations with older transmitters, at times hogged multiple wavelengths on the radio dial.[14]

The networks, too, were founded during this period, NBC in 1926 and CBS in 1927, and their purpose was to link stations via telephone lines so they could all broadcast the same show at the same time. It was especially sporting events—the World Series, boxing matches, the Kentucky Derby, evanescent events that took place in fixed locations—that made having networks so compelling to the audience. But the networks also led to precedent number two: Local programming would be eclipsed, especially during prime time, by shows produced in New York City and distributed across the nation. And broadcasting came under oligopoly control as the two networks dominated the airwaves.

The very public and heated debates about how to finance radio in the early and mid-1920s—and the denunciations of radio advertising as "full of insidious dangers" and an "unwarranted imposition on the public's time"—gave way first to what was called indirect advertising (no commercials but shows featuring the Gold Dust Twins and the Cliquot Club Eskimos) and then to precedent number three: Direct, grab-'em-by-the-lapels sales pitches.[15]

Thus the story is a familiar one in American history—bureaucratic centralization and increased corporate control of a technology that overly romantic writers had once predicted would bring Americans just the opposite. But away from the deliberations of the Federal Radio Commission, the network offices, and the ad agencies, what changes did radio bring to everyday people? What did radio listening mean during these early, heady years?

Beginning in 1920 several stations—8MK (later WWJ) in Detroit, 2XJ in Deal, New Jersey, and 2XB in New York—began broadcasting voice and music. But Frank Conrad at KDKA is generally credited with inaugurating, in the spring of 1920, the first regularly broadcast shows, initially called wireless concerts, which consisted primarily of pushing a Victrola up to a microphone and playing records.[16] Transmitting from his garage in Wilkinsburg, just outside Pittsburgh, Conrad and his sons also talked to fellow hams over the air and appealed for feedback on how well others picked up the music. As more and more hams tuned in and spread the word about the shows, Conrad became a local sensation. When his employers, the executives of Westinghouse, saw that a Pittsburgh department store was using the broadcasts to sell radio equipment, they decided to cash in on the fad themselves. They would manufacture apparatus suitable for amateur use and build Conrad a more powerful station at the Westinghouse plant in the city.

Westinghouse's inaugural, publicity-stunt broadcast was coverage of the incoming returns of the 1920 Cox-Harding presidential race, with the 100-watt KDKA on the air from 8:00 P.M. until midnight. The next day the Westinghouse switchboard was swamped with phone calls. After this debut the wireless concerts went out each night, from 8:30 to 9:30, to a growing audience. Boosting its transmitter to 500 watts and, in this very early period, facing virtually no competition on the air, KDKA could be heard in Washington, D.C., New Jersey, and Illinois. Early in 1921 KDKA expanded its offerings and featured the Sunday services of the Pittsburgh Calgary Episcopal Church.

In 1921, twenty-eight new stations were licensed to go on the air. Pioneers included WJZ in Newark, WBZ in Springfield, Massachusetts, and KYW in Chicago. The next year the floodgates opened: over 550 new stations began broadcasting, most on the same wavelength. Some featured speeches by educators and public figures on topics from Einstein's theory of relativity to the merits of the Boy Scouts, and others covered baseball games, college football, and prizefights. But the staple of early broadcasting—by some estimates three-quarters of all programming—was music. And radio took the middle classes—and the press—by storm. The radio boom was, according to Herbert Hoover, "one of the most astounding things that [has] come under my observation of American life." "People who weren't around in the twenties when radio exploded can't know what it meant," recalled the sportscaster Red Barber. "The world shrank, with radio."[17]

Figuring out why radio became such a sensation in the early 1920s is not as easy as it might seem. There are obvious explanations, but they remain not completely satisfying. For example, there was already an incipient broadcasting audience, made up of the tens of thousands of hams for whom radio had been an all-consuming hobby since at least 1910. Radio was the latest in a line of technically based entertainments—the phonograph, the nickelodeon—and its novelty alone guaranteed some success. The 1920s witnessed a 300 percent increase in spending on recreation, and between 20 and 30 million people each week went to the movies.[18]

But, with the exception of the movies and the nightclubs in urban areas, there also seemed to be the beginning of a shift in desire among some, especially in the middle classes, for the security, ease, and privacy of the home during leisure hours. Hurly-burly public entertainments—the theater, vaudeville, amusement parks, baseball, world's fairs, the circus—had exploded onto the national scene in the late nineteenth and early twentieth centuries, often bringing people of differing classes, ethnic groups, and neighborhoods into common public settings. There were pleasures here, and the cultural historian David Nasaw argues in *Going Out* that people loved losing themselves, and their anxieties about class and social position, in the crowds at Coney Island or darkened movie palaces.[19]

But he also describes the annoyances—the crowding and shoving, the unwanted advances, the noise, the often foul smells of small theaters—that undercut such public pleasures. So it is no surprise that fans began to write about how, with radio, listeners "do not sit packed closely, row on row, in stuffy discomfort endured for the delight of the music. The good wife and I sat there quietly and comfortably alone in the little back room of our own home that Sunday night and drank in the harmony coming three hundred miles to us through the air." Another wrote how radio always put him in the best seat in the house, instead of stuck up high in the gallery: "I enjoy the music just as well here by my fireside and I save a lot of climbing."[20] In the 1920s political isolationism seemed to intersect with, and possibly be driven by, the beginning of Americans' century-long retreat into the private, domestic sphere, with the help of technologies like radio. Technical novelty, the thrill of hearing voices and music from so far away, hunger for entertainment and diversion, and the emerging desire to withdraw from public spaces, all these fueled the boom.

I want to add another explanation: The turn to listening—especially to exploratory listening—was one of the important ways that some men and boys navigated the changing definitions of masculinity and their increased presence in the domestic sphere in the 1920s. From the start radio ownership was highest among the middle classes. But as the Harvard historian Lizabeth Cohen points out in her much admired history of the working classes in Chicago, many workers who interacted with factory machinery every day were not daunted by tackling radio technology at night. These men often made up in ingenuity and improvisation what they could not afford to buy in the shops, and one Chicago reporter claimed that "crude homemade aerials are on one roof in ten along all the miles of bleak streets in the city's industrial zones."[21] Radio listening in the early 1920s at first generally excluded women. So we should consider what special needs radio might have addressed in men.

Scholars have identified the 1910s and '20s as a time of great anxiety over what it meant to be a "real man" in America. Old ideals and new prescriptions collided, and many middle-class boys and men found themselves surrounded by mixed messages about whether to be vigorous, spontaneous, even "quasi-primitive," or to be genteel, urbane, and controlled. E. Anthony Rotundo in *American Manhood* and Gail Bederman in *Manliness and Civilization* note that by the turn of the century the Victorian middle-class model of "manliness," which emphasized honor, self-restraint, hard work, strong character, and the duty (and power) to protect those weaker than himself, seemed passé and irrelevant. Working-class and immigrant men, African American activists, entertainers and sports heroes, and the middle-class women's movement all challenged "white middle-class men's beliefs that they were the ones who should control the nation's destiny." This old model of manliness seemed "overcivilized" and effeminate, notes Bederman, and new epithets like "sissy" and "stuffed shirt" emerged to undermine it.

A new fascination with what Theodore Roosevelt would forever brand "the strenuous life" dominated popular culture, in the form of football, bodybuilding, Joseph Conrad novels, and the sensational success of Edgar Rice Burroughs's *Tarzan of the Apes*. Millions of men joined fraternal organizations that excluded women and men of other classes and races, and young men were urged to become more vigorous through the Boy Scouts and the YMCA.[22] Indeed, there was a major movement in the late nineteenth and early twentieth centuries to celebrate boyhood and to prevent boys from falling prey to "overcivilization." The first Boy Scout manual, which urged boys to be "handy with tools," warned them not to become "flatchested cigarette-smokers, with shaky nerves and doubtful vitality" but to be "robust, manly, self-reliant." Fathers, especially, were to take their sons in hand and train them to be competitive and physically hardy.[23] And it was not enough to be physically vigorous; men had to have forceful, commanding personalities as well.

At the same time it was clear that in the business world, physical strength mattered little: physical combat was a metaphor for other kinds of confrontations. And despite the prevailing mythology, much of the middle-class man's life was spent indoors, in urban areas, away from the enlivening and therapeutic tonic of the outdoor life. In reality, being the master of one's environment, or having mastery over other men, was for many simply not possible. "The expanding bureaucracy," writes Anthony Rotundo, "had a significant effect on manhood" because white-collar work—which had skyrocketed for men between 1870 and 1910—was "routine and required skills were limited." To succeed, a man had to fit in, cooperate, and be a team player.[24]

In these highly routinized, bureaucratic settings, many men worried that the chances for individual autonomy or personal distinction were disappearing. Movies in the 1910s and '20s, especially those featuring Douglas Fairbanks or Harold Lloyd, directly addressed the degradation of work while playing the onslaught of mechanization for laughs. They also, notes the film scholar Gaylyn Studlar, emphasized the ways men were supposed to learn how to select and then put on an appropriate masquerade of masculinity in the face of such depletions. The films of Fairbanks, Valentino, Barrymore, and the grotesque Lon Chaney emphasized "that men were made—not born," writes Studlar. Masculinity in these films highlighted transformation, the donning of manhood as a process. Studlar also notes that in the wake of female suffrage and the elevation of women as the nation's official consumers, there was increased anxiety that "the world is fast becoming woman-made."[25] Fairbanks, first in his host of "juvenile" roles and later as Zorro, a Musketeer, or the Thief of Bagdad, embodied an escape to more playful or exotic realms, where dealing with the new gender relations could be avoided or finessed.

Middle-class men were supposed to fit in, yet they were also supposed to rise above the herd, be noticed, stand out as distinctive. Books like *Poise: How to Attain It* and *Influence: How to Exert It*, and Dale Carnegie's 1920s lectures on "six ways to make people like you" all promised to help men walk that fine line between being "magnetic" and being overbearing. Bureaucratic imperatives, advertising copy that constantly harangued people about their first impressions and whether they fit in, advice books on how to influence people, the rise of Hollywood's star system with its charismatic matinee idols like Douglas Fairbanks and John Barrymore, all these insisted that men become "other-directed," obsessed with the approval of others, attractive commodities others would want to buy. T. J. Jackson Lears has described the rise, by the 1920s, of what he calls the "therapeutic ethos," a prevailing value system that urged

Americans to celebrate leisure, to focus on psychic revitalization and self-improvement, and to live for today instead of deferring gratification for some imagined hereafter. Conform but distinguish yourself: this was hardly an easy paradox to negotiate.

Linking hobbies pursued in private to such large-scale and seismic cultural shifts might seem a mismatch between the trivial and the grand, but I don't think so. Tinkering with radio (like tinkering with cars) was one way for some boys and men to manage, and even master, the emerging contradictions about masculinity in America, especially as some of them found themselves spending their increased leisure time at home. For a growing subgroup of American boys, these vivid yet often conflicting definitions of manhood and success were resolved in mechanical and electrical tinkering. Trapped between the legacy of genteel culture and the pull of the primitivism so popularized in the new mass culture, and certainly trapped between the need to conform and the desire to break out, many boys and men reclaimed a sense of mastery, indeed of masculinity itself, through the control of technology. What if you lacked "animal magnetism," weren't an energy-charged daredevil like Fairbanks, wanted challenge and adventure your job denied you, longed to escape from the confusions and resentment of changing gender relations? With the right kind of machine, there was escape, mastery, adventure, and knowledge few women, African Americans, or working-class men could have.

Popular culture in the 1910s and '20s glorified playing with technology as, more than ever, a young man's game. And few inventions—even the automobile—were more accessible to boys and men than wireless telegraphy. A new series of juvenile books—The Radio Boys—flourished in the 1920s. Just as articles giving instructions on building your own wireless set began appearing in all kinds of magazines, so did short stories entitled "Wooed by Wireless" or "In Marconiland," and adventure books named *The Wireless Man* dramatized the excitement awaiting any game and enterprising boy.

Romance, and the promise that you would have specialized, enviable knowledge, was not unimportant to stoking the radio craze: most radios in 1920 and '21 were homemade crystal sets with headphones, and they were extremely difficult to operate. Early tube sets were not much better, and they, too, were either homemade or home-assembled with great pride, as enthusiasts were guided by endless articles on how to build your own set, with titles like "Radio Broadcast's Knock-Out Four-Tube Receiver." Such "how-to" articles in newspapers and magazines, complete with circuit diagrams, were crucial, since early apparatus, designed for the knowledgeable ham, did not contain assembly instructions. One listener recalled spending $250 for a set in 1922 and being told simply to "sit down and turn the dials, you can't hurt it." Even four years into the craze, in 1924, few receiving sets were complete as sold. Over-the-counter sets usually contained tuning apparatus, wiring, and sockets for the vacuum tubes but not the tubes themselves, nor the batteries, the head-phones, or a speaker. *The Nation's Business* complained that with the number of radio manufacturers increasing from about thirty to five thousand in three years, "badly designed and carelessly manufactured products were dumped upon the market by the carload," further confounding potential enthusiasts.[26]

And here we see what kind of dedication was initially required for listening in. A shopping list provided by *Radio Broadcast* in 1924 included, among other things, "Two or three 1 and ½ volt dry cells for two tubes . . . a 6-volt, no. 80- to 120 ampere-hour storage battery . . . antenna wire, insulators, lightning arrestor, ground wire." And some manufacturers, amazingly, still didn't provide instructions on how to assemble the thing. Night schools and how-to discussions broadcast over local radio sought to help the aspiring tinkerer.[27] Tapping into the ethereal world meant conquering circuit diagrams; properly connecting tubes, coils, and transformers; and gaining a knowledge of electricity and electronics. It meant sorting out the reliable suppliers from the bad, and learning which, if any, repair people you could trust.

It also meant trying to fathom the workings of that recently discovered layer in the atmosphere, the ionosphere. Your set, warned *Radio Broadcast*, "may not produce music the first minute you get all the connections made. . . . Few sets do . . . a bit of experience is needed to determine the best battery voltages, and the proper positions of the dials for good volume without distortion." The Radio Press Service described radio as "a complicated maze of wires and controls which confuse women and discourage their use of it," something the press service hoped to change.[28]

Amalgams of unadorned and undisguised components and wires, early sets were distinctly unattractive, banished by some women to the attic, basement, or garage, tolerated by others only because of their novelty. The black box relied on both dry cell and storage batteries—it wasn't until 1924 that radios could be plugged into a wall socket, but these did not become affordable and widely available until 1927. Radio fans had to learn the difference between the three kinds of batteries that were needed to operate the new three-element vacuum tube. Successor to the crystal detector, the vacuum tube had three key components—the filament, the plate, and the grid—that transformed the high-frequency alternating current that oscillated up and down the antenna wire into a unidirectional current that acted as a carrier wave for voice and music. The grid amplified the incoming signal enormously. All three elements required power. A batteries heated the filament in the tube, B batteries charged the plate, and C batteries charged the grid. All these batteries had to be replaced or recharged frequently, which, unless you had your own charger, required lugging them to your local garage or subscribing to a battery-charging service. Batteries were also notorious for leaking battery acid onto—and wrecking—carpeting and furniture, and they often gave off noxious fumes. In addition, they were expensive: a B-type battery, which lasted only three months, cost ten dollars, plus an additional five dollars a month for upkeep.[29]

Since enthusiasts initially listened in on headphones, they had to be passed around from one person to the next if more than one wanted to tune in. As they sought to share their experience with others, men installed multiple headsets, since early loudspeakers mangled the sound of radio. Listeners thus sat around close to each other, all tethered by their headsets to the receiver. One worker in Chicago described improvising a kind of speaker by taking the headphones and putting them in a pot so the sound would be amplified.[30] Yet many switched to the gooseneck loudspeaker, a component considered especially hideous by most women, to try to make the pastime less exclusive.

Even store-bought sets required some assembly and, therefore, some technical expertise. Those with crystal sets had to master the cat whisker, the thin wire that provided the contact with the crystal. If it was placed on the wrong spot, the listener heard nothing. If the right spot was discovered, however, the listener's ears were suddenly filled with voices and music. The same was true for early tube sets, which required hairline calibrations to tune in different stations. Those without such expertise either acquired it or summoned the help of the neighborhood amateur operator. Money bought distance and amplification: while a crystal set with a 20-mile range cost between ten and twenty-five dollars in 1924, a three-tube set with a range of up to 1,500 miles ran anywhere from one hundred to five hundred dollars.[31]

Once you managed to get your set to work, there was no guarantee you would hear anything except auditory chaos. Not only receivers were crude, so were many transmitters, most of which in 1923 broadcast with less than 100 watts of power and failed to stick to one wavelength. And medium and lower frequencies, where AM is, are more subject to atmospheric noise than higher frequencies. Thus, static was a constant nuisance, as was blasting, a loud, grating noise that blew into your ears every time you changed from one station to another. And what listeners who had bought their apparatus in the winter didn't know until a few months later was that static was much worse in the summer, sometimes making the operation of a receiving set "practically impossible." Listeners were advised to reduce the length of their antennas in the summer and then lengthen them again in the winter, on the assumption that it was better to have a weak signal with less static than a strong one utterly marred by it. *The New York Evening Mail* offered detailed instructions on assembling your own loop aerial—a good "static eliminator"—by wrapping lamp cord around a 3-foot-square frame at the proper intervals and then connecting it to a variable condenser to provide for tuning.[32] Newspapers and magazines were filled, week in and week out, with often elaborate technical solutions to the vagaries of listening in.

Disturbances from electric light and power circuits also disrupted listening. *Literary Digest* noted that a new nomenclature of noise was emerging: " 'grinders or rollers' (a more or less rattling or grinding noise), 'clicks' (sharp isolated knocks) and 'sizzles' (a buzzing or frying noise more or less continuous)." *Century Magazine* commented that mixed in with sounds like the "hiss of frying bacon" was something resembling "the wail of a cat in purgatory." National snobbery came in handy when complaining about static. One magazine noted sarcastically that "in the United States it generally comes from Mexico, which some people might say is only what we might have expected."[33]

Interference was common, and in some places rampant, since between 1920 and 1922 radio stations were all assigned the same wavelength, 360 meters, or what would today be 833 on the AM dial. In 1921, 618.6 on the dial was designated for crop and weather reports. The next year the Commerce Department added a new frequency—400 meters, or 750 on the dial—for larger stations with greater power; these came to be designated Class B stations. But two frequencies could hardly handle the exploding number of stations, and many broadcasters simply moved to slightly different frequencies, where listeners would have to hunt them down. Tuning was a fine art, requiring endless patience and technical acuity as the listener adjusted four or five knobs to bring in stations. When these were adjusted improperly, he was jolted by earsplitting whistles and squeals.[34] And through the headphones of the crystal set, the human voice sounded like a distant, otherworldly squeak or vibration.

Even after the FRC assigned wavelengths in 1927 and 1928, some stations, especially those with antiquated transmitters, blanketed out all other stations within 40 kilocycles of their signals. So did the high-powered stations, some of which had boosted their power to 50,000 watts by 1929. As late as 1930 one disgruntled listener in Dallas wrote that seven different nearby stations "come in very well and clearly for a few seconds and then the next instant will fade far below the static level for twenty or thirty seconds then they come blaring back in like a local and then right back under the static again. It is this way all evening long." Another complained that just as he was getting ready to listen to *Amos 'n' Andy*, two stations interfered with KDKA, and the other stations he tried to tune in during the evening also interfered with each other.[35] Fans wrote to magazines itemizing the ongoing interference and begging for information on how to reduce it.

Nor was there uniform euphoria over radio programming. Some complained as early as 1922 that there was "too much canned music and too many talks on what not to eat." Another noted with irritation that "proud parents flaunt the talents of their children before unseen audiences. There is too much of little Jesse's piano playing—too much because Jesse is only ten and therefore hardly competent to elucidate even 'Ripplings of the Mississippi.' " *Review of Reviews* argued for abolishing the current system of recruiting radio performers, "which is dependent on artists who are willing to display their talents for nothing." Many of these were sopranos or contraltos singing genteel recital music, "the sort of thing that every red-blooded American boy would instinctively sneak out of the back door to avoid hearing during his mother's afternoon teas."[36]

So why bother? What was so compelling about the ethereal world? One commentator at the time went so far as to cast the skyrocketing demand for radio receivers as "abnormal," since the amount of time, sweat, and swearing that went into assembling them only led to more frustration when trying to tune in something. Some, in fact, abandoned listening in altogether because they couldn't get their sets to work, and when they did they heard mostly noise. "Construction without instruction," noted *Radio Broadcast*, "has done much to make the word 'radio' connote 'nuisance' in many quarters."[37]

But for men and boys of many ages in the early 1920s, tinkering with radio combined technical mastery with the chance to explore another strange but compelling dimension inaccessible to those without expertise and determination. Anyone could go to the movies or a vaudeville show, or thumb through a magazine. Plus these media gave you already produced glossy surfaces. With radio you *entered* something, cracked open the elements. Listeners could be in control of nature one minute, by riding the airwaves, yet at its mercy the next, after being hurled off the wave into some etheric riptide. There was no physical danger here, but there were challenges, victories, and defeats, depending not on physical strength or appearance but on how you used your mind and hands. And the terrain one entered, the ether, was, at the time, one of the few untamed, unpredictable, and uncommercialized realms left.

Here was one technology that some men felt *they* could control. Early enthusiasts took great pride in custom-designing their sets so they were distinctive and bore the maker's mark. "Installing a home set is a short cut to neighborhood fame," wrote one commentator in 1923, "a sure way to become known as a mechanical genius." According to the *Literary Digest* in 1924, the approximately 30 million set owners "get almost as much pleasure out of making and remaking [their sets] and putting them together in different kinds of circuits as they do in hearing the programs." Radio became an extension of many men's identity. "Your wits, learning and resourcefulness are matched against the endless perversity of the elements," wrote the author of "It's Great to Be a Radio Maniac."[38]

This is doubtless one reason that the early years of radio listening were dominated by what was called DXing—trying to bring in distant stations—and the farther, the better. (DX was early ham code for "distance," just as CQ was shorthand for "seek you.") Certainly there were many radio fans who simply found a local station they could tune in reliably and stuck with that.[39] But discursively and imaginatively, DXing was the practice that infused radio with its sense of romance, magic, and potential for nation building.

DXing defined early radio: it was why many people listened in, despite all the interference, and it shaped how they listened and what they listened for. Susan Smulyan, who has written warmly about this phenomenon, notes that these aficionados were called distance fiends; another nickname was DX hounds. Because AM propagation and reception are superior at night, and because this was what men did after work, DXing was a nocturnal activity. Content was irrelevant to DXers—in fact, it was a nuisance, "the tedium between the call letters." As the self-confessed radio maniac put it, "It is not the *substance* of communication without wires, but the *fact* of it that enthralls. . . . To me no sounds are sweeter than 'this is station soandso.' " Some complained when announcers failed to enunciate clearly and read the call letters too quickly, "like breath was too precious to use," and chastised stations for not giving the call letters more frequently.[40]

These early listeners indulged in what we today call channel surfing. Once they heard the call letters, they moved on. Truly dedicated souls had a United States map on the wall next to the radio that showed the locations of broadcast stations across the country, and they marked each time they reeled one in. They needed to materialize, with their own maps of listening, their sense of the nation. Many stations, and various of the new radio magazines, provided radio logs with the call letters, locations, and power of every station in the country so listeners could keep track of which station they heard when. Many people, even those who were not die-hard DXers, listened this way, filling in their logbooks throughout the night. Fishing metaphors were rampant in the press, as enthusiasts spoke of "bringing in" or "landing" stations. Ads for receiving sets asked, "How Far Did You Hear Last Night?" or boasted "Concerts from 14 Cities in One Evening." Avid DXers added up their total mileage and boasted of the tens or even hundreds of thousands of miles they had logged. The DX club of Newark, New Jersey, ranked DXers from junior (100 stations) to ace

...ations and verification from 10 stations more than 2,000 miles from the point of reception).[41] As noted earlier, some cities in the early 1920s designated one night a week as a "silent night": local stations stopped broadcasting so listeners could more easily capture stations from around the country.

DXing at night was possible because of the particular qualities of the AM band. Because AM transmissions benefit from both ground-wave and sky-wave propagation, and at night are "bounced back" to earth by the ionosphere, they can "land" hundreds, even thousands, of miles away from the transmitting station. So distances not possible during the day could be achieved at night, but you could never be sure which stations you might snatch. One listener, for example, recalled WBT in Charlotte, North Carolina, coming in throughout the West. Because the ionosphere itself is constantly moving and billowing, both horizontally and vertically, making the reception of some frequencies, from some locations, crystal clear one night and silent the next, DXing was a real adventure in mastering the unpredictable.[42]

More expensive sets had receiving ranges of 1,000, or even 1,500, miles; people who had never made a long-distance telephone call or sent a telegram more than a few miles could now listen in to Chicago, Havana, or San Francisco, all by "the slight crooking of one finger." One-upmanship also fueled the practice, which fit in well with a culture—especially a masculine culture—that used numbers and statistics like weapons to gauge prowess, achievement, and determination. As one enthusiast recalled, "It wasn't then a boast that you could get the Philharmonic in good tone and with full range of frequency. It was much more to your credit if you could say, for instance, that you had picked up twenty-five stations ranging from New York to Los Angeles—as often happened."[43] As early as 1922 the new magazine *Radio Broadcast* sponsored "How Far Have You Heard" contests. Another thrill was finding a station just recently on the air before anyone else did. The sheer immediacy of the auditory world, its fleeting quality, was gripping too—you either caught the sound at that moment or lost it forever, like a prize marlin.

This was not passive listening. Nor was it the kind of grooved, regular listening to favorite shows that would characterize the 1930s. The pleasure of exploratory listening was not predictability but its opposite, surprise. The nature of anticipation of exploratory listening was psychologically different from the anticipation of tuning in to Burns and Allen. With the latter, memory of the show's pleasures—the predictability of the format and the stars' personas—coupled with the surprises of that week's jokes, shaped the anticipation of hearing something known and familiar. But with DXing the anticipation rested on *not* knowing who or what you would hear, or from where: this was the delight of using your ears for discovery.

Radio provided out-of-body experiences, by which you could travel through space and time mentally while remaining physically safe and comfortable in your own house. Time and again the historian finds comments like "I can travel over the United States and yet remain at home" or "With that magic knob I can command the musical programs and press news sent out from a dozen broadcasting stations."[44] It's tempting to gloss over such remarks as the quaint yet fervid gushings of an antique time when people were technologically deprived—and naïve—and romanticized what would quickly become a huge industry. But look at the sense of mastery exploratory listening seemed to provide, the sort of narcissism it stoked, in which one defied gravity, had the country laid before one's feet, and, most important, enjoyed a seemingly unmediated access to other people and other parts of the nation.

Note the use of the word *command*, the extent to which those who wrote about DXing needed to emphasize the autonomy and privilege such listening brought. This was not insignificant in an era known for its increasing bureaucratization and routinization especially, but not exclusively, at work, and people's real sense of a decline in individual autonomy.[45] There was also the pleasure of eavesdropping, and the simultaneous sense of superiority and freedom from responsibility that accompanied listening in on others without their knowing who you were, or even that you were there. You could be taken out of your life, however briefly, and feel the liberation of anonymity. Like voyeurism, eavesdropping brought a sense of control over others, the power to judge them without them being able to judge you. In a culture as persistently judgmental as America, this was no small pleasure, and no small relief.

Remember that DXing antedated the networks: radio programming, such as it was, was locally produced for local audiences. And it was not uncommon for labor unions, churches, and fraternal orders to produce shows for ethnic and working-class listeners. Despite the fact that many stations in these early years played similar music—Gilbert and Sullivan, solos from *La Bohème,* or renditions of "Let Me Call You Sweetheart" and "Down by the Old Mill Stream"—many stations adopted slogans and audio stunts that boasted of their geographic distinctiveness. So it really was possible to listen in for difference, even through what was often mediocre or regionally indistinct music. An Atlanta station was "the voice of the South," one in Minneapolis "the call of the North," and another in Davenport "where the West begins." A Chicago station's trademark was playing taps on a set of bells; a Georgia station identified itself with the sound of a locomotive whistle; a Louisville station signed off every night by playing "My Old Kentucky Home." Some were more simple: "This is WHB, the Sweeney Automobile School, Kansas City" or "This is WDAP, the Drake Hotel, Chicago." Before the advent of the networks and their homogenizing effects on language, pronunciation, and programming, hearing the regional accents of announcers affirmed how far the listener had traveled, and how different other parts of the country were. Yet despite these differences, they were all Americans, enjoying this common experimental project of radio, eager to hear and be heard by others across the miles. Understanding this appeal, one ad touted its radio as the "ears to a nation."[46]

Nearly every commentator in the 1920s who wrote about radio and speculated on its impact predicted that radio would foster national unity. Here we see a class-bound wish, articulated by these white, middle-class men, that somehow radio would instill the "Anglo-conformity" they clearly thought would bring about social order and peace. These predictions contain a much more harmonious notion of the nation than actually existed. In a *Collier's* article titled "Radio Dreams That Can Come True," the author saw radio "spreading mutual understanding to all sections of the country, unifying our thoughts, ideals and purposes, making us a strong and well-knit people." One writer sought to make this transformation as concrete as possible:

> Look at a map of the United States . . . and try to conjure up a picture of what radio broadcasting will eventually mean to the hundreds of little towns that are set down in type so small that it can hardly be read. How unrelated they seem! Then picture the tens of thousands of homes . . . not noted on the map. These little towns, these unmarked homes in vast countries seem disconnected. It is only an idea that holds them together—the idea that they form part of a territory called "our country." . . . If these little towns and villages so remote from one another, so nationally related and yet physically so unrelated, could be made to acquire a sense of intimacy, if they could be brought into direct contact with one another! This is exactly what radio is bringing about. . . . It is achieving the task of making us feel together, think together, live together.[47]

In reality, DXing brought contradictory pleasures: the smugness of regional superiority blended with the pleasure of imagining a national entity, something grand, with a life of its own, of which you were part. It affirmed both hopes, that America was some kind of culturally cohesive whole but one that resembled a jigsaw puzzle of unique, definable pieces. It allowed the listener to cultivate a love-hate relationship with both regionalism and nationalism, homogeneity and difference. Cultural unity, while reassuring, could also be boring. Cultural diversity, while discomfiting, could be exciting and entertaining. Imagining a nation, and one's place in it, consisted then not only of conceiving of some unity; it also involved picturing *difference* and imagining that the difference of which you were a part was superior to—or at other times inferior to—that supposed unity. Radio established itself early on as a machine that would speak to the desire for both of these national features to be held, somehow, in a happy if imaginative suspension.

DXing was, of course, not the only way people listened to radio in the early 1920s. In fact, communal listening was not uncommon. One woman from a small town in South Carolina remembered that "the select few who had these first radio receiver sets entertained the whole town. We had a large discarded church bench in our back yard that was moved to the porch of a neighbor who had radio. All the spare chairs available throughout the neighborhood were collected. We would gather there in the evening to listen to all the music and talk beamed to us from Pittsburgh." A man in Maine recalled going to a neighbor's to listen to one of the Dempsey-Tunney fights, but they could barely hear the broadcast through the speaker. So the neighbor put the speaker in a wash-tub to try to amplify the signal, and they all huddled around the washtub together, straining to hear the fight. In Pelzer, South Carolina, the local druggist propped a ladder next to the store, climbed to the top with his crystal set and headphones, and called out the play-by-play to the crowd gathered below.[48]

But despite the pleasures of DXing, the interference listeners experienced in the early and mid-1920s was maddening, and they were demanding better audio quality from radio. The proliferation of stations meant that by the mid-1920s DXing was becoming more difficult. And DXers were coming to be outnumbered by those who wanted more predictable listening, who were more interested in program content than in miles logged, and who wanted to listen with others to music, speeches, and stories. More comfortable and conventional modes of listening were edging out exploratory listening. This desire interacted with technological developments in the middle and end of the decade. Manufacturers large and small wanted to cash in on the boom, and to do so they had to make receivers that were more user-friendly. This meant, first and foremost, making tuning easier, upgrading the appearance of receivers, and improving sound amplification and fidelity.

By 1922 tube sets had replaced crystal sets in popularity because their reception was better. But these early tube sets, known as regenerative sets, were hardly trouble free. Often, they actually interfered with themselves and with other nearby receivers because, in the hands of the less technically astute, they didn't just receive radio waves but also generated them. In other words, listeners could inadvertently turn their receivers into transmitters, producing horrible squeals and howls that made their neighbors furious with them. *Radio Broadcast* denounced the regenerative set as "radio's greatest nuisance. In the vicinity of the large cities, evenings were filled with such a collection of hums and whistles that a large and active swarm of bees would have been put to shame."[49] Nor could these sets be kept in adjustment. One night, after painstaking tuning, you would lure in a station only to discover that the next night, having left your dials in exactly the same spot, the station was nowhere to be found.

There was heated competition to improve these tube sets, and in 1924 E. Howard Armstrong introduced his revolutionary superheterodyne set. The principle behind the superhet, as it was familiarly called, was "heterodyning," which involved mixing two waves of different frequencies so they would generate a third, lower frequency that was much more audible and thus easier for the radio receiver to detect and amplify. One frequency came, of course, from the radio station, but the other had to be generated locally, in the receiver itself. The third, combined frequency was then amplified and filtered in the set. Signals previously too faint to pick up could now be reeled in. The superhet made the crystal set obsolete and opened up radio listening to many more people, especially women and children. It included two stages of audio amplification, featured a speaker instead of a headset, and was easy to tune. Most important, the sound quality was superior to that of both earlier sets and the phonograph. Despite one listener joking that the superhet was "at least ten feet long and had about fifteen tubes," the new models became so popular that the holiday season of 1924 was labeled the "radio Christmas." More than ten times the number of tube sets were manufactured in 1925 than just two years earlier, and four times as many speakers as in 1923.[50]

But it wasn't just the technical complexities that listeners wanted simplified. By 1925 music listening, not DXing, was what people turned to radio for, and they were getting increasingly critical of tone quality, especially since by then many stations broadcast live performances instead of phonograph records. Listeners wanted more faithful acoustical reproduction; they wanted to hear everything from "a whisper to a torrent of sound" and all this "without the slightest indication of distortion." Many also preferred listening with others to share the experience: they didn't like passing the cumbersome headphones around and having to take turns. By 1925 the quality of loudspeakers had improved dramatically, eliminating radio's "tinny" sound as the "cone-type" loudspeaker with a vibrating surface 15 inches in diameter replaced the horn speaker, whose insensitive metal diaphragm was no larger than 3.5 inches across. In 1927 Americans were finally treated to one-knob tuning, then to the loop aerial, which eliminated the need to string wire throughout and outside of the house.[51]

The shift from DXing to program appreciation was manifested in the radio magazines of the decade: in the early 1920s many were dominated by technical articles on how to build and improve your set. By the end of the decade, these were eclipsed by celebrity profiles and articles about programs, and it was possible for a listener to write, "I don't know a thing about the technicalities of radio, so I want a magazine that isn't devoted to that."[52]

The "Voice of the Listener" section of *Radio Digest* reveals the extent to which listeners were divided over whether radio should be local or national. Despite the familiar narrative that radio fans came to favor the networks because their program quality was superior, the fragmentary evidence indicates that many listeners preferred their local and independent stations, and loved announcers, singers, storytellers, and readers of the news whose names and fame have not survived in radio's highly ephemeral historical record. Even in 1930, ten years after the start of the radio boom, there was still not one "mass" audience, despite the success of shows like *Amos 'n' Andy*. Rather, there were many listening publics with ongoing, warring ideas about how to listen and what to listen to.

The question was one, in part, of regional pride and identification: New York, the center of chain broadcasting by 1930, was not necessarily where all listeners wanted to be transported to. In fact, some resented New York's shouldering out other cities as the self-proclaimed capital of radio entertainment. The other issue was homogenization and standardization. Listeners used to DXing and hearing all kinds of programming bemoaned the fact that so many stations, having affiliated with one of the networks, now played exactly the same thing at the same time, thereby reducing choice and variety. One listener warned in 1930 that "unless we watch our step, the chain stations will be the Czars of the Air." Added another, "The chains . . . have nearly complete control of the air. We feel sorry for the future of Radio if this chain business gets any worse." The term *chain broadcasting* resonated unfavorably with the controversy surrounding the spread of "chain" stores like A&P, which some people blamed for bringing on the Depression and putting local shops out of business. In fact, one very popular and controversial broadcaster was W. K. Henderson, on his station KWKH in Shreveport, Louisiana (self-proclaimed "Voice of the People"), who editorialized passionately against the spread of chain stores and was heard as far away as Michigan. His fans didn't miss the connection about the dangers of cultural monopolies. As one put it, "I hope the day will not come when we will be forced to listen to these rotten chain programs that fill the dial."[53]

There was enormous support and affection for what one listener called the "home talent" at local stations. "We always will have a warm spot in our hearts for the 50- and 100-watt stations," noted a letter signed "Dial Twister," because "some of the most interesting things . . . have been brought to our home by the small stations." Added another, "I want the voices of the local performers." Whether they were hearing local or national talents, listeners wanted to be able to see the faces that went with the voices they heard so regularly and intimately. *Radio Digest* specialized in making the invisible visible by printing photographs of radio personalities and stations from around the country, and readers would write in begging for features about their favorite on-air personalities from Cincinnati or Little Rock or Dallas. As one fan put it, "We certainly want to see and know them 'In Person' as well as 'In Spirit.' "[54]

The amateurs, however, were elsewhere, cognitively and culturally, with a rift developing between them and BCLs—broadcast listeners—over what kind of listening was superior. By the early 1920s, when the amateurs were back on the air but consigned to 200 meters, they had no choice but to see what the allegedly worthless shortwaves could do. Although the Radio Act of 1912 had restricted the amateurs to 200 meters or lower, the Commerce Department interpreted the law quite literally, and assigned them all to 200 meters. In March of 1923, Herbert Hoover, then secretary of commerce and father of an avid ham, let them roam between 150 and 200 meters.

What they—especially those called boiled owls because they stayed on the air until all hours, getting bags under their eyes—were discovering was that they were picking up, or being heard by, stations in Australia and New Zealand or, in the other direction, stations in England and France. Amateurs reported spanning distances as great as 10,000 miles—unthinkable back then—and Australia and New Zealand were described in the fall of 1923 as "a bedlam of Yankee signals."[55] And a major breakthrough came just after Thanksgiving of 1923. Moving to even shorter waves, 100 meters, Leon Deloy of Nice, France, and two Americans, John Reinartz and Fred Schnell, established two-way, nighttime transatlantic communication. Amateurs were actually carrying on a back-and-forth exchange over 4,000 miles. More important, they were doing it on 100 meters, a wavelength considered even more worthless than 200 meters.

This was not supposed to happen, and at first amateurs and scientists weren't sure how it did. More perplexing was how the 200-meter wave seemed to die out at 150 miles, only to reappear again, as strong as ever, at a greater distance. Amateurs were generating more perplexing data for scientists, adding to the questions posed by a more established inventor like Marconi. In 1901, when Marconi claimed to send the letter *S* across the Atlantic, the feat dumbfounded scientists who had presumed that radio waves, like light, traveled in a straight line and would never follow the curvature of the earth.

In the wake of Marconi's achievement, Arthur Kennelly of the United States and Oliver Heaviside of England hypothesized in 1902 that there was an ionized layer in the upper atmosphere that reflected radio waves of certain lengths or frequencies back to earth. But in 1923 the properties of this undulating, unpredictable layer 50 to 400 miles above the earth's surface were still barely known, and hardly anyone thought it would affect shortwaves.

The amateurs showed that it did, in at least two ways. It turned out that the shorter the wavelength, the more dramatically its direction could be refracted by the ionosphere, especially at night, when the lower layers of the ionosphere, which absorbed these frequencies, dissipated, and the upper layers mirrored them back to faraway stations. Some shortwaves bounced up and back repeatedly as they made their way around the globe. Others got trapped between the layers within the ionosphere, careening for thousands of miles in that medium like billiard balls before returning to the earth. Amateurs called the no-man's-land between where the signal went up into space and where it was reflected back skip distance. Skip distance could vary from night to night (even hour to hour) depending on the ebbing and flowing of the ionosphere, whose behavior was dramatically affected by sunspots. This meant that every night could be different for an amateur, every wavelength a new mystery and adventure.

While scientists, corporations, and military officials were fascinated by the amateurs' push into short- and then ultrashortwaves, the general public could have cared less. They were discovering broadcasting—often with the help of local hams—which meant that they were also discovering interference. Much of this interference, whether it came from the BCLs' own sets, static, other broadcasting stations, or nearby elevator motors, was blamed on the hams. Some were not particularly diplomatic in their responses. "I believe I speak for every amateur in America," wrote one, "when I say I hope the amateur may see the day when he can tromp on the grave of the nighthawk broadcaster, and kick his tombstone into perdition beyond recall."[56] This was a fight over how to listen and what to listen to, a dispute over which modes of listening should be cultivated and privileged, and which ones should be marginalized.

Fortunately for the hams, Herbert Hoover continued his support. He convened four national radio conferences in Washington between 1922 and 1925 and made sure to include representatives of the American Radio Relay League (ARRL). Their inclusion was testimony to their organization, their vociferousness, and their real and threatened political clout. Despite efforts by commercial broadcasters to eliminate the amateurs or appropriate their portion of the spectrum, the ARRL, firmly backed by Hoover, retained the amateurs' right to broadcast and their stake in the shortwaves, and these were written into the Radio Act of 1927, predecessor to the Communications Act of 1934, which established the Federal Communications Commission.

By the late 1920s music listening and story listening were winning out over exploratory listening. But it would be a mistake to suggest that DXing died out solely because of audience disinterest. DXing also died out because the FRC and the networks simply made it more difficult to do. When the FRC reallocated frequencies in 1928, the number of stations that were allowed to broadcast at night was reduced from 565 to 397. And 21 of the 24 stations granted clear-channel status and the right to boost their power, in some cases to 50,000 watts, were network affiliates, so many clear-channel stations were broadcasting the same thing.[57] And the last thing advertisers wanted was for listeners to tune in just for the call letters and then move on to another station. By the early 1930s the pleasure of using your radio to flit around the country and hear a range of independent local stations faced powerful auditory roadblocks. The tension between radio promoting local versus national culture remained, but the power was clearly with the networks and their advertisers, who wanted a national audience for national shows. The networks and their advertisers did not want many varied, regional, or subcultural listening publics. They wanted a "mass" audience, and they used popular music and comedy to forge it.

Tuning In to Jazz

"**F**ormerly the only music in a man's head, week-in-week-out, was the church organ on Sunday," boasted *Radio Broadcast*. "Now he hears several hours of assorted music a week." Magazines devoted to music gushed about radio's ability "to create a vast new army of music lovers in America." *Étude* predicted that "America is now on the threshold of one of the greatest musical awakenings the world has ever known." Walter Damrosch, the conductor of the New York Symphony who quit to establish NBC's national program of musical appreciation, said he was astounded by the thousands of letters he received "from people who pour out their hearts in gratitude for the opportunity to hear for the first time in their lives a wealth of concerts of great music. These people are amazed at the new worlds which the radio has opened to them."[1] However inflated and quixotic such prose might seem today, this unprecedented turn to music listening constituted an enormous perceptual and cultural realignment that reshaped the twentieth century.

Possibly radio's most revolutionary influence on America's culture and its people was the way it helped make music one of the most significant, meaningful, sought after, and defining elements of day-to-day life, of generational identity, and of personal and public memory. Obviously, people sang, danced, and listened to music long before the radio, sometimes at work, sometimes at home, and almost always in conjunction with ethnic and religious ceremonies of all kinds. Since at least the 1820s they had also gone out to hear music, in the theater, in concert halls, in town parks, and later in vaudeville. And, of course, there was the phonograph. But radio gradually made music available to people at most times of the day or night, and made music a more integral, structuring part of everyday life and individual identity. Through radio millions of people now established "new musical cultures."[2]

The piano had paved the way for this, with sales that skyrocketed between 1870 and 1910. Piano literacy, as the Columbia historian Ann Douglas puts it, was almost as high as print literacy among well-bred American women, and the sheet music industry made sure there was plenty to play. The phonograph was also critical to this change in American life—sales of phonographs rose from $27.1 million in 1914 to $158.7 million in 1919, and in 1921 Americans bought more than 100 million records, spending "more money for [records] than for any other form of recreation."[3] But within a few years radio supplanted the phonograph as the device people used to bring music into their homes. With radio listeners could have music on demand, and not just piano music or the same scratchy recordings, but that produced by the country's finest bands, orchestras, and singers. And while the music they heard might have been "canned" rather than live, they no longer needed to leave home to hear it.

Through radio, music became more fundamental to the American experience than it ever had been before. In fact, it began to structure social relations much more thoroughly and ubiquitously. The commonality of the experience was on an entirely new level: now more people listened simultaneously to the same bands and the same songs as they passed through their time in history. Within a few weeks radio could make a song a hit across the country. One study from the early 1930s showed that two-thirds of listeners "engaged in other activities" while listening to music on the radio, intertwining daily rituals and routines with particular songs and sounds.[4] Sometimes listeners concentrated totally on broadcast music; other times they danced to it; and other times they used it for background sound.

With radio, music played an enormous role in constituting people's emotions, sense of time and place, sense of history, and certainly their autobiographies.[5] After radio particular styles of music, and particular songs, were inextricable from people's memories of their youth, their courtships, their sense of separateness as a generation.

And this is why music on the air became controversial. By the mid-1920s African American music, particularly "hot" jazz, as performed by African American musicians, got on the air in certain places like Chicago and New York. Radio hastened the acceptance of this music among many who would not have heard it otherwise; the fact that radio brought such music into "respectable" people's homes also intensified traditionalists' reactions against jazz, with their calls to censor or at least tame it.[6] In the 1920s radio (along with phonograph records) opened a small crack between white and black culture, and Louis Armstrong, Bessie Smith, Duke Ellington, and a few others slipped through. By the end of the decade, most would agree that the newly founded radio networks and the white bands they rewarded had co-opted, domesticated, and often bastardized black jazz. But African American music crept into white culture and white subjectivity, and this was critically important for the enlivening of American music and for the long, slow struggle out of Jim Crow America.

It was not inevitable what kinds of music would predominate on radio. Audience preferences and hatreds—which were, of course, wildly heterogeneous—interacted with station and then network notions about what was and was not appropriate to broadcast. And stations were notoriously averse to criticism, so they played it safe most of the time. In the decade forever labeled the Jazz Age, classical music and opera were brought to more listeners, on a regular basis, than ever before. So were hymns, waltzes, male quartets, brass bands, light opera, hillbilly music, and song and patter groups. While Hadley Cantril and Gordon Allport in their 1935 book *The Psychology of Radio* admitted that "the nation . . . is not about to be transformed into a vast Handel and Haydn Society," they noted that listeners, through their letters to stations, were demanding "better music" over the air and were moderating their notion that classical music was "toplofty." They concluded that "a new form of aesthetic desire is appearing in [listeners'] lives" because of radio.[7]

Although phonographs, which by the 1910s had become fixtures in most middle-class homes, had brought people Caruso as well as ragtime, we must remember that talking machines were still hand-cranked, and the maximum playing time on each side of a record was about four minutes. Nor was there any such thing as a record changer. To listen to Beethoven's Fifth Symphony, for example, the listener would have to put on and remove five records while keeping the phonograph cranked up. Audio quality left much to be desired. Listeners responding to a survey done by the Edison Company in 1921 complained about the scratchy surface noise of Edison records and their tendency to warp.[8]

Until the mid-1920s, when electrical recording, which used microphones and acetate masters, became the standard, recording was done by the "acoustic" method. Performers sang or played into a tin horn connected to a hose, which was in turn connected to a needle. The needle turned these sonic impulses into grooves on a wax disk. The process turned high and low notes into noise, and percussive sounds from drums, pianos, or musicians tapping their feet knocked the needle off the wax. If such a mistake occurred, the band would use gas jets to melt the wax and then rerecord. *Radio Broadcast* complained self-servingly,

"The ordinary record is a pretty poor imitation of the human voice; practically all of them give a very disagreeable scratchy noise and even when they don't the enunciation is seldom distinct enough for one to understand the words of a song, for example, unless it is repeated many times."[9] Radio, because of its superior amplification process and its use of microphones, eliminated such nuisances. And while the quality of music as heard on crystal sets couldn't compare with that on phonograph records, the new superheterodyne tube set produced sound superior to that of the talking machine.

As fledgling radio stations struggled to fill the broadcast day in the first years of the boom, they either played phonograph music or brought in singers, professionals and amateurs alike, who were expected to perform for free or in exchange for publicity in the local paper. The radio craze seriously undercut the sales of phonographs, and in 1923 ASCAP, which represented those who made their living selling records and sheet music, forbade radio stations from playing phonograph music without paying royalties. This prohibition was onerous, especially for smaller stations, some of whom simply ignored it, or, more ingeniously, played phonograph records but asserted that it was live music. But it was also the case that live singers—at least those who weren't the third-rate "screeching sopranos" loathed by so many—sounded better than records, and most stations preferred local talent to records.[10]

At first most performers came to the stations to sing or play in studios dripping with velvet curtains to soften the acoustics. But alliances quickly grew between radio stations and hotels, who competed over which dance bands or orchestras they could book. The stations got live music—some of it the finest of the period—and the ambience of a glamorous nightclub, and the hotels got free publicity. Some shows were fed by telephone lines back to the station for broadcast (this was called a remote), but others, exploiting the fact that hotel buildings were some of the tallest in town, put a transmitting tower on top and broadcast from the hotel itself.[11]

The singers most heavily favored at first by stations were female sopranos, who sang arias from operas or what one program director called "potted palm music," the sort of straitlaced, high-culture recital music played in conservatories or hotel lounges. Contraltos also appeared frequently. These choices reflected many stations' own sense of their mission, that radio be culturally uplifting and proper. To ensure that the medium was respectable, and reinforced the cultural values of an educated bourgeoisie, many stations in radio's early years deviated only rarely from "salon" music. Songs from operettas and musicals were acceptable, as were old standards like "After the Ball Is Over" and "In the Good Old Summertime." In fact, some of the audience's most preferred songs were "old-time favorites" like "The Old Oaken Bucket" because people had sentimental attachments to songs their parents had loved, songs from their own youth.[12]

But safety had its price. *Radio Broadcast* complained in 1924 that these "singers programs" were "monotonous" because the same songs were performed "night after night" on "all kinds of stations," and that contraltos were especially irritating because they "slow down the tempo until they get on the listener's nerves."[13] These performances were alternated with piano or violin solos. Pianists played Chopin and Liszt most frequently, followed by Rachmaninoff, Beethoven, Mozart, and Grieg. One can imagine the reception this fare must have gotten among the generation F. Scott Fitzgerald was immortalizing in his novels. For out in the streets people—most notably African Americans—formed lines that stretched around city blocks to buy jazz and blues records, or what quickly came to be called race records. By the mid- and late 1920s many whites were fans of this music as well, and they wrote or called in to have it played on their radio stations. They also wanted classical music, waltzes, religious music, and dance bands.

This struggle over what kind of music should be played on the radio led to a major shift in the kind of music one heard in 1922, and the kind one heard just six years later. And the record suggests that, with important exceptions, the years 1924 and '25—the same years that DXing began to drop off—marked the point when stations moved away from "potted palm music" and toward variety that included symphonic performances, opera, and, yes, more jazz.

The technical properties of radio itself influenced what kind of music to broadcast. In the early years, with crystal receivers and headphones, or the distorting and tinny gooseneck loudspeaker, symphonic music was especially mangled. Instruments that produced musical tones of either very high or very low frequencies—violins and oboes on one end, cellos on the other—were scarcely heard. Other instruments—the piano, the clarinet, the saxophone—came across especially well given radio's early lack of fidelity. (Here, jazz would have a distinct advantage on the radio.) Singers—especially sopranos—accustomed to projecting their voices on a stage often blew the tubes on radio transmitters when they used the same vocal force in front of a microphone. Hence the development of crooning, pioneered by Vaughn de Leath, "The First Lady of Radio," who performed frequently on WJZ in Newark in the early 1920s. De Leath developed a soft, cooing approach to her singing that was less stage oriented and more intimate, and that didn't do violence to transmitters.[14] This style was emulated with great success by male singers, most notably Rudy Vallee and Bing Crosby, who exploited radio's technical limitations to their own ends.

By the late 1920s and early 1930s, radio had made certain bands and singers nationally recognized stars, with male and female fans. The Coon-Sanders Nighthawks, who played jazzy dance music, were initially heard over WDAF in Kansas City, and their fans argued with those who loved Guy Lombardo and His Royal Canadians over which band was the best. The bandleader Ben Bernie was known around the country for his "yowsah, yowsah, yowsah" catchphrase. And Rudy Vallee, radio's answer to Rudolph Valentino, became a sensation with female listeners.

Radio disseminated classical music, blues, and jazz in an etheric patchwork that, for some, resembled a war marked by illegal but frequent fraternizations. Here, certainly, was one of the precursors of postmodern life, in which people came to take for granted the musical pastiche of "high" and "popular" culture they could now sample at will. Would radio be an agent of respectability or of impudence? Would it "elevate" people's tastes by showcasing opera, classical music, and music appreciation shows, or would it "degrade" public taste by pandering to the popular? These were the questions posed by the intelligentsia, who wanted radio to educate and uplift "the masses." But those on the other side, especially many young people, wanted radio to repudiate such cultural hypocrisy and to be the agent of rebellion, "truth," and a grassroots cultural authenticity. They wanted jazz.

Debates quite familiar to us today, about whether popular music corrupts American values, began in earnest in the 1920s. Music became politicized, reflecting racial and class tensions. Many stations, seeing their role as part educational, began musical appreciation shows in which commentators intoned that "Bach brushed aside the narrow ideas of his predecessors and boldly strode out on new and unbroken paths" before playing a Bach selection. Some stations provided opera and jazz; others announced who they were by featuring one and shunning the other. (Opera enjoyed an enormous resurgence of popularity because of radio.) Yet given the way music in the 1920s became increasingly freighted with political and cultural baggage, it is important to remember that the divide between popular and classical music was much smaller then than it is today.[15]

What mattered most was the new importance music assumed in people's lives. This wasn't true just for cultural elites or the intelligentsia: it was true for people of all walks of life. And it was especially important for men. Musical appreciation had, in the nineteenth and early twentieth centuries, been one of the "womanly arts." In 1922 women constituted 85 percent of music students and 75 percent of concert audiences, prompting magazines like *Current Opinion* to ask, "Is Music an Effeminate Art?" And evidence suggests that while men indeed were attached to and used their phonographs, it was often women who bought the records and put them on to soothe people's feelings and end fights in the household.[16]

Radio, by initially linking technical mastery with music listening, helped make the enjoyment of music more legitimate for men. Increasingly, men felt they had permission to intertwine their personal histories, their emotions, their identities as men with song. Studies in the 1930s documented this change and showed that men welcomed it. One man, who had moved out west, where there were virtually no symphonies or concert halls, felt keenly deprived. But with radio, he told a researcher, "we are making up for the twenty-odd years we missed. It is like being born again."[17] Because there is such a powerful relationship between music and emotional arousal, radio provided both public and private ways for men to indulge their emotions and their aesthetic impulses.

The technical virtuosity and cultural clout of classical music (especially as emphasized by the various music appreciation shows) and the vibrancy and rebelliousness of jazz (as well as its virtuosity) helped overcome earlier prejudices about music appreciation being for women and girls. But Rudy Vallee in particular complicated men's relationship to broadcast music. Vallee was, by 1929, radio's first matinee idol, with women swooning and sighing over him both in public performances and in front of their loudspeakers. It was his conversational and seductive style of singing—as opposed to the more declamatory style of opera and light opera singers—that made one woman write, "It is a relief to have a man sing like a human being and not like an hydraulic drill." People said that his voice "has It"—meaning sex appeal—and "makes love so democratically to everyone." Women also described his voice as "restful" and "sweet."[18] Meanwhile, much press commentary was sarcastic and dismissive of "the boy," as if his wild success (especially on the heels of DXing) threatened to feminize the airwaves themselves. As men used radio to embrace music appreciation, many of them emphatically disdained Vallee as having ventured too far into female territory.

The war between classical music and jazz was especially dramatic in a city like Chicago, which was, arguably, the radio capital of America in the 1920s. As early as 1921, KYW broadcast all the afternoon and evening performances of the Chicago Civic Opera Company, making it an all-opera station and reportedly winning huge audiences.[19] At the same time, because of the wartime migration of nearly 60,000 African Americans to Chicago, a migration that included some of New Orleans's finest musicians, thrown out of work when the navy—as a "wartime precaution"—closed down the city's red-light district, Chicago became a major jazz center. Its recent arrivals may have been a benighted minority, but they also became something else: a market. And what they wanted was blues and jazz. So the airwaves in Chicago were, in these early years, marked by musical extremes: opera, the sine qua non of cultural elitism, and jazz, the exemplar of bottom-up cultural insurgency.

The radio boom coincided with the birth of jazz, a coincidence that would fuel the rebellion of a generation. The word *jazz* was imprecise and covered a wide range of music, from the "hot," New Orleans–inspired jazz played by what were then called colored bands to songs like "I'm Just Wild About Harry." And various successful white band leaders and performers—Paul Whiteman, the Original Dixieland Jazz Band, Bix Beiderbecke—appropriated and toned down black jazz to make it more acceptable to white audiences. Some writers were also referring to the blues when they used the word *jazz*. But despite its imprecision, the word, and most of the music it referred to, was enormously controversial throughout the early part of the decade. For example, that Louis Armstrong or Bessie Smith—probably the most popular singer of her time—was banned from many radio stations in the early 1920s is now unimaginable.

While radio did remove and "contain" a "black presence on the airwaves," some African American performers nevertheless became household names by the end of the decade. Because of radio, black culture—or at least those narrow, fetishized slices of black culture forced to represent the whole—"became part of mainstream American expression."[20]

It is in radio's relationship to jazz that we see the beginnings of this invention's nearly century-long role in marrying youthful white rebellion to African American culture. Now African American music would play an increasingly important role in constituting the identities not just of blacks but of whites as well. As a result of this marriage, middle-class cultural repression was challenged. But over the radio African American music was also tamed by white musicians, as well as by industry executives, co-opted, made safer for white audiences. Radio has, simultaneously, forced black musicians to be accommodationists and allowed them to be innovators and iconoclasts. This process has been especially heightened at roughly thirty-year intervals, with jazz in the 1920s, rock 'n' roll in the 1950s, and rap in the 1980s and beyond.

While the "Big Three" in the phonograph industry—Edison, Victor, and Columbia—struggled to stay afloat in the face of radio by continuing to record classical music and Tin Pan Alley songs, small independent companies, looking for new music and new markets, recorded jazz and the blues. They also marketed phonographs to urban blacks. It was these listeners who, in February of 1920, made Mamie Smith's "Crazy Blues" a smash hit that sold 8,000 records a week.[21]

Suddenly "race music" became big business, and it is widely agreed that Bessie Smith, who signed with the nearly bankrupt Columbia in 1923, single-handedly saved the company's fortunes by selling approximately 6 million records in the next six years. At first these kinds of sales came primarily from the black community, which bought at least 6 million records a year. But by the end of the decade white fans flocked to jazz and the blues too, finding in both a skepticism, a sexual vitality, and a revolt against repression and propriety missing from, say, "Sweet Adeline." For many jazz was protest music. And certainly many whites, whose adoration of black music was deep and powerful, projected onto this music a range of fantasies about whiteness and blackness. As Amiri Baraka (formerly LeRoi Jones) wrote of white listeners' attraction to jazz and blues, "Americans began to realize for the first time that there was a *native* American music as traditionally wild, happy, disenchanted, and unfettered as it had become fashionable for them to think they themselves had become."[22]

The hysterical, rabid denunciations leveled against jazz by the nation's self-appointed moral guardians in the 1920s resonate with later condemnations of rock 'n' roll and rap, and of radio's role in popularizing such music. The word *jazz* itself had, in some quarters, referred to sexual intercourse, and that's exactly what critics claimed it encouraged. To support this contention, they cited the scandalous new dances—the Charleston, the fox-trot, the shimmy, and other "lewd gyrations"—that people performed while listening to jazz bands. Given its associations with brothels, dives, and African Americans, its reliance on the sinfully suggestive saxophone, its often earthy lyrics, and its insistence that listeners let loose their backsides to shimmy and shake, critics saw jazz as the major indication that American society was going down in flames.

"Jazz," the *Ladies' Home Journal* warned its readers, "originally was the accompaniment of the voodoo dancer, stimulating the half-crazed barbarian to the vilest of deeds." In a subsequent issue the magazine lectured that jazz led to a "blatant disregard of even the elementary rules of civilization" and insisted the music caused an increase in the nation's illegitimacy rates. As one writer noted wryly in *The Atlantic Monthly*, "It is alleged that the moral corruption worked by jazz is vastly more calamitous than was the material havoc wrought by the World War." Jazz was "unhealthy" and "immoral," an "abomination" that had to be "absolutely eliminated."[23]

By the late 1920s various groups pushed for censorship of "lewd, lascivious, salacious, or suggestive" titles and lyrics, and the National Association of Orchestra Directors appointed a "czar" to police hotels and nightclubs for "the kind of jazz that tends to create indecent dancing." The National Association of Music Merchants condemned the proliferation of "smut words" in jazz and demanded that Congress act to permit the censorship of music. Congress didn't oblige, but section 26 of the 1927 Radio Act provided that "no person within the jurisdiction of the United States shall utter any obscene, indecent or profane language by means of radio communication," a provision adopted by the FCC in 1934. By the early 1930s the networks had imposed internal censorship, and within ten years NBC had blacklisted 290 songs.[24]

The discourse surrounding jazz was, of course, a discourse about race, about fears of miscegenation, pollution, and contamination. Even articles praising jazz referred constantly to "the jungle," "savages," and "primitivism," noting how staid, white, European culture was being forced to respond to more exotic, feral influences. This was also a battle about what was more important to concentrate on and appreciate in music: melody and harmony, or rhythm.[25] Rhythm seemed to be winning out with many, and to those threatened by this shift, rhythm equaled Africa.

It is not surprising that such attitudes, coupled with the race hatred and segregation of the times, would at first keep black singers and musicians off most radio stations. But several white bandleaders began to adapt various elements of jazz and incorporate them into white music, producing what some called "sweet jazz." Paul Whiteman was the most successful of these; he earned the title King of Jazz—and a gross income of over $1 million in 1922—by appropriating and diluting black jazz (without, one might note, hiring any black musicians) and selling it as "the real thing" to whites. Others included bands led by Victor Lopez and Ted Lewis. Beginning in 1921 Lopez broadcast from the Pennsylvania Grill in New York City every Friday night and became enormously popular, and Whiteman remained on the radio for twenty-five years.[26]

Despite the denunciations against jazz—and certainly in part because of them—this music's enormous popularity escalated through the 1920s and beyond. As early as 1924 the *Outlook* reported, "You can scarcely listen in on the radio, especially in the evening, without hearing jazz." *Étude* added, "Tap America anywhere in the air and nine times out of ten jazz will burst forth." What they meant, of course, was everything from Whiteman's symphonic-jazz hybrids to the music of Fletcher Henderson. Eventually jazz, in its various forms, dominated radio, nearly uprooting "potted palm music" and eclipsing classical. By 1926 the *Literary Digest* proclaimed "the whole world" as "jazz mad." "Jazz," wrote Gilbert Seldes, one of the first white cultural critics to embrace the music, "is our current mode of expression, has reference to our time and the way we talk and think."[27]

What this meant was that more black performers began getting airtime. It is not surprising, given the 1920s' epidemic of lynchings, spread of the Klan, and new restrictions on immigration, that segregation and discrimination would block African Americans from being on radio. What *is* surprising is that they got on at all—but some of them did. As Walter Barnes wrote in his column "Hittin' High Notes" for the African American newspaper *The Chicago*

Defender, "When the radio was first put into use there was no dream of ever hearing a race orchestra over the air." That quickly changed. "At first our bands were heard for ten or fifteen minutes over some local station, and a small one at that."[28] Barnes himself and his band, the Royal Creolians, were eventually heard nightly on a Chicago station.

Possibly one of the earliest radio appearances by African Americans was a duet by Earl Hines and Lois Deppe on KDKA in 1921. Hines went on to broadcast from Chicago's Grand Terrace and was the first African American bandleader from Chicago to get network play. In 1922 a concert at New Orleans's Lyric Theater featuring Ethel Waters, backed up by Fletcher Henderson's jazz band, was broadcast by WVG and was reportedly heard in at least five states and Mexico. Waters was, according to one paper, "the first colored girl to sing over the radio." Bessie Smith, whose classic "Empty Bed Blues" was banned in Boston, had her music broadcast over WMC in Memphis and WSB in Atlanta as early as 1923. Audiences of both stations were almost entirely white (that was who could afford radio in the South in the early years), and on occasion they flooded the stations with requests for her to repeat songs like "Outside of That." In 1924 WCAE in Pittsburgh broadcast one of her concerts to accommodate the thousands who had been unable to get tickets to see her, despite a one-week extension of her booking.[29]

By 1925 the African American music critic Dave Peyton could report in *The Chicago Defender* that there was actually a "great demand for race musicians." As this demand increased stations did more remotes, broadcasting live from nightclubs where popular bands were performing. WHN in New York City was especially noted for seeking out black bands and putting them on the air. So was the city's socialist station, WEVD, which featured "hot jazz." Duke Ellington and his band the Washingtonians appeared as early as 1924 over WHN in New York City, as did Fletcher Henderson and his band, who were performing at the Club Alabam on Forty-fourth Street in Manhattan. This led to live broadcasts of Henderson's band from the Roseland Ballroom in New York. And here Henderson was joined by the incomparable Louis Armstrong. The band was hugely popular between 1926 and 1928, when they were on WHN three times a week and WOR once a week. By 1927 Duke Ellington became famous nationally as a result of his nightly broadcasts from the Cotton Club over the newly formed network CBS, and so did Cab Calloway. Fats Waller's *Rhythm Club* premiered on WLW in Cincinnati and by the early 1930s originated from WABC in New York. The 1930 census indicated that 43 percent of Chicago's black families owned radios, and the city pioneered in featuring black talent on the air. Jack L. Cooper, considered the first black disc jockey, began hosting the *All Colored Hour* in 1928 or '29 on Chicago's WSBC and played recordings by Louis Armstrong, Ethel Waters, Fletcher Henderson, and Ida Cox.[30]

At the same time it is true that the networks refused to hire black studio musicians until the late 1930s. And the music of black jazz bands was more likely to be censored by the networks. Black musicians realized that they had to be more polished, more deferential, more circumspect to get bookings—both in white clubs and on the air—to overcome the barbed stereotypes that sought to keep them out of white preserves. Tuxedos with tails, mirror-shiny shoes, crisp white shirts, and an air of reserve became the "dress uniform" for those seeking to combat the old bromides that blacks were, as Dave Peyton complained, "unreliable, barbaric and huge liquor indulgents." Smiling a lot and appearing grateful to white audiences and employers was essential. Here began the ongoing dilemma of becoming a crossover star. Crossing over was good for the music, the performer, the race; but it could also corrupt the black artist's musical and personal integrity, bring charges of diminished authenticity, and force the musician to assume a highly constricting, dishonest masquerade.[31]

A critical symbiotic relationship began between African American music and radio. The timbre and tempo of jazz made the most of the limited fidelity and sound ranges of radio in the 1920s; more to the point, two-beat and four-beat jazz enlivened radio. Writing about the effect Louis Armstrong's bluesy yet swinging cornet playing had on Henderson's band at Roseland, the historian Philip Eberly comments, "One can only guess at the reaction of listeners, heretofore accustomed to tuning in Roseland broadcasts featuring conventional dance music, now hearing on WHN a joyous, new, stomping kind of music, thanks to Armstrong's New Orleans injections."[32] Armstrong was a genius at combining African American rhythms, vocalization, and blues chords with Western harmonies, embodying the quixotic notion that black and white music—and thus culture—could happily coexist. These were the kinds of black musicians who fared best on the radio. And radio, of course, gave Armstrong, Duke Ellington, and others exposure to a huge audience they would never have had otherwise. Radio made them international stars.

But jazz and swing historians agree that the radio industry—particularly its very wary advertisers—required standardization and slower tempos and preferred the smoothness of jazz orchestras to the impertinence and heat of the smaller combos. Once the networks and advertisers began to control programming in the early 1930s, segregation on the air became more pervasive and rigid, preventing Fletcher Henderson from appearing on shows like NBC's Let's Dance. As Variety noted, network radio was a "punishing 'courtroom for jazz' . . . that encouraged 'melody stuff over hot breaks and tricks.' " The elevation of jazz to a national musical form gave whites inordinate power to shape its evolution—at least in the mainstream. Whites also controlled the marketing of African American bands. So it is true that radio reined in black jazz. But it is also true that even in the mid- and late 1930s, on nonsponsored shows and late-night broadcasts from clubs and ballrooms, listeners could hear Count Basie, Jimmie Lunceford, or Earl Hines on the air. Radio took the music of African America into the heart of white America and made it our first genuine national music and one of the most important cultural exports of the century.[33]

Why did so many people who turned on their radios in the mid- and late 1920s tune in to hear jazz bands? While there are no data on audiences from this period, there was no lack of contemporary commentary on the subject. Some argued that jazz was "the product of a buoyant spirit. It is exuberant America expressing itself in sound." Indeed, one listener recalled that when he first encountered jazz on the radio, "it was the most joyful music I had ever heard." Jazz was not sentimental, but it was played from the heart. "Jazz is a joyous revolt from convention, custom, authority, boredom, even sorrow—from everything that would confine the soul of man and hinder its riding free in the air," exclaimed J. A. Rogers in the *Survey*. Describing jazz as "musical fireworks," he added, "it is a release of all the suppressed emotions at once, a blowing off of the lid." Another writer found "the employment of syncopation, in rhythm and melody . . . is quite as fundamental as the circulation of the blood, the beat of the heart, or the pulse." While black critics have rightly noted that whites, in the face of increased mechanization and bureaucratization, projected onto this music self-serving and erroneous notions of black primitivism and innocence, it remains true that these projections mattered deeply to whites' love of and gratitude for jazz.[34]

Certainly the physicality of the music, its insistence that you get up and move, made jazz listening an intensive experience for the body and the mind. The rhythm both created and resolved physical tension.[35] With radio in the home, and jazz on the radio, people used their bodies differently in their own houses, to dance in groups or alone, to move in syncopated beat to the music.

But what may have been the most important thing about jazz was the way it established bridges, however shaky and temporary, across the divides of race, class, and especially gender. If radio had made musical appreciation acceptable for men, jazz was a primary reason. As the *Outlook* noted, "It is the music which for the first time has seized hold of the great mass of American young men as something more than a mere feminine or effeminate accomplishment." It did so because this music spoke to the enormous rebelliousness against Victorian, bourgeois culture many young men were feeling. The iconoclasm of the syncopation, the phallic brashness of the saxophone and drums, the unpredictability of the improvisation, upended the feminized conventions of parlor piano music. Girls playing "Nearer, My God, to Thee" on the piano were one thing. But girls playing the trumpet, the trombone, or the bass guitar? Unthinkable. Jazz, unlike the blues, was a deeply masculine enterprise, showcasing male virtuosity and celebrating the overthrow of everything sedate and soothing in music. It made the performance of music masculine.[36] For all these reasons male fans flocked to it.

It was Gilbert Seldes, in his writings for *The Dial*, who captured how jazz spoke to the cultural contradictions of the 1920s, and to the confusions and warring impulses ricocheting around in its listeners. Jazz was "half-instinctive and half-intellectual," celebrating both careful planning and spontaneous improvisation. There was a tension in the music, as the different instruments talked back to one another, copied one another, then dropped out of the conversation for a while, only to reappear in some surprising, impudent riff. There was often musical discord, a dissonance that wasn't necessarily resolved. So the music enacted an ongoing American drama about how to reconcile the needs of the individual with the needs of the group.[37] The band played tightly together, but then the solos burst out (Louis Armstrong was the pioneer here), had their moment in the spotlight, and receded back into the group. Here individuality actually flourished because it was made possible by and was part of a group.

Just as many Americans, especially the young, thumbed their noses at middle-class conventions in the 1920s, the music they loved "attack[ed] . . . the perfect chord" through the slides of trombones, clarinets, and even of singers' voices. Seldes delighted in songs that spoke to different emotions simultaneously, that seemed to celebrate opposite personas. "Beale Street Blues," for example, expressed "simplicity, sadness, irony, and something approaching frenzy." The voice of the saxophone was especially equivocal, for it was "a reed in brass, partaking of the qualities of two choirs in the orchestra at once." Seldes described "Runnin' Wild" as a "masterpiece" that evoked "two negro spirits—the darky (South, slave) and the buck (Harlem)." He praised Negro jazz at length and admitted to its special fascination for whites. "In their music the negroes have given their response to the world with an exceptional naiveté, a directness of expression which has interested *our* minds as well as touched our emotions."[38] Yes, the unconscious racism of these remarks is all too clear now. But the desires and anxieties they embody should inflect our understanding of whites' genuine enthusiasm, and need, for this music.

Radio was the agent through which this African American music, for the first time on a mass scale, helped define the rebellion of young whites. Old photographs and footage of the era, with flappers and their young men doing the Charleston, fail to convey the importance of black music to white rebellion. As the jazz historian Marshall Stearns put it, "Jazz . . . involves conflicting attitudes that seem to be made-to-order for the adolescent," for with jazz "he can have his cake and eat it too." Dancing and listening to jazz allowed young people to rebel against their parents and mainstream culture while conforming to each other and forming an oppositional but cohesive generational culture. Listening to jazz on the radio in the 1920s tied you to other listeners you couldn't see but knew were out there, people like you who set themselves apart from a vapid culture that managed to find merit in "potted palm music." So radio provided "the double illusion of independence and safety."[39] It also fanned both a sense of narcissistic individualism, the desire to be above the herd, and a sense of belonging to a community.

The coincidence of jazz and radio married an aural technology with the fruits of a primarily oral culture. It wasn't just that the lyrics of Duke Ellington's "Baby, Ain'tcha Satisfied?" or Louis Armstrong's "Butter and Egg Man" simulated conversations about lost or promised love, referred to the great migration of blacks to the North, and conjured up the excitement and loneliness of city life. The music itself was full of information, and Armstrong especially displayed the vocal qualities of his instrument, the trumpet. In the oral culture of African Americans, this music—including instrumental techniques that evoked speaking, crying, moaning, and laughing—conveyed histories large and small, and invested them with powerful emotions.

The radio was the perfect vehicle for this storytelling, setting off such oral traditions as vibrant, authentic, even legitimate. Ben Sidran, in *Black Talk*, argues that jazz and the blues didn't simply "reflect" the African American experience; rather the music itself became the basis on which black culture was built and evolved. Radio played a key role in making this the case during the African American diaspora, when music that used to be shared live came increasingly to be shared through mechanical reproduction. In spite of all the restrictions placed on black musicians and the dilution of their music by whites, radio showcased the galvanizing, communal nature of African American oral culture and made it enviable to whites. The great irony here was that it was through a new electronic invention, radio, that whites, when listening to jazz, could pretend they were escaping from the alienation and routinization of an increasingly technological world.[40]

Through African American music on the radio, whites have often imagined themselves invited to a place less inhibited, more honest and spontaneous, and less boxed in by prevailing rules of decorum than Main Street, USA. They could play hooky in the safety of their own homes, far away from the ghettos, brothels, and gin joints that produced such music, such truancy. For

African American musicians, this medium without images, the medium that didn't constantly remind the audience of their darker skin, allowed fleeting moments of a pureness of exchange between performer and listener when, again, for moments here and there, either race didn't matter, or being black was actually an advantage. With radio as auditory turnstile between cultures, there were enormous enrichments, illusions, and delusions for both sides.

And Ben Sidran does not want us to overlook the connections between the rise of jazz and the blues, and the spiritualism craze of the 1920s. Openly displaying their roots in Negro spirituals, in funeral marches, and in the emotional suffering of slavery and Jim Crow, jazz and the blues spoke deeply to the "spiritual vacuity" of America after the Great War. "Black music can, and did, exist as a nonideological spiritual outlet" because, in part, of its emotional honesty, which seemed "an overt alternative to mainstream values." The eager appropriation of jazz elements by white musicians is further testimony to the recognized need for an infusion of such defiant and uncompromising honesty. And despite the dilutions of black jazz imposed by the networks, advertisers, and Tin Pan Alley, argues Sidran, "the introduction of black music into the American experience . . . indicated the need for, and recognition of, a spiritualistic element of a much higher order."[41]

Ann Douglas argues that the 1920s saw a reaction among many against "the pseudo-religious trappings of late-Victorian culture," a concern that sanctimonious but ultimately false religious posturings and institutions "had made real religious life impossible." The blues especially, Douglas notes, spoke to people's mysterious ability to survive, often with grace; they confirmed the existence and power of the soul. And they sang about what many recognized to be "universal and absolute truth."[42] Here was black music on the radio reassuring listeners that commercial culture could actually be redeeming.

As William Kenney has argued, the phonograph introduced Americans to new musical experiences while simultaneously "resurrect[ing] and repeat[ing] older, more familiar ones."[43] Radio throughout the century cultivated these opposites because it was profitable to nurture nostalgia through old favorites just as it was profitable to cater to the new and different musical tastes of young people. Music became more deeply assimilated into everyday life and cultural memory than ever before, something which Americans profoundly understood. That is why there were battles throughout the century over what kind of music should and should not be on the air.

As early as the 1920s, when the phenomenon of radio music listening was still quite new, people understood that concentrated music listening—memorizing lyrics, putting dance steps to certain songs, trying to copy chords or harmonies on one's own instrument at home—shaped individual and group identity as never before. Cultural elites, of course, were happy to have Handel and Mozart constituting people's emotional lives, their aesthetic sensibilities, their collective memories. But Louis Armstrong was another story. Much of the white bourgeois panic about jazz was based on this understanding—however unarticulated—of how powerfully music listening was constituting identity, and that now, at least with black jazz and blues, some of that identity, especially among the young, would be constituted in and through black culture. This emotional identification with African American culture, however partial and complicated by racism, spawned fears of psychic miscegenation, and informed the reactions against white youths' using radio to tap into black music in the 1920s, 1950s, and 1980s.

For men, radio colonized and reinforced new and old territories of masculinity. Tinkering with machines was nothing new for men, but radio brought such tinkering into the safety and comfort of the domestic sphere and of leisure time. It made being a nerd almost glamorous. Being able to embrace music emotionally, on such a daily basis, was new for men, and it helped bring them, however imperceptibly, closer to women, some of whom, in the 1920s, were trying their damnedest to be more like men. Radio as a trapdoor for men into new realms of gender pleasure, and as a trapdoor between the races—if open only a crack, and in the imagination more than in everyday life—these were real changes in the subjective life of the country. Desire, rebellion, self-image, behavior—all these were being reshaped by music as broadcast on the radio.

Radio Comedy and Linguistic Slapstick

When Ronald Reagan used the statement "Go ahead; make my day" in 1983 as a warning to Congress that he would veto, with glee, any tax increase it might pass, he was extending a tradition begun fifty years earlier in radio. A former radio announcer, he had an instinct for this. He borrowed a scrap of pop culture dialogue heard by millions (in this case, in a Clint Eastwood film) and used it in a completely different sphere of American life, national politics, to instantly bond himself to his audience. He knew intuitively that this macho comeback allowed him to inhabit, however temporarily, the skin of a tough, larger-than-life fictional cop with whom many of his listeners had identified. Being a creature of Hollywood, he grasped that such media catchphrases help produce a sense of solidarity, a sense of us-versus-them, of who's in the know and who isn't, of who gets the joke and who doesn't. Reagan, Eastwood's character, and Americans who envied this defiant retort were bonded through language, standing tall against a bunch of cowed spendthrifts. They were all real men. All this through five words.

There are many tacks one could take in writing about one of American popular culture's most beloved genres, radio comedy in the 1930s. The central role of advertising agencies in the making of popular entertainment was a key departure: networks didn't produce radio shows, ad agencies did, with particular products, like Jell-O, sponsoring particular comedians, like Jack Benny. One could focus on a few shows or stars, or on how radio created comedy factories manned by teams of writers who developed huge files reportedly containing up to 200,000 jokes they could feed into the ever needy maw of broadcasting.

I'd like to explore what radio comedy did with and to the American language. Usually we take language use for granted, rarely thinking about how transparent a window it is onto the values, hopes, and anxieties of society. But language and social order are braided together so tightly that, unless we untangle them, we can overlook what language tells us about history. And since radio pushed the use of language to the center stage of American life, we should explore what these words enacted. For when we think about the impact of radio on American life, we are thinking primarily about the impact of language on people's thoughts and cultural perceptions. Story listening evolved through radio comedy in important ways, and comedians like George Burns and Gracie Allen, Fred Allen, and Jack Benny added a visual, dimensional element to the standard joke repartee of vaudeville. It wasn't enough to laugh at some one-liners; now listeners were asked to see Gracie sliding down a banister, to go down to Jack's infamous vault, to stroll along Fred Allen's alley. These performers asked listeners to enter a common, imagined space, and they had to develop audio signposts to help the listeners along.

With millions of Americans from the late 1920s onward hearing the same often humorous phrases simultaneously, comments like "I'se regusted" and "Holy mackerel" from *Amos 'n' Andy* became embedded in the everyday language of ordinary people. Radio reshaped the spoken word in America, but not only by giving people new catchphrases to use. Just as silent films had relied on physical slapstick to make up for the absence of the verbal, radio made up for the absence of the visual by showcasing and inflating linguistic slapstick. In the 1930s, with the rise of comedy as the most popular genre on the air, radio enacted a war between a more homogenized language on the one hand and the defiant, unassimilated linguistic holdouts on the other. Wordplay reached new heights, but it was circumscribed by a new, official corps of language police, who determined and enforced what kind of English it was proper to speak on the air before a national audience. Decorum and insubordination took turns, and they worked hand in hand.

What radio did was provide an arena in which very different kinds of verbal agility could duke it out. The radio language wars were on, seemingly inconsequential and played for laughs. But language wars are never inconsequential. When we look at these battles, we are witnessing struggles over power, pecking order, and masculine authority. All societies are ruled by language, and nearly every society grants high status to those with deft verbal skills.[1] There are always rivalries between language users in a culture; when a mass medium caters to the ears alone, such rivalries assume central symbolic importance. Who says what to whom and how speaks volumes about who has power, who doesn't, and how that power is both challenged and maintained.

And questions about who should and should not have power were at the fore-front of thought and politics in Depression America.

Radio in the 1920s brought the disembodied voices of politicians, educa-tors, celebrities, and announcers directly into people's homes for the first time. By 1923 millions of listeners had heard Warren Harding, Woodrow Wilson, and Calvin Coolidge address the nation over radio. "It is incomparably more interesting to hear the message delivered than to read it in the next morning's paper," observed *Radio Broadcast*, because the voice conveys emotion, empha-sis, sincerity (or lack thereof), and personality. It quickly became clear that lis-teners, with the voice as their only clue, used a combination of their imaginations and social knowledge to ascribe all sorts of traits to an unseen speaker. Herta Herzog, a pioneer in audience research, found that listeners pic-tured the speaker's age, social status, appearance, and personality all from his or her voice. In addition, listeners made all sorts of assumptions about a speaker's intelligence, honesty, compassion, generosity, and competence sim-ply based on accent, as well as on tone of voice and delivery. Thus were those on the radio, the famous and the unknown, now "judged by vocal standards alone."[2]

Radio, like other mass entertainments, was a site of class tensions and of the pull between cultural homogeneity and diversity. So language use over the air became controversial by the late 1920s. The pronunciations of entertainers and announcers on radio were "as varied as their origins," with listeners won-dering whether one pronounced *tomato* "tomayto" or "tomahto" and *vase* "vays," "vayz," or "vahz." Radio, observed one writer, had made Americans "pronunciation conscious," prompting them to turn a book like *Thirty Thou-sand Words Mispronounced* into a best-seller and to flock to correspondence courses on how to speak. Were radio stations really going to permit people to go on the air who pronounced *birds* "boids," *avenues* "avenoos," and *God* "Gawd"? asked *The Commonweal*. Radio had to provide a model of good dic-tion, the magazine insisted. *The Saturday Review* asserted that the strict audio limitations of the device itself would compel the professional broadcaster "to become a careful speaker. The Southerner in America begins to pull his vowels together for the radio, and the Londoner sometimes makes *a, e, i, o, u* sound like those letters; while the slovenly New Yorker and the careless Chicagoan begin to articulate as the English do, because they have to, if they are to be heard."[3] Those with nasal voices were extremely unpopular, and critics asserted that women's higher voices didn't sound as good as men's over the ether.

In 1929 the BBC imposed a single standard of pronunciation for all its an-nouncers, who had to be phonetically trained and conform precisely to BBC usage. While *The Saturday Review* feared that "those in control of broadcasting will try to make us all talk alike," many critics urged the adoption of an official standard of radio pronunciation in the United States. As one argued, the "universal leveling of dialects . . . will go far to promote sectional and national and international understanding."[4] But the subtext of these recommendations acknowledged the powerful role that language plays in defining and reinforcing class, ethnic, racial, and gender differences, and insisted that language continue to perform this function. Malapropisms, wrong pronunciations, overly thick regional accents, and dialects marked the speaker, rightly or wrongly, as ignorant, stupid, and low-class.

By the 1930s the fully established networks and the advertisers who controlled much of radio programming *did* impose a standard of radio pronunciation. Diction contests on the air set norms for announcers and listeners, and one fan wrote that "not only the youth of today but many older people have received much help and inspiration toward correct speech from radio announcers." Announcers had to learn the proper pronunciation of words rarely used in everyday speech, easily mispronounced names and words like Chopin, Goebbels, Wagner, *chorale,* and *mazurka.*[5]

But the contest between linguistic homogeneity and diversity found a fascinating territorial compromise, one that quickly became highly ritualized. Announcers for shows and those who read the commercials were indeed the custodians of "official" English in America, as were newscasters and dramatic actors and actresses. Some complained that these announcers promoted "a stereotyped style of toneless expression, accurate, monotonous and stiff"; they "seem to wish to teach us all to talk like mechanical dolls or robots." This style of announcing bracketed everything, music, talks, and plays. It was "the norm to which the waves must always return . . . as inevitable as the hour-end chimes and more insistent."[6] But Americans were not going to abide such obvious, top-down, anti-individualistic verbal encasements. For in comedy shows—and *Amos 'n' Andy* was the harbinger here—linguistic rebellion, even anarchy, reigned supreme. Radio comedians, in contrast to their linguistically staid, even pompous announcers, ran wild with the American language. Yes, radio would have standards and impose them. But "nonstandard" English on the radio was where the laughs—and the profits—were.

Radio critics at the time bemoaned language use on the radio, particularly the way many advertisers and programmers seemed to "talk down" to the audience, reinforcing what many of these critics saw as a connection between the spread of mass culture and the dumbing down of America. Gilbert Seldes, in *The New Republic,* chastised Alexander Woollcott's broadcasts as "the Early Bookworm," because they "had none of the virtues of his written work." Needling Woollcott for saying that certain written treasures "caught these old eyes," Seldes remarked that "most of the rest of Mr. Woollcott's anatomy grew old as he spoke" and added that he sounded like "an English squire who detests intelligence."[7] By the mid-1930s many intellectuals felt that radio, with its over-explanation of scenes, its low comedy, and its wordplay, was infantalizing the audience.

Amos 'n' Andy was radio's first great national program, the one that got people into the habit of listening to a specific program at a fixed time every night.[8] It was the broadcast that demonstrated most forcefully the way radio was starting to determine how people divided up their time at home and matched their schedules to the schedules of the broadcast day. It showed vaudevillians—whose success was being undercut by movies and radios—that comedy over the air worked and was profitable.

The two thousand vaudeville theaters that had thrived at the turn of the century had been reduced to fewer than one hundred by 1930. By the early and mid-1930s, with advertisers and networks searching for similar shows with national appeal, a host of vaudevillians—Joe Penner, Will Rogers, Ed Wynn, Burns and Allen, and Jack Benny—signed up to do their own radio shows. And what they did was comedy that elevated the wisecrack, the witty comeback, the put-down to an art. "Because of radio," noted *Literary Digest,* America was becoming "a nation of wisecrackers."[9] Now, commentators noted, the air was filled with puns, malapropisms, insults, quips, and non sequiturs. Obviously, in this nonvisual medium, words, tone of voice, and sound effects carried all the freight.

Some have opined that radio comedy's main function was to cheer people up during hard times. Surely we can do better than this. For the nature of the linguistic acrobatics that went on over the airwaves in the 1930s, the centrality of verbal dueling, suggests that radio comedy was enacting much larger dramas about competition, authority, fairness, and hope during the greatest crisis of American capitalism, the Great Depression. Certainly Freud insisted that we regard comedy as something much more complicated and revealing than it appears on the surface. It often expresses barely articulated beliefs and fears, basic passions, and an ongoing contest between the infantile and the rational, in which the rational wins out—we "get" the joke—but up until then nonsense has a field day.

Jokes often express violence and aggression, frequently against the constraints we feel are imposed on us by institutions, indeed, by adulthood itself. It is in part our "infantile greed for disorder" that is manifested in people's love of wordplay, in our delight in breaking free and razzing the rules. Sociolinguists emphasize, in fact, that "ritual" insulting—insults as part of a game, done for laughs—occurs most frequently during times of cultural stress.[10]

Most important, I think, is that this dueling also reflected the crisis in masculinity and traditional male authority that the Depression precipitated. Let's remember that from 1929 to 1933 gross national product dropped by 29 percent, construction by 78 percent, and investment by 98 percent. Unemployment rose from 3.2 percent to a staggering 24.9 percent. Just one look at the enormously popular Shirley Temple films of the period, with their lost daddies, dead daddies, or blind daddies, drives home the enormous anxiety about the threatened collapse of patriarchy. Individual reaction to this catastrophe ranged from acquiescence, self-recrimination, and a sense of personal failure to outrage and a determination to find scapegoats and restructure society. In 1934 alone—the same year that radio comedy, with all its insults and linguistic battles, established its primacy over the airwaves—nearly 1.5 million workers participated in 1,800 strikes. As the historian Robert McElvaine succinctly puts it, "Class conflict reached the point of open warfare."[11] Workers were fighting back, often in the streets, sometimes with weapons and violence, against privilege, exclusion, inequity.

The enormous popularity of all kinds of verbal deviance suggests how anger, defiance, and rebellion were given voice, while also defused, over the airwaves. It is not enough to note that people wanted a good laugh during the Depression. When a particular culture at a particular moment invests enormous amounts of time, energy, and money into verbal dueling, we need to ask why.[12] What were these bloodless, cathartic battles stand-ins for?

The unspoken but understood rules of speech—of who says what to whom and how—both reflect and reaffirm any culture's established social order. When one man addresses another by his first name, while the other man uses "Mr." and a last name, we know right away who's boss. The most striking features of one's social environment—class, region, educational level, gender, and race—are all marked, in how one speaks.[13] Proper grammar, correct forms of address; polite, inoffensive commentary; a modulated tone of voice, neither too high nor too low; a neutral accent, not overly marked by geography or ethnicity—all of these govern middle-class speech, how someone who wants to be accepted and doesn't want to stand out is meant to talk.

Violating any of these rules, especially more than one, signals that the speaker isn't going to play by the rules, either because he or she doesn't know better or because he or she refuses. Not knowing better makes you pathetic and even contemptible. Refusing, however, sets you apart from the herd, and can make you scary. It can also make you funny. Most endearing of all, as radio comics learned, was violating staid linguistic conventions while appearing oblivious to the fact that you were doing so. This way the audience could laugh at you and feel superior to you while also wanting, on a psychological level, to take you under its wing, protect you, and thank you for the momentary relief from linguistic lockstep.

Radio comedy's reliance on linguistic slapstick was an auditory exaggeration of what had gone on in vaudeville for years. Vaudeville had popularized a new kind of humor, a humor like gunfire, more brash, defiant, and aggressive, more reliant on jokes and punch lines than on tall tales or monologues. It threw verbal pies in the face of Victorian gentility: it showcased hostility, not politeness; misunderstandings, not conversations; and it acknowledged that disorder, not order, governed everyday life. Its argot was slang, dialect, malapropisms. The wisecracks often took deadly aim at the gap between the sunny myth of success and the more overcast, unyielding realities of urban and industrial life. This was the humor of resentment and retaliation and, with the enormous influence of Jewish comics and minstrelsy, was the humor of the underdog trapped by verbal misunderstandings and barricades, tripped up by verbal codes he could never completely crack. Some of its roots could be traced to minstrelsy, in which actors in blackface mangled "proper" English, and to burlesque in the late 1860s and 1870s, in which women, often dressed as men, used puns to lampoon much that bourgeois culture found sacred.[14]

Although there was plenty of slapstick for the eyes—bizarre costumes, exaggerated facial expressions, and pratfalls—it was wordplay that was central to vaudeville humor. Indeed, wordplay was central to the country's sometimes raucous theatrical history. And while vaudeville managers did much to attract females to their shows in the 1890s and after, in cities like New York nearly two-thirds of the audience was still male in the 1910s.[15] This humor spoke especially to working-class men, to their frustrated ambitions and wounded pride, their respect and need for quick-wittedness, and their need to get even, if only verbally, with a system that rewarded some men at the expense of others. Radio didn't just continue this tradition of linguistic slapstick. The properties of the machine itself ensured that wordplay would be enshrined as a central cultural feature of American life at midcentury. And the conditions of everyday life ensured that wordplay would become heavily laden with other, much less frivolous freight.

The pioneering show here was *Amos 'n' Andy*, whose main characters were played by Freeman Gosden and Charles Correll. As Gilbert Seldes noted at the time, the show fused two successful pop culture genres, blackface minstrelsy and the "story comic strip."[16] Most of the humor came from the pair's mangling of conventional English, from the incessant malapropisms, inadvertent puns, and total misunderstanding of regular terms and phrases.

Thus it is important to move beyond the "was it racist or not" questions surrounding the show. Of course it was racist. Of course it took the most demeaning aspects of minstrelsy and enshrined them on the air. And it was hardly an exception. As the media historian Michele Hilmes reminds us, radio revived minstrelsy in shows like *Two Black Crows, The Dutch Masters Minstrels,* and *Watermelon and Cantaloupe.* But *Amos 'n' Andy* was one of the few situation comedies that didn't cast blacks solely as servants. And as Melvin Patrick Ely argues in his definitive study of the show, millions of white listeners were not glued to it every night at 7:00 simply so they could laugh at the stupidity and naiveté of black folks. Rather, through the dialogue the show "jumped back and forth across the color line in a manner both cavalier and surreal," in a way that ultimately caused that line "to blur altogether."[17] White listeners weren't simply laughing at black folks; they were also laughing at an only slightly exaggerated version of themselves. All too many white listeners, although most would never actually admit it, identified with *Amos 'n' Andy.*

Amos 'n' Andy became a network show in August 1929, just a few months before the stock market crash. It quickly grew to be the most popular program on the air, reaching an estimated 40 million listeners, or approximately one-third of the population. It was a national addiction: hotel lobbies, movie theaters, and shops piped the show in from 7:00 to 7:15 so as not to lose customers. Telephones remained still, toilets weren't used, taxis sat unhailed while the show was on.[18]

Certainly the show played on stereotypes about the incompetence, duplicity, and shiftlessness of black men. But its power came from the way it dramatized the collapse of paternal authority in the home, in the government, in the marketplace. White culture has often projected onto "stage Negroes" its worst fears about itself. And this was certainly true of *Amos 'n' Andy,* in which black men (portrayed by white men) struggled to earn a living, conquer bureaucracy, and retain some shred of masculine dignity in the face of breadlines, an indifferent government, and uppity women. Using what the writer and editor Mel Watkins has called "racial ventriloquism," white men put into the mouths of blacks their sense of helplessness in a world where all too many men suddenly felt superfluous, stymied, throttled.[19]

Amos (played by Gosden) was the more earnest, gullible, and hardworking partner of the Fresh Air Taxi Company, Incorpulated, while Andy (played by Correll) was the more cocky, lazy, and self-important of the two. The Kingfish (also played by Gosden) was the unscrupulous bunco artist who inducted the two into the fraternal organization the Mystic Knights of the Sea and constantly conned Amos and Andy out of what little money they had. As Melvin Patrick Ely has noted, the show, despite its reinforcement of a host of racial stereotypes, also evoked a rich and complex portrait of an urban black community during the Depression.

One of the pleasures of the show for whites came from its racial voyeurism, the eavesdropping the show pretended it allowed onto another speech community with ridiculous and fascinating attributes. There was, in the 1920s, with the popularity of jazz, the Harlem Renaissance, and the ongoing black migration in America, a renewed fascination with Black English, a distinctive language with rules all its own, indigenous to America yet nonstandard. *Amos 'n' Andy* was a hybrid, a bastardization of Black English by white men. But the use of *d* for *th* (as in "dese" and "dat"), the dropping of final *g*'s ("huntin' ") and final *r*'s ("heah" for *here)*, and the use of *done* as a substitute for the verb "to be" ("I done go now") marked the speech as authentically black. Here was a more lively, seemingly genuine dialect not roped in and confined by schoolmarms, intellectuals, or bourgeois codes of decorum. The fact that so many catchphrases from *Amos 'n' Andy* were used by millions of white listeners is testimony to people's affection for the show's version of Black English: people borrow linguistically from those they admire, not those they scorn, however forbidden it is to admit that admiration.[20]

The linguistic mutilations of the show allowed listeners to feel superior to these illiterate, verbally stumbling men, whose language deficiencies were meant to reflect cognitive deficiencies. But the malapropisms also ridiculed mainstream, white America, especially the arbitrariness and high-handedness of government bureaucracy and big business. Letters Andy "de-tated" to Amos were addressed to the "secketary of de interior o' labor," and nationally known figures were renamed J. Ping-Pong Morgan and Charles Limburger. Executives discussed "propolitions," the economic crisis was "de bizness repression," and garbled explanations of the causes of the Depression were not all that far from the incomprehensible and reckless machinations of Wall Street manipulators. This use of blacks—or faux blacks—to attack the pretensions, snobbery, and frequent inhumanity of the upper classes had begun in minstrel shows, in which the Dandy Jim caricature lampooned not just the urban black dandy but also the prissy and pompous upper-class *white* dandy.[21]

Andy—greedy, selfish, and always on the make—straddled those deeply contradictory feelings about businessmen after the crash. On the one hand, they were despicable and had ruined the country; on the other hand, without more entrepreneurs hustling to make it, the country would never recover. The suspicion that all too many businessmen were not just greedy but incompetent to boot was given full play in the show, as was the sense that most people were being buffeted about by economic forces way beyond their control.

And it was the wordplay that conveyed this. The Kingfish explained what had happened to small investors in Wall Street: "Ev'ybody knows de inside on de stocks, yo' see—dat's what dey tell yo', so den you buy it an' it just look like dey waitin' fo' you to buy it, 'cause de minute you buy it, it goes down . . . de fust thing you know it gits cheaper, den you lose." Andy asks what makes stocks go up. "Well, some o' dese big mens down on Wall Street git in a pool, an' when dey git behind de stocks, dey say dat's whut make it go up."[22] They weren't just stereotyping black incomprehension of complexities like the economy. They gave voice to *white* incomprehension—admittedly safely projected onto blacks—and to the deep resentment white working folks had toward those white elites who may have precipitated, yet remain unscathed by, the current disaster.

One of the most common story lines in the show featured the con man and the mark, in which an ambitious and/or well-intentioned and naïve type is duped by a more calculating, sophisticated shyster. Here a string of shimmering verbal mirages serves as the lure for the more credulous. *Amos 'n' Andy* insisted that language was fun, but it also acknowledged that it was dangerous, especially for plain, trusting folk. There was an identification that transcended race when Amos and Andy lost their money in the Kingfish's schemes, were hounded by unsympathetic creditors, or got in trouble with the IRS or other bureaucracies because they had failed to fill out forms too complicated for them to understand. And while Amos embodied the work ethic and insisted it remained *the* foundation to success in America, Andy repudiated the merits of hard work, personifying the sense that a lot of people *had* worked hard, and look where they were now.

This ambivalence about the merits and future of capitalism was intimately connected with dramas about the nature of masculinity and the ongoing battles of the sexes. Andy, of course, was totally cynical about women and love. When Amos describes marriage as requiring "give an' take," Andy agrees, saying that the husband must "give de money an' take de back-talk."[23] Andy specialized in macho braggadocio about the importance of keeping women in their place, and his exaggerated bombast about his mastery over women was deflated by Amos, female characters, and the plot lines. Amos was on the other end of the spectrum, respectful of and deferential to his girlfriend, Ruby, and not above crying when he got too emotional about his love life. Using stage Negroes, the show stripped away certain pretensions about masculinity—its self-importance, its seriousness, its coherence, its strength.

Here, language was also revealing. Ruby, the woman Amos loved, and Sapphire, the Kingfish's acid-tongued wife, both spoke standard English. It was the women who had mastered proper English. The men, by contrast, were constant victims of the way white people spoke and wrote. In one episode Amos and Andy struggle to sound out the word *acknowledge* and come up with *acna-o-wheel-dij*. In countless other episodes, they attempt the simplest mathematical calculations by "mulsifyin'," "revidin'," "timesin'," and "stackin' 'em up" (adding).²⁴ The humor here, the crisis in masculinity, came from the fact that the boys didn't get the better of the language, the language got the better of them. In the early 1930s the dynamic between male radio characters and the language became more complex. But this did not necessarily mean a rescuing of American manhood. With linguistic slapstick there was redemption, but there was also the enactment of utter failure.

While *Amos 'n' Andy* came out of a seventy-year tradition of minstrel shows in America, subsequent radio comedy drew from vaudeville. And vaudeville specialized in ethnic humor, in comedy teams of "the straight man" and the stooge, and in insults, puns, wordplay, and punch lines. But vaudeville was also a visual medium, and comics often relied on clownish costumes, mugging, and physical slapstick to get laughs. With radio this was impossible.

A radio comic had to do what other successful entertainers did—develop an identifiable and pleasing "personality." The show, of course, could refer to the clothes the comic wore, his face and body movements. In fact, radio had to overdescribe everything in a way you never would in real life—"Oh, look, here's Jack coming into the room now"—which made its discourse uniquely quaint. But for the most part the comic had to rely on his voice and his words to set himself apart from the others. So most radio comics early on developed "vocal trade-marks" by which they were known, including "Vas you der, Scharlie?" "Don't ever do that," and "Some joke, eh boss?" What helped the audience at home was the institutionalization of the studio audience, who helped comics time the delivery of their jokes and let those at home visualize themselves as part of a larger, public audience in which it was perfectly fine—even expected—to laugh out loud, in front of a box in your living room.²⁵

It was in the 1932–33 season that Ed Wynn, Fred Allen, Jack Benny, and George Burns and Gracie Allen all made their debuts on radio. Eddie Cantor had gone on the air the year before, Joe Penner would debut the year after. Separately and together, they made linguistic slapstick a central feature of American life in the 1930s. The comedy formats they designed—using the deep-voiced, well-spoken announcer or orchestra leader as the "straight man," playing ethnic types for laughs, making themselves the butts of jokes and insults—became so ritualized and durable that they persist in varying forms to this day. It was the contrast between types of voices, with different timbres, accents, and affectations, that was key to radio's humor—the jokes lay as much between the sounds and pronunciations of different voices as they did within the voice of one character. And central to these jokes, insults, and linguistic rituals was a debate about the sanctity of male authority in an economic system that certain male authority figures had nearly ruined because of their greed and carelessness.

Successful male comics set themselves up as self-inflated egoists in desperate need of deflation, often by women and ethnic minorities but also by their white, male straight men. Other men squealed and whinnied, their vocal cross-dressing central to their jokes and their on-air personalities. Still others had wives who refused to speak the official (male) language properly and used the double-jointedness of the English language to slip out of official linguistic handcuffs and to render their husbands helpless. Gracie Allen may have played the airheaded ditz, but it was George who, week in and week out, was the benighted chump.

Because his popularity was short-lived, Joe Penner is probably the least remembered of the famous radio comics. But in 1933 he was an overnight sensation when he hosted the half-hour variety show *The Baker's Broadcast*. In June of 1934, Penner was voted the best comedian on radio. His trademark was his exaggerated, squeaky, seemingly preadolescent voice—a precursor to Jerry Lewis—and his inane, "yuk yuk" horse laugh. Penner's careening, skidding voice shot up octaves into falsetto giggles and squeals. He elongated individual words as in "woooe is me," pulling the middle *o* up and down as if he were playing it on a clarinet. Through catchphrases repeated every week—"you nah-h-sty man," "Don't ever doooo that," and "Wanna buy a duck"—Penner masqueraded as a woman, a gay man, a child, an idiot, and, not insignificantly, a eunuch.

The humor of these expressions eludes us today, because such humor is so tied to its historical moment. But Penner and comics like him seemed to appreciate, however unconsciously, that catchphrases help cultivate an us-versus-them, insider-outsider mentality. Phrases like "you nasty man" were, as *Literary Digest* put it, "done to death by every street urchin."[26] The use of such broadcasting argot served as a password into a club, a code only the initiated could decipher.

Penner and his contemporaries also reveled in puns and other forms of wordplay. Proficiency with language was admired in 1930s America, as it was in most societies, but a deftness that came from wealth and class privilege was suspect, especially in the aftermath of the stock market crash. By playing such proficiency for laughs, and linking it to buffoonery and self-deprecating humor, radio comics could be above the less facile hoi polloi but one of the people at the same time. Most important, radio comics, most of whom had had limited formal education, used their oral displays instead of diplomas to make it in America. They showed that other kinds of verbal agility, not just that which came from a college degree, could move one up a few rungs on the social ladder.

There was with Penner and Ed Wynn, another giggling, falsetto type known as the Fire Chief, a sheer love of playing with language. One survey in 1933 reported that Wynn's show was the most popular on radio, with 74 percent of listeners on Tuesday night at 9:30 tuned in to him. Like most comics Wynn relied on the gag, usually a quick, two-line joke that did not depend on the context of the show to produce laughs, and he reportedly delivered sixty such gags every broadcast. Penner also played with the language itself rather than creating particular comedic situations. In an exchange between Penner and his girlfriend, she chastises him for failing to call her at 8:00 as he had promised. "I wanted to call you up to call you down for not calling me up," she chides, "but I couldn't do it because the phone company just installed a French phone and I don't know how to speak French."[27]

Ed Wynn loved puns and announced on the air, "You notice tonight I'm almost pun struck." As radio researchers noted at the time, "Puns are the *pièce de résistance* of radio humor." Most of these puns were real groaners. "The darnedest thing happened," reported Wynn. "I was just carrying a jar of jelly wrapped in newspaper when it fell on the floor and broke. You should see the jam Dick Tracy is in today." Puns also served as punch lines in exchanges between Wynn and his straight man–announcer, Graham McNamee, who also became one of radio's first important sportscasters. Repetition, which is key to oral cultures, helped with the cadence and timing of the jokes and made sure the audience was ready for the wordplay to follow.[28] McNamee, setting an example for Ed McMahon and other sidekicks thirty years later, was in a perpetual state of merriment, giggling constantly during his exchanges with Wynn, to cue the audience that a big laugh was coming. "How's your aunt?" McNamee would ask, and then giggle. "A mess, Graham, just a mess." "A mess," repeated McNamee, giggling. "Yes, a mess," responded Wynn. And then the jokes would proceed, and McNamee would let loose and laugh at the punch line.

Such grooved rhythms helped pull people into the flow of the show and set up the verbal surprises to come. Wynn would say to McNamee, "Graham, I had a friend of mine down to my farm the other day, and I served him some beer. I served him some beer, Graham, and do you know what he said?" "No, Chief, what did he say?" "He said, 'I don't want that! Bring me a whole stein. Bring me a whole stein!' So you know what I brought him?" "What did you bring him, Chief?" asked McNamee, again giggling, of course. "A cow!" giggled Wynn. In another exchange, Wynn said that his aunt went into a dry goods store and said, "I want some material. I want to make pillowcases. I don't know what kind of material I want for pillowcases." Then Wynn giggled. "The clerk said,

'You need muslin.' My aunt said, 'If I do, it'll take a bigger man than you to do it.' " Although puns are usually regarded as a low form of humor, they expose the loopholes in the language, the ways in which it is possible to disobey or deliberately ignore certain rules, and they celebrate the language's elasticity. They also show how language can move us—trap us—in a place we don't want to be. And puns, of course, work best when they are heard, not when they are read.[29]

Like Penner, Wynn played the vocal eunuch—he sometimes sounded like Tiny Tim—frequently interrupting his straight man with falsetto giggles and high-pitched interjections of effeminate comments like "fancy that" or "my goodness." Sometimes he affected a lisp. Like Penner, Wynn got laughs because he was an emasculated clown.

Eddie Cantor's *Chase and Sanborn Hour* premiered in September 1931, and within a year one of the fledgling ratings services estimated that over 50 percent of Sunday night's listeners tuned in to hear him. In 1933 and 1934 Cantor's show was the highest rated program on the airwaves. The variety show featured singers and a violinist, but the main focus was on the humor, which consisted of sketches and stand-up routines. Cantor's ethnic jokesters included the Mad Russian (played by Bert Gordon) and the Greek character Parkyakarkus (Harry Einstein). These players with exaggerated accents did double duty: their inability to master proper English marked them as men still outside the fold, yet their ability to zing Cantor verbally showed that recent immigrants could hold their own. The banter between Cantor and his straight man, as well as between him and the show's ethnic stooges, was combative and insulting, as the men ridiculed one another's appearance, competence, and especially their manhood. These insults were typical of banter not between grown men but between male adolescents. This same form of humor was used when famous guests appeared on the show. In an exchange with John Barrymore, Cantor says, "When I'm with my kids, I'm always acting funny." Barrymore retorts, "What a pity a microphone could stop all that." When Barrymore's wife appears, Cantor kisses her and announces, "Your wife kisses beautifully. My wife doesn't kiss like that." Barrymore's wife, Elaine, shoots back, "No wonder, look what she's got to practice on." In another show featuring Tallulah Bankhead, Cantor proposes doing a passionate love scene with her. "Stop kidding yourself, Eddie," she answers, "you haven't got enough fuel to give me a hot foot."[30]

The rapidity of the repartee, and the speed of the cutting comeback, was key to this humor. You had to be quick on the uptake. Insults establish a pecking order, and the one insulted must respond quickly and effectively or lose status instantly. Such oral dueling was inherently competitive; it reaffirmed that the competitive spirit was still thriving in America and that its pleasures—the laughs—were greater than its costs—the injured pride. Radio comics had to simulate spontaneity—hence their file boxes full of jokes. And offstage, joking insults are allowed only between people pretty familiar with each other, like brother and sister or husband and wife. So the very reliance on insults simulated a feeling of familiarity between those on the air, and between them and their audience.[31] Cantor treated his audience as if the show was a collaboration between speaker and listener, and as if they were all part of the same dysfunctional family.

While many of the jokes ridiculed masculine self-delusions, the pace, delivery, and tone of the humor reaffirmed verbal agility and quickness as a distinctly male trait. On Cantor's show masculinity was exposed as a masquerade that a lot of men, like Cantor, couldn't carry off. Men's conceits about their attractiveness and sexual prowess, about their intelligence and general mastery over life, were pricked into flaccid, deflated balloons. But at the same time masculinity was recuperated, its resilience, toughness, and instant ability to respond to a challenge celebrated week in and week out.

On Cantor's show and other comedy-variety shows like it, the listener was moved sometimes rapidly between modes of listening. There might be a series of jokes, then a vocal performance, then a skit, then a commercial, then an instrumental by the band. Each segment called for varying, nuanced levels of attention and for different emotional registers. Some invited imagining a particular scene and people, others didn't. Often at the same time you'd be rooting for Cantor yet eagerly anticipating his put-down. One song would bore you, the next would trigger all sorts of memories. Just as linguistic slapstick moved you between being the underdog and being the victor, between being a humbled man and a cocky one, these variety shows encouraged listeners to be many persons, with various stances, all at the same time.

The comedy teams that pushed wordplay to new and often subversive extremes were George Burns and Gracie Allen, and Jane and Goodman Ace. The Aces are not as well remembered today as Burns and Allen because they didn't make the transition to television (the TV version of their show lasted only six weeks). But they became enormously popular after their show premiered in 1930.

In both *The Burns and Allen Show* and *Easy Aces,* the wives were scatterbrained, upper-middle-class women who, on the surface, played into stereotypes about women being dumb, irrational, obsessed with the trivial, and unable to comprehend even the most basic rules of logic. But the humor and the roles were much more complex. For despite the fact that George Burns and Goodman Ace personified male logic and reason, their radio wives consistently got the better of them, maneuvering them into linguistic and cognitive labyrinths they couldn't begin to find their ways out of. Thirty years later, in the 1960s, TV wives who were really witches or genies had magical powers that turned the male world of business, technology, and logic upside down.[32] But in the 1930s, on radio, language was what these women used to demonstrate that male authority—especially the authority that came from *their* language, *their* logic—was totally arbitrary and extremely fragile. When these women spoke the seemingly crystalline nature of male reasoning was shattered into a million unretrievable pieces.

Jane Ace was especially known for her malapropisms and misquotes, known as Janeacisms. Like Gracie Allen, Jane appeared to be a scatterbrain, but language was putty in her hands as she reshaped existing clichés into double entendres and pointed jokes. "We're insufferable friends" and "Time wounds all heels" made fun of the tensions in interpersonal relationships, while a comment like "I was down on the Lower East Side today and saw those old testament houses" had a more biting undercurrent. So did "we're all cremated equal." Others, like "up at the crank of dawn," "working my head to the bone," and "you've got to take the bitter with the badder," breathed new life and meaning into outworn bromides.[33]

Gracie Allen, with her slightly nasal, high-pitched voice, was also a master at exposing the way male rules of language weren't as ironclad as they might seem, especially if you just looked at things a little bit differently, took things too literally, or not literally enough. Burns and Allen knew exactly what they were doing, and they referred to Gracie's worldview as "illogical logic." Because of the way she misread words and their meanings, Gracie made preposterous statements she believed to be true, and she convinced the audience to see things her way, if only for a second. In one of their earliest routines, she reports to George that on the way to work, a man said, "Hiya, cutie, how about a bite tonight after the show?" She answered, " 'I'll be busy after the show but I'm not doing anything now,' so I bit him." In another exchange, George asks, "Did you ever hear silence is golden?" to which she responds, "No, what station are they on?" "It's an adage," insists George, "you know what an adage is." "Oh sure," answers Gracie, "that's where you keep your old trunks." In another show she asks the straight man Bill Goodwin what she should get George for Christmas. Goodwin recommends silk pajamas with George's initials on the front and a dragon on the back. "A drag in the back," she muses, "that's just the way his pajamas fit him right now."[34]

Herman, Gracie's pet duck, was a stock feature of the show, and on one Christmas show Gracie taught him all about American history. In this version, Santa Claus came to America in 1492 with five reindeer, Dancer, Prancer, Niña, Pinta, and Santa Maria. Santa put on a red coat and rode around telling every-

one Paul Revere was here. After that Santa freed all the slaves while he was flying a kite in a thunderstorm, and that's why he's called the father of our
country.[35]

Gracie was also capable of the comic put-down. "You ought to live in the
home for the feebleminded," advises George, to which Gracie shoots back, "Oh,
I'd love to be your houseguest sometime." In one of his many expressions of
exasperation at Gracie's logic, he says, "Gracie, all I have to do is hear you talk
and the blood rushes to my head." "That's because it's empty," she replies.[36]

But most of all it was Gracie's unruliness—her absolute refusal to obey orders, her defiance of instructions, her willful misunderstanding of the language—that was legendary. In one routine George asks her, as part of a new bit,
simply to ask him the exact question he has just asked her. "If I should say to
you, 'Why are apples green?' all you have to do is just repeat the same thing. You
say, 'I don't know, why are apples green?' " After Gracie assures him that she's
got it down, George asks, "What fellow in the army wears the biggest hat?" Gracie responds, "I don't know. Why are apples green?" "Now don't be silly, when
I say, What fellow in the army wears the biggest hat? you must say, 'I don't
know. What fellow in the army wears the biggest hat?' " After Gracie assures
him she really does have it this time, George asks, "All right now, what fellow
in the army wears the biggest hat?" and Gracie answers, "The fellow with the
biggest head." By misunderstanding—and flouting—George's instructions,
Gracie is also the one to get the laughs. Gracie subverted male authority, as embodied and given power through the word, over and over.

The mix in the early 1930s of girlish, giggling, falsetto men like Ed Wynn
and Joe Penner; of insults and verbal sparring that put radio stars in their
place; and of the deflation of men by women all fused in the radio persona of
Jack Benny, probably the most popular radio comedian of all time. Benny went
on the air in 1932 and by 1933 had established the format of his show, a precursor to the situation comedy. Instead of relying on a series of vaudeville jokes
and stand-up routines, Benny's show featured a regular cast—Don Wilson, the
announcer; Mary Livingstone (Benny's wife); Phil Harris, the orchestra leader;
Kenny Baker, the tenor; and Eddie "Rochester" Anderson. The show constructed an on-air personality for Benny, and it was this personality that drove
the humor and skits. By 1934, when Jell-O took over sponsorship of the show,
listening to Jack Benny on Sunday night was a national ritual.

The Benny persona targeted masculinity and upper-class pretensions:
Benny assumed a series of traits, and "the gang" ridiculed these week in and
week out. It is interesting that, except for his notorious stinginess, most of
these traits were feminine. He was vain, especially about his age and appearance; he was coy; he loved playing the violin; he specialized in catty remarks;

he lacked an aggressive sexual desire for women; he was prissy; he had a high-pitched giggle; and one of his most famous retorts was the effeminate and ineffectual "Now cut that out." "The minute I come on," observed Benny, "even the most henpecked guy in the audience feels good." His trademark swishy walk, which viewers of his TV show could see, was turned into a joke even on the radio. "Who was that lady I saw you with?" Joe Louis asks Mary Livingstone on a 1945 broadcast. "That was no lady," says Mary, "that was Jack—he always walks that way."[37] Here was a projection of man's feminine side, extracted, exorcised, and sent into exile. And this dreaded femaleness was carried off on the back of its opposite, male acquisitiveness run amok. That Jack Benny linked people's hatred of Scrooge with the fear one might be too much like a girl to succeed was, frankly, nothing short of brilliant in the 1930s. He spoke to men who blamed themselves and blamed the system, and to women who blamed their unemployed husbands yet couldn't blame them at all.

Jack's role was to be the butt of everyone's jokes and insults, and what drove every show was the determination to displace this man—conceited, miserly, self-deluded—as the center of attention, power, and authority.[38] It was a dethroning the cast members pursued with glee and the audience relished. Here was a pseudoaristocratic skinflint who refused to own up to—or even recognize—any of his rather obvious flaws. For while Jack always believed he was an irresistible Don Juan type, calling himself the "Clark Gable of the air," and was repeatedly and sarcastically introduced by Don Wilson as a "suave, sophisticated, lover type," in reality his manhood was always provisional.

Benny's radio character was a personification of paternalism gone bad, of manhood undercut by narcissism, pride, and overweening avarice. The Jack Benny penny-pincher jokes, especially his use of the infamous vault to hide his money, and the contrast between his self-inflated masculine pride and the cutting remarks by Livingstone and other women remain funny even today. But this brilliant displacement of political criticism about the hypocrisy and collapse of paternal capitalism, this lampooning of failed manhood, had to have had special resonance during the Depression. When everyday people were writing letters to national leaders complaining about the "overly rich, selfish, dumb ignorant money hogs" whose parasitic behavior had ruined the country and millions of Americans, Jack Benny's rabid materialism lanced a rather large boil. The scene in which a mugger demanded "Your money or your life" and after a long pause, Benny replied, "I'm thinking, I'm *thinking*," produced one of the biggest laughs he ever got. In a job market where men over forty knew they couldn't compete for work with men in their twenties—as one man put it, "A man over forty might as well go out and shoot himself"—Benny's refusal to declare any age over thirty-nine let people laugh at the desperate realities of ageism for men.[39]

There was, and remains, considerable debate over Rochester, played by Eddie Anderson, who was the first black to land a regular part on a radio program. He became one of the most popular characters on the show. At first, with constant jokes about Rochester's drinking and carousing, devotion to "African badminton"—craps—and addiction to watermelon, African Americans criticized the show's perpetuation of the negative stereotype the character reinforced. Gradually, Benny and his writers abandoned these stereotypes, and despite the fact that Rochester was in a servile position, he almost always got the better of his boss, just like everyone else, hurling impudent rejoinders to Benny that were both good-natured and sardonic.[40]

In one episode Jack reports that he ran into some poor fellow who asked for a dime and announces, "I gave him fifty cents." The next sound we hear is of a tray of dishes crashing to the floor, and the audience cracks up. Jack asks, "Rochester, why did you drop those dishes? All I said was I gave a man fifty cents." Then there is another crash and more laughter. "Rochester, you didn't have to push that second stack off the drain board." Answers Rochester, "I didn't touch 'em. They jumped off by themselves." Here, an irreverent, even cocky black man talked back to and made fun of his white boss, and the fact that he too deflated Jack's ego made the impaling of white male pretensions even more thorough. In a time when "black *males* who challenged white authority were simply not seen in mainstream media," notes Mel Watkins, this was "a revolutionary advance."[41]

One of Jack Benny's most successful publicity stunts was his long-running "feud" with Fred Allen, which started in 1936, when Allen, on his show *Town Hall Tonight,* ad-libbed a joke about Benny's pathetic violin playing. Benny responded on his next show, and the feud was on. Allen, like Benny, preferred more sophisticated humor than Penner's or Wynn's and skewered upper-class pretensions. Allen was a virtuoso at wordplay, coining new, irreverent nicknames (the American eagle was "patriotic poultry"), exposing the pomposity of overblown words, and inventing maxims. "There's an old saying," offered Allen, "if all of the politicians in the world were laid end to end they would still be lying."[42] Some of the more famous characters on his show included Portland (Allen's wife), yet another squeaky-pitched, daffy type who played with language herself, Allen's characterization of the famous Chinese detective One Long Pan, and other stock types portrayed by the Mighty Allen Art Players. Later, Senator Bloat and Senator Claghorn, moronic yet bombastic southern politicians; Mrs. Nussbaum, a Jewish housewife who called Mississippi "Matzos-Zippi" and the famous Swedish actress "Ingrown Bergman"; Ajax Cassidy, the heavy-drinking Irishman; and Titus Moody, the New England hayseed, became radio icons in *Allen's Alley*, Fred Allen's show from 1942 to 1949.

The "feud" between Benny and Allen was irresistible to listeners. It pulled them into an inner circle of celebrity friendship, insider jokes, and deft but harmless jousting that combined intimacy with competition, affection with irritation. This way everyone was in on the joke, and the insults could be savored without discomfort or concern. It was essential that listeners know the feud was fake, that in "real life" Allen and Benny were good friends. But the feud also mirrored the twin needs for men, particularly working-class men, in the 1930s: their emotional need for each other's friendship and support, and their economic need to cooperate and organize, juxtaposed with their need to compete with each other and to regard each other as rivals.

The feud was quickly labeled the Battle of the Century in the typically modest terms the media choose for such events. After months of sniping the two met face-to-face on a broadcast from the Hotel Pierre in March 1937, and the show had one of the largest listening audiences in radio history. The insults on this and subsequent shows focused on the men's age and appearance, their sincerity, their cowardice and bullying of those weaker than they (especially children), their pretensions about their talents, their capacity for lying and for self-defeat, and their general integrity. Building on a previous insult, turning what was, for an instant, a barb that hit the target exactly where it hurt back on the man who had hurled it, was essential to the game. When Allen appeared on Benny's show after months of berating his violin playing, Benny warned, "Now look here, Allen. I don't care what you say about my violin playing on your program, but when you come up here, be careful. After all, I've got listeners." "Keep your family out of it," answered Allen.[43] This was key: using the man's own words to disarm him. For not only had you gained something but you had taken something away from him, made him less of a man than he was before.

By the time Edgar Bergen and Charlie McCarthy went on the air in the spring of 1937—at the height of the Benny-Allen feud—the speed of radio repartee had increased, and the insults were even more personal and cutting. That a ventriloquist act became such a smash hit on radio, where listeners couldn't even *see* whether Bergen was convincing at throwing his voice, remains almost laughable today. And the fact that Charlie was a wooden dummy, and a child, gave him even more license to express antisocial, adolescent sentiments in a comparatively uncensored form. Whether people took him to be the not-so-successfully repressed alter ego of the soft-spoken, conventional, and fatherly Edgar Bergen we can never know. But the dummy, not the dad, gave voice to male impudence, insolence, and rebellion.

It was Charlie who refused to study, to work hard, to respect his elders, to

behave properly around women. It was Charlie who could make suggestive remarks to Rita Hayworth or Mae West in a way flesh-and-blood men couldn't
on the radio, and in a way that was, frankly, creepy, given that he was supposed
to be a boy. W. C. Fields, another caricature of a man, the bulbous-nosed drunk
who loathed children and dogs, was Charlie's most formidable verbal opponent. "Tell me, Charles, is it true that your father was a gateleg table?" asked
Fields. "If he was, your father was under it," snapped back Charlie. Fields constantly threatened to carve Charlie up into shoe trees, to sic a beaver on him,
to saw him in two. Charlie, in turn, threatened Fields that he would "stick a
wick in your mouth and use you for an alcohol lamp."[44] Here was the Oedipal
drama writ large but, for safety's sake, acted out by a puppet and a clown, by a
parody of a father and a son.

At first on radio there was a clear demarcation between the linguistic antics of comics and the more staid, self-important announcements from advertisers. Comedians could be goofy, make fun of themselves, and turn the
language upside down, but commercials would not. This was where the sanctity of corporate America, male authority, and correct English interlocked into
one impregnable edifice of overseriousness. But the success and contagious-
ness of linguistic slapstick eventually colonized advertising as well. After an intense debate in the mid-1920s about how radio should be financed—with
advertising being one of the least popular and most vilified options—something called indirect advertising took hold by the late 1920s. Direct sales
pitches and prices were verboten; instead, performers took on the name of the
sponsor, as with the Cliquot Club Eskimos and the Happiness Candy Boys.

But such restraint didn't last long, and sonorous accounts of the merits of
Lux soap and Chevrolets soon bracketed most broadcasts. The contrast between the looseness and freedom of radio comedy and the zipped-up tightness
of the ads was irresistible to comics like Ed Wynn. He began spoofing Texaco
gas commercials and interrupting Graham McNamee with asides like "fancy
that" and "is that so" as McNamee delivered the latest ad.[45] At first sponsors had
no sense of humor about this, but as they saw sales increase, they lightened up.
By the mid-1930s advertisers—who also produced these shows—came to recognize that being the butt of jokes, and being willing to take a joke, endeared
whoever was on the radio to the audience. The jokes also helped the audience
recall who the sponsor was. Not only did ad-libbed jokes about the sponsor become tolerated, but scripted repartee about the product was worked into most
shows.

We forget today the extent to which Jack Benny, Burns and Allen, Fred
Allen, and others hawked their sponsors' products repeatedly. They had to be
shills, and they knew it: if sales didn't go up they would lose their shows. And

they made this more palatable to themselves and no doubt to the audience by embedding the ads in the same kinds of wordplay rituals they used during the rest of their shows. In the same show in which Gracie Allen is wondering what to buy George for Christmas, their straight man, Bill Goodwin, says he's trying to come up with a Christmas card to send out. This discussion is woven right into the skits and the main dialogue. Bill says he's thinking of something like, "Season's greetings from Bill Goodwin and Swan, the new white floating soap that's eight ways better than old-style floating soaps—something simple like that," he notes self-mockingly. Gracie suggests he send out a song and does her own version of "Jingle Bells." "Season's greetings to you and yours/and all of my best wishes/and don't forget, for goodness sakes/use Swan to wash your dishes." Bill then picks up the song: "Swan gives loads of suds/Swan is white as snow/You'll find that Swan suds twice as fast . . . ," and then Gracie blurts out the last line, "even in the hottest water." When Bill points out that *water* doesn't rhyme with *snow,* Gracie quips "H_2O."[46]

On Ed Wynn's show too the ads became embedded in the discourse and pace of the show, as Wynn and McNamee bantered about the merits of Texaco gas. McNamee might start by saying, "Hey, Chief, this is going to be a great year for touring," and then bring up the merits of Texaco. After some back-and-forth, Wynn would say, "I know it's powerful, Graham. Why, last week a man filled his car with Fire Chief gas" so he could tour American cities. "It went so fast he had to get a stenographer to take down the names of the towns in short-hand." Finally, McNamee would add the tag line—"Buy a tankful tomorrow"—which would signal that they were moving back to the show.[47]

Jack Benny began his broadcasts, "Jell-O, everyone," and it was a running gag that Don Wilson tried to slip in references to the product throughout the show. Shameless self-promotion, done in this highly self-conscious way, was funny, even endearing. The audience came to expect it, anticipate it, and laugh at—and with—it when it appeared. During their feud Allen referred to Benny as "an itinerant vendor of desserts" and "a gelatin hawker." His obvious refusal to say the brand's name only added to the sense that knowing about Jell-O, knowing it was Benny's sponsor, was what truly made someone in the know.

This linguistic embrace of the sponsor was essential to the increased commercialism of everyday life that radio accelerated and reinforced. Once you can be made fun of, once people play with your name in teasing ways and sing or chat about you in silly rhymes, then you're really part of the gang. Certainly plenty of Americans bemoaned what was, by the mid-1930s, the shameless, blaring commercialization of radio. But bringing commercials linguistically into the fold legitimized not just their existence but their purpose as well.

Commercialization became associated, however subtly, with spontaneity, happiness, freedom itself.

Probably the best-known piece of linguistic slapstick from the old radio days is Bud Abbott and Lou Costello's routine "Who's on First?" Abbott was the brittle, even-voiced, mustachioed city slicker, the straight man (in so many senses of the term). Costello was perennially prepubescent, short and still larded with baby fat, his voice wailing up and down octaves like a tantrum-throwing child's when he was frustrated or confused. The notion that any grown woman would find him attractive was preposterous, yet he slobbered over women like Goofy. Bud knew about women, not Lou. Each was a caricature of masculinity, the one so crass and unfeeling you couldn't imagine him as a father or husband, the other so vulnerable, so prone to hysteria, so gullible he was, well, like a girl. And "Who's on First?"—a routine so popular it was, for a while, performed nearly weekly on the radio—displayed how mastery over language separated the men from the boys, and, by implication, from the girls as well.

The exchange is about baseball, a male pursuit, and builds on the unusual nicknames many ballplayers had. Bud is introducing a team and says these members have silly nicknames too, and he wants to let Lou know who's who. Lou awaits the roster. But the players' names are all pronouns, like *who* or *what*, or conjunctions like *because* or *why*. Bud tells Lou that "Who is on first." Yes, Lou asks, "Who is on first?" "That's right," insists Bud, with increasing testiness, "Who *is* on first." And so it goes around the bases.

Lou struggles in vain to enter the linguistic domain that Bud so effortlessly masters. He takes everything too literally; he just doesn't understand. He wails and pouts with frustration and exasperation; at times he becomes hysterical. Bud, by contrast, gets impatient (as men often do in the face of overwrought emotions) but is always calm. The voices, their tones, their registers, are a study in contrasts: it is a parody of a fight between a man and a woman, a father and a child.

The routine is delicious; it is hard to tire of it; at times it seems addictive. It makes fun of and speaks to us about so many things: the connections between the ability to name things and the access to power; the ability to follow accepted, male logic, however convoluted; the anxiety about being part of the gang, the team; and, of course, the delight we take in hearing skilled people show how the linguistic rules we live and die by can be toyed with, stretched, broken. For the audience, the pleasure comes, in part, from seeing the logic of both men's positions, of understanding Bud's nomenclature and Lou's complete confusion in the face of it. We are inside and outside the power of language. We respect and balk at its tyranny, we laugh at the utter arbitrariness of words. We see the pleasures and stupidities of the coded argot of sports. Knowing how language includes and excludes us every day, in all kinds of realms—from business and politics to friendships, clubs, and families—we recognize how words alone give us power and take it away.

Radio comedy was revolutionary and conservative, insubordinate and obedient, attacking conventional authority yet buttressing it at the same time. Its befuddled, hapless men invited listeners' sympathies *and* their ridicule, bolstering the self-esteem of those in the audience, who recognized all too well what it was like to be confused and intimidated in the face of power yet were assured they would do much better than Lou Costello. At the same time these shows and their displays of male verbal agility also insisted that the resistance and persistence, aggression and energy of American manhood had yet to be doused, despite the ongoing economic catastrophe.

Linguistic slapstick acknowledged that America was a nation of subgroups, many of them antagonistic to one another, some of them deserving of ridicule. But it also suggested that, despite those differences—and maybe even because of them—America was on the rebound. Linguistic slapstick asserted that America was as vibrant, pliable, inventive, absorptive, defiant, and full of surprises as its language. And it claimed that that vibrancy came from the bottom up, not from the top down. Sure, radio cheered people up during the Depression. But it did so because it gave men an imagined preserve where they could project their own sense of failure onto others, hear acknowledgments that successful masculinity was a hard mantle to keep on, yet also hear that even benighted men, through their wits alone, were still going to land on top, if only for a few minutes.

The Invention of the Audience

A man stood before a microphone and opened his mouth. He felt self-conscious, even silly, and he wondered: Who am I talking to? Who is hearing me? How many of them are there? Do they like what they hear?

These were the questions that went through the heads of announcers, singers, and other radio performers in the 1920s as the radio boom increased in size and scope. Being sequestered in one of those velvet-drape-lined studios and projecting into a microphone was quite disconcerting to those accustomed to live audiences, to their laughs, their murmurs, and their applause. With radio there was no one to see and nothing to hear—just silence.

As people's voices became disembodied and were sent out over the airwaves, the growing questions about how the "invisible audience" reacted to these emanations stemmed from curiosity, vanity, and a fear of embarrassment or rejection. But by the late 1920s, when advertisers began sponsoring more shows, these became not only metaphysical questions but also economic ones. Curiosity about who was listening turned into calculations about how much these listeners were worth.

Beginning in the 1920s, and escalating to a fevered hysteria today, the corporate obsession with the tastes and preferences of the broadcast audience has produced a nationwide, technologically instantaneous network of audience surveillance. This is a system most Americans do not encounter directly on a daily basis. Indirectly, however, it shapes the entire media environment in which we live. It determines who will anchor the nightly news or host a talk show, what our children will get to watch on Saturday mornings, and which political opinions we will and will not hear on our radio or television. Today this system integrates a range of technologies—telephones, computers, Nielsen boxes, audience measurement devices like the program analyzer—with other inventions—like the focus group, the questionnaire, or the survey—and a host of technically sophisticated mathematical approaches to assessing media appeal and effects. Back in the 1930s all this had to be invented.

This system got its start in 1929, when Archibald Crossley developed a ratings service that relied on telephoning people and asking them what they had listened to the night before.[1] It was a crude method and left critical questions unanswered. Why did people listen to some shows and not others? What shaped their tastes? Could you convert listeners from listening to Rudy Vallee to listening to the New York Symphony? This was where Paul Lazarsfeld came in.

Paul Lazarsfeld, an Austrian émigré, was the father of market research in America as well as one of the founders of communications research, and anyone who watches TV, reads a magazine, or listens to the radio has been affected profoundly by his work and that of his countless protégés. This work showed broadcasters and advertisers how to invade, and colonize, the American psyche. It also paved the way for the systematic study of media effects that was, at times, quite critical of that colonization.

Lazarsfeld had no idea, when he left Vienna for the United States in September of 1933, that his career was about to be hijacked by a machine. Nor did he know that he would never return to live in his homeland again. A thirty-two-year-old psychology professor at the beginning of his life's work, Lazarsfeld sailed to New York preoccupied by one major question: What happens inside the mind at that moment when a person makes a choice? For several years he had been investigating why people decide to do one thing but not another (such as choosing an occupation) and trying to develop a systematic method for analyzing this psychological process. Now, under the auspices of a fellowship from the Rockefeller Foundation, he came to exchange ideas with American social scientists about this emerging field, social psychology.

Lazarsfeld came to a country in which a new technological system, the vast network of radio stations and receivers controlled by corporations rather than the government, was reshaping almost every aspect of life, including American politics, musical tastes, and language. Lazarsfeld confronted radio broadcasting, but he soon helped establish its less visible mirror image: the network of people and machines that provided audience research for networks and their advertisers. Over several decades this system linked up gadgets like his and Frank Stanton's program analyzer, audimeters, and Nielsen boxes with telephone lines, radios, TVs, and computers to monitor what Americans were tuning in and what they were turning off. It was a network that put Americans' tastes and preferences under increasing scrutiny.

Given his early history, Lazarsfeld seems an unlikely architect of such a system. He came of age in a city so dominated by the Socialist Party that it was known as Red Vienna. During and after the First World War, when he was in his teens and twenties, Lazarsfeld was an active and highly idealistic Socialist. He was especially drawn to the party's mission of educating and uplifting the working class, by making knowledge more available and by making intellectual pursuits a more regular, habitual part of working-class life. He often gave lectures to workers on topics like how to read a newspaper or on the history of revolutions, successful and failed.[2]

Lazarsfeld was also an intellectual trained in the Austro-Marxist tradition, earning his Ph.D. in applied mathematics from the University of Vienna. He combined a talent in mathematics with his interest in how and why people make crucial choices to pioneer in the quantification of group behavior and attitudes. It was at one of his political meetings that Lazarsfeld asked what he later regarded as a life-changing question. Otto Kanitz, a leader of the Vienna Working Youth, presented the results of a questionnaire that he claimed amply documented how miserable young factory workers were. "Did you count how many were miserable?" asked Lazarsfeld. Kanitz regarded this as an absurd question but turned the questionnaires over to Lazarsfeld to let him count them. Lazarsfeld compared the nature of the complaints by age; he was thus launched on his lifelong project of categorizing people and comparing how different groups behaved. He was committed to moving beyond description and anecdote to offering results that could be expressed in percentages as well as sentences. He would rely on interviews, which asked people a range of questions about their choices, then offer a statistical summary of the results.

One reason Lazarsfeld became interested in psychology, he later reflected, was that the socialist mission he was so dedicated to was less zealously embraced by the workers he was hoping to uplift. Few research projects drove this home more dramatically than his first study of radio listeners, which Ravag, the board that regulated and managed Austrian radio, commissioned Lazarsfeld to conduct in 1931. Over 110,000 radio listeners responded to questionnaires, which Lazarsfeld tabulated and summarized. The Socialists' worst fears about what this emerging mass medium was doing to people's tastes and leisure time were confirmed. It turned out that nearly half of the listeners were workers and employees, and they overwhelmingly preferred "light entertainment," including popular music and comedies. The least popular radio fare was chamber music, literary readings, symphony concerts, and lectures about music. As the historian Helmut Gruber notes wryly, "The sixteen items in the negative category contained virtually every program preferred by the Socialist Democratic Party of Austria for its worker listeners."[3]

Lazarsfeld and his fellow Socialists had hoped not just to improve the material conditions of life for the working classes. They sought nothing less than to create a proletarian counterculture opposed to what they saw as the consumerism, intellectual vapidness, and political complacency of bourgeois culture. Workers who succumbed to blandishments of the dance hall, the beer garden, the movie theater, and the department store were, in the Socialist view, buying into a commercial culture that ultimately co-opted them politically and narcotized them intellectually. Instead, workers should spend their leisure time reading, listening to "good" music, attending lectures, and organizing themselves politically.[4]

But there was a crucial contradiction here. Many of the socialist-sanctioned pursuits were those favored by the educated bourgeoisie, the very class Lazarsfeld and his comrades disdained. Being of middle-class origins themselves, and members of the intelligentsia, however, they prized certain bourgeois values, particularly those that promoted self-improvement, and they indulged in bourgeois rather than working-class pastimes.[5] In their efforts to transform the hearts and minds of the workers, Socialist leaders tended to denigrate most of their leisure activities and seemed blind to their need for diversion, escape, frivolity, and catharsis. Elitist in their cultural tastes, puritanical in their attitudes toward the amusement park, the saloon, and spectator sports, and generally paternalistic toward workers they too often saw as childlike and inadequately civilized, Lazarsfeld's Viennese circle began to run into resistance from workers about transforming their private lives and leisure time. In the late 1920s Lazarsfeld increasingly sought refuge in intellectual work.

At the same time he discovered that American businesses were hiring psychologists to ascertain which brand of a particular product people bought and why. "Market research," Lazarsfeld remembered, "was then completely unknown in Austria," but this kind of work was an instant revelation. "I remember the immediate feeling that this is a perfect conjunction; (a) you can get money for research, (b) you can find out why people do something." He also saw consumer choice as a more simple process than occupational choice, providing him with a decision easier to measure and quantify.[6]

This was the man—a Socialist politically and a Marxist intellectually—who arrived in New York in September of 1933 with his Rockefeller grant. His background, riddled as it was with conflicting desires to uplift the masses, pursue the life of the mind, and make a living in an increasingly hostile environment in Austria, set the stage for the schizophrenic mixture of optimism and pessimism, idealism and cynicism that informed much of the radio research in America. It is important to understand these contradictions because they crossed the Atlantic with Lazarsfeld and left their mark on radio research and on conceptions of the radio audience.

America was itself in the midst of a major psychic transformation, in which radio was playing an important but as yet poorly understood role. The Great Depression, now in its fourth grim year, had turned some of the most basic assumptions, ideas, and practices of the 1920s upside down. What had defined America, at least in its national mythology, was its freshness, its sense of limitless possibility, its robust optimism, and its success. Had all this been a conceit, an illusion? With the depth and breadth of the economic collapse, many Americans seemed to be experiencing a cultural identity crisis.

It was the anxiety, argued cultural historian Warren Susman, that inspired one of the most significant trends of the 1930s: "the most overwhelming effort ever attempted to document in art, reportage, social science, and history the life and values of the American people." The rise of photojournalism, of documentaries, a slew of books on American culture and the American character, and the establishment in 1935 of George Gallup's American Institute of Public Opinion to provide statistical evidence of how people thought and felt were all part of this desire for self-knowledge.[7] In addition, there was an explosion in academic psychology, so that by 1933 American publications in the field were triple those being written in Germany, where it had been born. The social sciences in general, which until 1929 had been the "poor relations of the natural sciences," were now assuming increased importance because they sought to ascertain how "the human factor" had "spoiled the American dream."

Radio made this quest for self-knowledge more vexing and more pressing. The radio boom, which some had dismissed as a passing fad, was by 1933 an established feature of everyday life in the United States. In 1925, 10 percent of American households had a radio. By 1933 the proportion had jumped to 62.5 percent, double that at the beginning of the Depression. Already there were 599 stations broadcasting in the country, with three networks—CBS, NBC-Red, and NBC-Blue—offering national programs.

Contradictions about national identity abounded in the constellation of shows to which listeners tuned in. In a segregated country, in which racism was woven into the entire fabric of the culture, the most popular show on radio was about two black men in Harlem. In a country known for its periodic outbursts against papacy and immigrants, the Irish-Catholic priest Father Coughlin was a national demagogue, drawing an estimated 30 to 45 million listeners a week and often receiving more mail than FDR. The NBC Symphony had an avid, national following; so did *Major Bowes' Original Amateur Hour.*

Who was listening most regularly to all this? What did these unseen listeners make of what they heard? This new technology raised a host of questions about what the act of listening to emanations from "the ether" was doing to the nation and the individual. In the early 1920s pundits predicted a massive cultural uplift through radio, with opera and lectures brought to the most isolated and uneducated in the country. But was that what was happening? Or were people forsaking books and newspapers in favor of Walter Winchell and Joe Penner?

These twin possibilities for American technology—progress and dehumanization—had been of central concern to intellectuals in the 1920s, and they became more pronounced during the Great Depression. The advent of radio and the uses to which it was being put stimulated renewed optimism and pessimism about the possibilities for spiritual and intellectual transcendence in the face of industrial change. For example, in the widely read sociological study of Muncie, Indiana, *Middletown,* Robert and Helen Lynd (who were some of the first scholars to befriend Lazarsfeld) emphasized how industrialization had undermined traditional neighborhoods and communities and had accentuated a sense of technological determinism among people, that they were the victims of forces beyond their control. Even those technologies dedicated to enhancing leisure time, like the radio, the automobile, and the motion picture, were said to discourage community and to promote social isolation.[8] In the process they "standardized" people's habits and attitudes, promoting conformity and a less thoughtful and creative approach to life.

The intellectual milieu that Lazarsfeld entered was filled with speculations, predictions, and advice about technology and the human spirit, about machines and the evolution of consciousness.[9] But what he quickly learned in his adoptive country was that questions about technology and consciousness or, more specifically, about what radio was doing to the American psyche were also of deep interest to businessmen and American corporations, as well as to the radio networks. And not incidentally they were willing to pay for their research, a nontrivial factor during the Great Depression. Their goals were quite pointed: they wanted to get a more detailed profile of this new entity—the vast, invisible broadcast audience—so they could understand better what role radio played in influencing whether consumers bought Product A or Product B. The evolution of consciousness was not their concern; the art of persuasion was.

Lazarsfeld's Rockefeller grant lasted for one year, but it was extended for one more in 1934 in light of the political turmoil back in Austria. As a Jew and a Socialist, Lazarsfeld found it an increasingly dangerous prospect to return home, and he decided to stay in America. During these years he visited various universities to see what other social psychologists were doing, and he spent a good part of his time seeking out those who worked in market research. He visited the research departments of NBC and CBS, and met Frank Stanton, a recent Ph.D. in psychology from Ohio State, who was setting up—from scratch—CBS's audience research department.

At the time, Lazarsfeld recalled, "American market research was based mainly on rather simple nose-counting." The question of *why* people bought what they did was still unexplored, and Lazarsfeld sought to change that. He spoke at professional meetings and wrote four chapters for *The Techniques of Marketing Research,* published by the American Marketing Association. He spent two months at the University of Pittsburgh, where he organized studies entitled "How Pittsburgh Women Decide Where to Buy Their Dresses" and "How Pittsburgh Drivers Choose Their Gasoline."[10]

This was a far cry from organizing a socialist youth movement or studying the effects of unemployment. Yet Marie Jahoda, Lazarsfeld's first wife, insists that he had not sold out. In Austria the "overwhelming social data" came from people's often passionate engagement in politics and political parties. "To come as a socialist to the U.S. and to look for socialism and the debating of Marxism would have been foolish," she notes. What mattered in America was consumerism. Unlike Vienna, where political parties were major forces in people's lives, in America what was "desperately important" was "what you bought."[11]

Despite the fact that radio had become a major cultural, political, and economic force in American life, there were only a few isolated studies of the invention's impact. The Rockefeller Foundation sought to change that. It awarded a major research grant to Frank Stanton and Hadley Cantril, the Princeton University psychologist who had coauthored the pathbreaking 1935 book *The Psychology of Radio.* But neither Stanton nor Cantril had enough time to supervise the project, so they approached Lazarsfeld, and the Office of Radio Research was born. Although nominally headquartered at Princeton, the bulk of the work took place in Newark. In 1939, after Lazarsfeld and Cantril had a falling out, the project moved to New York.

If the challenge was to get at what radio was doing to people's heads—as individuals and as members and shapers of a society—how would they proceed? It wasn't just that researchers were unsure about radio's impact on thoughts and actions; they didn't know which techniques and approaches might come close to producing answers. These would have to be invented. Lazarsfeld and Stanton devised one set of approaches; Hadley Cantril, Gordon Allport, and Herta Herzog (Lazarsfeld's second wife), another; and theorists like Theodor Adorno, a third. Still other researchers and pollsters developed additional approaches to studying the audience. All overlapped, yet most were in conflict. And over the next sixty years they would influence complementary and antagonistic methods of studying the broadcast audience for academic and commercial purposes.

The object of this scrutiny—the audience—was itself an invention, a construction that corraled a nation of individual listeners into a sometimes monolithic group that somehow knew what "it" wanted from broadcasting. But the most important thing to remember is something we now take totally for granted: how the audience spent its leisure time was up for study and study, in fact, became a hugely profitable industry. Everyday, ordinary people would find themselves, by the end of the century, embedded in a high-tech system designed to monitor their relationship with and reactions to another technological system, American broadcasting. Lazarsfeld's first task was to break down this notion of "the audience" into subsets of listeners differentiated by sex, age, and socioeconomic position.

The first important study of how radio was creating "a new mental world," as the authors put it, was Cantril and Allport's *Psychology of Radio*, published two years before the ORR was founded. A sense of wonder suffuses the book: the authors knew they were dealing with something that was a revolutionary cultural *and* sensory phenomenon. More than any other study of the audience in the 1930s this book tried to burrow into what radio was doing to the life of the mind. Seventy-eight million Americans were already habitual listeners, and Cantril and Allport couldn't emphasize enough the "tenacious grip radio has so swiftly secured on the mental life of man." Weekly attendance at the movies in the early 1930s was approximately 70 million; "our countrymen spend approximately 150 million hours a week before the screen, but nearly one billion hours before the loud-speaker." Of the estimated 37 million radio sets in the world in 1932, Americans owned nearly half. There were twice as many radio sets in America as there were telephones.[12]

It is critical to emphasize the sheer enthusiasm, breathlessness, even at times bravura of Cantril and Allport's meditation on the impact of radio. Only fifteen years later studies of the audience would become much more systematic but desiccated summaries of who likes to listen to what when. And, of course, the apparatus of monitoring and studying the audience would become a huge technological system. But with *The Psychology of Radio* we see the authors trying all kinds of approaches. They skip around, studying radio content and listeners' practices, observing students as they listen to people speaking who are hidden behind a curtain. Sometimes they seem to be, well, making it up. Often the made-up part is the most provocative—and right on the money.

We see two researchers fascinated by this device and trying pretty much every-thing they could think of to assess its impact on the life of the mind—and the nation.

Take, for example, their opening vignette, "An Evangelist and His Voice." In the early 1930s a "well-known evangelist" visited Boston and drew an overflow crowd. The hall hired for his speech couldn't hold everyone, but there was an auditorium one floor below the one in which he was meant to speak. The man-ager of the event installed a microphone on the speaker's podium, put a loud-speaker in the lower auditorium, and let the overflow crowd sit there so they could at least hear the sermon. "Here was an ideal occasion for the social psy-chologist to begin his observations on the psychological effects of radio," Cantril and Allport wrote. What this meant was that the "social psychologist" stood on the stairwell between the two floors, sometimes running up, some-times down, to monitor and take notes on the different reactions in the crowd that could see the speaker and the crowd that could only hear him.[13] And what did he find? That the crowd who could actually see the evangelist was much more responsive, singing along with hymns, laughing, raising their hands when asked to, and so forth, while the downstairs crowd was more passive, re-sistant, nonparticipatory, even sullen.

Does this mean that "radio is a complete failure as an agency in forming crowds"? Not at all. Effective radio speakers address their listeners differently than do those with a live crowd, working with the fact that they are invisible, consciously inviting the listeners' participation. Allport and Cantril acknowl-edged the skill of someone like Huey Long, who opened a radio address with "I have some important revelations to make, but before I make them I want you to go to the phone and call up five of your friends and tell them to listen in." "Such a clever opening makes each member of the audience a fellow con-spirator," Cantril and Allport wrote admiringly, "and does much to guarantee friendly attention for the duration of the speech, especially if the discourse throughout is kept on an equally informal plane." This was crucial. "Colloquial language and homely American allusions help. . . . Senator Long does away with all formality and awe. The people are elevated to a position of equality with high officials, or else the high officials are reduced to the common level. 'They are,' Senator Long assures us in plebeian tones, 'like old Davy Crockett who went to hunt a possum.' "[14]

Cantril and Allport were among the few radio researchers in the century to actually confront what it meant to have a medium that addressed only the ears, and what that did to public discourse over the airwaves. "Suddenly deprived of the sense of vision, we are forced to grasp both obvious and subtle meanings through our ears alone." Because people had to provide their own imagery, they were relearning the art of visualization, restoring in adults "the keenness of imagery dulled since childhood." The radio listener especially has "an imaginative sense of participation in a common activity. He knows that others are listening with him and in this way feels a community of interest with people outside his home." Allport and Cantril felt that the printed word simply didn't have the same effect as radio, which was to "fill us with a 'consciousness of kind' which at times grows into an impression of vast social unity."[15]

What challenges were posed by the fact that isolated listeners tuned in to some invisible and distant speaker? The radio listener must "have a lively 'impression of universality.' Each individual must believe that others are thinking as he thinks and are sharing his emotions." How does the skilled "radio spellbinder" achieve this effect? He reminds his audience that millions are listening, that he has already received millions of letters from those people. In other words, he paints a picture of a vast, unified, national audience of which each individual is part. He reiterates his main points, uses vivid examples—Father Coughlin, for example, painted bankers as "grinning devils" and said communism had "a red serpent head." Sincerity is absolutely crucial. "Sincerity is an unmistakable attribute of the voice," Cantril and Allport insisted, adding, "Whether to sound 'sincere' must correspond to inner conviction or whether it may be a pose is another question."[16]

Listeners, for their part, were liberated from the etiquette of the concert hall and lecture room. In his living room, noted Cantril and Allport, "the listener may respond in any way he pleases . . . he can sing, dance, curse, or otherwise express emotions relevant or irrelevant." He could talk back, and he was freed from the influences and reactions of others in the crowd. At the same time, however, he was constrained, because he was often listening with family or friends, and because radio, which came into the home (and was supported by cautious and conservative advertisers), was a "more moral agency" than film. "The radio dares not violate those attitudes fundamental in the great American home." In the darkened movie theater, by contrast, away from "the parlor lamps and the critical eyes and ears of the family," the spectator is "free to drift into the succulent fantasy of the screen." But both media, the authors emphasized, were playing a critical role in standardizing not just people's tastes and habits but their very inner fantasies.[17]

Cantril and Allport also offered a statistical portrait of the early audience. While radio ownership went up with income—90 percent of those earning over $10,000 a year owned radios, whereas only 52 percent of those earning under $1,000 a year did—studies showed that upper-income people listened the least while those of middle and lower incomes listened the most. Radio ownership was most prevalent in the Northeast and lowest in the Southeast, with only 24 percent of Mississippi homes equipped with radio. One study of listeners in Minneapolis found that nearly 40 percent of the audience listened three hours a day or more. Over three-quarters of the audience restricted their listening to three stations. They overwhelmingly preferred network to local programming and preferred to get the news over the radio rather than from the newspaper. Women listened slightly longer than men because they listened more during the day while they worked in the home. Music was the most popular form of program, especially for women, followed by comedy shows and dramas. Sports were the favorite program for men. Even then radio played a role in activating nostalgia for preradio days, as "old song favorites" were the most popular kind of program on the air. And while listeners had already begun to complain about advertising and wish there were less of it on the air, nearly three-quarters of those polled said that they would rather listen to ads on the air than have to pay a two-dollar-a-year tax to have programs without advertising.[18]

Early radio also generated tens of thousands—sometimes hundreds of thousands—of fan letters a week. Some of the mail responded to sponsor offers of coupons or booklets, other letters suggested programming changes or praised a recent show, and still others sought answers to personal problems. Early studies of this fan mail suggested that it came primarily from those of a lower socioeconomic group who lived in rural areas and small towns. "Fan mail from both children and adults pours into the studios particularly after sad broadcasts," noted Cantril and Allport, who argued that such letters helped listeners achieve emotional closure after having been upset.[19]

Cantril and Allport's fascination with how people processed this distinctly aural medium was showcased in their chapter "Voice and Personality." People hadn't thought that much about what a powerful indicator voice alone could be in providing all kinds of information about the speaker. What about a person did listeners conjure up, just from hearing his voice? Cantril and Allport recruited twenty-four men to serve as speakers; some of them spoke over WEEI, while others spoke from behind a curtain in a laboratory setting. In the lab students served as judges; over the air listeners did.

The task was simple—using only the man's voice as an indicator, the judges were to guess his age, height, and other aspects of his appearance, occupation, political affiliation, and personality type (introverted or extroverted, submissive or assertive). The judges were even asked to match the voice with a handwriting sample and a photograph. Recognizing that speech patterns provide information about an individual's class and geographic origin, they chose only speakers from Boston and had them read a uniform script—excerpts from Charles Dickens or Lewis Carroll. While some guesses based on the speaker's voice—like his height or general appearance—were not very accurate, Cantril and Allport found that listeners made pretty good guesses about age, occupation, and political preferences, and excellent guesses about personality. Although "the natural voice is somewhat more revealing of personal qualities than is the radio voice," radio listeners, the authors concluded, were "quite successful in 'hearing through' the inevitable burr which accompanies a mechanical transmission of the human voice."[20]

"Many features of many personalities can be estimated correctly from voice," they wrote in italics. More fascinating was this: while listeners might project the wrong characteristics onto a speaker based solely on his voice, these erroneous impressions were shared by large, disparate groups of listeners. Stereotyping through the voice alone was commonplace; listeners felt, quite strongly, that the voice was a clear window into a person's character.[21]

In the early 1930s listeners did not want those voices to be female. Simply put, 95 percent of listeners told the researchers that they would rather hear a man than a woman over the radio, although they couldn't say exactly why. The one reason they did offer was that men seemed more natural over the radio, while women seemed more affected, as if they were "putting on" a radio voice. Certainly the announcing staffs at nearly all radio stations were male. Why was it, asked Cantril and Allport, that "women who are freely employed as singers or actresses on the radio are virtually barred as announcers?" Conducting experiments with listeners, Allport and Cantril noted that when they actually listened to different voices, audience members preferred male voices for political talks, weather reports, and commercials while they preferred female voices for poetry, discussions of psychology, and passages of philosophy. Women's voices were often rated "more attractive." Much of the listeners' initial hostility, then, to women announcers, as expressed in quick questionnaires, stemmed from simple prejudice about who was supposed to do what kind of speaking over the air, reinforced by the practices in the industry. But listeners were especially hostile to women who had too much of an air of "cultivation and refinement"; they also hated " 'high-pressure' saleswomen." They didn't want to hear women who sounded upper-class or too aggressive. By contrast, "popular comediennes . . . have voices that are not only low in pitch but likewise, as a rule, vulgar and uncouth in sound."[22] Altos were preferred over sopranos. Women, in other words, who weren't too prissy, who seemed like the guys, did fine over the air.

Cantril and Allport ended their study by noting how crucial radio was in allowing listeners "to gain access to the outside world without seriously interfering with the demands of their immediate environment." People's environments were extended in unprecedented ways, and this was especially true for non-elites. "It is the middle classes and the underprivileged whose desires to share in the world's events have been most persistently thwarted, and it is these classes, therefore, that are the most loyal supporters of radio." For them radio is "a gigantic and invisible net which each listener may cast thousands of miles into the sea of human affairs" and then pull in what he or she wants. It was this extension of people's "social horizons" and the new sensory flexing that radio demanded of listeners that seemed especially revolutionary—and welcome—to Cantril and Allport.[23]

What wasn't welcome was radio's rampant commercialism. Cantril and Allport insisted that "radio should be removed from the dictatorship of private profits." They were particularly concerned that "millions of children in the nation—radio's most loyal listeners—are being exploited (no other word will serve) by a handful of profit-makers." The profit motive was simply not conducive to "the highest standards of art, entertainment . . . or even to basic freedom of speech." While acknowledging that political control had, in certain European countries, turned radio into a tool of propaganda, they also used the word *propaganda* to describe much of advertising and the radio fare it supported.[24] Like most educators and reformers of the time, Cantril and Allport were deeply disappointed that this device had been taken over so quickly by corporate interests to maximize profits rather than to reduce ignorance and promote social justice.

In 1937, when Cantril, Stanton, and Lazarsfeld established the Office of Radio Research, these same concerns dominated their studies. But Stanton was working for CBS, and market considerations were first and foremost for him because CBS was the smaller network trying to catch up with NBC. The ORR, then, started with a mixed agenda—to conduct academically defensible and interesting studies of radio's impact on America, and to figure out which audience members liked which shows—and why—so the networks could become more profitable.

As Cantril, Lazarsfeld, and Stanton set to work, they confronted a crude technological system. Audience research relied on two flawed devices: telephone surveys and human memory. The first ratings service, the Cooperative Analysis of Broadcasting, started by Archibald Crossley in 1929, involved telephoning between 1,500 and 3,500 people in cities around the country and asking them to recall who in the household had listened to which stations and programs during the previous twenty-four hours, and which of these programs family members preferred. They also asked if listeners remembered who the sponsors were. By the 1930s the CAB checked in with listeners at regular times: 9:05 A.M., 12:05 P.M., and 5:05 and 8:05 in the evening, and asked only what they had listened to in the previous two hours. There was a class bias here;

only 41 percent of households had telephones, so many working-class and ethnic listeners were excluded from the surveys. Even as late as 1948, only 58 percent of homes had phones.[25] Respondents also misremembered what they had heard the day before: there were lapses, false reports, and deliberate misrepresentations. Still, with public opinion polling yet unknown in America and with the radio audience a vast but still mysterious phenomenon, the Crossley ratings, as they were called, provided a rough glimpse of American tastes, and people were fascinated to know what these were.

Ratings thus became newsworthy in their own right, cited by gossip columnists like Walter Winchell and Ed Sullivan. In 1931 *Amos 'n' Andy* was the highest rated show. But why? In 1934 a new research firm, Clark-Hooper Inc., which eventually came to be known as the Hooper ratings, inaugurated the "coincidental telephone interview." Those called were asked to report what they were listening to right then, and on which station. This avoided the recall problem, but now, in the midst of the Depression, the number of households with telephones had declined to 31 percent, further biasing the results.[26] Eventually advertisers subscribed to both services, since the coincidental method conveyed how many people were listening to one show over another at any given time, while the "recall" method—which assessed memory, in part— helped suggest how big an impact a particular show had. There were often discrepancies between the ratings provided by the two services, especially after you got past the top five ranked shows. Neither Crossley nor Hooper provided any insight into radio's impact on the other mass media, on purchasing patterns, on politics, on cultural tastes and preferences, or on the life of the mind.

Stanton and Lazarsfeld were determined to systematize the study of the audience and to develop a mechanical means to measure what went on in people's heads when they heard a broadcast. To do this, they married two technologies: the techniques of survey research with a device they called the program analyzer or, more familiarly, Little Annie.

Stanton invented Little Annie on a dare. He recalled, "One Saturday afternoon, we were having one of these three-way meetings between Cantril, Lazarsfeld, and me at Princeton. Lazarsfeld described a technique for finding out what parts of a program held particular appeal for the audience. He recounted some experiments he had done in picking popular tunes for, I believe, a phonograph company in Vienna." He wanted to determine what made a popular song a hit. The "contraption," as Herta Herzog called it, required that the test subjects mark the portion of the music they liked with a fountain pen while the song played on the phonograph.[27] They had to turn the pages of a pad, and each page corresponded to a small section of the song. As the listener marked those pages before him that appeared when he liked the music, a metronome coordinated the turning pages with the movement of the song. So the test subject's response was complicated by his having to turn the pages of the pad and mark the pages when he liked the music, all over the constant tick of the metronome.

"When Paul was describing this, I kidded him about the looseness of the technique," Stanton remembered. "He challenged me—in a friendly way—to improve it. I told him it ought to be possible to minimize the interference with the enjoyment or the involvement with the program . . . by giving someone a way to register yes or no without having to turn pages and make check marks and so forth. I wanted to let people react to the program. So I built the first of the program analyzers."[28]

Stanton already had considerable mechanical and electrical experience building devices such as this. He had been a tinkerer since he was a child and got interested in radio when his younger brother became a ham operator in the 1920s. As a graduate student gauging what people were listening to, Stanton built, from scratch, an automatic recording device that he could attach directly to a radio. It anticipated what the A. C. Nielsen Company would later label the audimeter. Inside the device was a paper tape and a stylus; whenever a station was tuned in, the stylus marked the tape, providing a record of what program was listened to and when. He recalled, "I wasn't satisfied that asking somebody what they had done the day before necessarily gave you an accurate record of what had taken place." Indeed, when Stanton compared the record on the tape with listeners' memories of what they had heard, he found their memories faulty.[29]

What came to be known as the Stanton-Lazarsfeld program analyzer was a box with two buttons, one green and one red. Interview subjects were each given one as they gathered in a room to listen to a radio show. When they liked what they heard, they pressed the green button; when they didn't, they pressed the red. If they were indifferent, they were not to press anything. The buttons were connected by wire to a device not unlike a polygraph, which was in an adjoining room, invisible to the listeners. In the polygraph a paper tape moved continuously under paired sets of pens. Each red button activated the red pen, which swung down, marking a valley of dislike on the tape. Each green button activated the black pen, which marked the peaks of listener pleasure. The tape itself was also marked with a time line that showed exactly where in the program each reaction was so that a positive reaction to an announcer could be clearly distinguished from a negative reaction to the crashing, melodramatic organ music that followed him. Each seat in the room was numbered, as were the pens, so researchers could also tell which people were responding in which way to which parts of the program. Little Annie could test as many as eleven people simultaneously.[30]

Follow-up interviews, based on carefully designed questionnaires that could be statistically coded, explored why listeners liked or disliked what they did. Little Annie recorded only a shift in opinion, not why it occurred; thus, skillful interviewing was essential to the process. Stanton scoffs at the notion that today's focus groups constitute some major innovation. "I used to laugh when people in political research would use the term *focus group*. Hell, we were doing focus groups with the program analyzer."[31]

One of the most skillful interviewers was Herta Herzog, who, unlike her husband, was fascinated by the meanings people made of the shows they listened to. Her trick was to play dumb, never revealing that she already knew exactly which people had pressed the red and green buttons when. Because she had an Austrian accent and was a recent immigrant, the respondents felt they had to explain the semiotics of radio production very carefully to her, sometimes calling her Dearie. Herzog, a Ph.D. from the University of Vienna, had been studying radio for five years, yet she exploited the respondents' presumption of her ignorance and naiveté to get them to open up.[32]

Obviously Lazarsfeld and Stanton wanted to get clean responses, devoid of ambivalence, clear in their implications about programming preferences. This was especially true for Stanton, whose insistence on a yes/no, either/or binary model stemmed from his need to provide potential advertisers with definitive data about CBS listeners and programs. But look at what was assumed. The show in question was a given. The red-green response of the audience was a given. The notion of the audience member as someone with coherent, uncontested responses to the medium and to discrete sections of each show was a given. And, of course, the need to quantify, understand, and sell to this audience was a given. Yet despite these biases and the limitations of some of the Office of Radio Research's work, much of what they found is rich and provocative and merits reconsideration, in part because of the mess they could *not* explain away.

Herzog was one of eight or so people who initially worked in the ORR. Lazarsfeld organized and conducted research as part of the Rockefeller grant, but he also did market research for CBS, NBC, Roper, ad agencies like McCann-Erickson, and the Market Research Corporation of America. His plan was to conduct such studies for corporate clients and use the proceeds to subsidize academic studies. He called this activity Robin Hooding.[33] He hoped, in other words, to have it both ways. Lazarsfeld was a disaster with money—he always spent it before the project at hand was completed, raising deficit spending to an art form. So money from new contracts was always being funneled to finish previous obligations, and the ORR was always in debt.

By the spring of 1939, when the ORR's Rockefeller grant was up for renewal, Lazarsfeld had to produce some record of achievement to get continued funding. He and the staff pulled together their studies under the title *Radio and the Printed Page* and delivered the manuscript to the Rockefeller office on July 1, 1939, the deadline for grant submissions. The grant was renewed and *Radio and the Printed Page* published in 1940. Lazarsfeld also arranged to serve as guest editor of an issue of the *Journal of Applied Psychology* in 1939 and 1940, and a variety of the ORR's findings appeared there. Two subsequent collections, *Radio Research 1941* and *Radio Research 1942–43*, which Lazarsfeld and Stanton coedited, presented further ORR studies.

These publications are rarely checked out of libraries today—even libraries in schools where media studies is taught. They molder in the stacks, providing faded snapshots of a bygone audience—and antiquated research methods— that few care to dust off. Yet together these journals and books provide an incomplete yet fascinating portrait of a society and many of its subcultures coming to terms with a revolutionary technology.

Lazarsfeld, Cantril, Stanton, Herzog, and others used multiple approaches in the ORR, from more open-ended interviewing and analysis of radio content to statistics, charts, and graphs. Lazarsfeld wanted to measure the audience in a variety of ways and introduced several new approaches, which by today's standards seem boringly obvious and crude. But they were the first steps in developing what Lazarsfeld hoped would be a "science" of audience research. The former Marxist and socialist also remained interested in class as a determinant of social behavior, and this was one of the first factors he introduced into the intellectual construction of the audience. Lazarsfeld advanced several new techniques—the "secondary" study of data collected by others, the panel study that repeatedly questioned the same group of respondents about their opinions, the focus group, and survey research, which extrapolated national habits and attitudes from a sample of the population. The secondary studies allowed the ORR to correlate data from the ratings services with data from George Gallup's public opinion polls, as a way to get a better profile of the audience and its listening habits.

Radio and the Printed Page embodies all the tensions inherent in finding messy, contradictory responses among the audience while seeking clear-cut findings. Lazarsfeld was not some mindless number cruncher; he was deeply interested in often unanswerable questions: What kind of music engages our desire and why? Why do people choose one radio show and not another? And he was determined to break people's subjective processes down into definable, measurable components and moments, as if one really could develop an equation, some statistics, a questionnaire, that would codify the relationship between sensual stimuli and individual longing. On the surface *Radio and the*

Printed Page is orderly, establishing correlations between class, gender, age, and listening practices. But as Herzog especially found out, the "audience" was an elusive, even mythological construct that defied categorization, especially when individual respondents revealed highly contradictory responses to the same program.

Radio and the Printed Page focused, simply enough, on "who listens to what, and why." It opened with a note of concern that today remains all too familiar. People's lives were being shaped by "specialized technical or business experts far away from the scene of our own activities" while Americans, overwhelmed by increasingly complex problems, were "becoming progressively illiterate today in handling life's options." They also seemed highly impressionable, inundating Washington with telegrams after listening to one or another radio demagogue. Was this what radio was doing—turning people into easily manipulated lemmings?[34]

The book consisted of six chapters that studied radio's impact on reading (which was cast as the "intellectually more mature leisure-time activity"), analyzed the appeal of a game show called *Professor Quiz,* and correlated preferences in programming with economic and social class. The book's guiding question was whether radio, with its ability to send classical music, political talk shows, and educational programming out to millions, was "uplifting" the masses, reaching those who didn't necessarily read the newspaper or books, or go to museums or symphony halls.

This was a central issue for John Marshall, the grants officer at the Rockefeller Foundation who supervised the ORR project and thought most radio programming was mindless junk. Yet it resonated with Lazarsfeld's earlier proselytizing for the Socialist Party in Vienna, as well as with his own elitism about American popular culture. Thus, the book argued that "serious listening," which meant listening to political discussions and classical music, had to be "institutionalized." Throughout the book there was enormous emphasis on inculcating elite tastes among the masses. As Lazarsfeld put it, "Progress is the result of efforts originated by small, advanced groups and gradually accepted by the population."[35] Ironically, this comment ignored groups like the working classes who Lazarsfeld had sought to ignite and who, at various times, had been critically important agents of "progress."

This agenda coupled with a methodological one: the importance of finding statistically significant differences in any survey or set of data, of finding breaks and contrasts between groups and finding unity within groups. The study was filled with the either-or model: radio listeners versus readers, newspaper readers versus radio news listeners, listeners to serious broadcasts versus listeners to popular entertainment. While such categorizations were extremely helpful in teasing out how different groups of people used and responded to radio, they also imposed a bifurcation of the audience that was, in fact, too neat.

Radio and the Printed Page, in an effort to develop more sophisticated studies based on social stratification, focused almost exclusively on class. Lazarsfeld and his collaborators defined class in terms of four "cultural levels," A being the highest and D the lowest, with each level determined by income, education, and phone ownership. (Because they were relying on data provided them by a ratings service, there was a heavy bias toward urban listeners.) Class was posited here as a unified, relatively coherent category. Race was ignored and gender dealt with in a more ancillary fashion. For example, in one study of listenership to a political speech, the classification system for men was based on occupation. Since most women couldn't be classified in the same way, they were simply excluded from the study.

In an extensive statistical study of "serious broadcasts," especially classical music and public affairs programming, the ORR found that those from a "high cultural level" were more likely to be "serious listeners," while those from low cultural levels were not. What the ORR found was that listeners from the highest cultural levels, whose rents were highest and who were college educated, listened the least to radio, while those from the lowest cultural levels (with the exception of the very poor) listened the most. This discrepancy was especially pronounced for daytime listening.[36] Those from the highest cultural levels preferred reading to listening to the radio and preferred getting their news from the newspaper. While these findings are hardly earth-shattering, it was important to document what may have seemed like common sense at the time.

The study included a chart that emphasized that those from the highest cultural levels were most likely to listen to "serious broadcasts," like the Metropolitan Opera and the General Motors Symphony, while those from the lowest cultural levels were not. "The programs ... which are definitely preferred by people lower in the cultural scale, are those which can be characterized as of definitely bad taste." These included *Amos 'n' Andy, Major Bowes' Original Amateur Hour, Gang Busters, Lum and Abner,* and, of course, soap operas. Radio, the study maintained, did not bring serious culture to levels of the population previously unreached by the symphony hall or the library. The study documented that the percentage of airtime given to serious, public affairs programming was small. The ORR concluded that "people of lower cultural level ... are less concerned with serious subject matter" and added, "The idea that radio is at this moment a tool for mass education ... is groundless."[37] Left without comment was the more disruptive finding that there was a high correlation between "serious listening" to political shows and union membership.

In other words, these correlations were a little too pat, and Lazarsfeld was too concerned with getting clear-cut findings, too focused on what he saw as the inverse relationship between income and radio listening. As a result, he failed to explore people's contradictory relationship to radio, or to examine the ramifications of having this pastiche of "high culture" and kitsch broadcast into people's homes in a patchwork that sought, simultaneously, to pander and to uplift.

For example, the chart demonstrating that those from level A most preferred "serious broadcasts" also revealed that more listeners from this elite group listened to *Major Bowes' Original Amateur Hour* (11.4 percent) than to the NBC Symphony (10.4 percent). And one of their guilty pleasures was *Gang Busters,* which drew in more listeners from the highest cultural levels than did *Amos 'n' Andy.* In addition, those lower down the cultural scale, at level C, listened as much to the General Motors Symphony (10.4 percent) as they did to *Lum and Abner* (10.7 percent). Even more striking is that about the same proportion of these folks listened to the opera (11.9 percent) as did to a cornball, melodramatic, down-market serial called *Today's Children* (11.1 percent).[38]

Here is where the historian hungers for excerpts from interviews done with real listeners, to hear how they talked about crossing such cultural borders—either "up" or "down"—as they listened in, to hear what pleasures the upper classes got from a show that was the 1930s version of *The FBI* or *America's Most Wanted.* It is interesting that, except for the academic experts who were quoted in the book, and did their own readings of programming content, those from the highest cultural levels were not scrutinized, interviewed, studied, or quoted to nearly the same extent as were those from the lower classes. This was another aspect of the ORR's elitist bias: it was taken for granted that those from the lower levels needed to be put under the microscope but not those from the same educational and economic level as the interviewers themselves. Members of this latter group were too much like the broadcasters, and it was Lazarsfeld's lifelong mission to study the consumers, not the producers of media content.

The studies in this and subsequent volumes were highly varied. Some of them were statistically based and addressed yes-no questions like "Does radio reduce newspaper reading?" Others, like Theodor Adorno's spectacular exemplar of Frankfurt School pessimism and elitism, "The Radio Symphony," relied almost entirely on theory and speculation to argue that radio broadcasts—because of the very act of mechanical transmission—trivialized and eviscerated classical music.

Yet there was a chapter on "how to build audiences for serious broadcasts among people of lower cultural levels." Radio also offered "a rich opportunity for the promotion of reading." Here again is the schizophrenia of the educated bourgeoisie, who had strong, normative notions of what culture should be and how leisure time should be spent. On the one hand, their worst suspicions about the mass media and the degradation of popular tastes and the public imagination were confirmed. On the other hand, they still held out hope that radio would and could elevate such people. People's own contradictory relationship to radio, and the overlap between high culture and low culture, was not addressed.

This is where Herta Herzog's contributions to *Radio and the Printed Page* were so crucial. Because Lazarsfeld became such a giant in the field, and because Herzog did not find work in academics, her contributions to audience research have been overshadowed. It's time to correct this. Herzog preferred the qualitative side of audience research and enjoyed thinking about the richness and messiness of the responses she got. And she foregrounded—even reveled in—the contradictions she found. As a result Herzog was decades ahead of her time in anticipating how poststructuralism, feminism, and postmodernism would inform media criticism and analysis by emphasizing people's ambivalent relationships to media content that was itself filled with contradictions.

At the beginning of the chapter titled "Why Do People Like a Program?" we learn that those from the lower cultural levels did listen to shows they considered educational; but they just weren't *America's Town Meeting* or speeches by Supreme Court justices. Instead, they were what the ORR labeled "service programs"—home economics shows, hobby programs, and series like *The Voice of Experience,* a radio advice column in which letters from listeners were answered on the air, or *The Goodwill Hour,* which interviewed people in trouble and then offered advice. These "psychological programs," which addressed proper behavior, self-improvement, public and private morality, and the possibility of upward mobility, were in fact regarded as educational programs by millions. Herzog was fascinated to find that this attitude extended to soap operas.

Here we get the dirt—accounts from the listeners themselves about what radio meant to them. The melodramatic narratives and strong female characters of daytime serials—coupled with the intimacy of the medium—provided powerful points of identification, when listeners projected themselves into the situation at hand and then took guidance from the voice of radio. Interviewees told Herzog that the soap opera "teaches me as a parent how to bring up my child." Women said that the soap opera made them "know how other girls act" and gave them "an idea of how a wife should be with a husband." Referring to a male character who was "a good diplomat," another noted that "I can use some of the things he does in my own home. . . . On the radio they have problems with children and they do certain things and I can do it too then." Soaps provided listeners with moral and behavioral yardsticks against which to measure themselves. More important, while cultural elites like Lazarsfeld and his male cohorts sneered at soaps, these shows actually reinforced the cultural and social norms heavily promoted by the educated bourgeoisie and packaged them in a way that was extremely effective. As *Radio and the Printed Page* noted, "The interest of some listeners lies more in being given orders than in the special content of the information. They enjoy the opportunity to obey an authoritative voice."[39] This may seem self-evident today, but Herzog appears to have been one of the first to get it back in the 1930s. More important, she appreciated that people liked to talk back to the radio and feel superior to the people on it. In other words, she saw audiences using radio to rebel against yet acquiesce to the power and authority of cultural elites. Lazarsfeld encouraged Herzog to study soaps and quiz shows because they had become such popular genres on the radio. But it was her ability to empathize with individual interview subjects that sets her work apart from her husband's.

Herzog's study of *Professor Quiz*, the first radio quiz show, is nothing short of brilliant. Methodologically, it is skimpy, nearly indefensible by Lazarsfeld's standards. Herzog interviewed only eleven people (eight women and three men) for her article, and apologized that this made the study inherently inconclusive. But off she went, milking these interviews for all their richness. *Professor Quiz*, which went on the air in 1936 and became enormously popular, spawned the quiz show craze, including *Information Please* and *The Quiz Kids*, which showcased children classified as geniuses. *Professor Quiz* asked contestants questions like "name a heavenly body with a tail and one with rings" or "identify the shortest verse in the Bible" ("Jesus wept"), and listeners who sent in questions that were used on the show won twenty-five dollars.[40] The winner won twenty-five silver dollars.

Quiz shows had "a multiple appeal," argued Herzog, with different aspects of them appealing to different people. Most compelling for listeners was the participatory nature of the shows: it was almost impossible *not* to interact with the voices on the radio, and the audience loved being invited in to give the show its public and private meanings. Listeners inhabited multiple personas as they tuned in: they competed with the on-air contestant, they competed with their imagined community of other listeners, and they competed with—and often showed off in front of—admiring family members or friends. They were above the contestants; they were beneath them. They felt, as they listened, that they knew more than they thought they did yet less than they should.

Listeners simultaneously competed with the on-air contestants and felt solidarity with them. They sympathized when a contestant blundered yet also enjoyed and sometimes laughed at these blunders. The contestants, if they were unsuccessful in their answers, bolstered listeners' self-esteem. But successful contestants, especially "college graduates," aroused class antagonisms and feelings of inadequacy, as well as resentment against those with social advantages. Once those antagonisms were aroused, however, the show managed and relieved them. In fact, it seemed to reassure some that "you don't have to be a college graduate" to know the answers and win the game; the show enacted a public fantasy that educational level and class position were not the only avenues to success, that such barriers could be finessed.

Listeners preferred the contestants to be "average people," and when they rooted for someone in particular, they chose the contestant who, they said, "is most like myself." Herzog shrewdly noted that "a listener chooses the person 'like myself' apparently not to increase his own chances of winning but, through identification with the average man, to participate in the college man's defeat."[41] In an age when advertising, movies, and magazine articles insisted that first impressions matter, and that being a good, quick judge of people is essential to success, quiz show listeners delighted in choosing the potential winner after hearing contestants answer just a question or two. If they chose correctly, their self-esteem swelled, and their authority was enhanced among friends and family members.

Unlike the other ORR researchers, Herzog did not simply assume that listeners had some pat, coherent relationship to radio programming. She found them simultaneously passive and active ("semi-active," as she termed it), eager to participate vicariously at some moments, willing to withdraw at others. If they didn't know the answer to a question, they could always say, "I knew it, but couldn't get it past the tip of my tongue" or "I didn't hear it clearly enough," and thus they could "salve defeat." The show also allowed them to look down on the on-air contestants as "exhibitionists," never acknowledging the pleasure of their own displays in their homes. "Radio," wrote Herzog, "allows for participation in a 'public event' in the complete privacy of the listener's four walls." She saw radio substituting for, supplanting, the public sphere.[42]

Nor did listeners regard *Professor Quiz* with the same condescension that Lazarsfeld did; they felt they learned a lot from the questions, even if what they acquired were, as Herzog put it "scattered and unrelated bits of information." The show didn't cultivate in lower-income listeners a desire to read or to acquire a broader frame of reference. Instead, it flattered its listeners into thinking that learning discrete infobits was just as valuable as having a formal education.

Herzog saw the quiz program as a "lucky combination": "The Puritan attitude toward pleasure is still influential in this country," she noted, "so if recreation can be combined with serious effort, people feel less guilty about spending time in recreation." And she found the program to have a compensatory function, to make listeners feel smart and important just by the fact that *they* were being asked questions. The quiz show, by mimicking a school setting (while eliminating its risk) and by imparting bits of knowledge, relieved people of their guilt over not reading and failing to improve themselves. In addition, by replicating bygone school situations, with their quizzes and tests, yet giving the listener wide latitude in what she chose to answer, and by providing no punishments if she failed, the show "allow[ed] symbolically for a re-arrangement and mastery of difficult circumstances."[43] In this school failure could be hidden from the teacher and success exaggerated: the student controlled the judgment of her own performance.

One of the most important aspects of the quiz show was its role in helping the listener "finding out about myself." This desire for self-knowledge was repeatedly expressed to Herzog by the quiz show listeners, who loved to position themselves intellectually to "find out how dumb I am" yet to discover that "I know more than I expected."[44] To ensure that listening was satisfactory, listeners often underrated themselves just before the questions started so as to be "pleasantly surprised" by the end. "A good score is likely . . . to relieve one of a feeling of having been too indolent," she observed. More important, the show staged the contest over knowledge, merit, and success as profoundly individual. The roles of social structures, class positioning, race and gender biases were eclipsed as success and failure became totally individual dramas. This resonated with a powerful sense of the importance of luck, rather than merit, in shaping people's success on the show and, by extension, in life. We see among these fans the emergence of a culture of surrogacy, the culture of the vicarious life.

While Lazarsfeld demonstrated that radio was reinforcing preexisting class lines and patterns of consumption, Herzog shows us that this technology's impact was contradictory, and not always easy to quantify. Her study suggests that radio was accelerating the fragmentation of the self into many selves, each hailed at different times. *Professor Quiz* simultaneously activated and contained class antagonisms, helped listeners straddle the tensions between the work ethic and consumerism, allowed them to feel both passive and active, and promoted the value of learning while reinforcing anti-intellectualism. Herzog concluded that "paradoxically, the programs from which people claim to learn most are put on the air by advertisers and not by educators." This Lazarsfeld found regrettable, and the last chapter of *Radio and the Printed Page* urged that educators work to use radio to induce more people to read. Librarians got advice on how to "stow away" messages about the pleasures of reading into radio shows like *Lum and Abner,* and the author hoped that the audience for "serious" music could be increased.

Except for Herzog's chapter on *Professor Quiz,* there was little suggestion in *Radio and the Printed Page* that audience members might talk back to or rebel against what they heard. There was no recognition that some people—especially those of the "lower cultural level" who, during the Depression, were all too aware of enormous gaps in class and income—might not listen to "serious" broadcasts in part because they knew these broadcasts, like fancy art museums, weren't about or for them. There was little acknowledgment that working-class listeners might be "serious" or political: instead they were posited as the unsophisticated masses who wasted their time listening to Eddie Cantor. By the time the ORR had been established, the two greatest American radio demagogues, Huey Long and Father Coughlin, were dead or discredited. Yet in the early 1930s their populist attacks on corporate capitalism had activated an enormous audience who regarded their broadcasts as serious indeed. These were listeners who very much recognized the lines of cultural exclusion, yet they do not appear as active, self-aware subjects in the ORR's first book.

Stanton and Lazarsfeld argued in their books that radio had limited effects, that it was embedded in larger social and economic systems and had little power, on its own, to effect social change. Yet they also saw it as a "stupendous technological advance with a strongly conservative tendency in all social matters." They argued that each individual responded differently to radio depending on his or her social positioning and thus sought to divide the audience by class into measurable blocks whose tastes and preferences could be predicted. They averted their gaze from radio's role in promoting a dominant, consumerist ideology, and they neglected the female audience. Except for Herzog, they didn't confront these and the many other contradictions they found in radio listening and in radio programming. Radio worked especially well when a program located a major cultural contradiction, opened it, revealed it, reveled in it, then sutured it up nice and neat by the program's end. This is what Herta Herzog found. And this is what Paul Lazarsfeld failed to pursue.

Yet Lazarsfeld's legacy is considerable. He was a mentor to scores of scholars who institutionalized communication studies in America's universities. His model of audience research remained unchallenged until the late 1960s in the United States. Yet despite his support for qualitative and quantitative approaches to studying the impact of radio, his ambivalence about the audience—uncultured, anti-intellectual know-nothings who nonetheless deserved on-air cultural missionary work—and his emphasis on refining research methods ironically legitimized a patronizing stance toward media audiences by elites that helped retard, for decades, the qualitative study of the mass media in the academy.

Lazarsfeld did encourage the work of cultural critic Leo Lowenthal, who found that radio was playing a role in a major shift in values in America. Previously, Americans had idolized heroes of production, like Andrew Carnegie, Thomas Edison, and Henry Ford. Now they were more gripped by heroes of consumption, especially movie and radio stars. Radio shows emphasized status and prestige rather than knowledge and accomplishments. Radio seemed to be accelerating the rise of what Christopher Lasch would call, forty years later, the "culture of narcissism," with its emphasis on other-directedness, the desire to be envied, the desperate need for the approval of others, and a shift away from deferred gratification and spiritual redemption to immediate gratification and psychic fulfillment in the here and now.

One year after the first the ORR issued its second compendium, *Radio Research 1941*, edited by Lazarsfeld and Stanton. Three of the six chapters focused on radio and music, and they included Theodor Adorno's withering attack on the broadcast of classical music, "The Radio Symphony." The other chapters included "Radio Comes to the Farmer," "Radio and the Press Among Young People," and an analysis of whether foreign-language programs over American radio stations threatened national security. "At a time when the country is most interested in speeding up the assimilation of its national minorities who have recently immigrated," it was crucial to determine whether broadcasts in Spanish, Italian, German, Polish, or Yiddish promoted nationalistic feelings about America—or about the old country.[45]

This publication, too, was divided in its assessment of radio's impact, especially radio's effect on music and on musical tastes. On the one hand, song "pluggers" could take the basic building blocks of a pop song, put them together, and convince broadcasters to keep playing the song, announcing it was a new hit until it became one. "When the man in the street finally decides upon his favorite song, he has no idea that he has simply fallen in line with something which had been prescribed for him many weeks before." On the other hand, people who had not had access to or even known about "good" music became music lovers—and not just of Tin Pan Alley—through broadcasting. "Here are people whose interest in good music would never have developed had it not been for radio."[46] Again, musical elitism and disgust with radio's cynical, standardizing tendencies intermixed with that bourgeois optimism that radio could convert listeners from the Mills Brothers to Haydn. But the main finding here, class-based aesthetic anxieties aside, was how effortlessly and totally radio had enabled people to interweave music into everyday life.

Simply put, the chapter "Invitation to Music" documented that the very ability to listen to and appreciate music had been revolutionized by radio. This was especially true for men. For them radio made music listening, especially listening to classical music, more available and more permissible. The change was also dramatic for people over thirty, who in preradio days "had very little likelihood of ever developing an interest in music." It wasn't just that radio allowed them to indulge in a pastime they already had; radio "initiated" their interest. This was also true for people of lower economic status. Before radio family background, education, and income had determined access to symphonies and recitals. Geography and segregation kept jazz, the blues, and "hillbilly music" the province of some Americans and out of reach of others. Of course, in keeping with the ORR's tradition, this chapter was mostly concerned with "serious music," which constituted 12 percent of all musical broadcasts. Edward Suchman, the author of the chapter, sent out questionnaires to listeners of WNYC, New York's municipal, noncommercial station, noted for its show for classical music lovers, *Masterwork Hour*. Fifty of the respondents were then interviewed. Over half reported that radio either initiated or cultivated their current love of music.[47]

"How would I have known there was such a thing as good music without the radio?" asked a young male clerk with a high school education. *"Music had to be brought to me. Radio did this,"* noted Suchman in italics. One listener reported that being able to listen to classical music on radio was "like being born again." A fifty-two-year-old grocer admitted, "I couldn't live without music. I mean it—just as I need to eat to live. *I love more than anything else to close my eyes, sit back, and dream while listening to a great symphony.*" For such a man, Suchman enthused, again in italics, *"Radio is the heart of his musical being."* Suchman concluded provocatively that "radio tends to even out sex differences" since it had made men more interested in music and women more interested in the news.[48]

What was striking was that radio was "more than three times as important for men as for women in initiating an interest in music." Suchman was especially surprised by this, given that in America "musical activity" had traditionally been "a womanly grace." Part of the reason had to do with sheer availability, and the fact that you didn't have to go out to a concert hall anymore to hear such music. As one lawyer confessed, his wife was a music lover, "but I just couldn't get myself to make the necessary effort and go to concerts with her." But the radio was *"the opposite of the concert hall—restful and relaxing."* Added another man, "I can sit back in a soft chair, smoke a cigar and dream without being disturbed." Other men linked their love of radio music with the economic privations of the Depression. *"Music is all I have now. The* radio is more important to me than my business, which is bad." Some reported that radio listening prompted them to buy a phonograph so that they could then listen repeatedly to the music they had first heard over the air. Indeed, after an industry low in 1932, by 1940 record sales had increased 500 percent. But others felt that radio brought them much more choice and variety: *"I would be foolish to tie myself down to the victrola again,"* observed one enthusiast.[49] Nor were people dependent on concerts or on their own playing: because of radio people attended concerts and played their own instruments less than they had in the past.

For many the fact that they could hear classical music repeated over and over on the air until they learned to recognize specific symphonies or concertos eased them into a sense of knowledge and mastery. And radio commentators who explained the significance and history of the music provided listeners with immediate cultural capital previously reserved for the educated. Music appreciation became intertwined with male friendships and community. Some men were like the laborer who heard his druggist friend listening to classical music and thought, *"If he listens there must be something to it."* Another young man became a fan as a result of his high school friends constantly discussing the symphonies they heard on the radio. Other men, like aspiring doctors, listened as part of their hopes for upward mobility, or what Suchman called the "prestige" motivation.[50]

Under the snobbish influence of Theodor Adorno, Suchman maintained that those who were introduced to serious music primarily through radio didn't "understand" it as well and didn't have as good taste as did those who turned to radio to gratify an already cultivated interest. Too many of the radio initiates liked Rimsky-Korsakov and Dvorak (ranked "not as good" by "25 musically interested individuals") instead of Bach and Brahms, because, explained Adorno in an appendix, the former composers' music relied on "emotional appeal" and "Slavic melancholy," and was derivative of "folk tunes." Thus, while radio was creating new music listeners, theirs was a "pseudo-interest" in which "signs of real understanding [were] lacking."[51]

This elitism, for which Adorno was to become legendary, intersected with concerns about the standardization of taste and the crass, calculated manufacturing of music that radio both demanded and made possible. In his study "The Popular Music Industry," Duncan MacDougald traced the life cycle of a typical "hit," from its creation to the point when the proverbial man on the street could be heard whistling it. Here he was discussing songs like "Deep Purple," "Sunrise Serenade," "Jeepers Creepers," and "Beer Barrel Polka," as well as the music of Cole Porter, Irving Berlin, Glenn Miller, and Benny Goodman.

MacDougald wanted to make it clear from the beginning that this was an industrialized process; that, Tin Pan Alley conceits aside, a song's success had almost nothing to do with the "spontaneous, free-will acceptance of the public because of the inherent merit of the number." He wanted his readers to understand that pop songs that might stir the emotions, enhance a love affair, or offer temporary transport from everyday life were, at their base, products constructed and designed to sell. And the industry was basically controlled by fifteen publishers. Eight of these were, in turn, owned or controlled by Hollywood studios. Indeed, by 1938 only 18 percent of the top radio songs were published by houses not affiliated with Hollywood.[52]

Musical pleasure and profitability were mutually exclusive for MacDougald. So were musical quality and popular success. MacDougald could barely contain his disdain for the fact that pop songs required multiple contributors—one person to write the music, another to write the words, yet another to arrange the song. In fact, lack of musical training and ability among these creators was a badge of honor. "That Irving Berlin, for instance, must use a specially constructed piano because he can work in only one key, has already become part of the great American legend." What mattered wasn't talent, it was money, for promoting the record and the sheet music: the cost of making a hit was anywhere from $5,000 to $15,000 in 1940. "Any 'romantic' notion of the creative artist must be excluded in order to arrive at an understanding of 'how a song is written.' " Forget the muse on the shoulder; forget "inspiration"; this was a "cold-blooded process" in which songs were "hacked out" using roughly the same procedure one might use to solve a jigsaw puzzle.[53]

For example, the title of the song had to be incorporated "on the nose," meaning in the first line, then repeated in subsequent lines so that its trademark was quickly established. The melody had to be simple, the lyrics romantic, the song thirty-two bars long. Sometimes executives in the publishing houses would change the lyrics. Once the song was arranged, it went into the hands of the most important person of all: the song plugger, whose job it was to "persuade, wheedle, cajole and implore band leaders and singers to 'do' their songs." He tracked down performers in clubs, on the road, as they were about to go on the air, and the nagging and the "artificial build-up" began. His main goal—to get performers to do the song on national radio. And which songs did performers choose? According to Artie Shaw, " 'Few leaders play a new song solely because they think it's good. They play it only when a publisher assures them it will be the firm's No. 1 tune—the tune the publisher is going to work on and put money behind. They take no chances of introducing a tune and then having it die on them.' "[54] *The Enquirer,* then a trade publication, had a weekly column praising the success of pluggers in moving songs up the charts, prima facie evidence for MacDougald that the mechanics of the industry, not the intrinsic qualities of the song itself, determined what people thought they liked.

The shelf life of a hit in 1940 was about twelve weeks. Hits were measured by sheet music and record sales. Before radio a hit song would sell between 50,000 and 2 million copies of sheet music and stay a hit for as long as eighteen months; radio had slashed sheet music sales and speeded up the rate at which hits rose and fell. Hits were also "played to death" on the radio—one of them, "Says My Heart," was played 258 times over three of New York's radio stations during a four-week period—for an average of 9.2 times a day.[55] Of course this also meant that now millions of Americans around the country knew the same hit, hummed it to themselves, and would, later on, immediately return to 1940 when they heard it again.

We take for granted today the existence of a national musical culture, drivel and all, but this was a striking new national and cognitive phenomenon in the 1930s. For MacDougald, the fact that "Boots and Saddles" and "You Must Have Been a Beautiful Baby" became big hits was testimony to the standardization and degradation of American tastes, and to the listeners' inability to muster "active resentment and critical interest" toward such musical slop. Through radio, he argued, good taste was being eradicated. The fact that people buying sheet music told ORR interviewers that they, too, were fed up with the "sameness" and "banality" of music lyrics was relegated to a footnote.

In the very next chapter of *Radio Research 1941* we get to Adorno himself, whose 1941 essay "On Popular Music" is notorious among academics (if nowhere else) for its condescending, wrongheaded, and no doubt racist dismissal of jazz. Yet his overarching critique of what he and Max Horkheimer labeled the Culture Industry contains a great deal of truth. Adorno had been rescued from certain Nazi arrest and death by Lazarsfeld, who helped get him over to the United States and employed by the ORR. While Adorno certainly must have been grateful, you would not have been able to tell it by his essay in *Radio Research 1941*, "The Radio Symphony."

This was no lapsed Marxist like Lazarsfeld; Adorno saw radio as deeply implicated in the fetishizing of commodities and of "pseudo-individuation," the production of endless songs, radio shows, and movies that seemed different on the surface but were really the same old shows or songs, just in new clothes. Pseudo-individuation was narcotizing, training the audience to accept and expect the same standardized, mass-produced pabulum, stunting the audience's ability to imagine or accept anything new.

And Adorno had no patience with recent quixotic blather about radio bringing music never heard before "to the overburdened hypothetical farmer in the Middle West." In "The Radio Symphony," he complained that the mechanical transmission of symphonic music wrecked it, period. Worse, it produced "retrogressive tendencies in listening." Thus, the ORR's basic techniques—using questionnaires, ratings, interviews—were worthless because the listener who has never heard a symphony live has no ability to say anything substantive about the pleasures of such music. His or her answers just can't be trusted or accepted at face value because "the symphony is changed the very moment it is broadcast." As Adorno began his tirade, he admitted that "the social analyst must risk being castigated as a misanthrope if he is to pursue social essence, as distinct from the facade."⁵⁶ And since his piece was the only theoretical essay in a collection otherwise based on polls and experiments, he subtitled it, wryly, "an experiment in theory."

Adorno focused specifically on "the fate" of a Beethoven symphony when transmitted over the air. First, it was wrecked by commentators who helped listeners identify the basic elements and themes; now listeners regarded the symphony mechanistically, as a mere assemblage of parts rather than as a cohesive entity. Adorno was hardly the first to deride what *The New Republic* had blasted as "Crutches for Broadcast Music." In an effort to "sell" serious music, shows like Columbia's *Symphonic Hour* didn't just play concertos or symphonies: they set the stage for listening by providing biographical information about the composer, the performer, or both, and they lectured about the significance of the music. Thus, a Brahms concerto was preceded by this: "This famous work presents Brahms at his happiest, the noble dreamer and inspired romanticist, meticulous in his craft, and of amazing fertility of musical ideas." What was billed as a performance of Handel's *Water Music* was actually a play about the composer's relationship with George I; while the music played in the background, the radio actor playing the king uttered dialogue like "I feel transported to an unearthly realm" and "By my soul, that is sweet music, Baron. Listen to the dainty measures." An announcer for CBS, in his introduction to *En Saga* by Sibelius, divulged, "When I hear this music I avow a carnal desire to discard the soft, fat ways of life; to set out in oilskins, or something, for somewhere, to discover a desperate polar bear bent on conflict!"⁵⁷ This sort of drivel made Adorno insane.

But the real travesty for Adorno was that symphonies were never meant to be heard over some small box with tinny sound reproduction in one's living room. Instead, as Adorno noted in a metaphor that mixed sex and religion, the listener attending a live performance "entered" the symphony as he would a cathedral, which "absorbed" him totally. Only in the live performance did the listener truly experience what Adorno called "symphonic space." With radio "the sound is no longer 'larger' than the individual. . . . The 'surrounding' function of music also disappears," especially since radio at the time was monaural. The symphony was reduced to nothing more than a piece of furniture in someone's private room. And because the tonal range and volume on radio are limited, the Beethoven symphony "is reduced to the medium range between piano and forte" and thus "is deprived of the secret of origin as well as the might of unveiling." The work thus becomes "bad chamber music."[58]

Through radio a grand and complex symphony becomes "trivialized and romanticized at the same time." The sound alone over the radio undermines the symphony's ability to truly cast a spell. But because symphonic music on the radio is simply one small part of a broader system of broadcasting, the symphony falls prey to how that system organizes time and constructs knowledge. The music is hyped, and the listener is not trusted enough to simply sit back and listen on his own. In Adorno's most provocative critique of what radio had done to such music, he noted how quiz shows in particular insisted that people know how to "quote" from great books or songs. On musical quiz questions contestants were given a few bars of a symphony—some extractable theme—and asked to identify it.

Thus listeners were urged to regard symphonies—and here he singled out Beethoven's Fifth—as a series of individual, semi-independent, identifiable moments, "musical atoms." And it was not uncommon for music appreciation programs to play only a selected movement from a symphony, or even to extract briefer portions, thereby turning the symphony into "a set of quotations from theme songs." Some commentators attributed to Mozart what had been written by Beethoven and told the listener what to picture: "The symphony soars to the skies. It is the laughter of a Titan who elected for the moment to make play with the stars and the planets"; or the commentator saw "dwarves and pixies and elves all scampering away to their private haunts." Listeners can't possibly appreciate symphonic music under these circumstances. Rather, they become deeply anxious about their ability to "recognize the so-called Great Symphonies by their quotable themes" because they need and want to "identify themselves with the standards of the accepted and to prove themselves to be small cultural owners within big ownership culture."[59]

Radio Research 1941 and other such studies were deeply concerned about the homogenization of musical tastes, political views, entertainment, and the very way that radio seemed to impose a schedule onto people's daily lives. Cantril and Allport saw the contradictions in a medium that brought more cultural, musical, and even political variety into people's homes on an unprecedented level while standardizing and stereotyping their "mental life." Current affairs were neatly categorized into pro and con positions, as radio speech demanded "clear-cut positions." "One must take sides," observed

Cantril and Allport, "prohibition or repeal, Republican or Democrat, pro-strike or anti-strike, Americanism or Communism, *this* or *that*. One would think that the universe were dichotomous."[60] And because American radio was punctual, with shows starting precisely on the hour or half hour, it routinized the timetables of millions who now scheduled their private, daily routines around the radio.

As Americans stood poised, whether they knew it or not, to enter World War II, the ORR analyzed the extent to which foreign-language broadcasts pro-moted—or undermined—that crucial element for waging war, nationalism. This study, the first chapter in *Radio Research 1941,* is especially revealing of the extent to which some programs kept national unity and more particular ethnic and regional identities in quite delicate suspension. Historians have noted repeatedly radio's role in promoting a sense of national unity. This study is utterly transparent in exposing how anxious so many—including re-searchers—were that radio achieve exactly that: identification with a national culture, a national purpose, Americanism.

Rudolf Arnheim (author of his own book on radio in 1936) and Martha Collins Bayne, along with ORR researchers, listened in mid-February 1941 to stations across the country—in California, Arizona, and Texas, in Milwaukee, Detroit, and Chicago, and in New Haven, Boston, and New York—that broad-cast in Italian, Polish, Spanish, Yiddish, German, and Lithuanian. They didn't tell us which stations these were, whether they had any network affiliation, or what their broadcast range was. What they did document was the extent to which all foreign-language broadcasts nurtured powerful and nostalgic ties to "the mother country." Most of the listeners to these programs, they inferred, were older, didn't speak English well, and were not as well assimilated into American life as the younger generation of immigrants.

Even here the power of music was front and center. Most of what these sta-tions broadcast was music, but it was what the authors called "national" music, meaning popular tunes, sentimental ballads, marches, and waltzes from the old country. Songs with lyrics, rather than instrumentals, predominated. Many of these songs, the authors editorialized, especially those from Germany about mothers-in-law abandoned in the forest and corpses rescued from "suicide canals" in Berlin, were "of a deplorably low level of taste." "There are almost no good folk songs at all," they lectured, adding, "The melodramatic romance of the worst type prevails."

Nonetheless, these songs activated powerful emotional associations for their listeners by allowing "a dreaming back to that Germany or Poland or other homeland that the listeners left many years ago, and which by virtue of that distance has become to them some sort of earthly paradise." The music takes them back to "the beer-cellars, the men's choral societies, the rifle-clubs, the birthday parties" of their youth. To make sure that "the memory tie is fastened," announcers make the associations explicit: " 'Imagine yourself to be on the market square of a small German town and to be listening to the piece "Sparrows on the Roofs." ' " With listeners of such a "low cultural level," noted the authors, it was not surprising that "influences of an emotional character will generally prove to be more efficient than, say, intellectual reasoning."[61]

The ads were just as bad, if not worse. Ads for coffee or spaghetti or cigars or wine constantly emphasized the listeners' foreign identities. Commercials would "remind the audience of the good old days in the old country," hype cigars as "the kind you smoked in your own home town in Italy," hawk "old country sausage" as having "the same taste you are used to getting in Poland." Many ads also stressed that at their shops the clerks offered "service in your own language." In fact, they urged listeners to identify more closely with immigrants from their own country than with others, exhorting them to feel that "they and the sponsor form an in-group" in which ethnic groups should stick to their own kind instead of trusting outsiders. "The tavern-keep is a genuine Berlinian," offered one ad; "the owner . . . is the only such dealer who is a Lithuanian," confided another; "a Mexican will always get better values from another Mexican," advised a third.[62]

Drawing inspiration from American advertising, which sought to construct peer pressure for using a particular product by announcing that "most Americans," or, better yet, "discriminating Americans," used such-and-such a product, these foreign-language ads painted a picture of a larger community of Italians or Poles of which the listeners would surely want to be a part. Ironically, this was a critical element in the way advertising promoted nationalism over the air, by emphasizing that something was American made, or used by most Americans, or recognized around the country as the best of its kind. Here listeners were invited to see themselves as part of a vast and unified community of consumers who could see the tangible fact of "America" every day in the commonality of products they and their neighbors used. But on foreign-language programs, when appeals went out over the air boasting that "many Mexicans" or "the majority of Poles" or "discriminating Italo-Americans" preferred a particular product, they inverted the equation between consumerism and nationalism. On these stations the techniques of national advertising were appropriated to sell subcultural, ethnic identifications that resisted the pull of assimilation.

The other thing these stations did was help keep alive the public life of ethnic Americans. They served as bulletin boards—promoting dances, parties, picnics, music and cultural festivals, foreign-language films, and club meetings—reiterating dates and times, and urging their listeners to attend. Stations also invited listeners to write in, offered musical dedications, and aired jokes submitted by listeners. Some also gave information on filing income taxes or applying for citizenship, and they urged listeners to vote, sometimes giving instructions on whom to vote for. German-language stations had as sponsors many travel agencies that sent money, food, and supplies to family and friends back in Germany. At the same time these stations celebrated the United States, and their listeners' freedom of speech and religion and right to vote. Nonetheless, all these elements of foreign-language broadcasts "[completed] the group's artificial independence of the outside world."

What exactly should be done, asked Arnheim and Bayne, about "radio programs which, by their present policy, may hamper the further amalgamation of large groups of immigrants?" After all, these shows had "a tendency to maintain the status quo of the listeners' stage of assimilation" or, worse, "to drive him back to a setting of life which he left beyond the ocean many years ago." Such shows could simply be banned. But that would be too harsh, and besides immigrants often found themselves isolated. Instead, these stations should be encouraged to feature English-language courses, to air translations of current American songs and of political speeches, especially those of the president, to broadcast dramatizations that "create understanding of everyday American life," and to offer "employment hints."[63]

In 1939, the same year the ORR was analyzing how, or whether, radio could be used to promote greater musical sophistication and more serious reading and listening, advertisers were becoming increasingly dissatisfied with the CAB (recall) and Hooper (coincidental calling) ratings services. The findings of the two did not match, and the listeners telephoned were not always reliable—they could forget, or lie about what they had heard. At the same time advertisers remained keenly obsessed with how popular particular radio shows were. As *Newsweek* reported, " 'How's your Hooper?' became almost as frequent a greeting in radio circles as 'how are you?' " Noted *Business Week* prophetically in 1938, "The next development . . . is certain to be some sort of mechanical device attached to a radio set that will record when the set is turned on, the station it's tuned to, when the dial is switched, and to where."[64]

A. C. Nielsen in Chicago, refining an invention by Louis F. Woodruff and Robert F. Elder of MIT, was indeed testing just such a device—its audimeter. The audimeter mechanically recorded on a piece of tape every time the radio dial was changed and where it was changed to. When the tape was compared with the day's broadcasting schedule, Nielsen could see which shows were listened to and for how long. The Nielsen company already provided indexes to food, liquor, and drug companies that showed how their products sold against the competition. Now Nielsen was going into broadcasting.

Preliminary tests with 200 of the devices indicated, for example, that some shows got two-thirds of their audiences from homes with no telephones, meaning CAB and Hooper never even counted these listeners. The CAB and Hooper ratings, which concentrated more on urban listeners, also underestimated the number of small town and rural listeners to particular shows, and thus artificially depressed their ratings. The audimeters also showed something the phone calls never could: the degree of station switching that went on as listeners tuned out commercials or moved between segments of different shows. "Guinea Pig" homes, as *Business Week* called them, allowed monthly inventories of their kitchens and bathrooms so that Nielsen could assess the effectiveness of advertising on particular shows. And since Nielsen was careful to rank these homes by income level as well as locale, the company was able to provide preliminary demographic information about listeners. Critics and competitors complained that with the audimeter, all you knew was that the radio was on—you had no evidence that anyone was actually there listening to it. *Business Week* estimated that to install audimeters in 5,000 homes and then send men out once a month to retrieve the tapes would probably cost, in the beginning, ten times as much as the telephone surveys. But with so much money at stake on the radio, the magazine didn't think Nielsen would have trouble selling the system.[65] It was right. The company began offering its system in 1942, and in six years 63 percent of the country was represented by audimeters.

By 1947 the CAB was out of business, with most advertisers signed up with Hooper, which was then grossing about $1 million a year. The company's phone interviewers in thirty-six cities made 1,500 calls an hour, working their way through the phone book. But the battle of the rating systems was on. Nielsen was on the verge of covering 97 percent of the country through a systematic selection—with help from the Census Bureau—of 1,500 representative homes. One tape in the audimeter could simultaneously track four radios in the house. Nielsen would provide weekly reports, not just bimonthly ones representing only the cities, as Hooper did. In 1947 CBS backed the Nielsen system as superior, not surprising since the Nielsens gave CBS shows higher ratings than did Hooper, putting four of them, instead of just two, in the top fifteen. Sponsors and the other networks also subscribed to Nielsen's service. Within three years it was over. Hooper sold his ratings company to Nielsen in 1950 for $600,000. By 1959 A. C. Nielsen, which had, of course, also expanded into television ratings, was grossing $26.8 million a year.[66]

This research was a far cry from Cantril and Allport's *Psychology of Radio*.

Nielsen could have cared less about the quality of the listening experience, about what radio was doing to a sense of imagined communities. Nielsen delivered numbers, about what kinds of people listened to (or watched) what kinds of shows when, so that a station knew what it could charge Coca-Cola for ad time. The trend in audience research, given who was going to pay for it, was in upgrading the technical capabilities of the system to make it more foolproof. While it was never Paul Lazarsfeld's intention to produce a ratings service for the industry, his work with Frank Stanton pioneered in producing more systematic and mechanical ways of analyzing audience preferences that were indeed helpful to sponsors. A. C. Nielsen simply elaborated on these beginnings and produced a surveillance system of audience behavior that today is so instant and so seemingly thorough that it decides the fate of television programs within a few weeks. Program analyzers, in conjunction with focus groups, are still used to pretest movies and TV shows. All of us now are enmeshed in a technological system we rarely see or participate in directly that still seeks to codify our dreams and desires and all our messy ambivalences about the mass media into yes-no, hit-cancellation, pro-anti- divisions. Certainly this is one of the main legacies of radio research: encouraging us to think we are unified individuals with clear, stable identities and preferences while at the same time recognizing and pointing out that our experiences in the flow of broadcasting socialize us into being just the opposite.

World War II and the Invention of Broadcast Journalism

You could hear it in the very way that H. V. Kaltenborn, in 1939 and 1940, reported the news from Europe: he used words like *lugubrious, salient,* and *temporize;* he pronounced *at all* "at tall," and *chance* "chahnce." Yet in the next breath he would become much more colloquial, saying of the Germans, "All their stuff is censored," or that French lines were holding except for "a couple of unimportant spots." He frequently prefaced information from foreign communiqués with "what this means is" or "what this shows." Upper-class pedant or guy next door—what should the radio newscaster be?

When people listen to old-time radio, they don't listen to old news shows; most are lost forever. Only CBS seems to have made a systematic effort to preserve their war coverage (which they did on acetate disks, magnetic tape not yet having been invented), and you've got to go to the National Archives to hear the full collection of broadcasts.[1] With the exception of Edward R. Murrow, television reminds us of *its* history with the news: John Cameron Swayze, Huntley and Brinkley, Walter Cronkite. And as Stanley Cloud and Lynne Olson point out in *The Murrow Boys,* their rousing account of the invention of broadcast news at CBS, CBS itself did little, after the advent of television, to keep the memory of its own pioneer radio correspondents alive.

Yet by the fall of 1938 radio coverage of the Munich crisis had rendered the newspaper "extra" all but obsolete—people didn't run out to the street for the news; they tuned their dials, and they listened. "Radio," wrote Kaltenborn, "became of itself one of the most significant events of the crisis." More radio sets were sold during the three weeks in September that radio broadcast the crisis than during any previous three-week period. One year later over 9 million new sets were sold, a new industry record. In 1935, 67 percent of American families had radio; by 1940, 81 percent did. "Glued to the set" became a national cliché.[2]

With the seemingly endless documentaries made, and still being made, about World War II, and the success of the History Channel (nicknamed by some the Hitler Channel), we tend to think of this as a highly visual war, experienced by Americans back home primarily through pictures. And certainly, with 85 million people going to the movies each week, Americans saw the progress of the war through newsreels, as well as through photographs in newspapers and magazines. But the way we have come to remember the war—through this visual record—misrepresents how people followed and imagined this war on a daily basis. This was a war that people *listened* to. The media's collective memory of this war, which serves the programming needs of television, suggests that the visual was more important than the auditory, when just the opposite was true. And especially with the advent of gasoline rationing, radio listening increased as people were forced to stay closer to home. World War II was a radio war.

With the loss of so many news broadcasts, it is not easy to write about what was, quite simply, a total revolution in American life: the bringing of national and international news, with the actual sounds of political rallies, air-raid sirens, or gunfire, right into people's living rooms, bedrooms, and kitchens. Broadcasts included daily accounts of the Lindbergh trial, commentary on the New Deal, sentimental human-interest stories like the funeral for a blind man's Seeing Eye dog, and, of course, World War II. Listeners were transported to different places and times by radio. As *Popular Mechanics* gushed in 1938, "The rapid strides of radio during the past few years have made possible world-girdling hook-ups which, in the space of an hour, will take you into yesterday, today and tomorrow."[3]

Fortunately, some commentators wrote memoirs about the emergence of broadcast news. Still, there is so little left to *listen to* today, to *hear* what it actually sounded like. So much has been lost or destroyed that radio news from the 1930s remains severely underrepresented in histories of the press, and in histories of the period. Major books on the period, like Paul Fussell's *Wartime* or Alan Brinkley's recent analysis of the New Deal, *The End of Reform,* don't even have the word *radio* in their indexes. Miraculously, enough has survived from transcriptions made at the time that we can get some idea of the invention of broadcast news.[4]

And this is what we hear: a struggle over how men would deliver the news—which included a struggle over radio oratory—and a pushing out of horizons as listeners added new maps to their mental geographies. There were experiments with the use of sound—the use of ambient sound from the scene of the news story, the more contrived use of sound effects in the studio—to convey a sense of immediacy and urgency. News listening on the radio, as broadcasting styles were being invented, moved people between cognitive registers—informational listening, which was more flat and less imaginative as people took in brief, factual reports, and dimensional listening, as people were compelled to conjure up maps, topographies, street scenes in London after a bombing, a warship being dive-bombed by the Luftwaffe. We also hear certain radio reporters subtly leading public opinion toward a less isolationist stance, a worldview more sympathetic to mobilization and, eventually, engagement. They weren't supposed to do this, however, and most historical accounts of the rise of radio news in the late 1930s emphasize reporters' objectivity and network policy against editorializing.

But if you listen to the news broadcasts from 1938 on, you hear an insistence that Americans become much more aware of the world around them and understand that democracy itself was at risk. The Munich crisis as broadcast on radio made Americans much more interested in and knowledgeable about news from Europe: a public opinion poll from November 1938 asserted that this story was twice as interesting to the public as any other event of the year. Radio news in the 1930s and '40s played a central part in shaping a new vision of America's role in world affairs, a vision with considerable consequences for American foreign and domestic policy since World War II. As the radio historian David Culbert put it, "Radio emerged as the principal medium for combating isolationism in America."[5]

Indeed, Kaltenborn had no compunctions about asserting in *I Broadcast the Crisis*, the collection of his Munich crisis broadcasts published in the fall of 1938, that radio made "the blind, head-in-sand isolationist view of foreign affairs . . . no longer tenable." More to the point, after June 1940—after Churchill became prime minister of Britain and approached Roosevelt for help, after Dunkirk, after the fall of France—radio commentators supported Roosevelt's "preparedness" policies, helping to sway public opinion toward support of American intervention abroad. They implied and helped construct what seemed like a consensus about U.S. involvement in the war.[6] What we hear, as part of the radio industry's conscious and unconscious efforts to construct a sense of nationhood and national unity in the 1930s, is the evocation by commentators and newsmen of the national "we," the "we" that was united despite our differences, the "we" that was allegedly monolithic in its outlook and will.

At the same time, during this decade we hear the evolution of what would become the standards for objectivity in broadcast news. Although such standards began to be more firmly encoded in the print media during the 1920s, especially with the separation of commentary from news stories, they did not instantly, or even easily, migrate to radio.[7] Radio also sparked special concerns about the dangers of opinion or bias, because it was felt that the timbre and tone of the human voice alone could be used to unduly influence listeners. With the sainthood accorded Edward R. Murrow, and the loss of so many of the news broadcasts that preceded his legendary reports, it's easy to think of "objectivity" as appearing, somehow full-formed, out of the CBS studios in 1939. It's equally easy to forget that radio news and commentary were, for ten years before that, anything but "objective." Demagogues flourished on the air in the late 1920s and early 1930s, and news commentators—who were in the mid-1930s more common than actual broadcast reporters—felt no compunction to be unbiased or neutral. Father Coughlin and Huey Long were not the only men with strong opinions on the air. Much of early radio commentary was openly partisan, as when Boake Carter referred to administration officials as "fat New Dealers" while Walter Winchell fawned all over FDR. By 1945 what counted as objectivity, what the public and opinion leaders accepted as objectivity, became established in broadcasting. Newsmen, the networks, the government, and advertisers battled over what exactly constituted objectivity, until the fight spilled onto the front pages in 1943.

During the 1930s, when broadcast news was being socially constructed and fought over, we hear a genre being invented, and we hear that male archetype—the newsman—being designed as well. Only a few women—Dorothy Thompson, Mary Marvin Breckenridge, Betty Wason—got on the air in a deeply sexist industry in which it was gospel that people did not like and would not trust the female voice over the air. Radio commentators and war correspondents became national celebrities—sometimes overnight stars—their voices instantly recognizable, their public images often carefully crafted. In the evolution from the pretentious announcer Boake Carter—who actually said "Cheerio" at the end of his broadcasts—to the no-nonsense and conversational approach of Ed Murrow, Bill Shirer, and Bob Trout, we hear men who sounded like they came from middle America dethroning their pseudoaristocratic predecessors. Scribner's in 1938 reported Murrow as saying that he wanted CBS's foreign broadcasts "to be anything but intellectual. I want them to be down to earth, in the vernacular of the man on the street."[8]

We also hear these men praising simple heroism and denouncing cowardice during World War II, and reaffirming the centrality of American manhood to the survival not just of the nation but of the world. After the giggling of Ed Wynn, or Jack Benny's effete pretentiousness, or Edgar Bergen's being put in his place by a prepubescent dummy, or George Burns's frustration at being trapped by Gracie Allen's illogic—all played for laughs, of course—here were serious men sometimes risking their lives to deliver the news, men confident in the American man's place in the world, men affirming that knowledge, rationality, stoicism, courage, and empathy, and an utter disdain for upper-class pretentiousness, were what made men "real" men. By 1941 the apotheosis of American manhood wasn't Boake Carter or Eddie Cantor, it was Edward R. Murrow, the radio version of Humphrey Bogart's "Rick" in *Casablanca.*

Few events in the history of radio have been more notorious than the Halloween Eve broadcast of *The War of the Worlds.* Even people who know absolutely nothing about the history of radio know about this episode: people fleeing their homes around the country to escape the invading Martians so realistically portrayed by the Mercury Theatre that Sunday evening in 1938. We don't have reliable figures on how many people actually fled, but Hadley Cantril, Herta Herzog, and Hazel Gaudet in their study of the panic, estimated that about 1 million Americans were scared by the broadcast.[9] Orson Welles, director and star of the program, had to hold a press conference the next day to apologize and insist he meant no harm. Dramatizations of simulated news bulletins became verboten. And the broadcast was taken, in many circles, as an indisputable demonstration of the "hypodermic needle" theory of radio's power to instantly inject an unsuspecting people with unchecked emotions that would produce irrational responses. There is good reason to believe that the panic was less extensive than initially sensationalized in the press; after all, it made for great headlines. In the first three weeks after the broadcast, newspapers around the country ran over 12,500 stories about its impact.[10] But what mattered was the new perception of radio's power. And many in the industry took the panic as evidence of the intellectual simplicity of much of the audience, and the need therefore to speak to them in simple language.

It has become a commonplace to explain the panic as a result of people's newfound dependence on radio news, which, in the fall of 1938, had been bringing Americans increasingly urgent and disturbing bulletins about Hitler's conquests in Europe and particularly about the Munich crisis and Neville Chamberlain's capitulation. This explanation still makes sense. After all, *War of the Worlds* aired just one month after the crisis had been temporarily resolved, one month after Americans had been glued to their radio sets, used to having programs interrupted by the latest news from Germany. But how had radio news evolved, and why did a dramatic rendering of an alien invasion resonate so with it? What were people hearing on the radio that was different from what they read in the papers, and how did listening to the news—as opposed to reading it—reorient Americans toward current affairs?

KDKA's "inaugural" broadcast was a news program—coverage of the presidential election returns of 1920. But news remained an afterthought in early radio, which was dominated by talks, music, and fledgling variety shows. Listeners could hear the Democratic and Republican conventions on the air in 1924, and WGN in Chicago paid $1,000 a day for a telephone line to Dayton, Tennessee, so it could provide intermittent coverage of the Scopes "Monkey" trial. And radio was able to scoop the newspapers on the progress of Charles Lindbergh's flight and his safe arrival in France. But as the networks formed, and advertisers came not just to sponsor but also to produce radio shows, the overwhelming emphasis was on entertainment. One of the earliest quasi-news shows was Floyd Gibbons's highly popular *The Headline Hunter*, which premiered on NBC in 1929. Gibbons didn't report the news; with an orchestra backing him up, he recounted his adventures covering past news stories. Probably the most popular "news" program of the early 1930s was *The March of Time*, in which actors impersonated famous newsmakers like FDR, Huey Long, or Benito Mussolini. As late as 1938 a CBS executive would assert that "none but the most urgent or important news would displace temporarily a program designed to entertain."[11]

Nonetheless, with major breaking news, such as election returns, radio brought instantaneous coverage of the latest tallies, making such stories irresistible to the networks and their listeners. And even listening to something as dull as a Hoover campaign speech in 1932 was much more gripping on the radio. It wasn't just that the announcer evoked the scene by telling you that "more than 30,000 people packed and jammed every available seat" in this auditorium in Cleveland—you heard the sounds of people milling around, talking, yelling, and applauding. When the announcer described the "huge audience, standing as one man, greeting the president," you heard the ovation and the rousing band music. Listening on the radio brought you to the hall and allowed you to participate vicariously in this large event, to be part of this crowd, and to envision a thriving public sphere consisting of thousands of everyday people.[12]

Two events in 1932 proved to be turning points in the evolution of broadcast news. At 11:35 on Tuesday night, March 1, WOR in New York interrupted its programming to announce that the Lindbergh baby had been kidnapped. Forty minutes later CBS interrupted a dance program on its network with the same bulletin. By the next morning CBS and NBC had both established special lines to reporters in Hopewell, New Jersey, near the Lindbergh estate. Both networks kept a constant vigil for seventy-two days until the baby's body was found.[13] On-the-spot radio reporting had been established technically and journalistically. That November the networks' coverage of the Hoover-Roosevelt election returns scooped the nation's newspapers. What came to be known as the press-radio war was on.

Meeting at their annual convention in April of 1933, the American Newspaper Publishers Association voted to stop providing the networks with news bulletins and to discontinue publishing daily schedules of radio programs unless the stations paid for them, as if they were advertising. At this time NBC and CBS had skeletal news staffs and only a few regularly scheduled news programs. In 1930 *Lowell Thomas and the News* premiered, airing on NBC in the eastern half of the country and on CBS in the western half, and moving to NBC the following year.[14] H. V. Kaltenborn, an editor at the *Brooklyn Eagle* who had been doing weekly commentaries on WEAF since 1922, signed with CBS in 1930. These men read and commented on the news, drawing from newspapers and the wire services. After the ANPA resolutions, both NBC and CBS began building their own news departments, with CBS's efforts being especially ambitious. Newspapers began a CBS boycott, which included a publicity blackout of many of its sponsors.

The media historian Robert McChesney gives the best behind-the-scenes account of this "war," which, as he emphasizes, was not between radio and newspapers so much as it was between some newspapers and others. Many radio stations were owned by newspapers, and those that weren't were often affiliated with a paper in their town. One-third of the stations in the CBS network, for example, were by 1932 owned by or affiliated with newspapers, which were more interested in cooperation than in war. Network executives, for their part, were concerned about an ongoing campaign by educators and reformers to limit—or even eliminate—advertising over the air, a campaign some newspapers had already endorsed because they felt radio was stealing clients from them. Broadcasters did not want to give any newspapers reason to support such regulation, especially as Congress was preparing to deliberate over what would become the landmark legislation governing broadcasting, the Communications Act of 1934.

In December of 1933, broadcasters signed on to the Biltmore agreement, in which they pledged not to broadcast any news that was less than twenty-four hours old. The news agencies would supply the networks with brief news items, which would be broadcast in two five-minute newscasts daily—one after 9:30 A.M., the other after 9:00 P.M., to "protect" the morning and evening papers. Each broadcast had to end with the line "For further details, consult your local newspaper." Commentators were not allowed to touch spot news. And CBS was to disband its fledgling news-gathering organization. Kaltenborn described this as a "complete defeat for radio," and the chairman of the Scripps-Howard chain was congratulated for coming out of the negotiations "with the broadcasters' shirts, scalps, and shoelaces."[15]

Such postmortems were premature. Once the Communications Act was passed, and the commercial basis of American broadcasting was assured, broadcasters had little to fear from the press. Besides, the public hadn't liked the outcome of the war, telling pollsters in 1934 that they wanted more news over the air. Renegade stations, like WOR in New York, had refused to honor the agreement and aired the very sorts of news broadcasts the agreement forbade.[16] And several upstart news agencies, most notably Transradio Press, began competing with the wire services to provide breaking news to radio stations. Within a year the Biltmore agreement was being widely ignored, and radio news was poised for revitalization.

Besides, in January of 1935, radio was all too happy to provide coverage of one of the decade's most sensational stories. The media circus in the mid-1990s surrounding the O. J. Simpson trial—including the endless hype that it was the trial of the century—made it hard to remember that another trial, equally shameless in its exploitation by the press, remains a contender for that title. The Lindbergh kidnapping trial was the first nationally broadcast murder trial, and it made relatively unknown announcers national celebrities. Boake Carter was, in 1932, a print journalist who was also doing two five-minutes-a-day broadcasts over Philadelphia's WCAU. His boss, the owner of WCAU, was also William Paley's brother-in-law and persuaded CBS to send him to Hopewell, New Jersey, to cover the kidnapping. The exposure helped Carter land a daily program of commentary on the CBS network. Gabriel Heatter, another unknown, also became a star through his coverage of the trial, especially when, on the night Bruno Hauptmann was put to death, he was forced to ad-lib on the air for fifty-five minutes because of a delay in the execution. In a five-year period he went from making $35 a week to earning $130,000 a year.[17]

But one of the biggest radio stars of the trial was Walter Winchell, who had been on the air since 1930 and in 1932 had begun his *Jergens Journal,* which aired on Sunday night at 9:30 on NBC-Red (one of NBC's two networks) and made him one of the highest rated commentators on the air. Listeners recalled being able to walk down the street at night and hear Winchell's trademark rapid-fire "flashes" coming out of nearly every house on the block.[18] Winchell had made his name as a gossip columnist for the New York *Graphic* and then the *Mirror* and, as his biographer Neal Gabler emphasizes, turned gossip into a commodity that coexisted on the same pages—or in the same broadcast—with news. In the process, then, he helped—for better or for worse—to redefine what *was* news and stirred up heated debate about who had the right to shape listeners' tastes in and expectations of broadcast news. Here was another contest over the invention of broadcast news in the 1930s—would it be information, entertainment, or some hybrid of the two?

Since the "radio boom" of the early 1920s, educators, reformers, and commentators in the press had envisioned the social impact of radio through a utopian lens, seeing a future in which "the masses" were "uplifted" through radio, made better educated, more appreciative of classical music and intellectual engagement, more rational and deliberative. These were class-bound, bourgeois hopes, and in many ways they would be dashed. For they were countered by another vision of radio—as a profit-making vaudeville house on the air—which corporations and federal regulators ensured would be institutionalized.[19] This was the vision Walter Winchell brought to the air, and his intuitions about how to translate his newspaper column to radio were brilliant.

Already Winchell had seized on the post–World War I delight in slang, lacing his column with gaudy, inventive wordplay: "made whoopee" meant "had fun"; "Reno-vated" or "phffft" meant "divorced"; "Adam-and-Eveing it" meant "getting married." On the air—at 200 words a minute—such language intermixed with sound effects and Winchell's personal, direct address to the audience. Gabler perfectly captures Winchell's voice—"clipped like verbal tap shoes"—and reports that his voice went up an octave when he was on the air. Winchell opened the show with the urgent tapping of a telegraph key, which wasn't really tapping out anything resembling the Morse code but which did signify news "hot off the wire." "The big idea is for sound effect," Winchell noted, "and to set the tempo." The tapping bracketed the beginning and end of each story, and was coded to let the listener know what was coming: low-pitched clicks for domestic news, high-pitched beeps for international news. Winchell then greeted "Mr. and Mrs. America and all the ships at sea," suggesting, in his classic telegraphic form, that his broadcasts spanned oceans and that Mr. and Mrs. America was a national category all his listeners fit into. "I want to create as much excitement as a newsboy on the streets when he yells, 'Extry, extry, read all about it,' " he declared.[20]

At first the program focused almost exclusively on celebrity marriages, divorces, and love affairs, but gradually it combined a mix of celebrity and gangster gossip and national and international news. Winchell would open with an urgent "flash," often a train wreck, murder, or other disaster story. An assistant combed foreign newspapers for his "By Way of the High Seas" segment, which he introduced with the beeping sound of wireless dots and dashes.[21]

Critics of "mass culture" past and present have emphasized its appeal to the emotional, its cultivation of the irrational, its emphasis on romance, lost love, and melodrama in general. In other words, they have—sometimes quite consciously, sometimes not—derided mass culture as "feminine" and as contaminating more elite, allegedly intellectually based, masculine culture with feminized values and attributes. His contemporaries leveled such criticisms at Winchell, who was attacked for being too emotional and too corny, and for bringing gossip into the realm of serious journalism. After all, his program was sponsored by Jergens, and his news items were interspersed with messages about "the importance of charming hands to a girl." But if we accept these cultural constructions of what is "feminine" and what is "masculine," Winchell did represent a different kind of radio commentator than Kaltenborn, or Lowell Thomas, and certainly Murrow. Winchell fused male power, authority, and interest in the political with hysteria, irrationality, and an interest in the interpersonal and romantic. His appeal came in part from his emotionalism and urgency, from the permission he gave men to be passionate and even irrational about issues and events. Gabler very rightly points out that the controversies surrounding Winchell in the 1930s stemmed from class-based biases about who had the right to shape the nation's cultural agenda, an educated intellectual like Walter Lippmann or a scrappy rabble-rouser from New York's Lower East Side like Walter Winchell. But there were also tensions here about masculinity, about what kinds of *men* deserved such power, and about what kinds of things such men should discuss and how they should discuss them. These tensions, too, shaped the evolution of broadcast news in the 1930s.

By the time of the Lindbergh trial in 1935, Winchell had become a national celebrity, and he claimed that several of his broadcasts had helped police apprehend Hauptmann. With the Biltmore agreement ban on radio news all but defunct, and with over 100 photographers and between 300 and 350 reporters swarming over Flemington, New Jersey, the Lindbergh trial marked another turning point in radio news. It also embodied the term *media circus*. The local sheriff sold tickets to the trial; vaudeville impresarios offered witnesses contracts to go onstage; tourists by the busload descended on the small town. There was daily coverage of what went on in court, and NBC, the network that carried Winchell, struggled to prevent him from convicting Hauptmann on the air. Winchell ignored the network's directives and insisted that he was not "partial or biased" but simply in possession of the facts, all of which pointed to Hauptmann's guilt. In the courtroom he was as much an actor as a reporter, giving tips to the prosecution, mouthing comments to Hauptmann, sitting next to Hauptmann's wife during testimony. After this trial, writes Gabler, "the media would be as much participants in an event as reporters of it . . . turning events into occasions, national festivals."[22]

In none of these stories was Winchell a dispassionate, unbiased conveyor of information. His notorious staccato style conveyed a barely repressed hysteria. He was a shameless self-promoter, determined to make the news as well as announce it. By the early 1940s, the announcer for the show opened the *Jergens Journal* by reminding listeners that Winchell's column was "in 725 newspapers from New York to Shanghai." Winchell positioned himself, whenever possible, as omniscient. In kidnapping stories he appealed to the kidnappers on the air; in murder stories he implied he might have evidence for the police. "Ladies and gentlemen, here's the absolute lowdown," he would announce, and he often referred to predictions he had made that had turned out to be true—"I was right"—or speculative tips he had passed on that were subsequently verified, to reaffirm his credibility and access to inside sources.[23]

Nor was Winchell politically neutral. Roosevelt had called him to Washington for a brief meeting shortly after the 1932 election, and Winchell became a die-hard fan, always praising FDR in his broadcasts. He also began advocating economic social justice by berating the way the police and petty bureaucrats often harassed and discriminated against the poor and unemployed. By the late 1930s the administration fed Winchell news tips, inside information, and angles on FDR's policies, which Winchell happily translated into his rat-a-tat-tat, everyman's argot, wrapped up in a pro-Roosevelt spin.

Winchell was, much earlier than other commentators, an outspoken critic of Hitler and the Nazis, and a harsh critic of Chamberlain's appeasement. Yet he was at first opposed to U.S. involvement in another European war because Europe was "morally bankrupt," a frequent charge of isolationists at the time. He did, however, support U.S. preparedness. And after the fall of France he changed from isolationist to interventionist and made this clear on the air. So in 1940, with the country still divided between isolationist and internationalist sentiments, Winchell advocated a military buildup, expansion of the navy, and increased aid to the Allies. He also attacked isolationist congressmen on the air as Nazi sympathizers and announced, straight out, "I believe [the] Senator is wrong." He called his isolationist listeners "Mr. and Mrs. Rip Van Winkles" and taunted their complacency: "Don't worry about it happening over here. . . . Don't forget we have two lovely oceans—one on each side. . . . To drown in." By early 1941 he was mocking critics of his interventionist stance with the "Walter Winchell War Monger Department." He broadcast the names and addresses of people like "Maj. Johnnie Kelly" from New Jersey, a "dear, dear pal of the Nazis" or "a rabble-rouser with the initials D.S.—who really does the dirty laundry for big-name Nazi lovers in the U.S."[24]

Once France and England declared war on Germany, Secretary of State Cordell Hull and Assistant Secretary Adolf Berle, knowing Winchell's politics, asked his assistant if Winchell might "help prepare the country for war," which he happily did, continuing to take the lead from the administration. Winchell's assistant also fed him propaganda and intelligence supplied by the British Security Coordination office, a front for a covert propaganda organization designed to help bring the United States into the war. This is hardly insignificant, since by late 1940 Winchell was tied with Bob Hope for the highest rated program on radio. Thus Winchell, as one of radio's most popular commentators, helped "to destroy the opposition to preparedness and soften the public toward intervention."[25]

Winchell had proven indispensable to the Roosevelt administration. Boake Carter—Mr. "Cheerio"—had not. By the late 1930s Carter, sponsored by Philco on CBS, had developed a national following of people who tuned in specifically to listen to his broadcast at 7:45. In 1936 he was heard over twenty-three CBS stations; the next year he was heard on sixty. In Boston and Cincinnati in 1938, nearly a third of the radio audience listened to him, while over half of those in St. Louis did. In larger cities like Chicago and New York, with more stations to choose from, he was less popular, but still one-fifth tuned in to Carter. Evidence suggests that he was more popular among lower-income and rural listeners, and he was favored by Republicans and isolationists. By this time Carter—whose publicity photos featured him in jodhpurs and riding boots—broadcast from his studio-equipped estate outside of Philadelphia. Larry LeSueur, who would soon become one of the "Murrow Boys," was the poor guy back at CBS who fed Carter information about the day's events from a Teletype machine in New York.[26]

Carter had the classic deep radio voice, and he affected upper-class pronunciations, as when he pronounced *military* "mili-tree." He asserted that Arthur Morgan, the head of the TVA, had been fired for being "contumacious." Purple prose and clichés often dominated his reports: "Thus when the shadows of two mailed fists etched their dark outlines across war-torn, fire-ridden Madrid today, there stretched another dark shadow across the whole of Europe." His reading of the news was rapid, urgent, and dramatic, yet filled with the appropriate timing and pauses, as if he were reading a story to a bright child. Then he would segue into reading an ad for his sponsor, first Philco and then Post Toasties, as if there was no distinction between performing the news and performing a commercial. Another famous news commentator of the time, Edwin C. Hill, billed as "the best dressed newspaper man in New York," wore pince-nez with a black silk ribbon fluttering from them.[27] These were faux upper-class fops who did no reporting but who often voiced strong opinions.

Carter can be thought of in some ways as the Rush Limbaugh of the 1930s. He was popular, in part, because he was controversial. He hated Roosevelt and liberal politics, views he happily shared with his radio audience. In addition to reading predigested news, Carter repeatedly unburdened himself of his anti–New Deal and isolationist sentiments on the air, even supporting, for example, Nazi Germany's invasion of Austria in March of 1938, the *Anschluss*, as a welcome corrective to the Versailles Treaty. In the Russo-Japanese border dispute in 1938, he sided with the Japanese.[28] But, most important, whatever the international crisis, he advocated that America focus on itself and stay out of foreign affairs. Carter accused the president of trying to pay less income tax than he owed and of causing a senator's fatal heart attack. The Roosevelt administration, whose members referred to him as "Croak Carter," were incensed by his increasingly virulent attacks on New Deal initiatives.

But Carter's partisanship wasn't his only problem. His commentary was often filled with "innuendo, invective, distortion, and misinformation" instead of facts, and by the winter of 1938 he sounded not like a newsman but like a shrill demagogue. He didn't act as a reporter; he didn't check his sources; he often deliberately misinformed his audience. This didn't upset just those politically opposed to him. It upset important General Foods stockholders, government officials, and other corporate leaders.[29] Like Father Coughlin, Carter became more extreme in his views, and more deluded about his invulnerability, the longer he stayed on the air.

By 1937 the White House had three agencies investigating Carter, and administration officials put pressure on William Paley to pull him off the air. That same year, during the Little Steel strike, Carter began attacking the CIO, and the union responded by voting to boycott Philco products. Philco canceled its contract to sponsor Carter in February 1938, but CBS received so many angry letters from listeners that when General Foods—whose chairman of the board hated the New Deal *and* organized labor—offered to step in as sponsor, Carter got a temporary reprieve. Now the administration went straight to Paley, suggesting that it might be time for the FCC to seriously investigate monopoly practices in the broadcasting industry. Paley pulled Carter off CBS for good in August 1938.[30]

The timing could not have been better for CBS. The kind of news that was gripping the nation's attention now was breaking news about the crisis in Europe, news that required reporters to be on the scene and witnessing with their own eyes what was going on in Poland, Vienna, Berlin, and London. In August, as Hitler made it clear that the Sudetenland belonged to Germany, Chamberlain warned that an invasion of Czechoslovakia would mean world war. As the crisis evolved in September, Americans were riveted to their radio sets. As Sudeten Germans held mass rallies in favor of union with the Reich, and 20,000 rallied in Madison Square Garden in support of the Czechs, Chamberlain met with Hitler on September 15 and again one week later, finally signing the Munich accord on the thirtieth.

By this time listening to the radio was the nation's favorite recreational activity, according to a *Fortune* poll. And nearly a quarter of the respondents now got most of their news solely from the radio, while another 28 percent relied on both radio and newspapers. News broadcasts were listeners' third favorite type of program, and "the combined popularity of the two leading commentators, Boake Carter and Lowell Thomas [this was just before Carter's sacking], nearly equaled that of the two leading entertainers." These news commentators had national audiences, and each was "capable of becoming the most potent voice in the land." "By an inflection of the voice, a suggestive pause, he may nearly as effectively color the meaning of the news as by rigorous editing of the script from which he reads." In another poll published in 1940, *Fortune* reported that when asked, "Who is your favorite radio commentator?" 38.0 percent said they had no favorite. Of those who did, Lowell Thomas was the favorite; he was chosen by one-quarter of all those polled. H. V. Kaltenborn was next, chosen by 20.0 percent of respondents, but he was the favorite of those from the upper-income brackets and the professional classes. Carter, once so popular, was now chosen by only 6.0 percent of those polled and was beaten by Edwin C. Hill (9.3 percent) and Walter Winchell (6.8 percent), who was chosen as people's favorite syndicated columnist, especially if they were lower middle class or poor. The audience for news shows was greatest on the Pacific coast, with those in the Northeast coming in second, and these listeners often listened to more than one news show. Those in the "isolationist Midwest," as *Business Week* put it, were the least likely to tune in to the news.[31]

Those who preferred radio news offered the obvious reasons: they got the news more quickly, it took less time to find out what was going on, and they found it more interesting and entertaining. As *Fortune* wrote, those who in the past might have gone out for a newspaper extra now "are likely instead to watch the clock for the hour to turn on the world's routine news. . . . And what they hear," enthused the magazine, "is likely to sound so authentic, and personal, and vibrant, and final, that the next day's paper will seem like warmed over Monday hash not worth bothering with. This is an aggressive faculty of radio that is not likely to weaken with the years."[32]

In *Radio and the Printed Page*, published in 1940, the ORR also examined the extent to which radio news might be supplanting newspapers. By this time there were regularly scheduled fifteen-minute news shows, plus five-minute news bulletins. The study reminds us how much of this history has disappeared—while it's possible to hear a few surviving broadcasts of the major network reporters and commentators, the local newscasters, who dominated the air in the late 1930s, are lost to us. So it is important to remember that there were four times as many locally originated news programs as national ones: 80

percent of news reports came from local stations and featured local commentators. Of the more than nine hundred stations on the air in the early 1940s, 43 percent were not affiliated with any of the networks, and three-quarters used 1,000 watts or less.[33]

By 1939, according to the ORR, 61.5 percent of Americans listened regularly to radio news shows and were deliberately tuning in to them. Radio had not yet replaced the newspaper, but people were using a mix of both to get their news. As the war in Europe intensified, most people were poised between two media with distinct but overlapping qualities. Radio had obvious advantages: it was often first with breaking news, it was "free," you could get the news while doing something else, and listeners often felt transported to the scene of the event. Newspapers, by contrast, provided pictures of many people and events, allowed readers to pick and chose what they wanted to read, and choose the time to read as well, provided more in-depth coverage, and offered specialized coverage of financial news, society, and so forth.

Again, using class as a way to categorize listeners, ORR researchers found that radio news was preferred over newspapers as the listeners' economic status went down, and women greatly preferred hearing the news over the radio. So did young people, who constituted the first "radio generation," and those who lived in rural areas. The ORR also found that over 50 percent of high-income and professional men listened to political radio commentators, but only 37 percent of unskilled workers and men on relief did so. *Fortune,* in its 1938 survey, put it slightly differently: "News is welcomed by twice as many of the poor as of the prosperous. . . . Housekeepers (who like to listen while they work), wage earners, and the unemployed rank by occupation at the head of radio news fans."[34] While researchers sought to neatly demarcate those who preferred getting their news from newspapers and those who preferred radio, they found considerable overlap, especially during political campaigns, when radio seemed, to voters, "to give more clues about the personality of a candidate."

Using Cincinnati as one case study, the ORR documented that by the late 1930s radio was giving much more attention to international news than newspapers did, and more than 90 percent of those the ORR polled said that radio news had increased their interest in foreign affairs. Another study, of listeners in Buffalo, found that the five commentators people listened to most were Boake Carter, H. V. Kaltenborn, Lowell Thomas, Edwin C. Hill, and Walter Winchell. As the CBS commentator Elmer Davis heard from his friend Bernard De Voto, who was traveling in the West, "Everybody was listening to you, learning from you, and applying you. The radio had completely repaired the failure of the press, which appalled me . . . the war news in the local papers would average between a half and three quarters of a column." Radio listeners, he reported, "had the most astonishing amount of information about the war."[35]

Without images, there was a need for the newscaster to use his voice to dramatize events, and this often made broadcast news more emotional. The ORR claimed that in radio news there was an emphasis on conflict and more focus on crime and its prosecution. Radio, of course, was ideally suited to breaking news about natural disasters and accidents, and about the latest events in the European and Sino-Japanese wars.

Broadcast news created a sense of intimate participation in "a larger world." "The radio signals, coming instantaneously often from the very scenes of events and entering directly into the home, gave listeners a feeling of personal touch with the world that possibly no other medium could provide."[36] Radio relieved suspense about "what happened" in the course of a news story's narrative, and it did so faster than newspapers. Thus it intensified excitement about the news. One thing was clear: radio cultivated, especially among women, people of lower-income levels, and those living in rural areas, a greater interest in the news, and for many of these groups an interest they didn't previously have.

By 1938, especially in the aftermath of the *Anschluss,* NBC and CBS were competing to scoop each other with breaking news in Europe. (By comparison, radio before 1941 devoted very little coverage to China, Japan, and the rest of Asia.)[37] This was a very new development—"news," such as it was, directly from Europe had previously consisted of coronations, debates at the League of Nations, or speeches and concerts transmitted from abroad. The job of the foreign correspondent was to find and book such events. But now the networks were setting up news divisions: CBS hired Edward R. Murrow, who in turn hired Bill Shirer, Larry LeSueur, Eric Sevareid, and the others who came to be known as the Murrow Boys.

Max Jordan of NBC, known as Ubiquitous Max, had signed exclusive contracts with various state-owned radio systems, including those in Germany and Austria, which gave NBC access to their broadcast facilities. CBS responded by initiating, in March of 1938, the first of its news roundups, which brought the reports of foreign correspondents directly into Americans' living rooms. By 1940 MBS—the Mutual Broadcasting System, established in 1934— devoted much of its evening programming to news. NBC provided at least seven news summaries through the day, from 7:55 in the morning until 1:57 the following morning. And now, on a regular basis, Americans could hear, live, speeches by Hitler, Mussolini, Chamberlain, or Daladier, translated on the spot, if necessary, by network announcers. Fifty years later listeners recalled vividly what it was like to hear Hitler's frantic, sometimes screaming voice live on the radio, often, given the time difference, first thing in the morning as they were going to work, and how the sound of his voice alone convinced them that danger was ahead.[38]

Shortwave transmission, pioneered by the hams, was now invaluable to the networks: it was the only way such news bulletins could travel from Berlin or London to New York. The networks also had "shortwave listening posts" in New York, where those fluent in foreign languages monitored international shortwave broadcasts. NBC correspondents in London, Paris, Berlin, Rome, and Geneva broadcast via shortwave to RCA's enormous receiving facilities at Riverhead, Long Island. If the correspondent wasn't in or near a studio, he would phone in his report, which was then carried by phone lines and possibly even cables to the shortwave transmitter before crossing the Atlantic.[39] From Riverhead the reports were sent by telephone line to a master control room in Radio City, from where they went out by wire to NBC affiliates around the country. Those affiliates then broadcast the transmissions on the AM band.

CBS's technical challenge in doing the news roundup involved even more than getting the shortwave broadcasts across the Atlantic; technicians also needed to connect the various correspondents to one another. Murrow in London, Shirer in Berlin, Trout in the New York studio, and the others had to be able to hear one another—which required multiple shortwave channels—but not to hear themselves, which would have produced lag and interference. The frequency that each correspondent would use—a CBS report from Berlin in 1938, for example, broadcast on 25.2 meters, or 11,870 kilohertz—had to be cabled to New York in advance.[40] Everything had to be timed to the second as New York shifted from one European city, and one frequency, to another.

But shortwave transmission had its problems. Precisely because shortwaves were reflected back to the earth by the ionosphere, they were subject to its seasonal, weekly, even hourly vagaries as the ionosphere billowed, ebbed and flowed, and responded to magnetic pushes and pulls no one could see or predict. Engineers would test and clear a frequency only to find that, a few hours later, transmissions no longer came through. Shortwave sounded tinny and remote. Worse, it was subject to interference from bad weather and sunspots, and was sometimes accompanied by whines and crackles. Some correspondents sounded like they were underwater. Or there was an undercurrent of quasi-musical tones that sounded like slowed-down and muted jack-in-the-box music. Often a constant undercurrent of high-pitched Morse code accompanied the broadcast. Sometimes the broadcasts didn't come in at all, or cut off in the middle. Trout, from the studio in New York, would introduce a report from Finland by saying, "Go ahead, Helsinki," only to hear nothing in reply. "This is Bob Trout calling Helsinki, go ahead Finland."

Nothing. "Apparently we shall be unable to contact Finland." This was not an unusual occurrence. During the Munich crisis, Bill Shirer broadcast for two days from Prague, only to learn later that Atlantic storms, as well as government interference for official messages, prevented nearly all of his dispatches from coming through.[41]

This actually heightened the romance of hearing the New York announcer's voice imploring the ether with "America calling Prague; America calling Berlin; come in, London" and to hear Shirer answer, "Hello, America, hello, CBS, this is Berlin," as if the announcer embodied the city itself. The very auditory drawbacks of shortwave made this news listening all the more compelling as an auditory experience. You were inclined to lean closer, to try to use your body to help pull him in yourself. And listeners came to understand a semiotics of sound, as different sound quality itself signified the genre, the urgency, and the importance of the broadcast. Between 1933 and 1937 the sales of "all-wave" receivers, which allowed listeners to tune in European broadcasts for themselves, had soared from 100,000 to over 3 million.[42]

What did listeners to the first CBS roundup hear on March 13, 1938? They heard an act of interruption—"We interrupt our regularly scheduled broadcast"—that broke up the easy, patterned flow of radio entertainment and announced the urgency of the news program, the importance of world affairs, and the credibility of the reporters standing by. In the wake of the *Anschluss,* Bob Trout in New York announced, "The program of *St. Louis Blues,* normally scheduled for this time, has been canceled." Instead, "To bring you the picture of Europe tonight, Columbia now presents a special broadcast which will include pickups direct from London, from Paris, and other capitals in Europe." His tone was urgent yet conversational. "Tonight the world trembles, torn by conflicting forces. Throughout this day, event has crowded upon event in tumultuous Austria. . . . News has flowed across the Atlantic in a steady stream." His language was straightforward and anchored in facts as he outlined troop movements and anti-German demonstrations in London, but he shifted easily to the colloquial, as when he noted that Chamberlain and his aides "put their heads together" to consider the crisis. And Trout's language was hardly neutral. "Right at this moment, Austria is no longer a nation. . . . Austria and Germany are being welded together under one command . . . the Nazis are driving with all their might to bring Austria under complete Nazi domination." He announced that Jews and Catholics were being jailed.

He used language that helped listeners see and even hear what it had been like, and related the recent events to those that Americans might remember or have participated in. "The Associated Press says you have to visualize what happened in every city, town, and hamlet of the United States in 1918 on Armistice

Day" to get a sense of the celebrations that accompanied the Nazi march into Vienna. "Masses of shouting, singing, flag-waving Viennese milled around, marched through the streets saluting and yelling the Nazi call 'hail victory' [which Trout delivered as a cheer]. Truckloads of men, women, and children— there were even mothers with babies in their arms—rolled through the streets setting up a terrific racket. It seemed as if the whole population was in the streets." How did the takeover sound? There was a "switch of coffeehouse music from the old, graceful Viennese waltzes to new, German, brisk martial airs." Trout acknowledged that it was hard to know how the Austrians really felt and told his listeners that the Nazis had taken over the press and radio: "They are out to control everything."[43]

"And now," announced Trout, "Columbia begins its radio tour of Europe's capital cities, with transoceanic pickup from London. . . . We take you now to London, England." The word *tour* suggested a visual experience and *transoceanic* an almost physical vaulting over the Atlantic. Throughout the war the network made a point of presenting itself as *the* agent of transport to Europe, to the site of news in the making, as its announcer declaimed, "We take you now to . . ." Bill Shirer, who had witnessed the *Anschluss* and had just flown in to do the broadcast, compared what he'd seen in Austria and London. "What happened was this," the easygoing translator explained. Describing the anti-German demonstrations in London, Shirer noted, "I must say, that after the delirious mobs I saw in Vienna on Friday night," the demonstrations in London "looked pretty tame." After Edward R. Murrow's report from Vienna, from which he promised an "eyewitness account" of Hitler's entry into the city the next day, he said, "We return you now to America."

As the war spread, with the Nazis conquering Czechoslovakia in March of 1939 and Poland that September, and France and England immediately declaring war on Germany, radio correspondents became reporters and teachers, providing essential instruction in geography and in how to read and deconstruct government communiqués. This was especially critical because all the news coming out of Germany was heavily censored.

And while we may know these reporters today as Edward R. Murrow, William Shirer, or Robert Trout, on the air they introduced themselves, at least at the beginning of their radio careers, before they became institutions, as Ed, Bill, and Bob—regular guys who didn't need or want pretentious names like Boake or Edwin or Gabriel. And, tellingly, the New York anchor, when introducing Murrow or one of the others from overseas, did not say "Here's our correspondent in London" but rather "Here's our man in London, Ed Murrow." According to Stanley Cloud and Lynne Olson in *The Murrow Boys*, Murrow was determined that CBS newsmen *not* come across as upper-class pedants, or as breakneck-speed hysterics selling an artificial sense of urgency. They were to be neither in the mansion with Carter nor in the gutter with Winchell.

These men spoke to and for everyday Americans in a conversational, personal style, often using *I*, which some of their counterparts in the print media could not. Murrow's hallmark, and the one he wanted his "boys" to adopt, was to create concrete mental images—of what shopping for food was now like, or sleeping, or crossing the street—of how the war was affecting everyday people. Such details made a story told with words but not pictures more vivid and immediate; they also cultivated identification and empathy in the listener. Murrow especially hated purple prose and instructed one reporter, "Don't say the streets are rivers of blood. Say that the little policeman I usually say hello to every morning is not there today."[44] Nor did their voices have to be standard radio issue—Shirer's voice was actually somewhat thin and nasal by radio announcer standards, but by the standards of how a lot of everyday men sounded, his voice was refreshingly natural. Nor did Eric Sevareid have the classic baritone radio voice. As he and Shirer broadcast from European capitals in the throes of war, the very timbre of their voices affirmed the bravery of regular guys.

Although these men were becoming experts in European politics and warfare, they made it seem normal to discuss such things in everyday terms. They used the first and second person to address their listeners directly and involve them in what the war felt like. Shirer, whose account of his broadcasts from Germany, *Berlin Diary,* became an immediate best-seller, was the most adept at and comfortable with assuming a relaxed and intimate style of reporting. He told listeners that the Germans' bombing an undefended town in Poland "reminded me of the coaches of champion football teams at home, who sit calmly on the sidelines and watch the machines they created do their stuff." You could hear papers rustling and a chair creaking in the studio during his broadcasts, yet you felt he was really chatting, not reading a script. "I'm afraid I cannot arouse much interest by going through the German press with you tonight," he told his listeners on November 1, 1939, referring familiarly to his ritual of sharing with Americans what was being reported in the German newspapers so they'd understand what government control of the press meant and how thorough the Nazi propaganda machine was. Shirer introduced reports with "Incidentally" or "Well" or "What happened was this," just as you would at the dinner table. He spoke to the audience as if they were equals, explaining what they couldn't know because they were in the States but also addressing them as informed adults, with asides such as "the official position, as you know . . ."[45]

Murrow could be informal too, and, like Shirer, he often reported what was being said in the British press. Citing an item from the newspaper he was about to read, Murrow admitted, "I don't know why I give it to you, it just caught my eye. Here it is," as if he were reading it to you in your living room. Murrow also moved between being a teacher and acting as if his audience was already well-informed. He would preface his reports with "You're already aware" or "As you know." But he also educated. For example, he explained that there was a possibility in England of compulsory evacuation of people and animals; "in other words, if the government says 'go,' you've got to go whether you like it or not." Compulsory billeting meant that if "you had a house in the country with an extra room, the government might billet, without your consent, two or three people in that room." In commenting on Soviet foreign policy, Murrow noted, "Those surprising Russians keep handing out surprises." The Murrow Boys' broadcasts were sophisticated and simple at the same time. They were also simultaneously ethnocentric and international in their language and viewpoint. And Murrow himself couldn't resist reminding his listeners of what CBS was providing. "I'm not boasting when I tell you that you're getting as much information as the average Britisher."[46]

By the standards of Boake Carter, these broadcasts were much more objective. And Ed Klauber, William Paley's personal assistant, had imposed certain guidelines for CBS news. In the aftermath of the Carter contretemps, Paley asserted that CBS "must never have an editorial page." Klauber elaborated: "Columbia . . . has no editorial positions about the war." Thus, its reporters "must not express their own feelings." Commentators should "not do the judging" for the listener. The voicing of opinions should be confined to political round tables and other similar broadcasts where opposing views could be aired. "An unexcited demeanor at the microphone should be maintained at all times," added Klauber.[47] He was especially emphatic about emotionalism in the news: this was a male preserve, and real men did not show their emotions; they conveyed "the facts" without revealing what might be in their hearts.

Again, such standards did not emerge from any high-minded ideals about objectivity. FDR had hardly ignored the fact that in the 1936 campaign most of the country's editorial pages had opposed his reelection. Support for him and for the New Deal had been achieved very much through his administration's adroit and calculated use of radio. But by 1940 more than one-third of the country's radio stations were owned by newspapers. FDR regarded this as a direct threat to his policies. The FCC in 1938 began an investigation into monopoly practices—what was called chain broadcasting—in the industry. Privately, the president in 1940 asked the new FCC chairman, Lawrence Fly, "Will you let me know when you propose to have a hearing on newspaper ownership of radio stations?" Publicly, through his press secretary, Steve Early,

Roosevelt told broadcasters that "the government is watching" to see if they air any "false news." Radio, Early warned, "might have to be taught manners if it were a bad child." Network executives understood "false news" to be news critical of the administration's policies.[48]

Commentators were now called analysts, and they were not to indulge in editorializing on the air. Nor were CBS reporters to reveal any emotion or bias. They were not supposed to say "I believe" or "I think" but instead to use phrases like "it is said" or "there are those who believe" or "some experts have come to the conclusion." Nonetheless, Bill Shirer "made radio history," *The New York Times* noted in 1943, "by editorializing in his broadcasts from Nazi Germany." And H. V. Kaltenborn, who thought the distinction between "commentator" and "analyst" preposterous, continued to express his opinions. He couldn't say "I think" or assert that some German communiqué was an out-and-out lie? Well, then, he would say, "No one who has the slightest idea of the facts of this war believes these German propaganda claims." Kaltenborn also got pressure from his sponsor's ad agency to tone down his opinions so as not to alienate listeners.[49]

Once France and Britain declared war on Germany in the fall of 1939, the networks agreed that their commentators would not discuss how the United States should respond to Hitler. In May of 1941 the FCC, in what came to be called the *Mayflower* decision, ruled that "the broadcaster cannot be an advocate," thereby forbidding editorializing on the air. In practice this was impossible, especially as Shirer, Kaltenborn, Murrow, and others were deeply antifascist and anti-isolationist. They didn't have to say "I think" to convey a very decided point of view. Happily for the networks, their views supported Roosevelt's policies. But even tone of voice was to be regulated: Eric Sevareid was reprimanded when his voice cracked during a broadcast. The CBS newsman, warned Paul White from New York, should not "display a tenth of the emotion that a broadcaster does when describing a prizefight," even if thousands had just died.[50]

The struggle over what objectivity meant and how it was to be achieved constituted an ongoing experiment during the years before America's entry into the war. And let's keep in mind that it wasn't just government officials, network executives, and reporters who participated in this struggle—so did politicians, owners of local radio stations, the general public, and, notably, sponsors. Corporate executives who had their products advertised on the air were more likely to be conservative than liberal, and they were extremely wary of antagonizing listeners with isolationist attitudes. When they didn't like the opinions or slant they heard on "their" newscast, they first tried to reason with the newsman and his bosses. If that failed they would simply terminate their contract to sponsor the show, which often meant that the newsman in question lost his time slot.

What counted as opinion, and which kinds of opinions were more acceptable on the air, plagued newsmen who had been to Europe and felt they had a crucial perspective that most Americans did not. Eric Sevareid, after he returned from Europe in late 1940, found that his anti-isolationist bias provoked repeated outcries from congressmen, station managers, and his bosses. Edward R. Murrow confessed to a friend as early as 1938 that "I am finding it more and more difficult to suppress my personal convictions." On the air he insisted that he and Shirer in Berlin were "both trying to do the same thing. Trying to bring you as much news as we can, avoiding so far as is humanly possible being too much influenced by the atmosphere in which we work."[51] So, while bowing to the ideal of objectivity, he also suggested that any reasonable person would find it impossible to maintain a stance of pure unbias under the circumstances.

One way Murrow got around the rules was to read to his American listeners excerpts from the British newspapers, which he carefully chose as Congress launched its neutrality debate in the fall of 1939. For example, on September 20 he read an editorial from the *Evening Standard* predicting that England and France could be facing a "Nazi-Bolshevik Bloc stretching from the Rhine to the Pacific Ocean. If this is so, we shall be justified in hoping that the rest of the civilized nations, and among them, the greatest, who want us to destroy this menace, will lend us aid more material than their prayers." During the same broadcast Eric Sevareid reported how the French, once armed with "the new, fast, American planes, the Curtis planes with the Pratt and Whitney motors," were able to down German Messerschmitts, thus flattering Americans into seeing the merits of military aid. David Culbert in *News for Everyman* argues that the period between September 1939 and September 1940 marked a crucial turning point in what was considered objective. In 1939 the networks refused to allow the broadcast of an air-raid alert because it was "unneutral." One year later, in one of his most famous broadcasts from London, Murrow took his microphone outside so that Americans could hear the sirens warning of another imminent bombing by the Luftwaffe. *Variety*, ridiculing some of the rules governing broadcast objectivity, asked, "Who doesn't want England to win?"[52]

American correspondents in Berlin before America's entry into the war had their scripts previewed at least thirty minutes before broadcast by censors representing the military, the German Foreign Office, and the Ministry of Propaganda. Because CBS, NBC, and Mutual broadcast from the same tiny studio, a fourth censor in the control room, following their preapproved scripts, could cut them off the second they deviated from the text. Nonetheless, broadcasts critical of the Nazis got through. Bill Shirer, reporting from Berlin in January of 1940, read an official German communiqué—a common practice for correspondents—announcing that a Dutch airplane had "violated German territory." Shirer, as usual, addressed his audience as if he and they were sitting in a living room together. "Reading this communiqué a few minutes before I went on the air this morning, I was struck by that last sentence," he said, letting listeners in on his own thoughts. "Note that the communiqué does not specify whether the Dutch plane was a military or a civil machine," he instructed his listeners. He gave those back home a geography lesson, describing the alleged flight plan of the plane. He tried to get clarification, but "being a Sunday, it was difficult to contact" German officials. Listeners felt they were getting an inside, eyewitness account. Shirer had to struggle not to yell "bullshit" into the mike after reading most German communiqués.[53]

When he was done, Bob Trout in New York suggested, "Now let's call in our correspondent in London for a report." Here listeners heard the famous introduction "This [pause] is London." Murrow was interviewing an RAF pilot who, for security reasons, could not give his name. Murrow's purpose was clear—to showcase the bravery and endurance of the British military, particularly of the pilots, whom Murrow held in special awe, and to bring alive what American supplies meant to the British a full year before Lend-Lease. The pilot described his engagement with German planes, several of which he downed. He told his American audience that he was especially happy with the plane he flew, which was American and heated. Murrow then praised the pilot's "sheer gallantry and courage." Murrow was an internationalist who believed America had moral obligations to democracies abroad. He was up against a recent poll in which 66 percent of respondents had answered no to the question "Do you think the United States should do everything possible to help England and France win the war, even at the risk of getting into the war ourselves?"[54]

By the fall of 1940 Murrow was less circumspect and insisted that America become Britain's "fighting ally." Yet he also made periodic efforts to conform to the network's guidelines about objectivity. In December of 1940 he reported that the British overwhelmingly had wanted Roosevelt to win the election and, more to the point, wanted the country to abandon its neutrality since most agreed that victory couldn't be achieved without American help. "There are no indications that any British minister is going to urge you to declare war against the Axis," advised Murrow, but the British believed that "a democratic nation at peace cannot render full and effective support to a nation at war." Of course, this is what Murrow believed. But he added, "As a reporter I'm concerned to report this development, not to evaluate it in terms of personal approval or disapproval." Nonetheless, at the height of

Murrow's coverage of the Blitz, public opinion had turned around, with 52 percent favoring more aid to Britain.[55]

Until 1940, when Kaltenborn moved to NBC, the news roundup was followed by his commentary and analysis. Although Kaltenborn had been a regular commentator on CBS since 1930, it was his round-the-clock coverage of the Munich crisis in September of 1938 that made him famous. In eighteen days he made somewhere between eighty-five and one hundred broadcasts, bringing thousands of new listeners to CBS and receiving 50,000 fan letters. Kaltenborn was also known for his simultaneous translations and analyses of Hitler's speeches to the Reichstag as they came to America live via shortwave. He so embodied the archetypal radio commentator that the following year he played himself in *Mr. Smith Goes to Washington*. Kaltenborn, along with Raymond Gram Swing at Mutual, added another element to the construction of journalistic objectivity on the air: unlike Boake Carter and Gabriel Heatter, they refused to read the commercials sponsoring their shows. They insisted that the news be separated from the ads, and that a newsman could not be expected to report a fact-based story one minute and sell a product the next.[56] Since Murrow and his "boys" were foreign correspondents, writing and reporting the news and not, at first, tied in with sponsors, the separation of the news from sales pitches became institutionalized by the early 1940s.

Although he was raised in Milwaukee, Kaltenborn had just the slightest hint of what sounded like a Scottish accent, which added a tone of authority without sounding upper-class. He sometimes rolled his *r*'s, and Russia became "R-rush-shee-ia."[57] His broadcasts had a rhythmic cadence to them, and his language constantly moved between the academic and lofty on the one hand and the conversational and colloquial on the other. His approach was to have his listeners hear him sort out the wheat from the chaff, as when he would introduce a story with "Here's an important piece of news."

On June 3, 1940, after the Germans had conquered Belgium and the Netherlands and were on their way to Paris, which they would occupy on the fourteenth, Kaltenborn analyzed the meaning of a rumor that Hitler was ready to talk peace with France. An official communiqué from Berlin denounced the rumor as absurd. "What this suggests," instructed Kaltenborn, was the existence of a faction in the government or the military that did want peace and sought to leak it as a possibility. "All their stuff is censored," he explained. "When they talk peace over the radio, or over the cables, it's because someone in Germany *wants* them to talk peace and *lets* them talk peace." Each communiqué or government statement was followed by an explanation, which began with "What this shows" or "it means," so that listeners understood behind-the-scenes strategies, learned how to see beyond the surface content of communiqués, and grasped the often subtle ways propaganda worked.[58] Kaltenborn then discussed Charles Lindbergh's recent neutrality speech, which he cast as "unfortunate," and reported that "reaction in the United States was not favorable." To drive home his point, he read an extensive denunciation of the speech by a U.S. senator.

As the Germans advanced on Paris, Kaltenborn (now on NBC) drew the audience in. "Hitler has no time to lose, that's the thing to bear in mind," he instructed. While the Allies—which Kaltenborn pronounced "Al-*lies*"—still had time on their side, Kaltenborn lectured, "Obviously, they don't have as much time as they thought, and certainly we know now that they did not utilize their time to the greatest advantage." Then he really built up steam and raised his voice: "They *wasted* it in keeping a man like *Chamberlain* in office who continued to temporize and hope for the best while the situation was developing." He added hopefully that "man for man, the French army is as good, if not better, than any in the world," and thus France wouldn't collapse overnight the way Poland and Czechoslovakia had. Relying now on a direct, personal address to his listeners, he said, "Don't expect to get the same decisive results that we got in the earlier part of the German drive on the western front when they were, after all, tackling an enemy very much inferior to themselves."

Newsmen drew maps in listeners' heads, describing the geography of a region to help people understand where they were. French pronunciations were sometimes mangled, as when Seine was pronounced "sane" or Le Havre became "Le Hah-vera." But what mattered was the way these countries became less remote, less easy to push out of one's mental landscape. Kaltenborn—who gave away maps of Europe to listeners so they could locate the places he mentioned on the air—described where the Somme was in relation to the English Channel, and after mentioning the town Noyon added, "That's only sixty miles north of Paris." He adored radio's capacity to induce a powerful feeling of psychic and geographic transport. In *I Broadcast the Crisis,* he wrote to his audience, "I look upon most of you who are reading this book as old traveling companions. We traveled far together in September."[59] Newsmen would lay out the route of the Loire River and describe "the ancient and picturesque city of Rouen." When an announcer said, "I return you now to Columbia, New York," he was the listeners' vehicle of transport.

Commenting on the recent tax increase to support the defense effort, Kaltenborn chastised his countrymen, but note that he used the third person instead of the second, so that *his* listeners were not implicated. "Americans are rather insensitive to what's going on in the world, a great many of them. Perhaps if they can begin to feel it in their tax bills immediately they may become a little more concerned, a little less sure that we can do what we please in the new world without paying attention to the old." By June of 1940 many of Kaltenborn's broadcasts urged more U.S. aid to Britain.[60]

It was commentary like this that led isolationist groups in America to attack Kaltenborn for trying to stir up war hysteria. America First, one of the premiere isolationist groups, reportedly approached his sponsor to try to mute his opinions. The isolationist magazine *Scribner's Commentator* charged that "his broadcasts are as packed with Go To War jingoism as any on the airwaves."[61]

Before U.S. entry into World War II, Murrow, Shirer, and Kaltenborn adhered narrowly to network directives or developed their own methods to appear objective. But what they chose to bring to the nation's attention, and their subtle but persistent assumption of a "we" that shared a national consensus naturalized an internationalist point of view as obvious. When Kaltenborn announced, during the Lend-Lease debate in Congress, "We are committed irrevocably to helping the British cause—that is a major fact," he wasn't just stating his opinion. He was asserting the existence of a national consensus and embedding that consensus in a framework of "common sense."[62]

This was, of course, radio's first war, and once the Japanese bombed Pearl Harbor, the government was going to have to figure out its relationship with broadcast news. The timing was rotten. Industry-government relations were at a new low: in May of 1941 the FCC issued its *Report on Chain Broadcasting*, an attack on monopoly conditions in the industry. Among other things the report ordered that RCA, which operated two networks, NBC-Red and NBC-Blue, divest itself of one. It gave stations more power when negotiating with the networks they were tied to: an affiliate could reject any network show it felt did not serve the public; affiliates were bound to a network for only a year at a time, instead of five as previously mandated by the networks; affiliates could air programs from other networks if they wanted. The networks were also forbidden from owning more than one station in the same "service area," which meant that NBC would have to sell stations in New York, Chicago, Washington, and San Francisco. The networks were outraged, claiming the new rules would "threaten the very existence of present network broadcasting service." NBC and CBS filed suit in October to have the regulations struck down.[63] (In 1943 the Supreme Court upheld the FCC.) In this acrimonious atmosphere, two months later the industry and the government found themselves in the first radio war.

It was radio that flashed the news across the country on that Sunday afternoon less than three weeks before Christmas. Sunday afternoon programming usually consisted of public affairs shows and classical music. NBC-Red, for example, was about to broadcast its *University of Chicago Roundtable*. CBS had just finished a talk about labor sponsored by the CIO. Fans listening to the

Dodgers-Giants football game over Mutual got the news first, at 2:26. At 2:31 John Daly broke into the CBS network, stumbling over the pronunciation of Oahu as he announced, "The Japanese have attacked Pearl Harbor, Hawaii, by air, President Roosevelt has just announced. The attack was also made on naval and military activities on the principal island of Oahu." At 2:39 Albert Warner, at CBS's desk in Washington, announced the attacks on bases in Manila. Stations all over the country abandoned their scheduled programming, many staying on the air around the clock. CBS continued airing its Sunday concerts but interrupted them incessantly. The FCC immediately ordered the shutdown of all amateur stations, and some stations on the West Coast went off the air for fear their broadcasts could be used by the enemy to home in on targets. The Naval Observatory stopped broadcasting weather forecasts. Some stations hired extra guards to protect their transmitters. On Monday 79 percent of all homes in the country tuned in to hear Roosevelt's famous "day that will live in infamy" speech, requesting a declaration of war. The next day an estimated 60 to 90 million Americans—the largest audience up to that time—listened to Roosevelt's fireside chat as he told the country, "We are now in this war. We are in it—all the way."[64]

Given that radio was indispensable to getting out urgent information, to generating and sustaining support for the war effort, and to keeping up morale, how would the government handle its management? The precedents set during World War I by the Committee on Public Information, America's first ministry of propaganda, had not been happy. Then the government took over all commercial wireless stations. Censorship of journals and magazines, especially as imposed by the overzealous postmaster general, Albert Sidney Burleson, was draconian. News was tightly controlled by the government, and the CPI manipulated information as it saw fit, leading George Creel, its director, to write a book in the early 1920s boasting *How We Advertised the War*. Postwar revelations about the distortions and lies involved in British propaganda, and about the cynical way the CPI represented the progress of the war to Americans, meant that a similarly tightfisted control now would actually be counterproductive.

Despite the fears of many in the industry, the government did not take over radio but instead sought a close, cooperative relationship based on voluntary codes of censorship. The National Association of Broadcasters developed such a code, which included instructions not to broadcast anything "which might unduly affect the listener's peace of mind." And CBS updated the Klauber guidelines of 1939, insisting on an "unexcited demeanor" before the mike. Yet obviously pretenses to strict objectivity were silly now; on the contrary, as one CBS memo advised its news staff, the American people must constantly be reminded that "this is a war for the preservation of democracy," and listeners must "always be kept vividly aware of this objective."[65]

In January of 1942, Roosevelt appointed Elmer Davis, a news commentator for CBS, as head of the Office of Censorship; that June, Davis became head of the Office of War Information, which was meant to coordinate the efforts of a range of media—film, advertising, radio—in the selling of the war, and particular war initiatives, to the public. Newscasts were, of course, subject to military censors, who were at first deeply anxious that radio reporters not inadvertently give valuable information to the enemy.[66] Walter Winchell, for example, whom the army had tried to remove from the air for fear he would reveal sensitive military information, had his scripts reviewed by his own assistant, two attorneys for Jergens, his sponsor, and one attorney for the network. They sought to delete not just sensitive military information but politically biased stories as well, an effort Winchell vehemently fought.

But this was also, as Paul Fussell reminds us, a war very much guided by shrewd public relations, and having radio reporters covering action in war zones dramatized the heroism of GIs and officers alike. Military brass and government officials—not just American but British as well—wanted stories that would boost public morale and the image of the armed forces and that were not at odds with stated foreign policy. In theory this seemed fine, but in practice many of these reporters found that government news management really meant censorship of the truth. It is important for us to remember that such censorship—what was left out—also played a key role in the evolution of what would come to be thought of as objectivity in radio news.

Between 1940 and 1944 the hours devoted to news increased by 1,000 a year, up 300 percent. By 1944 news specials and newscasts constituted nearly 20 percent of the networks' program schedules. The number of "pundits" increased too, to approximately sixty on the four networks by 1943. Listeners tuned in, on average, for four and a half hours every day. And the men they listened to—Eric Sevareid, William Shirer, Charles Collingwood, Cecil Brown—became heroes and celebrities, stardom fusing with journalism, and not without help from the networks' own ruthlessly efficient public relations departments. Advertisers, too, wanted to capitalize on the success of radio news and began sponsoring regularly broadcast shows. The first sponsor of CBS's *World News Roundup* was Sinclair Oil, which paid each correspondent a seventy-five-dollar bonus every time he appeared on the air. By late 1943 on CBS, it was not "We take you now to London" but "General Electric takes you now to London."[67]

Listeners moved between informational and dimensional listening, sometimes being compelled to shift cognitive gears quickly, often inhabiting both listening modes at the same time. Robert Trout, for example, in his December 7, 1941, broadcast from London, began his report with a rundown of events in Europe and of British efforts to monitor Japanese movements in the Pacific. He then moved to a consideration of recent criticisms that Britain's war machine didn't employ the same "modern war techniques" that Germany's did. Suddenly, we are taken into the war. There had been complaints, reported Trout, "that while British tanks in the desert lay up at night like a defensive circle of covered wagons out west, the desert darkness is lit up with the flares of the Panzer repair squads patching up damaged German tanks for the next day's battle." This we visualize—the depth, the lights, the dark. Then a straight, factual deadline or report would move the listener out of this mode.[68]

As a result of the Munich crisis and, later, the Battle of Britain, Edward R. Murrow's name was, as *Variety* put it, "up in lights for the first time." In December of 1938, *Scribner's* ran a profile and described just what kind of a man he was: "tall without being lanky, darkish without being swarthy, young without being boyish, dignified without being uncomfortable." More important, he was a well-educated man who nonetheless had "no tea-time accent and no curl to the small finger. He's more a Scotch-and-story man." Yet "he knows what the big words mean."[69]

Murrow's wartime broadcasts, especially his coverage of the Blitz, became legendary for the way that they conveyed what the war meant to everyday people in England. His signature opening "This . . . is London," and his emphasis on details of everyday life that listeners could see and feel were shrewdly designed for an auditory medium that encouraged listeners to imagine themselves in other situations, in other people's shoes. As Archibald MacLeish put it in a speech honoring Murrow in November of 1941, "You burned the city of London in our houses and we felt the flames that burned it. You laid the dead of London at our doors and we knew that the dead were our dead . . . were mankind's dead."[70]

What is also striking is how simply and vividly Murrow's broadcasts showcased masculine courage and defined the basic elements of enviable manhood. There was a honey-hued, Frank Capra sensibility here, romantic while appearing to be antiromantic. RAF pilots were "the cream of the youth of Britain." As they discussed an upcoming bombing raid, "There were no nerves, no profanity, and no heroics. There was no swagger about those boys in wrinkled and stained uniforms." The firefighters who doused the flames after bombs had hit were equally unflappable and businesslike, focused on the job at hand. "Those firemen in their oilskins and tin hats appeared oblivious to everything but the fire," even though many of them risked and lost their lives in the course of duty.

In his famous rooftop broadcast in September 1940, Murrow described seeing one of the spotters watching for incoming bombs. "There are hundreds and hundreds of men like that standing on rooftops in London tonight, watching for fire bombs, waiting to see what comes down," evoking again the simple, quiet, unseen courage of so many everyday men.[71]

In another broadcast in 1940 from the outskirts of London, Murrow talked about "the little people . . . who have no uniforms and get no decorations for bravery" and who had to deal with their houses having been bombed. "Those people were calm and courageous. . . . There was no bravado, no loud voices, only a quiet acceptance of the situation." A few moments later he added condescendingly that "even the women with two or three children around them were steady and businesslike." And he was impressed by watching the Women's Auxiliary Air Force drill in formation. But Murrow was, as many of his friends noted, a "man's man," and the heroism he celebrated was almost exclusively male.[72]

One of his most famous—and stunning—broadcasts described an RAF bombing mission over Berlin that Murrow went on in December of 1943. The heroes here were barely men, "the red-headed English boy with the two weeks' old mustache" and "the big Canadian with the slow, easy grin." Jock, the wing commander, was calm and quiet, even in the face of deadly attack. Once up in the air and over the German coast, the gunners and the wireless operator "all seemed to draw closer to Jock in the cockpit. It was as though each man's shoulder was against the other's. The understanding was complete. . . . The whole crew was a unit and wasn't wasting words." Courageous, taciturn, working in sync as a team—these were the young men of the war in Murrow's eyes. Murrow then described the hair-raising mission over Berlin and stated that many men, including two journalists, did not make it back. "In the aircraft in which I flew, the men who flew and fought it poured into my ears their comments on fighters, flak, and flare in the same tones they would have used in reporting a host of daffodils."[73] Murrow confessed his own fright during the mission, but primarily as a way to emphasize the sangfroid of the young airmen. Besides, listening to his now steady, deep voice, you couldn't help but think he was being overly modest.

While it would be heresy to suggest that Murrow sought, in his broadcasts, to showcase his own heroism, his accounts of what he and his colleagues witnessed and experienced contributed significantly to the image of the foreign correspondent as a daredevil with nerves of steel, defying danger to come his way. Physical courage was of utmost importance to Murrow, who expected it of his newsmen and praised it on the air. Describing his and Larry LeSueur's drive through London while an air raid was in progress, Murrow told his listeners that "an antiaircraft battery opened fire just as I drove past. It lifted me from the seat and a hot wind swept over the car."[74]

Murrow was hardly alone in celebrating the courage of everyday American men. In December of 1942, Charles Collingwood, covering the African campaign from Algiers, noted that there was not much official news. "I'm just as glad, because I just got back a few hours ago from Tunisia, and I want to tell you all about it." Collingwood had visited an impromptu airfield set up in the desert, where he encountered "some of the finest American boys I've ever met." The lucky ones slept in tents; the others, under the stars. "These boys, these fresh-faced American kids in flying jackets, are up against the cream of the German Luftwaffe," Collingwood warned. The pilots flew from the airfield to Tunis and Bizerte; "it's just about as hazardous a trip as you can make these days, and that's why the boys call it the milk run. . . . It's a very tough war these men are fighting," he reported; "it's cold, it's muddy, and it's windy, and lots of things they need aren't there." He reminded listeners that there was "nothing gay or romantic about life at the front," but that these boys were "fighting it well."[75] In reports like this, these were everyone's boys; ethnic and class divisions were eradicated, invisible.

Webley Edwards, on the six-month anniversary of Pearl Harbor, gave an account of the mood in Honolulu two days after the Japanese's catastrophic defeat in the Battle of Midway. His mixture of mid-American slang and praise for the sailors' courage was very much like the hokey, faux-conversational newsreel narration people heard in the movies that sought to define the war, rhetorically, as everyman's war. The war was "this scrap"; at Midway "our forces threw everything in the book at them, yes, and some things that weren't in the book. The Jap couldn't take it." But it was Edwards's equation of national prowess—"might," as he repeatedly called it—with masculine achievement that was so striking. His incessant use of the word *hard,* and his emasculating language when describing the Japanese, made it clear that manhood and nationhood were one. After Midway, Japanese cruisers and transports "went limping off to find a place to die." The Japanese "crumbled"; they "couldn't take it." "We still poured it out, with men gritting out harsh words between their teeth, as they struck vengeance for Pearl Harbor." In Honolulu " 'let 'em come' seemed to be the general opinion" toward a possible strike by the Japanese, " 'we'll handle 'em.' "[76]

Gripping eyewitness accounts from the front combined dimensional listening—you were vividly transported into the scene of the fighting—with portraits of male heroism. Cecil Brown gave one such account via shortwave from Singapore when he described the sinking of the British battle cruiser *Repulse* on December 7, 1941. "Nine Japanese bombers flying at 10,000 feet dropped twenty-seven bombs. I stood on the flag deck amidships and watched them streaking for us . . . bombs exploded all around us . . . the flashes were blinding, the guns deafening." The gunner trying to shoot down the Japanese bombers "was something like a cowboy shooting from the hip." Brown continued with a blow-by-blow description of the attack until he, like everyone else, had to abandon ship. "I jumped twenty feet into the thick oil surrounding the ship. When I was fifty feet away, the *Repulse* went down, its stern kicked up into the air, then disappeared."[77]

With history-making events like D day, the listeners were right there, hearing and imagining the invasion, before they saw newsreel footage. By all accounts this was one of the most complicated and spectacularly successful newscasts in American history. Newsreels, and all those "World at War" documentaries, have made us forget this. George Hicks of NBC-Blue (which became ABC during the war) recorded from a warship his eyewitness account of German planes attacking the Allies' landing craft; it became an instant classic, airing on every network for days after the event.[78] What's striking is how much the account resembles the play-by-play of a ball game. Hicks describes everything he can as it's happening; gives a sense of distance, location, and trajectory; and pauses to let listeners hear the battle. We hear the low roar of airplane engines, and Hicks tells us, "That baby was plenty low." "Tracers have been flying up . . . the sparks just seem to float up in the sky," and we hear distant gunfire. Then, back to that German plane: "It's right over our heads now," he announces, and we hear the plane engine, the bombs, and the gunfire. "Here comes a plane!" and we hear men yelling. "There's very heavy ack-ack now," and instantly you hear it, but you see it, too: the explosions, the men rushing to shoot down the German plane, the ship rolling in the sea. "The sound you just heard," he tells us, came from 20-mm and 40-mm guns.

Hicks is brave, but he's also human. After a close call with the first German plane, he says, utterly conversationally and personally, "If you'll excuse me, I'll just take a deep breath for a moment and stop speaking." In the pause we hear more shots and explosions. Now Hicks is much more excited, sounding not unlike Red Barber when someone on the Dodgers hit a homer. "There we go again," he yells, "another plane's come over, right over our port side. Now it's right over the bow and disappearing into the clouds. Tracers are still going up," and he pauses so we can hear the shots. "Looks like we're going to have a night tonight," he notes, which includes the listeners in the "we." "Something's burning, it's falling down through the sky," he reports; "they got one!" and we then hear men cheering. "The lights on that burning Nazi plane are twinkling in the sea and going out," he concludes. Then, "to recapitulate," he gives an instant replay of what just occurred, including bringing some of the gunners to the mike to tell their names and where they are from.[79]

The image of these correspondents was of tough, competitive individuals who did what it took to get the story and who seemed, to the public at least, to enjoy vast reserves of physical courage. They were defiant, too, taking on censors, border guards, military police. But unlike the Nazi brutes who seemed incapable of seeing those they conquered as human beings, the newsmen were deeply empathetic with the victims of the war without being schmaltzy. They were, in a word, noble. When the famous print reporter Ernie Pyle died in April of 1945, the on-air obituary delivered by Robert McCormick emphasized how Pyle forced himself to ignore his fears. Pyle had a premonition that he would die in the war just as so many GIs he had covered. "He'd tell me how frightened he was in Europe," McCormick reported, and how he hoped he would never see any more combat. But he went to the Pacific because "he felt it was his job to be here. He never pretended to be a fearless hero, he never pretended he liked shots and shells. . . . But he sincerely believed he had a duty to the 11 million enlisted men . . . to tell Americans how they felt and acted during the worst days they would ever go through . . . he kept at it because he felt it was his job to keep at it."[80]

This was the romantic image of the GI that would be so celebrated in popular culture for decades after the war: the strong, brave, everyday guy who was a team player and not a prima donna, understated instead of a braggart, altruistic and selfless to a fault except where American achievement was at stake. Soldiers interviewed on the air, like Sgt. Herbert Brown of New York, also modestly yet stoically cast warfare as work: "We have a job to do over here, and the quicker we do it, the quicker we get home."[81] But the correspondents had another crucial element of masculinity: financial success.

This mantle of perfectly calibrated masculinity fell handsomely over the shoulders of the new radio correspondents, but it did not just drop fully spun from the ether. Every time a correspondent made history and then came home for a brief rest, the network publicity departments made sure he got a hero's welcome. Eric Sevareid had covered the fall of Paris and, fleeing through southwest France, was the first to break the story that France had surrendered to Germany. When he returned to New York in the fall of 1940, he found himself hounded by autograph seekers, reporters, and photographers, all pumped up by CBS press agents' tales of hair-raising adventure and brushes with death. CBS arranged a national lecture tour for him accompanied by a brochure that made him sound like Superman. In 1943, after he had been forced to jump out of a C-46 flying over Burma and live among headhunters while a rescue party located him, CBS feted Sevareid again, featuring him for two weeks straight on

Dateline: Burma, making sure his derring-do became synonymous with the network's own image.[82]

The same treatment awaited Bill Shirer when he returned from Germany in 1940: receptions, parties, a lecture tour, and a book contract for *Berlin Diary,* which became an immediate best-seller. Cecil Brown's leap from the *Repulse* turned him into an overnight celebrity, with Random House and Knopf vying to land a book contract with him. Random House won the bidding, and *Suez to Singapore* also became a best-seller. *Motion Picture Daily*'s list of top radio stars now included journalists like Brown. He even got Elmer Davis's prime news slot of 8:55 to 9:00, for which he earned $1,000 a week, when Davis joined the OWI.[83]

But Brown quickly became a very public casualty in the struggle over objectivity in radio news. He was an especially outspoken critic of government censorship—early on he was kicked out of Italy for his ridicule of Mussolini and fascism. After his repeated efforts to report—quite accurately, it turned out—how defenseless British-controlled Singapore was against the Japanese, British authorities revoked his press credentials.[84]

Reporters were learning that it wasn't just information about troop movements and the like that they couldn't report. Government officials wanted happy news about how well the war was going—even if it wasn't—and they wanted no critical accounts, however accurate, of America's allies. Sevareid, whose stay in China in 1943 convinced him that Chiang Kai-shek's regime was corrupt and exploitative of the Chinese people, found that *Reader's Digest* would not publish a piece to this effect because State Department officials refused to clear it. Nor, in 1944, was he allowed to describe the miseries that American soldiers endured in the Italian campaign because he would allegedly hurt troop morale—which Sevareid already knew to be at rock bottom. Sevareid and others developed a deep contempt for the various generals whose personal staffs were top-heavy with public relations officers. GIs, too, complained to the correspondents they met about the rather glaring gap between their experiences and what they heard over the radio. "Soldiers have huddled in foxholes under heavy aerial bombardment while their radios told them that U.S. forces had complete control of the air over that sector," reported *Time.* "They have come out of action, blind with weariness, just in time to get a cheerful little radio earful about what they had just been through." As a result, many felt they couldn't trust radio's coverage of the war.[85]

Brown, however, made anticensorship a personal crusade, and one tactic was to continually push the envelope in his new prime-time newscast by interlacing the news with his own analyses, warnings, and advice. Brown was especially concerned about American complacency and, worse, about an erosion of public support for the war. In a two-month tour of the country in the spring of 1942, in which he broadcast reports from different cities, Brown castigated his listeners for a "dangerous and serious overoptimism in the United States" and was especially appalled to hear, repeatedly, that people thought the war would be over by Christmas. This resulted from "hangover propaganda from non-interventionists." In commentary that could hardly have warmed hearts in the Hoosier State, Brown asserted on the air that "such optimism is not justified by any of the facts, but a good many people in Indianapolis do not seem to be concerned with the facts."[86] From St. Louis he spoke on behalf of "the people," saying, "They want to wipe Tokyo off the face of the earth. They want a second front. They want an invasion of Europe. . . . They want an invasion of Germany and, if necessary, the extermination of the German people." Some felt this wasn't exactly the unanimous will of "the people."

What Brown hadn't counted on was the increased clout that advertisers had over radio news now that it had become such a glamorous and profitable commodity. By 1943 news programs were second only to dramatic shows in drawing advertising. When commentators lost their sponsors, as Kaltenborn did in 1939, when General Mills dropped him after Catholic listeners protested his attacks on the Church of Spain, the networks became even more adamant about prohibiting the airing of opinion. Cecil Brown's sponsor, Johns-Manville, unhappy in part with commentary that its executives found too pro-Soviet, withdrew their sponsorship of Brown's news program in the summer of 1943. Paul White, the head of CBS news and an adamant opponent of any editorializing by newscasters, was also unhappy with Brown's continued harangues against alleged American apathy over the war. After a confrontation with CBS executives over his failure to keep his own opinions to a minimum, Brown resigned in September of 1943, asserting he was a victim of censorship.[87]

The firestorm of controversy that surrounded Brown's resignation revealed that debates about what journalistic objectivity was or should be on the air were hardly settled, especially when the main censor seemed to be corporate America. Magazines, newspapers, and NBC's *America's Town Meeting of the Air* all showcased the dispute. On the one hand, executives like CBS's White, sensitive to criticisms from listeners, advertisers, and government officials, insisted that commentators' opinions be ruthlessly expunged from broadcasts. He asserted this emphatically in a speech before the Associated Press, and CBS even took out full-page ads in newspapers announcing, "We will not choose men who will tell the public what they themselves think and what the public should think." This sounded high-minded but really sought to blunt mounting criticism, including from the FCC chairman himself, Lawrence Fly, that sponsors were exerting too much control over which kinds of stories and views got on the air. (White was no doubt made especially nervous by Fly's suggestion that sponsorship be eliminated from newscasts.) Kaltenborn, founder and head of the newly formed Association of Radio News Analysts, whose code of ethics opposed censorship, responded derisively to White with, "No news analyst worth his salt could or would be completely neutral or objective." *Time* agreed. "If radio becomes guilty of making its commentators take sides—or pull their punches—in order to curry favor with advertisers, it will have much to account for. But it will also have much to account for if it abandons all editorial views in order to put on a false front of impartiality." But *Time* also concluded that "much of the output of U.S. radio pundits is pontifical tripe."[88]

Despite denunciations from Walter Winchell, Kaltenborn, *Variety,* and even FCC Chairman Fly, CBS refused to compromise with Brown, in part, it seems clear, because Brown had become an insufferable prima donna. Four years later, when William Shirer's sponsor withdrew from his news program, there were new allegations that advertisers were wielding too much ideological clout over radio news. Stanley Cloud and Lynne Olson in *The Murrow Boys* maintain that this was exactly the case—that both men, however irritating to CBS, would have kept their jobs had they kept their sponsors. But with the new stardom and wealth accorded radio newsmen—Brown and Shirer were earning over $50,000 a year, a staggering amount in the early and mid-1940s— there were strings. By 1943 the CBS newsman Quincy Howe, writing in *The Atlantic Monthly,* noted that liberal commentators were being replaced by conservatives and that "sponsors snap up the news programs with a conservative slant as they never snapped up the programs with a liberal slant."[89] Advertisers had indeed emerged as the most powerful censors of broadcast news, a point that would become even starker during McCarthyism.

As broadcast news was invented on the radio, listeners had the world put before their feet, and they jumped around the country and the globe at will in a way that flattered a certain sense of omniscience and omnipresence. The dimensional listening that Kaltenborn, Collingwood, Brown, Murrow, and the others insisted upon in their broadcasts compelled people, in their minds' eyes, to look outward. Radio news, then, played a central role—both in its content and focus, and in the kind of listening it encouraged—in shifting American public opinion away from isolationism and away from self-absorbed parochialism.

The radio war also powerfully reaffirmed middle-class, American masculinity as intrinsic to the nation's identity and to its geopolitical successes. The manhood that had seemed so provisional, so fragile, so in danger of feminization in the comedy of Ed Wynn, Joe Penner, and Jack Benny was powerfully recuperated by the drama of the war and the men who reported it. The RAF pilots and the GIs that Murrow, Collingwood, and George Hicks portrayed for listeners were not shaken by warfare; they didn't complain; they were stoic; they were everyday guys; they were united in purpose; they obeyed orders from above yet proved their dominance over the enemy; they didn't brag, but they won. It is here on the radio, through the stories and voices of the newscasters and their construction of a sense of consensus, that this image of middle-class masculinity seemed to absorb and stand in for men of all classes (but not yet men of all races).

Objectivity, as it evolved on radio news, was embodied in stories that did not routinely displease the White House and those that did not routinely displease corporate sponsors. The war brought public relations and news management into broadcast journalism, and the success of radio news imposed commercial considerations on reporters and network executives alike. For the networks, the ideal of objectivity sounded worthy enough, but it was a very effective tool for disciplining uppity newscasters, keeping further regulation at bay, and keeping the sponsors happy. CBS stuck with its policy, which wasn't dramatically breached until 1954, when Edward R. Murrow on *See It Now* voiced his famous denunciation of Joe McCarthy. But that was the exception, not the rule.

At the same time—the late 1930s and 1940s—that radio news was helping to redirect listeners' attention outward and, in the process, promoting a sense of national identity and purpose within, Americans, particularly the men, were congregating around the radio to listen to an equally important nation-building genre: sports broadcasting. Here, images of disciplined men, standing alone or together to vanquish opponents, resonated powerfully with news of the war in a way that reaffirmed that, despite the Depression, this was a country of real men, of good men, after all.

Playing Fields
of the Mind

"**B**anished by bedtime to my second floor room, I lay beneath the blankets, a transistor wedged beside my ear," recalled Curt Smith. "I turned to baseball like a heliotrope turns toward the sun."[1] "How many of us . . . fell asleep at night with the radio on as the game was called?" asked Tom Snyder nostalgically on his radio show. Smith's and Snyder's warm, enfolding memories are shared by millions, most but hardly all of them men and boys, who fell asleep, or mowed the lawn, or tinkered at a workbench, or drove around while listening to baseball on the radio. Smith, a baseball historian, has written the definitive book about baseball broadcasting, *Voices of the Game,* and it would be hard to improve upon his account of the announcers who defined and redefined the art of the play-by-play.

But no book about radio listening would be complete without including a meditation on listening in to sports, especially boxing and baseball, which John Dunning rates in his *On the Air: The Encyclopedia of Old-Time Radio* as "the front burner radio sports." "At the beginning of radio," he continues, "baseball held the attention of the public to a degree that can barely be imagined" today. Sporting events were among the first live events that radio brought into people's homes, and they quickly became some of the most popular broadcasts of the decade. Fans in the 1920s flocked to the shop or home of a friend or neighbor who had radio so they too could hear the World Series or a Jack Dempsey fight. Boxing in the Depression assumed special metaphorical power when, out in the streets, real workers were often fighting with real cops or other agents of management over their livelihoods and "hard times" indeed involved direct physical conflict.

Approximately 8,000 professional boxers entered the ring in the 1930s in the hope that this sport would provide their financial deliverance, and nationally broadcast fights helped revitalize the sport. By the early 1940s listening to the World Series on the radio was a national ritual. It was estimated that 25 million listeners tuned in to the 1942 Series, which was also broadcast via short-wave to U.S. military personnel overseas so they could feel connected to the national pastime. *Radio Digest* was "tempted to say that baseball broadcasts are more potent than music, more productive of speculation than foreign or political situations, and are more widely heard than any other daytime program in the summertime. Radio has really made baseball the national game."[2] Sports on the air may have been the most important agent of nationalism in American culture in the 1920s and 1930s.

The marriage between radio and sports occurred at the end of a nearly fifty-year process in which a national sporting culture became one of the centerpieces of American life. By the 1920s baseball was "the national pastime" and a commercialized spectacle, sports had become embedded in school curriculums, the Olympics had been revived, basketball had been invented, and the middle classes were taking up golf and tennis. None of this had been true in 1875. Various reformers and public figures had, at the turn of the century, advocated the establishment of a "sporting republic" to revitalize American manhood and republican values. National sporting broadcasts began to occur just when all these trends had become solidified in post–World War I America.[3]

National sports broadcasts also began during yet another crisis about what an "American" was. Was there really something that could be considered a national identity in the 1920s when so many people were foreign-born and had come from so many different countries? Various commentators, concerned about the need for "Americanization" of all those immigrants and worried about the prospects for national unity in the face of so many ethnic and racial divisions, saw sports as a powerful "social glue" that could provide common ground, as well as assimilation to a more Anglo-American norm.[4] Over the years baseball and boxing on the radio dramatized this Americanization, as Italians, Swedes, Germans, Poles, Irish, and then African Americans, on their own or more frequently as part of a team, became embodiments of American will. And listening in to prizefights, ball games, or the World Series gave one, immigrant or not, a sense of belonging to a larger American community where there were clear rules, and where the ideal of "fair play" seemed to characterize the nation.

Of all the modes of listening that radio devised and nurtured, few may be as rich, as cognitively absorbing, or as transporting as listening to a sport like baseball. The announcers were often notorious for their wordplay, especially their facility with similes and their concrete and vivid descriptive styles. They showcased, as a masculine skill, agility with the language, and this was under pressure, during the unpredictable highs and lows of a game or match. They exploited the orality of the medium, requiring people to listen, concentrate, and imagine sights, smells, emotions through words alone.

Baseball listening was dimensional listening: the announcers conveyed the geometry of a ballpark and compelled listeners to reconstruct those lines and angles in their minds. The sports announcers—all men—were at one moment experienced, trained, dispassionate observers of the game and at the next yelling, screaming, emotionally overwrought participants with the crowd. They transported listeners from their private, domestic realms into the teeming public sphere of the ballpark or arena.

This transport, of course, moved two ways. For now masculine pastimes like boxing and baseball, which took place in public forums dominated by men, were also brought into the home, inflecting the domestic sphere more with male public culture. And sporting events, especially heavyweight championships and the World Series, which emphasized that they were being heard from coast to coast, linked images of manhood and masculine competition to the very notion of what animated the country. They demonstrated that America was a meritocracy founded on fairness in which the best man won. And indeed, when two-thirds of its radios tuned in to the 1949 World Series,[5] it was not just an illusion that the country—as an imagined, national entity—was bound together through imaginings of physical male competition.

The first broadcast of a baseball game was over KDKA in 1921 and was announced by Harold Arlin. That fall the opening game of the World Series was broadcast; in 1923, when Graham McNamee announced the Series over WEAF in New York, the station was flooded with mail. The first sports event broadcast in the New York area was the eagerly awaited and highly publicized Dempsey-Carpentier fight, also in 1921. By the late 1920s football games, tennis matches, the Kentucky Derby, and of course baseball and boxing had become staples of broadcasting.[6] And previous unknowns, like Ted Husing and Graham McNamee (who also served as Ed Wynn's ever-chuckling sidekick and as an announcer for Rudy Vallee), became national stars. McNamee became such a sensation that he was asked to cover everything—from baseball, football, and boxing to the Republican and Democratic conventions and presidential addresses to Congress.

As Red Barber reminds us in *The Broadcasters*, college football was covered regularly and followed avidly on the radio from the early 1920s on. In addition to the Army-Navy game, Ivy League contests, and games between powerhouses like Ohio State and Notre Dame, the Rose Bowl and its imitators became annual aural spectacles over radio. In fact, the sportscaster Ted Husing helped invent the Orange Bowl in the mid-1930s by hyping, as a major sporting event, a game played before a crowd of 3,500 who sat in makeshift bleachers. With radio you could get away with such things. But despite the concentrated coverage football got—for years all three networks often covered the same games so the airwaves were saturated with the sport—it is baseball on the air that people are most nostalgic for.[7]

Some have suggested that this is because the pace of baseball was especially well matched to an aural medium. Curt Smith, for example, argues that the pace of a game like basketball is too frenetic to imagine, but the pace of baseball allows you to imagine not just the play-by-play but the ambience and layout of the ballpark. "There's no radio sport better than baseball to do stream-of-consciousness," adds the announcer Lindsey Nelson.[8] And football's spectacular transition to television seems to have helped obliterate wistful memories of its coverage on the radio.

But just as important, baseball over the radio wasn't a once-a-week showdown: it accompanied people and interlocked with their daily lives in three out of four seasons and so got powerfully structured into people's associative memories. As Curt Smith emphasizes, baseball was "less an event than a fact of life." And this has produced biases in what gets remembered and celebrated about sports announcing on radio. Gary Cohen, announcer for the Mets, sees baseball as a male soap opera, "a daily saga of victories and defeats and triumphs and losses." As in soap operas, in baseball "every day connects with the day before and every day connects with the next day and one year connects with the next,"[9] with the dull, repetitive, or disappointing games becoming worthwhile when the team finally ends up in first place.

Smith's book gives a detailed chronology of baseball and its announcers, and there's no need to repeat him. Rather, I want to select various examples of the art of sports broadcasting from the 1930s through the 1950s, focusing on boxing and baseball to explore more deeply why sports announcing was so compelling, how it cultivated dimensional listening, and what kinds of models of manhood and nation it celebrated over the air. For African Americans, some of the most important broadcasts of the 1930s were the matches of Joe Louis, whose victories over white opponents galvanized black pride and spirit and suggested that, even in a deeply racist society, black men could occasionally embody the national will. When Louis had his rematch with the German Max Schmeling in 1938 (after having lost to Schmeling in 1936) and clobbered him in one round, it wasn't just a victory for blacks, it was a victory for America.[10]

Sports announcing was crucial to radio's early history because it revolutionized radio announcing. Early radio talks and speeches were delivered in a declamatory style that was often stiff or oratorical rather than conversational and intimate. And a lecture on oral hygiene or the value of the Boy Scouts was not likely to be animated. But when Graham McNamee announced the World Series, he injected emotion, pace, and an intimacy with the listener into his play-by-play. A "strong, surging personality," as Red Barber remembered it, came through the country's headphones and speakers.[11] Sportscasting thus set the precedent for a more relaxed, colloquial, and emotionally inflected form of announcing that influenced radio advertising, announcing for entertainment shows, and radio news in the 1930s and beyond.

Sportscasting did not spring forth as an already established technique; like newscasting it had to be invented. One of the reasons Barber so admired Mc-Namee was that he developed a mode of announcing with no established procedures or precedents. He couldn't see his audience, and his audience couldn't see the sporting event. Nor did he have time to watch a game or match and then write it up: he had to make it vivid, react to its instantaneous ups and downs—often just nanoseconds before the crowd reacted—"wring every drop of drama" from the event, report accurately, and all this with no script.[12]

What McNamee invented was the combination of the blow-by-blow or play-by-play with what came to be called color, the telling, visual details about how the event looked and felt. He reported the event as it occurred, but he also dramatized it, so listening to the broadcast was often better than going to the game or match itself. Grantland Rice, an accomplished newspaperman, was so exhausted by the demands of play-by-play that he quit during the third game of the 1923 Series and turned the mike over to McNamee. After the 1925 Series, McNamee received 50,000 letters. Said one, "I thought I was there with you." McNamee realized that in the 1920s listeners especially wanted drama, "to be brought close to the scene." By the 1930s fans, network executives, and Judge Landis, the baseball commissioner, were all placing more emphasis on accurate play-by-play, without, of course, losing the color.[13] Such nuanced changes influenced the evolution of announcing and of listening.

Between the 1930s and the 1950s, a wide range of styles of sportscasting emerged, from the rapid-fire blow-by-blow of Graham McNamee to the conversational, reportorial style of Red Barber to the florid, emotionally unleashed approach of Harry Caray and Gordon McLendon (a master of the re-creation). There was even room for Dizzy Dean, whose malapropisms were legendary (e.g., "He stood confidentially at the plate" or "The runner just slud into third safely, but he was awmost throwed out, the lucky stiff").[14] Ted Husing, CBS's major sportscaster, trademarked the rapid-fire delivery that went so well with boxing matches and horse racing. These men had considerable latitude in how they covered the sporting event and in the types of on-air personalities they developed; they weren't tied to specific camera angles, broader corporate agendas, or a rigid sequence of commercials, and their listeners' imaginations were more free to roam as well.

One is especially struck, when listening to what survives on tape of past boxing matches and ball games, by the power of sounds alone to transport one into the hubbub of the arena or the ballpark. From the 1920s through the mid-1930s, there were no radio booths at the ballparks. Announcers sat in box seats in the crowd, with a plank in front of them to hold the mike. Red Barber described Ebbet's Field as such an intimate ballpark that "you could see the perspiration on the players' faces, you could hear what they said." And that's how it and the other old ballparks sounded: not like huge stadiums with announcers and undifferentiated crowd noise in the background but like places with layered soundscapes. You could hear individual fans yelling "all right!" and hawkers calling, "Wanna buy *ice*? Wanna buy *ice*?", audio filigree punctuating and floating above the general din.[15] You not only heard the bat hitting the ball but also heard the ball going into the catcher's mitt. At boxing matches you heard the ref yelling in the ring, the crowd milling around and then yelling and cheering, the bell between rounds, and all of these sounds pulled you into a public event and connected you to a larger community.

At the same time, and this was particularly true of baseball, the sounds of the game over the radio intermixed with the sensory experiences of everyday life, the smell of the barbecue grill, the feel of the summer air on your skin, the sight of dusk, the sounds of kids yelling in the neighborhood or of lawn mowers—usually manual—clattering over lawns. Announcers often deepened these connections. "Oh man, it couldn't be a nicer afternoon," began Red Barber during a game. "This is the one we've been waiting for. This makes it feel like it's spring and baseball and no more measles and free tickets to the circus."[16] It is this sensory intertwining of private and public life, of being simultaneously at home and out with a crowd, that made baseball listening so delicious, and ensured that it would be forever wired into many people's most powerful associative memories of summer, youth, and America's past.

Boxing matches, by contrast, were rare spectacles. While sportscasters rightly look back fondly to radio as being much less commercialized than televised sporting events, advertisers were quick to latch on to such contests, and to suggest that it was they who were truly responsible for bringing the match or the game directly into people's living rooms. B. F. Goodrich was "happy to bring you" the June 1934 match between the challenger Max Baer and Primo Carnera. More to the point, "The fight is the outstanding sporting event of the year, and for six weeks the B. F. Goodrich Rubber Company has been completing arrangements to bring this description to the loud-speakers coast-to-coast from Canada to the Gulf of Mexico over the most extensive hookup ever used for a sporting event." Thus there was the image of the nation, despite its differences, bound up as one through this most manly of sports, prizefighting, all made possible by a tire company. Graham Mc-Namee continued to rhapsodize about this technological achievement: "I can tell you, that's big, it just covers the world just like a blanket. We're not only broadcasting here from the ringside, but it's also being broadcast to Italy in Italian by shortwave." In this context, B. F. Goodrich made sure to emphasize to its primarily male audience that it sold "big, rugged tires" that weren't subject to blowouts like other brands and truly allowed a man to protect his family. One year later, when Baer fought Jim Braddock, it was the Gillette Safety Razor Company that "for eight weeks . . . has been completing arrangements to broadcast this . . . outstanding pugilistic event of the year . . . coast-to-coast over a nationwide hookup."[17]

By one estimate 50 million listeners tuned in Graham McNamee's account of the 1927 Dempsey-Tunney match. In the two weeks before the match, one department store claimed to have sold $90,000 worth of radio equipment, most of it to hear the big fight. (*Radio Digest* reported that 127 fight fans "dropped dead during McNamee's tense descriptions.")[18] Boxing was a much faster-paced game to announce than baseball, and McNamee had to describe every swing, flick, and punch, plus keep the listener aware of how the two fighters were moving and where they were in the ring, all with barely a pause to swallow. At the end of each round, McNamee did a complete verbal instant replay, recounting how many times the fighters went into the ropes, where in the ring they were at particular moments, how they had moved in that round.

But McNamee also had to embellish on the "it's a left, it's a right" commentary and add color and visual description to bring the match to life. He breathlessly described Carnera, who was six feet six inches tall. "Boy, that man Carnera is big, Carnera is so big that your mind refuses to accept what you saw the last time you saw him. And you get that same sense of surprise the next time you see him—he really towers over Baer." When one of the fighters landed a solid punch, McNamee yelled out the news. "Oh boy! Oh boy! These boys are fighting!" He then described how Baer stopped to sneer at Carnera and began laughing at him. A punch wasn't just a punch; rather, "Baer swings a haymaker again right up from his toes." McNamee made you see it: "When Carnera received that terrific left hook to the body his mouth sprang open." But Carnera pressed on. "Talk about nerve," yelled McNamee into the mike. "He'll fight till he's *dead*, that man! He'll fight till nothing can stop him!" McNamee, like any avid fan, celebrated the aesthetics of hitting as an art by constantly describing ferocious punches as "beautiful" and referring to a slug-filled round as "that honey of a round."[19]

There were powerful similarities between sports announcing and newscasting, as men sought to give exciting eyewitness accounts of what they were seeing while the event unfolded. "All this panic you hear around here," reported NBC's Clem McCarthy before the Joe Louis–Jim Braddock fight in 1937, "is newsreel photographers and flashlight photographers trying to get as close as possible to the scene of action." And, of course, in a tradition that remains robust in American broadcasting, sports and war metaphors easily commingled in news and in sports announcing. Thus, in commentary at the opening of Joe Louis's fight with Jack Sharkey, Ted Husing asked, "Has the Brown Bomber reloaded that Big Bertha that helped him reblaze a sensational knockout trail along heavyweight avenue or has the flame been spiked by Max Schmeling?"[20]

Louis was the first black heavyweight champion since Jack Johnson, who scandalized much of white America by beating the defending champion Jim Jeffries in 1910. Jeffries, like his predecessor John L. Sullivan, had refused to fight any black man and retired in 1905. In 1908, the reigning champion Tommy Burns agreed to fight Johnson, who had repeatedly challenged Jeffries and then Burns. Johnson pummeled him and became the champion. Fans and journalists alike begged Jeffries to return to the game and "remove that smile from Johnson's face." Jeffries finally agreed, explaining that "I am going into this fight for the sole purpose of proving that a white man is better than a Negro." But he couldn't do it. When Johnson thrashed him in 1910, race riots broke out around the country as white men attacked and sometimes tried to lynch black men who were celebrating the victory. At least eighteen people died, and hundreds were injured. When it became known that he was consorting with white women, the government came up with trumped-up charges against Johnson, who fled the country in 1913 rather than face jail. After that there were no more black heavyweight champions. Blacks who got into the ring in the early 1930s were expected to be "stumblebums"—to throw a fight by eventually lying down.[21]

And then came Joe Louis. After winning the National Amateur Athletic Union light heavyweight title in 1934, he turned pro. He was a sensation: in his first six months he won all twelve of his fights, ten of them by knockout. With the help of white management, he got a showcase fight in 1935 against Mussolini's favorite, Primo Carnera, whom he beat. A few months later he beat Max Baer in a fight broadcast around the country and to Europe over shortwave. It was the most important mixed-race fight since the Jackson-Jeffries match. "In New York's Harlem, Negroes who had listened to radios in taxicabs, saloons, restaurants, pool-rooms and private homes surged through the streets, blew horns, turned hand springs, paraded, swarmed onto buses," reported *Literary Digest*. The same thing happened in Detroit, Louis's hometown.[22]

The fight revitalized prizefighting and "brought the million-dollar gate back to boxing." It was covered by more than 1,000 newspapermen, and "the total of 131 reserved telegraph-wires was the largest in history for a sports event." Thirty-three African American newspapers had ringside seats. The radio and telegraph facilities and the number of reporters "topped every previous fight and the 300,000 words of domestic news and 11,000 of cable kept tabulators busy until 6:00 A.M. in the Western Union Offices." The Associated Press named Louis Athlete of the Year. As with so many black talents, Louis became the object of white envy and admiration, and of white resentment and fear. Celebratory songs about him—mostly blues and swing—intermixed with revolting cartoons and caricatures. And the white press was obsessed by his race, referring to his punches as "dark dynamite," insisting on calling him "coffee-colored" or "the Tan Tornado."[23]

But his fights on the radio made boxing profitable again. In fact, Joe Louis prizefights, reported *Time* in 1941, attracted the largest audiences in U.S. radio history, with the exception of two prewar addresses by FDR. It wasn't just that white fans were eager to see which "great white hope" might take him out, although clearly many were. James T. Farrell, writing for *The Nation* in 1936, reported that many white fans were rooting for Schmeling during their first bout, yelling, "Kill him, Max," and cheering wildly when the German beat Louis against heavy odds.[24]

But witnessing the defeat of black strength was not the only motivation white fans had for tuning in to a Louis prizefight. Louis was a gifted fighter, incredibly fast and impressively composed, and he made many whites accept him as their champ. Some actually became fans. This was especially true in 1938, during his rematch with Schmeling, the only man who had ever beaten Louis, which he did in twelve rounds in 1936. In 1937 Louis beat James Braddock to become the world heavyweight champ. This fight had actually been arranged because there was fear that Braddock would lose to Schmeling, whom he was scheduled to fight in 1937. But hundreds of thousands of Jews and members of other religious groups threatened to boycott the fight rather than allow a Nazi to take the title back to Germany, and Braddock agreed to fight Louis instead. In other words, many Americans had reached a critical pass: better to have an African American world champ than a Nazi world champ.[25]

By 1938, with Nazi aggression a reality, the symbolism of the Schmeling-Louis fight was obvious (especially with Jesse Owens's victories in the 1936 Olympics), made more salient by the fact that Schmeling was a favorite of

Hitler. The weight of racial and national pride were on Louis. Before the fight President Roosevelt felt Louis's biceps and said, "Joe, we're depending on those muscles for America." Sixty-four percent of American radio owners tuned in to hear this rematch. When Louis trotted into the ring and knocked Schmeling out before he knew what hit him, defeating him in two minutes and four seconds, Louis, a black man, embodied America's conceits about its national strength, resolve, and ability to come back from defeat. Was America still the world's most vigorous, virile nation, despite the Depression, despite Hitler's conquests? Joe Louis's fists said yes. Louis's victory unleashed "a night of rejoicing in both the black and white neighborhoods of America." The fight was recorded and the knockout replayed on the air over and over.[26]

White manhood had, for decades, been predicated in part on its ability to keep black men subjugated and servile. White nationalism had been built, too, on the country's success in subjugating African Americans, Mexicans, and Chinese at home and various people of color abroad. Joe Louis's victories, especially in the service of national pride, deeply complicated these equations, for here was a black man standing tall for all men, all Americans, against the Hun. He personified that trait so central to conceptions of American whiteness—self-sufficiency—and he embodied the common good. German fascism, which promoted the ugly doctrine of racial superiority, prompted many white Americans to embrace Louis as evidence of their, and their country's, alleged tolerance. By 1941 Joe Louis was on the cover of *Time* magazine, hailed inside as the "Black Moses." When he enlisted in the army during World War II, still at the height of his career, he emphasized yet again that black men were a crucial component of American nationalism. When he spoke before 20,000 at Madison Square Garden in 1942 and predicted the United States would win the war because "we are on God's side," he inspired a poem that was nationally broadcast, "Joe Louis Named the War." In 1943 he persuaded many of the 65,000 white patrons of the Tam O'Shanter golf tournament to buy $933,000 worth of war bonds.[27]

Joe Louis provided, for many black listeners, an essential antidote to black minstrelsy, or invisibility, over the radio. Blacks flocked to radios to hear his fights; some bought their first radios for the purpose. Remembered one fan, "In many cases other people would come to your house and have a real party whenever Joe Louis would fight—this man not only represented himself but indeed represented a whole race of people." "Joe was our avenging angel," remembered the actor Ossie Davis. Given the spate of barbaric lynchings in the 1930s, in which black men were strung up naked and found with their ears, fingers, and penises cut off, Louis "stated our capacity to defend ourselves if given half a chance." Davis continued, "He was spiritually necessary to our sense of who we were, to our manhood."[28]

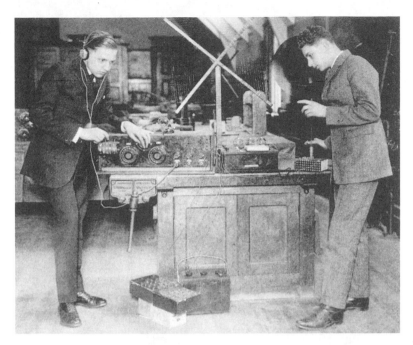

ABOVE: Radio hobbyists, known as "amateurs" and, later, "hams," pioneered in exploratory listening and demonstrated in the 1920s that shortwaves, previously thought useless, could travel thousands of miles. © *FPG International* BELOW: Graham McNamee was the first great radio announcer. Legendary for his sportscasting of baseball, football, and boxing, he was also the announcer for several variety shows, most notably *The Fire Chief* with Ed Wynn. *UPI/Corbis*

His voice shot up octaves as he whinnied and giggled, and his jokes relied heavily on wordplay, especially puns. Ed Wynn's vocal cross-dressing enacted larger setbacks to American masculinity during the Depression. *Corbis/Bettmann*

In 1933 and 1934, Eddie Cantor had the highest rated show on radio. His humor showcased verbal agility, in which various characters insulted each other, especially about their manhood. *FPG International*

George Burns and Gracie Allen elevated linguistic slapstick to an art form, in which George was constantly trapped by Gracie's refusal to enter the realms of male logic and language. Here they posed with "Spammy," who supposedly helped them promote Spam as "the meat with 1,000 uses." *Movie Still Archives*

LEFT: In their long-running "feud," Jack Benny and Fred Allen relied on verbal one-upmanship as the perfect weapon for deflating male egotism and misplaced vanity. © *Archive Photos* BELOW: Probably the most delicious exemplar of linguistic slapstick on the radio was Bud Abbott and Lou Costello's routine "Who's On First?" *FPG International*

At 200 words a minute, Walter Winchell intermixed gossip with news as he announced the next "flash" to "Mr. and Mrs. America and all the ships at sea." To his right are the telegraph keys he tapped to suggest that the news was "hot off the wire." *FPG International*

Edward R. Murrow played a pivotal role in inventing broadcast journalism during World War II. During his graphic accounts of the Battle of Britain, Murrow got out of the studio and transmitted the sounds of war—bombs, sirens, gunfire—right into Americans' living rooms so they could imagine the plight of the British more vividly. *Archive Photos*

William L. Shirer, who provided eyewitness accounts of the Nazi's conquest of Europe, excelled at a highly personal, conversational reporting style that demystified government communiqués and transported listeners across the Atlantic into the heart of the war. *Corbis/Bettmann*

By the early 1940s, more people were getting their news from radio than from any other source. Here people gathered around a radio outside the Capitol to hear President Roosevelt's Declaration of War on December 8, 1941. *UPI/Corbis*

ABOVE: More radios were sold in America during the three weeks of the Munich Crisis than during any previous three-week period in radio's history. World War II was a radio war, one people *listened* to. *UPI/Corbis* BELOW: Red Barber, famous as the "voice of the Dodgers" and then of the Yankees, interviewed Joe Louis, whose boxing matches in the late 1930s attracted the largest audiences up to that time in radio history, second only to two radio addresses by FDR. *FPG International*

ABOVE: When Joe Louis beat the German boxer Max Schmeling in 1938—a prizefight that nearly two-thirds of radio owners tuned in to hear—African Americans poured into the streets to rejoice. *UPI/Corbis* BELOW: Baseball listening was dimensional listening, as fans imagined the geometry of the ballpark and the arc and trajectory of the ball. Especially during the World Series, fans gathered together to listen, as they did here in a New Jersey soda shop in 1945. *UPI/Corbis*

ABOVE: Legendary sportscasters like Mel Allen used the play-by-play to compel listeners to pay attention to the fine details of the game, and developed audio signatures like "Three and two, what'll he do?" and "Going, going, gone." *Archive Photos* BELOW: Known for his exuberant announcing for the St. Louis Cardinals from 1947 to 1968, Harry Caray was *the* voice of baseball in the Midwest. The exclamation "Holy cow!" became his trademark. *UPI/Corbis*

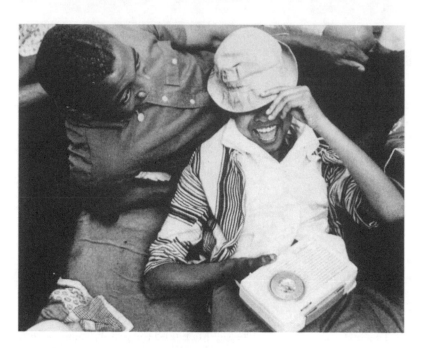

ABOVE: After World War II, African Americans became an increasingly important market, and more radio stations began playing rhythm and blues, gospel, and spirituals to attract these listeners. Gradually white listeners tuned in as well. © *FPG International* BELOW: Nat D. Williams was the first black DJ on WDIA in Memphis, the pioneering station that featured an all-black on-air staff and focused on the African American community. *Courtesy Library of American Broadcasting*

Rufus "Bear Cat" Thomas, a DJ at WDIA and a performer, was brilliant at rhyming and jive, which white DJs like Dewey Phillips sought to imitate. *Courtesy Library of American Broadcasting*

The self-proclaimed "Father of Rock 'n' Roll," Alan Freed introduced millions of white teenagers to rhythm and blues and black rock 'n' roll artists. An outspoken defender of teenagers and their music, Freed received thousands of letters and telegrams, many of which he read on the air. *Movie Still Archives*

"Hooked on sound" is how *Life* magazine described teenagers once they got their hands on a transistor radio. By the mid-1960s, Americans were buying twelve million transistors a year. *Ralph Morse*/Life *Magazine © Time Inc.*

ABOVE: In a still from *Beginning of the End*, with Peter Graves and Peggie Castle, we see how listening to rock 'n' roll on the radio while bombing around in your car was thought to heighten teenage rebellion—and lust. *Movie Still Archives*
BELOW: "I'm a guy who was born white," recalled Wolfman Jack, "but soon got captivated heart and soul by black American culture." Like other white DJs, the Wolfman was a racial ventriloquist who tried to sound black. Many fans didn't know he was white until they saw him, here, in *American Graffiti*.
Movie Still Archives

LEFT: Murray the K, the highly successful DJ on WINS in New York, used slangy rhymed couplets like "Murray the K, all the way" to sound cool to his teenage audience. In 1964, he declared himself "the fifth Beatle." *Archive Photos* BELOW: The FM revolution, a repudiation of AM radio's rapid-fire DJs and tight playlist, was championed by college stations around the country in the late 1960s and 1970s. *FPG International*

In the early 1970s, surrounded by huge stereo speakers or headphones, listeners could indulge in fidelity listening on FM radio in which jazz, rock, folk, and the blues were often played together in long, uninterrupted sets marked by the DJ's quest for the perfect segue. *Archive Photos*

Exemplar of the moniker "shock jock," Howard Stern revolutionized radio discourse in the 1980s. Appearing with Lisa Sliwa of the Guardian Angels in 1987, Stern wore prison stripes to dramatize that the FCC had made him a "prisoner of censorship."
UPI/Corbis

Don Imus, the original shock jock, has vastly expanded his influence by focusing on politics, books, and music, and by skewering the hypocrisies of the news media and celebrity culture. © *Todd France/Corbis*

The male hysteric who insisted it was necessary for men to become
emotionally explosive about politics, Rush Limbaugh was at the
center of an on-air backlash against feminism and liberal politics.
UPI/Corbis

Garrison Keillor's *A Prairie
Home Companion* brought a
knowing, even self-mocking tone
to an equally fond nostalgia for
old-time radio and the innocent
world it often represented. The
show, as well as other programming on National Public Radio,
has addressed many Americans'
ongoing desire to use their ears
to imagine a larger world.
UPI/Corbis

Because he was black *and* a heavyweight, Louis represented a threat to whites that his managers were all too aware of. For Louis to succeed, not just for himself but for his race, he had to assuage white anxieties about black male strength. Reading 1930s press accounts of him today, one is struck by the zeal with which his handlers constructed a counterstereotypical image utterly at odds with that of Jack Johnson. In the wake of white sportswriters casting him as a "jungle killer," Louis's handlers portrayed him as a humble, Bible-reading, soda-pop-drinking innocent devoted to his mother. Louis was also taciturn and lacked a formal education, so it was easy to suggest that intellectually he was simple, which muted the threat he posed and revived other stereotypes about black men. And for the most part the white media bought it. "Straight-living" was one of the most frequent adjectives used to describe him. "A debauch to the Negro hero," reported *Newsweek*, "means chewing four packs of gum a day, playing a game of pool, or studying arithmetic and history with his private tutor." Added *The New Republic*, "He was once taken to a night club, and it is reported that within ten minutes he wanted to go home." Lancing prevailing stereotypes even further, the magazine noted that "he suggests a gorilla or a jungle lion about as much as would an assistant professor at the Massachusetts Institute of Technology." Earl Brown, an African American journalist working for *Life*, wrote that Joe Louis "has probably done more than anyone since Booker T. Washington to create respect and admiration for his people."[29]

Because prizefights were singular events, there wasn't much fear that radio coverage would hurt tickets sales; indeed, the broadcasts clearly helped. But the dailiness of baseball, the need to bring people into the stands week in and week out, initially prompted concerns about ongoing radio coverage. While the Chicago Cubs owner William Wrigley saw radio coverage of Cubs games as one of the best promotions for the sport, many owners in cities like St. Louis, Philadelphia, Boston, and New York feared that radio would keep people at home and reduce attendance at the ballpark. In some cities with two teams, home games would be broadcast but away games wouldn't, on the assumption that fans of the out-of-town team would listen to the away games, and owners "didn't want to provide any excuse for fans to stay home and listen to one team while another might be playing a couple of blocks away." All three teams in New York banned baseball coverage altogether in 1934 (except for the World Series) for fear radio would hurt attendance, and they didn't lift the ban until the 1939 season, when Larry MacPhail took over the Dodgers and refused to continue with the boycott. "What you had, it's incredible, really," said Mel Allen, "was baseball taking off on radio all around the country while here in New York—the communications capital of the world. . . . You couldn't hear a game."[30]

Away games also weren't broadcast live in the 1930s because it was deemed too expensive to send an announcer off with the team and to pay the AT&T line charges to send the transmission back home. This economic decision led to one of the most impressive acts of broadcasting in any genre: the re-creation of the ball game using only Western Union dispatches. (Stations that didn't use the Western Union service sometimes hired "spotters," who found good vantage points on tall buildings near the ballpark.) For twenty-five dollars a game, recalled Red Barber, Western Union placed a telegraph operator in the ballpark and another at the radio station, who would sit at a typewriter with headphones on and translate the Morse code message into a coded account of the game. Barber stood behind the operator, looking over his shoulder as he typed. First, the weather conditions and the batting order came in. Once the game started the message from the ballpark would read B-1-L for "ball one, low" or S-1 for "strike one." But the announcer didn't know what kind of a strike it was—a call, a swinging strike, or a foul. Out of the sparest of information, announcers like Barber would re-create the game in the studio. When the code came in that there was a single line drive to right centerfield, the announcer had to remember who was in right centerfield and had to assume that he threw it to the second baseman. Baseball lore is filled with stories by announcers who were in the middle of a game, only to have the Western Union line go dead. At such a moment the announcer might have a batter hit nine foul balls, invent some diversion in the stands, or announce a sudden cloudburst until the wire got going again.[31]

Gordon McLendon, known for helping to invent Top 40 and other formats in the 1950s, made his mark in radio by re-creating ball games in the late 1940s and early 1950s. (Later he produced B movies such as *The Killer Shrews*, in which he dressed dogs up in shrew costumes and had them terrorize America.) Known as the Old Scotchman, he made re-creations that were sometimes more popular than live broadcasts because, as Curt Smith put it, McLendon "could make spring training sound like Armageddon." There was a massive and eager audience for such re-creations in towns and cities, especially in the West and Southwest, where there was no local franchise and no network feeds of games. "When you went west of the Mississippi and south of, say, Virginia, there was practically no way people could hear major league baseball," recalled Lindsey Nelson.[32]

McLendon, whose father bought him KLIF in Dallas, quickly built the Liberty Broadcasting System, a network of stations in the West and Southwest that agreed to affiliate with Liberty in part so that they could finally get baseball games. Using Western Union's play-by-play summation, McLendon re-created the "Game of the Day" and sent it out over land lines to all the Liberty stations.

By 1949 his baseball network included over 300 stations; one year later there were 431 affiliates, and McLendon added a "Game of the Night." He worked with Les Vaughn, who added sound effects like crowd noise, the ball hitting the bat, and the roar of the crowd when there was a hit as McLendon read from a ticker tape. He also invented local color moments, as when he told listeners that a foul ball hit a woman's parasol and she picked the ball up and threw it back to the umpire. The effect was highly realistic. "Here's Bobby . . . waiting . . . Bobby hits it!" he yelled as Bobby Thompson's home run in the bottom of the ninth clinched the pennant for the Giants in 1951. "Going, going, gone," he continued as Vaughn pumped up the crowd sounds. "The Giants win the pennant," he yelled, and you were convinced that you and he had seen the live game. McLendon had a simile writer, who gave him lines like "He's as happy as a cow in a Quaker Oats factory" or "This team has been colder than an igloo's basement"; an injured player "came up bloodier than a butcher's apron."[33]

A good announcer was an enormous asset to a ball club. Red Barber was credited with catapulting the Dodgers to a new level of popularity and respect through his announcing in the late 1930s and early 1940s. By 1941 attendance at Dodgers games hit an all-time high. Fans worshiped Barber as much as they did the players, and at one point, when the Dodgers won the pennant, they mobbed Barber and pulled out some of his hair for souvenirs. Barber was consistently voted best baseball commentator in the United States. *The Saturday Evening Post* described him as a "ladies favorite." Before Barber, according to the magazine, Dodgers games "resembled a For Men Only preview." After Barber as many as 15,000 women would attend one game.[34]

Many fans insisted, once portable radios and then transistors were available, on bringing a radio with them to the game so that they could watch it with two sets of eyes: their own and those of the announcer they knew and trusted, who often observed more than they did. If you were watching a ball game, and a batter came up to the plate, and walked a certain way, planted his feet a certain way, and scratched his head or set his shoulders before swinging, you might not register all of these discrete acts. You would not necessarily provide an internal narration to the scene. But a good announcer forced you to pay attention to the details. He took a series of fluid motions and broke them down into their nameable component parts.

By putting into words exactly what was happening moment by moment, an announcer brought you into a more attentive and analytical cognitive mode, the mode of the reporter who observed and named what others didn't and, thus, usually remembered things better and longer. The sportscaster Ernie Harwell credited this approach especially to Barber, who pioneered in "studying the players, supplying information, and taking folks behind the scene." He simply drew attention to little things you wouldn't necessarily comment on to yourself, like the fact that Dominic DiMaggio, in the 1941 All Star game, was the only player wearing glasses and that he wasn't nearly as big as his brother Joe but spread his feet even wider when he was at bat. Barber—the first broadcaster, along with Mel Allen, to be inducted into the Baseball Hall of Fame—appreciated that he needed to give the listener as many visual details as possible to help him "see" the game, but in doing so he and others like him helped forge a kind of radio listening that was much more imaginatively rich than listening to popular music or a political speech. When Harry Caray said to his listeners of Stan Musial, "Remember the stance, and the swing . . . we're not likely to see his likes again," Caray simply assumed that, through radio, fans could see the player. Fans felt this way too. Wrote one, in 1929, "The truth is that we can see the whole scene much better than we could were we on the field."[35]

The pace of the announcing also mirrored the pace of the game, which was characterized by lulls, interruptions, and eruptions. There was a rhythm and cadence to the announcing, as a slow description, marked by pauses and the sounds of the crowd, instantly revved into high gear when there was a hit or an amazing catch. Here's Red Barber, for example, unpacking Joe DiMaggio's turn at bat: "DiMaggio, with those feet . . . [pause] . . . widely spaced . . . [pause] . . . , his bat held w-a-y back, the pitch is"—and then the instant speed-up and increase in volume—"there's a swing and a line drive deep into left center." And note Vin Scully's attention to detail as he describes Sandy Koufax pitching: "Sandy backs off, mops his forehead . . . runs his left index finger along his forehead, dries it off on his left pants leg . . . now Sandy looks in . . ." Barber was also known for pausing to let the radio audience hear the roar of the crowd and the other ambient sounds of the ballpark. This was not, at first, a deliberate strategy. Barber severely strained his vocal cords during the 1942 World Series and vowed never again to yell against the crowd. So he developed an understanding with his engineer that he would lean back until the engineer signaled it was OK to return to the mike.[36]

Today, on television, there are cameras everywhere to provide every view, from the wide-angle establishing shot of the ballpark to the close-up of the pitcher's face. There is instant replay. There are the endless visual displays of statistical information. On radio, the announcer had to provide *all* of this, from the weather conditions and mood of the crowd to the play-by-play and instant replay. It required great observational skills, a sharp memory, and, during lulls, changeovers, or rain delays, the ability to tell stories. "An announcer must above everything else concentrate," wrote Red Barber. "Seventy-five to ninety percent of a play-by-play broadcast is done before you get to the booth . . . done by deep and thorough pregame preparation."[37] This mattered because

he was the listener's only source of information; the listener was utterly dependent on him for everything as he or she imagined the game—what kind of
pitch was thrown, what the count was, how the batter swung, where the ball
went in the field, who caught it and how, and whether someone was safe or out.
The listener had to work, too, imagining the width, height, depth of the ballpark, the configuration of the bleachers, the trajectory of the ball. When an announcer described an outfielder going "back, back, back, back," the listener
zoomed in on the ball, its motion, its arc.

In the early and mid-1950s, the St. Louis Cardinals were the westernmost
team in the country. For the millions who could reel in the 50,000-watt
KMOX, Harry Caray, the voice of the Cardinals from 1947 to 1968, before he
moved to Chicago, was *the* voice of baseball in the Midwest, and he made the
Cardinals "a regional obsession." The 120-station Cardinals network also ensured that the games were heard in at least nine other states. "I'll never forget
the sound of his gravelly voice cutting through the humid, hot air of an
Arkansas night," recalled Bill Clinton, "when I as a boy listened to Cardinals
games on my radio. . . . Harry Caray made those games come alive." Caray was
much more unbridled and passionate than Barber or Allen or Curt Gowdy of
the Red Sox. As he himself admitted, "I liked screaming at the top of my lungs."
He was emotionally excessive and extravagant. And he was wildly popular. He
yelled; he was a fan; nearly every call had multiple exclamation points behind
it. "There's a drive!! Way back!! It's gonna go to the wall!! Holy cow!!" Then you
heard relieved, excited laughter. "I can't believe it. Roger Craig hit the left centerfield wall! The Cardinals are gonna win this pennant," he predicted, correctly. He also celebrated the emotional outpourings of the crowd, insisting
that listeners take note of how wild the fans were going. Caray embodied, in
the words of Curt Smith, "barroom joviality." This was no nonpartisan: he
rooted for his team. When he moved to Chicago, and eventually became the
voice of the Cubs, Caray announced after a tying run that "The good Lord
wants the Cubs to win."[38]

"Holy cow!" will always be associated with Harry Caray. Mel Allen, the
much beloved voice of the Yankees, whose sponsor was Ballantine beer, was
known for his "going, going, gone" and then, "How about that!" if the Yankees
hit a home run, and his labeling of a hit as a "Ballantine Blast." If a batter had
a full count, Allen might rhyme, "Three and two, what'll he do?" Harry Caray,
watching a hit turn into a homer, yelled, "It might be, it could be, it *is!*" Russ
Hodges's home run signature was "Bye, bye baby." Rosey Rowswell, voice of the
Pittsburgh Pirates, whom his fellow announcer Bob Prince referred to as "the
Edgar Guest of baseball," called a strikeout by a Pirates pitcher "the old dipsy
doodle." He developed a famous routine when he thought the Pirates might

have hit a homer; he'd yell, "Get upstairs and raise the window, Aunt Minnie." This was accompanied by the sound of shattering glass simulated by a tray of nuts and bolts clattering to the floor.[39]

Most announcers had their trademarked catchphrases and took pride in their verbal agility and descriptive powers, which moved between wonderfully visual metaphors and simple, declarative phrases and words. Tune in and hear, "It's the Ol' Redhead up here in the catbird seat, where the bases are F.O.B.— full of Brooklyns," and you knew you were with Red Barber. When a new pitcher came in, Barber said he was "assuming the ballistic burden."[40] His nickname, these code words, suggested you were with a friend or a member of the family.

Barber quickly discovered that his colorful yet literate style was a special if unspoken point of pride for Brooklyners. "When somebody would say, 'I'm from Brooklyn,' everybody would laugh." Indeed, movies like those featuring the Bowery Boys, various radio comedians, heavies in films, all made fun of Brooklyn and its infamous accent. So it was crucial that the voice of the Dodgers *not* have that accent, and, during lulls in the game, Barber would talk about something he had read that day in *The New York Times*. Many fans in Brooklyn found in their ball club's victories, and Red Barber's enormous popularity, a way to fight back against and even feel superior to those in Manhattan and Hollywood who ridiculed their linguistic deviance. Nonetheless, Barber was referred to jokingly as the Verce of Brooklyn.[41]

As in the invention of broadcast news, debates about objectivity and editorializing shaped sportscasting. Ted Husing, CBS's star sportscaster, felt he had a right to comment on the performance of players and officials, and incurred the wrath of Harvard when he described one of their halfbacks as playing a "putrid" game. Harvard barred him from announcing their games until William Paley forced the university to reconsider. Husing wasn't so lucky with baseball. During the 1934 World Series he criticized the officiating of the umpires, and Judge Landis, the iron-fisted commissioner of baseball, barred him for life from announcing the Series. Landis, in fact, was adamant about sportscasters adhering to the ideal of objectivity and avoiding either criticism or praise in their commentary. In other words, Landis did not want sportscasters to editorialize any more than newscasters.[42]

Red Barber emulated this model. Although he was the voice of the Dodgers, and then the Yankees, he saw himself first and foremost as a reporter whose job it was to describe the game, not advocate for his own team. He always disapproved of a famous moment in baseball broadcast history when Russ Hodges, the announcer for the New York Giants, yelled at the end of their play-off with the Dodgers in 1951, "The Giants win the pennant! The Giants win the pennant!" at least five times. But others, of course, embraced partisanship and felt that announcers like Barber were too low-key and dispassionate. In Chicago, for example, "fans expect their announcers to get involved, to be part of the show. They want 'em to fit into a certain mold—exuberant, gung ho, go get 'em Cubs."[43]

As baseball announcing evolved between the 1930s and the 1950s, there was an increased use of and reliance on statistics, and this became especially true with the rise of television coverage. Red Barber and others had brought more statistical information into broadcasting in the late 1930s, but it was mixed in with detailed play-by-play and anecdotes. By the mid-1950s some complained that statistics had become so fetishized that they were cramming out decent play-by-play and color. Ball games, wrote one listener in 1954, sound "more like summaries of a cost accountants' convention." He also felt, as he watched the announcers on television, that "their eyes are not so much on the field below as on their score cards and record books."[44]

But with television, the power of observation, the ability to describe small details and make them metaphors for broader trends and tensions in the game were not as relevant. So some broadcasters turned from mastering words to mastering numbers. And what was counted multiplied geometrically. No longer was it enough to have batting averages and RBIs. Now there were statistics on how many runs the batter hit at home and how many on the road, how many hits he had against a particular pitcher, how his stats for this year compared with those from last year. Complained one fan, "It gets so bad that when someone belts one out of the park, we have to listen to several minutes of statistics (his sixth of the year, second at home, first off McDermott, first since June 14, and third against a left-hander) before we find out if anyone happened to score ahead of him."[45]

Although it is difficult to pinpoint a specific date, by the mid-1960s television had become the major deliverer of national sporting events. Radio still covered baseball, but no longer did two-thirds of the nation follow the World Series through radio and their imaginations. By 1971 *Sports Illustrated* was complaining about the "sea of blandness" that characterized baseball announcing on television. "The sins are easily catalogued," noted the magazine, "repetitive small talk about matters already deathlessly familiar; sugar-coated explanations for poor play; nice-Nellyisms about umpires who are never wrong and ballplayers who are, each and every last one, great guys in their own right." Especially irritating was the repeated use of "some kind of" as in "this is some kind of crowd" or someone was "some kind of player."[46]

"It might be that baseball is the only sport which television does nothing for artistically," wrote Harry Caray in 1970. "As a spectacle, baseball suffers on the tube."[47] Red Barber was another announcer who was never happy with the transition from radio to television. As he told Bob Costas in an interview, "In radio, the broadcaster is the supreme artist. The listener gets nothing that the broadcaster does not give him . . . as though he were a painter. On radio you paint the whole canvas any way you want to paint it. On television you don't do that. On television you're the servant of the director, who watches any number of monitors and orders which pictures come up. The broadcaster has to synchronize with that picture, otherwise it's a mismatch . . . so you wait for the next picture and speak in short phrases."

Barber also missed the days when there were three commercials for an entire nine-inning game, so the announcer could provide local color and features. The hypercommercialization of baseball on television reduced the amount of time the broadcaster had to tell stories: "You don't have the opportunity to be a personality." Harry Caray felt that television, and the telegraphic, nondescriptive announcing it required, "probably hurts the game more than anything." He also felt that television required announcers to be less emotional, more "indifferent," which someone with Caray's emotional registers surely deplored. "These guys were on their own—like writers," recalled the sportswriter Ken Smith. "They weren't hamstrung. No production trucks, no directors yelling in your ear, nothing. They could be creative, just let 'er rip." The announcer Bob Wolff adds that as more former players got into baseball broadcasting, they emphasized content about players and the game over the use of language and words. "Great calls now are more loaded with emotion than with words." Former players are also, noted *Sports Illustrated,* "notorious for crimes of omission, for avoiding saying anything that hints of criticism."[48]

By the early 1970s such requiems for radio sportscasting occurred within a culture that was powerfully divided over race relations, the status of women, and the conduct of the Vietnam war. The nostalgia for hearing "Three and two, what'll he do?" or "Raise the window, Aunt Minnie" was intertwined with a longing for times when, on the surface at least, the country seemed united through radio while still proud of its regional differences. Baseball listening allowed fans to feel a national identity and a fierce, elevated, local one at the same time. A Yankees fan felt himself to be quite distinct from a Red Sox fan and to experience, through radio, the pleasures of a deep, localized community membership. But both men were also baseball fans and, thus, Americans, bound up through their differences, even their hatreds, into something larger and more meaningful. Sports on the radio, by hailing people as members of different, often antagonistic clans who competed physically against each other, encouraged listeners to take on those multiple identities—individual, player fan, team fan, baseball fan—that made them feel part of a large, abstract thing called a nation yet utterly anchored in a specific locale with real people, concrete neighborhoods, particular rituals, loyalties, and animosities. Class animosities, which were especially grave during the Depression, could be effectively displaced onto team identifications and loyalties. Baseball on the air insisted that merit, not social status, mattered in this country.

Baseball and boxing on the radio in the 1930s, like radio journalism at the end of the decade, reaffirmed that, despite the Depression, there was still an equation between maleness and power. The resonances between newscasting and sportscasting, in which the nation's will and destiny were embodied in brave but simple middle-class men, meant that radio played a crucial role in revitalizing American manhood as a complex of noble traits. Sports on the radio gave men multiple, contradictory models of masculine prowess. There were prizefighters, with their brute force, who epitomized physical strength and violence as basic, structuring elements of manhood. There were ballplayers who, through natural talent and endless practice, personified the importance of quick instincts, studied physical skills, and the ability to combine long-term and short-run strategies. And there were the announcers, who demonstrated that men with none of these skills were still very much men because they had mastery over the language, over numbers, over the technology of radio, and over the sport itself. On the air the special fusion of physical prowess with the mental aspects of the game produced a balance in which sometimes how you used your body was crucial but at other times it was how you used your brain. As they identified with the athletes and the announcers, listeners could try on obedience to rules and deference to one's superiors, as well as initiative and self-sufficiency; they could be aggressive and moderate; free agents yet members of a team; fiercely competitive yet dedicated to fair play.[49] Listening to sports together on the radio was one of the ways men bonded with their sons (some, with their daughters too), so this became part of the initiation into manhood.

The announcers also represented the range of emotional registers that men could express and still be men, from low-key dispassion to barely repressed hysteria. And it wasn't just that one announcer, like Red Barber, embodied one extreme and another, like Harry Caray, the other. In individual broadcasts, from moment to moment, these men ranged over a broad emotional terrain in a way that simply wasn't permitted in the office or on the shop floor and that offered men a variety of personas to inhabit. Ironically, in listening to something rugged like sports, an act which in itself confirmed one's manhood, one could let loose and verbally and physically express joy, elation, worry, hope, despair, and a deep attachment to others without becoming feminized.

On the air sports became, week in and week out, *the* exemplar of American national character. Through baseball and boxing, listeners were reminded that the nation known as America was defined by male achievement. By tuning in on a regular basis, listeners could rehearse, usually unconsciously, through "recurring, unpredictable scripts," the deeply satisfying way that America was presented as reconciling the interplay between individual will and talent on the one hand and cooperation and obedience to rules and authority figures on the other.[50]

The national devotion to the World Series in the 1940s is just one example of what radio listening had done to American culture in just twenty years. In 1925 there were no networks, no nationally broadcast news, no national programs, and only an occasional national sporting event. By 1945 the majority of Americans had imagined, at exactly the same time, the bombing of London, a trip to Jack Benny's vault, Joe Louis pounding Max Schmeling to the mat, and D day. These were not just events people heard or read about at different times. Millions were engaged, simultaneously, in the same cognitive and emotional work: to create a mental representation of a history-making occurrence. Certainly it was this common activity, as well as living through the same times, that created a sense of a national culture.

By the mid-1950s the sort of dimensional listening cultivated by radio drama and comedy, and by gripping eyewitness newscasts was rarely demanded of Americans anymore. The one remaining outpost of true dimensional listening was ball games on the radio. People are so nostalgic for this type of listening because it was so cognitively rich yet didn't seem like work at all. Informational, dimensional, and associational listening came together powerfully with baseball listening, and what emerged was this: a cognitive delight that intersected with possibly the most flattering and reassuring representations of what manhood and America were all about.

The Kids Take Over: Transistors, DJs, and Rock 'n' Roll

I t was supposed to be all over. By 1954 that futuristic novelty television, which David Sarnoff had showcased as if it were his firstborn son at the 1939 World's Fair, was in over 26 million, or 56 percent, of America's households. The number of television stations had soared, from 6 in 1946 to 354 in 1954. Who was going to listen to sound alone when this new box brought you voice, music, and pictures, right in your own living room? Now you could see Burns and Allen, see the coronation of Queen Elizabeth, see the Army-McCarthy hearings, see the Dodgers at bat. No contest.

Yet in 1973, already nostalgic baby boomers flocked to the country's movie theaters to see a film that replayed, all too precisely, the soundtrack of their teenage years, a soundtrack straight out of radio. Made for $700,000 in a breathless schedule of twenty-eight nights by an aspiring and then un-known filmmaker, George Lucas, *American Graffiti* captured how crucial radio had been to young people in the 1950s and '60s, as they blasted Wolf-man Jack out their open car windows while cruising the strip, desperately looking for some excitement, some escape, some liftoff from suburbia. The movie showed how teens—especially boys—used their cars and their radios to stake out their own insolent, rebellious turf in public spaces meant for more orderly, aurally circumspect adults. And the movie showed how piv-otal rock 'n' roll music, and the often outrageous DJs who broadcast it, were to American life in the age of television. These kids weren't home watching *The Lawrence Welk Show* on Saturday night. They were listening to "Little Darlin'" and "Chain Gang" on the radio. And Wolfman Jack was living like a pasha in Beverly Hills. What had happened? What kind of a culture, and what kind of a medium, produces a public figure like Wolfman Jack?

By the early 1950s radio *was* thought to be dead, a victim, like the movies, of television. The famous "talent raids" of 1948–49 lured stars like Jack Benny, Bing Crosby, and Ozzie and Harriet away from radio to television, inaugurating the death knell. "Within three years," proclaimed NBC's president, Niles Trammell, in 1949, "the broadcast of sound or ear radio over giant networks will be wiped out."[1] Trammell was right: by 1954 network radio, with its prime-time programming that brought national stars to a huge national audience, *was* all but gone.

But radio was hardly dead. Some histories of broadcasting might suggest that radio became the shriveled appendix of the national media, but those of us who lay in bed at night listening to it, or walked around with a transistor earplug, or drove to it, later plunged ourselves into the lush, stereophonic dimension of FM radio know different. So did the advertisers, rock 'n' roll stars, DJs, and station owners who made careers, and often fortunes, from that durable old box in the corner of the room or the dashboard of the Chevy.

In fact, article after article in the late 1950s and early 1960s noted with some incredulity that radio was "alive and kicking" or that, as *Business Week* put it, "Radio's New Voice Is Golden." Each year in the 1950s and '60s showed increased advertising revenues from the year before, and sales of radio sets— especially portables and sets inside cars—continued to increase. Unlike during the 1930s and '40s, listeners now tuned in to stations better known for their local, rather than national, identification. In 1948 there had been 1,621 AM stations in America; by 1960 that number had more than doubled, to 3,458.[2] Listeners included housewives, people driving to and from work, truck drivers and cabbies trapped in their vehicles all day, and, in increasing numbers, teenagers. As one woman put it, "To me, when the radio is off, the house is empty. There is no life without the radio being on. As soon as I get up at 6:30, the first thing I do is turn it on." Another woman noted, "When you are home with children the day seems to have no beginning and no end, and radio really helps to break it up a little." Added a truck driver, "If I didn't have the radio, I'd go batty."[3]

Radio structured people's days, waking them up in the morning, punctuating their routines, separating the afternoon from the evening, and putting them to sleep at night.[4] It provided audio markings of time and space, an aural signifier of people's schedules. It was still, in the 1950s and early 1960s, the major source of news for most people. The patterns of radio listening had changed, slumping during TV's "prime-time" hours from 7:00 to 11:00 P.M. but soaring during what was first known as "traffic time" and later as "drive time" and holding steady in the early morning, during the day, and then later at night as people turned in.

The contours of programming had changed dramatically for most stations by the mid-1950s. No longer would one station offer a variety of formats—soap operas during midday, children's programming right after school, drama or comedies for the family at night. Rather, with the enormous success of Top 40, which offered the same programming all day and all night, stations increasingly went to one format targeted at a particular demographic segment. Programmers sought to develop station loyalty while offering shorter segments of music or talk geared to listeners who now tuned in for fifteen minutes here and half an hour there. Segmentation—the division of station output into "self-contained bites"—dominated postwar radio.[5]

For millions of Americans radio still mattered. What kept it mattering, aside from listener needs and loyalty, was a combination of major demographic changes during the war that had relocated and produced new, recombinant audiences, progressive government legislation, technical innovation, and shrewd changes in programming and format. The invention of the transistor in 1947 meant that by the mid-1950s increasing numbers of Americans were participating in what the industry called "out-of-home" listening. At work, in the car, on the beach, people—especially the young—brought radio with them and used it to stake out their social space by blanketing a particular area with their music, their sportscasts, their announcers.[6] With transistors, sound redefined public space. The other invention that compelled listeners to identify with particular stations, and often eased and even celebrated a new merger between black and white culture, was the disc jockey, known everywhere as the DJ. Between roughly 1948 and 1956, the radio industry was in flux as television stole away prime-time evening listeners, and executives and station owners tried to figure out how to respond. With corporate strategies and structures uncertain, experimentation on the air had room for a while to flourish.

In this climate repertoires of listening became even more complex and contradictory. Modes of listening were increasingly tied not just to *what* you listened to but to *where* and *how* you listened—while falling asleep in your bed, making out on the beach, and especially driving around in the car. While listeners might have a favorite station, they also shopped around, often moving among three stations with different formats depending on their spirits, the time of day, and what they were doing. The push buttons on car radios especially encouraged this. According to "The Moody, Ever-Changing Radio Listener" in *Broadcasting*, a listener in a "good mood" seeks out programs that "make him think" but seeks retreat, often in music, when he is "out of sorts." The realization that "listening preferences vary according to individual moods" confirmed the more private, individualistic ways in which many were now turning to listening.[7] One mind-set radio increasingly nourished was young people's urge to rebel against their elders and desire to conform with their peers. And after the racial stereotyping or blackout of African Americans on the radio during the late 1930s and early 1940s, radio listening in the 1950s and '60s meant that the identities of young people could once again be constituted, in part, by black culture.

While television was the new mass-market medium, radio, which became more local and decentralized, led the way in market segmentation in the 1950s. Competition over markets *within* markets led to the staking out of the youth market, which was, of course, growing exponentially in the 1950s and '60s. DJs, in an effort to earn listener loyalty, cultivated a distinct generational identity among teenagers, addressing them as cool, different, in opposition to those who would blanket the airwaves with Mantovani and his orchestra. DJs had to get the first television generation to want to turn to radio mindfully and eagerly, to expect to enter and inhabit a happy mood of belonging. DJs, particularly those who embraced black music and slang, promoted breakout listening: a mode of listening to patter and music that required concentration on the music and its lyrics, and identification with the music and talk as a form of generational and racial rebellion against the status quo. Breakout listening involved a conscious turn away from mainstream, adult, white culture and an eager, often defiant entrance into an auditory realm in which a fairly new species—the teenager—was welcomed, embraced, and flattered. Because of the interaction among the baby boomers, rock 'n' roll, and the invention of the DJ, a new generation of Americans still turned to listening to constitute their identities and their histories in quite powerful ways.

Radio listening became highly politicized in the 1950s. The reason was simple—this technology had particular qualities at the time that made it an agent of desegregation. Radio—more than films, television, advertising, or magazines in the 1950s—was *the* media outlet where cultural and industrial battles over how much influence black culture was going to have on white culture were staged and fought. Increasingly, teenagers' music was written or performed by African Americans, and many of the announcers they loved, who were white, tried to sound black. (A few others, of course, actually were black.) It wasn't so much that in the postwar period there were more radio outlets featuring black music, which panicked many older white Americans. It was that whites themselves—the DJs, the performers, and their fans—embraced a hybridity that confounded and defied the existing racial order. And it was precisely because of radio's invisibility that such hybridizations could flourish. From Dewey Phillips to Wolfman Jack, there was a renewed form of interracial male bonding on the air as white men, through their voices, assumed black selves.[8] This racial cross-dressing provoked a vicious backlash against rock 'n' roll and AM radio, and, as I'll explain later, a witch-hunt against DJs in the form of the "payola scandals."

We cannot understand the changes in—and, I would suggest, the survival of—radio in the 1950s and beyond if we don't place radio in the context of changing race relations, the rising aspirations of African Americans in the postwar period, and the often powerful reactions against those aspirations. Let's remember that the jobs created during World War II prompted approximately 1.2 million African Americans to leave the rural South and move to cities like Detroit, Los Angeles, and Mobile, Alabama, to work in wartime industries. Membership in the NAACP soared from 50,000 in 1940 to 450,000 in 1946.[9] The arrival of so many blacks in cities where the demand for scarce resources like housing and transportation was already high prompted racist responses from whites, as evidenced in the racial violence on Belle Isle in Detroit in the summer of 1943, to cite just one example.

But this new proximity did more than incite hatred, resentment, and contempt; it also aroused, among some whites, renewed curiosity, desire, even envy, albeit in often masked forms. Because of the wartime migrations, and despite segregation, working-class blacks and whites mixed more frequently on and off the job, and whites bought Louis Jordan records and flocked to see rhythm and blues performers like Bull Moose Jackson.[10] While television in its early years first reactivated minstrelsy, with *Beulah* and *Amos 'n' Andy*, and then, after protests against such stereotypes, ignored African Americans altogether (with the exception of a few singers like Nat "King" Cole), many radio stations provided a trading zone between the two cultures. And what we hear going on in this zone tells us as much, possibly even more, about the emptiness and forced conformity of white culture (especially under the influence of blacklisting) as it does about the new ambitions of blacks.

This trading zone was made possible by the proliferation of small, independent stations, which by 1948 were more numerous than any other kind in the country. The fact that the number of television stations increased a whopping sixtyfold between 1946 and 1954 obscured the fact that during the same time period the number of AM stations tripled, from 948 to 2,824. Some of this increase was the result of the FCC's *Report on Chain Broadcasting*, issued in 1941, which had prompted certain congressmen to vilify the then chairman of the FCC, Lawrence Fly, as "the most dangerous man in Washington."[11]

In the deregulatory and merger-obsessed atmosphere that suckled the telecommunications industry in the 1980s and '90s, we can barely imagine an FCC chairman like Fly. For starters, he was determined that the airwaves provide more intellectual and ideological diversity. A New Dealer deeply concerned about the dangers of monopoly control of the airwaves, Fly had a passion for trust-busting that intersected nicely with his boss's political agenda. It has, of course, become a commonplace to note that Franklin Roosevelt needed to use radio as well as he did because so many newspaper publishers—New Deal–loathing conservatives—regularly bashed his policies in the pages of their papers. But by 1940 more than one-third of all radio stations were owned or controlled by newspapers. In nearly one hundred towns the only radio station was also owned by the town's only newspaper. This did not escape the attention of the president, who asked Fly in 1940 to take stock of newspaper ownership of radio stations."[12]

Fly subsumed this concern under his broader attack on monopoly control of radio, which the FCC had been investigating since 1938. The resulting *Report on Chain Broadcasting* staggered and infuriated CBS and NBC. It forbade NBC from operating two networks (RCA still owned NBC-Red and NBC-Blue), and it gave local affiliates much more power when dealing with the networks over programming, advertising rates, and the length of time affiliates were bound to the networks. The FCC also launched an investigation into the co-ownership of newspapers and radio stations.

The resulting attacks on Fly and his newly activist commission were relentless. *Collier's* identified the agency, preposterously, as "public enemy number one." Congressman Eugene Cox of Georgia charged Fly with turning the FCC into "a Gestapo."[13] Cox was hardly a disinterested party. He had, it turned out, illegally accepted $2,500 (stupidly paid by check, no less) in exchange for helping a Georgia station get its license. Cox, well anticipating the tactics that would make Joseph McCarthy famous, accused the FCC of harboring subversives, succeeded in having their pay withheld, and announced his intention to impeach Fly. But Cox was forced to back off when one of the newest commissioners, Clifford J. Durr, circulated copies of the canceled check for his bribe through the Washington press corps. Two years later, in May of 1943, the Supreme Court upheld the provisions in the chain broadcasting report. RCA sold NBC-Blue to Edward Noble, the owner of WMCA in New York and the man who had made millions from the novelty candy Life Savers.

Another less inflammatory provision of the chain broadcasting report promoted the growth of smaller, local stations by reducing the required bandwidth distance between stations in 1946, thus allowing more stations to inhabit adjacent frequencies. Between 1946 and 1951, the number of small stations, between 200 and 1,000 watts, increased by 500 percent. And their proliferation coincided with the collapse of network radio and the explosive rise of small, independent record companies, many of which were not based in New

York. The geography of sound began to change as music played on many small radio stations reflected more local, grassroots influences.[14]

What we see after the rise of television is the devolution of radio, a reversal of the centralization that gripped the industry in the 1930s and '40s. Hundreds of stations disaffiliated from the networks, finding their audiences and their advertising revenues in local markets. Between 1946 and 1958 advertising on radio by local businesses quadrupled.[15] Stations also became more specialized, developing distinct personalities and catering to specific market segments by playing "beautiful music," airing talk shows, or repeating the Top 40 over and over. What would eventually be called narrowcasting began as stations targeted teens, or Christians, or country and western fans, or African Americans with particular music and focused advertising, all presented by distinctive announcers. And radio listening, especially in the home, became a less communal and a more individualized activity.

Gone were the days when families would cluster around their Philco listening to Jack Benny. Now, just like in the early 1920s, listening was more often than not a personal affair, done in the privacy of the kitchen, the bedroom, the car, even the bathroom. Spurred in part by the industry's postwar campaign slogan, "A Radio in Every Room," Americans bought even more radios so that different family members could listen to different programming at different times. By 1954, 70 percent of American households had two or more radios, and 33 percent had three or more.[16] Listeners developed personal bonds with the personification of postwar radio, the disc jockey. And what they turned to radio for most was music and news. Things had come almost full circle.

No invention was more essential to radio's survival in the age of television than the transistor. Developed by John Bardeen, Walter Brattain, and William Shockley of Bell Labs in 1947, the transistor performed most of the functions of the electron tube but was much smaller and required a fraction of the power to operate. It was about the size of a kernel of corn, and using tiny crystals of germanium or silicon it rectified and amplified radio signals when placed in an electrical circuit. The transistor represented a return to and refinement of the crystal detector that had so transformed radio between 1906 and 1924. Discarded by most radio listeners after the improvement in tube receivers, the cat whisker and crystal found a crucial new function during World War II: as a detector of extremely high-frequency waves in the new system called radar.[17]

By the end of the war few scientists talked about crystals. Instead, there was a new field, solid-state physics, and a class of solids called semiconductors. Studying the physical behavior of solids, especially in electrical and magnetic fields, had led to the realization that some crystals were neither conductors of electricity nor insulators: they were somewhere in between, behaving like conductors at high temperatures and like insulators at low temperatures. Their conductivity could be manipulated to create devices that could pass, strengthen, or block electric current. When these semiconductors were used in radio receivers, they did what crystals couldn't: amplified the incoming signals enormously.[18] After years of dealing with expensive, fragile, short-lived tubes that consumed a great deal of power, the transistor was an improvement in almost every way. It lasted longer than the tube, generated less heat, took up less space, was more rugged, and cost less.

Transistorized sets did not come onto the market until 1954, and at first they were relatively expensive, costing from fifty to ninety dollars. But competition from the Japanese drove both the size of the sets and their price down, so that by 1961 one could get a transistor set for under ten dollars. That meant that young people—even as young as eight or nine—could have their own radio sets. That year alone 9 million transistors, as the small, portable sets were known, were sold in America, and by the mid-1960s they were selling at a rate of 12 million a year.[19] Transistor sets initially weighed about five pounds, an improvement on early portables double that weight, but by the late 1950s some weighed less than a pound.

The transistor also made car radios more selective, easier to install, and more durable. In 1946, 9 million automobiles, or nearly 40 percent of American cars, had radios. But the 1950s saw an explosive growth in the wedding of these two transporting technologies, so that by 1963, 50 million cars—60 percent—were radio-equipped. And car radios often had a feature that radios in the home didn't—push-button selection, so the listener could hop easily between stations, exerting instant control over which stations he or she tuned in to when. By 1963 *Advertising Age* reported that especially in West Coast cities during certain time periods, "radio listening in autos is two to five times as high as in-home listening." That same year out-of-home listening accounted for 15 to 30 percent of the total radio audience. When A. C. Nielsen reported in 1964 that radio listening had increased over the previous year, the gains were attributed to increased listening to portable sets—now owned by nearly 50 percent of American families—and to car radios.[20]

In 1956 *Life* noted the rise in portable radios in an article featuring a photo section captioned "They will have music wherever they go," which pictured the family unit out on picnics or at the beach, listening in. With each year in the late 1950s and early 1960s, out-of-home radio listening increased. But by the early 1960s the portability phenomenon was linked more directly to the young. *Life* then described "teeners and sub-teeners" who were "hooked on sound . . . eleven-year-olds hiding the local disk jockey under the pillow." The "transistor addict" or the "bleatnik," as *Time* labeled such listeners, "can't stand silence."

"As a result of transistors with earplugs," the magazine complained, "red-eyed little tykes come to the table snapping their fingers and lisping *Tossin' and Turnin'.*"[21]

Time was hardly alone in its concern about what was happening between young people and radio. With the enormous success of Elvis Presley in 1956 and the explosive rise in rock 'n' roll, many stations had turned to a rock and pop format, at least for the after-school and evening hours. One ad agency executive complained in the trade journal *Broadcasting* that "a baby-sitting society has taken over the musical programming of hundreds of American radio stations," and that "a minor portion of the population is exerting disproportionate pressures on a mass-medium." In 1962 Newton Minow, chairman of the FCC and the man who would soon refer to television as a "vast wasteland," described the radio industry as a "clamorous Casbah" in which too many radio stations had turned themselves into "publicly franchised jukeboxes." Mitch Miller, fuddy-duddy host of the sappy *Sing Along with Mitch,* was even more pointed. He told attendees at the first annual disc jockey convention in 1958, "You have abdicated your programming to the eight to fourteen-year-olds, to the pre-school crowd. . . . Much of the juvenile stuff pumped over the airwaves these days hardly qualifies as music."[22]

While Miller's charge that adults could barely find anything to listen to on the radio was hyperbolic, he did identify a major trend in radio and many adults' reaction to it. By the late 1950s teenagers were buying more records than adults, and they were not buying "Good Night, Irene." They were bringing huge new profits to the industry: record sales nearly tripled in five years, from $213 million in 1954 to $613 million in 1959.[23] Radio stations, of course, had started out in the 1920s by relying heavily on phonograph music, but that had changed with the rise of the networks, which showcased live music. The crash of 1929 nearly destroyed the phonograph industry as people turned to radio as their main source of music. But by the late 1930s a renewed symbiotic relationship began between the two industries, especially when the country's 162 nonnetwork stations (almost one-quarter of all AM stations in the country) were exempted from the deal struck between the American Federation of Musicians and the networks that restricted the use of mechanically reproduced music on the air.

These smaller stations became outlets for the 400 new recording companies started during the 1940s. Now local stations could produce regional, even national hits, and new ties—which were later to become problematic—developed between record company representatives and DJs. The "battle of the speeds" between Columbia Records, which in 1948 had introduced its more expensive 33⅓ rpm long-playing album, and RCA Victor's much cheaper 45 rpm singles format, inadvertently also pitched the adult against the youth market. The cheaper records—which could be played on a small box phonograph that sold for $12.95—were simply more affordable to kids on allowances, and they allowed the kids to sample a variety of musical styles, especially early rock 'n' roll.[24]

Teenagers' musical preferences and growing economic clout spurred the growth of Top 40, much to the chagrin of many advertisers, broadcasting executives, and editors of the industry trade journals. In sheer numbers of stations, those that featured "easy listening" or "beautiful music" or "golden records (oldies)" or mainstream pop by Frank Sinatra, Doris Day, or Perry Como easily outnumbered those that played rock 'n' roll (which included rhythm and blues, rock and pop, and other hybrids). Studies in the late 1950s confirmed that housewives listened to radio four and a half hours a day on average, favoring morning news and information shows like the enormously popular *Don McNeill and the Breakfast Club*. Other studies asserted that rock 'n' roll was actively hated by many listeners over the age of twenty-one.[25] So it is inaccurate to foreground this new constellation between the young, radio, and rock 'n' roll given what predominated on the air. But the controversies this new constellation generated, the new forms of racial cross-dressing it made possible, and the cultural and social changes it magnified and accelerated all tend to hog the historical spotlight.

There were, in fact, many advertisers who refused to advertise on Top 40 stations because they didn't want their products associated with *that* kind of music. *That* kind of music, just like the jazz of the 1920s, had started out as race music. Once again, this time in the form of rhythm and blues and then rock 'n' roll, it was African American music that spoke to the cultural alienation, rebellion, and sexual energy of the younger generation. One teenage-dance promoter reported that rhythm and blues was, especially among the young, "a potent force in breaking down racial barriers." And just like jazz the music was condemned as lewd and dangerous, and many stations actively censored certain records or banned the music entirely.[26]

Because the popularity of this music coincided with and gave sustenance to an increasingly robust civil rights movement in the 1950s, rock 'n' roll was even more threatening to established race relations. Nonetheless, the Top 40 format became immensely popular and profitable—in some markets gaining between 40 and 60 percent of the radio audience—and the stations and DJs that played this music became generational touchstones to the kids of America. Ed Ward, Geoffrey Stokes, and Ken Tucker in *Rock of Ages* capture how it felt to lie in bed and be addressed by the disc jockey as one of the late people:

"Late people"—what a concept! here you were, an insignificant teenager, bumbling your way through school, filled with teenage anxieties and problems and fears of the opposite sex, and here was this guy—a white guy, at that—playing weird records with sort of dirty lyrics, talking into your ear, like a co-conspirator. He knew who you, all of you, were—the "late people" who stayed up to hear that show, to groove on this weird stuff. It was your own secret society![27]

Tony Pigg, who began his own career as a disc jockey in 1960, remembered how a rhythm and blues station he listened to as a kid provided him with a psychic escape hatch from Sacramento, which was to him "this deathly, middle-class place." "I was seized with how phony white culture was in the 1950s. It wasn't *Happy Days* for me, it was awful, horrible. . . . I thought I had to grow up to be like Dennis the Menace's father or Ozzie." Listening to Clyde McPhatter or Bobby Bland on the radio, and to the hip, unrepressed DJs of the Bay Area offered a vision of liberation, of a way out of the traps that seemed poised for him and so many other kids. Wolfman Jack echoed this desire in strikingly similar language: "I wanted an alternative world to live in, someplace more to my own liking. Radio and records gave me a cool world to belong to."[28]

It was DJs—most, although not all of them white—who used their voices, slang, sound effects, and music to conjure up such a cool world. The DJ was a postwar phenomenon, as transforming of 1950s radio as the transistor and the automobile, and a critical money-saving and marketing device. Certainly there had been versions of the DJ as early as 1932, when Al Jarvis created his "Make-Believe Ballroom" on KFWB in Los Angeles. Using phonograph records, which were disdained by the networks as déclassé compared with live music, Jarvis inexpensively created the illusion of a live musical broadcast. His counterpart in New York, WNEW's Martin Block, brought the Make-Believe Ballroom to the East in 1935. On WSBC, the country's first African American DJ, Jack L. Cooper, reportedly used this format as early as 1931. But it wasn't until the late 1940s and 1950s that the DJ became ubiquitous and essential to the survival of local radio. By 1958 *Broadcasting* admitted that the disc jockey "has emerged as the big business factor in today's new concept of radio."[29]

Every DJ's job was predicated on selling, which meant developing a magnetic personality on and off the air. Using only his voice, a particular style and pace of talk, and certain trademark words and turns of phrase, the DJ worked to create a distinctive identity. Since this was an aural medium, the shrewd DJ developed endlessly repeated verbal "identity marks" that the audience associated only with him. Successful wordplay, an agility and deftness with the language, was once again crucial to masculine success on the airwaves as DJs devised their own updated version of linguistic slapstick that drew from the jive talk of hipsters and jazz musicians.[30]

DJ talk had to be invented and had to serve—and mediate between—very particular cultural and corporate interests. It was a monologue that had to sound like a dialogue. The talk had to dramatize and personify the station's identity, and it had to make the audience feel personally included in the show, feel sought out and enfolded into a special, distinct community. In a study done for WMCA in New York in 1962, the Psychological Corporation found that listeners had strong impressions of their co-listeners. This image was highly positive and self-flattering. The other listeners were "their kinds of people": active, young or young-at-heart, liberal, and "hep." There was a strong sense of in-group identification, and the study emphasized that listeners "need to be in close association with others."[31] Listeners were made to feel that they and others were mutually present during the show, that even though they were invisible to each other, they constituted a vibrant, energetic community that mattered to the DJ and that, right then and there, shared a basic, elemental zeitgeist. The DJ achieved this through language and music alone.

The DJ's talk, his mode of address, was different from that of the funny man host or emcee of the "golden years," who spoke and joked to a studio audience and whose listeners were invited into that imagined space in New York. DJs' talk was directed to the audience "out there." So the mode of address and the reception weren't mediated by others; DJ talk went—and was meant to go—straight to you.[32] Unlike many newscasters in the postwar period, who spoke in the past tense and usually used the third person, DJs created intimacy by moving between *you* and *me*, while often speaking in the present or future tense. DJs usually made a point of emphasizing the closeness and familiarity between them and the audience by acknowledging that "I" the DJ try to deliver what "you" the audience like or request, and implying that "I" the DJ know and care a lot about "you." References to "you" were multiple and overlapping, as when he spoke to "any of you having a birthday today" or to "anyone out there in love." The DJ also identified listeners by their communities or neighborhoods, hailing "anyone listening in Garfield Heights" or "all of you in New Jersey." The listener was, simultaneously, a distinct, unique individual and a member of a like-minded group.

Most DJs took on nicknames, which were also key to the construction of intimacy. The DJ often asked direct questions of the audience; of course, they couldn't really respond, but questions also suggested conversation and exchange. The main strategy was to ensure that listeners felt they were participants in the show and members of the community hailed by this DJ. Once Alan Freed began taping his show for WNJR in Newark in 1953 while also serving as a DJ in Cleveland, he welcomed "all of our thousands of friends in Ohio, Ontario, western New York, western Pennsylvania, and West Virginia," then added that "joining us will be thousands of listeners in New York and New Jersey." He wanted his listeners to understand how many of them there were, and he wanted them to feel located on a common map. When he moved to 1010 WINS in New York, he read telegrams over the air from one listener to another. These too conjured up a mapped community, as Bobby from Rye had Freed tell Judy from Bronxville, "The feeling is still the same." He was the verbal bulletin board of love, friendship, and community, and read a long list of names—Gail S., Nicky A., Ginny M., Bob R.—of kids who were planning a high school dance or who simply wanted to say hi to another group of kids. It was Freed's voice, and his status, the fact that *he* chose which messages to read that gave them their special aura. DJs around the country became switchboards on the air for their young listeners, making themselves privileged conduits within their listeners' imagined communities. Being directly addressed as "you," as someone with a birthday, as a resident of Brooklyn, as someone going through a breakup, did double duty. It constituted listeners as in on things together, as sharing a common experience on the air, while it acknowledged that the audience was not monolithic, not some "mass" the way TV often treated it, but made up of individuals with their own particular autobiographies.[33]

Freed especially forged loyalty among his listeners by frequently naming the ways teenagers were being stereotyped and vilified by the mainstream press and movies. He interrupted the highly regulated cadence and song-ad, song-ad format of his show during a 1956 broadcast on 1010 WINS in New York to announce a fund-raising dance sponsored by kids at a local high school, describing it as "another worthy project undertaken by a fine bunch of teenagers." Then the tirade began. "You know, it just goes to show you how much a lot of these wonderful kids do for other people all the time and have to take the brunt of all these attacks. And the most sickening thing I've seen in a long time is a marquee of one of our prominent Broadway movie theaters showing the picture *The Blackboard Jungle* . . . called 'the bold story of a teenage terror,' and I think it's probably the most sickening thing I've ever seen." Emphasizing his personal ties to young people, he added, "Teenagers, I've been dealing with them for thirteen years, and they're the greatest, most wonderful age-group in America. Since when has it become a crime to be a teenager?"[34]

The DJ often used different vocal registers, slang, tone of voice, even whoops and howls, to give listeners multiple versions of himself to latch on to. Murray the K, the highly successful DJ on 1010 WINS in New York, constantly addressed his audience as "baby" or "babe" and used slangy rhymed couplets like "Murray the K, all the way" and "our swinging soiree is gonna come your way" to show his playful dexterity with the language. A verbal riff like "If you think you're going ape" was impressively economical: it cemented the me-you bond, showed his ease with the latest slang, and suggested that he had effervescent, uncontrollable impulses, just like his listeners. Repeated use of the word *hey* hailed the audience in the way kids would call to each other at school.

George "Hound Dog" Lorenz of Buffalo's mighty 50,000-watt WKBW, which at night could be heard hundreds of miles away, emphasized that listeners were "right here at the people's choice" and insisted, "I got a lot of goodies for you, baby." Jack Armstrong at Chicago's WIXY, "movin' and groovin' with you," let his voice soar as he yelled to his audience, "It's your leader." DJ talk, then, was neither a purely commercial or purely popular indigenous form of speech, but a brilliant hybrid of both.[35]

Listening to this kind of music and patter evoked a powerful sense of associations, with others near and far away, with the DJ and his cool world, and with your own past, especially when a "golden oldie" or "flash from the past" was played. Audiences practiced informational listening too, about the news, the weather, concerts, products, and new songs. While listeners did not have to sustain dimensional listening as they had when tuning in to baseball or "golden age" storytelling, many songs, especially those that told a story ("Maybellene," "Wake Up, Little Susie," "Jailhouse Rock"), depicted exotic places ("Under the Boardwalk," "Up on the Roof," "Spanish Harlem"), or described great parties ("At the Hop," "Party Lights"), compelled listeners to imagine specific locales and actions often as powerfully as folks had imagined Jack Benny's vault. The AM format, just like the variety format of the 1930s and '40s, rapidly moved listeners among these modes and emotional and cognitive registers, and listeners became adept at interacting with this format, often to manipulate their own feelings of pleasure, desire, longing, transport, and self-pity. Listening still mattered powerfully.

Not only did the DJ have to sell himself on air as the irresistible personification of the station but off air he had to sell time to advertisers. As many national advertisers abandoned radio in favor of television, the DJ had to persuade local merchants that his show was the best vehicle for them to reach their desired local market. He also had to convince them that their ads wouldn't sound amateurish next to the slickly produced spots for Coke or Marlboro that aired on radio. Often it was his own reading of the ad copy, or his personal introduction of the spot, that provided special credibility and a contrast to "the impersonal and polished style of national commercials."[36]

In the romance surrounding DJs like Alan Freed, it's easy to forget how much selling they did on the air, and how hard-sell the pitches were. In a surviving 1956 tape from Freed's *Rock 'n' Roll Party Time* on WINS, New York, the standard format was song-ad, song-ad. And the ads were not short. Virtually all of them were delivered by Freed himself in his high-voltage, hyperventilating style, and he combined direct, personal appeals with the hard sell of the used-car vendor. The ads were also explicitly gendered, with most of them, except for, say, the Barbizon School of Modeling, directed at boys and men. "Say, fellas, I just discovered the best auto wax," he would announce conspiratorially, letting his listeners in on his unique finds and expert judgments. "Believe me, it's just what you've been waiting for . . . believe me, guys, it outshines them all." All the ads insisted that here, finally, the listener would really save money and get a great deal. "Never before, guys, have you been able to take advantage of sensational discount savings like these!" Everything was "unbeatable" and "unbelievable." The I-you mode of address and the personal structure of the direct question were clearly meant to modulate the intensity of the pitches. "Say, Dad, did you know you could own a beautiful, brand-new 1955 Mercury, the car of your dreams? How? It's simple!" And on he would go.[37]

Competition between stations was fierce: the postwar proliferation of lower-power stations meant that stations' listening audiences, on average, had dropped from 60,000 to 30,000, and thus there were more stations vying to sell smaller audiences to local advertisers. The guy who made his station number one commanded a high salary and considerable prestige. He also often worked like a dog after hours, attending Masons, Elks, and Moose lodge meetings, serving as the emcee for charity events, giving speeches at local functions, and in certain markets meeting with record company executives, staging live shows, and scouting and even managing talent. It was essential to his ongoing success that the DJ be seen prominently outside the studio, as an intrinsic part of the community, an enviable celebrity and a respected altruist.

In the early years especially, successful DJs enjoyed considerable autonomy—in the music they played, in what and how much they said over the air, in the personalities they assumed, even, sometimes, in the way they pitched their sponsors' products. Part of the appeal of the job was that "behind a microphone you can become exactly what you would like to be."[38] Many of them broke the rules on and off the air. As employees many either were helping to invent a station's identity or were already so popular that they didn't have to listen to the station manager or program director. On the air those addressing teenagers and playing rock 'n' roll exemplified a new kind of masculinity, and a new kind of racial hybridity.

No discussion of the invention of DJ talk can proceed without emphasizing the enormous contributions made by African American slang and music to this genre of public discourse. The few African American DJs in the late 1940s and early 1950s, like Maurice "Hot Rod" Hulbert, Rufus "Bear Cat" Thomas, and Jocko Henderson, brought a rhyming and rapping style to the air widely imitated by many of their white counterparts. It was DJs, black and white, at large and small stations, and their young listeners, who brought an end to segregation on the airwaves. Before the great wartime migration of African Americans, those few radio stations that programmed to blacks were primarily in Chicago, or in the South. In 1949 the trade publication *Sponsor* warned broadcasters that they were missing out on a $12 billion market by ignoring African American consumers. After all, between 1940 and 1953 black median income rose 192 percent, and black home ownership increased by 129 percent. In most regions of the country, especially in cities, 90 percent of African Americans now owned radios.[39] In the postwar period, with the increased availability of radio licenses for small local stations, the networks' gradual abandonment of radio in favor of television, and the discovery that African Americans were an important new niche market—*Ebony* had begun publication in 1945—certain independent stations began courting the black audience.

One of the most famous was WDIA in Memphis, which started out with 250 watts and in a few years was up to 50,000 watts, blanketing much of the mid-South with black music. WDIA was the first station in the country to feature an all-black on-air staff that programmed directly to African American listeners. Chicago's WVON—"Voice of the Negro"—became, in 1947, the nation's first black-owned station. By 1955 more than 600 stations were programming to black audiences in thirty-nine states, and 36 of these stations devoted their entire schedules to black-oriented programming. In gradually increasing numbers white listeners discovered these stations and tuned in to hear something vibrant, hip, and forbidden. By 1952, for example, the Dolphin Record Store in Los Angeles sold over 40 percent of its R&B records to whites.[40]

Although African American singers and musicians had broken the color barrier on the air by the mid-1920s, the homogenization of radio fare by the early 1930s—and the persistent racism of the industry—meant that rigid and ridiculous conventions circumscribed the representations of blacks on radio. As *Billboard* noted in 1943, when the race riots in Detroit had once again made the treatment of African Americans a national issue, "Radio still has a rule that a Negro cannot be represented in any drama except in the role of servant or as an ignorant or comical person." Nor could "Negro artists" be introduced "with the appellation of Mr. Mrs. or Miss preceding his or her name."[41] Nonetheless, some black musicians did have their own shows, appeared on network variety shows, and began to get jobs as studio musicians.

The war heightened the need for national unity and the importance of defining America in stark opposition to Hitler's fascism, thus prompting a series of shows designed to counter "race hatred" in the United States. One month after the Detroit riots in 1943, CBS featured "An Open Letter on Race Hatred" with the former presidential candidate Wendell Willkie warning of the dangers to democracy posed by racism. *America's Town Meeting of the Air* addressed the need for racial tolerance on several of its shows, and stars like Edward G. Robinson appeared on shows like *Too Long, America,* which attacked racial prejudice. That icon of wartime patriotism Kate Smith warned listeners on *We, the People* in 1945 that "race hatreds—social prejudices—religious bigotry—they are all the diseases that eat away the fibers of peace." She insisted that everyone had to work to exterminate race hatred. "You and I must do it— every father and mother in the world, every teacher, everyone who can rightfully call himself a human being."[42] No one would suggest that these gestures marked the end of racist depictions on the air. But they did signal a recognition among some whites that blacks had been denigrated as citizens and overlooked as a market.

During World War II, as Michele Hilmes reports in *Radio Voices,* there were two star-studded variety shows broadcast to American troops overseas: *Command Performance,* which featured primarily white stars like Frank Sinatra, Bob Hope, and Judy Garland, and *Jubilee,* the "Negro variety show" with stars like Duke Ellington, Lena Horne, and the Mills Brothers.[43] Hilmes sees *Jubilee* as a defeat: an institutional affirmation of separate but equal, a stubborn failure of radio to integrate black voices, music, and perspectives into mainstream broadcasts. But we can also see *Jubilee* as a beginning, with its irresistible elements of what would define Top 40 radio in the 1950s: a cool, hip, jive-talking host; bebop, blues, and jazz; a celebration of black language, music, and culture.

"Like sugar from the maple, like honey from the bee, the stuff we got is pure and mellow and it's here on *Jubilee.*" From the introduction of the host— "Here's your emcee, that walkie-talkie butterball Ernie—'The Q' for cute— Whitman"—the slangin', jivin', and wordplay defined the pace, tone, and voice of the show. Listening to tapes of these broadcasts fifty years later, it's hard to know if you've heard right, since the emphasis of the banter is on rhyming, not on making sense. Ernie Q starts off with "Much water's passed under the oil tower trestle of this fessel vessel since we made with the riffs." He then introduces a "hepster with the hottest licorice stick in town"; little Ida James is "a chick" who sings "Shoo-Shoo Baby"; the pianist Art Tatum "will manipulate the eighty-eights." "Man, we're gonna be saturated by some solid solos," he promises, and Jimmie Lunceford and his band are "gonna treat us to some crashing cadenzas." Modes of address, to the performers and the audience, include "papa," "brother," and "cats." He signs off, "Dig you later. So long and good luck."[44]

There wasn't much distance between this and the radio show *Red, Hot and Blue* with Dewey Phillips, a white DJ impersonating a black man and playing black music for a predominantly African American audience over WHBQ in Memphis in the early 1950s. (Phillips would later become known as the first DJ to play Elvis's early recordings.) He called the station WH-Bar-be-Que, and his sponsor was Omega flour and cornmeal, which Phillips pitched to his black audience as making the best biscuits ever. He sang along with some of the songs he played and cut into "Hey You Ever Been Booted" with "Hey, she better notta booted me." Phillips addressed his listeners personally in a rapid-fire delivery, with phrases like "Man, I'm tellin' you" and "You would go flat crazy" and, in pushing a free promotional brochure from Omega, "it don't cost you one red copper." He would dedicate one song to as many as twenty listeners— "This one's for Willie, for Ida Mae, Thelma, Jimmy," and so on—and thus cultivated a sense of a large community of listeners bound together by his show. Blacks had never heard their names on the radio before; now they heard theirs and those of their friends. Jivin' Jerry on WLCS in Baton Rouge in the early fifties had a nearly identical show, also sponsored by a flour company. This flour was "what people are talkin' and shoutin' about." Biscuits made from Levy flour will "make you feel so glor-ee-fied." He advised his women listeners to "make [your man] a pie and make him cry for joy." His program featured "Jim Jam Jumpin' Jive music."[45]

Like Phillips and later Wolfman Jack, a host of white DJs imitated their black counterparts. This represented a conscious turning away from the official "announcer speak" that had been institutionalized since the early 1930s: deep-voiced, bell-shaped tones in homogenized English that policed the boundaries of acceptable public address by men. Instead, these DJs showcased jive, the hipster talk based on black rhyming games that began to circulate more widely in the 1940s. *Ebony* reported that by the end of 1947 there were 16 African American DJs on the air (out of 3,000), most in and around midwestern cities like Detroit and Chicago with large black populations, others in Philadelphia, Washington, D.C., and New York. And *Ebony* was quick to point out that shows like *Ravin' with Ramon* in Philadelphia, and DJs like Jack Gibson on WCFL in Chicago, had interracial audiences. Gibson, in fact, claimed that 90 percent of his fan mail was from whites. Listeners who could get Jack L. Cooper on Chicago's WSBC could choose from thirteen shows he aired, many of them specializing in "hot wax and jivey patter." By 1950 several New York stations—WMCA, WNEW, WLIB, and WWRL—were broadcasting as much as twenty-two hours a week of black-oriented programming, and several had studios in Harlem.[46] In 1954 WNJR, servicing Newark and New York, specialized in black-oriented programming and hired several black DJs.

But it was WDIA, 1070 on the AM dial in Memphis, that was really the pioneer, and it still hasn't gotten the credit it deserves in revolutionizing not just black radio but white radio as well. After all, putting black DJs and primarily black music on a 50,000-watt station—in the South no less—was unheard of. While the station was not black-owned, it hired—and made stars of—a host of African American DJs that whites like Dewey Phillips then mimicked. And it was the first station in Memphis to make $1 million. Nat D. Williams, who joined the station in 1948, hosted the *Tan Town Jamboree* and later *Brown America Speaks*. Williams did not foreground the slangin', jivin' talk of many of the DJs he hired, but he showcased a hip, poetic language and celebrated both African American music and his largely black audience. And he emphasized a first-person, second-person mode of address that instantly constructed an imagined—and a real—community. "Now folks, here we are, smack dab at the end of another day of broadcasting and right on the tiptoes of still another one." To close the show he reminded his listeners that "we have tried to fill your hours with an earful of tunes; the indigo notes of the blues, tunes with a swing, tunes with beauty and deep earthy sentiment, tunes to make you smile and chuckle, and tunes with deep religious fervor." And why did WDIA do this? "We did this for you, the WDIA listener, the finest people in the world. And we want to thank you for being our good friends." Each show began and ended with his deep, trademark heh-heh-heh-heh laugh, the audio signal that copyrighted his show. The DJ Martha Jean "The Queen" Steinberg, who also got her start at WDIA, remembered that they couldn't use the words *black* or *Negro*, so they referred to their shows as "sepia time" or "brown time."[47]

With Williams's growing popularity, he was able to hire other African American DJs. Maurice "Hot Rod" Hulbert, who joined WDIA in 1949 and went to Baltimore two years later, became famous for his imaginary spaceship, which would take him and his listeners to outer space. It was great for a song to "Get the Nod from the Rod," and his rhymin' and patter often featured a sultry cornet in the background. His listeners were "mommio" and "daddio," and they were "the greatest people in the world." His other trademark maxim was "If I tell you a mosquito can pull a plow, don't ask me how; hitch him up . . . and take a ride to the moon." As mystifying to us today as Joe Penner's "Wanna Buy a Duck," this aphorism signaled that the listener was entering a distinct, privileged worldview that was, simultaneously, rural and futuristic. More important, this wordplay that built on slang and folklore assured the listener that Hulbert could be trusted; he was the genuine article.[48]

Rufus "Bear Cat" Thomas, who replaced the then DJ B. B. King at WDIA in 1950, hosted the *Hoot 'n' Holler* show, in which he said he was "gonna try to make you rise and swing." He opened each show with "I'm young and loose and full of juice. I got the goose, so what's the use." He was brilliant at rhyming promotions of the show and notices of upcoming concerts. And then there was Theo "Bless My Bones" Wade, who played gospel and was also known as Brother Wade. There is little doubt that he was one of the WDIA DJs Dewey Phillips was especially trying to imitate. Here is his ad for Martha White's flour. "Say, you eveh had, eveh had a biscuit baptizin'? Heh, heh, heh, listen, let Bless My Bones tell you somein', let me tell you 'bout a biscuit bap-TIIIZIN' [with *baptizin'* emphasized and drawn out]. Here's what you do. You bake your biscuits with Martha White's self-risin' flour, an' when them Martha White's biscuits come oudda the oven, you jus' grab 'em up an' budda 'em. You baptize 'em in budda, and you talkin' 'bout good eatin'. You sop your way onto the promised lan' after the baptizin', you got it?"[49]

Note the direct, neighborly, but instructional mode of address and the playful transformation of cooking into a religious experience. Jocko Henderson, who started at WHAT in Philadelphia in the early 1950s and quickly became one of the most sought after DJs in town, has been labeled by some the "first original rapper" because of his trademark "rhythm talk." Al "The Swingmaster" Benson in Chicago introduced his *Swing and Sway* show in the late 1940s with "Here I am, all ready and all set to bring you thirty minutes of red hot, beat me down, bring you up swing tunes of today."[50] This was the cool patter, the smooth facility with language that was playful, hip, and irreverent that white DJs sought to emulate as they created their on-air identities.

Chicago had also been a center for African American programming, particularly through WSBC, which had, since the 1920s, catered to the city's various ethnic groups. And two of its most renowned DJs in the late 1940s embodied the dilemma for some African American broadcasters. Did you adhere to the King's English and show that, contrary to media stereotypes, African Americans actually could speak the official language? Or did you embrace and showcase the linguistic playfulness, creativity, and distinctiveness of Black English, or at least black slang, at the possible cost of further reinforcing racial marginalization? Such linguistic choices, of course, embodied thorny debates about assimilation versus maintaining one's distinct ethnic or racial cultural identity. And both approaches prevailed, often on the same station.

As early as the mid-1920s, Jack Cooper, on WSBC, became the first black DJ with a commercially sustained show, and in 1929 he hosted an all-black variety hour. He put gospel music on the air, introducing listeners to Mahalia Jackson. He did remotes from bars where African American bands were playing and broadcast the Negro league baseball games until 1946. By the mid-1940s he was earning six figures. Cooper had a deep voice and spoke straight, proper English. By contrast, his fellow Chicagoan Al Benson "slaughtered the

English language" according to many blacks who listened to him: he mispronounced words, spoke with a lisp and a deep southern accent, ate food while
he talked on the air, and often stumbled over words like *monthly,* which he pronounced "mont-ly." But he played Billie Holiday, Lloyd Price, the Platters, and
other music no one else was playing in Chicago; he knew how to rhyme his ads
("Every hour of the day, you can hear people say, 'Drink Canadian Ale' "), and
he was an enormous success with black audiences. Other disc jockeys, black
and white, sought to imitate his style.[51]

Stations specializing in black programming also served as models for how
to use radio to build a sense of community, something that would be essential
to the success of white DJs on AM radio in the 1950s. With Chicago as one of
the top destinations for blacks during the great migration, Jack Cooper began
an on-air missing persons service in 1938 to help family and friends find people who had moved up from the South. These broadcasts allegedly helped locate thousands of people in a fifteen-year period.[52] WDIA, being "the goodwill
station," had a variety of community service announcements, including an on-
air lost and found service, and no item was too ridiculous or too trivial to locate, from farm animals gone astray to false teeth lost on Beale Street. When
the lost teeth couldn't be found, listeners sent money in to the station to help
their owner get a new set. Linguistically and musically, these stations acknowledged that much of the community's identity derived from a distance from
mainstream, white, bourgeois culture, a distance that white DJs would mimic
and cultivate to great profit.

Time and again we see white DJs who themselves became harbingers—and
icons—of psychic escape through music identifying powerfully with African
American music and language. As Martha Jean Steinberg, who started her
radio career in 1954, put it, "Everybody was trying to sound black." She also
claims that it was blacks—or at the very least whites trying to tap into and draw
from black culture—who started the cult of personality on the air. The Smithsonian Institution, in its 1996 radio documentary on the history of black radio,
devoted an entire program to the phenomenon of "sounding black" because it
was so pervasive in early 1950s radio. WLAC, for example, a 50,000-watt station in Nashville, featured "Daddy" Gene Nobles, Bill "Hoss" Allen, and "John
R." Richbourg, all of whom were white men who sounded black and played
rhythm and blues, reaching audiences as far away as Texas and Virginia, sometimes even hitting New England. Allen recalled that "most people, white and
black, thought that John was black, and that I was black." He said that when listeners called the station to ask if they were black or white, Allen would reply,
"Does it make a difference?" Alan Freed—aka "the Moondog" when he became
famous as Cleveland's preeminent DJ in the early 1950s—promoted himself as

a one-man advocate for the popularization of rhythm and blues to white audiences. Hunter Hancock successfully passed for black as the hipster host of *Huntin' with Hunter* on KGFJ and *Midnight Matinee* on KMPC in Los Angeles, playing jazz, blues, and spirituals targeted to the audience in Watts.[53] New Orleans had Jack "The Cat" Elliot, and Atlanta had "Daddy" Sears.

New Orleans, in fact, provides a fascinating account of the deliberateness, in some quarters, of this racial ventriloquy. No station in town in the immediate postwar era would hire a black DJ. But WJMR wanted to tap into the black market, and Vernon Winslow, an African American newspaperman and college professor, wanted to break into radio. So WJMR hired Winslow to teach its white DJs how to sound black, and to write and direct a show called *Jam, Jive and Gumbo* that featured a black-talking DJ nicknamed Poppa Stoppa and played by a white man. Winslow chose the music, wrote the scripts for the white DJs, and laced them with phrases like "Don't worry 'bout nothin', man" and "Wham bam, thank you, ma'am." Finally, in 1949, Winslow got his own show; he went on the air as Doctor Daddy-O and stayed on until the 1980s.[54]

We don't have much information on how African Americans regarded such impersonations, once they discovered the masquerade. Certainly some felt that whites were simply trying to exploit black listeners to make a quick buck, and of course this is true. At the same time, however, black musicians like B. B. King, James Brown, and Aaron Neville felt grateful to such DJs because they gave black music a much wider audience; exposed blacks and whites to gospel, rhythm and blues, boogie-woogie, and jazz; and often gave these same musicians their first break. As James Brown put it, "John R. meant so much to Afro-American people. He did as much to help blacks as any white I know, and more than most. Because he made us aware, and he made our music important."[55] And ironically, white DJs trying to sound black opened up jobs—although certainly not as many as should have been—to black DJs.

Wolfman Jack, a New York City WASP named Bobby Smith from West End Avenue, couldn't flee from his roots into this racially hybrid world fast enough. "I'm a guy who was born white," he recalled, "but soon got captivated heart and soul by black American culture." In the early 1950s, when he was in his early teens, Bobby Smith got a fancy transoceanic radio from his dad, capable of picking up weak and distant signals. Holed up in his basement away from his folks, Bobby was not trying to pull in the BBC news. Instead, he was reeling in WLAC from Nashville and WDIA from Memphis. The DJs he heard spoke like "hepcats," their patter laced with "hey man," "baby," "cool cat," and sexual innuendo. The grown-up Bobby, rechristened Wolfman Jack, recalled how exciting it was to tune past Eddie Fisher, Patti Page, and the Four Freshmen to hear Jocko Henderson call to his audience, "Hey Mommio, hey Daddio, this is your spaceman—Jocko! Three, two, one—blast-off time," followed by the Clovers singing, "Down in the alley, just you and me, we're goin' ballin' till half past three." Or he could tune in Tommy "Dr. Jive" Smalls, who was also black, from Harlem. DJ John R. on WLAC, Wolfman Jack recalled, called himself "the blues man" and yelled to his listeners, "Yeah! Have mercy, have mercy," with a vocal quality Smith said "radio people call 'a big set of balls.' " Young Bobby Smith also pulled in XERF, the 250,000-watt powerhouse just over the border in Ciudad Acuña, Mexico, which featured one Big Rockin' Daddy from midnight on who played Ike Turner and his Kings of Rhythm and Louis Jordan doing "Fatback and Corn Liquor." "We were seeing another universe," Smith recalled, "a very attractive one, and we wanted to go there like crazy."[56]

Why did white kids, and especially boys like Tony Pigg and Bobby Smith, want to "go there like crazy"? And why was it that so many white DJs, from Alan Freed as "the Moondog" to Bobby Smith as "Wolfman Jack," assumed these on-air personas that combined racial ventriloquism with an almost tribal animalism? George Lorenz, on Buffalo's 50,000-watt WKBW, was "the Hound Dog" and opened his broadcast with the sound of werewolves howling. Robin Seymour in Detroit was "the Big Bad Bird." Joe Niagra at WIBG in Philadelphia was the "Rockin' Bird." Others didn't follow this odd totemism but were known as "Mad Daddy" (Pete Myers on WHK in Cleveland) or, simply, "the Screamer" (Dick Biondi, over various midwestern stations). What exactly were these white DJs and their listeners seeking?

Part of the answer lies with the suffocating, phony, surface conformity that threatened to suck all the spirit and individuality out of a white, middle-class boy the minute he grew up. Both David Riesman's *Lonely Crowd* (1950) and C. Wright Mills's *White Collar* (1953) portrayed white, middle-class masculinity as deadened and flaccid, overly obedient to the conformist, homogenizing demands of bureaucratic America. A lemming rather than a rugged individualist, anxious about pleasing others instead of confident and aggressive, this postwar man was, as Mills put it, a "small creature who is acted upon but who does not act, who works along unnoticed in somebody's office or store, never talking loud, never talking back, never taking a stand."[57]

What young boy would want this for his future? Raised on independent, brave pop culture heroes like the Shadow, the Lone Ranger, and even the goody-two-shoes Hardy Boys, all of whom had serial adventures and were never stuck behind a desk sucking up to some boss, American boys were torn, urged to be aggressive, distinctive individuals yet urged to obey authority figures and behave themselves.

What they were definitely not supposed to do, especially as they entered their teens, was indulge in any behaviors that might mark them as "juvenile delinquents." The JD, as Michael Kimmel points out, was the polar opposite of Mills's white-collar worker. He flaunted authority, did what he wanted when he wanted, had no respect for sexual mores or public decorum, and was completely uninterested in the future or deferred gratification. He wanted his kicks now, and getting kicks, by definition, involved getting into trouble.

Juvenile delinquency became a media-driven obsession in the 1940s and '50s, as panics about sweet, middle-class boys morphing into leather-jacket-clad wiseasses with motorcycles, DAs (the "duck's ass" haircut), and a love of vandalism gripped women's magazines, the press, and the movies. These kinds of boys would not do at all—how would they ever learn to succeed as organization men? And since academic studies and media imagery virtually defined working-class adolescence as automatically deviant, physical segregation from the lower orders seemed the best solution. The real fear, of course, was that middle-class boys would be contaminated by lower-class hostility or indifference to bourgeois values. Conscientious middle-class parents would get their boys out of the cities and into the suburbs, away from hoods and punks who thought that the best way to have fun was to get into trouble.

Of course, there simply wasn't much thought that white boys would look to black men with envy or admiration. Yet for all too many boys in the 1950s, that was exactly what happened, not necessarily directly with real black men but through radio, which simply ignored carefully crafted residential boundaries. As the cultural historian George Lipsitz has argued about white resistance to increased regimentation and conformity in the late 1940s and early '50s, "White Americans may have turned to black culture for guidance because black culture contains the most sophisticated strategies of signification and the richest grammars of opposition available to aggrieved populations." With "everything so sterile," recalled Martha Jean Steinberg, "being black was so unique, it was like hidden treasure. We were havin' a good time," she added, and "if you start havin' a good time, everybody want to know *why* you havin' that good time."[58]

We also have to remember that there is a history in this country of white men impersonating black men, going back at least to the 1830s with the popular theater and minstrel shows. And as Eric Lott, Nathan Huggins, and other scholars remind us, this has always been a much more complicated act than simply trying to make fun of your alleged inferiors. The blackface tradition allows white men, however unconsciously, to bridge the gap between the races, to become racial renegades, and to try on a thrillingly different, freer black self. There is a forbidden form of male bonding here, in which white men, in however convoluted a fashion, admit their envy of black manhood and their desire to get to know black men more intimately. Lott suggests that such blackface comes to the fore in our culture at those moments when racial divisions seem especially stark and unmovable yet when there is simultaneously a collective desire to break down those divisions.[59] The 1940s and early 1950s was such a time, as the pervasiveness of racial ventriloquy on the radio powerfully reveals.

At a time when white men performing in blackface was becoming increasingly passé and taboo, racial cross-dressing through the appropriation of black slang and black music became a rage on radio for teens. The black DJs and musicians Freed and Wolfman Jack emulated and admired were completely different from C. Wright Mills's bland, emasculated corporate cog, but they weren't delinquents. They were better than both: they were cool.

Despite segregation—probably because of it—some whites were able to project onto blacks romanticized notions about the freedom from constraints that many whites craved, or thought they did. At the same time, according to Ben Sidran, a masculine ethos was developing among urban blacks, and it revolved around being "cool" and having "soul." A new, sometimes halting, sometimes quite assured sense of self-definition accompanied critical victories like the desegregation of the armed forces, Jackie Robinson's breaking of the color barrier in baseball, and *Brown v. Board of Education of Topeka* in 1954. This self-definition insisted, as had jazz in the 1920s, that blacks had a history that was rich, authentic, and pertinent to the rest of America, and that this history was embodied in black music and black slang.

"Feeling" was something everybody had, but black folks, as a result of their history and culture, had "soul." Soul was a mystique; it seemed to be "a distinct characteristic of colored folks," and it "posed an emotional center of black cultural experience . . . which was at peace with itself, 'positive' and 'complete.' " Certainly white masculinity was not "at peace with itself," nor was it supposed to have a visible "emotional center." Soul, then, was a challenge to the technocratic rationalism threatening to enslave white men and their sons. And black music in the 1950s, observes Sidran, "was a negation of Western analytic process . . . that posited a near mystical naturalness, reaffirming biological priorities and denying the Puritan ethic of middle America." As America became more repressive in the 1950s, with the grip of conformity and McCarthyism tightening, black music became especially attractive to the young "because it could generate emotional release" and because it promised a kind of commentary about life ignored or frowned upon in the schools, in the family, and on television. Many white men had also, for years, associated black masculinity with the especially powerful currents of sexual desire that emerge in adolescence. As Leslie Fiedler famously put it, "Born theoretically white, we are permitted to pass our childhood as imaginary Indians, our adolescence as imaginary Negroes, and only then are expected to settle down to being what we really are: white once more." But white DJs who drew from black culture didn't settle down: they were in a state of arrested adolescence and suggested their listeners could be too. They and the music they played insisted that people had a right to pleasure.[60]

Black hipster slang signaled membership in a special, outcast community that seemed to laugh at and be above those clueless, cookie-cutter, tightassed white folks. Wolfman Jack remembered the radio banter of black DJs he worked so hard to imitate, and the banter of those whites trying to pass. "They were a lot cooler than even the toughest hood in the toughest street gang around. They had such command, just by being quick-mouthed and entertaining, they took control of the room.[61] Once again in radio verbal agility was the mark of a real man, although here, as DJ, one operated without a script—or a net. So the racial cross-dressing had to be very convincing indeed, especially to young people often eager to detect and reject phoniness.

The totemism of DJ culture, in which DJs added to their identities the spirit of the hound dog, the moondog, the wolfman, or birds, intermixed with this racial ventriloquism. DJs hailed their listeners as kinship groups, who were meant to identify with a particular animal figure. What are we to make of this pattern, one that appears to have been largely unself-conscious, highly imitative, and confined to this particular medium during this particular era? Without studying, say, Inuit culture, Freed, Wolfman Jack, and others seemed to understand that the ritualistic nature of radio listening they were promoting would be well served by tying listeners together through a totem that the DJ himself personified, inviting them to feel a kind of mystical bond of unity because the figure that brought them together embodied a wild, animal-like spirit, and often a spirit of the night. "Away we go, howling at midnight," Freed called to his otherwise roped-in listeners.

As a totemic figure the listeners worshiped, this "wolfman," this "hound dog" reinforced an identity in themselves as a group almost biologically apart from that in which some plain old human like Arthur Godfrey held sway. The DJ's feral, hybrid persona reminded them of their bond with one another as part of a subcultural group too wild for stations playing Rosemary Clooney, indeed, too wild for much of America. Even DJs who weren't wolves or birds but were screamers or mad daddies appreciated the need to be wild, to suggest the irrational, to embody the possibility of utterly losing it at any time. And this, in turn, reinforced the image of the DJ as a man who refused to grow up, who instead insisted that it was perfectly reasonable, even desirable, to see adolescence not as some transitory stage but as a destination, a permanent way of being.[62]

It was extremely important for many teenagers to associate themselves with the idiosyncratic, to feel they were individualizing their media consumption, especially in the face of so much homogenized mass-cultural output. Of course, they also wanted to fit in and belong. WMCA's in-house report noted this contradiction: young people wanted to be self-assertive, but they also looked "to others (radio stations among them) for cues and advice regarding [their] own behavior."[63] The DJ allowed listeners to feel that others might be suckered in by mainstream, bourgeois mass culture but not them. Indeed, people feel compelled, when they meet DJs they grew up with, to tell them, "I used to listen to you all the time when I was a kid." What people are really telling the DJ is how he is an intrinsic part of their personal histories; his voice and personality shaped their identity at a crucially formative period.

If the black ventriloquism of white DJs was seductive to Wolfman Jack, Tony Pigg, and Alan Freed, to others it was an outrageous transgression against American civilization itself. Here were white men furthering the mainstreaming of black music and language that was much more impertinent than anything that had been offered on network radio by Duke Ellington or Ella Fitzgerald. As men who could become invisible and inhabit the voices of black men, voices that went out in the lush darkness to white teen bedrooms, these DJs, to their enemies, personified miscegenation let loose on a whole new scale. Just at the moment when so many white, middle-class parents had spirited their families off to the safe, segregated suburbs, the kids were imbibing forbidden music, language, and attitudes from the cities through that box in the corner that ignored geographic demarcations. Listening in from a safe distance, kids could accept yet subvert segregation at the same time.[64]

This threat was especially strong in the early 1950s, when DJs often enjoyed considerable autonomy in the control room. Of course their top mandate was to create and hold the largest audience possible rather than to indulge their own tastes or hunches, but they still chose what they played. Their "market research," such as it was, was based on informal surveys of local record store owners, jukebox operators, and the record distributors, as well as the charts; they had the latitude to play and push records they believed would be hits. As late as 1958, when the autonomy of DJs was beginning to erode in the face of a more rigid Top 40 format, 50 percent of those polled at the first annual Pop Music Disc Jockey Convention claimed that their personal tastes, interacting with the lists of best-selling records, determined what songs they aired. Only 21 percent cited "station management directive" as shaping their choices.[65] This already represented wishful thinking, a clinging to how things had been at the start of the decade.

Few men better embodied this intersection between the autonomy of the DJ, a love of African American music, and a celebration of youth culture than

Alan Freed. And few DJs were as obsessed as Freed with their self-promotion and with securing their place in history as "the father of rock 'n' roll," which Freed sought to do through his radio shows, the live concerts he hosted, and movies like *Rock, Rock, Rock! Mr. Rock and Roll,* and *Go, Johnny, Go!* He used these films to burnish the myths he created about himself, especially about his paternal role in bringing R&B to white audiences. What were these stories Freed insisted on telling about radio and the rise of rock 'n' roll, and why were they so important to him? Can they tell us something about some white people's investment in blackness in the 1950s and how that investment shaped radio and American culture?

According to the myth, Leo Mintz, who owned the Record Rendezvous on the edge of Cleveland's African American district, invited Freed into the shop in 1951 to witness the spectacle of white teens buying records by Fats Domino and LaVern Baker. This prompted an epiphany, which led Freed to start playing R&B for his white listeners on his late-night show *The Moon Dog House Rock 'n' Roll Party,* and rock 'n' roll was born. Freed wasn't claiming to be the only white DJ in America playing R&B, he was claiming that it was *he* who brought this music to effusively grateful white teens.

In reality, according to Freed's biographer John Jackson, Mintz—who was offering to sponsor a whole show of R&B music as a way to bolster sales among his established African American clientele (there were nearly 130,000 blacks in Cleveland in the early 1950s)—had to cajole Freed into hosting such a show. Nonetheless, Freed clearly fell in love with the music and held a deeply felt indignation over racial prejudice that stemmed, in part, from a close high school friendship with an African American boy. The early audiences for his radio shows and his infamous "Moondog Coronation Ball" were primarily African American. The crucial transition years, in which young white audiences also began to tune in, buy such music, and attend concerts featuring African American performers were from 1952 to 1956, the year Elvis became king. Nonetheless, Freed's successful construction of himself as the father of rock 'n' roll, as the man who brought black music to white kids, meant that he would be singled out for special opprobrium as the culture wars around race escalated in the late 1950s.

What began to emerge in the early 1950s and led to the invention of the Top 40 format was "programming by the charts"—basing what was played on the air on record sales and jukebox plays. This was nothing new—as early as 1935, *Your Hit Parade* offered performances of the top ten hits, and by the early 1950s stations like WDSU in New Orleans boasted tag lines like "the Top 20 at 1280."[66] What this often meant was that DJs simply chose what to play from *Billboard's* list of rankings. Listening to Alan Freed in 1956, one is struck by the variety of R&B and independent label music he played and by the absence of a tight rotation of the same hits. He played Bo Diddley and Frankie Lymon and the Teenagers but also gave airplay to the Charms, the Five Keys, the Three Chuckles, groups rarely played today on "oldies" stations. "Refined" Top 40 was something else—the repeated playing of the biggest hits much more often than other songs on the list.

As with all inventions, there are disputes about who thought of Top 40 first; the two most frequently cited inventors are Todd Storz, who owned a string of stations by the mid-1950s, and Gordon McLendon, the former sportscaster and founder of the Liberty Broadcasting Network, which eventually consisted of over four hundred stations. Clearly both men, as well as others, crafted Top 40 into what would become by the early 1960s, a nearly ossified format. But in the mid-1950s, Top 40 was a programming breakthrough that brought huge profits to many stations. It foregrounded rock 'n' roll, but it also meant that you would hear Fats Domino, Connie Francis, and the Beach Boys all on the same station.

The Top 40 strategy reportedly relied on Storz's casual ethnography of watching how people listened to popular music in public spaces. He was struck by the way people would keep playing the same song on the jukebox. Just as customers in a diner, or kids in a soda shop, played the same song on the jukebox over and over, the reasoning went that these listeners would tune to the radio station that played these hits in frequent rotation. The DJ should not be the one to pick the music, argued Storz, because "he is usually above the audience mentally and financially [and] is not representative of the public . . . his own preferences are a dangerous guide."[67]

It was Storz who reportedly came up with the idea of the "pick hit" of the week, and with the decision to play the number-one song once an hour. But it was McLendon, regarded by many in the radio business as an entrepreneurial genius, who, through KLIF 1190 in Dallas, introduced the promotional jingle, with the call letters sung repeatedly, as the signature for a station and who placed overturned cars on the freeways leading into Dallas with "I just flipped for Johnny Rabbit" painted on them to promote one of his station's new DJs. Or, as bongo drums sounded the alert, a woman announced, "KLIF presents the world's greatest disc jockey, Ross Knight!" Then Knight cut in with "All right, Baby, this is Ross Knight, the weird beard, the savior of Dallas radio."[68] McLendon brought a new intensity of promotion to AM, living by the motto that you told your listeners constantly that you were about to do something, that you were now doing it, and then that you had done it. In one stunt he rented a room on the top floor of a Dallas hotel and dropped balloons with money taped to them out the windows at 5:00 in the evening, paralyzing the city with gridlock. He introduced mobile news units that would report "cliff news" straight from the streets and advertised "news on the hour, every hour."

Other ploys were less successful. KTSA in San Antonio was doing poorly in the ratings, and since the town had a high military presence, McClendon decided to change the call letters to the snappy and patriotic KAKI. What McClendon failed to factor in was that the call letters now sounded exactly like a Hispanic slang word for excrement, which made the station something of a laughingstock in a town with such a large Latino population.[69]

Both Storz and McLendon brought cash giveaways to AM radio as a way to build audiences. And both ensured that the hit station would offer predictability—the same songs, a regular stable of DJs—the listener could turn to day or night and be reassured that he would encounter an utterly familiar audio environment. This meant more centralized control of the playlist by management.

The introduction of jingles, many of which sounded like variations on the theme song for *The Flintstones,* helped establish musical trademarks for Top 40 stations. "KLIF—Where the action is," "KLIF—it's a legend—yes, indeed!" "KLIF—Makes the week go fast, makes the weekend last and last." Other jingles introduced a "solid gold" hit, the weather report, and all the DJs, provided brief but insistent sing-along reminders of which station was *your* station, which station was the best station, which station brought you exactly what you wanted and when. The jingles became increasingly irritating over the years, but they also effectively established powerful auditory associations among listeners, the music they loved, and the station.

The real purpose of the Top 40 format, argues Martha Jean Steinberg, was to minimize the threat posed by the R&B disc jockey, who had potentially enormous influence over young people during a time of racial and political unrest. Certainly many of these DJs were either black themselves or avowedly antiracist whites. By 1956 Top 40 and tight playlists were becoming more common, and the DJs themselves rebelled against the format at their first annual conference in 1958, demanding "greater programming freedom."[70] But the imminent payola scandals—in which DJs admitted taking money or other gifts from record companies in exchange for playing their songs—ensured that, until the rise of FM and progressive rock, programming freedom would be even more restricted.

Paying prominent performers to sing or play one's song dated back to the Civil War, and song plugging dominated the radio business in the 1930s and '40s, so the practice was hardly new. Rather, the payola scandals, argue Peter Fornatale and Joshua Mills in *Radio in the Television Age,* must be understood as an outgrowth of the often racist reactions against rock 'n' roll. Anyone who has seen the various documentaries about rock 'n' roll recalls some fulminating, balding white man (usually a member of the Klan) attacking this "nigger music" and scenes of bonfires in which rock records were torched. A predictable coalition of religious leaders, schoolteachers, more conservative disc jockeys, politicians, and newspaper editors denounced the music as corrupting trash. Press coverage of rock typically demonized it by focusing on and sensationalizing concerts accompanied by unruly behavior. Members of the southern White Citizens' Councils denounced rock as "a means by which the white man and his children can be driven to the level with the Negro." Not that the North was any more progressive. Boston's Very Reverend John Carroll warned that rock inflamed teenagers "like jungle tom-toms readying warriors for battle." By 1955 authorities in Bridgeport, Hartford, and Washington, D.C., either banned or tried to ban rock 'n' roll concerts and dance parties.[71]

Rock posed two major threats. First, all the evidence indicates that there was, in fact, more racial mixing as a result of the kind of music played on the radio. Between 1955 and 1963 the number of black artists with Top Ten pop hits on the air increased by more than 50 percent. Many DJs sought to boost their ratings with teenagers by hosting dance parties, which often resulted in integrated crowds. Whites' embrace first of R&B and then of black rock and pop stars disrupted the old patterns of segregated shows, and this was especially revolutionary in the South, where segregated facilities were commonplace. Now blacks and whites would enter the same building to hear the same R&B group they had heard on the radio, but they were separated from each other by ropes or other dividers. Once everyone started dancing, however, these barricades often fell, and there they would be, dancing together. Freed's dances and concerts were especially scandalous in this regard. Not only did he encourage white teens to join with blacks in coming to listen and dance to black music but he also kissed black female performers on the cheek, embraced black men as they walked offstage, and was even seen sharing a cigarette or a drink with these performers after the show.[72]

Anxiety about increased infusions of black culture into the white mainstream escalated after 1956, when growing numbers of white boys like Elvis Presley and Jerry Lee Lewis took on black performing styles. Before Presley's success and his fusion of R&B, country, and blues, virtually all the R&B music that white listeners heard on the radio was performed by black artists. But once white performers began imitating blacks in their music, and performing with greater physicality onstage, it was clear that black music was constituting the identities of a significant group of white teens. Hollywood added to the panic about what racial hybridization was doing to white society with the release of

The Blackboard Jungle, which fused the image of teen delinquents with the sounds of "Rock Around the Clock."[73]

The second major danger to the Jim Crow conventions of America was the fact that rock music posed a financial threat to established white music interests in the industry. The American Society of Composers, Authors, and Publishers (ASCAP) had since the 1920s done battle with radio over the payment of fees to its members for songs played on the air. By the late 1930s the networks sought to counter ASCAP's monopoly over music and formed a competitor, Broadcast Music, Inc., or BMI. Since BMI was starting from scratch in 1939, and since it had a fee structure that paid all musicians equally for the playing of their music (ASCAP paid more to older, more established members), it especially attracted younger musicians. By the 1950s BMI controlled the majority of R&B, blues, and rock 'n' roll music, and ASCAP was determined "to use all their resources to destroy rock 'n' roll."[74] This combustible combination of racial phobia and economic aggression domesticated various aspects of AM broadcasting in the late 1950s and early 1960s, thwarting the rebellions of the early '50s and setting the stage for the FM insurgencies of just a few years later.

In 1959 the revelation that television quiz shows like *Twenty-One* and *The $64,000 Question* had been rigged and clean-cut, highly respectable contestants like Charles Van Doren had cheated provided ASCAP with the wedge it needed. With high-profile members like Frank Sinatra accusing alleged straight arrows like Mitch Miller of accepting kickbacks for pushing BMI songs, ASCAP representatives insisted that the House Legislative Oversight Committee expand its quiz show investigations to include a wider look at "corruption in broadcasting."[75] The May 1959 disc jockey convention in Miami, which the press cast as an orgy of "booze, broads, and bribes," gave the ASCAP proddings a boost. All this negative publicity, coupled with the press's hostility to rock 'n' roll, ensured that the public stage was well set for the disciplining of Top 40 radio.

As the record and radio industries became more mutually dependent in the early 1950s, and as DJs like Alan Freed gained the power to make or break a song, record company reps offered a variety of incentives to play their records on the air. These incentives included alcohol, women, and money. Others involved giving the DJ writing credit on a song so that he could collect royalties in perpetuity, a practice foisted disproportionately on African American artists. (This is why Alan Freed was listed as a cowriter of songs like Chuck Berry's "Maybellene.") Some DJs were hired as "consultants" to record companies, and others, like Dick Clark, had investments in a variety of performers and companies in the music business, which wasn't illegal but certainly raised issues of conflict of interest.[76] But to suggest that what came to be called pay-ola was new with DJs and rock 'n' roll was ridiculous—song plugging and bribery had been around for decades. Only now it was undermining the hege-mony of white, middle-class and upper-middle-class culture and economic in-terests, and favoring black culture, working-class culture, and youth culture.

ASCAP's goal was simple: dethrone the disc jockey and rock 'n' roll and re-build the adult audience for the sort of "high-quality" music that predomi-nated in ASCAP's stockpile of songs. Although no one put it this way at the time, this was a massive fight over listening, over the barely articulated under-standing that radio listening was playing a central role in shaping the identities of millions of young people. This was a recognition that despite the highly vi-sual nature of American culture, especially with the ubiquity of television, radio was addressing and cultivating young people in a way that television didn't dare. The Special Committee on Legislative Oversight took testimony on payola, and Alan Freed and Dick Clark were singled out as exemplars of the problem. Clark divested himself of many of his financial holdings in the music industry (which he figured cost him $8 million), while Freed refused to com-ply with various face-saving efforts, including signing an affidavit claiming he'd never taken payola, saying, "What they call payola in the disc jockey busi-ness, they call lobbying in Washington."[77] WABC in New York immediately fired him.

Freed's firing in November 1959 was front-page news in New York; "The type was the same size when World War II ended," quipped one of the owners of Birdland when he saw the Daily News and the Post. Within hours a nation-wide purge of DJs began. Many resigned rather than get fired; some left the business for good, others moved to different stations, especially those on the West Coast, which were more removed from the fracas. Sensationalized press coverage and threats of license revocation from FCC Commissioner Robert E. Lee contributed to the witch-hunt atmosphere. Freed, who became a national scapegoat, found himself pursued by a range of federal agencies, including the IRS, and he died broke in 1965 at the age of forty-three.[78]

In hearings that opened in February 1960, DJs testified that they had ac-cepted payola to play certain records, and legislation prohibiting payola fol-lowed. But the real impact of the hearings was the further erosion—some might even say elimination—of DJ autonomy in favor of programming by committee, meaning increasingly by management, who followed the lists of best-selling records.[79] For Top 40 stations, this meant the tight playlist com-bined with jingles, on-air promotions, ads, and the rapid-fire patter of a DJ with a trademark nickname like "Big Dan" Ingram or Murray the K. Small, in-dependent labels were hurt, since there were fewer opportunities for their songs to be played. And black music was tamed. With Elvis Presley in the army, Jerry Lee Lewis blacklisted for marrying his thirteen-year-old cousin, Chuck Berry under arrest, falsely accused by the FBI of transporting a teenage girl "across state lines" for "immoral purposes," and Buddy Holly, Ritchie Valens, and the Big Bopper dead, radio gave listeners Frankie Avalon, Paul Anka, and Bobby Vee.

The further reining in of Top 40 came in the form of the widely imitated Drake format, named after the programmer Bill Drake and showcased by KHJ in Los Angeles in 1965. Although technically still Top 40, the Drake format gave DJs even less time to talk and made them hew to a thirty-record playlist. In reality, however, rotations emphasized the top six to eight records, playing the hits over and over and over.[80] One study of Top 40 in the 1960s found that an hour of airtime on a typical station consisted of twenty-two commercials, seventy-three weather, time, or contest announcements, fifty-eight announcements of the station's call letters, one three-and-a-half-minute newscast, and twelve songs.

Fortunately, even after the payola scandals, radio also brought teenage listeners Maurice Williams, the Shirelles, Jackie Wilson, Otis Redding, the Ronettes, and the Marvelettes. Berry Gordy's Motown, founded in 1960, emphasized crossover music that was "clearly black, but not threatening, and very danceable."[81] DJs like Dick "the Screamer" Biondi on Chicago's WLS or Cousin Brucie on WABC abandoned the totemism of moondogs and the like, and the black slang and jive talk of the early and mid-1950s was replaced by more generic youth slang like "sockin' it to you" and "groovy." Nonetheless, much of AM was now decidedly the aural outpost of the young, and they knew it: this was their medium, and they were going to use it in the ongoing battles between young and old.

Top 40's talent for making the national—even the international—seem local reached its apogee with Beatlemania. At night, of course, kids could pull in those distant 50,000-watt stations, but for the most part they listened to local stations rooted in and speaking for their particular locale. As a result, many large Top 40 stations around the country were able to claim that they had a special relationship with and access to the Beatles. Murray the K in New York billed himself as the "fifth Beatle," and WABC instantly morphed into W-A-Beatles-C. KRLA—"first in fun, first in music"—announced the time as "KRLA-Beatle Time." KLIF in Dallas claimed to be the first station in the country to capture Beatlemania with its "exclusive Beatle interviews" and "exclusive Beatle hits, weeks ahead of other Texas radio stations."[82]

With rock 'n' roll broadcast over car radios and transistors, it was the mobility of the music, not its fidelity, that mattered. The explosive growth in car sales in the 1950s, and the industry's emphasis on planned obsolescence, meant that by the early 1960s there was a plethora of used cars, and many of these were sold or handed down to teenagers. One 1961 survey estimated that by the spring term of their senior year in high school, almost half of all boys had a car.[83] Those who didn't used their parents' cars.

The powerful fusion of cars, young people, rock 'n' roll, and the radio meant that teenagers could—and did—use broadcast music to become squatters: they claimed territory that wasn't really theirs by blanketing that space with rock 'n' roll. They did this while driving around small towns, cruising up and down certain strips, blasting their radios in Laundromats and candy stores, or staking out portions of beaches and parks. At nights and on weekends especially they occupied public spaces reserved for grown-ups, for business, for the orderly conduct of all kinds of commerce, and used the sounds of radios and cars to defy that orderliness. They reclaimed districts where they were supposed to be seen but not heard as loud, unruly kid space, where their sensibilities took precedence.[84]

By the mid-1960s Top 40 radio was deeply woven into teenage life and daily practices. It summoned up teens as a distinct social group, apart from their parents yet united across geographic boundaries and differences. It accompanied driving around, making out, doing homework, working summer jobs, and going to sleep. During the 1950s it had become the most racially integrated mass medium in the country. In 1964, when the landmark Civil Rights Act was passed, even as Beatlemania gripped America, ushering in the nearly all-white "British invasion," black artists retained their hold on teenage hearts and imaginations. Martha and the Vandellas, the Four Tops, the Temptations, Smokey Robinson and the Miracles, and the Supremes, to name just a few, had top ten hits, adored by white and black fans alike. And the Beatles themselves repeatedly cited American R&B artists as their inspiration and did covers of "Please Mr. Postman" and "Roll Over, Beethoven."

What the rabid antirock forces of the 1950s had feared had come to pass: white kids, lying in their beds at night or necking with their boyfriends or girlfriends, were having their dreams, hopes, and anxieties—their very autobiographies—constituted in part by black culture through some of its music. Radio once again had become a turnstile between white and black cultures. African American performers—most of whom never got the royalties they deserved—gained entry into white homes through radio. Whites gained access to black music and language, which invigorated their own sense of America and of the possibilities for opposing mainstream culture.

There is, at this point, too little evidence to sustain the suggestion that AM radio's embrace of first R&B and then rock 'n' roll and soul encouraged some white kids to be more sympathetic to and supportive of the civil rights movement. We simply need more data, from public opinion polls, from oral histories, possibly from audience surveys at the time, to document such a claim. But we do know that various white DJs took the lead in the late 1940s and early 1950s in promoting integration through music, and that many of their listeners followed. When white DJs promoted black artists, their record sales increased significantly among white listeners. White musicians and DJs, including Johnny Otis, Alan Freed, and Joe "Butterball" Tamborru, a popular Italian American DJ in Philadelphia who got his start on a black radio station, were antiracist activists who served as role models to many young whites. And by dancing to and singing aloud with "Dock of the Bay" or "Tears on My Pillow" or "You Don't Know Me," some white kids, as Martha Jean Steinberg put it, were able to feel "I understand who you are, although you might be black, you created it from your soul, and I feel what you said."[85]

By the mid- and late 1960s, the Top 40 format, with its tight rotation of hits, rejectable at the touch of the push-button radio on the dashboard, had cultivated a more selective style of listening than provided in the early 1950s. There were so many jingles, ads, and promos to tune out. There were too few songs played too many times—how often could one stand hearing Bobby Goldsboro's "Honey"? Top 40 had become highly predictable and routinized. Yet embedded in that routine was still surprise, a surprise you knew was coming, you just weren't sure when. Then, there it was—your favorite song. Up went the volume, and often up went your voice—*this* song you were going to pay attention to, to really feel. The pleasure of Top 40 lay in anticipation, in knowing you would hear what you wanted, but having that pleasure seem spontaneous and unexpected.[86]

The homogenized programming of Top 40 on AM sought to co-opt, routinize, and commercialize youthful rebellion, and ultimately became so predictable, and so cynical, that young people started turning away, especially as that rebellion became much more politicized. New albums, like *Sgt. Pepper's Lonely Hearts Club Band* or the Doors' debut album, featured long, metaphorical, musically layered songs in stereo that weren't played on the AM format and that commented more pointedly on social conditions. By the late 1960s, especially in cities and college towns around the country, groups of disaffected DJs, music lovers, and community activists rediscovered FM and used this thirty-year-old invention to stage another technological and cultural insurgency in radio. And these FM DJs asked their audiences to start listening again with undivided attention, to cultivate and foreground a new mode of listening, fidelity listening.

Why are so many baby boomers still nostalgic for Wolfman Jack, Dick

Biondi, Alan Freed, Cousin Brucie? Because, despite the taming of the AM format by the early and mid-1960s, people associate listening to those DJs, and the music they played, with that time in their life when they could imagine escaping from what they saw their parents trapped by: "bureaucratic careerism and programmed suburban consumption."[87] Television in the early and mid-1960s rarely gave voice to the possibility of such escape, but that was what Top 40 radio was all about. *American Graffiti* captured the exhilaration of bombing around in your car with the radio turned up, living absolutely in the present, and using that radio to announce and cement a group identity at odds with and hostile to official, grown-up America. At the end of the film, when the closing text tells us that those previously free kids, who spent their evenings in such abandon, were now insurance salesmen or casualties of the Vietnam war, the contrast between the world we imagined, and sometimes created, by listening to the radio and the one we later had to live in was stark indeed. *Leave It to Beaver* or *The Munsters* may indeed take baby boomers back to their youth. But hearing air checks of the Wolfman or Cousin Brucie, intermixed with "Higher and Higher" by Jackie Wilson or "My Girl," because of the way music and sound are so intrinsic to associational memories, opens up a door to the heart, where rebellion, hope, and a furtive racial mixing defined what it meant to be young.

The FM Revolution

I t was nothing like Top 40. A voice as rich and slow as aged honey read the poetry of the Soviet dissident Yevgeny Yevtushenko as rock music played in the background. Then the Doors played for nineteen minutes straight. Another DJ played Bob Dylan's "Subterranean Homesick Blues" and reflected on how its symbolism compared with that in Saul Bellow's *Mr. Sammler's Planet.* The news was read over the guitar strains of Telemann. "Let it happen," urged the quintessentially cool, reassuring voice of Rosko, " 'cause it's gonna happen anyhow . . . reality, eeeemmm-brace it. The mind excursion . . . the true diversion . . . the hippest of all trips . . . join me." If you tuned in to 102.7 on the FM dial in New York City after October of 1967, you heard a new WNEW, and a new format, called free form, underground, or progressive rock.[1]

With our CD players, Walkmen, in-car stereos, and the like forming a taken-for-granted audio environment, it's easy to forget what a complete auditory revolution so many of us experienced in the late 1960s and early 1970s. There was that moment when someone got a new stereo system—maybe you, maybe a friend—and you listened to the lush, layered sound quality and said, "Wow." The new breed of FM DJs on the East and West Coasts were responding to the fact that their listeners—mostly college and high school kids—had started to listen to music differently. But they also pushed their listeners, taught them to hear more carefully, to think about how seemingly different music might go together, and to consider how listening helped achieve a higher level of consciousness. So free form wasn't just a new format. It was a complete repudiation of AM's ceaseless commercials, jingles for "W-A-Beatles-C," and tight rotation play of "Mrs. Brown, You've Got a Lovely Daughter."

This was the FM revolution, another moment in radio's history when uncertainty and flux in the industry allowed for experimentation on the air. The FM revolution was, of course, about many things: changes in technology, stagnation in the industry, regulatory initiatives, the rise of the counterculture in America, and the readiness and desire among young people to hear more challenging and complex music. But at its heart the FM revolution was about an intensified quest for deeper, richer, more nuanced listening. From the end of World War II onward, a subgroup of American men pushed first the phonograph industry and then radio to pay attention—really pay attention—to the aesthetics of listening. When both industries were slow to respond, these men pushed the quest forward themselves. They staged yet another technological insurgency that redefined radio design and use.

Why there was such a hunger among many men in postwar America to hear music in a richer, clearer, more complex fashion is not easy to say. Part of the answer lies in the coming of age of the baby boom. Studies show that as people get older and their listening skills improve, they prefer increasingly complex music, and thus by the late 1960s there was an enormous cohort of people who were ready to move from hearing "Big John" on monaural AM to hearing the Beatles' "A Day in the Life" on stereo FM.[2] But this sensory hunger started earlier, in the late 1940s, and it transformed radio and phonograph equipment, DJ styles and personas, on-air formats, the technology of transmission—in other words, an entire industry. One man, in the 1930s, developed the hardware for this new audio system and another, in the 1960s, invented the software, the programming.

Except for the fact that they both died before their time, the two men could hardly have been more different. E. Howard Armstrong, electronics prodigy and inventor, was a tall and punctilious man, precise and proper in his dress, reserved and often aloof in his manner, a social conservative and a loner. Tom "Big Daddy" Donahue, by contrast, was a 350-pound, long-haired, pot-smoking, bearded bohemian, a social rebel, an irreverent and gregarious man who surrounded himself with people and thumbed his nose at convention. They never met. In January 1954, when Tom Donahue was twenty-nine years old, playing rhythm and blues on AM, Armstrong, then sixty-four, jumped out of his thirteenth-floor apartment to his death in New York.

Yet Armstrong and Donahue were tied by their love of FM radio. Their visions for FM were quite different, even, one could presume, antagonistic. But between the two of them, and with the help of many others, they succeeded in bringing FM out of the shadows where it had been kept (with considerable effort by David Sarnoff and RCA) for over thirty years. Armstrong, after nearly ten years of intense work, invented his system of frequency modulation in the early 1930s. Donahue took this form of radio in 1967 and in the utopian, anti-establishment, and drug-enhanced atmosphere of San Francisco used it to pioneer free-form radio, the revolutionary format that catapulted FM into serious competition with AM and eventually led to AM's displacement.

FM radio, and the new stereo systems that showcased it, represented at that time the ultimate use of technology to magnify, extend, and deepen the capabilities of the human ear. The new technology separated sounds, highlighted how they were layered, made the components of music more distinct and pure. When young people tuned in to certain FM stations in the late 1960s, they entered a brand-new auditory, political, and cultural world. And they went there specifically to indulge in a newly heightened, much more concentrated mode of listening, fidelity listening.

Gone were the AM jocks with their rapid-fire delivery who called listeners "baby" and "cousin," hyped H.I.S. pants and station contests, and played the same twenty songs every hour. Instead the lush, stereophonic sound made possible by the new transmitters and receivers allowed listeners to concentrate on the layering of instruments, voices, and sound effects in a song like the Chambers Brothers' "Time Has Come Today," which stations like KSAN in San Francisco played in its full nine-minute version. The few ads were, quite literally, revolutionary: "Darling, where else would I shop for my records? Only Leopold's has X-69. Now, when I spend my record dollar, I don't want it sitting in the pocket of some fat capitalist, I want it recycled! And that's what X-69 does—it recycles the money into the pockets of community groups. So take it from me, darling, I wouldn't be caught dead in another record store no matter what hypes they used."[3] Sadly, much of this audio revolution has been lost or destroyed.

The long-delayed success of FM built, in part, on the success of the transistor, and also on the postwar hi-fi craze, which eventually led to the unpacking—and enlarging—of radio and the phonograph into stereo components. And it was the interaction between these inventions and the baby boom generation that played a major role in redefining how radio would be used in the late 1960s and early 1970s. The final success of FM in the late 1960s was not just a technical reaction against AM; it was a cultural and political reaction as well.

After over thirty years of marginalization, the trade journal *Broadcasting* announced in September 1973 that "Major Armstrong's baby is a baby no more." Continuing the unfortunate metaphor, it added,

> It is past the toddler days when licensees owned FM stations for their subcarriers which allowed them to beam a Muzak service to area stores. It is

past the pre-teenage days when only the rich and educated knew about FM and could afford to buy a set. It is even through with its period of adolescence when it weathered its identity crises by proving that it was *not* AM through over-blown subjectivism and under-developed selling and production techniques. FM is symbolically twenty-one years old now. It is old enough to drink and suffer the pitfalls of excesses. It is old enough to pay its own way. And, more and more, big enough to do its own thing.[4]

This is the sort of pronouncement Edwin Howard Armstrong had desperately dreamed of reading ever since the 1930s. Now, twenty years after his suicide, the radio industry was marveling at the FM boom of the early 1970s.

A few figures only begin to convey the magnitude of the FM revolution. In 1964 total net FM revenues were $19.7 million. Ten years later that figure had increased thirteen times to $248.2 million. In 1962, according to the FCC, there were 983 commercial FM stations on the air; in 1972 their number stood at 2,328. Four years later there were nearly 3,700 FM stations on the air. By 1972, in cities such as Chicago and Boston, it was estimated that 95 percent of households had FM sets.[5] A few years later that figure was true for much of the country. And soon more people were listening to FM than to AM. After the infamous and tragic fight to the death between Armstrong and Sarnoff over the dissemination of FM radio, Armstrong, at last, had won. Why did FM finally become so appealing? What was it about FM broadcasting that slowly but surely stole listeners away from AM?

While technical refinements, overcrowding in the AM band, and regulatory changes were obviously critical factors in the FM explosion, it was primarily the emergence of a profoundly anticommercial, anticorporate ethos in the 1960s that caused FM to flower. And it was marked especially by a new passion for listening, in particular for fidelity listening, which had been spreading since the late 1940s. This ethos rested on a contempt for what had come to be called mass culture: a disdain for the "vast wasteland" of television and for the formulaic, overly commercialized offerings of radio, and a scorn, first on the part of older intellectuals and later on the part of the counterculture, for the predictability and mindlessness of mainstream popular music.[6]

The quest for fidelity, in other words, was not only a technical quest driving the improvements in FM transmitting and receiving. It was also a cultural and political quest for an alternative medium marked by fidelity to musical creativity and cultural authenticity. The quest for fidelity meant the reduction of noise not just from static but from the hucksterism of America's consumer culture. Once again in radio's history, white middle-class men and boys who were expected and eventually compelled to integrate into institutional bureaucracies, yet who were yearning to defy and postpone such integration, put radio to oppositional, antiestablishment uses.

Certainly FM, itself invented by a man torn by the desire to rebel and to succeed, was one of these technologies. Howard Armstrong had made his fortune in the 1910s and '20s as the technical golden boy of RCA, especially with the success of the superhet receiver in 1924. He and David Sarnoff, then executive vice president of RCA, became friends, and Sarnoff complained frequently about the static that accompanied, and compromised, AM transmissions. Armstrong too, as early as 1922, saw the elimination of static as "the biggest problem" confronting radio.[7] Wasn't there some way to achieve staticless radio? Armstrong, a truly gifted inventor who had been trained in electrical engineering at Columbia, set to work on this problem between 1928 and 1933, when his basic FM patents were awarded.

As its name indicates, FM involves modulating the frequency, rather than the amplitude, of a radio wave. Radio waves themselves carry no information: sounds like voice or music must be superimposed on them, and this was initially achieved by varying—or modulating—the amplitude, or strength, of the carrier wave. Such a wave then fluctuates in amplitude in correspondence with the fluctuations of the music or voice. The problem was, however, that naturally generated electrical disturbances like lightning are produced by similar waves that also vary in amplitude, so they break into and mix easily with AM waves. "Lightning creates radio energy on the same frequency as AM radio," explains Rick Ducey of the National Association of Broadcasters. "So if you are listening to an AM station during a thunderstorm, you hear lightning." As Armstrong's biographer put it, "Any device that passed amplitude variations, passed static." The only other way to vary radio waves was to modulate their frequency—the number of wave cycles radiated per second. Efforts to do this in the early 1920s had produced nothing but distortion.[8]

Armstrong persisted, however, and first developed refined transmitters and receivers that gave him more control over modulating frequency. But he was still working with the transmission model developed for AM, which emphasized confining each signal to as narrow a band of fixed frequencies as possible to reduce interference and heighten the ability to tune between frequencies. In AM broadcasting, for example, there was only a 10-kilohertz spacing between channels: this is a narrow bandwidth, the width of the sound signal that is superimposed on the carrier wave.[9] By 1932 Armstrong abandoned this model and decided to try using a much wider band of frequencies for radio transmissions. The principle was simple: the wider band of frequencies provided a higher signal-to-noise ratio, meaning a stronger signal and minimal interference, and it allowed for high-fidelity sound reproduction and greater suppression of static. Armstrong increased the bandwidth to 200 kilo-hertz, a twentyfold increase over the AM model. Conceptually and technically, this was a total departure from accepted wisdom and practice. And it worked, brilliantly.

This move to a significantly wider bandwidth was undoubtedly Armstrong's most important discovery in his work on FM. He achieved a level of clarity and lack of static interference unattainable with AM. In fact, the new system was virtually immune to atmospheric and man-made interference, as well as to interference from other stations operating on the same frequency.[10]

But to have the space he needed for FM, Armstrong had to move up the spectrum to the VHF (very high frequencies) region, 30 to 300 megahertz. (Remember that AM was in the lower, medium-wave frequencies of 550 to 1600 kilohertz. FM would have worked in the AM band, but luckily it was already taken.) This move provided FM with advantages and disadvantages, all of which ensured its superior sound fidelity. The trade-off with VHF propagation is that there is less interference at these frequencies—lightning and sunspots, for example, don't create energy in the FM part of the spectrum—but the broadcast range is shorter, usually restricted to 60 miles or less. Because VHF transmission relies on ground waves, which follow a line-of-sight path and are not reflected or refracted by the ionosphere, FM signals don't travel farther at night, the way AM signals do. But then they also can't be interfered with at night by stations on the same frequency that might be a state or two away. Some have argued that if AM had been moved to the VHF band, and had wider channels like FM, it could have achieved much of the sound fidelity success that FM did.[11]

Armstrong first demonstrated FM to Sarnoff, now president of RCA, in 1933, and the next year RCA gave him space at the top of the Empire State Building to continue his experiments. Antenna height was especially important in FM transmission, because it increased the distance to the horizon and thus the station's range, and Armstrong reportedly succeeded in broadcasting over 80 miles from the top of what was then the tallest building in the city. But in 1936 Sarnoff asked Armstrong to remove his equipment and devoted the Empire State site to the development of television. Sarnoff was determined that RCA be first with television, a breakthrough technology that he believed would supplant radio. A corporate shift to FM would have required everyone to buy new radios, hardly a welcome prospect during the Depression, when disposable income had plummeted. If NBC switched to FM but CBS and Mutual didn't, RCA's sales and legal departments feared that people, not wanting to invest in a whole new system, would simply stick with or turn to the competition. And if RCA pushed for FM instead of television, Sarnoff feared the company would be scooped by its competition, which he would not tolerate.[12]

But Armstrong didn't see things this way and spent the rest of his life advancing a conspiracy theory about RCA quashing his invention. Armstrong assumed that Sarnoff was simply trying to protect AM against competition from FM, and, worse, he saw Sarnoff as trying to suppress a superior method of broadcasting. By 1935, with Armstrong's technical vision and Sarnoff's corporate agenda moving in opposite directions, Armstrong's attitude toward his erstwhile corporate benefactor soured. With RCA's decision that year to spend $1 million developing television while doing much behind the scenes to ignore and even, at times, thwart FM, Armstrong took an increasingly anti-industry stance.

This stance was not without its contradictions. Armstrong wanted to expose what he saw as the technical myopia and cynicism of the corporate giant RCA; he was willing to do this, however, with the help of other established corporations such as General Electric and with the upstart Yankee Network of New England. In the summer of 1939, when Armstrong began broadcasting FM on a regular schedule from W2XMN in Alpine, New Jersey, the Yankee Network established experimental stations near Worcester, Massachusetts, and then on Mount Washington in New Hampshire. General Electric publicly endorsed FM and began manufacturing receivers. And Armstrong launched a one-man public relations and marketing campaign, touring the country and speaking to a variety of groups on the superiority of FM. In 1939 the FCC allocated thirteen channels to FM, and in 1940 it designated the FM band at 42 to 50 megahertz. By the fall of 1939 the commission had received 150 applications for FM stations; three years later over forty FM stations were in regular operation.[13] Some of these were independent; others were owned by AM stations. And so, despite a withdrawal of financial support, public denigration of FM's performance, and lobbying with the FCC to keep FM out of the spectrum, RCA failed to stop FM completely.

In 1945, however, after a year of hearings, the FCC moved FM to a higher position in the spectrum—to its current allocation of 88 to 108 megahertz, so that the 42- to 50-megahertz slot could be freed up for television. Debate still continues on how great a role the warring parties RCA and CBS played in this shift, with some scholars arguing that RCA was simply looking out for its television interests and wasn't paying much attention to FM. But Armstrong and his partisans saw the reallocation as yet another effort to thwart his invention. What this meant, of course, was that all prewar transmitters and the approximately half a million receivers owned by enthusiasts were now obsolete.[14] In addition, the FCC ruled that television would use FM for its sound transmission, but RCA—unlike Westinghouse, GE, and Zenith—refused to pay Armstrong royalties for using his invention. Armstrong sued, and the protracted and nasty legal battle, coupled with FM's slump in the early 1950s, prompted his suicide in 1954. So from the beginnings of its technical, business, and regulatory history, FM was an antiestablishment technology marginalized by vested corporate interests. It is not surprising, then, that FM's renaissance would be pioneered by those very much outside of—even at odds with—the media culture those corporations had created.

The immediate catalyst for the FM explosion in the 1960s came from the FCC. Since the late 1940s many FM outlets owned by AM stations simply broadcast the same programming their AM parents did. But by the early 1960s FCC Commissioners Robert E. Lee and Kenneth Cox argued that frequencies had become so scarce in the face of increasing demand that duplication was "a luxury we can't afford." In 1962 the FCC had ordered a freeze on AM license applications while it tried to address the overcrowding in the spectrum. The solution it chose was to promote more aggressive commercial exploitation of the FM band. In May of 1964 the commission issued its nonduplication ruling, which was to take effect in January 1967. In cities of more than 100,000 people, radio stations with both AM and FM could not duplicate more than 50 percent of their programming on both bands simultaneously. Although the edict affected only 337 of the country's 1,560 commercial FM stations (and of these, 137 had already been programming separately), it nonetheless helped promote much more enterprising exploitation of the medium. Between 1964 and 1967, 500 new commercial FM stations and 60 educational stations took to the air.[15]

Obviously, the FM boom was not prompted by these regulatory changes alone. Technological and economic factors played a role as well. In the late 1940s and early 1950s, about 80 percent of the FM stations were owned by AM stations in the same market. Because of the programming duplication then allowed, FM sounded just like AM; the only differences were that there was no static and the receivers cost more. The few independent FM stations broadcast either background or classical music and featured few if any commercials. By 1957 there were only 530 FM stations on the air, 86 fewer than five years earlier. The FM audience consisted primarily of those devotees to the classical music stations that broadcast in the country's largest cities. As *Business Week* noted, "The exclusiveness of the programming and the high cost of FM receivers kept audiences small."[16]

These early FM devotees were usually hi-fi fanatics, a subgroup of electrical tinkerers that emerged in the late 1940s and 1950s. They gave top priority to two things: technical one-upmanship and the richest audio fidelity possible.

By January of 1957—a bit late, given the ten-year history of the fad—*Time* sarcastically exclaimed that "a new neurosis has been discovered, audiophilia, or the excessive passion for hi-fi sound and equipment." Sufferers were usually "middle-aged, male and intelligent, drawn largely from professions requiring highly conscientious performance." Six years earlier *The New Yorker* had described the hi-fi craze as the fastest growing hobby in America. As early as 1952 sales of hi-fi equipment to audiophiles had climbed to $70 million a year, and sales figures were still soaring. And this was before corporations began to manufacture and market sets for the general, nontinkering public. By the mid-1950s the phonograph industry, which had, according to a September 1957 article in *Business Week*, "once looked down on hi-fi fans as mere fanatics," was scrambling to meet the new demand.[17]

The hi-fi craze of the late 1940s and 1950s had been started by tinkerers dissatisfied with the sound quality available in commercially manufactured phonographs. They began assembling their own "rigs" out of separate components, paying special attention to and customizing the wiring that connected the parts into a whole. The proper matching and balancing of components was critical to success. The goal was to reproduce in one's living room the way classical music sounded in a concert hall. The most sensitive human ear can hear sounds ranging from 20 to 20,000 cycles per second. Most old 78 rpm records could play up to only 7,500 cps, and AM radio could reach a maximum of 10,000 but usually broadcast at 5,000 cps. Audiophiles wanted to push beyond these ranges, which cut off the highs as well as the lows of most music. "Hi-fi is, in fact, an attitude," reported *Time*, "a kind of passion to reproduce music exactly as it sounded in its natural setting."[18]

This quest for fidelity gained impetus from several key developments just during and after World War II. The wartime shortage of shellac, the principal ingredient of records at that time, prompted research into other materials. The result was the introduction in 1946 of the vastly superior Vinylite. Columbia records used the material to introduce its new 33⅓ rpm long-playing record in the spring of 1948. Using considerably finer grooves than the 78 rpm, the LP provided three to four times the playing time with considerably reduced surface noise and additional range and clarity. The LP could record up to 12,000 cps, twice the range of the shellac 78 record. In addition, the shift to magnetic tape in the late 1940s dramatically enriched the quality of recording. Yet most existing phonographs failed to do justice to the new LPs.[19]

During the war many servicemen and civilians were trained in the fundamentals of electronics in order to participate in the manufacture, installation, and operation of radar and other communication equipment. Those stationed in Europe, especially in England, became acquainted with the striking superiority of sound engineering abroad and the significantly higher quality of music reproduction and phonograph equipment. After the war some of these men brought imported audio components home, while others bought surplus amplifiers and other kinds of electronic gear from the government. Small electronics companies also began to improve amplifiers, speakers, and other components. Armed with their recent training, soldering irons, miles of wires, and a host of experimental circuit designs, these men formed the initial core of the hi-fi enthusiasts who sparked the skyrocketing component parts trade of the late 1940s and early 1950s. The custom-built sets they assembled often provided twice the fidelity of reproduction that one could get from the most expensive commercial system, and for one-half to one-third the price. Magazines from *Popular Mechanics* to *The Saturday Review* began to run regular features on hi-fi construction, musical developments, and the intense technical debates that raged among hobbyists. In 1951 a new quarterly called *High Fidelity* began publication, and in one year its circulation leapt from zero to 20,000.[20]

The hobby's rate of growth was breathtaking, producing enormous sales for the small companies willing to cater to audiophiles by selling high-quality components. By 1953 approximately one million Americans had invested in custom-built sets. Firms such as Fisher Radio Corporation and Altec Lansing reported that sales had increased by twenty times between 1947 and 1952. The quality of sound on these sets often produced instant converts: once people heard a record on a custom-built hi-fi, they had to have a set of their own. For those incapable of building their own sets, small firms such as Electronic Workshop would install a customized set. One repeatedly noted characteristic of the audiophile was that he was never satisfied; he was constantly striving for greater fidelity and spent endless hours and hundreds of dollars a year trying to approximate perfection. He was also completely disdainful of corporate America's audio offerings.[21]

As with amateur radio operators, there were barriers to entry to this hi-fi fraternity. Technical knowledge separated outsiders from those in the know. So did language, as a whole new vocabulary containing words like *woofer, tweeter, preamp,* and *equalizer* made discussions among enthusiasts unintelligible to outsiders. Especially alienated were women, who were not just excluded from such technical activities but had to put up with obsessive monomaniacal tinkering that filled living rooms with boxes and wires and covered rugs with gobs of solder. Women began publishing articles such as "The High Fidelity Wife, or a Fate Worse than Deaf" and "I Am a Hi-Fi Widow."[22]

While some hi-fi enthusiasts spent more time tinkering with their rigs than listening to the music they produced, what bound many of these men together was an obsession with musical authenticity. There were, of course, many audiophiles whose interest in music was minimal; it was the tinkering alone that mattered to them, and after hours of work they would celebrate how accurately they had made a train whistle sound on their rigs. But the hi-fi craze also defined musical appreciation as a masculine enterprise best cultivated by those with specialized, often technical knowledge who could truly discern good music, not just with their hearts but with their heads. Hi-fi enthusiasm allowed men to retreat from the wartime application of technology to cultural destruction and use their electronic expertise in the service of beauty and cultural preservation. Through this hobby, so firmly embedded in the masculine province of electronics, men could indulge in the pleasures of music while warding off suggestions of effeminacy. With charts, circuit diagrams, and potentiometers, enthusiasts could quantify music, move it from the emotional to the rational realm, make its appreciation objective. Although the composing, conducting, and performing of music had always been dominated by men, there was, simultaneously, an association for American men between the love of certain kinds of music—especially opera and classical music—and effeminacy. The strong strain of anti-intellectualism in American culture that regarded the "egghead" as effete contributed to the sometimes uneasy position of the musical devotee. For men who loved music but were eager to avoid such associations, technical tinkering was one way to resolve the contradictions.

The connections such devotees made between the feminine and the inauthentic and, therefore, the inferior became clear when the more entrenched manufacturers such as Magnavox and RCA sought to sell preassembled hi-fis to the general public and, particularly, to women. Entering the market belatedly in 1953 and 1954, these companies enclosed their hi-fis in finished cabinets that matched existing furniture designs such as French provincial or colonial. Audiophiles denounced the new equipment as overpriced, inferior, too dedicated to appearance, and not even meriting the label hi-fi, because it didn't come close to the rigid specifications of enthusiasts.[23]

Hi-fi enthusiasts began to tinker with FM, and others bought the newly available sets, especially imported ones. An FM channel's capacity was twenty times that of an AM channel, and it allowed for a tripling of sound fidelity, from AM's 5,000 to an unprecedented 15,000 cycles per second. These early listeners to FM stations were generally more educated than the average American and tended to have "high culture" tastes, preferring FM's music, intellectual fare, and lack of commercialism to the usual AM programming. Another characteristic many of these enthusiasts shared was a deep aversion to television. A study done for the National Association of FM Broadcasters in the winter of 1963–64 concluded that "FM penetration and FM listening both increase as household income and head-of-the-house education increase." Those homes that accounted for the bulk of FM listening also watched the least amount of TV and, in fact, listened to FM rather than watched TV during the evening prime-time hours.[24]

Early FM listeners were concentrated in major metropolitan areas such as New York, Chicago, Los Angeles, Washington, and Boston. They listened primarily to "middle of the road" music, from Frank Sinatra and Mantovani to Dave Brubeck. But in the largest metropolitan areas there was greater diversity in programming and a devoted listenership to classical music.[25] Again the quest for fidelity really was twofold: the technical quest for purer, richer sound reproduction was deeply intertwined with an aesthetic, cultural quest for an alternative media outpost, a refuge that maintained fidelity to imagined precommercial values. This mind-set, which was adopted and reshaped by the next generation of rebellious young men, helped spawn a new group of audio outlaws, the underground FM programmers of the late 1960s and 1970s.

In the immediate aftermath of the FCC's reallocation of the FM band in 1945, sales of FM receivers fell, and in 1949 over 200 FM stations went off the air. Beginning in 1958, however, FM experienced a resurgence. The number of stations began to increase, and so did the audience. The AM spectrum had gotten so crowded, especially in major cities, that by the late 1950s there were few or no slots left. The only way to start a new station was to use FM. The slackening of the TV boom made investment money available for FM. And the reduced price and improved quality of FM receivers, particularly those imported from Germany, and later Japan, made FM more accessible and attractive to potential listeners. Between 1960 and 1966 the annual sales of FM radio receivers increased more than fivefold, and by 1967 over one-third of all radio sets sold were equipped with FM reception. In 1960 there were approximately 6.5 million households with FM; by 1966 that number had soared to 40 million.[26]

Increasing numbers of FM stations also had a compelling new feature: they were broadcasting in stereo. In 1961 the FCC authorized stereo broadcasting of FM, and 57 stations tried it. By 1970, 668 FM stations broadcast in stereo. (The first FM car radios made their debut in 1963.)[27] This desire for a more pure, lifelike sound, for a sound that could replicate actually listening to a symphony or a quartet or a soprano live, drove one of the major technological revolutions of the 1960s and '70s, the transformation of the phonograph into the stereo system, which delivered two channels of sound. When albums were recorded in stereo, technicians divided the music between two tracks, each of which ran along the grooves of the record. Each track then came out through a separate speaker. With, say, the horns on the left track and the piano on the right, listeners got a more geological sense of music: it had levels, certain seams stood out, the bedrock wasn't uniform, all the layers mattered.

This revolution was deeply interconnected with the proliferation of FM listeners and stations, because these new stereos featured extremely sensitive FM receivers that were now connected to two separate and often large speakers. Instead of radios or phonographs, listeners now had sound *systems,* each of which consisted of an amplifier and a tuner, a turntable, the speakers, and sometimes a tape player as well. Those who really wanted to be encased in music could also buy stereo headphones. Now listeners could feel music reverberating from all sides, and the controls for treble and bass, monaural and stereo, balance, loudness, and so forth gave them much more ability to customize the sounds they heard. A masculine, hi-fi aesthetic won out in terms of how these systems looked: performance was critical, and such sets "made little concession to style." No encasement in French provincial cabinetry here: systems were series of flat metal boxes connected by wires that advertised the importance of achieving audio fidelity over conforming to suburban decorating sensibilities.[28] The workshop defied, and moved into, the living room.

Another major factor would transform FM's content and appeal: the rise of 1960s youth culture. Bound by rock and folk music, contemptuous of the commercialization that seemed to infuse and debase every aspect of American culture, and hostile to bourgeois values and the profit motive, members of that loose yet cohesive group known as the counterculture were revolutionizing almost every aspect of American culture. And music was central to their individual and generational identity, their sense of having a different, more enhanced consciousness about society, politics, and self-awareness.

It is important to emphasize that like the other FM listeners of the early 1960s, many of the young people who turned to FM in this period also scorned television and watched very little of it. They too were contemptuous of what had come to be called mass culture. Separated by age and possibly by political orientation, these early devotees of FM nonetheless shared a vision of what culture, and radio, should and should not be. They also shared a devotion to musical fidelity, whether they preferred listening to Mozart or Jimi Hendrix. But they would come to be pitted against each other, as competition over FM stations and over the disposable incomes of young people began, in certain markets, to push classical stations out in favor of rock stations.[29]

Particularly hateful to these young people was what they saw as the lockstep conformity of American life, which made everything from work to popular music joyless, unspontaneous, and false. They wanted their lives to be less programmed, less predictable. They wanted to see and hear things in a much less mediated yet sensually heightened fashion. To achieve this transcendence of bourgeois constraints on lifestyle and the senses, many began doing drugs, most frequently marijuana and hashish but also psychedelics.

At the end of the twentieth century the official demonization of all drugs (and of the '60s) has imposed a censorship on any discussion of drugs that isn't negative. But with radio (and in other areas as well), drugs helped make history, and in this case history for the better. The use of marijuana and psychedelics increased the appreciation of and demand for improved clarity and richness in sound reproduction. *The New York Times* reported in 1970 that "drug use was central to the listening experience" of the free-form audience.[30] And the sounds these young people were listening to, especially folk music, blues, and rock, gave expression to their critique of mainstream culture rarely heard on television or radio. It is no surprise that when some of these young people, primarily men, worked their way into FM radio stations they deliberately used their positions to challenge every aspect of what people heard and how they heard it on the dominant medium, AM radio.

At this time AM radio was characterized by incessant commercials, songs no longer than three minutes, and repeated promotional jingles. Tom Donahue, one of the maverick pioneers of underground radio, summed up the counterculture assessment of such broadcasting: "The bulk of popular music radio programming in this country is devoted to absurd jingles . . . babbling hysterical disc jockeys. . . . The tempo is Go! Go! Go! The air is replete with such blather as 'here comes another twin spin sound sandwich' and 'here's a blast from the past, a moldy oldie that'll always last.' Top 40 radio, as we know it today and have known it for the last ten years, is dead, and its rotting corpse is stinking up the airwaves." He added, "How many goddamn times can you play Herman's Hermits and still feel good about what you do?"[31]

Donahue is generally credited as being the "father" of free-form FM. Tony Pigg, who had the choice 6:00 to 9:00 P.M. slot on KYA before he, too, moved to free form, suggests that Larry Miller, who was doing a late-night free-form show on KMPX in 1967, also deserves credit as a pioneer of the form. A former AM DJ known as "Big Daddy," Donahue had been one of those white DJs in the late 1940s and early 1950s who played rhythm and blues, initially in Washington, D.C. Forced to quit a job in Philadelphia because of the payola scandals, he ended up in San Francisco, where he had also become a major Top 40 radio star on KYA. A story told by Donahue's widow, Raechel, and their friends from the time describes an evening in 1967 with people sitting around, stoned, listening to the Doors' first album. Donahue asked why people couldn't hear that kind of music on the radio. More to the point, he wondered, why didn't DJs play records the way people listened to them, instead of playing record, commercial, commercial? "We gotta go paint the sky blue for someone, baby," Raechel recalls his saying.[32]

The next day Donahue called all the FM stations in town until he found one whose phone had been disconnected. He located the owner and reminded him that there, in San Francisco, they were at the center of the counterculture movement, where thousands would turn up for a Grateful Dead concert yet where no radio station catered to that market. On April 7, 1967, Tom and Raechel Donahue brought four cardboard boxes filled with their albums to KMPX and went on the air. Donahue opened the show with "This is Tom Donahue, I'm here to clear up your face and mess up your mind."[33] Donahue played "sets" of three or four songs in a row, and he didn't talk over the beginnings or endings of the records as AM DJs often did, because that corrupted the music and the listening process.

Some of the earliest of these "underground" or "progressive rock" stations, as they were called, that went on the air between 1967 and 1969, in addition to KMPX and then KSAN in San Francisco, were KPPC in Pasadena, KMET in Los Angeles, WOR and WNEW in New York, and WBCN in Boston. The underground stations threw all the conventional industry rules and responses out the window. They eliminated advertising jingles, the repeated announcing of call letters, and the loud, insistent, firecracker delivery of AM disc jockeys. They repudiated conventional market research, which sought to identify the "lowest common denominator" and thus reinforced the predictable repetition of Top 40 AM. As one program director of a progressive rock station acknowledged, his market research consisted of seeing who was appearing at the Fillmore in San Francisco and "asking around among college students." DJs segued from one song to the next, also "unheard of in those days," recalled Tony Pigg, since on AM you spoke or played a jingle after every record. Instead, they organized a series of songs into sets (like bands in a club did) or "sweeps," some of them thirty minutes long. At the end of the set there were long "backsells," or recaps of all the songs, performers, and album titles. Then they would "double-spot"—playing two to four commercials back-to-back, a "cardinal sin" on AM. College stations around the country, not surprisingly, pioneered and embraced the underground format, which in many ways wasn't really yet a format since it allowed for so much experimentation. Listeners—most of whom were educated, affluent young men—were extremely loyal to such stations.[34]

Underground radio, in the words of one industry analyst, "was the first really new programming idea in ten years."[35] Instead of being required to play only from a tight playlist determined by a programming manager, disc jockeys on progressive rock stations were given wide latitude to play what they wanted. They also sought and responded to listener requests in a more spontaneous fashion. They avoided most Top 40 music and the playing of singles. Instead, a low-key, at times somnambulant voice talked to the audience in what was called a "laid-back" and intimate fashion in between long segments of music that included album cuts of rock, blues, folk, jazz, international, and even, on occasion, classical music.

Once again styles of radio announcing changed as these DJs sought to cultivate a more genuine, less stilted form of address. The affectations, swooping voices, screams, faux slang, and pumped-up vocal projection of Top 40 DJs ("the stilts," as they were called) that had once seemed so rebellious, youthful, and intimate on the air now seemed contrived and phony. As WBCN's Charles Laquidara put it, "We didn't think of ourselves as radio announcers or deejays. We were ourselves, guys who communicated as individuals, not radio personas. Deejays were those fucking hype-heads on AM Top 40." But in their efforts to become "anti-announcer announcers," these DJs developed their own very particular and somewhat set style. The pace was slow and subdued, and the DJ spoke into the mike as if he were chatting with you in bed. It was very important to sound "mellow," as listeners came to identify this vocal quality as being the most authentic. More to the point, many sounded—and were—stoned, and the inside jokes about how especially great a song sounded or having the munchies brought knowing listeners in on the secret. Cousin Brucie wrote that "the best FM announcers sounded like they'd been awakened from a deep sleep, as if they could hardly concentrate long enough to read a spot before they nodded off. . . . Where the most successful jocks on AM sounded like they'd love a piece of your bubble gum, the rising stars of FM sounded like they knew where you kept your stash of pot."[36]

Progressive FM stations especially delighted in playing the longer cuts of songs, some of them as long as twelve or twenty minutes, for an audience who could hear such music nowhere else on the spectrum. These listeners were usually also the fans of new rock and folk groups such as Richie Havens, Big Brother and the Holding Company, the Grateful Dead, and Cream, whose albums were selling well and concerts selling out but who couldn't get airplay on AM. Some programs were self-consciously cerebral, citing poetry and literature, commenting on contemporary politics, analyzing the structure of the music.

DJs delighted in indulging in auditory surrealism when they juxtaposed two pieces of music that normally would never be played on the same station together, not to mention back-to-back. The free-form DJ Jim Ladd, in his memoir *Radio Waves*, emphasizes that many of the DJs and their listeners regarded the format as an auditory art form. "I held the medium itself in a kind of sacred regard. . . . It was a wondrous time of learning and adventure without restriction, a time of total freedom on the air." DJs like Ladd created their shows by listening to one song or a set of songs and concentrating on what would be the best song to play next. "Once you tapped into the muse, you could play your radio show like an instrument. You could make your own music, choose just the right tune to strike a specific chord, find that certain combination of lyrics that tied the songs together in a thematic way. . . . I immersed myself in the music and let it carry me away."[37]

These DJs had to have a highly developed aural memory for pitches and tones and be able to draw from this aural catalog at will to produce sound combinations that were simultaneously surprising and not jarring. Keeping such a vast musical library in your head and drawing from it while you were on the air required both concentration and playfulness. Rosko of WNEW emphasized how he played music "for sound . . . to create an audio picture." Segues were often based on how the closing notes or mood of one song fit with the opening notes of another. For example, Rosko acknowledged thirty years after the height of free form that few DJs would follow Dylan's "Subterranean Homesick Blues" with the Supremes' "You Keep Me Hangin' On." But Rosko did because he felt that the opening guitars of the Supremes' song provided a great tonal transition from the Dylan song and shifted the mood, but not too radically. Rosko reportedly didn't put a record on the second turntable until the first record was already playing so he could listen and think about what would be an exciting auditory match. "That's working without a net," noted Pete Fornatale admiringly; "that's an artist."[38]

Tony Pigg, who started at KSAN in 1967, recalled this process with palpable fondness: "I'd sit there while a record was playing and say, 'What's gonna sound good after this, what's gonna take this feeling further or embellish this or change it in a way that I want it to change?' And it was just so much fun to do that." Especially successful segues would give him chills and goose bumps. Audiences felt the same way. What are we to make of such reports, of such pleasure in creating audio montages that matched tones, instruments, rhythms, harmonies? People who imitated these DJs at home by making their own audiotapes know, viscerally, this joyous satisfaction.

What Tony Pigg describes is how essential anticipation and repetition are to pleasurable music listening. Active, engaged listening is led by anticipation, and we anticipate only what we already know: our brains reach out and latch on to the elements of music that are familiar. Once the auditory system is excited by certain pitches, it activates the limbic system, which governs our emotions. The limbic system wants to sustain this pleasurable, newly heightened state, so it asks for similar sounds. So there seems to be a cognitive pleasure when a song that ended with mandolins is immediately followed by a song that begins with mandolins. Even moving between songs with common bass lines—which many listeners don't consciously pay attention to—is pleasurable because bass lines carry the energy and are the foundation on which songs are built. One song would set up musical anticipations in the DJ and his listeners; the next song satisfied them. At the same time, research has shown that cognitively people also like surprise; we like music that somewhat defies our expectations, that is slightly challenging. Without studying cognitive psychology, Pigg and others knew this: their rule was that "if you were going to play a bunch of stuff that was new, you had to include something familiar or you'd drive people away."[39] So the joy in putting together the perfect segue that Tony Pigg, Jim Ladd, and others describe is the pleasure in finding this seemingly perfect balance between the familiar and the unexpected, and when such matches occur we celebrate cognitively and emotionally.

Ladd freely acknowledges that smoking pot between sets helped inspire his choice of music and give psychic and artistic direction to the night's program. He also insists that listening to this music stoned provided a powerful point of connection between himself and FM listeners. "Having listened to the Jefferson Airplane after visiting the psychedelic pharmacy myself, I not only had an alternative point of view, I had a bond of sorts with everyone else who had heard 'White Rabbit' as something more than just a nice three-minute song with a good beat." Getting stoned altered people's modes of emotional and cognitive processing; it allowed listeners to wipe the sensory slate clean. You broke away from all those daily tasks—planning meals, getting to work or school on time, balancing your checkbook—that required so much automatic and overlapping processing, and focused more intensely on a single processing mode, the pure act of listening to music.[40]

Progressive rock stations also specialized in information on the antiwar movement and countercultural activities in general. Here is a news broadcast from Tom Donahue on KSAN: "The news today, friends, is obscene, dirty, immoral, filthy, smutty news. But if you cook it up in a brownie, it doesn't taste all that bad. Meanwhile, the Viet Nam war is still going on and man, that's obscene." There was also a strong emphasis on community issues affecting the young, and the news and public service announcements emphasized the station's organic relationship to its locale. KSAN also offered, as a public service, paraquat alerts and drug testing: listeners could send samples of their drugs to Pharm Chem, then call up and find out if the drugs were tainted with the herbicide used to kill off marijuana plants. At other times listeners were urged to "go to Golden Gate Park at 10:00 A.M. to sign a petition" promoting the legalization of marijuana. "If you're in the Venice area and haven't learned the scene," advised B. Mitchell Reed on KMET in Los Angeles, "there's free food in Venice Beach at the first pagoda in Venice, bring your own utensils." Bob Coburn on WDAI in Chicago talked about different men's names and how it was handy to have shorter versions, like Bob for Robert. "Richard is the best, 'cause you can be Richard or Dick, which is good because, after all, our president is a dick."[41]

The ads were, well, mind-blowing by today's standards. One record shop in LA, the Music Revolution, advertised that it gave out free rolling papers to everyone who came in, whether or not they bought something. Jeans West was "a fun place to drop by and get it on." Another ad, for Leopold's records, wasn't really an ad at all. "We at Leopold's sell records," it began, "not just to move plastic, but as a means to an end, to get funds to help worthy projects in Berkeley and the Bay Area. To the same end, the Bangladesh concert was put on. There's a serious question whether the funds raised ever got to Bangladesh, to the people who were really suffering and who are still suffering," the ad warned. It then asked listeners to write to Ron Dellums and ask for a congressional investigation of what happened to the $30 million raised. It gave out Dellums's address and asked that listeners "please help."[42]

Fidelity listening—a new, avid, artistic celebration of sound itself—was what FM DJs promoted and what listeners sought. The sheer, sensual pleasure of diving into music, not just to memorize lyrics or dance to a beat but to concentrate on particular tones, on the interplay between instruments, on the layering of the sounds, was at the heart of free-form radio. DJs emphasized the centrality of the ear to listeners' cognitive, emotional, and political lives. Al Collins on KMET in L.A. said he was ready with "some sounds for your translucent lobes." Tom Donahue introduced "Darkness, Darkness" by the Youngbloods with "I'm looking forward to the day I can hear this in stereo, 'cause it must be unreal." Record stores and stereo companies were the primary FM advertisers, and DJs urged their listeners to buy eight-track systems for their cars because "there's no reason to deprive yourself of the very best music while you're on the road." With the new equipment, "you'll be adding a lot of great sound to your life." One of the main purposes of listening was to achieve a higher, more intense level of consciousness, to go on what Rosko at WNEW in New York called "the mind excursion, the true diversion, the hippest of all trips."[43]

The FM revolution coincided with—and promoted—the remasculinization of rock music, which relied in part on a celebration of male musical virtuosity, especially with the guitar. One must be careful here, because there has been, in rock criticism, an equation made between overcommercialism and the "feminization" of rock versus "real" rock, which involves male singer-songwriters, eschews selling out to the mass market, and is allegedly more authentic. Music of special appeal to adolescent girls, like the girl groups of the early 1960s or the Spice Girls of the 1990s, has been routinely dismissed by rock critics, not explicitly because it involves female performers (although that's clearly key) but because it is allegedly crassly commercial and overly concerned with love and relationships. What is ignored, using the "authenticity" criteria, is how such music speaks to girls' lived experiences in patriarchal societies. And why anyone might think that "Nowhere to Run" or "Will You Love Me Tomorrow?" is commercially crass but "Stairway to Heaven" isn't remains a mystery to me. So I am hardly interested in reproducing hierarchies that insist that male rock is at the top of some imagined artistic pyramid.

Rather, what I think is important to note about the marriage between FM radio and rock is the way that it further sanctioned musical appreciation for men and allowed them to claim the skills of musical artistry (including writing lyrics) and fidelity listening as distinctly masculine. The obsession among some men over the size of their speakers—some of which approximated walk-in freezers—suggested that more than audio fidelity was at stake. Certainly rock 'n' roll had become "a man's world" in a way that marginalized and often exploited women. The music scholar Simon Frith notes how "the male-ness of the world of rock is reflected in its lyrics, with their assertions of male supremacy, narcissism, and self-pity." The new rock world, with a few exceptions like Janis Joplin and Grace Slick, was dominated by male rebels and iconoclasts—Jimi Hendrix, Jim Morrison, Eric Clapton, Bob Dylan—who personified the equation between musical creativity and unconventionality. Women, argues Frith, were seen as the "embodiment of convention," who represented the home, being tied down, and the suffocation of the male rocker's independence. Male rock stars, and the free-form formats that featured them, celebrated detachment from the daily routines that trapped most people in predictable lives.[44]

At the same time, of course, one of the reasons these male rock stars were so successful was that they frequently plumbed the depths of their emotions in their music while also writing often surreal or, at the very least, highly metaphorical lyrics. FM free-form stereo radio insisted, through the way its DJs talked about and played this music, that the emotional and the cerebral could be, and needed to be, fused through the act of listening.

Powerful contradictions about masculinity, which were careening around the culture at the height of the Vietnam war, were finessed on free-form radio, and an alternative version of manhood radiated from the format. This kind of radio rejected the dominant definitions of masculinity enshrined in John Wayne movies and the rhetoric of William Westmoreland. Men were still men, of course: in much of the discourse of free-form radio and rock, men were seen as more technically masterful, intellectually superior, politically more astute, and aesthetically more developed than most women, even though little of this was ever explicitly stated. Men were the alienated artists who saw and expressed the truth; women were the audience that appreciated them. And heterosexual male prowess was, more than ever perhaps, the centerpiece of male mastery.

Yet traditional male attributes, such as physical strength, the desire to fight, the violent assertion of mastery over nature, acquisitive and competitive individualism, and hyperrationality were all repudiated in the fusion of rock and free-form radio. Of course, such countercultural reformulations of masculinity circulated throughout the culture in movies, books, and television. But FM radio, with its personal address to the listener, its overwhelmingly male roster of DJs and musicians, and its insistence that you consciously access and link your emotions and your thoughts through fidelity listening, provided, I would argue, an especially powerful site for the reimagination of masculinity in the late 1960s and early 1970s.

By the 1970s this proliferation of stations and upheavals in program formats drove owners of FM stations to make a profit and then to maximize that profit. It is important to remember that the FM spectrum in the late 1960s was inhabited by nonprofit college stations, by independent underground stations, by other independent stations run by those much more interested in profits than politics, and by the networks with a bottom-line mentality and stockholders to please. They all faced a vexing economic and cultural tension surrounding FM. FM had become so popular, after all, because of its fewer commercials, so determining how to maximize profits was tricky. As *Broadcasting* noted in October of 1974, FM accounted for one-third of all radio listening but only 14 percent of all radio revenues.[45] And as FM stations proliferated in the early 1970s, there was increased competition for the same audiences.

One reason that so much experimentation had been possible with FM was precisely that advertisers exerted very little influence over the medium. Prejudiced by the notion that "FM listening was the province of eggheads and Hi-Fi buffs," advertisers had eschewed FM until the early 1970s, despite industry efforts to promote the FM audience as highly desirable because it was upscale. As one ad executive put it in 1967, "There is no real hard information on the FM audience, its composition or its buying power. For some time now it [FM] has been good for such things as airlines, luxury items and the like, but we still aren't sure whether we can risk selling soap or food in the medium." WNEW in New York knew its listeners were primarily students, and the station successfully convinced coffee companies to advertise to the all-nighter crowd. But this was based on instinct and visits to local campuses.[46] The incursion of more systematic market research into the FM industry to ascertain just who this audience was and how it could be captured began to rein in the diversity and experimentation of the late 1960s.

In fact, encouraging the proliferation of the more free-form underground format was deemed strategically unwise by network executives, many of whom regarded these as nothing more than "hippie stations." "We think we know how many people there are who want this kind of radio and statistically there aren't enough to make our stations profitable," noted an ABC executive. "We could not continue to operate at great losses by appealing to an audience that just isn't large enough to support a commercial radio station."[47] Nor did network execs or station managers want to grant so much autonomy to disc jockeys. And there remained a deep, culturally based hostility between many industry executives and rock music and culture.

Yet industry analysts had identified the major audience for many FM stations as young and affluent, and advertising agencies were already beginning to develop targeted advertising to audiences segmented by demographics and media. Commercial FM stations and advertisers alike wanted as large a portion of this market as possible. The youth market, alienated though some of it was, was nonetheless quite large, and it spent money on stereos, records, jeans and T-shirts, food and alcohol, and toiletries. As advertisers and owners of FM stations recognized this, more and more stations were converted to some type of rock format, thus edging out the early FM pioneers, the classical stations. By 1973, according to *Newsweek*, there were just over thirty full-time commercial classical stations, a decline of 50 percent since 1963.[48]

The industry sought to co-opt some of the stylistic innovations of underground while purging it of left-wing politics and too much musical heterogeneity. What such initiatives began to do was exploit some of the iconoclasm of FM in order to turn the anticorporate ethos to the industry's advantage. To appeal to the younger market, the ABC-FM network developed a hybrid format with the musical predictability of the AM format but the announcing style of underground. In 1971 CBS-FM did the same. Looking at its target audience of upper-income, college-educated people between the ages of eighteen and thirty-four, WCBS in New York played a mixture of rock, folk, and other popular music and restricted advertising to eight minutes per hour (many Top 40 stations had eighteen minutes of advertising per hour). WCBS also offered "bonus music periods"—101 minutes of music without commercials, to remind listeners that the station's dial position was 101. Promotional gimmicks, ironically, promoted anticommercialism. Progressive rock came to be the victim of its own success.[49]

Other successful progressive rock stations, like WBCN in Boston, buoyed by success, enlarged their staffs, bought more sophisticated equipment, and moved to posher facilities, in 'BCN's case the top of the Prudential Tower. This meant greater overhead, which required more ad revenues, which in turn required more reliable and robust ratings than progressive rock stations had been interested in producing. And now stations like 'BCN around the country had more competition, as the number of FM rock stations increased, all fighting over the same audience.[50]

By the end of the decade, with the collapse of the counterculture and the ravages of "stagflation," the pressures that came from the demand to maximize profits had straitjacketed FM into new, rigid formats targeted to very specific audiences. As early as 1972, for example, WCBS in New York had switched to a "tightly run oldies format" which had proved hugely successful with a large and varied audience.[51] Existing networks like CBS and ABC became strengthened in the 1970s, and new networks got established. Consolidation in FM soared, as more stations were taken over by corporations that owned multiple radio stations around the country.

In November of 1974, *Broadcasting* featured an article entitled "FM Rockers Are Taming Their Free Formats." It noted that many progressive stations were adopting one of the techniques of AM stations, the tighter playlist. It also noted the increase in market research, "more study of audience tastes as measured by sales and requests, more attention paid to national sales and airplay." As one FM programmer noted, "We're seeing a nationalization of tastes." Albums out of the mainstream, the mainstay of early FM, were now no longer given a chance at many stations. The playlist was agreed upon by committee or determined by the program manager, as it had been in AM during the 1960s.[52]

To put it simply, the assembly line had come to FM, breaking down freeform programming into its component parts, robbing the disc jockey of autonomy, and making the final product—the show—more predictable. Programming decisions became highly centralized, as fewer and fewer people controlled what music went out over the airwaves. Jim Ladd recalls the imposition of "the format," which "came to symbolize the antithesis of everything FM radio stood for." The format, developed by the station's program director or an outside consultant, was a blueprint for what music would be played when. It was based on sales figures, telephone surveys, demographics, and focus groups. The DJ came in to work and got a playlist with a sequence of letters on it, like C, A, F, B, A, and so forth. These letters corresponded to categories of songs like current hit single, new record, oldie, and so forth. Each song was noted on a three-by-five card and filed by category in a long metal box. The DJ saw that the letter *C* was first, pulled the first card in the C file, initialed it to verify that he had played it that day, and moved through the list in that fashion.

At WNEW-FM, assembly-line programming techniques came in initially via "the rack." The rack was a box of albums sorted into categories labeled as oldies, folk, and so forth, and the DJs were supposed to follow a menu of choices from the various categories. At first, like most workers in industrial settings confronted with new forms of routinization, they ignored the directions, or acted as if they forgot or didn't understand. And at first the pressure to program rigidly by the rack was only mild. But as the DJ Jonathan Schwartz put it, "The rack was the beginning of the end." Added Rosko, "Once we became successful, that's when the control set in."[53] The emphasis was on musical familiarity and predictability, so the listener would know exactly what he or she was in for and, finding a secure and predictable environment, would choose to stay tuned.

This A-B-C patterning was meant to ensure the proper rotation of different kinds of music and excluded songs programmers deemed "obscure." "No longer could we mix songs together in thematic sets, using lyrics to tell a story, or to try to make a point," noted Ladd. "These songs . . . were now merely random cogs in the great format wheel." But Ladd also acknowledges that DJs at first found ways to get around the playlist, and many took special delight in getting songs on the air that weren't on the format or were out of rotation. DJs also got "liner cards" with one-line station logos or catchphrases to promote station identification. "Instead of talking to our friends," Ladd lamented, "we were now supposed to sell to the sheep." Rosko bemoaned the resultant loss of feeling and artistry: "You must have the disc jockey sink or swim with what he creates on the show. If he's not doing that, he's playing someone else's show, and I don't think he can feel it."[54]

Just as the 1950s witnessed the invention of the disc jockey, the 1970s saw the invention of his behind-the-scenes successor, the radio consultant. Mention this term to most disc jockeys, especially those who were on progressive rock stations, and the revulsion is palpable. "Newly mutated life form" was the term Jim Ladd favored. For consultants routinized, standardized, and codified what DJs felt they did by instinct, and they returned FM to many of the conventions of AM that progressive rock had cast itself against. As Tony Pigg put it tellingly, "They stopped having the courage to listen with their ears and started listening with their research." Consultants relied on demographic data, purchasing habits, and ratings, and linked these to specific formats, depending on the demographic the station was going after. So many of these consultants also became de facto programmers, and they especially emphasized the importance of repetition of tunes, and music that was not too threatening or unfamiliar. They "imposed a statistical grid over the psychedelic counterculture."[55] They took the feeling out of FM programming, made it bloodless and allegedly scientific. Music, once so sacred to FM DJs, was now called "product."

Accompanying this trend toward homogenization was the adoption by different stations of a particular, tightly circumscribed format: oldies, soft rock, album-oriented rock, or country and western, with little if any overlap. Each station and its advertisers were, then, geared to a very specific fragment of the once "mass" audience. As *Advertising Age* noted in 1978, "With the increased emphasis on specific demographics, stations are finding it imperative to implement tight format control to ensure that the target audience is being reached. The day of the disc jockey who controls his individual program is quickly becoming a dinosaur." In the late 1960s and early 1970s, there were more than 300 progressive rock stations in the country; by the mid-1970s the number had shrunk to about 25.[56]

With the new, more systematic research and tighter formats came increased advertising revenue and, thus, increased success. By 1977 FM stations saw their revenues soar to $543.1 million, a nearly 30 percent increase over the previous year. FM receivers were now in 95 percent of all American households. And a new business was booming: automated programming services that sold syndicated formats to FM stations around the country.[57] The assembly-line techniques that underground DJs had deplored now very much informed FM programming.

As in other industrial practices, the assembly line often gave way to automation, which became greatly enhanced by computerization. As early as the mid-1970s, an estimated one-seventh of FM stations were automated, with the numbers continuing to grow. Automation meant that a station could stay on the air for hours with virtually no human intervention. The process was simple. The sequence of music was provided on tape, and prerecorded comments from DJs for a four-hour show (which they could tape in fifteen minutes) could be inserted at the appropriate times. Ads and even the time could also be interspersed throughout the "show." While "beautiful music" FM stations especially took advantage of automated services, so did FM rock stations.

What this meant for rock music was a new regimentation based on market research and a strict hierarchy of musical success. AOR (album-oriented rock) stations emphasized performers rather than singles and played album cuts by the most successful artists, such as Fleetwood Mac, Elton John, or Linda Ronstadt. It was very difficult for new groups or new music to get airplay on these stations.[58] Listeners heard less diverse music and fewer songs. This had implications for the record collections and musical tastes of many baby boomers, whose knowledge of much of rock 'n' roll stops in, say, 1976, when they switched to jazz or learned only of the most famous rock performers. It became harder for people in many radio markets, especially smaller ones, to learn about or sample new music. By the early 1980s the only national outlet for such new groups was a format still in its fledgling days: MTV. The initial success of MTV, which introduced Americans to ska, post-punk, new wave, and "world music," indicated how frozen, in both format and content, the once free-form and rebellious rock FM had become.

We also can't overlook the national political climate within which FM evolved. Certainly the counterculture claimed FM and shaped its development in many cities in the late 1960s and early 1970s. But at the other end of the spectrum, the Nixon administration's rather titanic paranoia about the media in general, and the news media in particular, was legendary, and Spiro Agnew made a minor theatrical career of touring the country and declaiming against the various outrages of newspapers, TV, and magazines. One such outrage was, of course, rock music, which he said was "brainwashing" America's young people into becoming drug addicts. The worst songs were "White Rabbit" by the Jefferson Airplane and the Beatles' "A Little Help from My Friends."

The Nixon administration, as we know, left very little to chance: its friend in the FCC, Barry Goldwater's 1964 campaign manager, Dean Burch, made sure that the commission sent a public notice to radio stations in 1971 reminding them of their duty to screen all songs for lyrics that tended to "promote or glorify the use of illegal drugs." There was no explicit consequence attached to the continued playing of, say, "One Toke over the Line," but the implication was clear: ignore this memo, place your license in jeopardy. In response, KSAN had an "all drug" weekend, during which it played every song it could find with possible references to drugs and read the Bill of Rights between sets.[59] As FM rock became more popular and pervasive, corporate owners became more cautious, and while "White Rabbit" was never banished from the air, ads for record stores that gave away free rolling papers were replaced by ads for Michelob.

In the 1980s FM achieved a dominance Howard Armstrong had only dreamed of. By 1979 FM stations in cities such as New York, Chicago, Boston, Detroit, Dallas, and Los Angeles were outstripping AM stations in popularity. In all of these cities five or more of the top-ten rated stations were FM, and nationwide FM accounted for more than half of all stations in the top-ten ranks of the top fifty markets. Ten years later it was AM that was scrambling to find new formats to attract the legion of listeners who had defected to FM. FM was clearly the dominant band for music; as *Broadcasting* noted, "Younger audiences . . . are not prone to tune to an AM station unless there's a tornado or something and they want to hear the news." In 1989 the fastest growing format for AM was the talk show.[60]

The audio revolution of the 1960s and '70s meant that fidelity listening could now really happen in the car. The more compact in-dash cassette decks gradually replaced eight-track systems in the 1970s, their success propelled by Ray Dolby's application of his revolutionary studio recording system to retail cassette players. The Dolby system, developed in the 1960s, relied on emphasizing certain higher frequencies, like quieter or higher-pitched sounds, during the recording process, then deemphasizing hiss, which is especially audible at high frequencies, during playback.[61] This noise reduction system, plus improvements in the quality and design of audiotape and the miniaturization of stereo speakers, meant that the fidelity listening so lovingly cultivated by a host of progressive rock stations could now be achieved without radio as people cruised along the highway. People could also be their own DJs, recording their favorite cuts on a tape and bringing that along. These technical enhancements to musical autonomy came just at the time when progressive rock was getting reined in, and those who turned to radio for variety and newness now felt that there was no station left for them.

The FM revolution, and the rise of fidelity listening, was a technological insurgency that seems to have been powerfully driven by men's desire to retreat from or rebel against war. I don't think it's mere coincidence that the hi-fi fad flourished in the immediate aftermath of World War II, or that free form was at its height during the worst years of Vietnam. Just as men have used machines to destroy, many have sought to use them to repudiate such barbarism and to gain access to supposedly feminine territory. And once again in radio's history, a subgroup of men defied how the industry was constraining the act of listening. At least with radio, technological insurgency has used traditionally male traits, like technical one-upmanship, to allow men to slip into more feminine, comfortable garb.

One of capitalism's greatest strengths, however, is its ability to incorporate the voices and styles of the opposition into a larger framework, and to adapt such opposition to its own ends. The cultural benefits are, of course, that mainstream culture is enriched and, at moments of technological uncertainty and cultural upheaval like the late 1960s, provides brief periods when diversity can really flower. But in the cyclical history of radio, this incorporation quickly leads to formulaic predictability, which is where the various FM formats—including most "alternative" stations—find themselves right now. The social construction of FM began with a nexus of technological, perceptual, and aesthetic insurgencies. But this was only the beginning of the process; corporations dedicated to producing known, predictable audiences for advertisers took hold of these rebellions and harnessed them to the bottom line.

It is also important, however, to emphasize that many listeners *did* want more predictability. They didn't necessarily want to hear Ravi Shankar after Neil Young and then jump to Yusaf Lateef. The DJs, many of whom regarded programming as a highly individualized art form, eschewed predictability. The corporate suits eschewed surprise. Maintaining a calibrated tension between the two makes great radio, and many of the free-form DJs achieved just that; others didn't. And while corporate imperatives deep-sixed free-form radio, so did demographic changes. One of the things that free-form FM required was the time to devote to fidelity listening. Once baby boomers got jobs and started families, the time available to lie on the floor between the speakers listening to Santana or Procol Harum shrank. But in the pursuit of more predictability, many new radio networks have eliminated surprise altogether, which has helped cut many boomers out of rock music listening, and which may set the stage for another programming revolution in the near future.

There remains among the DJs who were lucky enough to have worked in free-form radio, and among many of their former listeners, a wistful and bitter nostalgia for free form and fidelity listening. The DJs miss the autonomy, the creativity, the ability to play music for music's sake, and a more direct, less cynical and commercialized relationship with their listeners. And they miss the joy of creating the perfect segue. Listeners, in turn, miss learning about new music, the juxtaposition of genres, and the intimate, conspiratorial mode of address. Ideologically, many miss an outpost on the airwaves that was avowedly left-wing and anticommercial. But the longing is not just political or emotional, it is cognitive, too, as people miss the blend of familiarity and surprise, the challenges, the required attentiveness that fidelity listening demanded.

By the late 1970s another era of radio listening had come to an end: breakout listening, which in turn paved the way for fidelity listening, had been roped in and tamed and, except for a few independent or college stations, no longer existed. In fact, the biggest thing to hit radio in the 1980s wasn't a music format at all; it was built on controversy and total unpredictability. This was the rise of talk radio. This was where surprise, irreverence, and iconoclasm on the radio had gone.

CHAPTER

11

Talk Talk

I t was 1978. On the AM dial in New York City, from 11:30 at night until 5:00 in the morning, Bob Grant yelled, "You creep! Get off the phone!" or "You mealymouthed, pompous oaf," to listeners who called in to his show. He insisted on the mandatory sterilization of welfare mothers with more than two children, suggested that rude taxi drivers be shot, and referred to criminals—or people he didn't agree with—as "sickolas," "mutants," and "savages."[1]

Meanwhile, over on the lower-frequency portion of the FM band, *All Things Considered*, then in its seventh year, featured an essay by the Los Angeles commentator Joe Frank: "When you're a child, you're so alive to experience. The world dazzles you, especially the world of living beings. Do you remember how you felt about ladybugs? I loved them. Whenever a ladybug would land on your arm or your shoulder or the back of your hand, you'd be very careful not to scare it away by an abrupt movement and you'd count the spots on its back to see how old it was."[2]

These broadcasts couldn't be more different—in their tone, their focus, and what they tried to address and cultivate in their listeners. Political talk radio and NPR were still in their infancy, their influence and their importance to their listeners barely imagined in the late 1970s when television was bringing the mass suicides in Jonestown, the disaster at Three Mile Island, and then the Iranian hostage crisis into people's living rooms. And as talk radio and NPR became more established, and politically and culturally important in the 1980s and beyond, they continued, in form and content, to diverge in almost every imaginable way.

Yet I'd like to suggest that they were mirror-image twins, each speaking to a profound sense of public exclusion from and increasing disgust with the mainstream media in general and TV news in particular. They both became electronic surrogates for the town common, the village square, the general store, the meeting hall, the coffeehouse, the beer garden, the park, where people imagined their grandparents—even their parents, for that matter—might have gathered with others to chat, however briefly, about the state of the town, the country, the world. NPR and political talk radio both tapped into the sense of loss of public life in the 1980s and beyond, the isolation that came from overwork and the privatization of American life, and the huge gap people felt between themselves and those who run the country. They were also responses to changes in the network news and the newsmagazines in the 1980s, when news staffs were cut, stories became shorter, the sound bites allowed even presidential candidates shrank from just under a minute to about nine seconds, and in-depth reporting was eclipsed by celebrity journalism. "Talk radio and NPR have the same core values," notes Jim Casale, a consultant and industry analyst. "They give people an in-depth understanding of the news that they can't get elsewhere. They also get a perspective on the news—they get interpretation."[3]

As Bob Grant's vocal bullying and Joe Frank's ode to a ladybug indicate, talk radio and NPR also offered very different models of manhood on the air. While NPR built on and elaborated the more socially conscious, antiviolent, aesthetically appreciative versions of manhood as articulated on free form, talk radio provided a platform for what can best be called male hysteria, a deft and sometimes desperate fusion of the desire to thwart feminism and the need to live with and accommodate to it.

By the 1980s much of FM, once so vibrant and experimental, had been sliced up into predictable, homogenized formats that offered little surprise and no interaction. Beautiful music and soft rock were hardly going to get your blood boiling or your brain moving first thing in the morning. Simply put, much of FM stopped having any personality—and this in a medium where personality had been everything.[4] Formats were also predicated on intermittent, often distracted listening: you could dip in and out for fifteen minutes here, twenty minutes there; there was no beginning, no end. NPR and talk radio both sought to reactivate attentive listening and to develop programs with a flow that you entered and stayed with. They offered programs that, like earlier radio, established new daily rituals and new forms of dialogue through which people could build imagined communities on the air.

Efforts to reinvigorate radio in the 1970s and '80s coincided with two often contradictory trends: attempts by some to reactivate notions of citizenship and participatory democracy, and bids by others to use audience participation formats to rake in more viewers and boost ratings. As entertainment and news were merging in a variety of formats, including infomercials, newsmagazines, dramatic reenactments, reality-based TV, and talk shows, audience members and spectators were brought in as participants—as people with opinions, or problems, or videos to share. Talk radio and NPR led the way in opening up the airwaves to a range of voices, some of them quite unwelcome elsewhere. Talk radio and NPR, in different but also overlapping ways, provided entirely new venues, circumventing the gatekeepers to the culture on TV, for listening in on American attitudes and opinions flattened out by public opinion polls.

Talk radio and NPR also shared another trait: their celebration of sound as a medium and hearing as a sense. Much of talk radio—and this is particularly true of Don Imus, Howard Stern, and Rush Limbaugh—and NPR revitalized radio as a highly suggestive aural medium in which the calculated use of sound could create powerful mental images in listeners' minds. The early producers at NPR felt that most people had lost the art of listening to radio and believed that if they used sound creatively, to evoke atmosphere and feel, listeners could come again to embrace—and possibly even prefer—news on the radio. Bill Siemering, the creator of *All Things Considered,* believed that public radio should be "an aural museum," and NPR's mission statement cast the "aural esthetic experience" as one that "enriches and gives meaning to the human spirit." Jay Kernis, the creator and early producer of *Morning Edition,* wanted to revive the style of reporting developed by Edward R. Murrow during World War II, in which "pure sound could tell a story," as when Murrow laid his microphone on the ground so listeners could hear advancing tanks.[5] Both news shows on NPR came to specialize in reporting on location and used background noise, sound effects, and music to enrich their stories. There was a conscious effort, in other words, to reactivate dimensional listening.

Don Imus and Howard Stern, both of whom had ensemble casts of characters supporting them, used sound effects (not the least of which are those produced by the human mouth), voice impersonations, sometimes graphic descriptions of what was going on in the studio, and uncontrolled giggling and laughter to convey a clubby atmosphere of fun. Rush Limbaugh, while not quite as dramatic, used the bass guitar riff from the Pretenders' "My City Was Gone" to open his show, imitated the sound of a dolphin when trashing animal rights advocates, pounded his desk to make a point, and riffled his papers and clippings in front of the mike to evoke the feel and imagery of the studio.[6] This return to the image-making capabilities of pure sound, whether subtle or gross, set these radio genres apart from beautiful music and Top 40.

Talk radio began to make national headlines in the mid-1980s, when Howard Stern gained increasing notoriety and earned the moniker shock jock and Alan Berg, an especially combative talk show host in Denver, was murdered, presumably, by one of his infuriated listeners. In December of 1988, Ralph Nader called *The Jerry Williams Show* in Boston to protest a proposed 51 percent congressional pay increase that then Speaker of the House Jim Wright planned to push through without a floor vote. At approximately the same time, an anonymous caller phoned in the same protest to the talk show host Roy Fox in Detroit, and Mike Siegel in Seattle had also become agitated over the issue. Williams, Fox, Siegel, and a coalition of approximately thirty talk show hosts coordinated a major attack on Wright. Mark Williams, a host on the 50,000-watt XTRA in San Diego, got a call giving him the number of the fax machine in Wright's office, which Williams shared with his compatriots. Broadcasting their outrage—and Wright's fax number—to their listeners, these talk show hosts unleashed an avalanche of protest that scuttled the pay increase.[7] "Except for a few isolated markets, like Boston, no one knew we were out here," recalled Mark Williams. The Wright episode, and the resulting newspaper headlines, changed all that.

The number of radio stations with all-talk or a combined news and talk format quadrupled in ten years, from approximately 200 in the early 1980s to more than 850 in 1994. By the mid-1990s talk radio was one of the most popular formats on the air, second only to country music. Talk radio—and its particular version of radio populism—had arrived. So had NPR. Only 104 stations carried the first installment of *All Things Considered* in May 1971. By the early 1990s NPR's 520 stations could boast nearly 160 million listeners. Those who actually responded to the pledge drives and paid to be "members" totaled only 1.3 million by the late 1980s, but that was still more people than were members of the National Rifle Association.[8]

One of the inventions that especially fueled the popularity of call-in talk radio and shifted the demographics of the audience was the cell phone. Virtually unheard of as car accessories in the mid-1980s, cell phones had exploding sales between 1989 and 1992. During that period the number of subscribers to cell phone services increased by 215 percent; by 1993 there were 12 million cellular phones in use, with 10,000 new subscribers signing up each day; by 1995 there were 33 million subscribers.[9] And one of the things they did, as they drove to and from work or in between meetings, was call in to radio talk shows.

Like some of the most successful popular culture—one thinks of P. T. Barnum's early "museums," or *National Geographic,* or *60 Minutes*—talk radio entertained and educated, fused learning with fun, allowed people to be titillated and informed, and encouraged them to be good citizens and unruly rebels, all at the same time. Clearly the genre filled an array of needs for contact with others and for participating in and shaping public discourse.

There were various progenitors of the form. Listeners to WOR in New York in the 1960s tuned in to a chatty, meandering, and relentlessly genial morning show, *Rambling with Gambling,* in which talk reigned over music. Late at night, while falling asleep, they could listen to the often brilliant stream-of-consciousness reminiscences and reflections of Jean Shepherd. Neither show tackled political controversy or took calls from listeners, but they were important departures from music format shows and revealed how deeply listeners still identified with a disembodied yet familiar voice, one that reflected on the most mundane aspects of everyday lived experience. A few stations, like KABC in Los Angeles, KMOX in St. Louis, and KVOR in Colorado converted to the talk format in the early 1960s, but they were exceptions.

In Los Angeles in the early 1960s, Joe Pyne was already launching a much more in-your-face style of talk radio—he often told guests with whom he disagreed to "go gargle with razor blades." But it wasn't until the late 1970s and early 1980s that talk radio emerged as a distinct and popular format. As music programmers and listeners evacuated the AM dial in favor of FM in the 1970s, previously thriving stations were faced with a crisis. Some tried the all-news format while others clung to music, but by 1980 the talk format—whether the host was a sexologist dispensing advice or a political consultant fielding calls—was proving to be a solution to AM's abandonment. Talk radio didn't require stereo or FM fidelity, and it was unpredictable, incendiary, and participatory. On WOL-AM in Washington, D.C., for example, the audience increased by 48 percent between 1980 and 1981 in response to the talk show format.[10]

The initial problem with talk radio was that production costs were high, often quadruple those of a music format. The reason was simple: the format was labor-intensive, requiring the talkmaster, a producer, an engineer, a programmer, and a researcher. There were also costly telephone charges for long-distance interviewing. Because of these expenses, talk radio required a large urban market. The cost of conversion to all-talk sometimes ran up a station's expenses by 300 percent. But ratings could go up by anywhere from 25 to 250 percent. Station managers also discovered that talk show audiences were extremely loyal—once they listened and liked what they heard, many got hooked. This, of course, was what advertisers needed to hear. In fact, once the genre became established, stations discovered that some advertisers were willing to pay twice as much to reach the talk radio audience because of what were called its "foreground" aspects—people didn't use it for background noise, like they sometimes did with a music format. They paid closer attention; they concentrated on what they were hearing; and if a host with whom they especially identified, someone they trusted, read the ad copy, advertisers were convinced that sales were enhanced. "Thousands of AM stations, given up for dead in the

1980s, had nothing to lose by switching to talk," Michael Harrison of *Talkers* magazine reminds us.[11] Because of the stampede of consultants and marketing experts to FM, these AM stations were also freer to program by their guts instead of by the book.

Satellite technology, first used in radio broadcasting by NPR in 1978, also allowed some stations to maximize profits by distributing their shows nationally. Instead of relaying shows via telephone lines, satellite technology provided a much cheaper and technically superior method of transmitting a local broadcast nationally. Such technology in the 1980s would come to be Larry King's, Rush Limbaugh's, and Howard Stern's best friend. Ironically, it was the more politically progressive and polite National Public Radio that pioneered in using satellite uplinks and downlinks to reestablish a national network of simultaneous broadcasts that cut costs and expanded the audience.

By 1984 *Time* was able to feature a major story on the talk show format, titled "Audiences Love to Hate Them." There was a new dynamic here, one that had been developing since at least the late 1960s, in which certain radio shows sought to rile up their audiences, following the notion that fury equals—and begets—attention, and thus profits. Unlike TV in the 1950s and early 1960s, which sought to avoid controversy so as not to alienate its audiences, talk radio pursued controversy and, again in total contradiction to the earlier years, used this as a selling point to advertisers looking for loyal, large, engaged audiences. In other words, controversy and marketability were joined, so that talk radio developed a "financial dependence on sensation." By 1995 one general manager of a talk radio station was able to give the following explanation for why conservative hosts dominated the air: Liberals "are genetically engineered to not offend anybody. People who go on the air afraid of offending are not inherently entertaining."[12]

Most of the commentary about talk radio, whether journalistic or scholarly, has focused on two things: its rudeness—the threat it posed to civility—and its unrepresentative amplification of right-wing politics—the threat it posed to democracy. But what is obvious yet much less frequently discussed is talk radio's central role in efforts to restore masculine prerogatives to where they were before the women's movement. After all, over 80 percent of the hosts, and a majority of the listeners, particularly to political talk radio, are male.[13] Talk radio is as much—maybe even more—about gender politics at the end of the century as it is about party politics. There were different masculinities enacted on radio, from Howard Stern to Rush Limbaugh, but they were all about challenging and overthrowing, if possible, that most revolutionary of social movements, feminism. They were also about challenging buttoned-down, upper-middle-class, corporate versions of masculinity that excluded many men from access to power. The "men's movement" of the 1980s found its outlet in talk radio.

The talk on political talk radio, as well as the talk about talk radio, was, from the start, decidedly macho and loud. The imaginary audience, the one most hosts seemed to speak to, was male. And what these hosts and their audiences did was assert that talking over the phone, talking about your feelings and experiences, talking in often emotional registers, was no longer the province of women. These guys were going to take America's traditional assumptions of associating talk, or "chatter," with women and throw them out the window.[14] In fact, in the late 1970s many talk shows were therapeutic, featuring male and female shrinks, psychics, and sexologists—Dr. Ruth being the most famous—who focused on the personal, not the political. By the 1980s, while there were certainly famous female therapists and counselors like Dr. Toni Grant, Joy Brown, or Joan Hamburg on the air, it was the male culture of political talk radio that had become newsworthy. Various hosts were promoted successfully with the moniker radio's bad boy.

Characterizing most talk show hosts' abrasive style as "a verbal adjunct to street fighting," *Time* acknowledged that their success stemmed in part from the fact that "the decade's mood has become more aggressive." Talk radio hosts helped build imagined communities that made quite clear who was included and who was excluded. The guy nobody wanted was the new male pariah of the 1980s, the wimp.[15] No yes-men, mama's boys here, beaten-down types who obeyed too eagerly, who had responded too sympathetically to the civil rights or the women's movement. Hosts insulted and yelled at listeners like abusive fathers, and tough callers knew how to take it. In fact, talk radio proved to be a decidedly white, male preserve in a decade when it became much more permissible to lash out at women, minorities, gays, lesbians, and the poor—the very people who had challenged the authority and privileges of men, of white people, of the rich and powerful, and of heterosexuals in the 1960s and 1970s. Now it was payback time.

As the scholars Susan Jeffords, Yvonne Tasker, and Michael Kimmel among others have noted, the late 1970s was a period of greatly heightened anxiety about manhood in America. Indeed, one could argue that this was a true moment of crisis for masculinity. Feminists had made gender politics front-page news, and they had demonstrated how patriarchy undermined and threatened core American values, particularly democracy and equality of opportunity for all. And you didn't have to be a feminist to feel that it was, in part, warped masculine aggression and pride that had got the country into Vietnam, and kept us there too long. Various therapy movements emerged—in a decade awash in therapy crazes as it ended—to help men become more sensitive and emotionally expressive.[16] At the same time a panic about the legitimacy of America's patriarchal power structure took hold as the country watched one president resign in disgrace, his successor continually trip, stumble, and hit people in the head with out-of-control golf balls, and a third stand by helpless as Americans were held hostage by a "third-rate" military power. All of the presidents of the 1970s were perceived to have lost control, and control and mastery are central to most conceptions of true manhood. A new term—Vietnam syndrome—characterized American reluctance to engage in military action, as if this was an ailment or disease. Flaccid men had made for a flaccid foreign policy, according to Richard Nixon and other conservative critics.

Ronald Reagan, through his rhetoric, policies, and appearance, sought to change all that. Screw feminist politics and getting in touch with your feminine side, said the Reagan presidency. All that had done was make the country vulnerable and weak. It was time to reassert male supremacy. As if in response, Hollywood in the 1980s pumped out high-action, bloated-budget beefcake movies in which Sylvester Stallone, Arnold Schwarzenegger, Bruce Willis, and others used their tough, muscled bodies to remasculinize America's self-image, which played all too well into Reagan's efforts to pump a great deal of testosterone into America's foreign policy, the fight against crime, and the "war on drugs." Battalions of Afghan soldiers, armies of invading space aliens, cadres of lethal drug kingpins, were no match for these rippled, tough-talking guys.[17]

But Reagan and these "hard body" movies had hardly resolved the issue. The 1988 presidential campaign was all about manhood, with George Bush and his handlers working round the clock to jettison his "wimp" image, and Michael Dukakis getting pilloried in the press for looking like a little boy instead of a real man as he rode around in a tank and wore an oversized helmet. Wall Street insiders termed men with power "big swinging dicks." The fear that American men weren't "real men" anymore, and a determination on the part of many men to abandon certain traditional masculine behaviors and roles, coexisted with an insistence that some men were never going to respond to the women's movement, period.

But there were also genuine anxieties about and frustration with what came to be called political correctness toward women and people of color. Many men thought they were being genial when they kept telling a woman she looked nice or persisted in calling her honey—why were these women so sensitive all of a sudden? And just when white people thought that "blacks" was perfectly acceptable, they learned they should use the term "people of color" or "African American," but not Afro-American. Diversity training and sexual harassment workshops became de rigueur in many workplaces. So many white men came to feel that they were walking on eggshells, that they didn't know what was right and wrong to say anymore, that they wanted a place where they, too, could exhale. Talk radio gave them that refuge. As one talk show host put it, "Today, you have to hyphenate everything. People have no sense of humor. Talk radio allows people to break away from that. As a host I can be like Grandpa—you know, 'There goes Grandpa again'—I can say anything."[18]

On talk radio the trend was the same as in many mainstream films—to take over public discourse, purge it of conciliatory, bland, or feminine tendencies, and reclaim it for men. But not men like Peter Jennings, Dan Rather, or Tom Brokaw—well-groomed, decorous, polite types who told us the news without any passion and who, by their very demeanor, embodied goody-two-shoes men with money and influence, former presidents of the student council or captains of the debating team.

No, the masculinity on talk radio was different, fusing over the years some working-class politics and sensibilities with the language and attitude of the locker room. There were clear exceptions to this—the suave, urbane Michael Jackson in Los Angeles, and Larry King, who by 1984 was reaching 3.5 million listeners nationally with his interview show. But Don Imus, Bob Grant, Howard Stern, and their many imitators would become famous for their verbal dueling, or for assuming the persona of a horny, insubordinate twelve-year-old boy. Growing at first out of the bitterness of political and economic alienation of the late 1970s and 1980s, some talk radio—especially the version offered by Stern and Imus—was a rebellion against civilization itself, against bourgeois codes of decorum that have sought to silence and tame the iconoclastic, delinquent, and defiant impulses in which adolescent boys especially seem to revel and delight. Here the transgressions of the unreconstructed class troublemaker were packaged and sold to an audience of eager buyers. But Imus and Stern were not just mindlessly celebrating pubescent anarchy for its own sake, although certainly at times it seemed that way. They, and Limbaugh, spoke to many men on the wrong end of power relations, men excluded from the upper levels of America's social hierarchies, where restraint, rationality, good taste, good manners, and deference marked who was allowed in. They insisted there was a place—an important place—for disobedience, hedonism, disrespect, bad taste, and emotionalism.

In *Talk Radio and the American Dream,* the only book on those early years of the format, Murray Levin describes talk radio as "the province of proletariat discontent, the only mass medium easily available to the underclass."[19] Focusing on two political talk shows in New England between 1977 and 1982, including the highly successful *Jerry Williams Show,* Levin found that callers felt themselves marginalized from media versions of the political mainstream, deeply distrustful of political and business institutions, and profoundly anxious about the collapse of community and civility.

Levin cites the pollster Daniel Yankelovich, who documented various manifestations of Americans' escalating mistrust of a range of national institutions. "Trust in government," he reported in the late 1970s, "declined dramatically from almost 80 percent in the late 1950s to about 33 percent in 1976. Confidence in business fell from approximately a 70 percent level in the late '60s to about 15 percent today." The press, the military, and elite professionals like doctors and lawyers all suffered a similar sharp drop in trust, according to the polls. More to the point, noted Yankelovich, "A two-thirds majority felt that what they think 'really doesn't count.' "[20]

It was lower-middle-class and working-class men especially, Levin reports, who eagerly sought an outlet, a platform, for what they thought. And call-in talk radio shows, beginning in the late 1970s, provided access to such a podium while keeping the callers invisible and preserving their anonymity. While television news and talk shows like *Inside Washington* and *This Week with David Brinkley* favored as commentators, experts, and guests those who were well-spoken, well-educated, influential, or famous, the radio version invited those with poor grammar, polyester clothes, bad haircuts, and only a high school education to hold forth on national and local affairs. Levin argued that the absence of those stiff protocols that restrained a commentator's performance on television was key to talk radio's spontaneity and informality, which were, in turn, key to the format's appeal.[21]

Among callers—he taped 700 hours of talk radio—Levin found a discourse "preoccupied with emasculation," a belief that the proper order of things now seemed inverted, so that crime, blacks, rich corporations, women, and inept bureaucracies all had the upper hand.[22] The Iranian hostage crisis—and Jimmy Carter's failed efforts to overcome it—further exacerbated a sense that America had become weak, could be bullied, and was being compromised by soft-spoken new age guys. As with the linguistic slapstick of 1930s radio comedy, the "verbal martial arts," as Levin puts it, assumed center stage here. Talk radio was a linguistic battleground, and few callers had the skills, or the position of authority, to deflect the verbal salvos and put-downs of the host. Yet they kept coming back for more.

It was the participatory ethos of talk radio, its suggestion that it would reverse years of ongoing consolidation and centralization of power—especially in Washington—that was central to its appeal. The great irony is that this very kind of talk radio, with its new macho populism, was the product of government deregulation, merger mania, and corporate consolidation during the 1980s and beyond. Populism and participation were the public faces of radio;

they masked increased economic concentration and heightened barriers to entry for all but the very rich in the industry itself. But then again, that was the Reagan administration's great genius—selling the increased concentration of wealth as a move back toward democracy. And the verbal antics of Howard Stern or Rush Limbaugh were sexier news stories than the profound behind-the-scenes changes in the industry that made their phenomenal success as national radio personalities possible. While the business press and *The New York Times* did report the regulatory and corporate upheavals of the 1980s, in general television news and the newsmagazines gave scant coverage to the corporate colonization of the country's airwaves.

It was a combination of technological and regulatory changes that enabled Rush Limbaugh and Howard Stern to gain national followings. First, satellite technology transformed what was economically and technically possible in radio. It offered superior audio quality and increased program options to station owners and managers. Telephone lines, which had previously linked stations into networks, allowed the transmission of only one program at a time. With satellites, managers could choose what they wanted to broadcast and when from a variety of options, and all for less money than land lines. No more snail-mailing of audiotapes to stations—now the feed was electronic and instant. While stations downlinked one event or program to air, they could record another program to air at a later time. Satellite technology also changed from analog-based systems, which are more prone to interference, to digital feeds, which carry much less noise.

The push to develop satellite technology for global and domestic communications had its roots in the post-*Sputnik* hysteria, when the U.S. government vowed that the Soviets would not win the "space race."[23] The air force and the army launched experimental satellites, followed by AT&T's successful launch in 1962, an event impressed upon the youth of America by the Tornado's number-one instrumental hit "Telstar."

But these early satellites were nonsynchronous—they orbited around the globe at a different speed than the rotation of the earth and required multiple, expensive tracking antennas to follow their pattern. The true breakthrough came with geosynchronous satellites. These orbit at 22,300 miles above the earth, a distance that allows them to revolve in synchronism with the earth's rotation—meaning that since they turn as the world turns, they actually stay in the same "slot" in relation to the earth and appear to be stationary. It is the balance between the earth's gravitational pull at this height and the centrifugal force of the universe pulling away from the earth that keeps the geosynchronous satellite in place.[24]

Such satellites couldn't be launched until NASA had developed rockets and rocket boosters powerful enough to take them that far out into space. NASA's first geosynchronous satellite, *SYNCOM-II,* launched in 1963, led to other launchings in the 1960s, and the first satellite for domestic communications in the United States was Western Union's *Westar I,* which went up in 1974. RCA and AT&T immediately sought to compete with Western Union, and between 1980 and 1983 alone fourteen domestic communications satellites docked in slots aimed at America.

Satellites park roughly along the line of the equator, which is why, if you are in the Northern Hemisphere, you'll see satellite dishes facing south. Their "slots" are designated by longitude, and the FCC has mandated that there must be at least two degrees between each pair of satellites. Each satellite also has a "footprint"—the somewhat elliptical area on earth that best receives its signal. Frequently a satellite will have several antennas, each with a different footprint to cover different regions of the earth. Earth stations with those round, often white, dish-shaped antennas focus the broadcast signals and send them to the satellite, where transponders amplify the signals, shift their frequency, then send them through the satellite's antennas so they may be retransmitted to earth.[25]

The use of satellites led to a re-networking of radio, but with more networks than in the 1930s and with many of them dedicated to a single format, like talk, twenty-four hours a day. By 1979 NPR had a satellite-based radio network. Previously NPR programming had been distributed on a monaural phone line, one show at a time. Shows besides the news went through the mail, on tape. Now NPR transmitted several shows simultaneously, and member stations picked what to air and when. ABC, CBS, and NBC switched to satellites during 1983–84. The switchover to satellites coincided with the deregulation of the phone industry and the elimination of AT&T's monopoly privileges. Without the monopoly structure to support some less profitable services with those that were more profitable, AT&T's broadcast loops between stations became too expensive for many stations.[26] Satellites allowed for the inexpensive creation of new networks run by companies like Infinity Broadcasting and the transmitting of stock formats of syndicated programming, like oldies, beautiful music, or talk, to a national audience attractive to national as well as local advertisers.

Also, as early as 1981, Ronald Reagan's FCC, under the free-market stewardship of Mark Fowler, began deregulating radio. One of Reagan's great symbolic moments occurred during his State of the Union address, when he pointed to a tower of paper that represented an old, cumbersome, burdensome set of regulations, then held up a slim sheaf, about the size of a high school term paper, that represented the new, streamlined regulations under his administration. Fowler fit in perfectly with this ideology. His mantra during his tenure as chairman of the FCC was to "eliminate unnecessary rules and regulations." Specifically, his vision of the FCC was that it serve primarily as a "technical traffic cop," that otherwise it "get out of the way" to let issues of public service, programming content, equal time for opposing views, and the like be determined by the marketplace. The old model of the FCC as public trustee of the airwaves had been, according to Fowler, "very bad for the consumer."[27] The new FCC was very good for corporate America.

Radio stations, which for decades had had to reapply for their licenses every three years, saw that licensing period extended to seven years. The government suspended previous public service requirements, which had required stations to devote a certain percentage of their broadcast week to public affairs programming. The amount of time stations could devote to commercials was lengthened. In 1985 the FCC also expanded the number of radio stations any one entity could own outright, from seven AM and seven FM stations— known then as the rule of sevens—to twelve of each. (The same entity could also own twelve television stations.)[28]

Another FCC regulation, the "one-to-a-market" rule enacted in 1970, also bit the dust in 1985, in the aftermath of the sensational and largest media merger up to that time, the Capital Cities/ABC deal that took place in March of that year. Known more formally as cross-ownership rules, the one-to-a-market caveat meant that any person or company that already owned a television station in a particular market could not buy an AM or FM station in that market. But the Cap Cities/ABC behemoth presented a problem. It now owned radio and television stations in some of the biggest media markets in the country: Los Angeles, New York, Chicago, San Francisco. It did spin off some radio stations but argued to the FCC that, really, it should be "grandfathered," since the two previously separate entities owned TV and radio stations before the merger, and it would be unfair to have to spin them off now.

The FCC agreed and granted Cap Cities/ABC a "waiver" to the one-to-a-market rule. More to the point, since the FCC had done this for one corporation, it wouldn't be fair not to "look favorably"—in the commission's language—upon waiver requests by other entities. The waivers would apply specifically to the top twenty-five media markets in which there were at least thirty separately owned broadcast licenses or, to quote from the FCC again, "voices." Fowler was especially proud of "freeing up investors so that there is more flexibility permitted in investing in broadcast stations without running afoul of multiple ownership rules; that is, permitting capital to flow more freely into our great broadcast industry." He added that his theory was "free the businessman; let the businessman react in the marketplace; let the consumer, in other words, be sovereign."[29] In 1992 the FCC eased restrictions on ownership limits again, raising the number of radio stations that a single company could own to eighteen AM and eighteen FM stations.

With the passage of the Telecommunications Act of 1996, the government went whole hog and eliminated restrictions on the number of stations a company could own nationally. There were limits by market, but they were quite generous. In a major market like Los Angeles or New York, with forty-five or more commercial stations, one company could own up to eight stations. In a market with thirty to forty-four stations, a company could own up to seven; in a market with fifteen to twenty-nine stations, one company could own up to six. And in the smallest markets, with fourteen or fewer stations, a company could still own up to six of them. The interaction between such deregulation and satellite technology made possible a reversal of the trend that had characterized radio in the TV age—a de-networking and a focus on the local. Now there was a re-networking move, making the organization of radio look more like it did before World War II.[30] Investors formed new national radio broadcasting companies, like Capstar, Clear Channels, and Jacor, which by 1997 owned between two hundred and three hundred stations each. Rush Limbaugh and Howard Stern would cease to be locally confined—now they could, and would, become national phenomena.

Most significantly, the FCC suspended a 1962 regulation known provocatively as the antitrafficking rule. Designed to discourage station owners from making quick profits by selling stations they had just bought, the antitrafficking rule required owners to hold on to stations for at least three years. The rule was also intended to promote local community service. But in the 1980s, when the ideology of "the marketplace" as best arbiter of social policy reigned supreme, the antitrafficking rule seemed quaint. At the same time the FCC licensed more than 2,000 new radio stations during the decade.[31]

The radio rush was on. Many radio stations had been underpriced while revenues in the industry remained strong. With no restrictions on length of ownership, and with commercial and real estate speculation in general escalating to a frenzy in the mid-1980s, the prices of radio stations soared, and new conglomerates formed to purchase, link, and manage these stations. In the era of leveraged buyouts and junk bonds, borrowing money for such purchases was not difficult. Stations that had sold for $5 to $7 million during the 1970s sold for ten times that much by the late 1980s. In one year alone—1988— money spent on buying radio stations totaled $3.45 billion.[32]

Whereas NBC, Mutual, and ABC had once dominated radio, now new conglomerates like Infinity Broadcasting—which became famous for its battles with the FCC over Howard Stern's language—were big players, controlling stations in major markets around the country. Nearly all the major consolidators controlled multiple stations in any major market. Merger mania continued into the 1990s, culminated by Westinghouse/CBS's purchase of Infinity Broadcasting for $4.9 billion, making this new behemoth the largest radio company in American history, with approximately 170 stations nationwide and dominance in major radio markets like New York, where it now controlled seven stations, or San Francisco, where it owned eight. Two other competitors, Jacor and American Radio Systems, owned 92 and 94 stations respectively. By 1998, Chancellor Media Corporation had dwarfed these early giants by gaining control of 463 stations. The amount of time that many of these stations devoted to news, not to mention public affairs, declined, and one 1992 survey of 700 radio stations revealed that many music stations' hourly news slots were two minutes or less, and there were fewer news broadcasts than there had been in the past.[33]

The other significant deregulatory move in the 1980s was the abandonment of the Fairness Doctrine, which the FCC announced in 1987 it would no longer enforce.[34] This basic principle—that broadcasters had the obligation to address all sides of public controversy during the course of their broadcasting—was implied in the Communications Act of 1934 and made explicit by what came to be known as the *Red Lion* decision of 1969.

Back in 1934 there were only two national radio networks—NBC and CBS—and while large cities had multiple radio stations, many small towns had only one. The framers of the Communications Act—who were, after all, politicians—were concerned that radio stations, with their power to reach millions of voters, not favor one candidate or party over another during campaigns. So they stipulated that broadcasting stations provide "equal opportunities" to all legally qualified candidates for public office to speak to the electorate on the air. Time made available to the candidate of one party had to be made available to all other candidates on basically the same terms. This equal time provision was known in the industry as Section 315.[35]

The FCC expanded this principle of equal time in 1949, when it revoked the *Mayflower* decision of 1941. WAAB in Boston had begun, in 1940, to broadcast editorials and opinions in the name of the station about political candidates and current controversial issues. The FCC reacted against this practice and ruled that "the broadcaster cannot be an advocate." But in the face of widespread negative criticism, which charged that the *Mayflower* decision curtailed the public's access to commentary about public affairs, the FCC reversed its ruling. In 1949 editorializing was permitted, but the FCC required that stations doing it must present opposing views.

But it was the 1969 *Red Lion* case that made the terms of what had come to be known as the Fairness Doctrine most explicit.[36] Fred Cook, a writer for *The*

Nation and author of *Barry Goldwater: Extremist on the Right,* became the subject of a vitriolic attack in 1964 by the Reverend Billy James Hargis's *Christian Crusade,* broadcast over WGCB in Red Lion, Pennsylvania. When Cook learned of the broadcast, which included charges that he was a communist, he demanded equal time to respond. The Reverend John M. Norris, owner of WGCB, countered by demanding that Cook pay for the airtime or prove that he was unable to do so before he went on the air. Cook filed a complaint with the FCC, and the FCC notified the station that it had to let Cook respond, for free if necessary. The doctrine, emphasized the FCC, pertained specifically to damaging personal attacks and to issues of public importance.

Norris appealed, and the case eventually went to the Supreme Court, which upheld the FCC's original ruling. The public had a right to hear opposing viewpoints, and broadcast stations, as trustees of the airwaves, were obligated to treat controversial topics fairly. This formed the basis for Johnny Carson's enduring skit on *The Tonight Show* in which one Floyd Turbo, clad in plaid and utterly untelegenic, provided his own inarticulate response to a recent TV station editorial. Audiences around the country recognized the character, because TV stations most frequently responded to the Fairness Doctrine by allowing activists, local politicians, and everyday people to come on the air and respond to station editorials, usually offered by the station owner or general manager. Yet despite such conventions many stations—and citizens—were confused about what the Fairness Doctrine did and did not require, and in 1973 alone 2,400 fairness complaints were submitted to the FCC. In practice the doctrine was meant to do two things: require stations to cover controversial issues of public importance and provide differing points of view about such issues.

Early in his tenure Mark Fowler announced his opposition to the Fairness Doctrine and Section 315, insisting that the FCC "must get out of the content regulation business."[37] He argued that in the era of cable and satellite transmissions, the spectrum scarcity argument no longer held up. He also maintained that broadcasters should enjoy the same First Amendment protections those in the print media enjoyed, meaning they had the right to broadcast what they wanted, when they wanted, free from government guidelines. In August of 1987 the FCC simply announced that it would no longer enforce the Fairness Doctrine. Congress responded in September by passing a bill that would have reinstated the doctrine, and President Reagan promptly vetoed it. There has been no Fairness Doctrine since.

What this means, in part, is that a radio station can air Rush Limbaugh followed by G. Gordon Liddy, and it is not required then to air a liberal talk show or to bring on anyone who might challenge or correct these guys' assertions. It was this powerful constellation of forces in the 1980s—satellite technology, deregulation, and a sense among many Americans, especially many men, that they were not being addressed or listened to by the mainstream media—that propelled talk radio into a national phenomenon, and a national political force. By 1992 the talk radio format claimed 875 stations nationally, up from 238 in 1987. In 1989 the first annual meeting of the National Association of Radio Talk Show Hosts consisted of 25 people; by 1992 the figure had jumped tenfold, to 250 hosts.[38]

The 1989 fax attacks on the proposed congressional pay raise alerted those out of the talk radio loop that something was afoot, but it was the 1992 presidential campaign, and the torpedoing of Zoe Baird's nomination for attorney general, that made talk radio, and Rush Limbaugh in particular, national front-page news. Ross Perot launched his 1992 presidential campaign on talk radio and TV, and Bill Clinton, eager to circumvent the mainstream press after reporters put him on the spot for his alleged affair with Gennifer Flowers, sought out radio and TV talk show hosts. Some listeners, already alienated by the network news, were turning increasingly to talk radio and political talk TV to get more thorough discussion of the issues. And in 1992 they were not disappointed. One study showed that television talk shows often featured three times as much substantive coverage of the issues as did the network news.[39] Poll respondents said they felt they learned things about the candidates from talk radio during the 1992 campaign that they didn't learn elsewhere.

As Kathleen Hall Jamieson, dean of the Annenberg School of Communications, noted in *Dirty Politics*, news coverage since the 1970s had shifted from issue-based to strategy-based, focusing on who's ahead and who's behind, and what strategies each candidate was using to try to position him/herself in the campaign. Actual policy coverage on the networks declined from 40 percent in 1988 to 33 percent in 1992. Thomas Patterson rightly dubbed this "horse race coverage." While such reporting gives a kind of "insider's account," it conveys little about the real issues and has made people cynical,[40] because voters are positioned as spectators of candidates who are performers instead of as citizens who must choose between their positions.

The seemingly explosive rise of talk radio prompted national polls and studies, and the *CQ Researcher* in 1994 devoted an entire issue to the question "Are call-in programs good for the political system?" In 1992 *Time* asked, in a major story, whether Limbaugh was a "Conservative Provocateur or Big Blowhard." Three years later, in the wake of the "Republican Revolution" in Congress, a cover story asked "Is Rush Limbaugh Good for America?" But by 1996 talk radio was barely a factor in the presidential race, and in a 1997 issue of the political magazine *George*, Neal Gabler asked whether Limbaugh was washed up. "Dr. Laura" Schlessinger, an antifeminist faux therapist with call-in analysands, was beginning to beat him out in various markets and had one of the highest rated shows in the country. Michael Harrison, the editor of *Talkers* magazine and an expert on the genre, calls 1987 to 1996 the "modern era" of talk radio, the period when it became an established form. He also thinks that it will be looked back at for years as the "golden era" of the form. "Years from now, nobody's going to be looking back at talk radio in 1998."[41]

Whether political talk radio was a political Roman candle or a new and enduring part of America's political landscape, its emergence raised a host of anxieties—as well as utopian hopes, especially among conservatives—about the transformation of public discourse and the relationship between the mainstream media and politics. In 1995 *Time* referred to talk radio as a "true hyperdemocracy." Recalling a now lost public sphere, the magazine noted, "Like the backyard savants, barroom agitators and soapbox spellbinders of an earlier era, Limbaugh & Co. bring intimacy and urgency to an impersonal age."[42]

Limbaugh, whom I'll discuss in detail shortly, became the poster boy for all of political talk radio. He boasted that in 1994 alone there were 4,635 stories written about him. Although his political influence was no doubt exaggerated, he raised fears that a conservative, activist minority was circumventing representative government, undermining the role of objectivity in the press, and imposing the will of an unrepresentative minority on public policy. While acknowledging that talk radio was "a needed jolt to sclerotic Washington," *Newsweek* cautioned that "it raises the specter of government by feverish plebiscite—an entertaining, manipulable and trivializing process that could eat away at the essence of representative democracy." As *Time* put it in 1989, "The current radio activism . . . has elements of a *Meet John Doe* nightmare." In part, of course, this was a potential nightmare for *Time* itself, and for newspapers and the network news, all of which were experiencing a decline in their audiences. Talk radio was a new, sexy competitor—for people's attention, for political influence, and for advertising dollars. And media coverage of talk radio, which was more often than not alarmist and negative, reflected these anxieties. In the aftermath of the Zoe Baird debacle, *Newsweek* did a cover story titled "The Power of Talk Radio." The blaring headlines were superimposed over an open, angry mouth that took up the entire cover.[43]

Much of the debate about the possible pernicious influences of talk radio stemmed from this very real threat that the new genre posed to its more established rivals. But the debate also reflected pronounced concerns about a decline of "civility" and the collapse of "civil discourse." These are debates about the public sphere, about how to reconstruct one and about just *whose* public sphere it's going to be, the educated bourgeoisie's or the rabble-rousers'.

Being threatened, especially from the academic and journalistic point of view, were middle-class, elite notions about the public sphere and citizenship, as well as established notions about journalism, commentary, experts, and who gets to be a source. These were hardly frivolous concerns, given that G. Gordon Liddy advocated the killing of federal agents, Ken Hamblin referred to James Brady as "that cripple," J. Paul Emerson of KSFO announced that he "hated the Japs," and Bob Grant called African Americans "sub-humanoids, savages."[44] Nor were journalists, who were compelled to fact-check everything, sanguine about many of these hosts offering their own, often misinformed opinion as fact, or about callers spreading the rumor that cellular phones cause cancer.

But many in the talk show business felt that the more outrageous types— Liddy, Stern, and Grant—were singled out to stand for all talk show hosts in a way that was alarmist about the genre. "There is much more diversity than the stereotypes suggest," insisted the industry analyst Jim Casale, adding, "we've been demonized." The talk show host Mark Williams also felt that the attention given to talk radio was "all out of proportion to its influence."[45] This was part of the ongoing battle in America over control of public discourse, a battle that has always been based on class, gender, and racial antagonisms. Talk show hosts were not just storming the media citadel; they were thumbing their noses at bourgeois conventions about political debate, public dialogue, and who deserves access to the soapbox.

In newsmagazine articles with titles like "Bugle Boys of the Airwaves," "Populist Radio," "Bad Mouth," and "Morning Mouth," writers speculated about who talk radio listeners were and what they got out of tuning in. "Callers are no longer lonely night owls," announced U.S. News & World Report; the audience was "as diverse as America." Callers—many of whom used their carphones to reach the stations—were "hardly the nation's disenfranchised."[46] Unlike Levin's portrait from the late 1970s of alienated working-class guys, anecdotal reports suggested a new audience profile. But who were these listeners, and how did this new brand of DJ reel them in?

No discussion of talk radio can proceed without considering the meteoric rise of Howard Stern and his archrival, Don Imus, both of whom worked for Infinity Broadcasting and each of whom claimed 5 million listeners by the mid-1990s. As the media critic Howard Kurtz notes, "Stern brought talk radio to the rock generation." He also helped pave the way for Rush Limbaugh's brand of stream-of-consciousness political diatribe. Stern's revisionist movie *Private Parts* sought to whitewash the depth of his racist, sexist, and vulgar remarks throughout his tenure on the air—his voice-over in the film kept claiming, "Everything I do is misunderstood"—but it was these very transgressions that made him a millionaire. So did his celebration of locker-room masculinity, bullying yet self-deprecating, working-class yet college-educated, quintessentially adolescent yet adult. "Listening to Stern," noted the former *Boston Globe* columnist Mike Barnicle, "is the electronic equivalent of loitering in the men's room of a bus terminal."[47] Apparently this was a place a lot of listeners wanted to go. The Stern of *Private Parts* was a mensch, like Woody Allen before Soon-Yi, who bemoaned the fact that he was "hung like a three-year-old," threw up after he was forced to fire someone, only wanted to be loved by the public, and whose main targets were pigheaded and autocratic broadcasting executives. The Stern on the air, however, was something else.

He was perfect for the Reagan years. The Reagan administration, with its attacks on affirmative action, "welfare queens," "bleeding heart" liberal politics, and abortion, and its celebration of greed, often used coded terms and loaded symbols to give Americans permission to be selfish, sexist, racist, uncharitable. There was nothing coded about Stern. Buoyed by this political climate, he took the gloves off and articulated in explicit terms what this new backlash politics was all about. At the same time he lashed out at the puritanism of the "family values" crowd. His DJ persona as a shock jock emerged on WWDC-FM in Washington, D.C., in 1981 and tripled the station's morning drive-time audience. He then went to WNBC-AM in New York and got fired three years into the job, presumably because of routines such as "Bestiality Dial-a-Date." Infinity's WXRK, known as K-Rock, quickly hired him for the morning slot, and his show soon zoomed to number one (beating out Imus, on in New York at the same time).

In 1990 Stern signed a five-year contract with Infinity reportedly worth $10 million, and by 1992 he was heard in ten cities around the country. He was the first local DJ to have a national drive-time audience, thanks to satellite technology. His core audience was white, often working-class men, aged eighteen to thirty-four,[48] but he also attracted others, including women, and many listeners had a love-hate relationship with him. His draw was that you'd never know which taboos he would violate next, what scandal he might commit.

How far would he go today? Would it be farther than yesterday? Stern was a linguistic stripper, teasing his audience that maybe today, maybe tomorrow, he would really take it all off, although it was often hard to imagine what boundaries were left to violate. He was also often very funny—not to my mind when he was humiliating women, people with disabilities, and blacks, although clearly others found this hilarious—but when he took on celebrities he thought were arrogant, hypocritical, or both. People with real distaste for many of Stern's routines adored his skewering of Kathie Lee Gifford, Bryant Gumbel, and Tom Hanks's bathetic acceptance speech when he won the Oscar for *Philadelphia.* Stern's populism emerged especially when he ridiculed the self-importance and mediocrity of a celebrity culture that the rest of the media profited from, promoted, and took all too seriously. With celebrity journalism spreading like anthrax and the Hollywood publicity juggernauts ramming through all the media, Stern just said no. This was the antithesis of the TV talk show host, who had to suck up to celebrities pushing their latest "projects." Stern gleefully flattened these hierarchies and exposed them as arbitrary and ridiculous.

Stern's on-air persona was that of the class troublemaker—and often the bully—in seventh grade, the guy who made fart noises during study hall and tried to snap girls' bra straps in the cafeteria. He was obsessed with sex and was also relentlessly self-absorbed. One of the adjectives most frequently used to describe him was *pubescent*. This is telling in more than the obvious way. Because Stern assumed different identities at different times—one minute the insecure, almost feminized boy, the next minute the mouthy, arrogant stud—he enacted those swings between masculine and feminine, confident and abject, that young men really experience. The sound effects he used and verbal signatures of his cast all signified adolescent rebellion. They laughed often and loudly, creating an audio environment that signaled fun.[49]

While it's true that his commentary seemed aimed at twelve-year-old boys, this characterization lets Stern off the hook. For his persona was also that of a grown man, a deeply cynical one at that, who hated liberal politics and who insisted that unreconstructed white men get back on top. He was antigovernment and anti-immigrant, and said the L.A. police were right to beat Rodney King.[50] He combined adolescent humor about toilets, breasts, penises, passing gas, and jerking off with politically reactionary jokes that harkened back to minstrel shows and burlesque. He was especially determined to defy the liberal sensibilities about race, gender, physical disabilities, and sexual orientation that had emerged from the social movements of the 1960s and '70s. He was also determined to expose the hypocrisy of a culture that is often prudish and pornographic at the same time.

Yet his libertarianism had decidedly liberal strains: he was a free speech absolutist, ardent foe of censorship, at times even feminist. This was a volatile and, it seems, deliberately incoherent combination of libertarian, liberal, and conservative sensibilities. He was pro-choice and, in what came to be one of his most oft-cited quips, suggested that any woman who voted for George Bush might as well mail her vagina to the White House. His defiance of all codes of decorum, his insistence that sex was something talked about in the open, and that nothing and no one was sacred made him very hip, very 1980s. Yet in his on-air comments to female and African American guests, he harkened longingly to the 1950s, when Jim Crow was still the law of the land and the objectification of women was both commonplace and celebrated. He told the

Pointer Sisters that he wished he could be their "Massa Howard." "The closest I came to making love to a black woman," he announced, "was masturbating to a picture of Aunt Jemima." Of newscaster Connie Chung, he said, "For an Oriental woman, she has big breasts."[51]

In other words, Stern embodied the edict "Question Authority" and challenged convention, tradition, and bourgeois morality every chance he got. Yet the framework within which this occurred could not have been more utterly conventional, more conformist to deep-seated American attitudes and prejudices about men, women, people of color, and the order of things circa 1952. So Stern's listeners could be, vicariously, iconoclasts and traditionalists at the same time, totally hip yet sticks-in-the-mud. They could luxuriate in the contradictions surrounding what was expected of men.

Stern was a brilliant Peter Pan. He created a space where men didn't have to overcome their socialization as boys—they didn't have to grow up, leave Never-Never Land, and go back to that stuffy, Victorian nursery—at least not until the show was over. Moms and middle-class mores said that you had to learn how to be a gentleman, be polite to girls and deferential to superiors, learn how to make a living, and become a responsible and civilized young man. Not on Stern's show you didn't.

Stern insisted that free speech be extended to the airwaves, a principle that, ironically, the FCC head, Mark Fowler, also advocated, although Fowler was thinking in political rather than sexual terms. Stern hit on one of the fault lines of free marketers—they want the marketplace to be unregulated, to be free of burdensome laws, yet they also want their representatives to monitor and even censor what's allowed in that marketplace. Unregulated markets can often be extremely profitable, and Stern went straight for this contradiction between a desire for profits and a desire for censoring the content that produces those profits.

Since 1934 the FCC had sought to restrict obscene materials on the airwaves, and as recently as 1976, in response to a George Carlin routine called "Filthy Words," it had established a list of "seven dirty words" that could not be uttered on the air. There were also restrictions on "patently offensive" material and on depictions of "sexual or excretory activities or organs." Beginning in 1986, with Alfred Sikes chairman of the FCC, the agency began warning Infinity Broadcasting about the indecency of Stern's broadcasts. Jokes about Woody Allen's penis and having sex with the puppet Lamb Chop enraged conservative activists, and attacks on women and blacks infuriated women's and civil rights groups, as well as white men with progressive politics. But it was Donald Wildmon's National Federation for Decency, which picketed outside the FCC for a month in 1986, that applied the most consistent pressure. The FCC notified

Infinity that Stern was violating the agency's standards for decency, and when Stern and Infinity refused to buckle under, the commission began fining Infinity; the penalties totaled $1.7 million by 1992. The next year the agency upped the ante, threatening to block Infinity's purchase of three major-market radio stations while it reviewed a new rash of complaints against Stern.[52]

Stern was justifiably furious and argued that he had been unfairly singled out, given the penchant of television talk shows to showcase sexual deviance, with programs on transsexual, S & M practitioners who dated their cousins and so forth. To many the FCC seemed on a vendetta. Infinity supplied the FCC with tapes from *Donahue* and other television talk shows to document that Stern's material was no more sexually explicit than what was airing on TV in the immediate after-school hours. But while Infinity awaited taking the case to court, it was unable to continue buying radio stations, and in 1995 it caved in and paid a fine sixty-eight times larger than any previous FCC fine.[53]

But this drama and defeat were crucial to Stern's presentation of himself as a hero of epic proportions. He went on a crusade about his battles with the FCC, and while Stern no doubt believed in the principles of his First Amendment battles, the showdown put the lie to his lament that he was a loser who was hung like a chipmunk. Here he was, refusing to knuckle under to federal authority, insisting on speaking his mind.

Stern's archrival was Don Imus, the real pioneer of the format. As early as 1971, when he was a DJ on WNBC in New York, Imus was offering irreverent, insulting humor between Top 40 hits. He became enormously successful, and *Life* magazine labeled him "the most outrageous disc jockey anywhere." But his alcoholism seriously hampered his work, and he was fired in 1977. He subsequently returned to WNBC but became addicted to cocaine. It was not until 1988, after Imus had gone through a rehab program and got a new show on his old WNBC-AM station, now owned by Infinity and redubbed WFAN, that he reemerged as a major figure in talk radio. Within three years *Imus in the Morning* was the third-ranked program among men between twenty-five and fifty-four, but he had more male listeners making over $100,000 than any other morning talk show.[54] Imus has not just been resilient; as he continues to recalibrate his on-air persona, his influence grows.

Imus has not escaped the adjective *juvenile,* and Dinitia Smith, writing for *New York* magazine in 1991, likened listening to *Imus in the Morning* to "being stuck in a classroom with a bunch of prepubescent boys while the teacher is out of the room. Imus lets the educated male who grew up in the sixties and was taught not to judge women simply by the size of their breasts to be, for one glorious moment of his day, an unreconstructed chauvinist pig." As with Stern, for Imus nothing was sacred, and his show was replete with the de rigueur breast and penis jokes, attacks on homosexuals and African Americans, and tasteless characterizations of women, especially famous ones like Madonna, who was referred to as a "two-legged yeast infection," and Monica Lewinsky, "the fat slut."[55] He was simultaneously infantile and autocratic; one of his favorite things to do was ban somebody "for life" from appearing on the show.

In a show from 1990 Imus and the gang pretended to have Mike Tyson on the phone and had the heavyweight's first utterance be a belch. In the safety of the studio, they all roared with laughter as someone imitated the champ speaking with a lisp. Then Imus turned to one of his favorite subjects, the people who run Simon & Schuster, his current publisher. One Judy Lee, who made the mistake of not returning Imus's calls, came in for a thrashing, as Imus insisted she should be home, because her husband works hard all day and when he gets home "he has to cook his own dinner." "What good is she?" demanded Imus. "She can't return a phone call or bake a tasty meat loaf." Wondering why Lee hadn't returned his calls, Imus guessed "maybe she was shaving." More recently, sidekicks have called in pretending to be an outraged Howard Stern.

But the difference between Imus and Stern was that Imus was more explicitly political. "Imus," notes the media critic Howard Kurtz, "meshed eighth-grade locker-room jokes with fairly serious talk from pundits and politicians." He featured commentary by Jeff Greenfield, Mike Barnicle, and Anna Quindlen; read and deconstructed items from the day's newspapers; and invited politicians on the show. He made national headlines when Bill Clinton, whom Imus had been trashing throughout the spring of 1992 as a "hick" and a "bubba," appeared on his show and charmed listeners—and, temporarily, Imus himself—by holding his own against Imus and quipping that "Bubba is just southern for 'mensch.' "[56] Imus expressed grudging admiration, and when Clinton won the New York State primary, some credited Imus's endorsement as helping push him over the top. Imus's stock as star-maker went up. By 1998 the show was less sexual and scatological, with much more emphasis on books, music, and political affairs. Journalists in particular feel that they can come on the show and say things about current affairs (especially the Lewinsky circus) that they can't on TV. By the late 1990s Imus was syndicated on over one hundred stations in cities around the country and could also be seen on MSNBC, reaching over 10 million listeners and viewers.

In focus groups Imus fans have said they especially like his parodying of public figures, bringing them down from their pedestals and stripping them of their aura. As one man put it, "He's not afraid to poke fun at people and poke hard," even with prominent political guests or media stars. This fan added, quite tellingly, that *Imus in the Morning* "gets me going real good." Fans like this were sick of spin and news management, weary of the deferential constraints that bond journalists and politicians together in their staged minuets, and eager for a deflation of decorum and pretense. They wanted hierarchies flattened, and Imus obliged. They couldn't say whatever they feel like at work; Imus could. Most TV morning show hosts, and certainly late-night talk show hosts, have to please and flatter their guests. Not Imus. The guest must entertain and inform *him* or be subject to his withering dismissals, and now that he has taken to plugging books he likes, single-handedly creating best-sellers, guests with books to sell are only too eager to please. For many of his listeners Imus has turned the tables on money, power, and entitlement, created a place where polite people in prestigious and influential jobs have to "suck up," as Imus put it, to a man who breaks all the rules of bourgeois decorum.

Imus in the Morning has also been a venue in which warring elements of masculinity spar, wound each other, and call a truce. Insults have been the primary form of jousting, and some of the most pleasurable moments in the show have come when Imus and one of his regular callers, like the *Meet the Press* host Tim Russert, take each other down a peg. Imus—who must, in real life, get sick of people "sucking up" to him—loves being razzed by men he respects. This verbal ritual of inflation and deflation is how manhood is most frequently tested these days, and Imus's show stages the costs and pleasures of winning some verbal duels while losing others. Imus's persona has been that of the unfeeling bastard, but his charitable work and oft-stated admiration for his wife show how insensitivity and empathy coexist in men. Nor does Imus present himself as a tough guy in control of his emotions. Although his tone is sarcastic, Imus insists that he handles stress poorly and is thrown into a bad mood when his friends are maligned, he doesn't get to see enough of his wife, or his charitable work is criticized. Since the birth of his son, Imus has also been unabashed in his celebration of the pleasures of fatherhood. Imus embodies the extremes of manhood, from s.o.b. to doting dad, and thus shows that men can, and must, cobble together a male identity that draws from so many conflicting norms.

Stern's and Imus's success as "shock jocks" raised alarm that radio was cultivating the worst in its white, male listeners by encouraging them to repudiate the achievements, however partial, won by women, people of color, gays and lesbians, and the disabled. But when the press itself, and much of the white male power structure in Washington, felt threatened by talk radio, this became a major story. And the man who made political talk radio a national concern, rightly or wrongly, was Rush Limbaugh. By the early 1990s all sorts of power was attributed to him, and he himself boasted that he was "the most dangerous man in America." When the former congressman Vin Weber introduced Limbaugh to freshmen Republicans in 1994, celebrating their takeover of Congress, he said, "Rush Limbaugh is really as responsible for what has happened as any individual in America."

Was he? In their study of talk radio, Michael Traugott and his research team at the University of Michigan found that, despite grand assertions about his power, there had been very little systematic research done on Limbaugh's impact on American political life. In fact, Traugott noted, we knew very little about the talk radio audience, period, and how it had changed over time. Different wordings of questions in different surveys of the audience produced different estimates of the talk show audience's size. Some questionnaires, for example, didn't distinguish between call-in shows on TV or radio, or didn't distinguish between political shows and, say, call-in shrink shows. Very little research had been done with the same respondents over time to see how—or whether—talk radio changed their attitudes.[57] The studies that had been done were especially concerned about Limbaugh and the national phenomenon of talk radio, and they thus underplayed the importance of local DJs and talk show hosts to listeners, many of whom listen to local *and* nationally syndicated hosts. Have the psychological gratifications of listening changed over time? Questionnaires provided few answers.

By 1993 the Times Mirror Center for People and the Press decided to do a systematic study of political talk show listeners and surveyed 1,500 people, including a representative sample of 112 talk show hosts in major markets, most of whom were highly critical of Bill Clinton. Titled "The Vocal Minority in American Politics," the study opens with a tone of alarm: "American public opinion is being distorted and exaggerated by the voices that dominate the airwaves of talk radio, clog the White House switchboard when a Zoe Baird stumbles, and respond to call-ins." These talk show voices, according to the study, exaggerated and "caricatured discontent with American political institutions," and were more conservative and more critical of Clinton than the average American. Republicans had "a louder voice" than Democrats in this venue.

How many people listened, and how frequently? It was hard to tell. The study's finding that "almost one half of Americans (42 percent) listen to talk radio on a relatively frequent basis" was pretty meaningless and overstated talk radio's influence, since survey respondents could answer that they listened "sometimes" without having to spell out how frequent "sometimes" was. After all, sometimes could mean three times a month. The more reliable finding indicated that one in six (17 percent) listened regularly, a figure that remained relatively consistent across other studies. Those who "never listened" were most numerous in the East. While 11 percent of Americans had tried to call in to one of these shows, only 1 percent had actually talked on the radio. Various reports described Limbaugh's audience, in particular, as overwhelmingly male, but Times Mirror reported that across talk radio there was only a slight gender gap, with 45 percent of men—as opposed to 38 percent of women—saying they listened regularly or sometimes. But men were far more likely to call in.

Conservatives were twice as likely to be regular listeners as liberals, and, in general, they opposed gays in the military, were highly critical of Congress, were less supportive of social welfare programs, and advocated school prayer. They hated Bill Clinton. Two years later conservatives outnumbered liberals almost threefold among regular listeners.

Talk show hosts in the late 1980s and early 1990s saw themselves as playing a significant role in shaping public opinion and as having an impact on politics and public policy. Three-quarters of those polled said they were "able to recall a case in the recent past when they or something that happened on their show had an impact on public policy or politics." Whether the hosts' campaigns had to do with repealing a state's mandatory seat belt law or protesting lax enforcement of America's immigration laws, they saw their role as bringing a local issue to the forefront and galvanizing their listeners to do something about it. "Try calling city hall and getting something fixed," demands Mark Williams. "The average guy on the street doesn't have much of a voice. Talk radio is a way for them to feel enfranchised, to reconnect."[58]

In a 1995 update study Times Mirror emphasized how attentive the talk radio audience was to the news; these listeners were greater consumers of all kinds of news and paid more attention to it than did the general public.[59] Talk radio listeners were more knowledgeable about world events and followed political and financial news more closely than most people. For example, they followed the failure of the balanced budget amendment at almost twice the average level but followed the O. J. Simpson trial at about average rates. (Placing a high priority on political news was a badge of honor for Limbaugh; during the summer before the Simpson trial, when much of the mainstream news media was awash in rumor, speculation, and stories purchased from any possible source, Limbaugh's motto was "No OJ, none of the time.") Michael Traugott argues, in fact, that listening to talk radio encourages listeners to become more dedicated news junkies, especially in relation to domestic news, and suggests that listening might prompt some to become more politically active.

The Times Mirror update documented that talk radio listeners were more politicized than the average American: they were more likely to vote and more likely to vote Republican. Regular listeners were highly vocal in contacting their elected officials. Limbaugh liked to brag that he played a critical role in spurring conservatives to go to the polls in '94 and bringing about the "Republican revolution." While not focusing specifically on him, the Times Mirror study agreed that talk radio had played a central role in the uprising of the much vaunted "angry white men." For despite the ranting and raving of Limbaugh, Liddy, and others against liberals, bureaucracy, politics as usual, and the evils of an overlarge federal government, their listeners were not alienated or resigned. On the contrary, they evidently felt they could do something—they were, in fact, optimistic about the possibilities for change.[60]

Both Times Mirror studies confirmed the journalistic portrait of the audience as more upscale and less working-class than previously thought. Research in the 1990s indicates that audience members are more affluent, better educated, and more issue-oriented than their nonlistening counterparts.[61] In fact, in 1993, 24 percent of regular listeners earned more than $50,000 a year, and an additional 17 percent earned between $30,000 and $49,999, so nearly half earned the median income or more. Twenty-two percent of the regular listeners were college graduates, and another 17 percent had attended college. Talk show hosts, as well, were very well educated and often quite affluent; 60 percent had a college degree, 33 percent earned between $50,000 and $100,000, and 30 percent made in excess of $100,000. Sixty-three percent of hosts, but only 18 percent of the public, had incomes over $50,000.

Why did people listen to talk radio? Looking at the results of telephone surveys, talking to listeners, and analyzing the programs themselves suggests that, first and foremost, the collapse of public life that seemed so dramatic by the 1980s left many people longing for an arena through which they could stay in touch with the opinions and attitudes of their fellow citizens and have an ongoing sense of what this nation called "America" was.

Seventy percent of people told the Times Mirror pollsters that they listened to talk radio to become informed about issues of the day and to find out what others think about these issues. Talk radio gave listeners a way to tap into the nation, into public opinion, into a community that they didn't have before, where they could hear viewpoints that had not been filtered and homogenized by the TV networks and their news anchors. In fact, by a two-to-one margin, listeners said they were more interested in the program when they were listening to someone with an *opposite* point of view than when hearing a view similar to their own. A majority also said that talk radio was "a good place to learn things that cannot be learned elsewhere." They also said they "pick up information that they can use in conversation with other people."[62] When small groups of listeners talk about their relationship to talk radio, it is clear that distinct features of radio itself—its intimacy; the fact that you can listen while doing other things, especially driving; its accessibility, particularly in comparison with television; and the anonymity it affords the listener—and many of the callers—make political talk especially compelling over this medium.[63]

Some found themselves politically isolated at work or at home, deprived of any forum for discussion or debate. Co-workers and family members were either politically apathetic and ignorant or of a different political persuasion, which meant that going back and forth with them about current affairs would be frustrating, even infuriating. But tuning in to talk radio, people could hear other points of view, even outrageous points of view, and they could take them in quietly, or scream back at the radio without fear of an altercation. As one woman reported with a certain glee, you "can talk back to the radio with impunity" whether it's to the caller or the host, and it becomes a crucial outlet. Unlike television shows, from *Dallas* to *The X-Files,* which often prompt "watercooler conversations" in which people talk about the previous night's programming, talk radio seems to address an absence of such exchanges, especially around politics and current affairs, which may not be safe topics at work.[64]

This ability to talk back to the radio, in utter privacy, while learning about other people's point of view was key to listeners, who consistently pointed to another thing they liked about talk radio: it made them flex their mental muscles. Talk radio "gets people thinking," as one fan put it, and listeners spoke animatedly about how they felt mentally more active while listening. Some felt especially revved up intellectually when their own views were challenged and they had to make a case for their side, even if just in their heads. They specifically liked being freed from the "visual distractions" of television. (This is particularly true for older listeners, who grew up with radio.) They especially enjoyed learning about "behind-the-scenes" aspects of news stories, insider information, more detailed background than television news gave them. Liberals liked to tune in to Limbaugh or Liddy to "see what the opposition is up to," while conservatives tuned in to liberal hosts for similar surveillance reasons and "to hear how dumb liberals are." These folks used TV to "trance out." Not talk radio.

While most surveys suggest that people still trust the mainstream news media, in the small setting of a focus group, people quickly volunteer that they are cynical about and disgusted with the mainstream news, especially television. We must remember that the network news programs lost viewers in the 1980s—according to the Nielsens, ratings dropped 8 percent between 1983 and 1988.[65] Telephone questionnaires, which allow respondents to choose only "very favorable," "mostly favorable," and so forth to describe their attitudes toward the network news, flatten out people's ambivalence, while focus groups provide much more free reign for griping. So the surveys may underestimate public frustration with the news, while focus groups may magnify it.

But clearly talk radio taps into some people's sense that they are being poorly informed, pandered to, and manipulated as an audience. As one man put it succinctly, "If the major media were doing their job, talk radio wouldn't exist." Some suspect that the network news has been so co-opted by corporate America that it can't possibly tell the truth; others, and this is especially true of Limbaugh regulars, feel the news is too sensationalistic, too liberal, too superficial, or all of the above. "I don't believe much of what I read in the newspapers," reported one man, "so I listen to talk radio." Another described the network news as "mostly fluff," and still another cast it as "shallow . . . you can't find anything out." The media are out to get conservatives, insisted a conservative listener, and are "full of interest groups trying to present the news with their slant." People understand that competition corrupts the news, that the networks news is "about ratings, about putting on a performance."

Others objected to what they saw as the arrogance of network reporters and anchors, who seem to position themselves above everyone else as insiders with superior knowledge. Phrases like "we believe" in a report grate on such talk radio fans, who regard these interjections as undermining claims to objectivity. Clearly, for some, there are class-based antagonisms to silk-suited millionaire anchors who seem to place themselves above everyone else. One man singled out Richard Jewell—whom the media unfairly cast as a suspect in the Atlanta Olympic bombing—as a classic example of someone who was tried by the media without adequate evidence. Many hated the local news' promotional techniques, especially the practice of hyping a story hours before the news comes on—"Watch at 5:00 to learn information that could save your life!"—and then, at news time, putting the hyped story at the end of the news and having it last only ten seconds. "If I need to know something, I want to know it now, I don't like being teased."

Others feel that they just don't know *who* to believe in the news and find talk radio more credible. As one listener put it, when he's watching TV or reading the paper, he might encounter one economist favoring one side of an issue, another favoring the opposite, and since this listener is not an economist, he has no basis for judgment—he can't determine which expert is right or wrong. He concluded that "you might as well read nothing" as watch the news. His comments support studies of public cynicism and the news, which suggest that with so much oppositional commentary on television and on the op-ed pages, the audience tends to drop out of the debate; every possible response to a problem is picked apart, so all solutions seem ineffective and worthless.[66]

Interviewing people about talk radio and the shows they tune in to, tends to put Limbaugh more in his proper place: while Dittoheads, as Limbaugh fans are known, are often one-man fans, many listeners dip into a mix of local and national hosts. Regional hosts have a more familiar, local identity, and because they often focus on issues close to home, many listeners feel less distant from them than they do national hosts who have become media stars.

Nonetheless, we can't ignore the Limbaugh phenomenon, and we need to consider why he became the megastar that he did. Limbaugh was to the early 1990s what Father Coughlin was to the early 1930s: a radio orator who made people feel that he gave voice to what they really felt but hadn't yet put into words. One fan especially liked Limbaugh because he "articulates things in a way they haven't been articulated before." Limbaugh "fills in the blanks." When conservatives hear Limbaugh, according to this listener, they say to themselves, "Why can't I say it like that?" and "Yes, that's the way I feel." While only somewhere between 6 and 9 percent of the population listened to him on a daily basis at the height of his influence, this still amounted to, by 1992, the largest audience in political talk radio, estimated at somewhere between 12 and 20 million listeners. In 1992 Limbaugh was heard on 529 stations; three years later 660 stations aired his show. He earned $1.7 million a year. And he had only gone national in 1988. Limbaugh did the unprecedented: he gathered a large audience in the early afternoon, a slot thought to be dead compared with morning and evening drive time. And he succeeded in having a New York–based show go national. "Rush may have saved AM radio in this country," notes Jim Casale. "He did what no one thought could be done."[67]

After having lost several radio jobs in the Midwest in the 1970s and early '80s, Limbaugh landed a job in 1984 as Morton Downey, Jr.'s replacement on a Sacramento station. Within a year his brand of irreverent political commentary had made him the hottest host in Sacramento. Four years later Ed McLaughlin, the former president of ABC radio who had recently started his own radio syndication company, brought Limbaugh to New York to go national. At first Limbaugh was on only 58 stations, and some listeners complained about his harangues. But within two years he was on over 300 stations, and many of those that picked him up saw their ratings soar. Some restaurants and bars opened "Rush rooms," so Dittoheads could gather and listen while having lunch.[68]

Most of his listeners were white, and many had a higher income than the general population. Nearly 80 percent of those who listened often to Limbaugh expressed Republican sentiments; two-thirds identified themselves as conservative. They often expressed significantly greater interest in politics and public affairs than nonlisteners. For example, a whopping 90 percent of those who reported listening often to Limbaugh said they voted in the off-year elections of 1994. His listeners were more likely to talk about politics and to engage in political activities.[69] So even though Limbaugh may have been preaching to the choir, the fact that this was an activist choir that could be mobilized to fax, write letters to Congress, and jam the White House switchboard gave him and his listeners considerable clout.

By 1990 Limbaugh had become a critically important opinion leader for many, who didn't necessarily have their positions changed by him but who learned how to think about particular issues after listening to him. The "Limbaugh effect," if there is one, was not in converting liberals into conservatives but in honing conservative listeners' opinions about particular issues and events, and in cultivating deeply negative attitudes about certain people, like Hillary Rodham Clinton, or political groups, like environmentalists.[70]

Limbaugh's brilliance was in bringing humor, irreverence, and a common touch to what had been a pretty laced-up form, conservative commentary. This was no William F. Buckley. He was particularly skillful in his use of metaphors and had a talent for distilling issues to their most simple elements. He delighted in conjuring up vivid mental images of environmentalists as wacko tree huggers and feminists as combat-boot-wearing, goose-stepping "feminazis." He zoomed right into signifiers of class privilege. Academics, for example, were the "arts-and-croissant, wine-and-brie crowd." He nicknamed the anchor of CBS Nightly News Dan Blather. Clinton was "the Schlickmeister."

Once Clinton became president—arguably, one of the best things that happened to Limbaugh—the show focused most frequently on health care reform, crime, the media, and the role of government in spending money and providing services. Evidence suggests that Limbaugh's tirades against the Clintons' health care plan contributed to its defeat by activating and inflaming his listeners' opposition. In September of 1993 he lambasted the plan as promising "the simplicity of the tax form, the efficiency of the post office, the bureaucracy of the Department of Agriculture, and the results of rent control." One month later, evoking a highly coordinated military action requiring group loyalty and teamwork, he added, "We want to isolate this plan, encircle this plan, cut off this plan's supply line, and then we want to kill this plan." He denounced Clinton's crime bill as "worthless and meaningless" because of programs like "midnight basketball in the inner cities." Limbaugh gave his listeners a simple peg—midnight basketball—as a way to ridicule an entire program.

Between 1993 and 1995 Limbaugh discussed the liberal, mainstream media on well over four hundred days, with utterances like "The dominant media doesn't portray the real truth of today's society." He drove home the term "liberal media" over and over, and castigated the press—rightly so—for their superficial and incomplete coverage of health care reform, and for their sensationalistic focus on the O. J. Simpson case. Limbaugh clearly hates the mainstream media, but by emphasizing that only on his show will you hear the *real* truth, he also promotes the insider status and veracity of his own show. He continues to emphasize that his is "the most listened to talk show, and deservedly so." "Why do you listen to this program?" he rhetorically asks his audience. "Let me answer this. You will hear analysis here that you won't get anywhere else."[71]

Another of Limbaugh's brilliant strokes was to provide an on-air political Elderhostel for those long out of the classroom who wanted and needed guidance in a media-saturated, spin-governed world. He labeled his show the Institute for Advanced Conservative Studies, and he addressed his listeners as if he sensed that they missed being educated, being privy to knowledge that others aren't. He offered the Limbaugh Letter, a syllabus one could study and review.

Limbaugh has been denounced for being a demagogue, but his real persona is that of pedagogue. He has brought his listeners into a spectral lecture hall and helped them see themselves as part of a literate community where everyday people, and not just elites, must have knowledge, because knowledge is power. And, as one listener indicated, "You have to listen to Rush over a period of weeks, and then you can see where he's coming from." This wasn't a one-shot class; this was an ongoing seminar in which you didn't just learn isolated infobits but acquired a broader framework that constituted a worldview. He would take often obscure, complicated stories and turn them into simple, easy-to-imagine overheads.

While the network news and the newsmagazines increasingly addressed their audiences as consumers, Limbaugh addressed them as citizens. He read to his audience from *The New York Times* and *The Washington Post,* quoted from the network news, and juxtaposed these excerpts with hot-off-the-press faxes that he received from "inside" conservative sources who allegedly had the "real" truth.

Limbaugh was also deft at flattering his audience. He encouraged listeners to see themselves as competent critics who could detect media bias, sensationalism, and superficiality. At the same time, they still needed a teacher. As he said in 1996, "I believe that the most effective way to persuade people is . . . to speak to them in a way that makes them think that they reached certain conclusions on their own." Yet his caller screening practices gave preference to sycophants who offered very high teacher evaluations on the air. As Limbaugh told Howard Kurtz, "The purpose of a call is to make me look good." Savvy callers knew it was important to play the courtier, and those who did usually didn't get dissed. These flattering remarks—"It's such an honor and privilege to talk to you"—laid lovingly before Rush's feet seemed to serve as "sacrificial offerings to win acceptance and entry" into the "discursive kingdom" presided over by the great professor.[72]

Of course, Limbaugh is a conservative activist, and it is his politics and their effect on national discourse—and national elections—that have received the most attention. But let's remember that his listeners were primarily male, with one study claiming that his core, die-hard audience was as much as three-quarters male. Another study reported that nearly one-third of all men listened to Limbaugh at least sometimes, compared with only 13 percent of all women. It wasn't necessarily true that women hated Limbaugh—although clearly many did—but they just didn't tune in.[73]

What else did Limbaugh offer these men? He was a gender activist, an ideological soldier in the war to reassert patriarchy, to reclaim things as they "ought to be." He himself lamented the state of masculinity in the 1990s. "On the one hand, we want men who are sensitive and crying, like Alan Aldas, and then, after so much of that, women finally get tired of wimps and say, 'We want real men again!' O.K., so now we gotta change, we've got to go back to tough guys, we're not gonna take any shit. And our memories tell us, we go back to high school, look at who the girls went for—the assholes! The mean, dirty, greasy sons of bitches."[74] The ads on the show, for hair loss products, memory enhancers, and health care organizations that seek to prevent heart attacks, impart a worried subtext about emasculation that can, and must, be reversed.

But Limbaugh is more than a throwback. He personifies a new kind of 1990s man, the antithesis of the allegedly new age, sensitive, feminized kind of guy. He is a male hysteric who skillfully uses his voice to signal the easy slide between rationality and outrage. Real men don't eat quiche; they have a point of view and voice it. So Limbaugh deftly *does* blend "feminine" traits into his persona, because he gives men permission to get hysterical about politics. Here is a man who is emotionally unchecked, yet simultaneously reasonable, combative, and avowedly antifeminist. There is no equivocation here, no "on the one hand, on the other hand," no genial, get-along stance. This is not the persona of the organization man who goes along with institutional idiocy because his boss says to. This is not some Dilbert forced to seethe in silence in his cubicle.

No, this man loses it, his naturally deep voice shooting up an octave as he denounces something he thinks doesn't make a lick of sense. When quoting from newspaper articles, especially a section he's about to mock, Limbaugh theatrically lowers his voice, parodying the paper's supposed aura of authority. As soon as his pitch zooms up, we know we're back to Limbaugh, who interjects comments like "Idiocy! Pure idiocy!" or "Get this!" or "That can't be!" Limbaugh, and many of his fellow hosts, attacked post-Vietnam media and corporate versions of masculinity; they attacked what Christopher Lasch labeled in the late 1970s the narcissistic personality, the bureaucratic operator desperately dependent on the approval of others who learns how to wear a variety of amiable masks to get by. Limbaugh's special talent is how he flexes his vocal cords to enact this critique. He understands that radio needs clear auditory signposts that instantly produce an emotional reaction. It was this delicately calibrated balance between letting go and holding on that staked out the male hysteric as not just a reasonable but an enviable persona, a man more authentic, more in touch with the connection between his feeings and his ideas than circumscribed TV reporters or political spin doctors.

Yet such an emotionally accessible and explosive guy has to maintain that he is still a real man. Hence the special importance of feminist bashing—for Limbaugh this is done through his regular "feminist updates" on the movement's alleged idiocies—to the presentation of the male hysteric as appropriating some "feminine" prerogatives while still not acquiescing to women's demands for equality. Because his hysteria requires that he come up with deliberately perverse assertions, he can charge, for example, that the controversy over smoking in the United States is really the fault of native Americans, since they grew tobacco here first.[75]

Limbaugh in particular has been cagey about how much political influence he has. Obviously, as a conservative he has a political agenda and wants to exert power. And he has hardly been reluctant to serve as a pundit on the Sunday morning TV talk shows or to revel in his role in the 1994 "Republican Revolution." But it has also been crucial for Limbaugh to deny that he has such power and to cast himself primarily as an entertainer. "My purpose is not to make America more like what I think it should be," he told *Vanity Fair*. "I simply want to be the best radio guy there is." In television interviews with Barbara Walters, he also insisted that he's just an entertainer, and "a pussycat" to boot. Clearly, Limbaugh must be publicly ambivalent about his power—his listeners want him to be a force to be reckoned with, but they don't want him to become an insider.[76] Limbaugh wants—and needs—to have it both ways: to be perceived as having power yet to be perceived as an outsider, a mere conduit of "the people."

With Stern, Imus, and Limbaugh, there is a very different kind of listener identification than there was with the Top 40 DJ, who flattered his audience and devised all sorts of rhetorical devices to fold listeners into a community in which they felt included and necessary. Many of this new breed of talk jocks, in fact, create an aura of exclusivity, of having a clubhouse many would not dare to enter in real life and wouldn't be welcome in if they did. You enter at your own risk and call in at your peril. Often audience members are cast, in part through the way the host treats callers, as lonely, isolated, even abnormal folks who need to get a life.[77] Why has defiant self-assertion and an adversarial stance been so important to the talk radio host, and why do listeners find this so compelling? A version of what media studies scholars have labeled the third-person effect seems to be operating here: the notion that the media affect *other* people in negative and manipulating ways but not us. Here, it is possible to think that it's the other folks in the audience who are jerks and losers, or others who think the fart and breast jokes are really funny. But it seems that such shows can be double-edged: they can create a community of, say, Dittoheads but also encourage many listeners to feel apart from, superior to, and antagonistic toward their co-listeners.

If talk radio was frequently aimed at conservatives, and at men, then where could women go on the dial to be informed? And what about those SNAGs— "sensitive new age guys"—that Stern, Imus, Limbaugh, and Liddy wanted nothing to do with, men with liberal, progressive, or even middle-of-the-road politics who had made accommodations with, or even embraced, the civil rights and women's movements? These people could turn to radio too and find there a community also rejected by the network news, people who wanted more background, more detail, and fewer sports and warfare metaphors in their evening news. They turned to National Public Radio.

By 1995 during a typical week between 10 and 11 million Americans tuned in to NPR news programming, with the largest audiences in big cities with long car commutes, like Los Angeles. (For comparison, each of the nightly network news shows has about 11 million viewers.) In Boston and San Francisco, *Morning Edition* was the number-one-rated drive-time show. If you had just met someone and learned that he or she, too, listened to Terry Gross's *Fresh Air,* or Click and Clack's *Car Talk,* or Ray Suarez's *Talk of the Nation,* let alone *All Things Considered,* you felt that you had met a kindred spirit, one who, like you, was part of a community quite different from that activated by Howard Stern. NPR constructed an imagined community as much as political talk radio did, and its ethos stood in stark opposition to the pugnacious—and often adolescent—pose of talk radio. As the political cartoonist Jules Feiffer put it when he first heard *All Things Considered* in 1979, "You feel like part of some underground network or some kind of conspiracy. It's like back in the sixties when you discovered someone else who'd heard Mort Sahl."[78]

After listening to Stern or Liddy, NPR seemed like a retreat to Amish country. Bill Siemering, the man who wrote NPR's original statement of purpose, wanted "something that was not, and is not, available in very many places on the radio dial," wrote NPR host Linda Wertheimer. "He wanted quietness. He wanted calm conversation, analysis and explication." Critics agreed that he achieved this. In 1979 *Time* referred to *All Things Considered* as "surely the most literate, trenchant and entertaining news program on radio."[79]

Like political talk radio, NPR's decade of dramatic growth was the 1980s, after satellite technology made linking up as a network more economical and efficient. While the audience was often stereotyped as consisting of upper-middle-class liberals—"elitists" as Newt Gingrich charged in 1995—surveys indicated that nearly half of NPR's audience lived in households with incomes below $40,000, that only one-third had a college education and were in professional or managerial occupations, and that one-third of the audience described itself as "conservative."[80]

NPR was actually an afterthought of the Public Broadcasting Act of 1967. The Carnegie Commission on Educational Television, which began work in 1965, recommended that Congress establish a Corporation for Public Broadcasting and that it be financed through an excise tax on the sales of new television sets. Instead the CPB was left beholden to government subsidies that Congress would approve, a method of funding that has plagued public broadcasting ever since. But the commission focused primarily on television—what FCC Chair Newton Minow had dubbed "the vast wasteland" in 1962. It was Lyndon Johnson—who himself owned a radio station in Austin and had other holdings in broadcasting—who added radio to the proposal, reportedly after heavy pressure from Jerrold Sander, head of the National Association of Educational Broadcasters.

To say that NPR got its start in the face of major financial and technical obstacles would be an understatement. Unlike PBS, which aired shows but wasn't required to produce all of them, NPR was obliged to produce *and* distribute national programming. And it received less than 10 percent of the public broadcasting budget—the rest went to television.[81] Its potential network of affiliates consisted of many low-power, community and college and university stations, some of which broadcast only during the day, were staffed by volunteers, and had shoestring budgets.

When the CPB drew up guidelines for minimum standards of eligibility to become a member station, they ruled out 80 percent of NPR's potential affiliates. The guidelines required that stations broadcast at least eighteen hours a day, 365 days a year, that they have a full-time professional staff of at least five and an annual operating budget of at least $80,000, that FM stations be at least 3,000 watts and AM stations 250 watts, and that they have adequate facilities for producing local programming.[82] Only 73 stations qualified. Despite these challenges the founders of shows like *All Things Considered* were determined to make their radio news more absorbing, more conversational, more immediate. By the mid-1970s *All Things Considered*, hosted by Susan Stamberg (the first female anchor of a national news broadcast) and Bob Edwards, had a core following of approximately 5 million listeners—the most widely heard noncommercial radio show in American history—and by 1979, 220 stations met the CPB membership guidelines.

The first installment of *All Things Considered* aired on May 3, 1971, one day before the anniversary of the Kent State massacres, when antiwar demonstrators hoped to block traffic around Washington, DC, and shut down the nation's capital. This was no standard, from-the-studio, rip-and-read news show. Instead the broadcast revived the sort of eyewitness account pioneered by CBS in the late 1930s and exploited ambient sounds and on-the-spot interviews to create a you-are-there feel. The reportorial style demanded dimensional listening. "Flying squads of police zigzagging on motor scooters moved in and out of the city with tear gas and nightsticks . . . and tried by charges and feints to break up the demonstrators." Then the announcer, Robert Conley, quite conversationally, told his listeners what would come next. "Rather than pulling in reports from all over town, we thought we might try to take you *to* the event, to get the feel, the texture of the sort of day it's been, through a mix of sounds and events." The next thing listeners heard was demonstrators chanting, "Stop War, Stop the War Now!" while helicopters circled overhead. Jeff Kamen, reporting on the scene, used the present tense and eavesdropped on everything he could. "Here come the police . . . one, two, three four . . . ," and you heard their motorcyles roar up. He then relayed two utterly conflicting accounts, one from a demonstrator, one from a cop, of a police motorcycle knocking down a demonstrator. When one policeman said a brick was thrown at him, Kamen told the audience he saw nothing thrown.

Over at the Pentagon, one protester described paddling across the Potomac in his kayak to get into town. Kamen then made sure his microphone was poised in the middle of an exchange between the demonstrators and a Pentagon official, who was insisting they leave immediately. Listeners could hear most but not all of the exchange, just as they would have had they been bystanders. Listeners heard sirens and yelling, while Kamen described Indiana Avenue as "choked with tear gas." After a series of eyewitness accounts of how the police had harassed or beaten peaceful bystanders because they looked like hippies, Kamen noted, "Today in the nation's capital it is a crime to be young and to have long hair." The eyewitness accounts of police brutality, coupled with descriptions of severe reactions to the tear gas, including people vomiting in the streets, were enormously powerful, because people were given time to describe in detail what they saw, their voices were filled with outrage, and you could picture it all vividly. "Today is another Saigon," a Vietnam veteran told Kamen.[83]

The report was emblematic of how *ATC* was going to do the news. Reporters got out of the studio whenever possible and consciously used the natural sounds of the scene to emphasize points and create a powerful mental image. They talked to more everyday people, and the show was filled with voices you hardly ever heard on TV, like those of African American witnesses and bystanders, some of them office workers trying to get to work. Toward the end of the broadcast, the show went to a barbershop to hear how barbers were faring in an age of long hair. This became another trademark: exploring pedestrian situations and locales that spoke to broader cultural shifts and tensions.

Many consider Frank Mankiewicz, who became president of NPR in 1977, the man who turned it into a truly national network with a national following. Mankiewicz had been, among other things, Bobby Kennedy's press secretary, and millions knew him as the ashen-faced man who had announced to the nation in June of 1968 that Kennedy was dead. Mankiewicz was an aggressive champion of public radio and succeeded in increasing its share of public broadcasting funding to 25 percent. Even though it took five years for *All Things Considered* to find 1 million listeners, under Mankiewicz NPR's budget grew from $3.2 million in 1973 to $12.5 million in 1979. The network made headlines in 1978 when NPR broadcast the Panama Canal Treaty debate live from the Senate floor with Linda Wertheimer—a woman—anchoring the broadcast. The coverage drew an estimated 25 million listeners, won the network a Du Pont–Columbia Award, and increased NPR's audience by 25 percent. This was the first time *any* network had covered the Senate live, in action, and it led to a tradition of NPR offering live coverage of such gripping national dramas as the Iran-Contra hearings and the Clarence Thomas confirmation hearings. In 1979 Mankiewicz got $4.0 million from CPB to launch *Morning Edition*. The network's audience doubled to approximately 9 million listeners by the early 1980s. NPR also sought to revive story listening by featuring *The Masterpiece Radio Theater* with productions of *Moby-Dick* and a drama series called *Earplay*.[84]

While Mankiewicz was a genius at network building, apparently financial management was not a commensurate skill. By 1983, with the country coming out of a recession and the Reagan administration cutting CPB's funds by 31 percent between 1981 and 1983, NPR found itself $9 million in debt. Although he survived two no-confidence votes, Mankiewicz resigned. But despite this, and the ideological and fiscal hostility of the administration, NPR continued to grow. The network faced a daunting prospect: reeducating people, especially those raised to turn to television for news and nonmusical entertainment, to turn to the pleasures of listening. Millions made the shift. But behind the scenes, to make this possible, NPR had begun to accept corporate underwriting, even to allow particular organizations to sponsor coverage of particular topics, something unheard of in the print media.[85]

By 1995 more listeners than ever were tuning in to NPR, and their contributions had increased from $40 million in 1985 to $95 million. In many markets NPR became people's primary radio news source, and its news shows had more listeners than *The New York Times* had readers. Some were responding, in part, to the threats by those same folks Limbaugh allegedly helped get elected—Republican congressmen—to slash and eventually "de-fund" the budgets for public broadcasting. While the television networks and newsmagazines experienced downsizing of their news divisions in the 1980s and '90s, NPR's news budget tripled, and it boasted a staff of 200. As the veteran NPR reporter Susan Stamberg noted, "With all the takeovers, with all the mergers, with all the bottom-lineness that has hit commercial television, this is the last bastion for electronic news reporting. We're what CBS News was in the 1960s."[86]

The hallmark of *All Things Considered*, in addition to the length and depth of its news stories, was its inventive and playful use of sound. Ambient sound—of distant gunshots, of sirens, of crickets at night, of children at a playground—were standard features of all stories, evoking place and mood. And because the show had ninety minutes to work with, it was not unusual to hear long, detailed stories, such as an eighteen-minute profile of Sen. Russell Long or a thirty-minute piece on people who had grown up in and would probably never leave the Appalachian Mountains of West Virginia.[87]

Stamberg and Edwards also had a sense of humor and drew from old genres, like radio drama or game shows, to play with the implications of a story. In the game show "Gimme Shelter"—"America's favorite tax-planning fun game"—Stamberg competed to see if she could correctly identify all the tax shelters available to rich people. Rising interest rates were explained through a mock opera, "Gross Interesso." A press release from the Carter administration listing the gifts bestowed on the president turned into an audio tour of the White House, replete with the sounds of squeaking doors and breaking glass. Many stories, like one on the hundredth anniversary of the banana or the "people mover" in the National Gallery of Art, as well as much of the essays and commentary, celebrated a wry, bemused outlook on contemporary American culture.[88]

But as the journalist James Ledbetter emphasizes in his terrific analysis of the commercial corruption of public broadcasting, *Made Possible by . . .*, NPR was always torn between two goals. Would it be an aural pioneer, offering listeners new audio experiences, or would it provide hard news in more depth and detail than television did? Often *All Things Considered* in the 1970s succeeded in addressing both desires, but more frequently this debate divided the staff, one side deriding the network's penchant for serving up nothing more than "ear candy," the other side condemning the trend toward sensory and political conformity.[89] By the mid-1980s the hard news advocates had won.

One of NPR's biggest hits was Garrison Keillor's *A Prairie Home Companion*, which began airing in 1974. By 1985 Keillor was on the cover of *Time*, and his book *Lake Wobegon Days* became a best-seller, with over 700,000 copies in print. Allegedly modeled loosely on the Grand Ole Opry, the show was an olio of songs and instrumental performances, fake commercials, and twenty-minute stream-of-consciousness monologues by Keillor about the fictitious Minnesota town Lake Wobegon, "where all the women are strong, all the men are good-looking and all the children are above average."[90] While Imus and Stern were making fun of women and minorities, Keillor went after middle-American white-bread culture and took aim at its often hollow center.

This was not a rapid-fire mode of stand-up comedy—Keillor didn't tell jokes. Instead, he sought to replicate the childhood experience of listening to a grown-up tell sometimes wry and sometimes poignant stories about what it was like in small-town America, before you were born. "Keillor," noted *Time*, "knows that childhood is the small town everyone came from," and his show provided listeners with "a time machine" to revisit their youth—real or imagined—and to revisit radio as a medium. Keillor revived the variety show and story listening. And he harkened to the old days of communal family listening to the radio. This was cornball country but with a twist. There was a worldly wise quality to Keillor's view of Lake Wobegon, a way in which he longed for this small town but also saw it as a place to be laughed at, and an unflinching sense of how small-town life can be both secure and smothering. The show was both deliberately square and hip about its squareness.

Keillor brought a knowing, even self-mocking tone to the show's nostalgia, especially for old-time radio. Taking listeners back to shows that "influenced me as a boy," he offered a "salute to early Minnesota radio" as he revived shows like "The Bud and Betty Show" or "Rusty, Boy Detective," from their "graveyard in the ether." Then, truly bad or inadvertently funny dialogue would make fun of old radio while longing for its calculated naiveté. "Why was I born Scandinavian?" asked one of the supposed male radio characters. "The food's lousy, and the religion enough to break a man's heart." The fake ads for Bertha's Kitty Boutique, Mr. Pickle's Swedish Salsa, and Chuck's Charities ridiculed what many, in their nostalgia for radio's "golden age," had forgotten: its overabundance of schlocky commercials that sought to turn everything into a commodity.

In Keillor's stories about Lake Wobegon, listeners heard about characters named Merle and Lefty, people who had managed to remain utterly unselfconscious amidst a culture of narcissistic self-absorption. He loved hick America; and he was relieved he had escaped it. As a band like the Night O' Rest Motel Orchestra played ragtime, the show evoked the America of outdoor bandstands and gazebos. Other singing groups evoked the 1940s, like the Andrews Sisters or the Mills Brothers. This was an America before TV, before rock 'n' roll, and certainly before Howard Stern. There were few good estimates of his audience's size—260 public radio stations carried the show in 1985, and Minnesota Public Radio guessed at 2 million listeners but wasn't sure—but they were absolutely devoted to this throwback to the old way of listening to the radio.[91]

Like talk radio, NPR in the 1990s remains much more interactive than the nightly news. People from around the country deliver op-ed pieces and essays on *All Things Considered,* and letters from listeners are read over the air every week. *Talk of the Nation* and *The Diane Rehm Show* offer live, nationwide questions and comments from callers and cover topics rarely, if ever, discussed on television. When listening to the news, one is urged to listen, concentrate, and imagine. Eyewitness accounts of disasters such as the August 1998 bombings in Kenya and Tanzania break an event into its gruesome but telling sequences, and listeners don't just see a flat, if horrifying picture. They relive how someone experienced the event and get drawn into its sensations: through hearing it is given dimension.

But like free form before it, the network has had its earlier freedom reined in. Pressure from conservatives in Congress and the need to use corporate underwriters have made shows like *All Things Considered* less likely to take risks, more inclined to showcase features about the arts instead of investigative political stories, and less likely to feature left-of-center commentary. After pressure from Sen. Bob Dole and the Philadelphia police in 1994, *All Things Considered* abrogated its contract for a set of commentaries by Mumia Abu-Jamal, a Peabody Award–winning journalist serving time on death row for allegedly killing a policeman. After the conservative commentator Fred Barnes wrote an infamous attack on the show titled "All Things Distorted," he was offered a regular commentator's slot.[92] *ATC,* while still providing some of the most in-depth news coverage anywhere on the airwaves, has moved through that cycle so familiar in radio history, from riskiness to safety. And safety eventually provokes a rebellion elsewhere in the radio spectrum.

As commercial radio approaches the turn of the century, it is a fragmented industry increasingly devoted to niche markets that is simultaneously highly consolidated and controlled primarily by four behemoths: Capstar Broadcasting, CBS, Clear Channel Communications, and Jacor. By 1997 the top four radio group owners controlled 90 percent of radio advertising revenues in the country.[93] And they are hardly finished with their shopping spree. A frequent analogy suggests that some cities are becoming like one-newspaper towns—the press is controlled by one owner, but the paper has different sections for different audiences. So Jacor might own eight stations in Cincinnati or Denver, but each station will be targeted to a different niche audience.

Talk radio has also become more controlled and contained, more reliant on technologies that bar or limit entry to the talk world. Call screening procedures now include delay systems, which postpone the airing of a call by four to seven seconds so the caller can be dropped if he or she uses profanity. New computers show the caller's name and give a brief synopsis of what he or she wants to talk about so the host can decide who to put on next—or at all. Potentially inflammatory callers are more likely to get on than those who might be more moderate or reasoned. New devices also allow for "call stacking"—putting some people lower and lower in the line of those who might get on the air until the show runs out of time, a strategy used especially against elderly voices.[94]

In 1997 over 1,200 stations were doing talk, and they needed to find new listeners, not just hang on to the ones they had. Those listeners would have to come from the group that turned to radio not for talk but for music. The business was fiercely competitive, with new hosts trying to break in and established hosts trying to hold on to their audience. And for AM talk stations, there was the still hard reality that 80 percent of radio listeners tuned in to FM. There was also powerful reaction against certain hosts' excesses on the air. After visiting the U.S.-Mexican border, the talk show host Jeff Katz suggested on a San Diego station that the solution to illegal immigration was to run Mexicans over at the border, and for doing so you could get a sombrero and a free meal at Taco Bell. Outrage and well-organized pressure from the Hispanic communities in California forced Katz off the air.[95]

Some fear that talk radio will go the way of FM in the 1980s—that the freedom of the hosts will be circumscribed by formulas and assembly-line production techniques.[96] They fear that as syndication takes over more and more stations, the opportunities for local hosts will dry up, and that to get on the air a host will have to demonstrate that he or she can lock up 100 stations and get into 50 percent of the top markets right away. Research may take over instinct, just as it did with AM and then FM. Talk show topics, for example, could be pretested with focus groups to assess their marketability ahead of time. Radio hosts could be tested for their "Q" ratings before they can get on the air. In short, the kind of spontaneity that has gotten various hosts in trouble—but also made the medium vibrant and unpredictable—may very well be squelched.

These are not just concerns about radio as a form. Talk radio and NPR are, political differences aside, about using the airwaves to reinvigorate democracy. They both stemmed from populist impulses on the right and the left that demanded, in the Reagan years and beyond, that the nonmonied classes have their say too. NPR and talk radio also insisted that Washington, D.C., was not the center of the universe, and that the centralization of the mainstream news media ignored the majority of America. Now that financial considerations are pressuring both genres, and consolidation in the industry threatens to reduce the number of voices in talk, the fear is that public discourse, even on radio, will shrink to fit inside narrower, more orthodox margins. These are valid concerns. But we must also remember that much of talk radio was also about reaffirming patriarchy, a value system utterly at war with democracy. "Dr. Laura" Schlessinger, a woman, may be beating out Rush Limbaugh, but her show is entirely about keeping women in their place.

Neither Imus and Stern nor *All Things Considered* plays with the possibility of sound as they once did. But talk radio and NPR, when the hold of television on audience attention seemed complete, tapped into that still vibrant desire among many to listen. Both forms of talk reminded Americans of radio's distinct power to forge group ties. In all of the anxiety about the influence of Limbaugh or Stern, pundits focused on the hosts, not on the medium. But it was the medium that allowed Stern's fans to imagine whatever they wanted when he talked about sex. It was the act of listening together simultaneously that made Dittoheads feel such camaraderie. With the glut of visual imagery more relentless than ever, it was radio, still, that formed imagined communities among subgroups of Americans and dramatized the connections between listening, emotions, and political engagement. As talk radio and NPR bow lower to the pressures of free market ideology, with formats more predictable than ever, and with increasing numbers of people turning to the Internet for news and information, what will happen to listening in the twenty-first century?

Why Ham Radio Matters

On March 30, 1992, on its front page, *The New York Times* announced the end of an era. "Before there were nerds . . . there were Heathkits, which let tens of thousands of ambitious amateurs and aspiring engineers build their own radios." But now, after forty-five years of production, the Heath Company was discontinuing the sale of its do-it-yourself kits. Ready-made radios were cheaper and had driven Heathkits out of the market. The *Times* regretted that this marked "the passing of an American institution that fostered learning-by-doing in its finest form." And the article quoted former Senator Barry Goldwater, builder of more than one hundred Heathkits: "It's just that people today are getting terribly lazy, and they don't like to do anything they can pay someone else to do." Goldwater wasn't just bemoaning the apparent decline in tinkering. He was also suggesting that certain key elements of twentieth-century masculinity—the insistence on mastering technology, the refusal to defer to the expertise of others, the invention of oneself by designing machines—all this was in jeopardy. Yet at the time of Goldwater's lament there were more licensed amateur operators—650,000—than at any other time in American history.[1]

Why include a chapter on the hams in a book about commercial radio? Because the hams didn't just start radio broadcasting in America. They also have consistently offered another model for how radio might be used and for how to listen. For over nine decades of the twentieth century, boys and men by the hundreds of thousands have learned about electricity and electronics by tinkering with radio. Because hobbies are pursued during leisure hours, often in private, and seem nonproductive in terms of the larger econ-

omy, they often get short shrift in historical accounts of America's technological evolution. This is a mistake. By ignoring hobbies—from men tinkering
with their Model T's to women working on their sewing machines—we miss
the critical history of the rise and fall of technical literacy in the United States.
And there is a critical relationship between the technical literacy of ordinary
people and a nation's ability to compete in increasingly high-tech international
markets.

Ham radio played a pivotal role in producing engineers who kept American industry, not to mention the American military, at the cutting edge of the
field. And for many the hobby also brought them into a distinctly American
subculture, a poorly understood and barely known fraternity known as the
hams. If we are going to think about the relationship between radio and masculinity, as well as how technological insubordination brings about technological progress, ham radio is clearly the place to start. Broadcast listeners may
love radio—or have loved it once—but the hams *really* love radio. For many it
is their passion, their religion, their family, their life.

The hams are one of the most important yet least visible subcultures in
America. They surface in the news periodically, when a natural disaster or political coup makes them the only source of instant communication between the
embattled spot and the rest of the world. When Hurricane Andrew devastated
portions of Florida in 1992, the hams, with battery-powered equipment—and
thus no need for electricity—handled the emergency communications for fire
departments, police stations, and rescue squads whose own radio and telephone systems had crashed. One of the first things to be set up in the shelters for
survivors is a ham station, which, after handling "life and death" traffic, sends
and receives "health and welfare" messages between survivors and their friends
and family far away.[2] Hams also handled huge volumes of traffic in the aftermath of the 1994 earthquake in San Francisco, when phone lines were first
down and then clogged. In situations like these we see for a brief moment a
cross section of an anthill, with all its teeming channels and chambers, working
constantly and without fanfare, to keep contact alive. Then the disaster abates,
the anthill gets covered up again, and everyone forgets about this intensive fraternity of public-spirited folks.

Most of the time, in fact, Americans pay little attention to these etheric ob-
sessives; when they do, they probably regard the hams as techno-dweeb odd-
balls driven to their hobby because they have all the social skills of robotics
equipment. As Steve Mansfield, the head lobbyist for the American Radio
Relay League put it, he is constantly battling a stereotype of hams as "old fat
guys sitting in their basements" whose hobby is irrelevant or silly. And reporters for the broadcast media, who used to provide much more coverage of

the hams' heroism during natural disasters than they do now, are less in awe of the hams' ability to step into the breach now that reporters themselves have satellite technology, cellular phones, and the capacity to do live remotes.

But the hams are not just inconsequential, idiosyncratic tinkerers, and it would be a mistake to see them as eccentric technophiles. They form a society over half a million strong, with its own language, mores, rituals, and ethos. And they should be thought of as a tribe—if we can manage to purge that word of its associations with the condescending word *primitive*—because they are a distinct collectivity whose history and anthropological characteristics have inflected the broadcast culture, and certainly the evolution of radio, in profound ways. One of their most important contributions throughout the century has been demonstrating that frequencies thought worthless were in fact extremely valuable. The other has been their role in developing "spectrum economizing" apparatus—radio equipment that needs less bandwidth and less power to operate over sometimes enormous distances.

More to the point, hams have always insisted that listening in be an active, participatory pastime and that Americans always have a portion of the spectrum reserved for *them*—everyday people. They have demanded and cultivated a commercial-free zone in the spectrum in which individuals—not just corporations and ad agencies—are allowed to transmit, to explore, and to connect with one another. Their vision of the spectrum, in other words, is that some of it forever remain undeveloped wilderness, a trust that is rightly the property of all Americans. Because of them, some portions of the radio spectrum—the short waves 160 meters and lower (remember, the shorter the wavelength the higher its frequency, so these are frequencies from 2 up to 1,300 megahertz)—remain democratic and unpredictable. We should especially take note of this vision now, as major corporate forces seek to undermine the idea that the spectrum is a common property resource and try to put it all up for sale to the highest bidder. Some of these same interests often try to snatch spectrum away from the hams, most recently for use by cellular phone or truck dispatching companies. It is a full-time job warding off such commercial encroachments.

The nickname *ham* used to be despised as a slur; now it is almost a badge of honor. While there has been much debate over the origin of the name, the safest hypothesis is that it is a carryover from telegraph days. Operators used to refer to those whose Morse code transmissions were sloppy as hams, which may have come from the ham-handed way they seemed to handle a telegraph key. When telegraph operators moved into wireless, they of course brought their language with them, and at first *ham* was a perjorative term applied to incompetent wireless operators. There was so much sensitivity about the term that it didn't come into accepted use until the 1950s, when *ham* replaced the more cumbersome (and often inaccurate) term *amateur operator.*[3]

The hams have a totally different relationship to the technology of radio and the forces of nature that made broadcasting possible than do the rest of us. They have constantly experimented with wavelengths and found, for example, that 40 meters (7 megahertz) achieves worldwide propagation at night and up to 1,000 miles during the day. Twenty meters (14 megahertz) offers excellent worldwide communication even during the day. Hams also came to learn that high sunspot radiation enhances the ionosphere's ability to reflect higher-frequency radio signals—the really short waves above 20 megahertz (16 meters or less)—back to earth. There are sunspot cycles, going from minimum to maximum radiation, some as short as seven years and some as long as seventeen, with the average at eleven years, and hams learned to track these cycles so they could get the maximum out of their sets. But even here there is surprise. During the solar minimum, isolated solar flares can burst through and, for a brief time, open up the higher frequencies once again to long-distance work. So while someone like me is watching the weather report on television to see whether it will rain the next day, the hams are monitoring sunspot activity. They closely follow the ever-changing behavior of the ionosphere, which I barely think about. Others may be listening to the radio waves that emanate from Jupiter and keeping track, via their own sets, as they did the summer of 1994, of that planet's much publicized collisions with a comet. Some have conversed with astronauts on the space shuttle.

While most folks chat on the phone with a friend from across town or even a few states over, there are hams in the United States talking to friends and acquaintances in Australia, Bulgaria, or Japan. Not until the spread of the Internet in the mid-1990s were other Americans able to communicate across the distances that the hams did. By maintaining contact with hams in Eastern Europe during the fall of communism, they talked to eyewitnesses and participants who actually knew something, while the rest of us had our information filtered through news anchors and highly uninformed "experts" safely sequestered in Washington. Hams can also listen in on air traffic controllers and Coast Guard transmissions. In the mid-1990s they followed a reading of numbers on the air that went something like "38 . . . 12 . . . 44 . . . 9 . . . 23" and was believed to be a secret espionage code (although no one knew for sure).

Hams get to hear things you're not really supposed to hear, whether they're military messages or the whines and howls of the universe. They speak most passionately about the friendships they've made and preserved on the air, about becoming part of a closely knit, mutually supportive community that exists not just in their hometown but all over the country, the world. The hams represent one response to the dislocations most of us face, forced to move from one place to another, leaving irreplaceable friends behind, struggling, sometimes in vain, to make new ones. They also represent a response to the isolation and privatization of American life that television in particular has accelerated and reinforced. Radio allows hams to transcend the barriers to friendship too often imposed by social class and distance, and to vault over the self-absorption, reticence, or lassitude that encourages us to keep too much to ourselves.

Eighty-five percent of hams are male, nearly all of them in America are white, and most of them are either in their forties and fifties or in their seventies and eighties. (This has begun to change dramatically since 1991, when one no longer had to know Morse code to get an entry-level license. Today approximately 40 percent of those applying for licenses are women.)[4] Hams are clannish: they have their own clubs and conventions, their own highly effective lobbyists in Washington, a strong sense of their traditions and history, and their own language, which consists almost entirely of abbreviations.

The rest of us are BCLs—broadcast listeners—QRN is static, VKs are Australians, 73 means best regards, and XYL (ex–young lady) is the wife. They address each other as OM, Old Man. They talk about "working" a wavelength, as in "I was working six meters last night," as if it were a furrow, a piece of earth that produces nothing without their intervention. An Elmer is a mentor who helps you get started with the hobby, and rag chewing is talking on the air. Every ham refers to his set as his rig, and the room housing the rig, no matter where it is or what it looks like, is a shack. A set of internationally recognized abbreviations, all beginning with the letter Q—QSO is contact with another station, QRS asks, "Shall I send more slowly?"—surmount language barriers. Many of the abbreviations are from the early Morse code days of ham radio, when message economy was critical. Now they form the amateurs' patois, the coded dialect that distinguishes members from nonmembers and identifies them as a separate speech community and, thus, a separate culture.

Even though there are more hams now than ever before, they are more invisible—or maybe the better term is *inaudible*—than they used to be. Despite their unstinting public service work, they don't get the media attention they once did. For decades the hams were both admired and resented by Americans, who appreciated their heroic work during disasters but also blamed them— often but not always wrongly—for interference on the broadcast band. One of the shrewdest subcultures in America, the hams recognized as early as 1910 the importance of good public relations and of deft, preemptive lobbying in Washington. As a result, they are the only hobbyists whose pastime is explicitly protected by both federal and international law. Protecting their foothold in the spectrum has required a blend of selflessness and self-interest that they have mastered brilliantly.

The communications network set up by the amateurs proved critical during a variety of natural disasters, notably the great flood of 1936 and the hurricane of 1938. During World War II the Selective Service questionnaire filled out by every draftee asked, "Is your hobby radio?" A yes meant you went straight into the Signal Corps. Over 25,000 hams served in the war, designing military equipment and working on radar stations. After the war was over, ham radio experienced another boom. Between 1954 and 1959 the number of amateurs increased nearly 80 percent, from 115,000 to 205,000.[5] In the late 1940s and early 1950s, the amateurs applied SSB—single sideband transmission—to radio, a development that revolutionized military communications. Since the 1950s there has been a convergence between ham radio and the space program so that now when NASA wants its astronauts to talk via radio from a space shuttle to some schoolchildren in a classroom, it is hams who handle the communications.

Communication—or, more accurately, *contact*—matters to hams on some almost mystical, metaphysical level. Ask any one of them about DXing, and off he goes. David Sumner, executive vice president of the American Radio Relay League, the oldest and largest amateur organization in the country, believes that when it comes to hams McLuhan was right, content is irrelevant, the medium is the message. When you make contact with a fellow ham in Bulgaria, it doesn't matter what you say to each other; what matters is that you connected. "At that precise instant in time, two men are doing exactly the same thing at the same time. In the time and frequency dimension we were brought together for *that instant*," says Sumner. More than one writer has described the initial call, *CQ*—which asks if there's anyone on the air who wants to talk—as the amateurs' "mating call."[6] While such a metaphor may liken the ham to some forlorn moose, it also inadvertently reveals the intense desire for coupling that drives ham radio. There *is* an eroticism here, but let me be quick to emphasize that this is a disembodied eroticism, not at all of the flesh but of the psyche. It is about a simultaneous intellectual and technical sense of communion. In a society that devalues intellectual pleasure and often bastardizes and exploits spiritual desire, ham radio structures a way—and a place—for intense yet nonphysical meeting of the minds and sharing of the human spirit.

What has been and is most compelling for hams is the inherent democracy of their hobby. And what enforces such democracy is the social anonymity, especially when sending code. Occupation, income, social standing, age, and appearance are irrelevant to success as a ham. What matters is speed and deftness as an operator, and skill as an engineer and experimenter.

Harper's noted in 1941 that in the world of the amateurs, "the social and monetary criteria of the outside world were tacitly barred. In New York City, the boys of the Bronx, using homemade condensers coated with tinfoil still redolent of Liederkranz cheese, compared notes over the air with the affluent members of the West Side—five miles distant, geographically, but a social light-year removed." Dave Sumner remembers that as an awkward and self-conscious adolescent, he could go on the air once he mastered Morse code and talk to any adult as an equal. There was no appearance, no voice to give away who he was—just the pureness of the code—which made his age, and everything else about him, unimportant.[7] This social invisibility of ham radio, its elevation of technical achievement over good looks, wealth, or charm, in a culture that too often overinflates the superficial and the material is, for many men, a profound relief.

Hams also take enormous pride in the altruism of their hobby. One weekend every June they hold a "Field Day," in which they take their equipment outdoors and simulate operation during a disaster. The goal is to set up temporary stations and make contact with as many others as possible. The "Amateur's Code," written in 1928 and still printed in large, bold letters in *The ARRL Handbook,* sounds like the Boy Scout pledge. The radio amateur is "considerate, loyal, progressive, friendly, balanced [radio never interferes with family or work], and patriotic." He offers "support and encouragement to other amateurs," is "always ready for service to country and community," and keeps "abreast of science." The "hallmarks of the amateur spirit" are providing "friendly advice and counsel to the beginner," "slow and patient operating when requested," and "consideration for interests of others."

And the thing is, hams mean it. Without this kind of stellar behavior on the air, they could jeopardize their protected preserves on the spectrum. Louts, loudmouths, and delinquents are "frozen out," ignored by other hams, who simply refuse to interact with them until they go away or reform. Cooperation is balanced by competition, which the ARRL has institutionalized and elaborated into a host of contests, each with its badges and awards. There are prizes for contacting every state in the Union, all the Canadian provinces, and one hundred countries around the world. As with American sports, the competition is over how much and how far. And also like most American athletics, ham radio seeks to cultivate the right balance in masculine culture between rugged, competitive individualism and cooperative, mutually beneficial teamwork.

It is not hard to be swept up in the romanticism of ham radio, even if you don't know a gigahertz from a golay encoder. So it is important to remember that the amateurs have always had their outlaws and misfits, their aerial delinquents, who, like some of the hackers and cyberpunks of today, thumbed their noses at governmental authority, deliberately interfered with their etheric neighbors, or goaded and harassed others on the air. This, in fact, characterized the early days of ham radio and gave it its energy as well as its visibility.

Both hams' transgressions and their heroism on the air have raised a key question about broadcasting, namely who "owns" the spectrum and who decides who gets what. For the amateurs have always operated outside of and often in opposition to the commercialism of mainstream broadcasting. Once they regarded their portion of the spectrum as a reservation on which they were trapped. Now they argue that it is much like national park land, a commercial-free zone that must be preserved for them and future generations. At a time when greater chunks of the spectrum are being auctioned off for use by cellular phone companies and other corporations, they are the only voice, aside from the military, to keep the notion alive that some of the airwaves, like the sea, are a common property resource in which everyone has a stake.

Just as the 1930s is regarded as the "golden age" of broadcast radio, it is referred to fondly by hams as their golden age. In the first four years of the decade, despite the Depression, their numbers skyrocketed from 16,800 licensed amateurs in 1929 to 46,400 in 1934: an increase of 300 percent.[8] The American Radio Relay League instituted all sorts of clubs and contests to promote improvements in apparatus and in speed and accuracy in sending. And another big change was the growth of "phone work," meaning voice instead of Morse code transmission. The sense of international solidarity that had begun in the mid-1920s was now an established feature of the amateur world.

It was in this decade that the hams especially showcased the lifesaving role they and their invisible networks play during natural disasters. An earthquake in New Zealand in 1931, a shipwreck off Newfoundland the same year, and the California earthquake of 1933—the first news of which came from an amateur station—prompted many of the hams to think of themselves in public service terms, as an army in reserve who needed to train and be in a constant state of preparedness. In 1935 the ARRL Emergency Corps was formed as the vanguard of this army. The Army-Amateur Radio System (AARS) became a cooperative venture between the ARRL and the Signal Corps to serve as the officially recognized amateur radio link between disaster areas and official relief agencies like the Red Cross and the army. "Far seeking amateurs," advised an article in QST, the leading amateur magazine, "are organizing in order that amateur radio will be prepared when the elements go on a rampage." In 1936 that rampage occurred.

It began with endless rain and melting snow that swelled the Conemaugh River and Stony Creek in Johnstown, Pennsylvania, putting the town under fourteen feet of water by March 17, 1936. Cars were completely submerged, and people panicked as the muddy waters lapped up to the second floors of homes, shops, and office buildings. The entire city was without lights, and most people could not use their phones, which were on the first floors.[9]

By the next day the flood waters, and the headlines, exploded. What was first thought to be a replay of the Johnstown Flood of 1889 became the "Great Flood" as it spread to twelve and then fifteen states, devastating cities from Pittsburgh to Hartford. More than a dozen cities were almost completely isolated, their normal communications facilities destroyed. Within four days a quarter of a million people were homeless, nearly two hundred dead, and the damage was conservatively estimated to exceed $300 million. The steel mills of Pittsburgh and the factories of the Merrimack Valley were at a standstill, as were rail, car, and air transportation throughout much of the Ohio Valley and New England. Pittsburgh and Hartford were without power, as were dozens of smaller towns and cities. In Pittsburgh water was as high as the loge sections in movie theaters, and one could barely see the tops of railroad freight cars. Hartford had a 9:00 P.M. curfew and was under martial rule. On the fifth day of the flood, a blizzard hit western Pennsylvania and northern West Virginia. Telephone and telegraph lines collapsed, and telephone operators, most of them women, stayed at their posts without food or heat, working by candlelight, until they were forced to flee.

The only lines of communications in and out of many of the devastated areas came from the hams, who brought a fresh, unpackaged, "you are there" feel to sensational news events. "Radio Amateurs in Flood Did Heroic Work as Vast Audience Eavesdropped," announced a headline in *The New York Times.* *QST* was even more effusive: "Amateur radio needs a poet laureate" to do justice to the amateurs' heroism.[10] Because of the communications networks they set up, the amateurs were able to expedite evacuation of people before the floodwaters got too deadly and thus helped save hundreds, perhaps thousands of lives.

Hams became reporters and rescue workers, relaying calls for help and news dispatches. Some went out in rowboats to gather information and returned to their rigs to relay the latest news. Many of them set up instant "nets" consisting of amateurs in various locations who could convey messages, most of them official. They worked with the Red Cross, local police, the National Guard, and other relief organizations, as well as newspaper and radio reporters, providing information on general flood conditions, on where people were stranded, who needed boats, or food, or clothing, or medicine, and giving directions to various locations. They set up communications links for local power companies struggling to restore electricity. Reporters camped out for days in those hams' houses that weren't flooded. The hams described changing water levels and provided regular updates on how particular dams were or were not holding up. This meant verifying rumors that dams had burst, warning people when they had, assuring them to remain calm when they hadn't. They relayed messages in and out of the disaster areas between friends and relatives desperately seeking information about loved ones. Joshua Swartz of Harrisburg set up a station in the state house so Governor Earle could supervise the broader aspects of relief and reconstruction work. Swartz handled well over one thousand messages.[11]

"The amateurs seemed never to tire," noted the *Times*. Joseph Vancheri of Punxsutawney stayed on the air for thirty-two hours without a break. Gerald Coleman was "the only outlet Johnstown had with the outside world," the paper reported. It was Coleman who sent the first message to Washington via Pittsburgh for relief: "Worst flood in history . . . we need everything." Another ham, Francis Duffy, handled messages for the National Guard for more than a week. The Radio Club at Carnegie Tech in Pittsburgh handled traffic for the Bell System, the Red Cross, and the local police, as well as giving news dispatches to NBC, CBS, and Hearst Radio. In Shelburne Falls, Massachusetts, Leland Wheeler, working closely with the state police, transmitted the message that resulted in the incredible two-hour evacuation of the lower river valley, "including the entire village of Hatfield—people, cows, pigs, chickens—in which place the river rose to a point where only the eaves were showing." Thousands of other amateurs contributed to the effort by staying off the air and keeping the lines open. In its "they also serve" editorial, *QST* praised this restraint, noting, "It is far harder to be silent than to join the babble when everyone else in creation is having a big time 'saving the world.'"[12]

Those BCLs who had "all-wave sets" could tune in on the shortwave band and get, as the *Times* put it, a "front row seat" for the disaster. The 75-meter band especially "pulsed with voices . . . there was never a quiet moment. Every hair breadth turn of the dial brought new voices into hearing." What listeners heard on the shortwave band was "drama, unscheduled and unrehearsed," and they could "eavesdrop on graphic eyewitness descriptions of the destructive deluge."

The networks wanted such drama on the broadcast band, and CBS had initially hoped to set up its own temporary broadcast stations in Johnstown but couldn't because there were no dry landing fields nearby. NBC was not daunted by this and arranged to pipe amateur transmissions into its coast-to-coast hookup so that broadcast listeners could get, as the *Times* put it, "a word-picture" of what was going on outside their tuning range. NBC interrupted regular programming on over fifty of its affiliates to go live to the flood locations. Joseph Vancheri was rebroadcast on the NBC network describing flood conditions and the work of the amateurs. One of the most dramatic moments came when cries of "The dam has burst! Everybody out for your lives! We're heading for the hills!" flashed across the nation from the telephone exchange building in Johnstown as radio and telephone operators were forced to flee. The *Times* called this "one of the most dramatic and brief bits of radio reporting ever heard in any emergency." Less than an hour later Gerry Coleman, who had stayed on the air serving as an eyewitness reporter of conditions in Johnstown for NBC, announced from his station at home, "The water continues to come up and I may have to get out of here and go to higher ground." Shortly after that, he did.[13] Coleman, Vancheri, and others became celebrities, praised by Walter Winchell and other radio commentators, featured in newsreels about the flood, and lionized in the press. The publicity for ham radio couldn't have been better.

In September 1938 the hams repeated this performance as the Northeast was slammed by one of the worst hurricanes in its history. Battering the coast from Cape Hatteras to Maine and hitting Boston with hundred-mile-an-hour winds, the storm especially devastated Long Island and Rhode Island, producing 6-foot tidal waves in the city of Providence. Other tidal waves along the coast were as high as 40 feet. It was Rhode Island's worst disaster. Trees were uprooted, power lines downed, telephone and telegraph exchanges flooded, and communications cut off. Even some of the major broadcasting stations in New York—WABC, WNYC, WEAF—went silent for anywhere from minutes to hours as they struggled with flooding and their auxiliary power sources. In many areas once again it was the hams who provided the only link between the disaster centers and relief organizations. Hams on Long Island, hearing the storm warning on the Coast Guard frequency, drove around frantically trying to buy batteries before the storm hit. One amateur reportedly lashed himself to his roof at the height of the storm so he could erect an emergency antenna. The vice chairman of the American Red Cross went on WJZ once its power was restored to "pay tribute to radio amateurs, for relaying relief messages and maintaining communication to and from the stricken areas." Because of the amateurs' work, the Red Cross, the Coast Guard, and other agencies were able to locate the most devastated areas and people and get aid to them as quickly as possible.[14]

Wilson Burgess, an amateur in Westerly, Rhode Island, provided the only contact the town had with the outside world for several days and gave the first accounts of how badly they had been hit. For a while his was the only signal emanating from the state. Returning home at the peak of the storm so he could go on the air, Burgess discovered that his antennas and the garage that held them up were gone. He determined to erect a new antenna, but while he was outside, the wind whipped a pair of pliers out of his hand. Burgess got an antenna up despite this and handled every word that went in and out of Westerly for the next fifty-six hours. After the storm had subsided, his pliers were found embedded in a tree.[15] He was awarded the Paley Prize, which CBS established in 1936 to honor outstanding service performed by an amateur.

Because of this determination to establish themselves as a public service army in reserve, the 51,000 hams operating in America at the outbreak of World War II provided ideal recruits for radio and radar work during the war, men with sophisticated technical expertise and the ability to work both individually and as part of a team. Except for a War Emergency Radio Service organized by the Office of Civil Defense, amateur radio was banned from the airwaves for the duration. And when amateur activity resumed after the war, enlivened by the availability of all kinds of surplus military equipment, a riveting expedition and worldwide media event caused their numbers to surge again.

This was the voyage of the *Kon-Tiki*, led by Thor Heyerdahl. The journey across the Pacific of six men in a balsa wood and bamboo raft held together only by ropes began off the coast of Peru on April 29, 1947. In the wake of the most technologically sophisticated and destructive war known to humankind, the vision of six men relying only on their instincts, their guts, and the weather to try to make history seemed almost like an act of contrition, a return to a time before all the aircraft carriers and atomic weapons. Heyerdahl, struck by the similarities between Polynesian and precolonial South American cultures, wanted to prove that it would have been possible for Peruvians to sail to the South Seas in the 1400s, and that the prehistoric settlers of Polynesia could have come from South America. According to Peruvian legend, such a journey occurred in 1470, when a group of Incas set sail for a year and returned with the news that they had discovered two islands. Polynesian legend was filled with stories of "mysterious white ancestors." But scholars dismissed the connection, alleging that the journey from Peru to any of the Polynesian islands would not have been possible in the vessels the Incas used. So Heyerdahl replicated the Incan raft, which navigated only by a canvas sail and a mango wood steering oar, organized his crew, and sought to ride the Humboldt Current, which sweeps from east to west just below the equator.[16] In the public imagination the trip quickly became not about some theory of Incan-Polynesian cross-pollination but instead about male heroics in the face of the awesome forces of ocean and wind. After a harrowing, magical, and extraordinary 4,300-mile trip that ended off the reefs of Raroia on August 7, Heyerdahl chronicled the adventure in his book *Kon-Tiki*. It became an instant and international best-seller, spawning TV shows like *Adventures in Paradise* and a rage for "tiki" dolls.

What the expedition also helped spawn was increased interest in ham radio, for the one modern appliance Heyerdahl allowed on the journey was a 10- to 15-watt shortwave radio set powered by dry batteries and a hand generator, which enabled them to stay in touch with the rest of the world. The aerial was, at first, elevated by a small balloon. After hitting a "dead spot" off the coast of Peru, the *Kon-Tiki* made its first North American contact on May 20 and by mid-June was working a range of American stations. Every night the vessel's two radio operators, Knut Haugland and Torstein Raaby, took turns sending out their reports and weather observations, and the lucky amateur who picked up these transmissions was elated, feeling himself part of the expedition too.

One night after days of no radio contact, a ham from Los Angeles who was trying to reach Sweden heard the *Kon-Tiki* instead, and after a series of exchanges assured the crew that he would let their families know they were alive and well. Heyerdahl wrote of the episode, "It was a strange thought for us that evening that a total stranger called Hal, a chance moving-picture operator far away among the swarming population of Los Angeles, was the only person in the world but ourselves who knew where we were and that we were well."[17] Hal and another Los Angeles ham named Frank helped save the day more than once. When the *Kon-Tiki* finally ran aground on a coral reef surrounding a desert island, the crew salvaged the radio equipment and began signaling their whereabouts and their plight. For a while no one heard them except for a ham in Colorado, who thought the message—"This is the *Kon-Tiki*. We are stranded on a desert island in the Pacific"—a prank. But then Hal reached the crew and was able to relay their message.

Once the crew moved to Raroia, they came upon a six-year-old boy with a 106-degree temperature and a painful abscess as large as a man's fist on his head. Haugland and Raaby described the boy's symptoms over the air to Hal and Frank, who in turn called a doctor. Frank signaled back the doctor's advice, which included lancing and sterilizing the abscess and treating the boy with penicillin from the *Kon-Tiki*'s first aid kit. Heyerdahl made it clear, through his brisk yet romantic prose, that without the help of these hams the boy would surely have died. To be able to participate in such history-in-the-making, in such selfless heroism, and to be praised in a huge best-seller: no wonder the *Kon-Tiki* drew in tens of thousands of new converts. The ARRL did not fail to capitalize on this: it published a quarter of a million copies of a little pamphlet titled *You Can Be There*, which it distributed at fairs, hobby shows, and other community gatherings. Between 1954 and 1959 alone the number of amateurs nearly doubled, from 115,000 to 205,000.[18] Jobs in electronics were plentiful in the 1950s, and these trends reinforced each other.

The postwar period also dramatized how the amateurs' ongoing grassroots tinkering continued to shake up conventional wisdom and to revolutionize institutional uses of radio. Even in the face of the rather formidable interlocking research and development labs of the military-industrial complex, many of which were focused explicitly on electronics, the hams continued to be a source of invention and innovation, some of it pathbreaking. In fact, many of those working in the electronics and aeronautics industries were hams, and having a boss who was unable or unwilling to promote innovation on the job often spurred the frustrated ham to prove, in his off hours, what he believed to be technically possible. *QST*, the ARRL's magazine, provided a place for hams to share technical information about new apparatus and new transmitting and receiving techniques, and experimentation was especially fevered and enterprising in the late 1940s with all the military surplus equipment to play with. Many hams had sold their receivers to the Signal Corps at the start of the war, so now they had to rebuild sets from scratch. Plus, there were two new interlopers, FM radio and television—both major spectrum hogs. Amateurs and TV viewers alike discovered that ham radio could interfere with TV reception. In addition, the high-frequency shortwave bands the amateurs used were getting more congested, especially in the face of increased demands by a military now fighting the Cold War, and by commercial users like the airlines, which needed reliable air-to-ground communications. It was another time in radio history when the hams faced powerful pressures to invent their way out of spectrum scarcity if they were to preserve their hobby and their ability to roam different tracts of the spectrum.

The late 1940s and early 1950s found the hams and their suppliers tinkering their way out of TVI—interference with television signals—and advancing a revolutionary method of radio propagation called ssbsc—single-sideband suppressed carrier transmission—or single-sideband for short. Early critics ridiculed single-sideband as "Donald Duck" transmissions because of their thin-toned, squawky voice quality. Sidebander pioneers responded by calling AM "ancient modulation." The sidebanders had the technical advantages: single-sideband transmissions require only one-fourth of the power that AM does and take up one-third of bandwidth space.[19]

With AM transmissions, the human voice or music is used to modulate a radio frequency wave—called the carrier wave—which, without modulation, would look like a flat bar on an oscilloscope and sound like a single tone on the air. Once the carrier wave is modulated, however, frequencies immediately adjacent to it are required to carry the full range of information—in the case of AM, a range of vocal and musical tones. These adjacent frequencies above and below the carrier—which is at the midpoint of a channel—are called the sidebands, and it is these modulated sidebands, not the carrier wave itself, that carry voice and music.[20]

Sidebands, however, are mirror images of each other, carrying the same information. So theoretically, if one sideband were suppressed, messages could still be conveyed. This hasn't been done with AM and FM, because the equipment required for a single-sideband mode that would maintain the level of audio fidelity would be much more expensive. For hams audio fidelity was not the priority it clearly had to be with broadcasters: the hams were consistently interested in distance, in economizing on power, and in using as little spectrum space as possible. If a fellow ham's voice sounded a bit crackly and thin but could be heard from farther away using fewer watts, that was technological progress for the amateur. Oswald G. Villard, Jr., of Stanford is the ham generally credited with successfully establishing single-sideband operation in September of 1947, working with Winfield G. Wagner on the 75-meter band. The January 1948 issue of *QST* devoted its cover, its editorial, and three articles to SSB. By the early and mid-1950s, a range of firms were supplying hams with SSB equipment, and in 1956 U.S. hams reported working every continent with SSB.

What the hams did, according to Perry Williams of the ARRL, was deliver to the military, and to the airlines, a much improved method of air-to-ground transmission. By the mid-1950s the high frequencies—2 to 30 megahertz— used for ground-air communications were extremely congested and subject to interference during adverse conditions. Remember that with the rise in air travel and tourism, and the military race for technological competitiveness during the Cold War, the demand for air-to-ground communication soared. SSB more than doubled the possible channels available and quadrupled the radiated power available from one's transmitter.[21] SSB was also perfect for military ground-to-ground communications when one station was at a fixed point and the other was moving—as might occur during maneuvers. According to ham legend, it was Gen. Curtis LeMay, then one of the most prominent cold warriors—and, coincidentally, a ham—who demonstrated the superiority of SSB to the air force by outfitting a small plane with SSB and maintaining contact with an American base from halfway around the world.

It is not surprising, given their ambivalence toward governmental presumptions about access to the air, that there were hams who refused to be left out of the U.S.-Soviet space race, or to remain mere spectators when the government launched dozens of satellites with names like *Explorer, Discoverer,* and *Pioneer* in the late 1950s and early 1960s. Hams who were Lockheed engineers by day decided they could build a satellite of their own that would signal back to hams on earth. The one thing they would need was a ride into space for their device. The ARRL, taking advantage of the fact that Curtis LeMay was a ham and had been a major proponent of SSB, persuaded the air force to let their device hitchhike a ride aboard *Discoverer XXXVI*. But the space they were allotted was irregularly shaped—somewhat like an accordion in its curved, playing position, and was only about two feet by three feet.

Working nights and weekends, these hams built a miniature ten-pound shortwave transmitter, operating on a tenth of a watt, that would circle the globe for several weeks, sending four dots and two dots—"Hi" in Morse code—back to earth. Using cast-off parts from the aerospace industry, this first nongovernmental satellite cost eighty-seven dollars. They named it Project Oscar, for Orbiting Satellite Carrying Amateur Radio, a name that helped get the attention of the press and cartoonists. The launch date from Vandenberg Air Force Base, December 12, 1961, marked the fortieth anniversary—to the day—of the first transatlantic shortwave tests between the United States and Scotland that demonstrated once and for all that shortwaves could achieve great distances.[22]

Hams around the world listened in on 145 megahertz—the 2-meter band, which was the international frequency assigned to hams—to hear *dit dit dit dit, dit dit*—which, in addition to spelling "Hi," was the ham's Morse code abbreviation for laughter. The dots actually conveyed Oscar's internal temperature—the more frequent and higher pitched they were, the hotter Oscar was—and when it lost altitude three weeks after the launch and reentered the earth's atmosphere, the hams heard it beeping faster and faster, at even higher pitches, screaming until it burned up and went silent. The hams made two exact replicas of Oscar, one of which hangs like a mobile from the ceiling of the ARRL headquarters, the other on display at the Smithsonian.

Since the 1950s ham radio has been less visible, all but eclipsed in the 1970s by the songs, movies, and lore about CB radio, often unacknowledged in the press even when hams play a critical role in the aftermath of floods and hurricanes. And many young men now prefer cruising the Internet to cruising the airwaves. But after a slackening of interest in the 1970s and '80s, ham radio is again on the rise. And today's ARRL is savvy about public relations, sending volunteers into schools with 2-meter equipment capable of receiving transmissions from orbiting space shuttles.

The hams' next major battle is the one they started with—preserving a portion of the spectrum for noncommercial, free transmission between regular people. The Republican Congress that came to power in 1995, with their aphorism that government regulation is bad and the "free market" is fabulous, was determined to apply this to spectrum management as well. Calling their work "spectrum reform," Congress eliminated the restrictions on how many radio stations a corporation could own, and that was just for starters. At the same moment that Bob Dole was publicly excoriating the media for flooding the country with "nightmares of depravity," in the cloistered chumminess of the Senate halls he was working to hand over much of the spectrum to corporate behemoths.

When it comes to deciding who might get dibs on some of the ultrahigh frequencies—waves as short as 3 meters to 3 centimeters—the favorite new mechanism is the auction. Earlier methods—the lottery, or endless administrative hearings at the FCC—were cast in disrepute as unfair and inefficient, and the auction had the added allure of raising cash for the federal government. Companies like AT&T, Sprint, and GTE covet portions of the ultrahigh frequencies for new cellular phone systems and for PCS—personal communications service—which will provide long-distance wireless telephone service. Other demands for these frequencies come from trucking companies that want better dispatching and tracking services to and from their fleets of vehicles.

All of this, of course, represents progress in the classic American sense of the term: machines conquering space and distance, businesspeople squeezing more out of our natural resources for the increased convenience of consumers. But the move to auction off chunks of the spectrum to corporations marks a revolutionary departure in how America conceives of and manages the airwaves.

When the *Titanic* sank in 1912, and people realized that proper use of the ether could have saved everyone's life, a conception of the airwaves began to take hold: that they were a communal resource, something in which all people had a stake, a realm that had to be protected and managed for the common good. Overpopulation—in this case, interference—wrecked the commons for everyone. And privatizing the commons—simply selling it to the highest bidder—meant it was no longer a commons. Like the ocean or wilderness areas, it was not something that could or should be owned by private, commercial interests.

As broadcasting emerged, of course, commercial interests *did* take over first the AM and then the FM band. But neither the stations nor the networks could own their frequencies. They got licenses to use them for several years and then had to demonstrate, when it was license renewal time, that they had served the "public interest, convenience or necessity." In reality, this was window dressing: very few stations lost their licenses because of challenges by irate citizens, and most stations did acquire de facto property rights to their frequencies.

But in America, ideals matter. Giving them up—however little they have to do with everyday practice—signals resignation and cynicism. Although too few would notice, it would be a major change—and loss—to admit that the spectrum is now nearly all privately owned, available to the highest bidder.

It is this idea, as much as the reality of a privatized spectrum, that the hams continue to fight. Of course they are self-interested—they have a hobby they've invested money, time, and their very identities in—and they want to be able to call whomever they want, when they want, without having to pay AT&T or anyone else. They want to continue to have that experience of sending out a call into the night and having it caught by someone else, halfway around the globe, someone also searching, also calling, also wanting to be found. So they are the last holdouts for the notion that radio can and should be participatory, and that encroachments onto this etheric preserve by the inexorable march of commercialization must be driven back.

Like many other sectors of American life, ham radio is getting feminized—more women are entering the subculture, getting licenses, learning Morse code, taking to the air. But ham radio has always been a place where men could simultaneously escape the constraints of conventionalized masculinity and preserve distinctly male traits and privileges. On the air, having muscle definition is irrelevant. Being overly aggressive and tough is inappropriate. Being a smooth bureaucratic player who knows how to wield power and to manipulate underlings and superiors alike is equally irrelevant. On the air men cultivate different facets of masculinity—the competition to go farther than the next guy, to be more technically expert, to do what others can't, hear what others haven't. Other nonham men, and certainly women, are barred from entry here by the most basic of obstacles—we can't understand what they're talking about.

But this competitiveness, honed by the exclusivity that marks all fraternities, is self-consciously tempered by cooperation, altruism, mutual support—traditionally more "female" traits. Hams are individuals yet part of a team. They explore and sometimes conquer the vagaries of nature. But they can also cultivate traits that John Wayne movies and Mickey Spillane novels ignored or repudiated for men—the desire to connect with others, to use machines to achieve forms of intimacy, to be dependent on other individuals or groups, to share and nurture rather than compete head-to-head. They could also repudiate the tendencies of more extreme masculinism—physical aggression, personal isolation, emotional repression, antagonism toward community norms.

Ham radio has been especially compelling to men who have felt frozen out of the increasing bureaucratization of America, who have found the hierarchies of the workplace frustrating and humiliating. Through their hobby they have, over the years, flouted authority, either by challenging the military, and then corporate interests, over access to the spectrum or by inventing techniques deemed impossible by the powers that be. Like their latter-day counterparts the computer hackers, they have shown through technological insurgency that highly centralized, hierarchical, corporate control of technological systems may produce vast profits but may also suffocate the very sort of innovation that keeps such industries ahead of the pack.

The hams also continue to show that, at least for some, the earliest visions about radio that now seem so quaint and naïve can still very much grip the human imagination. Behind the stereotype of "old fat guys in basements" are people who insist that radio be participatory, active, noncommercial, educational, personally liberating, and democratic, even if all hams are doing on the air is "rag chewing." They continue to hear the unearthly noises that remind us that radio waves, however encased they are in commercial culture, still come from nature. What the hams have sustained for over eighty years are the pleasures of exploratory listening that animated radio listening when it was new. Radio waves aren't energy sources that we harness only so they can deliver ads for cars and beer. Radio waves are something we ride to see where they take us—both in the world and in our minds' eye.

Conclusion: Is Listening Dead?

The disc jockey walks into the studio. Before him is a computer printout and often a computer monitor as well that tell him which songs will be played in which order throughout his shift. Pre-positioned on the printout, between the songs or sets of songs, are bullet points, some more scripted than others, that tell the DJ what he should say when about station promotions, upcoming concerts, or the music. The log also tells him exactly how long he has to talk. The program or music director, away in another office, has developed this list with the help of audience research, consultants, and computer software programs like Selector. Selector makes sure that musical sequences don't vary too much in tempo or mood, keeping "the music from becoming too depressing, too uplifting, or 'roller-coastering back and forth between the two.' " Also, if your audience is primarily male, Selector will regulate to a minimum how many female performers appear in any given hour. The computer draws from a tight playlist and helps determine the rotation of songs to assure the right sequence of new and repeated songs.[1] Welcome to the age of the mechanical DJ.

Out in the car is the mechanical listener, moving via the seeker button through a radio landscape he or she has come to know all too well. There is the smooth jazz station that repeatedly plays Kenny G, David Benoit, and Sade; a soft rock station with Elton John, the Eagles, and Steely Dan in tight rotation; fourteen country stations (currently the most numerous format in the country); alternative or modern rock stations that have played "Semi-Charmed Life" by Third Eye Blind and Alanis Morissette to death. We know that we can usually find NPR on the lower end of the FM band. And over on AM, there's Dr. Laura, sports talk, and, still, Rush. That's how it is most places. Whether you're in Providence or Albuquerque, the music on those formats is the same.

There are twice as many radios in America as there are people, and we listen, on average, about twenty-two hours a week, with radio's prime times occurring between 6:00 and 9:00 A.M. and 3:00 and 7:00 P.M. We're making a great deal of money for the owners of radio chains and many of their advertisers. But are we excited by what we hear? Or is radio, as one analyst put it, not something we really listen to anymore but something we just "sit in"?[2] Have all the older modes of listening vanished as most of us succumb to push-button listening?

There are currently something on the order of fifty officially listed formats, and the hairsplitting between them seems ridiculous to an outsider. What really is the difference between soft rock ("plays older, softer rock") and soft adult contemporary ("recurrents mixed with some current music")? Classic hits features " '70s and '80s hits from rock-based artists," while classic rock features "older rock cuts." Country—whose AM audience, according to the Katz Radio Group, is primarily fifty-five and over, has gotten carved up into hot country or young country on the FM dial to attract younger listeners, where its core audience is twenty-five to fifty-four. There are swing formats, farm/adult contemporary, and Hawaiian. Music from the 1970s and '80s (but not punk, ska, or anything else more troubling from these years) dominates most formats as the people who were teenagers then hit their thirties and forties.[3]

Industry spokespeople insist that, especially in large markets, there's more variety than ever, since the listener can choose from a host of carefully crafted and narrowly defined formats. But within the format of a particular station, variety is kept outside the door. In promotional ads listeners are assured, for example, that they won't ever have to hear heavy metal, rap, or anything unexpected on their station. Audience research indicates that many Americans want this kind of safe, gated-in listening. It goes with our increasingly insular, gated-in communities and lives. Indeed, in the 1980s listeners used new technologies, most notably the Walkman and the boom box, either to isolate themselves from others or to enact hostile takeovers of communal auditory space. Industry representatives also note that many people listen for only ten minutes at a time and move among six different stations; programmers are at the mercy of such habits, they emphasize.[4] Their point is that people have become more selfish and less tolerant listeners, and that stations must cater to this.

But in the last twenty years the radio industry itself has cultivated this kind of caution in listeners, so that many have lost—or never acquired—the patience and playfulness needed to learn about other music, especially the music of the young. Radio is no longer designed for music lovers, or for those interested in sampling rock, folk, jazz, and the blues. With the exception of a few crossover artists, formats are also highly segregated, and stations that used to include black music and artists don't do so anymore. So someone like me, who admittedly does not want to hear Anthrax or Ice T if I can help it, also doesn't get to hear Beck, Arrested Development, Salt-N-Pepa, or Ani Difranco on my "classic rock" or "contemporary hits" station. The radio industry and its advertisers, which successfully forged a national market in the 1930s, have now helped us see ourselves as members of mutually exclusive auditory niches, willing and able to listen in only a few ways. This has been enormously profitable. In fact, at the end of the twentieth century radio is the most profitable of all the media businesses.[5]

"Yes, we've gone and done it again—more stations!" boasts Jacor's Web page. These proclamations are accompanied by sketches of a kid exclaiming, "Looky, gee whiz, I got Tampa, Sarasota, and Venice," while another says, "Radical. I'm headed to L.A., yes!" "Click below to read about heap big Indians deal," the company suggests tastefully as you move to an announcement of its new Cleveland station featuring a grimacing, bright red warrior. "Like kids in a candy store, Jacor has been shamelessly opportunistic about its growth and acquisition," brags the remainder of the text, which is designed for investors, not listeners.

Jacor was one of the first radio consolidators to emerge out of the deregulation and merger mania of the late 1980s. But as of the fall of 1998, Jacor, which owns and distributes Rush Limbaugh's and Dr. Laura Schlessinger's shows and monopolizes markets like Cincinnati and Denver, has been dwarfed. It owns or operates just over 200 stations. That's nothing compared with Chancellor Media Corporation. At the end of August 1998, Chancellor, which already owned over 100 stations, primarily in major markets, merged with Capstar, which was formed only in 1996 yet already owned over 350 stations, primarily in midsized markets like Austin, Texas, and Wilmington, Delaware. (This was hardly a hostile takeover; Chancellor was run by Thomas Hicks, and Capstar was run by his younger brother, Steven.) Chancellor Media became the country's largest radio broadcasting company, with a chain of 463 stations in 105 markets and an estimated weekly listenership of over 65 million. Chancellor also owns billboard businesses and TV stations. Consolidators, whose goal has been to acquire and manage as many stations as possible, are different from networks: they don't supply these stations with the same programming, the way NBC or CBS did. Rather they seek to own stations with a variety of highly targeted formats so they can assure advertisers that they have a "portfolio" of stations, each designed to hit a different demographic bull's-eye. If an advertiser wants to saturate a particular market while tailoring its messages to different age-groups, the radio chains provide an excellent vehicle.

The business wire *Newsedge*, on the Web, noted predictably that "the new

Chancellor Media is expected to achieve significant operating and financial synergies." How are such "synergies" achieved? By making the on-air talent and programs of larger markets available to midsized and smaller markets. In other words, there will be less and less need for local DJs, talk show hosts, producers, and engineers. Why bother? It is technologically possible and financially much more efficient to run virtual stations, which have no announcers of their own but use the voices and programs of far-off, prerecorded talent.[6] Advertising sales forces can be consolidated too; fewer people are needed to promote one portfolio. Merger mania, and the excitement it generates on Wall Street, means downsizing back in the control booth.

How does such consolidation look from the studio, and from the corporate board? For Thomas O. Hicks, times could hardly be better. Hicks, who was chairman of the board of both Capstar and Chancellor, will naturally head the newly merged firm. He's also the chairman and CEO of Hicks, Muse, Tate & Furst, the leveraged buyout firm he helped found in 1989, which specialized in investments in radio stations. And he has proven himself brilliant at devising ways to maximize profits and reduce competition in the industry. Hicks's father, John, an advertising salesman for TV and radio stations in Dallas, began buying small stations in Texas in the 1950s and '60s. When he retired in 1980, Tom and his brother Steve bought three of these stations for $3 million and began purchasing other small stations. After revamping the formats or moving the transmission towers to better locations, the Hicks brothers were able to resell some of these stations for three times what they paid for them.[7]

When they began acquiring stations, they were restricted by the one-to-a-market rule, which forbade one entity from owning more than one AM or FM station in a market. (The FCC eased this restriction in the top twenty-five media markets in 1985, but it still applied to the smaller markets.) So Hicks devised what came to be called local marketing agreements, known in the industry as LMAs, meaning that a company would manage another station without owning it, and would pay the owner a predetermined fee for doing so.

Why own or manage multiple stations in the same market? According to Hicks and others, in the late 1980s competition among stations featuring the same format—say, album-oriented rock—meant that the hit stations made money and the others lost money but the less successful stations kept down the price of advertising spots for all of them. If one entity owned or managed several stations, it could program one station with a rock format but go after other "demos"—demographic groups—with the other stations by converting them to oldies, soft rock, or country. With one sales department representing all of these stations, the advertising rep now had several products with tightly defined audiences to sell to advertisers, who could choose what to advertise when and where.

Once the Telecommunications Act of 1996 eliminated restrictions on radio ownership, the Hicks brothers and others could push this strategy to the max. In 1998, for example, Chancellor boasted about the "wall of women" it delivered in New York City. Four of its five FM stations target women of different ages: Z100 for teenagers; WKTU, featuring dance music, for women twenty to thirty-two; Big 105, with "music from the eighties and nineties," for women from twenty-eight to thirty-eight; and WLTW, with soft "adult contemporary" for women from thirty-five to sixty-four. (It is unclear where these listeners are meant to go once they hit sixty-five.) One of Hicks's main competitors, Mel Karmazin, the president of CBS, delivers men, with shock jocks and sports programs. Nor has Hicks confined himself to the United States. In 1998 Chancellor acquired a 50 percent interest in Mexico's Grupo Radio Centro, Latin America's largest and most successful radio company. Radio has made Thomas Hicks a very, very rich man. In 1998, for the second year in a row, *Radio Ink* declared him "the most powerful person in radio."[8]

But how do those in the studio experience these changes? If you're one of the few national stars, like Howard Stern or Dr. Laura, you have a happy prospect; there's the possibility of getting into even more markets, and charging more to advertise on your show. But for the vast majority of DJs and other on-air talent, this is a time of great uncertainty, and of sadness at what's been lost. Pete Fornatale, one of the most successful "classic rock" DJs in New York, who got his start in college and progressive FM radio, has his own metaphor for what's happened to the DJ's autonomy, creativity, and relationship to his audience. "In the early days of this kind of radio, the lucky individuals allowed to invent it were great chefs cooking up exotic dishes with great flourishes, covering a lot of taste sensations. As the business aspect reared its ugly head, the great chefs became waiters: we had to carry out a centrally controlled vision of others, the music or program directors." Of course, there are many great waiters who take pride in their work and do it extremely well, adds Fornatale. But if you've been used to being the chef, it is very hard to make peace with being thrown out of the kitchen.[9]

Interviews with a range of DJs who preferred to remain anonymous reaffirmed that, from their perspective, a bottom-line mentality has so taken over radio that, as one put it, "No one today makes decisions based on aesthetics."[10] Instead, the interlocking interests of recording companies, Hollywood (with the explosion of the soundtrack CD), and the radio consolidators assure that only musically "safe" songs that are easy to categorize will get airplay. When asked what would happen if they went to work one day and suggested that a certain album cut get played because the DJ heard it and thought it was great, they assured me this was no longer possible except at a college station. Many feel they are playing too much mediocre music. They know they can't go three, four, or five cuts into an album anymore unless it's an enormous hit: there's the hit single, and that's it. One reported that many songs are tested before focus groups, who get to hear from ten to thirty seconds of a song, and if they don't like it on the basis of that instantaneous sampling, the song won't get on the air. Repeatedly they used the words *homogenized, bland, plastic,* and *lowest common denominator* in their discussions of the formats. "Heavily formatted radio is like wallpaper," noted one. "It's no longer like a painting that you would actually stop and look at." "Why can't I hear Beck on the radio?" I asked. "Because he doesn't fit into any of the neat categories," they replied. Many DJs used to work with one- to three-year contracts; now often there are no contracts, and if a station changes format, the DJ can instantly find himself or herself out of a job. Ageism affects this industry like all the others. Older jocks can find their shifts reduced and salaries cut, and if they protest know that, without a contract, they can easily be replaced by younger and cheaper talent.

Pete Fornatale recalled the day that WNEW, the pioneering free-form station in New York, removed a host of albums from the DJ's music library in the studio because management deemed them "no longer commercially viable." "I was despondent for days," he remembered, because he knew that no longer would the DJ be able to play Led Zeppelin and Joni Mitchell or Harry Chapin on the same show—eventually not even on the same station. Not only was the DJ's autonomy circumscribed but also all of the folk rock that had helped build the free-form FM movement was banished from major portions of the broadcast day. And DJs like Fornatale, who got into the business because they loved the music, had to hide that love away.

While sad, angry, or both about how the bottom-line mentality has limited what gets on the air, many DJs understand why there is so much reliance on research and consultants: they insulate management from responsibility in a time of enormous competition and provide props managers can lean on when profits and audience share fail to increase or, worse, fall. "If you make a decision based on your gut and you're wrong," noted one jock, "you can lose everything. Management has become very risk averse because their jobs and reputations depend on being right." With stations changing hands so frequently in the 1990s, program directors never knew when they would have a new set of bosses to whom they would have to prove, yet again, that they deserved to remain at the station. WNEW, according to Fornatale, had seven owners between 1987 and 1998. When it was owned by Metromedia, hardly a tiny company but not like the current behemoths, "you did have a feeling of belonging to a family," he noted. But one could hardly have that same feeling when every year or so a new set of bosses with a new set of proclamations about what works and what doesn't called the staff together for yet another lecture. Program directors have high-risk jobs; to keep them, they must use very cautious strategies.

The feeding frenzy in the radio industry—since the Telecommunications Act of 1996, nearly a quarter of the country's radio stations have changed hands—has bid up the price of stations nearly tenfold in three years. The debt burden of some of these stations is enormous, and the new owners are under great pressure to produce good profits immediately. As with so many other enterprises in the 1990s, the owners must think first about investors and later about their primary clientele and their employees.[11] This is simply not an environment in which experimentation can occur, even though it has always been experimentation, based on people's guts, love of music, and ties to their communities that has produced the greatest success stories in radio.

Central to these transformations in the industry has been the honing of audience research into an extremely well-oiled machine dominated by one company, Arbitron. Founded in 1965, Arbitron Radio contacts over 2 million listeners a year and claims to collect over a million "listening diaries" from them. When the diary arrives in the mail, the listener is required to account for every quarter hour of his or her listening for a week, writing in which station was turned on at what time of day, where the listening took place, and when the radio was off. All family members over age twelve are asked to respond, and to list their sex and age-group. Boxes like the ones Nielsen uses to monitor television viewing would be nearly worthless, since 70 percent of radio listening occurs outside the home, primarily in the car or at work.

Arbitron boasts that the diary eliminates the dangers of "interviewer bias" and that it is personal and portable. What they don't mention—and I speak here as a recent Arbitron respondent—is how easy it is to forget to fill it in, compelling you to try to remember as best you can what you tuned in when and, if that fails, simply to make it up. When the diaries arrive at Arbitron, they are scanned into a computer and reviewed to see whether they're complete enough to be used. Once they are in the system, station reps can use various computer programs to manipulate the data in a host of ways, grouping the respondents by age, sex, time of day they listened, and so forth. Results from the diaries can be combined with Arbitron's telephone surveys of people in particular zip codes that identify what kinds of cars, furniture, fast food, groceries, and beer those neighborhoods buy the most. To find even more precise niches, in 1994 Arbitron introduced "block group coding," which reduced the population to groups of 250 to 500 households within a zip code who share similar "lifestyle characteristics." Databases such as MapMAKER "can map the geographic location of a radio station's listeners and correlate their location with retailer trading areas." The company is developing a pocket people meter, based on "the latest military technology," designed to track radio listening electronically no matter where the person is and to eliminate the diary altogether.[12]

Arbitron's research allows the 2,300 radio stations that subscribe to its service "to customize survey areas, dayparts, demographics, and time periods to support target marketing strategies."[13] Listeners are categorized according to their loyalty. A P1 or First Preference listener tunes in to one radio station almost exclusively; having a lot of these is key to a station's success. P2s and P3s often have a favorite station, but they shop around more.

Research began in 1994 with Minneapolis as a test market to track listeners between the ages of two and eleven, lest children escape marketing surveillance. Parents had to fill out the diaries for the littler ones, but the older children were encouraged to fill out their own, and Arbitron interviewed a sample of them over the phone to further explore these customers' preferences.[14] If businesses can be convinced that children listen too, argues Arbitron, then stations can promote more radio advertising geared to kids.

So what has happened to listening in the 1990s? Once again, ossification grips radio music programming, which is one of the reasons that Howard Stern and Don Imus remain popular—at least they're often unpredictable, irreverent, and the antithesis of safe. With music radio such an assemblage of precision-tooled formats, much of radio listening has become mechanized too. We've learned to expect and demand instant gratification from radio stations. Don't like it? Push the seeker button. Our patience for different kinds of music has shriveled, as has our appreciation for how different genres of music influence and sustain one another. Formats allow us to seek out a monotone mood with only the tiniest surprises. In this age of niche programming, young adolescents between twelve and fifteen still turn to radio, but as they get older they turn to CDs and tapes to hear the variety they crave.[15]

The same device that worked so powerfully, through comedy and drama, sports and news, to forge a powerful sense of national identity in the 1930s is now working—along with cable TV, magazines, and niche advertising—to cultivate and encourage cultural segregation. In other words, changing corporate imperatives—first for national markets, now for niche markets—have influenced our sensory relationships to the outside world. And at the end of the century our modes of listening, once so varied and rich, are truncated. Story listening and news listening on the radio, with their requirements for dimensional listening and detailed imaginings, are virtually gone from the dial, except on NPR. People still listen to sports on the radio when they have to, but most now watch on TV, where there's no need, anymore, to imagine the arc of the ball or the geometry of the ballpark.

The ability to imagine, wildly and wonderfully, without limits, is something all children have. But it must be cultivated and developed so it remains a talent that, when we're older, extends beyond play. Radio did this for several generations of Americans. And it encouraged us, through its various discourses—linguistic slapstick, news reporting and commentary, the play-by-play, and DJ talk—to construct imagined communities of which we were part, some of them national, some of them regional, racial, or generational. The emphasis on wordplay required a concentration on language, on the richness of vocabulary and the rewards of verbal agility. Again, the content often may have been drivel; it was also at times sublime. But the point is that by compelling them to use their imaginations as part of the cultural work of being Americans, radio required people to engage in a cognitively active mode in the construction of mass culture's varied, multiple meanings.

I don't mean to suggest that radio listening made people smarter while TV viewing dumbed them down, although it's a tempting assertion, despite inadequate evidence. And I remain unclear in my own mind whether after this exploration I am trying to privilege the auditory over the visual. There is so much we have learned from and enjoyed about television that would not have been possible from radio—from seeing the path of a hurricane to seeing into outer space. But I do think that listening remains the richer form of cognitive processing. Radio, from the dramas of the 1930s up through free form, made people learn how to pay attention. There are contradictions here, because listening to many of the variety shows of the 1930s and '40s, and hearing how the listener was asked to move from listening to a three-minute song to laughing at a three-minute skit and so forth, one is struck by how radio did begin this electronically induced shortening of attention span. But so many of the shows also required prolonged imagining of a world beyond one's own and concentration on the complexities and slipperiness of language and music. This orality that radio foregrounded helped craft a culture in which many people learned to pay attention, not just to radio but to political speeches at rallies, to talks and lectures, to a variety of music. When I have asked young people to compare listening to *All Things Considered* with watching the news on TV, those who had never heard *ATC* before found that listening to the news was unfamiliar, often hard work for them; but they also found it a less frenetic cognitive and more powerful learning experience. Listening is a challenge today because so many of the other media work against it; it is a skill that is being rapidly eradicated in our culture, as any teacher can attest. This is a major cultural loss. For listening sets a standard for a more focused way of perceiving the world, and those who know how to lis-ten have a cognitive advantage over those who don't.

With the atrophying of communal imaginings comes reduced cognitive engagement, which leads to increased alienation from the concept of commu-nity itself. Radio did encourage people to feel connected to one another. Be-cause talk radio and NPR still do these things, they continue to have devoted audiences, however reined in they've become, because those audiences, with-out saying so, feel the connection between cognitive engagement and a sense of political and cultural community. At various key moments in this century, radio played a central role in bringing African American music, language, and cultural attitudes to a white audience in ways that often allowed whites to feel superior to yet envious of black Americans. Radio also gave many African American musicians access to a much larger audience than they would other-wise have had. In the 1950s and '60s radio was the most integrated of all the mass media, which I believe provided a subtle but crucial undergirding for support by many young whites for the civil rights movement. Today radio, be-cause of the formats, is heavily resegregated. This hasn't prevented legions of young whites from flocking to rap music. But with so many "soft rock" and "best mix" stations explicitly announcing that their listeners will never, ever have to encounter rap on their station, a musical apartheid gets promoted that in a corrosive, subterranean fashion legitimates geographic apartheid as well.

DJs differ in their sense of where things are headed. Some feel that the in-dustry is so powerfully centralized and consolidated, so in the grip of research, consultants, and investment groups, that insurgencies are no longer possible. They are pessimistic that radio stations will ever again regard listeners as music lovers instead of niche markets. They note that those, especially young people, who are looking for community-building communication technologies that allow for independent, unconventional expression, are deserting radio for the Internet. And they wonder whether people's repertoires of listening have be-come so impatient, so amputated, their lives so hurried and fragmented, that there may not be a market for the kind of music listening from the 1960s and '70s for which many of us are so nostalgic.

But I, and millions like me, don't have a radio station to listen to anymore. We don't have DJs we connect to. And we miss that. Of course there's NPR, and talk, but in music radio we don't have that realm we can enter where we hear a provocative mix of old and new music, new music by young people that we need to hear, and cultural and musical commentary that is intelligent and iconoclastic without being scatological.

This hole, this longing, is exactly why others think that, just as in the past, when the industry seemed to be in the grip of rigor mortis, a radio renaissance may be in the making. They realize this may be quixotic. But it was just at those moments when programming seemed so fixed—in the late 1940s and early 1950s, and again in the late 1960s and early 1970s—that off in the audio hinterlands programming insurgencies revolutionized what we heard on the air. When social movements and radio have intersected, previously forbidden and thus thrilling listening possibilities have emerged. In radio, as in so many industries, powerful centralized control means enormous profits and efficiencies for the corporations in charge. With the 1996 Telecommunications Act sanctioning corporate greed and the squelching of localism and diversity, we are probably in for a long aesthetic drought in the ether. In the face of this consolidation, micropower pirate radio stations have sprouted up around the country, arousing the ire of the FCC, which shut down 320 such stations between September 1997 and October 1998 alone.[16] But corporate control is never complete. And the growth of pirate radio suggests a new insurgency is afoot.

So a sigh is a corny, wildly naive way to end. But as baby boomers retire in increasing numbers in the early twenty-first century and have more time on their hands, and as the initial luster wears off the Internet as it becomes more commercialized and, I predict, "unbundled" into multiple nets, each of which will have ever increasing entry fees, maybe some renegades somewhere will turn their attention, once again, to radio. For boomers remain a huge market and a potentially powerful cultural force. And they will be nostalgic for their youth. Like their parents and grandparents before them, they will miss not only what they listened to but also how they listened to it, ways of listening that helped define them as a generation. Of course many will be perfectly satisfied with the formats, or will stick with talk and NPR. But it remains to be seen whether the modes of listening that defined overlapping generations throughout a century will be allowed to vanish or whether somewhere, when the suits aren't paying much attention, some defiant rebels, old or young or both, will revolutionize radio yet again and cultivate new modes of listening and new discourses yet to be imagined. Buried today as we are under the avalanche of visual slag, many people seem to want increased input in shaping the often top-down meanings of the media. I think we want our imaginations back. I think we want—and need—to listen.

Notes

INTRODUCTION

1. Claude Fischer, *America Calling: A Social History of the Telephone to 1940* (Berkeley: University of California Press, 1992), p. 22.
2. Andrew Crisell, *Understanding Radio* (New York: Routledge, 1994), p. 9; Frank A. Biocca, "The Pursuit of Sound: Radio, Perception, and Utopia in the Early Twentieth Century," *Media, Culture, and Society* 10, 1988, pp. 61–67.
3. Jacques Atali, *Noise* (Minneapolis: University of Minnesota Press, 1996), p. 3.
4. Constance Classen emphasizes this in *Worlds of Sense* (New York: Routledge, 1993). Scholars like Rick Altman, Jim Lastra, and others are challenging this emphasis on the gaze with their work on the development of sound on film. See Rick Altman, ed., *Sound Theory/Sound Practice* (New York: Routledge, 1992).
5. Paul Nahin, *The Science of Radio* (New York: American Institute of Physics, 1996), pp. xx–xxviii; Peter Fornatale and Joshua E. Mills, *Radio in the Television Age* (Woodstock, N.Y.: Overlook Press, 1984), p. ix.
6. The Freedom Forum Media Studies Center has sought to rectify this by devoting an entire journal issue to "Radio: The Forgotten Medium" *(Media Studies Journal,* Summer 1993). Exceptions include Susan Smulyan's *Selling Radio: The Commercialization of American Broadcasting, 1920–1934* (Washington, D.C.: Smithsonian Institution Press, 1994); Robert W. McChesney's *Telecommunications, Mass Media, and Democracy: The Battle for Control of U.S. Broadcasting, 1928–1935* (New York: Oxford University Press, 1993); Michele Hilmes's *Radio Voices: American Broadcasting, 1922–1952* (Minneapolis: University of Minnesota Press, 1997); and Tom Lewis's *Empire of the Air: The Men Who Made Radio* (New York: HarperCollins, 1991). And in Britain, Paddy Scannell has devoted considerable attention to radio. See his *Radio, Television, and Modern Life* (Cambridge, Mass.: Blackwell, 1996) and Scannell and D. Cardiff, *A Social History of British Broadcasting: Serving the Nation* (Oxford: Blackwell, 1991). Young scholars, including Derek Vaillant, Barbara Savage, and Jason Loviglio, will soon publish work that will fill existing historical gaps.
7. Sherry Turkle, *The Second Self: Computers and the Human Spirit* (New York: Simon

& Schuster, 1984) and *Life on the Screen: Identity in the Age of the Internet* (New York: Simon & Schuster, 1995).

8. Sandra Blakeslee, "The Mystery of Music: How It Works in the Brain," *New York Times,* May 16, 1995, pp. C1–C10.

9. Walter J. Ong, *Orality and Literacy: The Technologizing of the Word* (New York: Routledge, 1982), p. 34.

10. For a discussion of radio programming to women and its role in reinforcing gender roles over the air, see Hilmes, *Radio Voices.*

11. E. Anthony Rotundo, *American Manhood* (New York: Basic Books, 1993), p. 291.

12. Gail Bederman, *Manliness and Civilization: A Cultural History of Gender and Race in the United States, 1880–1917* (Chicago: University of Chicago Press, 1995), pp. 12–19.

13. Carroll Pursell, "The Construction of Masculinity and Technology," *Polhem* 11, 1993, pp. 206–17; Judith McGaw, *Most Wondrous Machine: Mechanization and Social Change in Berkshire Papermaking, 1801–1885* (Princeton: Princeton University Press, 1987); Ruth Schwartz Cowan, *More Work for Mother: The Ironies of Household Technology from the Open Hearth to the Microwave* (New York: Basic Books, 1983); Annette Kolodny, *The Land Before Her: Fantasy and Experience of the American Frontiers, 1630–1860* (Chapel Hill: University of North Carolina Press, 1984); Judy Wajcman, *Feminism Confronts Technology* (University Park, Pa.: Pennsylvania State University Press, 1991); Langdon Winner, *The Whale and the Reactor: A Search for Limits in the Age of Technology* (Chicago: University of Chicago Press, 1986).

14. Rotundo, *American Manhood,* pp. 247–51. See also Michael Kimmel, *Manhood in America: A Cultural History* (New York: Free Press, 1996).

15. Wiebe E. Bijker et al., *The Social Construction of Technological Systems: New Directions in the Sociology and History of Technology* (Cambridge, Mass.: MIT Press, 1987).

16. Hilmes, *Radio Voices,* p. xix.

17. Eric Lott, *Love and Theft: Blackface Minstrelsy and the American Working Class* (New York: Oxford University Press, 1995); Mel Watkins, *On the Real Side* (New York: Touchstone Books, 1994), p. 271; Hilmes, *Radio Voices,* p. 33.

18. See Neal Gabler's account of the Lindbergh trial in his superb biography *Winchell: Gossip, Power, and the Culture of Celebrity* (New York: Alfred A. Knopf, 1995).

19. Ben Sidran, *Black Talk* (New York: Da Capo Press, 1971), p. xxiv.

20. Merritt Roe Smith, "Technological Determinism in American Culture," in Smith and Leo Marx, eds., *Does Technology Drive History?* (Cambridge, Mass.: MIT Press, 1994), p. 13.

21. See Dorothy Nelkin, *Selling Science: How the Press Covers Science and Technology* (New York: W. H. Freeman, 1995); Daniel J. Czitrom, *Media and the American Mind* (Chapel Hill: University of North Carolina Press, 1982).

22. Fischer, *America Calling,* pp. 24–26.

1. THE ZEN OF LISTENING

1. Andrew Crisell, *Understanding Radio* (New York: Routledge, 1994), p. 10.

2. Anthony Storr, *Music and the Mind* (New York: Free Press, 1992), p. 26.

3. Benedict Anderson, *Imagined Communities: Reflections on the Origins and Spread of*

Nationalism (New York: Verso, 1983, 1991) pp. 6–7; Michele Hilmes also felt obliged to cite Anderson in *Radio Voices: American Broadcasting, 1922–1952* (Minneapolis: University of Minnesota Press, 1997), pp. 11–13.

4. Forthcoming work by the historian Derek Vaillant will document the role of such stations in Chicago in the 1920s.

5. Marshall McLuhan, *Understanding Media: The Extensions of Man* (New York: New American Library, 1964), pp. 263–64.

6. I am indebted to Dr. David Rosenbaum of Pennsylvania State University (interview, August 4, 1995) and Dr. Mark Tramo of Harvard Medical School (interview, July 8, 1998) for their help on this topic. The pioneering work on visual imaging was done by Stephen M. Kosslyn. See, for example, *Image and the Brain: The Resolution of the Imagery Debate* (Cambridge, Mass.: MIT Press, 1994). See also Roger Shepard, "The Mental Image," *American Psychologist*, February 1978, pp. 125–27.

7. Samuel A. Bobrow and Gordon H. Bower, "Comprehension and Recall of Sentences," *Journal of Experimental Psychology* 10, 1969, pp. 455–61.

8. Michael I. Posner and Marcus E. Raichle, *Images of Mind* (New York: Scientific American Library, 1994), p. 99; Dorothy G. Singer and Jerome L. Singer, *The House of Make-Believe: Children's Play and the Developing Imagination* (Cambridge, Mass.: Harvard University Press, 1990), pp. 187–89.

9. Robert Jourdain, *Music, the Brain, and Ecstasy* (New York: William Morrow, 1997), p. 245.

10. Ibid.

11. Ibid., p. 255. I am also grateful to Nick King in the History of Science Program at Harvard for insisting on this point.

12. Interview, Mark Tramo.

13. Don Ihde, *Listening and the Voice: A Phenomenology of Sound* (Athens, Ohio: Ohio University Press, 1976), p. 4.

14. Walter J. Ong, *Orality and Literacy: The Technologizing of the Word* (New York: Routledge, 1982), pp. 74, 136; McLuhan, *Understanding Media*, p. 88; Jourdain, *Music, the Brain, and Ecstasy*, pp. 328–29; Idhe, *Listening and the Voice*, p. 45; Storr, *Music and the Mind*, p. 7.

15. Stephen Handel, *Listening: An Introduction to the Perception of Auditory Events* (Cambridge, Mass.: MIT Press, 1989), p. xi; Ong, *Orality and Literacy*, p. 72; Edith Slembek, "The Vision of Hearing in a Visual Age," *American Behavioral Scientist*, vol. 33, November/December 1988, p. 150.

16. Rudolf Arnheim, *Radio* (London: Faber & Faber, 1936), p. 23; Hadley Cantril and Gordon Allport, *The Psychology of Radio* (New York: Harper & Brothers, 1935), p. 259.

17. Cantril and Allport, *Psychology of Radio*, pp. 232–33.

18. Idhe, *Listening and the Voice*, p. 137.

19. Crisell, *Understanding Radio*, p. 7.

20. Ibid., pp. 211–12.

21. Interview, Mark Tramo.

22. Sandra Blakeslee, "The Mystery of Music: How It Works in the Brain," *New York Times*, May 16, 1995, p. C10, citing especially the work of Jamshed Bharucha at Dartmouth; Jourdain, *Music, the Brain, and Ecstasy*, p. 319.

23. Jourdain, *Music, the Brain, and Ecstasy,* pp. xiv–xvii.
24. I am indebted to my colleague Kris Harrison for directing me to the mood management literatures. For a summary, see Roger Desmond and Rod Carveth, "Illuminating the Black Box: The Psychological Tradition in Media Studies," in Donald P. Cushman and Branislav Kovacic, eds., *Watershed Research Traditions in Human Communication Theory* (Albany: State University of New York Press, 1995).
25. For an overview, see Susan T. Fiske and Shelley E. Taylor, *Social Cognition* (New York: McGraw-Hill, 1991), chap. 8; J. R. Anderson, *The Architecture of Cognition* (Cambridge, Mass.: Harvard University Press, 1983). Vincent Price and David Tewksbury use this model to theorize about how people form associations while watching the news. See "News Values and Public Opinion: A Theoretical Account of Media Priming and Framing," in F. J. Boster and G. Barnett, eds., *Progress in the Communication Sciences* (Greenwich, Conn.: Ablex, 1997).
26. Jourdain, *Music, the Brain, and Ecstasy,* p. 263.
27. Hugh G. J. Aitken, *Syntony and Spark: The Origins of Radio* (New York: John Wiley, 1976), p. 50.
28. I am very grateful to Rick Ducey for this explanation. The following descriptions are based on my interview with him on May 14, 1998.
29. Sydney W. Head, *Broadcasting in America,* 3d ed. (Boston: Houghton Mifflin, 1976), p. 39; *The ARRL Handbook* (Newington, Conn.: ARRL, 1993), chap. 22, p. 2.
30. Head, *Broadcasting in America,* p. 39.
31. Interview, Rick Ducey.
32. Philip T. Rosen, *The Modern Stentors: Radio Broadcasters and the Federal Government, 1920–1934* (Westport, Conn.: Greenwood Press, 1980), pp. 136, 152; "The Problem of Radio Reallocation," *Congressional Digest,* vol. 7, no. 10, October 1928, pp. 255–86.

2. THE ETHEREAL WORLD

1. Constance Classen, *Worlds of Sense* (New York: Routledge, 1993) pp. 3, 121.
2. *New York Herald,* October 1, 1899, p. 7; P. T. McGrath, "Authoritative Account of Marconi's Work in Wireless Telegraphy," *Century Magazine,* March 1902, p. 782; *Popular Science Monthly* 56, 1899, p. 72.
3. Frederick Lewis Allen, *Only Yesterday* (New York: Harper & Row, 1957), p. 197; "His Visit Really a Success," *New York Times,* February 23, 1920, p. 12.
4. For a detailed and elegant description of Lodge's system and his patent, see Hugh G. J. Aitken, *Syntony and Spark: The Origins of Radio* (New York: John Wiley, 1976), pp. 130–42; W. P. Jolly, *Oliver Lodge* (Rutherford, N.J.: Fairleigh Dickinson University Press, 1975), p. 219.
5. Criticisms cited in Frank Ballard, "Immortality and Modern Science," *Living Age,* May 17, 1919, pp. 400–405; "Between Two Worlds—Oliver Lodge Answers Our Questions," *Independent,* March 13, 1920, p. 389; Oliver Lodge, "The Etherial World," *McClure's,* October 1920, pp. 10 ff; Oliver Lodge, "How I Know the Dead Exist," *McClure's,* November 1920, pp. 20 ff.
6. Joseph McCabe, "Scientific Men and Spiritualism: A Skeptic's Analysis," *Living Age,* June 12, 1920, p. 652; "The Ouija Board, Bolshevik of the Spirit World," *Literary Di-*

gest, January 31, 1920, p. 64; "Ouija, Ouija, Who's Got the Ouija," *Literary Digest*, July 3, 1920, p. 66.

7. B. C. Forbes, "Edison Working on How to Communicate with the Next World," *American Magazine*, October 1920, p. 10.

8. Frank Ballard, "Immortality and Modern Science," *Living Age*, May 17, 1919, p. 400.

9. Jolly, *Oliver Lodge*, p. 205.

10. Ibid.; cited in Ballard, "Immortality and Modern Science," p. 403; Joseph Jastrow, "The Case of Sir Oliver Lodge," *Review*, March 6, 1920, p. 226.

11. "Doyle Says Ghosts May Use the Radio," *New York Times*, May 5, 1923, p. 6.

12. Jolly, *Oliver Lodge*, p. 114; "Through the Dream Stratum," *New York Times*, January 17, 1920, p. 10; Lodge, "How I Know the Dead Exist," p. 20.

13. Ronald W. Clark, *Edison: The Man Who Made the Future* (New York: G. P. Putnam's Sons, 1977), p. 81; Evan Eisenberg, *The Recording Angel: Explorations in Phonography* (New York: McGraw-Hill, 1987), p. 57.

14. See William Kenney's excellent new book on the phonograph, *The Phonograph and Recorded Music in American Life, 1870–1945* (New York: Oxford University Press, 1999). Chapter 1 covers the reports of using the phonograph to "contact" lost loved ones. Quotation in unpub. ms. on p. 22.

15. Ray Barfield, *Listening to Radio, 1920–1950* (Westport, Conn.: Praeger, 1996), pp. 8–9.

16. Waldemar Kaempffert, "The Social Destiny of Radio," *Forum*, June 1924, p. 772.

17. Joseph K. Hart, "Radiating Culture," *Survey*, March 18, 1922, p. 949; A. Leonard Smith, Jr., "Broadcasting to Millions," *New York Times*, February 19, 1922, sec. 7, p. 6; Rudolf Arnheim, *Radio* (London: Faber & Faber, 1936), p. 15.

18. See Susan J. Douglas, *Inventing American Broadcasting, 1899–1922* (Baltimore: Johns Hopkins University Press, 1987), p. 231.

19. The most detailed and elegant discussion of Lodge's work on tuned circuits is in Aitken, *Syntony and Spark*.

20. For more detail on the early years of radio in America, see Douglas, *Inventing American Broadcasting*, and Hugh G. J. Aitken, *The Continuous Wave* (Princeton: Princeton University Press, 1986).

21. Erik Barnouw, *A Tower in Babel* (New York: Oxford University Press, 1966), p. 125; "The Long Arm of Radio Is Reaching Everywhere," *Current Opinion*, May 1922, p. 685; " 'Listening In,' Our New National Pastime," *Review of Reviews*, January 1923, p. 52; Waldemar Kaempffert, "Radio Broadcasting," *Review of Reviews*, April 1922, p. 399; *New York Times*, March 2, 1922, p. 20; Smith, "Broadcasting to Millions," sec. 7, p. 6.

22. *New York Times*, January 24, 1920, p. 10.

23. Barfield, *Listening to Radio*, p. 17.

24. William Burke Miller, "He Sends Thoughts Through the Ether," *Radio Digest*, November 1929, p. 43.

25. Barfield, *Listening to Radio*, p. 12.

3. EXPLORATORY LISTENING IN THE 1920S

1. "Astonishing Growth of the Radiotelephone," *Literary Digest*, April 15, 1922, p. 28.

2. Ibid.; Waldemar Kaempffert, "Radio Broadcasting," *Review of Reviews*, April 1922, p. 399.

3. See Susan Douglas, *Inventing American Broadcasting, 1899–1922* (Baltimore: Johns Hopkins University Press, 1987); Susan Smulyan, *Selling Radio: The Commercialization of American Broadcasting, 1920–1934* (Washington, D.C.: Smithsonian Institution Press, 1994); Robert W. McChesney, *Telecommunications, Mass Media, and Democracy: The Battle for Control of U.S. Broadcasting, 1928–1935* (New York: Oxford University Press, 1993).

4. The real pioneer was Erik Barnouw, whose three-volume *History of Broadcasting in the United States* has remained the standard for decades. For the 1920s, see his *Tower in Babel* (New York: Oxford University Press, 1966). Other fine works include Philip T. Rosen, *The Modern Stentors: Radio Broadcasters and the Federal Government, 1920–1934* (Westport, Conn.: Greenwood Press, 1980), and Smulyan's book, which is especially good on the emergence of the networks and broadcast advertising. See also Michele Hilmes, *Radio Voices: American Broadcasting, 1922–1952* (Minneapolis: University of Minnesota Press, 1997).

5. For more detail on the amateurs, see S. Douglas, *Inventing American Broadcasting,* chaps. 6 and 9.

6. Robert A. Morton, "The Amateur Wireless Operator," *Outlook,* January 15, 1910, pp. 132–33.

7. Cited in Clinton B. DeSoto, *Two Hundred Meters and Down: The Story of Amateur Radio* (West Hartford, Conn.: ARRL, 1936), p. 40.

8. S. Douglas, *Inventing American Broadcasting,* p. 299.

9. Kaempffert, "Radio Broadcasting," p. 398; cited in "The Radio Business," *Literary Digest,* May 5, 1923, p. 28.

10. Lynn Dumenil, *Modern Temper: American Culture and Society in the 1920s* (New York: Hill & Wang, 1995), pp. 224, 226–27; John Mack Faragher et al., *Out of Many: A History of the American People* (Upper Saddle River, N.J.: Prentice Hall, 1997), p. 742; Lawrence Levine, *The Opening of the American Mind* (Boston: Beacon Press, 1996), pp. 106–14.

11. Rosen, *Modern Stentors,* pp. 56–57.

12. Ibid., p. 93.

13. Ibid., p. 124; George H. Douglas, *The Early Days of Radio Broadcasting* (Jefferson, N.C.: McFarland, 1987), p. 95.

14. Christopher H. Sterling and John M. Kittross, *Stay Tuned: A Concise History of American Broadcasting,* 2d ed. (Belmont, Cal.: Wadsworth Publishing, 1990), p. 111; "Voice of the Listener," *Radio Digest,* January 1930.

15. Cited in G. Douglas, *Early Days,* p. 88; For more details, see Smulyan, *Selling Radio.*

16. Paul Nahin, *The Science of Radio* (New York: American Institute of Physics, 1996), p. xxix. For a more detailed account, see G. Douglas, *Early Days,* pp. 17–21.

17. Neil Leonard, *Jazz and the White Americans* (Chicago: University of Chicago Press, 1962), p. 92; " 'Listening In,' Our New National Pastime," *Review of Reviews,* January 1923, p. 52; *New York Times,* March 2, 1922, p. 20; "Astonishing Growth of the Radiophone," p. 28; cited in Nahin, *Science of Radio,* p. xxx.

18. Dumenil, *Modern Temper,* p. 76.

19. David Nasaw, *Going Out* (New York: Basic Books, 1994).

20. Orange Edward McMeans, "The Great Audience Invisible," *Scribner's,* April 1923, p. 411; Bruce Bliven, "How Radio Is Remaking Our World," *Century,* June 1924, p. 148.

21. Lizabeth Cohen, *Making a New Deal: Industrial Workers in Chicago, 1919–1939* (New York: Cambridge University Press, 1990), pp. 132–33.

22. Gail Bederman, *Manliness and Civilization: A Cultural History of Gender and Race in the United States, 1880–1917* (Chicago: University of Chicago Press, 1995), pp. 15–17; E. Anthony Rotundo, *American Manhood* (New York: Basic Books, 1993), p. 258.

23. Rotundo, *American Manhood*, pp. 255–62.

24. Ibid., pp. 248–49.

25. Dumenil, *Modern Temper*, pp. 86–93; Gaylyn Studlar, *That Mad Masquerade* (New York: Columbia University Press, 1996), pp. 249, 93; T.J. Jackson Lears, "From Salvation to Self-Realization: Advertising and the Therapeutic Roots of the Consumer Culture, 1880–1930," in Richard Wightman Fox and Lears, eds. *The Culture of Consumption* (New York: Pantheon, 1983).

26. Rosen, *Modern Stentors*, p. 113; John Brennan, "Radio Broadcast's Knock-Out Four-Tube Receiver," *Radio Broadcast*, September 1924, p. 379; "The Radio Business," *Literary Digest*, May 5, 1923, p. 28; "Voice of the Listener," *Radio Digest*, March 1930; William H. Cary, Jr., "How to Go About Buying a Set," *Radio Broadcast*, April 1924, p. 521.

27. Cary, "How to Buy a Set," pp. 522–23; Lizabeth Cohen notes in *Making a New Deal* that Western Electric in Chicago set up how-to classes for its workers, p. 132.

28. Cited in "Women and Wireless," *Literary Digest*, December 15, 1923, p. 25.

29. Rosen, *Modern Stentors*, p. 113.

30. Cohen, *Making a New Deal*, p. 133.

31. Cary, "How to Buy a Set," p. 521.

32. Cited in "The Pranks of the 'Static' Pest," *Literary Digest*, April 29, 1922, p. 25.

33. "The Demon in Radio," *Literary Digest*, August 2, 1924, p. 26; Bliven, "How Radio Is Remaking Our World," p. 151.

34. Sterling and Kittross, *Stay Tuned*, p. 87; Rosen, *Modern Stentors*, p. 113.

35. "Voice of the Listener," *Radio Digest*, September 1930, March 1930.

36. Joseph K. Hart, "Radiating Culture," *Survey*, March 18, 1922, p. 949; Kaempffert, "Radio Broadcasting," pp. 399–400; Waldemar Kaempffert, "The Progress of Radio Broadcasting," *American Review of Reviews*, September 1922, p. 305; G. Douglas, *Early Days*, p. 168.

37. Cary, "How to Buy a Set," p. 520.

38. G. Douglas, *Early Days*, p. 40; " 'Listening In,' Our New National Pastime," p. 52; "What Makes Radio Fans," *Literary Digest*, July 5, 1924, p. 27; Howard Vincent O'Brien, "It's Great to Be a Radio Maniac," *Collier's*, September 13, 1924, p. 16.

39. Lizabeth Cohen, for example, has described how ethnic and working-class listeners in Chicago reinforced these ties and identities by tuning in quite loyally to local stations that provided labor news, ethnic nationality hours, and ethnically based religious services. See her *Making a New Deal*, pp. 134–38.

40. O'Brien, "It's Great," p. 16; "Voice of the Listener," *Radio Digest*, January 1930.

41. Cited in Smulyan, *Selling Radio*, pp. 15, 16; "Voice of the Listener," *Radio Digest*, November 1929.

42. "Voice of the Listener," *Radio Digest*, December 1929; *The ARRL Handbook* (Newington, Conn.: ARRL, 1993), chap. 22, p. 2.

43. McMeans, "Great Audience Invisible," p. 412; "Music in the Air . . . and Voice on the

Crystal Set: Fifteen Pioneers Recall Their Adventures in the Early Days of American Radio," *American Heritage,* August 1955, p. 69.

44. Cited in Smulyan, *Selling Radio,* p. 16, and in Hilmes, *Radio Voices,* p. 15.

45. Dumenil, *Modern Temper,* p. 6.

46. McMeans, "Great Audience Invisible," pp. 412–23; " 'Listening In,' Our New National Pastime," p. 52; cited in Smulyan, *Selling Radio,* p. 15.

47. Stanley Frost, "Radio Dreams That Can Come True," *Collier's,* June 10, 1922, p. 18; Waldemar Kaempffert, "The Social Destiny of Radio," *Forum,* June 1924, pp. 771–72.

48. Ray Barfield, *Listening to Radio, 1920–1950* (Westport, Conn.: Praeger, 1996), pp. 4, 9, 10.

49. J. H. Morecroft, "1923 Passes in Review," *Radio Broadcast,* March 1924, p. 393.

50. G. Douglas, *Early Days,* p. 48; "Voice of the Listener," *Radio Digest,* December 1929; "The Growth of Radio," *Literary Digest,* November 20, 1926, p. 29.

51. "New Developments in Radio," *Outlook,* September 30, 1925, pp. 142–43; Barfield, *Listening to Radio,* p. 11; W. F. Crosby, "Keeping Pace with Radio," *Saint Nicholas,* March 1926, p. 538; Rosen, *Modern Stentors,* p. 114.

52. "Voice of the Listener," *Radio Digest,* February 1930.

53. Ibid., June 1930, March 1930, April 1930.

54. Ibid., April 1930, February 1930, March 1930.

55. DeSoto, *Two Hundred Meters,* p. 85.

56. Carl Dreher and Zeh Bouck, "Our Radio Amateurs," *Harper's,* October, 1941, p. 540.

57. G. Douglas, *Early Days,* p. 96.

4. TUNING IN TO JAZZ

1. All quotations cited in Frank Biocca, "Media and Perceptual Shifts: Early Radio and the Clash of Musical Cultures," *Journal of Popular Culture* 24, Fall 1990, pp. 5–8.

2. William Kenney, *The Phonograph and Recorded Music in American Life, 1870–1945* (New York: Oxford University Press, 1999).

3. Ann Douglas, *Terrible Honesty: Mongrel Manhattan in the 1920s* (New York: Farrar, Straus & Giroux, 1995), p. 365; Burton W. Peretti, *The Creation of Jazz* (Urbana: University of Illinois Press, 1992), p. 152; Neil Leonard, *Jazz and the White Americans* (Chicago: University of Chicago Press, 1962), p. 91.

4. Neil Leonard, "The Impact of Mechanization," in Charles Nanry, ed., *American Music: From Storyville to Woodstock* (New Brunswick, N.J.: Transaction Books, 1972), p. 48; Hadley Cantril and Gordon Allport, *The Psychology of Radio* (New York: Harper & Brothers, 1935), p. 219.

5. For a more detailed discussion of music and the inner life, see Anthony Storr, *Music and the Mind* (New York: Free Press, 1992).

6. Leonard, *Jazz and the White Americans,* pp. 95–99.

7. Cantril and Allport, *Psychology of Radio,* p. 219.

8. George H. Douglas, *The Early Days of Radio Broadcasting* (Jefferson, N.C.: McFarland, 1987), p. 158; Kenney, *Phonograph and Recorded Music,* p. 7 (ms.).

9. Peretti, *Creation of Jazz,* p. 161; J. H. Morecroft, "1923 Passes in Review," *Radio Broadcast,* March 1924, p. 390.

10. G. Douglas, *Early Days,* pp. 183–84, 168.

11. Philip K. Eberly, *Music in the Air: America's Changing Tastes in Popular Music, 1920–1980* (New York: Hastings House, 1982), p. 14.

12. Erik Barnouw, *A Tower in Babel* (New York: Oxford University Press, 1966); G. Douglas, *Early Days,* p. 168; Cantril and Allport, *Psychology of Radio,* p. 219.

13. *Radio Broadcast,* September 1924, p. 397; Jennie Irene Mix, "The Listener's Point of View," *Radio Broadcast,* May 1924, p. 16.

14. G. Douglas, *Early Days,* pp. 158, 170.

15. Cantril and Allport, *Psychology of Radio,* p. 220. *The New Republic* featured an article on this practice called "Crutches for Broadcast Music," on December 2, 1932; Storr, *Music and the Mind,* p. xi.

16. A. Douglas, *Terrible Honesty,* p. 377; Kenney, *Phonograph and Recorded Music,* chap. 1, p. 18.

17. Paul F. Lazarsfeld, *Radio and the Printed Page* (New York: Duell, Sloan & Pearce, 1940), p. 131.

18. Martha Gellhorn, "Rudy Vallee, God's Gift to Us Girls," *New Republic,* August 7, 1929, pp. 311, 310; "Riding the Crest," *Outlook and Independent,* September 11, 1929, p. 58; "Voice of the Listener," *Radio Digest,* July 1930.

19. G. Douglas, *Early Days,* pp. 155–57; Barnouw, *Tower in Babel,* pp. 88–90.

20. Michele Hilmes, *Radio Voices: American Broadcasting, 1922–1952* (Minneapolis: University of Minnesota Press, 1997), p. 79; Ben Sidran, *Black Talk* (New York: Da Capo Press, 1971).

21. Amiri Baraka, *Blues People* (New York: Morrow-Quill, 1963), p. 100.

22. Andre Millard, *America on Record: A History of Recorded Sound* (New York: Cambridge University Press, 1995), p. 77; Kathy J. Ogren, *The Jazz Revolution: Twenties America and the Meaning of Jazz* (New York: Oxford University Press, 1989), p. 91; Marshall W. Stearns, *The Story of Jazz* (New York: Oxford University Press, 1958), p. 297; Baraka, *Blues People,* p. 100.

23. Cited in Ogren, *The Jazz Revolution,* p. 157; A. Douglas, *Terrible Honesty,* pp. 377–78; Carl Engel, "Jazz: A Musical Discussion," *Atlantic Monthly,* August 1922, p. 183; Barnouw, *Tower in Babel,* p. 130.

24. Leonard, "Impact of Mechanization," pp. 52–53.

25. Robert Jourdain, *Music, the Brain, and Ecstasy* (New York: William Morrow, 1997), pp. 256–58.

26. Sidran, *Black Talk,* p. 69; G. Douglas, *Early Days,* pp. 173–74.

27. "Jazz," *Outlook,* March 5, 1924, p. 381; cited in Ogren, *The Jazz Revolution,* p. 102; "King Jazz and the Jazz Kings," *Literary Digest,* January 30, 1926, p. 37; Gilbert Seldes, *The Seven Lively Arts* (New York: Harper & Brothers, 1924), p. 84.

28. Walter Barnes, "Hittin' High Notes," *Chicago Defender,* January 9, 1932, p. 7.

29. A. Douglas, *Terrible Honesty,* p. 420; William Howland Kenney, *Chicago Jazz: A Cultural History, 1904–1930* (New York: Oxford University Press, 1993), p. 157; Eberly, *Music in the Air,* p. 43; Chris Albertson, *Bessie* (New York: Stein & Day, 1972), pp. 48, 52, 68–69.

30. Dave Peyton, "The Musical Bunch," *Chicago Defender,* October 31, 1925, p. 6; Eberly, *Music in the Air,* pp. 42, 45; Peretti, *Creation of Jazz,* p. 154; James Lincoln Collier, *Duke Ellington* (New York: Oxford University Press, 1987), pp. 54, 96; Mark

Newman, "On the Air with Jack L. Cooper," *Chicago History,* Summer 1983, p. 52; Jack L. Cooper Collection, Chicago Historical Society, "Biographical Sketch of Jack L. Cooper" and "Jack L. Cooper, First DJ, Is Dead," *Daily Defender,* January 14, 1970.

31. A. Douglas, *Terrible Honesty,* p. 420; Peyton, "Musical Bunch," p. 6. For the debates about crossover in the later part of the century, see Steve Perry, "Ain't No Mountain High Enough: The Politics of Crossover," in Simon Frith, ed., *Facing the Music* (New York: Pantheon, 1988).

32. Eberly, *Music in the Air,* p. 44.

33. Ogren, *The Jazz Revolution,* p. 87; Lewis A. Erenberg, *Swingin' the Dream: Big Band Jazz and the Rebirth of American Culture* (Chicago: University of Chicago Press, 1998), pp. 3, 42–43; Erenberg, *Swingin' the Dream,* p. 43. For the definitive discussion on the critical importance of African American music to the prestige enjoyed by American culture in the 1920s, see A. Douglas, *Terrible Honesty.*

34. "Jazz," *Outlook,* p. 381; interview, Jim Sibbison, March 1995; J. A. Rogers, "Jazz at Home," *Survey,* March 1, 1925; Darius Milhaud, "The Jazz Band and Negro Music," *Living Age,* October 18, 1924, p. 169. For a discussion of whites' projections onto jazz, see Sidran, *Black Talk,* p. 55.

35. Sidran, *Black Talk,* p. 9.

36. "Jazz," *Outlook,* p. 382. Ann Douglas, in her magisterial analysis of the rise of ragtime, blues, and jazz, sees this trend beginning with ragtime. See *Terrible Honesty,* p. 409.

37. Seldes, *Seven Lively Arts,* p. 86; Stearns, *Story of Jazz,* p. 305.

38. Seldes, *Seven Lively Arts,* pp. 96, 98, 99, 101.

39. Stearns, *Story of Jazz,* pp. 298–99, 300.

40. Sidran, *Black Talk,* pp. xxi, 54.

41. Ibid., pp. 55–56.

42. A. Douglas, *Terrible Honesty,* pp. 400–403.

43. Kenney, *The Phonograph and Recorded Music in American Life,* unpub. ms.., p. 3.

5. RADIO COMEDY AND LINGUISTIC SLAPSTICK

1. Elaine Chaika, *Language: The Social Mirror* (New York: Newbury House, 1989), p. 142.

2. J. H. Morecroft, "1923 Passes in Review," *Radio Broadcast,* March 1924, p. 386; W. P. Robinson, *Language and Social Behavior* (Baltimore: Penguin Books, 1972), p. 105; Janet Rankin Aiken, "Vays, Vayz or Vahz?" *North American Review,* December 1929, p. 716.

3. Aiken, "Vays, Vayz, Vahz?" p. 716; Francis T. S. Powell, "Radio and the Language," *The Commonweal,* April 10, 1929, p. 652; "Radio English," *Saturday Review of Literature,* October 16, 1926, p. 187.

4. Ibid., Aiken, "Vays, Vayz or Vahz?" p. 719.

5. "Voice of the Listener," *Radio Digest,* January 1930; Hadley Cantril and Gordon Allport, *The Psychology of Radio* (New York, Harper & Brothers, 1935), p. 210.

6. "Broadcasting English," *Saturday Review of Literature,* January 31, 1931, p. 1.

7. Gilbert Seldes, "Some Radio Entertainers," *New Republic,* May 20, 1931, p. 19.

8. "Blackout," *Time,* January 25, 1943, p. 51.

9. Arthur Frank Wertheim, *Radio Comedy* (New York: Oxford University Press, 1979), p. 87; "Pun and Punch: Radio Comics Supply Audience with Quip Reserve," *Literary Digest*, March 27, 1937, p. 20.

10. Scott Cutler Shershow, *Laughing Matters: The Paradox of Comedy* (Amherst: University of Massachusetts Press, 1986), p. 4; Chaika, *Language*, p. 167.

11. Robert S. McElvaine, *The Great Depression* (New York: Times Books, 1984), pp. 75, 81, 171, 225.

12. Peter Farb, *Word Play: What Happens When People Talk* (New York: Alfred A. Knopf, 1974), p. 124.

13. Robinson, *Language and Social Behavior*, p. 104.

14. I am indebted to Rob Snyder for reminding me to make the connection between radio comedy and vaudeville. Albert F. McLean, Jr., *American Vaudeville as Ritual* (Lexington: University of Kentucky Press, 1965), pp. 109–14, 123; Robert W. Snyder, *The Voice of the City* (New York: Oxford University Press, 1989), pp. 129–32; Robert C. Allen, *Horrible Prettiness: Burlesque and American Culture* (Chapel Hill: University of North Carolina Press, 1991), p. 103.

15. Snyder, *Voice of the City*, p. 105.

16. Seldes, "Some Radio Entertainers," p. 19.

17. Michele Hilmes, *Radio Voices: American Broadcasting, 1922–1952* (Minneapolis: University of Minnesota Press, 1997), pp. 29–33, 79–80; Mel Watkins, *On the Real Side: Laughing, Lying, and Signifying* (New York: Simon & Schuster, 1994), p. 283; Melvin Patrick Ely, *The Adventures of Amos 'n' Andy; A Social History of an American Phenomenon* (New York: Free Press, 1991), p. 63.

18. Wertheim, *Radio Comedy*, p. 48; Watkins, *On the Real Side*, p. 278.

19. See Nathan Huggins's brilliant discussion in *Harlem Renaissance* (New York: Oxford University Press, 1971), especially chap. 6; Watkins, *On the Real Side*.

20. See Ann Douglas's discussion of this in *Terrible Honesty: Mongrel Manhattan in the 1920s* (New York: Farrar, Straus & Giroux, 1995); Walter Brasch, *Black English and the Mass Media* (Amherst: University of Massachusetts Press, 1981), p. 223; Chaika, *Language*, p. 173.

21. Ely, *Adventures of Amos 'n' Andy*, p. 120; Allen, *Horrible Prettiness*, p. 173. See also Jules Zanger, "The Minstrel Show as Theater of Misrule," *Quarterly Journal of Speech* 60, 1974, pp. 33–38; and Alexander Saxton, "Blackface Minstrelsy and Jacksonian Ideology," *American Quarterly* 27, 1975, pp. 3–28.

22. Cited in Wertheim, *Radio Comedy*, p. 38.

23. Ely, *Adventures of Amos 'n' Andy*, p. 108.

24. Brasch, *Black English and the Mass Media*, p. 223; Ely, *Adventures of Amos 'n' Andy*, pp. 93, 94, 208.

25. Cantril and Allport, *Psychology of Radio*, pp. 222–23.

26. "Pun and Punch," p. 20.

27. "Listeners-In," *Business Week*, February 1, 1933, p. 12; Cantril and Allport, *Psychology of Radio*, p. 225; Museum of Television and Radio, "The Bakers Broadcast" with Joe Penner, May 13, 1934, R76: 0070.

28. Cantril and Allport, *Psychology of Radio*, p. 224; Wertheim, *Radio Comedy*, p. 106; Walter J. Ong, *Orality and Literacy: The Technologizing of the Word* (New York: Routledge, 1982), p. 34.

29. Museum of Broadcast Communications, "The Fire Chief," April 9, 1935, RA 19; Cantril and Allport, *Psychology of Radio*, p. 225.
30. Wertheim, *Radio Comedy*, p. 89; Museum of Television and Radio, *The Eddie Cantor Show*, June 6, 1938, R85: 0378 and April 23, 1941, R90: 0058.
31. Farb, *Word Play*, pp. 122–23; Chaika, *Language*, p. 167.
32. For more details, see Susan J. Douglas, *Where the Girls Are: Growing Up Female with the Mass Media* (New York: Times Books, 1994).
33. Wertheim, *Radio Comedy*, p. 194; quotations cited in J. Fred MacDonald, *Don't Touch That Dial! Radio Programming in American Life, 1920–1960* (Chicago: Nelson-Hall, 1979), pp. 134–35.
34. Wertheim, *Radio Comedy*, p. 198; Museum of Television and Radio, *The Burns and Allen Show*, R85: 0287.
35. Ibid.
36. Wertheim, *Radio Comedy*, p. 204.
37. Alexander Doty, *Making Things Perfectly Queer: Interpreting Mass Culture* (Minneapolis: University of Minnesota Press, 1993), p. 66.
38. Ibid., p. 64.
39. McElvaine, *Great Depression*, pp. 82, 172.
40. Watkins, *On the Real Side*, pp. 285, 286–88.
41. Museum of Television and Radio, "Black Radio: In the Beginning," 1996, R: 14496; Watkins, *On the Real Side*, pp. 285–86.
42. Wertheim, *Radio Comedy*, p. 176.
43. Ibid., p. 185; cited on p. 186.
44. Ibid., p. 363.
45. Ibid., p. 104.
46. "The Burns and Allen Show."
47. "The Fire Chief," April 9, 1935.

6. THE INVENTION OF THE AUDIENCE

1. Christopher H. Sterling and John M. Kittross, *Stay Tuned: A Concise History of American Broadcasting*, 2d ed. (Belmont, Cal.: Wadsworth Publishing, 1990), p. 126.
2. Paul Lazarsfeld, "An Episode in the History of Social Research: A Memoir," in Donald Fleming and Bernard Bailyn, eds., *The Intellectual Migration: Europe and America, 1930–1960* (Cambridge, Mass.: Harvard University Press, 1969), p. 273.
3. Ibid., p. 272; Helmut Gruber, *Red Vienna: Experiment in Working-Class Culture, 1919–1934* (New York: Oxford University Press, 1991), p. 140.
4. Gruber, *Red Vienna*, p. 114 ff; Hans Zeisel, "The Vienna Years," in Robert K. Merton et al., *Qualitative and Quantitative Social Research* (New York: Free Press, 1979), p. 10.
5. Here I follow Gruber's elegant analysis of the class tensions besetting "Red Vienna," pp. 7–8.
6. Everett M. Rogers, *A History of Communication Study: A Biographical Approach* (New York: The Free Press, 1994), p. 253; Lazarsfeld, "Memoir," p. 279.
7. Warren I. Susman, *Culture as History: The Transformation of American Society in the Twentieth Century* (New York: Pantheon, 1984), pp. 154–58.
8. For a summary see Richard Pells, *Radical Visions and American Dreams: Culture*

and *Social Thought in the Depression Years* (New York: Harper & Row, 1973), pp. 23–28; Robert and Helen Lynd, *Middletown: A Study in Contemporary American Culture* (New York: Harcourt, Brace, 1929), p. 265.

9. One of the more influential books on this topic was Lewis Mumford's *Technics and Civilization* (New York: Harcourt, Brace, 1934).

10. Lazarsfeld, "Memoir," pp. 295, 298.

11. Interview, Marie Jahoda, August 1993.

12. Hadley Cantril and Gordon Allport, *The Psychology of Radio* (New York: Harper & Brothers, 1935), pp. 3, 14, 38, 85.

13. Ibid., pp. 4–5.

14. Ibid., p. 7.

15. Ibid., pp. 10, 18.

16. Ibid., p. 72.

17. Ibid., pp. 15–16.

18. Ibid., pp. 85–93, 97, 103.

19. Ibid., pp. 96, 109–26.

20. Ibid., pp. 119–20.

21. Ibid., p. 125.

22. Ibid., pp. 127–38.

23. Ibid., pp. 259–62.

24. Ibid., pp. 269–72.

25. Hugh Malcolm Beville, Jr., *Audience Ratings: Radio, Television, Cable* (Hillsdale, N.J.: Lawrence Erlbaum, 1985), p. 4; "Checking Radio Checkups," *Business Week*, May 28, 1938, p. 36; "Modern Frankenstein," *New Yorker*, May 24, 1947, pp. 24–25; Arthur D. Morse, "Radio: Battle of the Ratings," *Nation*, October 2, 1948, p. 373.

26. Beville, *Audience Ratings*, pp. 7–11.

27. Interview, Frank Stanton, March 18, 1993; interview, Herta Herzog, August 29, 1993.

28. Interview, Frank Stanton.

29. Sally Bedell Smith, *In All His Glory: The Life and Times of William Paley and the Birth of Modern Broadcasting* (New York: Simon & Schuster, 1990), p. 130.

30. Jack N. Peterman, "The 'Program Analyzer,'" *Journal of Applied Psychology* 24, 1940, pp. 728–29.

31. Interview, Frank Stanton.

32. Interview, Herta Herzog.

33. Interview, Peter Rossi, March 1, 1993.

34. Paul F. Lazarsfeld, *Radio and the Printed Page*, (New York: Duell, Sloan & Pearce, 1940), pp. xi–xii.

35. Rogers, *A History of Communication Study*, p. 268; Lazarsfeld, *Radio and the Printed Page*, p. 94.

36. Lazarsfeld, *Radio and the Printed Page*, pp. 18–19.

37. Ibid., pp. 23, 26, 48.

38. Ibid., p. 22.

39. Ibid., pp. 52–53, 62.

40. Ibid., pp. 64–93; John Dunning, *On the Air: The Encyclopedia of Old-Time Radio* (New York: Oxford University Press, 1998), p. 555.

41. Lazarsfeld, *Radio and the Printed Page*, pp. 68–70.

42. Ibid., pp. 73–74.

43. Ibid., pp. 81, 86.

44. Ibid., p. 83.

45. Rudolf Arnheim and Martha Collins Bayne, "Foreign Language Broadcasts over Local American Stations," in Paul Lazarsfeld and Frank Stanton, *Radio Research 1941* (New York: Duell, Sloan & Pearce, 1941), p. 4.

46. Lazarsfeld and Stanton, *Radio Research 1941*, pp. ix–x.

47. Edward A. Suchman, "Invitation to Music," in ibid., pp. 142–51.

48. Lazarsfeld, *Radio and the Printed Page*, p. 131; Suchman, "Invitation to Music," pp. 151, 177, 183. Italics in original.

49. Suchman, "Invitation to Music," pp. 148–56, 158–59, 184–86; Duncan Mac-Dougald, Jr., "The Popular Music Industry," in Lazarsfeld and Stanton, *Radio Research 1941*, p. 70.

50. Suchman, "Invitation to Music," pp. 170–71.

51. Ibid., p. 179.

52. MacDougald "Popular Music Industry," pp. 74–77.

53. Ibid., pp. 66–67, 78.

54. Ibid., p. 95.

55. Ibid., p. 72.

56. T. W. Adorno, "The Radio Symphony," in Lazarsfeld and Stanton, *Radio Research 1941*, pp. 113, 136.

57. B. H. Haggin, "Crutches for Broadcast Music," *New Republic*, December 7, 1932, pp. 93–95.

58. Adorno, "Radio Symphony," pp. 119, 124.

59. Haggin, "Crutches for Broadcast Music," p. 95; Adorno, "Radio Symphony," p. 131.

60. Cantril and Allport, *Psychology of Radio*, p. 23.

61. Arnheim and Bayne, "Foreign Language Broadcasts," pp. 13–18.

62. Ibid., pp. 41–44.

63. Ibid., pp. 58, 63.

64. "How's Your Nielsen?" *Newsweek*, March 13, 1950, p. 50; "Checking Radio Check-ups," p. 36.

65. "Who Hears What?" *Business Week*, December 7, 1940, p. 38; "Listening Record," *Business Week*, April 29, 1939, p. 38.

66. "Modern Frankenstein," pp. 24–25; Arthur D. Morse, "Radio: Battle of the Ratings," p. 372; "Big Push for NRI," *Newsweek*, November 24, 1947, p. 58; "How's Your Nielsen?" p. 50; "A. C. Nielsen and the Things His Marketing Researchers Study," *Business Week*, December 12, 1959, p. 46.

7. WORLD WAR II AND THE INVENTION OF BROADCAST JOURNALISM

1. The National Archives Division of Sound Recording at the College Park, Maryland, facility has the most complete collection of CBS's wartime coverage. The Museum of Television and Radio in New York also has some of these broadcasts.

2. H. V. Kaltenborn, *I Broadcast the Crisis* (New York: Random House, 1938), p. 3; "Dean of Pundits," *Time*, June 28, 1943, p. 43; David Holbrook Culbert, *News for*

Everyman (Westport, Conn.: Greenwood Press, 1976), pp. 4, 73; "Radio's Biggest Year," *Business Week,* January 27, 1940, p. 30; Christopher H. Sterling and John M. Kittross, *Stay Tuned: A Concise History of American Broadcasting,* 2d ed. (Belmont, Cal.: Wadsworth Publishing, 1990), p. 197; Edward Bliss, Jr., *Now the News* (New York: Columbia University Press, 1991), p. 106.

3. Emile C. Schnurmacher, "Ether Jumpers Never Sleep," *Popular Mechanics,* November 1938.

4. Tapes of surviving broadcasts can be found at the Sound Recording Division of the National Archives in College Park, Maryland; at the Museum of Television and Radio in New York; and at the Museum of Broadcast Communications in Chicago.

5. Culbert, *News for Everyman,* pp. 74, 4.

6. Kaltenborn, *I Broadcast the Crisis,* p. 5; Culbert, *News for Everyman,* pp. 4–5, 11.

7. See Michael Schudson's now classic account of the rise of objectivity in *Discovering the News* (New York: Basic Books, 1978).

8. Robert J. Landry, "Edward R. Murrow," *Scribner's,* December 1938, p. 9.

9. Hadley Cantril, *The Invasion from Mars* (Princeton: Princeton University Press, 1940). Although the book was researched and written with the help of Herta Herzog and Hazel Gaudet, Cantril was the sole author listed.

10. Shearon Lowry and Melvin L. DeFleur, *Milestones in Mass Communication Research* (New York: Longman, 1983), p. 69.

11. Bliss, *Now the News,* pp. 17–20; John Dunning, *On the Air: The Encyclopedia of Old-Time Radio* (New York: Oxford University Press, 1998), p. 495; Culbert, *News for Everyman,* pp. 16, 19.

12. Museum of Television and Radio, 1932, R76: 0227.

13. Bliss, *Now the News,* pp. 31–32.

14. Ibid., pp. 27–28.

15. Robert W. McChesney, *Telecommunications, Mass Media, and Democracy: The Battle for Control of U.S. Broadcasting, 1928–1935* (New York: Oxford University Press, 1993), pp. 170–71; Erik Barnouw, *The Golden Web* (New York: Oxford University Press, 1968), pp. 20–21.

16. "Newscasters: Public Wants More Press Reports by Radio," *Newsweek,* July 21, 1934, p. 20; Sally Bedell Smith, *In All His Glory* (New York: Simon & Schuster, 1990), p. 166.

17. Bliss, *Now the News,* p. 36; "Hotter Heater," *Time,* January 13, 1942, p. 58.

18. Neal Gabler, *Winchell: Gossip, Power, and the Culture of Celebrity* (New York: Alfred A. Knopf, 1995), pp. 214, xii. Gabler's fine book is must reading for anyone interested in the rise of mass culture and celebrity journalism in the twentieth century.

19. For a more detailed discussion of the utopian hopes, see Susan J. Douglas, *Inventing American Broadcasting, 1899–1922* (Baltimore: Johns Hopkins University Press, 1987); see McChesney's powerful discussion of the profit-making process in the late 1920s and early 1930s in his *Telecommunications, Mass Media, and Democracy.*

20. Museum of Broadcast Communications, *Jergens Journal,* May 18, 1941, RA 292; Gabler, *Winchell,* pp. xii, 162.

21. Gabler, *Winchell,* p. 215.

22. Ibid., pp. 207–13.

23. Ibid., p. 216; *Jergens Journal,* May 18, 1941.

24. Gabler, *Winchell,* pp. 192–96, 282–83, 285, 289, 293; *Jergens Journal,* May 18, 1941.

25. Gabler, *Winchell*, pp. 297, 291.

26. Culbert, *News for Everyman*, p. 47; Paul Lazarsfeld, *Radio and the Printed Page* (New York: Duell, Sloan & Pearce, 1940), pp. 188–89; Stanley Cloud and Lynne Olson, *The Murrow Boys: Pioneers on the Front Lines of Journalism* (Boston: Houghton Mifflin, 1996), p. 14.

27. Museum of Television and Radio, broadcasts on May 24 and May 25, 1938, R79: 0034 and R79: 0035; Culbert, *News for Everyman*, p. 45; "Newscasters: Public Wants More Press Reports by Radio," p. 20.

28. "Biased News," *Time*, September 12, 1938, p. 67.

29. Culbert, *News for Everyman*, pp. 48–53.

30. Ibid., p. 48; Cloud and Olson, *Murrow Boys*, p. 16.

31. "The Fortune Survey," *Fortune*, April 1938, pp. 104–6; *Fortune*, January 1940, p. 92; "Radio Holds Gains," *Business Week*, August 30, 1941, pp. 40–41.

32. "Fortune Survey," p. 106.

33. Charles Siepmann, "American Radio in Wartime," in Paul Lazarsfeld and Frank Stanton, eds., *Radio Research 1942–43* (New York: Duell, Sloan & Pearce, 1944), p. 119.

34. Lazarsfeld, *Radio and the Printed Page*, p. 245; "Fortune Survey," p. 106.

35. Lazarsfeld, *Radio and the Printed Page*, pp. 211, 244; cited in Culbert, *News for Everyman*, pp. 24–25.

36. Lazarsfeld, *Radio and the Printed Page*, p. 201.

37. Culbert, *News for Everyman*, p. 6.

38. Cloud and Olson, *Murrow Boys*, p. 31; Culbert, *News for Everyman*, pp. 20–21; interview, Holmes Brown, November 1997.

39. Max Wylie, *Best Broadcasts of 1939–40* (New York: Whittlesey House, 1940), p. 327.

40. "Radio Goes to War," *Popular Mechanics*, February 1940, pp. 210–13; William L. Shirer, *Berlin Diary* (New York: Alfred A. Knopf, 1941), p. 106.

41. Cloud and Olson, *Murrow Boys*, pp. 38–39; Museum of Television and Radio, *The World This Week*, January 14, 1940, R76: 0227; "Trials and Tribulations of the Radio Reporter, a New Type of Correspondent," *Newsweek*, October 17, 1938, p. 32.

42. *Biennial Census of Manufacturers* (Washington, D.C.: GPO); "Long on Short Wave," *Business Week*, June 27, 1936, p. 31.

43. Museum of Television and Radio, March 13, 1938, R89: 0102; also in the National Archives, 200 G 136.

44. Cloud and Olson, *Murrow Boys*, pp. 63–64.

45. Ibid., pp. 59–60; *The World This Week*, January 14, 1940.

46. National Archives, *News of Europe*, September 7, 1939, 200 MR 992; National Archives, *European News Roundup*, August 28, 1939, 200 MR 988.

47. Bliss, *Now the News*, p. 107.

48. Barnouw, *Golden Web*, pp. 168–70; Culbert, *News for Everyman*, pp. 25–26.

49. John K. Hutchens, "The Columbia Network Tells Its Analysts to Keep Their Opinions to Themselves," *New York Times*, September 26, 1943, sec. 2, p. 9; Barnouw, *Golden Web*, p. 135; Museum of Television and Radio, H. V. Kaltenborn, "The Fall of France," n.d., R77: 0273; Culbert, *News for Everyman*, p. 27.

50. Barnouw, *Golden Web*, p. 137; Bliss, *Now the News*, p. 140. The decision gets its name from the Mayflower Broadcasting Corporation, which unsuccessfully challenged the license of WAAB in Boston for being too one-sided. Barnouw, *Golden Web*, p. 150.

51. Cloud and Olson, *Murrow Boys*, p. 142; A. M. Sperber, *Murrow: His Life and Times* (New York: Freundlich Books, 1986), p. 123; *News of Europe*, September 7, 1939.

52. National Archives, *News of Europe*, September 20, 1939, 200 MR 1012; Culbert, *News for Everyman*, pp. 27–28.

53. Bliss, *Now the News*, pp. 112–13; Cloud and Olson, *Murrow Boys*, p. 57.

54. Barnouw, *Golden Web*, p. 134.

55. Edward R. Murrow, *In Search of Light: The Broadcasts of Edward R. Murrow* (New York: Alfred A. Knopf, 1967), p. 42; Cloud and Olson, *Murrow Boys*, p. 92.

56. See, for example, National Archives, "Hitler Address to Reichstag," January 30, 1939; 200 MR 1059, and October 6, 1939, 200 MR 627–28; Culbert, *News for Everyman*, pp. 67, 73; Barnouw, *Golden Web*, p. 148.

57. Culbert, *News for Everyman*, p. 83.

58. Museum of Television and Radio, *The World Today*, June 3, 1940, R77: 0034.

59. Culbert, *News for Everyman*, p. 84; Kaltenborn, *I Broadcast the Crisis*, p. 4.

60. "The Fall of France," n.d.; Culbert, *News for Everyman*, p. 88.

61. Cited in Culbert, *News for Everyman*, p. 86.

62. Cited in ibid., p. 89.

63. Sterling and Kittross, *Stay Tuned*, pp. 190–91.

64. Ibid., p. 203; Bliss, *Now the News*, pp. 135–38; Barnouw, *Golden Web*, pp. 151–53.

65. Paul Fussell, *Wartime* (New York: Oxford University Press, 1989), p. 181; Bliss, *Now the News*, p. 139.

66. Sterling and Kittross, *Stay Tuned*, pp. 203–15.

67. Mitchell V. Charnley, *News by Radio* (New York: Macmillan, 1948), p. 31; Cooperative Analysis of Broadcasting, "Program Popularity in 1943," Library of American Broadcasting, no. 470; Sterling and Kittross, *Stay Tuned*, p. 215; "Dean of Pundits," p. 42; Fussell, *Wartime*, p. 181; Cloud and Olson, *Murrow Boys*, p. 61; National Archives, *The World Today*, November 13, 1943, 200 MR 2792.

68. Museum of Broadcast Communications, "Pearl Harbor Attack" (CBS Special), December 7, 1941, R 124.

69. Landry, "Edward R. Murrow," p. 9.

70. Cloud and Olson, *Murrow Boys*, p. 143.

71. Bliss, *Now the News*, p. 132; Murrow, *In Search of Light*, pp. 40–41; National Archives, *The World Today*, September 22, 1940, 200 MR 1484.

72. Murrow, *In Search of Light*, pp. 30–31.

73. Ibid., pp. 70–76.

74. Cloud and Olson report that Murrow could not really hide his contempt for those who showed fright during the war. See their *Murrow Boys*, p. 95; Murrow, *In Search of Light*, p. 35.

75. National Archives, *The World Today*, December 15, 1942, 200 MR 2415.

76. National Archives, *World News Tonight*, June 7, 1942, 200 MR 2212.

77. National Archives, *The World Today*, December 12, 1941, 200 MR 2008.

78. Dunning, *On the Air*, p. 498.

79. Museum of Broadcast Communications, "German Air Raid on U.S. Convoy," June 6, 1944, RA 209.

80. Museum of Broadcast Communications, "The Death of Ernie Pyle," April 17, 1945, RA 209.

81. National Archives, *The World Today*, May 25, 1942, 200 MR 2197.
82. Cloud and Olson, *Murrow Boys*, pp. 104, 177–84.
83. Ibid., pp. 147–50, 167.
84. Ibid., p. 152.
85. Ibid., pp. 183, 185–86; "The News, Unvarnished," *Time*, September 27, 1943.
86. *The World Today*, May 25, 1942.
87. "Program Popularity in 1943;" "Brown and White," *Time*, October 4, 1943, p. 70; Cloud and Olson, *Murrow Boys*, p. 169; Bliss, *Now the News*, p. 140.
88. "Should Newscasters Voice Opinion?" *Newsweek*, October 4, 1943, p. 86; "Brown and White," p. 70; "Dean of Pundits," p. 42.
89. Cloud and Olson, *Murrow Boys*, pp. 168–71, 270–76; Quincy Howe, "Policing the Commentator: A News Analysis," *Atlantic Monthly*, November 1943, p. 47.

8. PLAYING FIELDS OF THE MIND

1. Curt Smith, *Voices of the Game* (New York: Simon & Schuster, 1992), p. 1.
2. John Dunning, *On the Air: The Encyclopedia of Old-Time Radio* (New York: Oxford University Press, 1998), p. 627; Aaron Baker, "A Left/Right Combination: Populism and Depression-Era Boxing Films," in Aaron Baker and Todd Boyd, *Out of Bounds: Sports, Media, and the Politics of Identity* (Bloomington: University of Indiana Press, 1997), pp. 161–62; "50,000,000 Ears," *Time*, September 28, 1942.
3. Mark Dyreson, *Making the American Team: Sport, Culture, and the Olympic Experience* (Urbana: University of Illinois Press, 1998), pp. 7–31; For an overview of this transition, see S. W. Pope, *Patriotic Games: Sporting Traditions in the American Imagination, 1876–1926* (New York: Oxford University Press, 1997), pp. 3–10.
4. Pope, *Patriotic Games*, p. 10.
5. Smith, *Voices of the Game*, p. 114.
6. George Douglas, *The Early Days of Radio Broadcasting* (Jefferson, N.C.: McFarland, 1987), pp. 113–18.
7. Red Barber, *The Broadcasters* (New York: Da Capo Press, 1970), chap. 2, and pp. 50–52.
8. Museum of Broadcast Communications, *The Tom Snyder Show* (interview with Curt Smith), June 30, 1992, RA 544; quoted in Smith, *Voices of the Game*, p. 191.
9. *The Tom Snyder Show*, June 30, 1992; Museum of Television and Radio, "Baseball on the Radio," T: 46134.
10. Dunning, *On the Air*, p. 627; see "To Be Somebody," part of the PBS series *The Great Depression*.
11. Barber, *Broadcasters*, p. 20.
12. Dunning, *On the Air*, p. 627.
13. Barber, *Broadcasters*, p. 24; Dunning, *On the Air*, pp. 629, 630.
14. "Radio," *New Republic*, April 28, 1947, p. 39.
15. Barber, *Broadcasters*, p. 28; Museum of Television and Radio, World Series 1936, game 5, Giants v. Yankees, October 5, 1936, R: 4975.
16. Museum of Television and Radio, *Costas Coast-to-Coast*, R: 8699.
17. Museum of Television and Radio, Baer-Carnera Fight, June 14, 1934, R77: 0354; Museum of Television and Radio, Baer v. Jim Braddock, June 13, 1935, R77: 0311.

18. John Rickard Betts, *America's Sporting Heritage: 1850–1950* (Reading, Mass.: Addison-Wesley, 1974), p. 272; Benjamin G. Rader, *In Its Own Image: How Television Has Transformed Sports* (New York: Free Press, 1984), p. 25.

19. Museum of Television and Radio, "First Fifty Years of Radio," R85: 0558; Baer-Carnera Fight, June 14, 1934.

20. Museum of Television and Radio, Louis-Sharkey Fight, R76: 0179.

21. For details on Johnson and his significance to ongoing definitions of manhood and nationalism, see Gail Bederman's excellent *Manliness and Civilization: A Cultural History of Gender and Race in the United States, 1880–1917* (Chicago: University of Chicago Press, 1995), pp. 1–4; Earl Brown, "Joe Louis: The Champion, Idol of His Race, Sets a Good Example of Conduct," *Life*, June 17, 1940, p. 54.

22. "To Be Somebody," from the PBS series *The Great Depression;* "World at Ringside by Proxy," *Literary Digest*, October 5, 1935, pp. 32–33.

23. "World at Ringside by Proxy," p. 33; "Boxing: Bible-Reading Louis Takes Leaf from Book of David," *Newsweek*, July 6, 1935, p. 22; "Black Moses," *Time*, September 29, 1941, p. 60.

24. "Black Moses"; James T. Farrell, "The Fall of Joe Louis," *Nation*, June 27, 1936, p. 835.

25. "Boxing: Schmeling Commutes Across Atlantic—For What?" *Newsweek*, May 29, 1937, pp. 19–22.

26. Dominic J. Capeci and Martha Wilkerson, "Multifarious Hero: Joe Louis, American Society and Race Relations During World Crisis, 1935–1945," *Journal of Sport History* 10, Winter 1983, p. 10; "Black Moses"; Marc Pachter et al., *Champions of American Sport* (New York: Harry N. Abrams, 1981), p. 87; Rader, *In Its Own Image*, p. 25.

27. Capeci and Wilkerson, "Multifarious Hero," pp. 10–11, 19; "Black Moses."

28. "In the Beginning," *Black Radio . . . Telling It Like It Was*, Radio Smithsonian transcript, 1996; quoted in "To Be Somebody," from the PBS series *The Great Depression.*

29. Baker, "Left/Right Combination," p. 169; see, for example, "Boxing: Baer and Louis Sharpen Their Weapons for the Kill," *Newsweek*, September 21, 1935, p. 28; "Boxing: Louis Wins $47,000 and Puts His Camp on the Wagon," *Newsweek*, August 17, 1935, p. 24; "Boxing: Bible-Reading Louis Takes Leaf"; Jonathan Mitchell, "Joe Louis Never Smiles," *New Republic*, October 9, 1935, pp. 239–40; Brown, "Joe Louis: The Champion, Idol of His Race," p. 49.

30. Smith, *Voices of the Game*, pp. 14, 25, 26; *Costas Coast-to-Coast*, quoted in Smith, *Voices of the Game*, p. 38.

31. *Costas Coast-to-Coast*, Rader, *In Its Own Image*, p. 27.

32. *The Tom Snyder Show*, June 30, 1992; Smith, *Voices of the Game*, p. 112.

33. Smith, *Voices of the Game*, pp. 113–15; Museum of Broadcast Communications, "KVIL Special: Gordon McLendon," RA 924.

34. Richard G. Hubler, "The Barber of Brooklyn," *Saturday Evening Post*, March 21, 1942, p. 34.

35. Quoted in Smith, *Voices of the Game*, p. 28; *Costas Coast-to-Coast*, Museum of Broadcast Communications, "Harry Caray's Fiftieth Anniversary," RA 810; John R. Tunis, "Sport and the Radio," *Outlook and Independent*, October 16, 1929, p. 276.

36. *Costas Coast-to-Coast.*

37. Barber, *Broadcasters*, pp. 28–29.

38. Smith, *Voices of the Game*, pp. 148, 302; Rader, *In Its Own Image*, p. 27; "Caray's Fiftieth Anniversary."

39. "Baseball on the Radio"; Smith, *Voices of the Game*, pp. 4, 79, 77; "First Fifty Years of Radio."

40. Hubler, "Barber of Brooklyn," p. 64.

41. *Costas Coast-to-Coast*, "50,000,000 Ears."

42. Barber, *Broadcasters*, pp. 32, 82–83; Rader, *In Its Own Image*, p. 25.

43. *Costas Coast-to-Coast*, The only reason this survives on tape is that a fan taped the last inning and sent the tape to Hodges; see Smith, *Voices of the Game*, pp. 64–65, 90.

44. Arthur S. Harris, Jr., "The Baseball Experts," *Atlantic Monthly*, July 1954, p. 87.

45. Ibid., p. 88.

46. Jerry Kirshenbaum, "And Here to Bring You the Play by Play," *Sports Illustrated*, September 13, 1971, p. 35.

47. Cited in Smith, *Voices of the Game*, p. 300.

48. *Costas Coast-to-Coast*, cited in Smith, *Voices of the Game*, p. 29; "Baseball on the Radio"; Kirshenbaum, "And Here to Bring You," p. 38.

49. These oppositions in sports were laid out by Stephen Hardy and summarized in S. W. Pope, "Introduction: American Sport History—Toward a New Paradigm," in Pope, *The New American Sport History* (Urbana: University of Illinois Press, 1997), p. 6.

50. Ibid., p. 1; Dyreson, *Making the American Team*, p. 31.

9. THE KIDS TAKE OVER

1. Christopher H. Sterling and John M. Kittross, *Stay Tuned: A Concise History of American Broadcasting*, 2d ed. (Belmont, Cal.: Wadsworth Publishing, 1990), p. 262.

2. "Radio's New Voice Is Golden," *Business Week*, March 5, 1960, pp. 94–99.

3. "People Depend on Radio," *Broadcasting*, March 26, 1962, p. 70.

4. H. Mendelsohn, "Listening to Radio," in L. A. Dexter and D. M. White, eds., *People, Society, and Mass Communications* (New York: Free Press of Glencoe, 1964).

5. Andrew Crisell, *Understanding Radio* (New York: Routledge, 1994), p. 215.

6. I am indebted to Alex Russo's prize-winning senior thesis for this insight. Alex Russo, "No Particular Place to Go," unpub. ms., Wesleyan University, 1996, p. 80.

7. "The Moody, Ever-Changing Radio Listener," *Broadcasting*, February 5, 1962, p. 46.

8. For an analytical assessment of this phenomenon, see Eric Lott, "White Like Me: Racial Cross-Dressing and the Construction of American Whiteness," in Amy Kaplan and Donald E. Pease, eds., *Cultures of United States Imperialism* (Durham, N.C.: Duke University Press, 1993), p. 475.

9. John Mack Faragher et al., *Out of Many: A History of the American People* (Upper Saddle River, N.J.: Prentice Hall, 1997), p. 807.

10. George Lipsitz, *Rainbow at Midnight: Labor and Culture in the 1940s* (Urbana: University of Illinois Press, 1994), p. 320.

11. Philip H. Ennis, *The Seventh Stream: The Emergence of Rocknroll in American Popular Music* (Hanover, N.H.: Wesleyan University Press, 1992), p. 136; Sterling and Kittross, *Stay Tuned*, pp. 632–33; Erik Barnouw, *The Golden Web* (New York: Oxford University Press, 1968), p. 174.

12. Barnouw, *Golden Web*, p. 170.
13. Ibid., pp. 173–75.
14. John A. Jackson, *Big Beat Heat: Alan Freed and the Early Years of Rock and Roll* (New York: Schirmer Books, 1991), p. 40; Ennis, *Seventh Stream*, p. 99.
15. "Radio Volume Will Rise 50 Percent, Exceed $1 Billion by 1965, Says Sweeney," *Advertising Age*, May 5, 1958, p. 3.
16. Ennis, *Seventh Stream*, p. 132.
17. "Portable Transistor Radios," *Consumer Reports*, May 1956, p. 223; Ernest Braun and Stuart MacDonald, *Revolution in Miniature: The History and Impact of Semiconductor Electronics* (New York: Cambridge University Press, 1978), p. 17.
18. Braun and MacDonald, *Revolution in Miniature*, pp. 17–26; "Tubeless Radio," *Time*, October 25, 1954, p. 71.
19. Peter Fornatale and Joshua E. Mills, *Radio in the Television Age* (Woodstock, N.Y.: Overlook Press, 1984), p. 18.
20. Ibid., p. 20; "More Listen to Radio in Cars than at Home, Study Shows," *Advertising Age*, July 8, 1963, p. 28; "Pulse Data on Radio," *Broadcasting*, January 28, 1963, p. 36; "More and More People Are Listening to Radio," *Broadcasting*, May 18, 1964, p. 66.
21. "Listening Habits," *Broadcasting*, July 27, 1959, p. 42; "Transistor Craze—There's No Escape," *Life*, November 24, 1961, p. 23; "The Bleatniks," *Time*, August 11, 1961, p. 48.
22. Ernest Hodges, "Critique on Rock and Roll Radio: We're Not After the Twelve-Year-Olds," *Broadcasting*, April 14, 1958, p. 113; "Mitch Miller Raps Disc Jockeys, Stations, Time Buyers for 'Bad Programs Aimed at Non-Buying Teenagers,' " *Advertising Age*, April 14, 1958, p. 83.
23. Fornatale and Mills, *Radio in the Television Age*, p. 44.
24. Lipsitz, *Rainbow at Midnight*, p. 315; Ennis, *Seventh Stream*, p. 133.
25. "Radio—¹/₅ of Her Life," *Broadcasting*, October 12, 1959, p. 48; "At Last a Reliable Music Survey," *Broadcasting*, October 12, 1959, p. 55.
26. Jackson, *Big Beat Heat*, p. 95; Fornatale and Mills, *Radio in the Television Age*, p. 43.
27. Ken Barnes, "Top 40 Radio: A Fragment of the Imagination," in Simon Frith, ed., *Facing the Music* (New York: Pantheon, 1989), p. 11; Ed Ward, Geoffrey Stokes, and Ken Tucker, *Rock of Ages: The Rolling Stone History of Rock and Roll* (New York: Rolling Stone Press, 1986), p. 68.
28. Interview with Tony Pigg, February 18, 1994; Wolfman Jack with Byron Laursen, *Have Mercy* (New York: Warner Books, 1995), pp. 39–40.
29. Jackson, *Big Beat Heat*, p. 21; "Disc Jockeys," *Ebony*, December 1947, p. 44; "What Makes the Music Go 'Round?" *Broadcasting*, March 17, 1958, p. 88.
30. Paddy Scannell, *Radio, Television and Modern Life* (Cambridge, Mass.: Blackwell, 1996), p. 118; letter to the author from George Lipsitz, September 24, 1998.
31. This material on DJ talk is from the highly economical and helpful article "DJ Talk" by Martin Montgomery, in *Media, Culture, and Society* v. 8, 1986, pp. 421–40; "Listening to Radio Station WMCA: A Study of Audience Characteristics, Habits, Motivations and Tastes," Library of American Broadcasting, February 1962, no. 1918.
32. Montgomery, "DJ Talk."
33. DJ Airchecks, Rock 'n' Roll Hall of Fame, Cleveland; Museum of Broadcast Communications, *The Alan Freed Show*, 1956, RA 186; Montgomery, "DJ Talk," p. 432.
34. *The Alan Freed Show*, 1956.

35. I am grateful to George Lipsitz for bringing this point to my attention.
36. Ennis, *Seventh Stream*, p. 136.
37. *The Alan Freed Show*, 1956.
38. Scannell, *Radio, Television and Modern Life*, p. 118.
39. Jackson, *Big Beat Heat*, p. 39; "The Forgotten 15,000,000," *Sponsor*, October 1949, pp. 24–25; Russo, "No Particular Place to Go," p. 61.
40. Ennis, *Seventh Stream*, p. 176; Lipsitz, *Rainbow at Midnight*, p. 319.
41. Cited in Ennis, *Seventh Stream*, p. 173.
42. J. Fred MacDonald, *Don't Touch That Dial! Radio Programming in American Life, 1920–1960* (Chicago: Nelson-Hall, 1979), p. 354.
43. Michele Hilmes, *Radio Voices: American Broadcasting, 1922–1952* (Minneapolis: University of Minnesota Press, 1997), p. 263.
44. Museum of Television and Radio, *Jubilee*, 1943 and 1944, R90: 0099.
45. Museum of Television and Radio, "DJ Airchecks," R: 6987.
46. "Disc Jockeys," pp. 44–49; MacDonald, *Don't Touch That Dial!* p. 365.
47. Museum of Television and Radio, "Black Radio: WDIA, the Goodwill Station," 1996, R: 14499; DJ Aircheck, Rock 'n' Roll Hall of Fame; Museum of Television and Radio, "Black Radio: Yesterday and Today," 1996, T: 43092.
48. DJ Aircheck, Rock 'n' Roll Hall of Fame; letter from Lipsitz, September 24, 1998.
49. "Black Radio: WDIA, the Goodwill Station," 1996.
50. Museum of Television and Radio, "Black Radio: Jack Cooper and Al Benson," R: 14499.
51. Ibid.
52. Ibid.
53. Museum of Television and Radio, "Black Radio and the Roots of Rock 'n' Roll," T: 32815; Jackson, *Big Beat Heat*, p. 40; "Sounding Black," *Black Radio . . . Telling It Like It Was*, Radio Smithsonian transcript, 1996, pp. 4–8; Ward et al., *Rock of Ages*, p. 68.
54. "Sounding Black," pp. 11–15.
55. Ibid., p. 7.
56. Wolfman Jack, *Have Mercy*, pp. iv, 40–41, 47, 42.
57. Cited in Michael Kimmel, *Manhood in America: A Cultural History* (New York: Free Press, 1996), pp. 240–41.
58. Lipsitz, *Rainbow at Midnight*, p. 305; "Black Radio: Yesterday and Today," 1996.
59. Lott, "White Like Me," pp. 475–81.
60. Ben Sidran, *Black Talk* (New York: Da Capo Press, 1971), pp. 126–27, 129, 128; cited in Lott, "White Like Me," p. 480; letter from Lipsitz, September 24, 1998.
61. Wolfman Jack, *Have Mercy*, pp. 38–39.
62. Russo, "No Particular Place to Go," p. 12.
63. John Corbett, "Free, Single, and Disengaged: Listening Pleasure and the Popular Music Object," *October*, p. 81; "Listening to Radio Station WMCA: A Study of Audience Characteristics, Habits, Motivations and Tastes," Library of American Broadcasting, February 1962, no. 1918.
64. Russo, "No Particular Place to Go," p. 10; I am grateful to George Lipsitz for this observation about segregation.
65. "What Makes the Music Go 'Round"? p. 88.
66. Fornatale and Mills, *Radio in the Television Age*, pp. 26–27.

67. Cited in Barnes, "Top 40 Radio," p. 9.
68. Fornatale and Mills, *Radio in the Television Age*, p. 27; Museum of Broadcast Communications, "KVIL Special: Gordon McLendon," RA 924.
69. Museum of Broadcast Communications, "KVIL Special: Gordon McClendon," RA 924.
70. "Black Roots and the Roots of Rock 'n' Roll; "What Makes the Music Go 'Round?" p. 88.
71. Ennis, *Seventh Stream*, pp. 43–44; cited in Jackson, *Big Beat Heat*, p. 96.
72. Ward et al., *Rock of Ages*, p. 272; Jackson, *Big Beat Heat*, pp. 95–96.
73. Jackson, *Big Beat Heat*, pp. 94–95.
74. Ennis, *Seventh Stream*, p. 259.
75. "The Voice and Payola," *Time*, September 9, 1957, p. 76; Fornatale and Mills, *Radio in the Television Age*, p. 48.
76. Fornatale and Mills, *Radio in the Television Age*, p. 49.
77. Ibid., pp. 50–51.
78. Jackson, *Big Beat Heat*, pp. 250–55; Fornatale and Mills, *Radio in the Television Age*, p. 51.
79. Ennis, *Seventh Stream*, p. 265.
80. Barnes, "Top 40 Radio," p. 12.
81. Steve Chapple and Reebee Garofalo, *Rock 'n' Roll Is Here to Pay* (Chicago: Nelson-Hall, 1977).
82. Museum of Broadcast Communications, "Disc Jockey Clips," RA 1479; Museum of Broadcast Communications, *The Dave Gold Show*, RA 955.
83. Russo, "No Particular Place to Go," p. 19.
84. This is Alex Russo's main point, ibid., pp. 46, 80; see also Simon Frith, *Sound Effects: Youth, Leisure, and the Politics of Rock 'n' Roll* (New York: Pantheon, 1981), p. 216.
85. "Black Radio: Yesterday and Today," 1996.
86. Barnes, "Top 40 Radio," pp. 8–9.
87. Deena Weinstein, "Rock: Youth and Its Music," in Jonathan S. Epstein, ed., *Adolescents and Their Music: If It's Too Loud, You're Too Old* (New York: Garland, 1994), p. 13.

10. THE FM REVOLUTION

1. Museum of Television and Radio, "WNEW and the Free Form Format," T: 50942.
2. Robert Jourdain, *Music, the Brain, and Ecstasy* (New York: William Morrow, 1997), p. 260.
3. Museum of Television and Radio, "The Golden Age of Underground," KSAN-FM, T: 43091.
4. "The Rites of Passage Are All Over for FM Radio; It's Out on Its Own," *Broadcasting*, September 24, 1973, p. 32.
5. "Cox Says It's Nowhere but Up for FM Medium," *Broadcasting*, September 13, 1976, p. 50; "The FM Boom," *Newsweek*, May 22, 1972, p. 57; Christopher H. Sterling and John M. Kittross, *Stay Tuned: A Concise History of American Broadcasting*, 2d ed., (Belmont, Cal.: Wadsworth Publishing, 1990), p. 379; "The Rites of Passage," p. 31.
6. For such criticisms of mass culture, see Bernard Rosenberg and David Manning White, eds., *Mass Culture: The Popular Arts in America* (New York: Free Press, 1957); for the counterculture ethos, see Charles Reich, *The Greening of America* (New

York: Random House, 1970); Todd Gitlin, *The Sixties* (New York: Bantam, 1987); the classic intellectual critique of popular music is Theodor Adorno's "On Popular Music," *SPSS* 9, 1941, and "A Social Critique of Radio Music," *Kenyon Review* 7, Spring 1945; see also Simon Frith, *Sound Effects: Youth, Leisure, and the Politics of Rock 'n' Roll* (New York: Pantheon, 1981).

7. Lawrence Lessing, *Man of High Fidelity* (New York: Bantam, 1969), p. 159.

8. Interview, Rick Ducey, NAB, May 14, 1998; Lessing, *Man of High Fidelity*, p. 160.

9. Tom Lewis, *Empire of the Air: The Men Who Made Radio* (New York: HarperCollins, 1991), p. 250.

10. Lessing, *Man of High Fidelity*, pp. 161–65; Andrew F. Inglis, *Behind the Tube: A History of Broadcasting Technology and Business* (Boston: Focal Press, 1990), pp. 117–19.

11. Interview, Rick Ducey; Inglis, *Behind the Tube*, pp. 119–20.

12. For more details on the Armstrong-Sarnoff relationship and on Sarnoff's decision, see Lewis, *Empire of the Air*, pp. 261–62.

13. Lessing, *Man of High Fidelity*, pp. 188–203.

14. Ibid., p. 212. Gary Frost at the University of North Carolina argues in his forthcoming Ph.D. dissertation that the evidence does not support Armstrong's conspiracy theory.

15. "FM: It Has Arrived," *Broadcasting*, March 29, 1965, p. 88; "FM Gets a Shake-up," *Newsweek*, November 28, 1966; Sterling and Kittross, *Stay Tuned*, p. 633.

16. Sterling and Kittross, *Stay Tuned*, p. 323; "FM Radio Has to Change Its Tune," *Business Week*, September 24, 1966, p. 173.

17. "Audiophilia," *Time*, January 14, 1957, p. 44; *New Yorker*, November 24, 1951, p. 31; "High Fidelity: Next Year a $300,000,000 Industry," *Newsweek*, December 21, 1953, p. 64; "Everybody Gets in Hi-Fi Chorus," *Business Week*, September 21, 1957, p. 62.

18. "Hi-Fi Takes Over," *Time*, February 28, 1955, p. 64.

19. "Cashing In on Finicky Ears," *Business Week*, March 22, 1952, pp. 52–53. See also Oliver Read and Walter Welch, *From Tin Foil to Stereo: Evolution of the Phonograph* (Indianapolis: H. W. Sams, 1976), and Roland Gelatt, *The Fabulous Phonograph, 1877–1977* (New York: Macmillan, 1977).

20. "Cashing In on Finicky Ears," p. 54.

21. "High Fidelity," pp. 64–66.

22. Opal Loomis, "The High Fidelity Wife, or a Fate Worse than Deaf," *Harper's*, August 1955, pp. 34–36; A. Goodenough, "I Am a Hi-Fi Widow," *McCall's*, May 1954, pp. 11–12.

23. "Hi-Fi Takes Over," pp. 64–66; "High Fidelity," p. 65. I am grateful to Alexander Magoun, who is currently writing about the hi-fi craze, for reminding me that there were many audiophiles who were not music lovers.

24. Sydney W. Head, *Broadcasting in America*, 3d ed. (Boston: Houghton Mifflin, 1976), pp. 42–43; "Where FM is the dominant medium," *Broadcasting*, April 12, 1965, pp. 36–37.

25. Mort Keshin, "FM Now a Mature Medium," *Media/Scope*, May 1967, p. 12.

26. Head, *Broadcasting in America*, p. 150; Keshin, "FM Now a Mature Medium," p. 12.

27. Sterling and Kittross, *Stay Tuned*, p. 381; Peter Fornatale and Joshua E. Mills, *Radio in the Television Age* (Woodstock, N.Y.: Overlook Press, 1984), p. 124.

28. Andre Millard, *America on Record: A History of Recorded Sound* (New York: Cambridge University Press, 1995), pp. 212, 216–17.
29. Fornatale and Mills, *Radio in the Television Age*, p. 129; "FM Radio Has to Change Its Tune," p. 173.
30. Cited in Michael C. Keith, *Voices in the Purple Haze: Underground Radio and the Sixties* (Westport, Conn.: Praeger, 1997).
31. Quoted in Fornatale and Mills, *Radio in the Television Age*, p. 117; the study of AM radio cited in ibid., p. 127; Keith, *Voices in the Purple Haze*, p. 1.
32. Interview, Tony Pigg, February 18, 1994; John A. Jackson, *Big Beat Heat: Alan Freed and The Early Years of Rock and Roll* (New York: Schirmer Books, 1991), p. 41; Fornatale and Mills, *Radio in the Television Age*, p. 52; interview with Raechel Donahue in Museum of Television and Radio, "The Rise of Rock FM," T: 43091.
33. Interview with Raechel Donahue in "The Rise of Rock FM"; Jim Ladd, *Radio Waves, Life and Revolution on the FM Dial* (New York: St. Martin's Press, 1991), p. 9.
34. "The New Respectability of Rock," *Broadcasting*, August 11, 1969, pp. 46B, 46C; interview, Tony Pigg; Keith, *Voices in the Purple Haze*, pp. 56–57; Fornatale and Mills, *Radio in the Television Age*, p. 129.
35. "The New Respectability of Rock," p. 46B.
36. Cited in Keith, *Voices in the Purple Haze*, pp. 61, 63.
37. Ladd, *Radio Waves*, pp. 51, 23, 24.
38. "WNEW and the Free Form Format."
39. Interview, Mark Tramo, July 8, 1998; Jourdain, *Music, the Brain, and Ecstasy*, pp. 246–59; interview, Tony Pigg.
40. Ladd, *Radio Waves*, pp. 24, 26.
41. Interview, Mark Tramo; Keith, *Voices in the Purple Haze*, p. 68; Museum of Television and Radio, "The Golden Age of Underground," R: 5912; "The Rise of Rock FM."
42. Museum of Television and Radio, "The Golden Age of Underground" R: 10737.
43. "The Golden Age of Underground," R: 5912; "The Rise of Rock FM.", T: 43091.
44. Frith, *Sound Effects*, p. 87.
45. "Cox Says It's Nowhere but Up for FM Medium," p. 50; "The Upbeat Tempo of FM 1974," *Broadcasting*, October 7, 1974, pp. 41–42.
46. "FM Sniffs Sweet Smell of Success," *Broadcasting*, July 31, 1967, pp. 58, 62; "WNEW and Free Form Format."
47. "Switch hitting on ABC's FM's," *Broadcasting*, March 13, 1972, p. 51.
48. "Bach vs. Rock," *Newsweek*, March 19, 1973, p. 83.
49. "High on the Medium, Bob Cole Is Redoing CBS's FM Operation," *Broadcasting*, August 23, 1971, p. 67.
50. Fornatale and Mills, *Radio in the Television Age*, p. 140.
51. "Back Above Ground: How the Pressures Got to Two Progressive Rockers," *Broadcasting*, October 2, 1972, p. 42.
52. "FM Rockers Are Taming Their Free Formats," *Broadcasting*, November 25, 1974, pp. 47–49.
53. "WNEW and the Free Form Format."
54. Ladd, *Radio Waves*, p. 49; "WNEW and the Free Form Format."

55. Interview, Tony Pigg; Ladd, *Radio Waves*, pp. 236–37.
56. *Advertising Age*, May 29, 1978, pp. R1, R26; Fornatale and Mills, *Radio in the Television Age*, p. 142.
57. "Putting FM in Its Place in the Top 50," *Broadcasting*, January 22, 1979, p. 32; "Automated Programmers: The Pros with the Right Sound," *Broadcasting*, July 25, 1977, p. 74.
58. *Advertising Age*, May 29, 1978, p. R26.
59. Keith, *Voices in the Purple Haze*, p. 74.
60. "Putting FM in Its Place in the Top 50," p. 42; "Following the formats," *Broadcasting*, February 27, 1989.
61. Millard, *America on Record*, pp. 318–19.

11. TALK TALK

1. Cynthia Heimel, "The Man You Love to Hate," *New York*, May 22, 1978, p. 54.
2. Linda Wertheimer, *Listening to America* (Boston: Houghton Mifflin, 1995), p. 121.
3. Interview, Jim Casale, June 21, 1997.
4. Interview, Michael Harrison, June 20, 1997.
5. Mary Collins, *National Public Radio* (Arlington, VA: Seven Locks Press, 1993), pp. 24, 14; cited in James Ledbetter, *Made Possible by . . . : The Death of Public Broadcasting in America* (New York: Verso, 1997), p. 117.
6. Peter J. Boyer, "Bull Rush," *Vanity Fair*, May 1992, p. 159.
7. Wayne Munson, *All Talk: The Talkshow in Media Culture* (Philadelphia: Temple University Press, 1993), p. 93; interview, Mark Williams, June 20, 1997; Joe Klein, "Talk Politics," *New York*, February 27, 1989, p. 28; Richard Zoglin, "Bugle Boys of the Airwaves," *Time*, May 15, 1989, p. 88. By the end of 1989 Congress had voted in a 25 percent raise in pay, to $125,000, but banned all other honoraria.
8. "Talk Show Democracy," *CQ Researcher*, April 29, 1994, p. 375; Howard Kurtz, *Hot Air: All Talk, All the Time* (New York: Times Books, 1996), p. 257; Wertheimer, *Listening to America*, pp. xi–xx; Anna Kosof, "Public Radio—Americans Want More," *Media Studies Journal*, Summer 1993, p. 171.
9. *Statistical Abstracts of the United States: 1996* (Washington: U.S. Bureau of the Census, 1996), p. 565.
10. "Audiences Love to Hate Them," *Time*, July 9, 1984, p. 80; "Why AM Stations Are Talking Up," *Business Week*, June 15, 1981, p. 99.
11. "Why AM Stations Are Talking Up," p. 99; Munson, *All Talk*, pp. 39–40; interview, Michael Harrison.
12. Munson, *All Talk*, p. 42; Richard Corliss, "Look Who's Talking," *Time*, January 23, 1995, p. 24.
13. Kurtz, *Hot Air*, p. 259.
14. Munson, *All Talk*, p. 114.
15. "Audiences Love to Hate Them," pp. 80–81; Michael Kimmel, *Manhood in America: A Cultural History* (New York: Free Press, 1996), p. 294.
16. Kimmel, *Manhood in America*; Susan Jeffords, *Hard Bodies: Masculinity in the Reagan Era* (New Brunswick, N.J.: Rutgers University Press, 1993); Yvonne Tasker, *Spectacular Bodies: Gender, Genre and Action Cinema* (New York: Routledge, 1993);

R. W. Connell, *Masculinities* (Berkeley: Univeristy of California Press, 1995), pp. 206–7.

17. See Jeffords, *Hard Bodies.*

18. Interview, Mark Williams.

19. Murray Levin, *Talk Radio and the American Dream* (New York: Lexington Books, 1987), p. xiii.

20. Cited in ibid., pp. 4–5.

21. Ibid., p. 16.

22. Ibid., pp. 27, 147.

23. For more detail on the satellite revolution in communications, see Andrew F. Inglis, *Behind the Tube: A History of Broadcasting Technology and Business* (Boston: Focal Press, 1990), ch. 8, pp. 392–438.

24. Ibid., p. 393.

25. Ibid., p. 402.

26. Lynn Distler, Comrex Corporation, talk at the NARTSH convention, Los Angeles, June 20, 1997.

27. "Mark Fowler's Great Experiment: Setting His People Free," *Broadcasting,* April 30, 1984, pp. 116, 128.

28. "Deregulation's Architect Finds the Structure Sturdy," *Broadcasting,* December 23, 1985.

29. "Mark Fowler's Great Experiment," p. 118.

30. See Section 202, "Broadcast Ownership," of the Telecommunications Act of 1996; Vincent M. Ditingo, *The Remaking of Radio* (Boston: Focal Press, 1995), p. 17.

31. Ditingo, *Remaking of Radio,* p. 2; see also "Mark Fowler's Great Experiment," p. 122; Anthony Ramirez, "F.C.C. Eases Radio-Station Ownership Limits," *New York Times,* August 6, 1992, p. D1.

32. Ditingo, *Remaking of Radio,* pp. 3–4.

33. Richard Turner, "An Ear for the CBS Eye," *Newsweek,* December 16, 1996, pp. 58–59; Ditingo, *Remaking of Radio,* p. 16.

34. For a detailed discussion, see Patricia Aufderheide, "After the Fairness Doctrine: Controversial Broadcast Programming and the Public Interest," *Journal of Communication* 40, Summer 1990, pp. 47–72.

35. For overview information on the Fairness Doctrine, see Sydney W. Head, *Broadcasting in America,* 3d ed. (Boston: Houghton Mifflin, 1976), pp. 395–403.

36. For an overview of *Red Lion* and a conservative take on the Fairness Doctrine, see Thomas W. Hazlett, "The Fairness Doctrine and the First Amendment," *Public Interest,* no. 94–97, 1989, pp. 103–16.

37. "Dingell-Fowler Debate Highlights Press Forum," *Broadcasting,* March 22, 1983, p. 142.

38. Munson, *All Talk,* p. 4.

39. "Talk Show Democracy," p. 364.

40. Kathleen Hall Jamieson, *Dirty Politics* (New York: Oxford University Press, 1992); Joseph Cappella, Kathleen Hall Jamieson et al., "Public Cynicism and News Coverage in Campaigns and Policy Debates," unpub. ms.; Joseph Cappella and Kathleen Hall Jamieson, *Spiral of Cynicism* (New York: Oxford University Press, 1997).

41. Richard Corliss, "Conservative Provocateur or Big Blowhard?" *Time,* October 26,

1992, pp. 76–79; Corliss, "Look Who's Talking," pp. 22–26; interview, Michael Harrison.

42. Corliss, "Look Who's Talking," p. 23.
43. Margaret Carlson, "My Dinner With Rush," *Time*, January 23, 1995, p. 26; Howard Fineman, "The Power of Talk Radio," *Newsweek*, February 8, 1993, p. 25; Zoglin, "Bugle Boys of the Airwaves," p. 88; "Power of Talk Radio."
44. Corliss, "Look Who's Talking," pp. 22–24.
45. Interview, Jim Casale; interview, Mark Williams.
46. "The Changing Voice of Talk Radio," *U.S. News & World Report*, January 15, 1990, pp. 51–52.
47. Turner, "Ear for the CBS Eye," p. 59; Kurtz, *Hot Air*, p. 272; Mike Barnicle, "Allow Stern to Be Stupid," *Boston Globe*, January 13, 1994, p. 25.
48. Jeanie Kasindorf, "Bad Mouth," *New York*, November 23, 1992, p. 43; Kurtz, *Hot Air*, p. 274.
49. Paddy Scannell, *Radio, Television and Modern Life* (Cambridge, Mass.: Blackwell, 1996), p. 123.
50. Kurtz, *Hot Air*, p. 274.
51. Cited in Kasindorf, "Bad Mouth," p. 40; Richard Zoglin, "Shock Jock," *Time*, November 30, 1992, pp. 72–73; Kurtz, *Hot Air*, p. 275.
52. Kasindorf, "Bad Mouth," p. 44; Edmund Andrews, "F.C.C. Delays Radio Deals by Howard Stern's Employer," *New York Times*, December 31, 1993, p. D2; Kurtz, *Hot Air*, pp. 275–76.
53. Kurtz, *Hot Air*, p. 276.
54. Biographical material on Imus from Dinitia Smith, "Morning Mouth," *New York*, June 24, 1991, pp. 28–35, and Kurtz, *Hot Air*, pp. 278–83.
55. Smith, "Morning Mouth," pp. 30, 31; Ken Auletta, "The Don," *New Yorker*, May 25, 1998, p. 59.
56. Kurtz, *Hot Air*, p. 283; "Sacred and Profane," *New Yorker*, December 21, 1992, p. 47.
57. Michael Traugott et al., "The Impact of Talk Radio on Its Audience," unpub. ms.
58. Interview, Mark Williams.
59. "The Talk Radio Audience," Times Mirror Center for People and the Press, April 1995.
60. Kathleen Knight and David Barker, " 'Talk Radio Turns the Tide'? The Limbaugh Effect: 1993–1995," unpub. ms., 1996, p. 6.
61. Ibid.
62. "The Vocal Minority in American Politics," Times Mirror Center for People and the Press, Washington, D.C., 1993.
63. The following information comes from two focus groups Professor Michael Traugott and I conducted at the Marsh Center for the Study of Journalistic Performance at the University of Michigan, on January 28, 1997, and February 2, 1997.
64. I am grateful to Michael Traugott for this observation.
65. Munson, *All Talk*, p. 175.
66. Cappella, Jamieson, et al., "Public Cynicism," p. 26.
67. Marsh Center Focus Group, January 28, 1997; Boyer, "Bull Rush," p. 205; interview, Jim Casale.
68. Boyer, "Bull Rush," p. 206.

69. Knight and Barker, " 'Talk Radio Turns the Tide'?" pp. 10–11.
70. Ibid., pp. 12, 14, 15–16.
71. *The Rush Limbaugh Show*, July 9, 1998.
72. Cited in Knight and Barker, " 'Talk Radio Turns the Tide'?" p. 3; Kurtz, *Hot Air*, p. 237; Scannell, *Radio, Television and Modern Life*, p. 129.
73. Knight and Barker, " 'Talk Radio Turns the Tide'?" p. 10.
74. Cited in Boyer, "Bull Rush," p. 208.
75. *The Rush Limbaugh Show*, July 9, 1998.
76. Boyer, "Bull Rush," p. 159. As Munson puts it, talk show hosts "construct an ambivalent, deniable position with respect to power," see Munson, *All Talk*, p. 95.
77. Munson, *All Talk*, p. 118.
78. Marc Gunther, "At NPR, All Things Reconsidered," *New York Times*, August 13, 1995, sec. 2, p. 27; Karl E. Meyer, "Now Hear This," *Saturday Review*, July 21, 1979, p. 42.
79. Wertheimer, *Listening to America*, p. xix; "All the News Fit to Hear," *Time*, August 27, 1979, p. 70.
80. Wertheimer, *Listening to America*, p. xii.
81. Collins, *National Public Radio*, p. 23.
82. Peter Fornatale and Joshua E. Mills, *Radio in the Television Age* (Woodstock, N.Y.: Overlook Press, 1984), pp. 175–76.
83. Museum of Broadcast Communications, "All Things Considered," May 3, 1971, RA 705.
84. Meyer, "Now Hear This," pp. 42.
85. Ledbetter, *Made Possible by . . .* , p. 125.
86. Ralph Engelman, *Public Radio and Television in America: A Political History* (Thousand Oaks, Cal.: Sage Publications, 1996), p. 114; cited in Gunther, "At NPR, All Things Reconsidered," p. 27.
87. Roger Piantadosi, "Stamberg Considered," *New York*, October 22, 1979, p. 90.
88. "All the News Fit to Hear," p. 70; Meyer, "Now Hear This," p. 94.
89. James Ledbetter, *Made Possible by . . .* , pp. 116–19.
90. "Lonesome Whistle Blowing," *Time*, November 4, 1985, pp. 68 ff.
91. Ibid., p. 70.
92. Ledbetter, *Made Possible by . . .* , pp. 130–35.
93. Speech by FCC Commissioner Susan Ness, March 12, 1998, FCC News Report No. MM 98-3.
94. Munson, *All Talk*, pp. 46–47.
95. Comments by Ken Kohl at the NARTSH convention, Los Angeles June 20, 1997.
96. Interview, Mark Williams.

12. WHY HAM RADIO MATTERS

1. I am deeply indebted to Steve Mansfield, the manager of legislative and public affairs at the American Radio Relay League, for assistance with this chapter. He provided names of people to interview, books, manuals, videotapes, and invaluable information. All mistakes are, of course, my own.
2. Interview, Perry Williams, August 31, 1995.

3. Interview, David Sumner, June 29, 1994.
4. Interview, Perry Williams.
5. Carl Dreher and Zeh Bouck, "Our Radio Amateurs," *Harper's*, October 1941, p. 544; Jack Cluett, "Hobby Happy Hams," *Reader's Digest*, May 1950, p. 87; *Fifty Years of the ARRL* (Newington, Conn.: American Radio Relay League, 1981), p. 133.
6. Interview, David Sumner; Cluett, "Hobby Happy Hams," p. 87.
7. Dreher and Bouck, "Our Radio Hams," p. 538; interview, David Sumner.
8. *Fifty Years of the ARRL*, p. 69.
9. *New York Times*, March 18, 1936, p. 1.
10. Orrin E. Dunlap, Jr., "Flood Perils Afford Radio Some Realistic Drama," *New York Times*, March 22, 1936, p. 14; "The Editor's Mill," *QST*, May 1936, p. 7.
11. Clinton B. DeSoto, *QST*, May 1936, pp. 11–12.
12. Ibid., pp. 10, 17, 118.
13. "Flood Perils Told over Radio; Rail Traffic Halts," *New York Times*, March 19, 1936, p. 18.
14. Clinton B. DeSoto, "Amateur Radio Bests Triple Catastrophe," *QST*, November 1938, p. 16; "Scenes of Havoc Depicted on Radio," *New York Times*, September 23, 1938, p. 23.
15. DeSoto, "Amateur Radio Bests," p. 16.
16. "The Kon Tiki Adventure," *Life*, August 14, 1950, p. 91; "Westward Voyage," *Time*, April 21, 1947.
17. Thor Heyerdahl, *Kon-Tiki: Across the Pacific by Raft* (Chicago: Rand McNally, 1950).
18. *Fifty Years of the ARRL*, p. 133.
19. Ibid., p. 117; interview, Perry Williams.
20. For more detail, see Sydney W. Head, *Broadcasting in America*, 3d ed. (Boston: Houghton Mifflin, 1976), pp. 38, 50–51.
21. Philip J. Klass, "Military, Airlines Push Single Sideband," *Aviation Week*, April 30, 1956, pp. 62–64; interview, Perry Williams.
22. Interview, Perry Williams; "Ham Radio Robot Fired into Orbit," *New York Times*, December 13, 1961, p. 19; "Satellite for Radio Hams," *Science Newsletter*, December 23, 1961, p. 410.

CONCLUSION: IS LISTENING DEAD?

1. Keith Moerer, "Who Killed Rock Radio?" *Spin*, February 1998, p. 77; interview, Peter Fornatale, September 16, 1998.
2. Tony Schwartz, cited in Andrew Crisell, *Understanding Radio* (New York: Routledge, 1994), p. 3.
3. "Focus on Radio," Katz Radio Group Format Averages, Fall 1996. Information on formats from the Katz Radio Group Web pages, September 2, 1998.
4. Moerer, "Who Killed Rock Radio?" pp. 75–76.
5. Matthew Schifrin, "Radio-Active Men," *Forbes*, June 1, 1998, www.forbes.com, p. 1.
6. "Chancellor Media and Capstar Broadcasting to Merge, Creating Nation's Largest Radio Broadcasting Company with Enterprise Value of More than $17 Billion," *Newsedge*, August 28, 1998; Allen R. Myerson, "Riding Radio

Merge Wave, Chancellor Will Buy Capstar," *New York Times*, August 28, 1998, p. C4.

7. Schifrin, "Radio-Active Men," pp. 5–7.

8. Ibid., pp. 7–11; Business Wire, "Chancellor Media to Acquire 50 Percent Interest in Mexico's Grupo Radio Centro, Latin America's Most Successful Radio Company, for $237 Million," www.newsalert.com, July 10, 1998; PR Newswire, *"Radio Ink* Magazine Announces 40 Most Powerful People in Radio," www.newsalert.com, July 10, 1998.

9. Interview, Peter Fornatale.

10. Interviews conducted with several DJs in August and September 1998.

11. Moerer, "Who Killed Rock Radio?" p. 78.

12. "Block Group Coding," *BTR Radio,* Spring 1994; "Listening to Persons Listening to Radio," *BTR Radio,* Winter 1993.

13. "The Arbitron Company 1996 Profile," press release from Arbitron, April 1997.

14. "How Kids Listen to Radio," *BTR Radio,* Winter 1994, pp. 8–10.

15. Raymond L. Carroll et al., "Meanings of Radio to Teenagers in a Niche-Programming Era," *Journal of Broadcasting & Electronic Media,* 1993, pp. 159–76.

16. Phillip Taylor, "FCC vs. Low-Watt Radio: Does Limited Spectrum Justify Limited Speech?" The Freedom Forum online, www.freedomforum.org.

Index

Abbott, Bud, 122–23
ABC and WABC, 22, 93, 193, 251–52,
    295–98, 314, 338
    in FM revolution, 256, 277–78
Abu-Jamal, Mumia, 325
Ace, Jane and Goodman, 114–15
Adorno, Theodor, 131, 143, 149, 151,
    153–55
advertising, 10, 12, 15–16, 19–20, 54,
    346, 348
    AM radio and, 258–59, 266, 269–70
    in audience analysis, 124, 127,
        129–30, 134–37, 143, 146–48,
        157–60
    in broadcast journalism, 164, 166,
        168, 172–73, 182–83, 185, 189,
        196–98
    consolidators and, 349–51, 354
    DJs and, 220, 222, 227–28, 231–34,
        236, 238–39, 251–52, 254
    in ethereal world, 40
    exploratory listening and, 56, 62–64,
        67, 72, 82
    FM revolution and, 256, 258–59, 263,
        266, 268–70, 274, 276–78, 280–83
    ham radio and, 330
    in jazz listening, 94, 98
    and language usage on radio, 103
    music formats and, 348–49

NPR and, 324
payola scandals and, 251
radio comedy and, 100, 104, 114, 116,
    120–22
in radio-listener relationship, 5–6,
    11
regulation of, 224–25
sports broadcasting and, 203–5, 213,
    216
talk radio and, 286, 288–89, 295–96,
    301, 317
war propaganda and, 189
in Zen of listening, 24–25, 29, 31, 35
Advertising Age, 226, 280
African Americans, ix, 84–85, 87, 89–99,
    225, 356
    in audience analysis, 128
    DJs and, 221–23, 228–29, 233–46,
        248–49, 252, 254
    in exploratory listening, 66, 68
    language usage of, 108
    music of, *see* jazz; rock 'n' roll
    NPR and, 322
    payola scandals and, 250–52
    radio comedy and, 18, 56, 58, 71, 79,
        101, 103–4, 106–10, 116, 118, 137,
        142, 223
    sports and, 200, 202, 206–9, 238
    talk radio and, 291, 293, 302–5, 307–8

African Americans (*cont'd*)
  teenagers and, 242–44, 249–50,
    252–53
  in Zen of listening, 25
  see also race and racism
age, 357
  in audience analysis, 131, 141, 150,
    156, 353–54
  consolidators and, 349, 351–52
  FM revolution and, 264, 277
  ham radio and, 332–34
  talk radio and, 303
  see also teenagers
Alexanderson, Ernst, 50–51
All Colored Hour, 93–94
Allen, Bill "Hoss," 239
Allen, Fred, 3, 11
  Benny's feud with, 118–19, 121
  linguistic slapstick of, 101, 110,
    118–21
Allen, Frederick Lewis, 42
Allen, Gracie, 3, 15, 19, 26, 74, 165,
    219
  linguistic slapstick of, 101, 104,
    110–11, 114–16, 120–21
Allen, Mel, 209, 212–13
Allen, Woody, 6, 303, 305
Allport, Gordon, 30–31, 85
  in audience analysis, 130–36, 155–56,
    159–60
All Things Considered (ATC), 284,
    286–87, 319–25, 327, 355
"All Things Distorted" (Barnes), 325
amateurs, *see* ham radio
America Calling (Fischer), 21
American Graffiti, 219, 255
American Manhood (Rotundo), 66–67
American Radio Relay League (ARRL),
    60, 81, 329, 333–35, 340–43
American Radio Systems, 298
American Red Cross, 335–38
American Society of Composers,
    Authors, and Publishers (ASCAP),
    86, 250–51
America's Town Meeting of the Air, 144,
    196, 235

Amos 'n' Andy, 18, 56, 58, 71, 79, 137,
    142, 223
  linguistic slapstick in, 101, 103–4,
    106–10
AM radio, 177, 344, 347–48
  bandwidths in, 260–61
  consolidators and, 350
  DJs and, 220, 223, 227, 232, 237, 239,
    247–48, 258, 269–71
  in exploratory listening, 70–74
  FM revolution and, 256–64, 266–67,
    269–71, 277–79, 281
  ham radio and, 341–42
  NPR and, 320, 326
  and rock 'n' roll, 250, 253–55, 257
  talk radio and, 284, 288–89, 296–97,
    306, 314
  technology of, 36–39
  teenagers and, 252
  wavelength assignments for, 63
  in Zen of listening, 22–23, 35–36
Anderson, Benedict, 23
Anderson, Eddie "Rochester," 116, 118
announcers, 8, 21
  in audience analysis, 124, 134–35,
    138, 151, 154–55
  celebrity of, 189–90, 194–95, 197
  in language usage, 102–3
  in radio comedy, 112, 116–17, 120–21
  see also broadcast journalism; DJs;
    sports and sports broadcasting;
    talk and talk radio
Arbitron Radio, 353–54
Arlin, Harold, 201
Armstrong, E. Howard, 78, 257–63, 281
Armstrong, Jack, 232
Armstrong, Louis, 85, 90, 93–94, 96–97,
    99
Arnheim, Rudolf, 48, 156–58
Associated Press, 178–79, 196, 207
AT&T, 45–46, 56, 210, 294–95, 344–45
Atlantic Monthly, The, 91, 197
audience and audiences, 10–11, 100, 347
  Adorno on, 131, 143, 149, 151,
    153–55
  analysis of, 124–60, 221–22, 245, 247,

276–78, 280, 283, 302, 309–14,
  317–19, 348–49, 352–54, 356
in broadcast journalism, 165–66,
  172–75, 181–82, 184–86, 188–90,
  192–98
Cantril on, 130–37, 140, 155–56,
  159–60
and consolidators, 351–52
and DJs, 221, 228, 230–41, 244–48
in exploratory listening, 58, 61,
  63–65, 72, 75, 79, 82
and FM radio, 254, 263, 269–80, 282
Herzog on, 130, 137, 139–41, 144–48
in language usage, 102–4
Lazarsfeld on, 125–30, 136–49, 153,
  160
MacDougald on, 151–53
in music listening, 86–89, 93–95, 98,
  348–49
and NPR, 319–27, 356
and payola scandals, 251
and radio comedy, 105–8, 110, 112,
  114–15, 117–18, 120–23
and radio-listener relationship, 4, 11
in radio studios, 110, 124
and rock 'n' roll, 254
and sports, 199–201, 203–4, 208, 210,
  212–13, 216–18
Suchman on, 150–51
of talk radio, 124–25, 141, 284–90,
  292, 295, 301–3, 305, 307–19, 356
technological insurgencies in, 16–17
teenagers in, see teenagers
voices analyzed by, 134–35
in Zen of listening, 25, 39
audimeters, 138, 158–60

Bach, Johann Sebastian, 88, 151
Baer, Max, 204–7
Baird, Zoe, 300–301, 309
Baker, Kenny, 116
Baker, LaVern, 246
Baker's Broadcast, The, 111
Ballard, Frank, 44
Bankhead, Tallulah, 113
Baraka, Amiri (LeRoi Jones), 91

Barber, Red, 15, 65, 193, 201–4, 210–17
Barnes, Fred, 325
Barnes, Walter, 92–93
Barnicle, Mike, 303, 307
Barnouw, Erik, ix
Barry Goldwater (Cook), 299
Barrymore, John, 67, 113
baseball, 8, 10, 64–65, 199–205, 209–19,
  232, 243
basketball, 200, 202
Bayne, Martha Collins, 156–58
BBC, 102, 240
Beatles, 3, 252–54, 256–57, 281
Beck, 349, 352
Bederman, Gail, 13, 66
Beethoven, Ludwig van, 33–34, 85, 87,
  154–55
Bellow, Saul, 256
Benny, Jack, 3–4, 26, 31, 35, 164–65,
  197–98, 218, 220, 225, 232
  linguistic slapstick of, 100–101, 104,
  110, 116–21
Benson, Al "the Swingmaster," 238–39
Berg, Alan, 287
Bergen, Edgar, 6, 119–20, 164–65
Berle, Adolf, 171
Berlin, Irving, 151–52
Berlin Diary (Shirer), 180, 195
Bernie, Ben, 88
Berry, Chuck, 250, 252
Billboard, 234, 246
Biltmore agreement, 167–68, 170
Binns, Jack, 59
Biondi, Dick "the Screamer," 241, 252,
  255
Blackboard Jungle, The, 231, 250
Black Talk (Sidran), 97–98
Block, Martin, 229
Bogart, Humphrey, 165
book reading, 276, 307–8
  in audience analysis, 141–42, 147, 158
Boston Red Sox, 213, 216
boxing, 10, 63–64, 77, 199–202, 204–9,
  217–18
Braddock, Jim, 205–7
Brady, James, 302

Brahms, Johannes, 151, 154
Bride, Harold, 49, 60
Brinkley, Alan, 162
Brinkley, David, 161, 293
Broadcasters, The (Barber), 201–2
Broadcasting, 221, 227, 229
   on FM radio, 258–59, 276, 278, 281
broadcast journalism, 10, 161–98, 281
   of Carter, 164–65, 168, 172–75,
      179–81, 185
   DJs and, 230
   emotionalism in, 181–83, 188–89
   as entertainment, 166, 168, 174
   on Lindbergh, 162, 168–70, 186
   of Murrow, 161, 164–65, 170, 172,
      176–77, 179–85, 187, 190–92,
      197–98, 286
   objectivity in, 164, 181–89, 195–98,
      214
   on-the-spot, 167–68, 170, 176,
      178–80, 182–85, 189–95, 206, 218
   shortwave in, 177–78, 185, 192–93
   sports broadcasting and, 203, 206,
      214, 217–18
   talk radio and, 286, 301–2
   war between newspapers and, 167–68
   of Winchell, 164, 168–72, 174–75,
      180, 189, 197
   on World War II, 161–63, 165,
      171–73, 175–80, 182–98, 286
Broadcast Music, Inc. (BMI), 250
Brooklyn Dodgers, 209, 211, 214, 219
Brown, Cecil, 189, 192–93, 195–97
Brown, Earl, 209
Brown, Herbert, 194
Brown America Speaks, 237
Brown v. Board of Education, 243
Burch, Dean, 281
Burgess, Wilson, 338–39
Burleson, Albert Sidney, 188
Burns, George, 3, 15, 19, 26, 74, 165, 219
   linguistic slapstick of, 101, 104,
      110–11, 114–16, 120–21
Burns, Tommy, 206
Burroughs, Edgar Rice, 14, 66
Burumowska, Madame, 56

Bush, George, 291, 304
Business Week, 158–59, 174, 220, 263–64

cable companies, 41, 49, 51–52
Cantor, Eddie, 11, 148, 165
   linguistic slapstick of, 110, 113–14
Cantril, Hadley, 30–31, 85, 165
   in audience analysis, 130–37, 140,
      155–56, 159–60
Capital Cities/ABC, 296
Capstar Broadcasting, 297, 325, 349–50
Caray, Harry, 15, 203, 212–13, 215–17
Carlin, George, 305
Carnegie, Dale, 67
Carnera, Primo, 204–6
Carpentier, Georges, 62, 201
Carroll, John, 249
Carroll, Lewis, 134
Carson, Johnny, 299
Car Talk, 319
Carter, Boake, 164–65, 168, 172–75,
      179–81, 185
Carter, Jimmy, 291, 293, 323
Casale, Jim, 285, 302, 314
CBS, 6, 39, 93, 128, 154, 224, 235, 295,
      298, 315, 325, 337, 339, 349, 351
   audience research at, 130, 136, 139,
      154, 159
   and broadcast journalism, 161, 164,
      166–68, 172–73, 175–91, 194–98
   and FM revolution, 260–62, 277–78
   founding of, 63
   and NPR, 321, 323
   sports broadcasting on, 203, 214
celebrity journalism, 285, 304–5, 307,
      314
cellular phones, 287, 302, 330, 335, 344
Century Magazine, 42, 71
chain broadcasting, 223–24
   broadcast journalism and, 181, 187
   in exploratory listening, 56–57, 79
Chamberlain, Neville, 165, 171, 173,
      176, 178, 186
Chambers Brothers, 17, 258
Chancellor Media Corporation, 298,
      349–51

Chase and Sanborn Hour, The, 8, 113–14
Chiang Kai-shek, 195
Chicago, Ill., 238–39
  jazz broadcasts in, 84, 89–90, 93–94
Chicago Cubs, 33, 209, 213, 215
Chicago Defender, The, 92–93
Christian Crusade, 299
Chung, Connie, 305
civil rights and civil rights movement,
  228, 253–54, 290, 305, 319, 356
Clark, Dick, 250–51
Clark-Hooper Inc., 137, 158–59
classical music, 85, 88–90, 92, 169, 187–88
  in audience analysis, 126–27, 141–43,
    148–51, 153–55
  DJs and, 232
  in ethereal world, 40
  FM revolution and, 263, 266–68, 271,
    277
  jazz vs., 84–85, 88–90, 92
  in Zen of listening, 35
Clear Channel Communications, 297,
  325
clear channel (Class I) stations, 39, 82
Click and Clack, 319
Clinton, Bill, 213, 300, 307, 309–10,
  315
Clinton, Hillary Rodham, 315
Clooney, Rosemary, 244
Cloud, Stanley, 161, 179–80, 197
Clovers, 241
Coburn, Bob, 273–74
Cohen, Gary, 202
Cohen, Lizabeth, 66
Cold War, 341–42
Cole, Nat "King," 223
Coleman, Gerald, 337–38
college stations, 270, 276, 283, 320, 352
Collier's, 76, 224
Collingwood, Charles, 189, 192, 197–98
Columbia Records, 90–91, 227–28, 264
comedy, radio, 8, 10–14, 234, 354–55
  in audience analysis, 126
  broadcast journalism and, 164–65,
    197–98
  DJs and, 221

in exploratory listening, 56, 58, 62,
  65, 70, 72, 74, 77, 79, 82
imagination in, 101–2, 230–31, 237
linguistic slapstick of, 100–123
men and, 15, 101, 105–7, 109–20,
  122–23
radio-listener relationship and, 3–4,
  11
rise of, 101, 104–5
sports and, 122–23, 214, 218
talk radio and, 293
vocal trade-marks in, 110–11, 117
in Zen of listening, 25–26, 31, 34
Command Performance, 235
commentators, *see* announcers
Commerce Department, U.S., 62–63, 71
commercialism, *see* advertising
Communications Act, 81, 167–68, 298
communities, 225, 353, 355–56
  in audience analysis, 129, 145–46,
    151, 157, 160
  DJs and, 230–31, 233, 236–37, 239, 244
  in ethereal world, 40–41, 47
  ham radio and, 332, 334, 345
  imagined, 11, 23–25, 145, 160,
    230–31, 237, 290, 319, 327, 355–56
  on Internet, 20
  in jazz listening, 91, 97
  radio comedy and, 107–8
  sports and, 200, 204, 208, 216–17
  talk radio and, 290, 293, 311, 316,
    318–19, 327
  in Zen of listening, 22–25, 38–39
computers, 19, 346
  in age of mechanical DJs, 347
  in audience analysis, 125–26, 353
  in FM radio, 280
  NPR and, 326
  proliferation of, 55
  users' relationships with, 10–11
concentrated music listening, 33–35
Congress, U.S., 91–92, 100, 201
  broadcast journalism and, 167, 171,
    183, 186–87
  on Fairness Doctrine, 299
  on ham radio, 343–44

Congress, U.S. (cont'd)
  NPR and, 320, 322–23, 325
  on payola scandals, 250–51
  in radio deregulation, 343–44
  in radio regulation, 223–24
  talk radio and, 287, 299–300, 308–10,
    314
Conley, Robert, 321
Conrad, Joseph, 66
Cook, Fred, 298–99
Cooper, Jack L., 93–94, 229, 236, 238–39
Cooperative Analysis of Broadcasting
    (CAB), 136, 158–59
Corporation for Public Broadcasting
    (CPB), 320–22
corporations, 21, 58, 169, 350, 357
  in audience analysis, 124–25, 129,
    136, 139, 148
  in broadcast journalism, 173, 182–83,
    187, 196, 198
  in controlling radio, 46, 56, 62–64
  DJs and, 221, 230
  ethereal world and, 45–46
  in exploratory listening, 56, 62–64,
    67, 81
  FM revolution and, 259, 261–66,
    277–78, 281–83
  ham radio and, 60, 330, 335, 344–46
  in jazz listening, 90–91
  in man-machine relationship, 14–15
  NPR and, 322, 325–26
  radio comedy and, 108
  in radio-listener relationship, 6–7
  sports broadcasting and, 204
  talk radio and, 289–90, 293–94, 296,
    313, 317
  technological insurgency and, 15–16
Correll, Charles, 106–7
Costas, Bob, 216
Costello, Elvis, 3, 17
Costello, Lou, 122–23
Coughlin, Father, 25, 128–29, 133, 148,
    164, 173, 314
country music, 33, 40, 348, 350
Cousin Brucie, 5, 22, 252, 255, 271
Cox, Eugene, 224

Cox, Ida, 94
Cox, Kenneth, 263
Craig, Roger, 213
Creel, George, 188
Crosby, Bing, 87, 220
Crossley, Archibald, 125, 136–37
crystal sets, 58–59, 70–71, 225–26
  in music listening, 86–87
  replacement of, 77–78
Culbert, David, 163, 183
culture and cultural differences, x, 8–11,
    16–17, 19–21, 100–101, 354–56
  in audience analysis, 127–30, 137,
    141–44, 147–49, 151, 153, 155–58
  in broadcast journalism, 169–70, 194
  and DJs, 221–23, 228–30, 235,
    239–41, 244–46
  in ethereal world, 40–41, 46–47
  in exploratory listening, 55, 57, 59,
    61–62, 65–66, 68, 74–76, 79–80
  and FM revolution, 258–59, 263,
    266–70, 273, 275–79, 282
  in future, 357
  and ham radio, 329–30, 332, 334, 339,
    346
  importance of radio in, 9–10
  and language usage on radio, 103, 105
  in music listening, 83–90, 92, 94–99
  as national vs. diverse, 17
  and NPR, 322–24, 356
  and payola scandals, 251
  in radio comedy, 101, 104–7, 123
  radio in introducing new orality to,
    12
  radio-listener relationship and, 4, 6–7
  in rise of television, 19
  and rock 'n' roll, 253
  and sports, 200–202, 216, 218
  and talk radio, 284, 286–87, 303–4,
    356
  in technological insurgencies, 16
  and teenagers, 18, 242–43, 245
  in Zen of listening, 23–24, 26, 28–35

Daly, John, 188
Damrosch, Walter, 83

dance bands, 87–88
Darwin, Charles, 45
Dateline: Burma, 195
Davis, Elmer, 175–76, 189, 195
Davis, Ossie, 208
Dean, Dizzy, 203
De Forest, Lee, 50–51, 59
de Leath, Vaughn, 87
Dellums, Ron, 274
Deloy, Leon, 80
Dempsey, Jack, 62, 77, 199, 201, 205
Deppe, Lois, 93
Detroit race riots, 223, 235
De Voto, Bernard, 175–76
DiMaggio, Dominic, 212
DiMaggio, Joe, 212
Dirty Politics (Jamieson), 300
distance-signaling (DXing), 24–25, 38,
    333
  demise of, 78–79, 82, 87, 89
  in exploratory listening, 57–58, 61,
    73–82
DJs, 10, 12–14, 227–55, 355–56
  African Americans and, 221–23,
    228–29, 233–46, 248–49, 252, 254
  AM and, 220, 223, 227, 232, 237, 239,
    247–48, 258, 269–71
  autonomy of, 21, 245, 251–52,
    277–78, 280, 283, 351–52
  celebrity of, 231–32, 237
  consolidators and, 350–53, 356
  on FM, 254, 256–58, 269–80, 282–83
  intimacy of, 230–32, 236, 271
  in jazz listening, 93–94, 230
  mechanical age of, 347
  nostalgia about, 254–55
  in payola scandals, 223, 248, 250–52,
    269
  in radio-listener relationship, 5–6
  and rock 'n' roll, 219–23, 225, 228–29,
    231–33, 236, 239–41, 245–49
  talk radio and, 302–3, 306, 309
  teenagers and, 17–18, 219–22,
    227–40, 242–46, 249, 252, 254–55
  totemism, 244, 252
  in Zen of listening, 22–23, 32, 34–35

see also specific DJs
"Dock of the Bay," 26, 254
documentaries, 9–10, 128, 162, 193
Dolby, Ray, 282
Dole, Bob, 325, 344
Domino, Fats, 246–47
Donahue, Raechel, 269–70
Donahue, Tom "Big Daddy," 5, 257–58,
    269–70, 273–74
Don McNeill and the Breakfast Club, 228
Doors, 3, 254, 256, 269
Douglas, Ann, 84, 98
Downey, Morton, Jr., 314
Doyle, Sir Arthur Conan, 43, 45
Drake, Bill, 252
dramas, 11, 34, 218, 234, 354–55
  in audience analysis, 134, 142–45
  DJs and, 221
  in exploratory listening, 58
  NPR and, 322–23
  in Zen of listening, 25, 31, 34
drugs, 268–69, 271, 273–74, 281, 291
Ducey, Rick, 37, 260
Duffy, Francis, 337
Dukakis, Michael, 291
Dunning, John, 199
Durr, Clifford J., 224
Dylan, Bob, 256, 272, 275

Early, Steve, 181–82, 196–97
Earplay, 322
Easy Aces, 114–15
Eberly, Philip, 94
Ebony, 234, 236
economics, 12–13, 17, 20, 169, 349
  AM radio and, 344
  in audience analysis, 124, 127–28,
    130–31, 133–34, 136, 141–43, 146,
    148, 150–53
  broadcast journalism and, 171–72,
    175, 186–87, 196
  consolidators and, 350–51, 353–54
  DJs and, 220, 227–28, 234
  ethereal world and, 45–46
  exploratory listening and, 56, 61–65,
    69–70

economics (*cont'd*)
  FM radio and, 259, 261–63, 266–68,
    276–80, 282, 344
  in future, 357
  ham radio and, 334–35, 342
  importance of radio in, 9
  in jazz listening, 90–92, 94–95
  NPR and, 320, 322–23, 327
  payola scandals and, 250–51
  radio comedy and, 104–5, 107–9, 111,
    117, 119–23
  in radio-listener relationship, 6–7
  of rock 'n' roll, 250–51
  sports and, 200, 207, 210
  talk radio and, 288–89, 292, 294–97,
    305–6, 308, 310–11, 313, 315, 320,
    327
  of television, 19–20
  in Zen of listening, 24, 31
  see also advertising
Edison, Thomas, 43, 46, 149
Edison Company, 85, 90
education, 102, 126–27
  in audience analysis, 127, 129,
    141–44, 146–47, 150–51
  broadcast journalism and, 167,
    169–70, 181, 190
  DJs and, 221, 229, 231–32
  ethereal world and, 43
  exploratory listening and, 56, 63–64
  FM revolution and, 266, 270, 277
  ham radio and, 346
  and language use on radio, 105
  in music listening, 86, 88
  NPR and, 320, 322
  radio comedy and, 111–12
  sports and, 200, 209
  talk radio and, 287, 293, 302–3, 306,
    311, 316
  in Zen of listening, 31, 35
Edwards, Bob, 320–21, 323
Edwards, Webley, 192
Einstein, Albert, 26, 64
Einstein, Harry, 113
Eisenberg, Evan, 46
Elder, Robert F., 158

electromagnetism, 36–37, 41–42, 44–45,
  49–54
Ellington, Duke, 3, 10, 85, 93–94, 97,
  235, 245
Elliot, Jack "the Cat," 240
Ely, Melvin Patrick, 107
Emerson, J. Paul, 302
employment, *see* labor and labor
  movement
End of Reform, The (Brinkley), 162
Enquirer, The, 152–53
environmentalists, 315
ethnicity and ethnic groups, ix, 238
  in audience analysis, 128–29, 137,
    149, 156–58
  in exploratory listening, 61–62, 65, 75
  and language usage on radio, 103
  in music listening, 83
  in radio comedy, 106–11, 113, 118–19
  in radio-listener relationship, 5–6, 11
  sports and, 200
  in Zen of listening, 25
Étude, 83, 92

Fairbanks, Douglas, 67–68
Fairness Doctrine, 298–99
Farrell, James T., 207
Federal Communications Commission
  (FCC), 6, 10, 39, 62, 227, 357
  antitrafficking rule of, 297
  on broadcast journalism, 173,
    181–82, 187–88, 196–97
  in censoring music, 92
  consolidators and, 350
  establishment of, 81
  Fairness Doctrine of, 298–99
  FM revolution and, 259, 262–63, 267,
    281
  NPR and, 320
  one-to-a-market rule of, 296–97
  on payola scandals, 251
  in radio deregulation, 295–97, 350
  in radio regulation, 56, 223–24, 344
  talk radio and, 295–99, 305–6
Federal Radio Commission (FRC), 39,
  62–64, 71, 80, 82

Feiffer, Jules, 319
Fessenden, Reginald, 50–51
Fibber McGee and Molly, 4, 33
Fiedler, Leslie, 243–44
Fields, W. C., 120
"Filthy Words" (Carlin), 305
Fischer, Claude, 21
Fitzgerald, F. Scott, 87
Fleming, John Ambrose, 51, 59
Florida, 59
Flowers, Gennifer, 300
Fly, Lawrence, 181, 196–97, 223–24
FM radio, 10, 220, 248, 250, 254,
    256–85, 344, 347–48
  assembly-line programming
    techniques in, 278–80
  bandwidths in, 260–61
  consolidation in, 278, 280, 350–51
  consultants in, 279–80
  early devotees of, 263, 266–68
  free-form format of, 13–15, 17, 35,
    256, 258, 267, 269–83, 352, 355
  ham radio and, 341–42
  how it works, 260–61
  NPR and, 320, 326
  oldies format on, 278–79
  origins of, 257–70, 278, 281
  proliferation of, 259, 267–68, 276,
    278, 280–81
  stereo broadcasting on, 267–68
  talk radio and, 284–85, 288–89,
    296–97
  technology of, 36–38
  in Zen of listening, 34–35
folk music, 268–69, 271, 277, 279, 348
football, 64, 201–2, 214
foreign-language programs, 149, 156–58
foreign-language stations, 25
Fornatale, Peter, 248, 272, 352
Fortune, 174–75
Fowler, Mark, 295–97, 299, 305
Fox, Roy, 287
Frank, Joe, 284–85
Franklin, Aretha, 33
Freed, Alan, 5, 19, 230–33, 239–41,
    243–47, 249–51, 254–55

Fresh Air, 319
Frith, Simon, 275
Fussell, Paul, 162, 189

Gabler, Neal, 168–70, 300
Gallup, George, 128, 140
Gang Busters, 142–43
Gaudet, Hazel, 165
gender and gender differences, 8
  in audience analysis, 131, 141–42,
    147, 150, 353
  and exploratory listening, 67–68
  in jazz listening, 95–96
  and language usage on radio, 103, 105
  in man-machine relationship, 14
  in radio-listener relationship, 5–6
  and talk radio, 302–5, 310, 317
  in Zen of listening, 23, 35
  see also men and masculinity; women
General Electric (GE), 45–46, 189
  FM revolution and, 262–63
  in radio technology, 50–51
generations and generational identities,
    175, 355, 357
  in audience analysis, 156
  and DJs, 222, 228
  in ethereal world, 43, 46
  and FM revolution, 267–68
  and ham radio, 335
  in music listening, 83, 87–88, 90,
    96–97
  in radio-listener relationship, 5–8
  technological insurgencies in, 16
  in Zen of listening, 35–36
  see also age; teenagers
geography, 8, 12, 253, 356
  in audience analysis, 134, 150
  in broadcast journalism, 179, 184,
    186
  ethereal world and, 41
  in exploratory listening, 55–58, 75–76
  ham radio and, 334
  and language use on radio, 105
  in radio-listener relationship, 5, 11
  in radio regulation, 225
  in Zen of listening, 24, 39

geography (*cont'd*)
  see also distance-signaling
George, 300
Germany:
  broadcast journalism on, 161–63,
    165, 171, 173, 176, 178–80, 182–86,
    190–96
  sports and, 207–8
Ghost Hour, 53
Gibbons, Floyd, 166
Gibson, Jack, 236
Gifford, Kathie Lee, 303
Gingrich, Newt, 320
Godfrey, Arthur, 244
Going Out (Nasaw), 65
Goldsboro, Bobby, 254
Goldwater, Barry, 281, 328
golf, 200, 208
Goodman, Benny, 3, 6, 151
Goodwill Hour, The, 144
Goodwin, Bill, 115, 121
Gordon, Bert, 113
Gosden, Freeman, 106–7
Gowdy, Curt, 213
Grant, Bob, 284–85, 292, 302
Grateful Dead, 33, 270–71
Great Depression, 4, 13, 79, 102, 227
  addressing needs of men in, 15
  in audience analysis, 128–29, 137,
    148, 150
  broadcast journalism and, 198
  FM revolution and, 261
  ham radio and, 335
  radio comedy and, 104–5, 107–8, 111,
    117, 123
  sports and, 199, 208, 217
Greenfield, Jeff, 307
Gross, Terry, 319
ground waves, 37–38
Gruber, Helmut, 127
Grupo Radio Centro, 351
Guest, Edgar, 213
Gumbel, Bryant, 303

Hamblin, Ken, 302
ham radio, 11, 15–16, 138, 328–46

in battle to preserve spectrum space,
  343–45
behavior code of, 334
broadcast journalism and, 177
channel surfing on, 73
distances spanned by, 80
in exploratory listening, 56, 58–61,
  64–65, 68–70, 72–80
false messages sent on, 59–60
in *Kon-Tiki* voyage, 339–40
language and abbreviations in, 73,
  332
men and, 12–13, 15, 257, 259–60,
  264–70, 274–76, 281
during natural disasters, 329–30,
  332–33, 335–38, 343
origin of term, 330–31
proliferation of, 60–61, 335, 340
regulation of, 58, 60–61
social invisibility of, 334
ssbsc transmission of, 341–43
sunspot activity monitored by, 331
technology of, 16, 51, 58–59, 328–31,
  334, 341–43, 346
in Zen of listening, 34
Hancock, Hunter, 240
Hanks, Tom, 303
Happy Days, 229
Harding, Warren, 64, 102
Hargis, Billy James, 299
Harper's, 334
Harris, Phil, 116
Harrison, Michael, 289, 301
Hart, Joseph K., 48
Harwell, Ernie, 211
Haugland, Knut, 340
Hauptmann, Bruno, 168, 170
Headline Hunter, The, 166
headsets, 70–71, 87
Heatter, Gabriel, 168, 185
Heaviside, Oliver, 80–81
Henderson, Fletcher, 92–94
Henderson, Jocko, 234, 238, 240–41
Henderson, W. K., 79
Hendrix, Jimi, 268, 275
Herman's Hermits, 269

Hertz, Heinrich, 41, 49
Herzog, Herta, 102, 130, 137, 139–41, 144–48, 165
Heyerdahl, Thor, 339–40
"Hey You Ever Been Booted," 236
Hicks, George, 193–94, 198
Hicks, John, 350
Hicks, Steven, 349–51
Hicks, Thomas O., 349–51
hi-fi, *see* FM radio
"Higher and Higher," 255
High Fidelity, 265
Hill, Edwin C., 172, 174–75
Hilmes, Michele, 18–19, 107, 235
Hines, Earl, 93, 95
History of Broadcasting in the United States (Barnouw), ix
Hitler, Adolf, 234–35
    broadcast journalism on, 162, 165, 171, 173, 176–77, 179, 182, 185–86
    sports and, 208
"Hittin' High Notes" (Barnes), 92–93
Hodges, Russ, 213–14
"Honey," 254
Hoot 'n' Holler, 237–38
Hoover, Herbert, 62–65, 80–81, 166–67
Hope, Bob, 172, 235
Horkheimer, Max, 153
horse racing, 63, 201, 203
hotels, 86, 91–92, 95, 107, 119
Howe, Quincy, 197
How We Advertised the War (Creel), 188
Huggins, Nathan, 242
Hulbert, Maurice "Hot Rod," 234, 237
Hull, Cordell, 171
Huntin' with Hunter, 240
Hurricane Andrew, 329
Husing, Ted, 201–3, 206, 214
"Hymn to the Sun" (Rimsky-Korsakov), 56

I Broadcast the Crisis (Kaltenborn), 163, 186
imagination, 19–20
    in audience analysis, 133, 144–45, 160
    broadcast journalism and, 193

communities in, 11, 23–25, 145, 160, 230–31, 237, 290, 319, 327, 355–56
    DJs and, 230–31, 237, 255
    ethereal world and, 41, 44–47, 52–53
    in exploratory listening, 57, 73, 76–77
    FM revolution and, 267, 276
    ham radio and, 346
    NPR and, 319, 324
    in radio comedy, 101–2, 230–31, 237
    radio in stimulation of, 4, 8, 10–11, 17, 19, 27–29, 46, 52, 346, 355–57
    sports and, 201, 204, 212–13, 215, 218, 355
    talk radio and, 290, 303, 327
    teenagers and, 243–44, 255
    in Zen of listening, 23–31, 33, 39
immigrants and immigration, 92, 200
    in audience analysis, 128–29, 149, 156–58
    in exploratory listening, 61–62, 66
    NPR and, 326
    talk radio and, 304, 310
Imus, Don, 12–13, 35, 354
    meteoric rise of, 302–3, 306–8
    talk radio of, 286, 292, 302–3, 306–8, 318–19, 324, 327
"Incense and Peppermints," 34
independent stations, 24
    DJs and, 223, 227
    in exploratory listening, 57, 79, 82
    FM revolution and, 263, 276, 283
Infinity Broadcasting, 295, 297–98, 302–3, 305–6
Internet, 8–9, 16, 20, 26, 327, 331, 349, 356–57
Iran-Contra hearings, 322
Iranian hostage crisis, 284, 291, 293

Jackson, John, 246
Jackson, Mahalia, 238
Jackson, Michael, 292
Jacor, 297–98, 325–26, 349
Jahoda, Marie, 130
Jam, Jive and Gumbo, 240
James, Ida, 235
Jamieson, Kathleen Hall, 300

Jarvis, Al, 229
jazz, 12, 16, 18–19, 87–99, 108, 228, 235, 240, 243, 280, 347–48
  in audience analysis, 150
  birth of, 90
  classical music vs., 84–85, 88–90, 92
  criticisms of, 91–92
  DJs and, 93–94, 230
  FM revolution and, 271
  live performances of, 92–96
  symbiotic relationship between radio and, 94, 97–98
  in Zen of listening, 35
Jefferson Airplane, 273, 281
Jeffries, Jim, 206
Jergens Journal, 168, 170–71, 189
Jerry Williams Show, The, 287, 292–93
Jewell, Richard, 313
Jews, 129–30, 178, 207
  radio comedy and, 106, 118–19
Jivin' Jerry, 236
"Joe Louis Named the War," 208
John, Elton, 280, 347
Johnson, Jack, 206, 209
Johnson, Lyndon, 320
Johnstown Flood, 335–38
Joplin, Janis, 275
Jordan, Louis, 223
Jordan, Max, 176
Jourdain, Robert, 32
Jubilee, 235

Kaltenborn, H. V., 3, 33–35
  broadcast journalism of, 161–63, 167–68, 170, 174–75, 182, 185–87, 196–97
Kamen, Jeff, 321
Kanitz, Otto, 126
Karmazin, Mel, 351
Kasem, Casey, 40–41
Katz, Jeff, 326
Katz Radio Group, 348
KDKA, 39, 47, 64, 71, 93, 166, 201
Keillor, Garrison, 324–25
Kennedy, Bobby, 322
Kennelly, Arthur, 80–81

Kenney, William, 46, 98
Kent State massacres, 321
Kentucky Derby, 63, 201
Kernis, Jay, 286
Kimmel, Michael, 242, 290
King, B. B., 237, 240
King, Larry, 289, 292
King, Rodney, 304
Klauber, Ed, 181, 188
KLIF, 210, 247–48, 252
KMET, 270, 273–74
KMOX, 213, 288
KMPX, 269–70
Knight, Ross, 247
Kon-Tiki, voyage of, 339–40
Koufax, Sandy, 212
KSAN, 258, 270, 272–73, 281
Ku Klux Klan, 61, 92, 249
Kurtz, Howard, 302, 307, 316
KYW, 39, 64, 89

labor and labor movement, 223, 353
  in audience analysis, 126–27, 130, 133–35, 142–43, 150–51, 158
  and broadcast journalism, 171, 173, 175, 187
  in exploratory listening, 56, 68, 75
  and ham radio, 333
  in ideals of masculinity, 14–15
  in music listening, 83
  and NPR, 320
  and radio comedy, 105–7, 109, 117–19
  and sports, 199
  and talk radio, 285
  and teenagers, 241–42
Ladd, Jim, 271–73, 278–79
Lake Wobegon Days (Keillor), 324
Landis, Kenesaw Mountain, 203, 214
Laquidara, Charles, 271
Lasch, Christopher, 149, 317–18
Lateef, Yusaf, 283
Lazarsfeld, Paul, 125–30, 136–49, 153, 160, 174
Lears, T. J. Jackson, 67–68
Ledbetter, James, 323

Lee, Judy, 307
Lee, Robert E., 251, 263
LeMay, Curtis, 342–43
LeSueur, Larry, 172, 176, 191–92
Levin, Murray, 292–93, 302
Levine, Lawrence, 61–62
Lewinsky, Monica, 307
Lewis, Jerry, 111
Lewis, Jerry Lee, 249, 252
Liberty Broadcasting System, 210–11, 247
Liddy, G. Gordon, 299, 302, 311–12, 319
Life, 17, 209, 226, 306
Life on the Screen (Turkle), 11
Limbaugh, Rush, 9–10, 13, 26, 172, 347, 349
   talk radio of, 286, 289, 292, 294, 297, 299–302, 308–19, 323, 327
Lindbergh, Charles, 19, 162, 166–70, 186
Lipsitz, George, 242
listeners and listening:
   active, 27
   aesthetics of, 257
   associational, 34, 218
   breakout, 35, 222, 283
   as challenge and skill, 355–56
   changes over years in, 27–28
   communal, 5, 77
   complexities of, 26
   concentration on present in, 30
   dimensional, 33–35, 189–92, 197, 202, 218, 232, 286, 321, 354
   exploratory, 55–82
   extending environments of, 135–36
   fidelity, 35, 37, 254, 258–59, 264–68, 274–76, 282–83
   fragmentation of, 11
   habitual, 131, 133–34, 136
   hearing vs., 27
   importance of, 7
   informational, 33–35, 189–90, 218, 232
   linguistic, 33–34
   looking vs., 29–31
   magic in, 28

   modes of, 8–9, 11, 26–27, 33–35, 57–58, 77, 189–92, 200–202, 211, 222, 254, 258, 348, 354, 357
   patter, 35
   as personal experience, 5–6, 47
   physical responses elicited in, 29–30
   power of, 9
   push-button, 348
   reactive attentive, 285
   relationships between radio and, 3–8, 10–13, 17–19, 26, 28, 36, 40, 225
   routines of everyday life in, 32
   Zen of, 22–39
Liszt, Franz, 87
Literary Digest, 71–73, 92, 104, 111, 207
Little Steel strike, 173
Living Age, 44
Livingstone, Mary, 4, 116–17
local stations and localism, 16–17, 357
   in audience analysis, 134
   and broadcast journalism, 174–75, 182
   and DJs, 220, 227, 229, 232–34
   in exploratory listening, 57, 62–63, 69, 73–74, 79–80, 82
   home talent at, 79–80
   in jazz listening, 93
   and NPR, 320
   proliferation of, 224–25
   and talk radio, 295, 297–98, 309, 313–14
   in Zen of listening, 24
Lodge, Raymond, 44
Lodge, Sir Oliver, 42–53
London Blitz, 183–85, 190–92
London Times, 60
Lonely Crowd (Riesman), 241
Long, Huey, 132, 148, 164, 166
Long, Russell, 323
Lorenz, George "Hound Dog," 232, 241
Lott, Eric, 18, 242–43
loudspeakers, 70, 78, 87
Louis, Joe, 117, 202, 206–9, 218
Lowell Thomas and the News, 167
Lowenthal, Leo, 149
Lucas, George, 219

Lum and Abner, 142–43, 148
Lynd, Robert and Helen, 129

McCarthy, Clem, 206
McCarthy, Joseph, 197–98, 219, 224, 243
McChesney, Robert, 56, 167
McClure's, 49
McCormick, Robert, 194
McDonald, Eugene, 62–63
MacDougald, Duncan, 151–53
McElvaine, Robert, 105
McLaughlin, Ed, 314
MacLeish, Archibald, 190
McLendon, Gordon, 203, 210–11, 247–48
McLuhan, Marshall, 7, 25–26, 31, 333
McMahon, Ed, 112
McNamee, Graham, 112, 120–21, 201, 203, 205–6
McNeill, Don, 228
MacPhail, Larry, 209
MacRae, Gordon, 8
Madison Square Garden, 173, 208
Mailer, Norman, 18
Major Bowes' Original Amateur Hour, 11, 129, 142–43
Mankiewicz, Frank, 322
Manliness and Civilization (Bederman), 13, 66
Mansfield, Steve, 329
Mantovani, 222, 267
MapMAKER, 354
March of Time, The, 166
Marconi, Guglielmo, 16, 21, 41, 48–52, 58, 80–81
Marshall, John, 141
Masterpiece Radio Theater, The, 322
Masterwork Hour, 150
Maxim, Hiram Percy, 60
Maxwell, James Clerk, 26, 36–37
"Maybellene," 232, 250
Mayflower decision, 182, 298
Meet the Press, 308
men and masculinity, 100–101, 347
    in audience analysis, 134–35, 142, 144, 146, 150–51

in broadcast journalism, 164–65, 170, 190–92, 194, 197–98
and DJs, 241–43
in exploratory listening, 57, 59, 61, 66–69, 72–74, 76
and FM revolution, 12–13, 15, 257, 259–60, 264–70, 274–76, 281
and ham radio, 328–29, 332, 334, 345–46
in music listening, 88–89, 95–96, 99
and NPR, 319
in radio comedy, 15, 101, 105–7, 109–20, 122–23
relationship between machines and, 14–16, 20–21
and sports, 199–202, 205, 208–9, 211, 216–18
and talk radio, 285, 289–93, 300, 302–6, 308–11, 317–19
and teenagers, 219, 222–23, 229–30, 233, 243, 255
validating aesthetics and emotional needs of, 12–16
see also gender and gender differences
Mercury, Freddie, 3
Metromedia, 352–53
Middletown (Lynd and Lynd), 129
Midnight Matinee, 240
military, 81, 200, 248, 354
    broadcast journalism and, 171, 183, 188–94
    ham radio and, 59–60, 329, 331, 333, 335–37, 339, 341–43, 345–46
    talk radio and, 291, 293–94, 310
Miller, Larry, 269
Miller, Mitch, 227, 250
Mills, C. Wright, 241–43
Mills, Joshua, 248
Mills Brothers, 149, 235, 325
Minneapolis, audience research in, 354
Minnesota Public Radio, 325
Minow, Newton, 227, 320
minstrelsy, 208, 223, 242–43, 304
    in radio comedy, 106–8, 110
Mintz, Leo, 246

Mr. Sammler's Planet (Bellow), 256
Mr. Smith Goes to Washington, 185
Moby-Dick (Melville), 322
Morgan, Arthur, 172
Morning Edition, 286, 319, 322
Morrison, Toni, 18–19
Morse code, 41, 48–51, 53, 169, 210, 330, 332, 334–35, 343, 345
Motion Picture Daily, 195
Motown, 252
movies, 9, 11, 15–16, 19, 45–46, 100, 219–20, 222, 231, 343, 345
   in addressing needs of men, 15
   in audience analysis, 129, 131, 133, 146, 157–58, 160
   broadcast journalism and, 162
   DJs and, 246
   exploratory listening and, 56–57, 62, 65, 67–68, 72
   FM revolution and, 276
   imagination in watching of, 29–30
   nostalgia about, 25
   radio comedy and, 104–5
   sports broadcasting and, 214
   talk radio and, 291–92
   teenagers and, 242
   war propaganda and, 189
Mozart, Wolfgang Amadeus, 87, 155, 268
Munich crisis, 33, 161–63, 165, 173, 178, 185, 190
Murray the K, 231–32, 251–52
Murrow, Edward R., 3, 13, 15, 33–35
   broadcast journalism of, 161, 164–65, 170, 172, 176–77, 179–85, 187, 190–92, 197–98, 286
Murrow Boys, The (Cloud and Olson), 161, 179–80, 197
Musial, Stan, 212
music, 16–19, 83–99, 166, 343
   of African Americans, *see* jazz; rock 'n' roll
   in age of mechanical DJs, 347
   in AM, 341–42
   in audience analysis, 125–27, 134, 137–38, 140, 149–58

   as background sound, 33, 84
   censorship of, 91–94
   in ethereal world, 40, 46–47
   in exploratory listening, 55–58, 61, 63–65, 69–70, 72–75, 77–78, 81–82
   FM revolution and, 257, 259–60, 263, 265–83, 285
   in future, 356
   listeners' relationships with, 3–6, 8–9, 11–13, 32–36
   live performances of, 78, 83, 86–87
   NPR and, 325–26
   radio technology for transmission of, 51, 53
   talk radio and, 286–88, 298, 306–7
   technology in recording of, 85–86
   variety in choices of, 348–49, 354–56
   in Zen of listening, 22–23, 25–36
   see also specific styles of music
Music, the Brain, and Ecstasy (Jourdain), 32
musical appreciation programs, 34, 83, 88, 154–55, 275
Music and the Mind (Storr), 23
Mussolini, Benito, 166, 176, 195, 206
Mutual Broadcasting System (MBS), 176, 183, 185, 188, 261, 297–98
"My City Was Gone," 286
"My Girl," 32, 255
"My Old Kentucky Home," 75

Nader, Ralph, 287
Nasaw, David, 65
Nation, The, 207, 299
National Aeronautics and Space Administration (NASA), 294–95, 333
National Association of Broadcasters, 37, 260
nationalism, nationhood, and national broadcasts, 100, 220, 349, 354–55
   in audience analysis, 128, 131, 133, 140, 149, 153, 156–57
   in broadcast journalism, 168, 172, 174–75, 183, 187, 192, 194, 197–98
   and DJs, 220, 232, 234–35

nationalism, nationhood and national
broadcasts (*cont'd*)
in exploratory listening, 55, 57–58,
62, 66, 73, 75–77, 80, 82
and FM revolution, 278, 281
and ham radio, 338
in jazz listening, 94–95
and language usage on radio, 103
and NPR, 320, 322, 325
and radio comedy, 104, 116
and sports, 200–205, 207–9, 215–18
and talk radio, 285, 289, 293, 295,
297–98, 300–303, 309, 313–14,
317–19
in Zen of listening, 23–25, 31
National Public Radio (NPR), 10, 19,
26, 34, 319–27, 347, 354–57
eyewitness reporting on, 321–22, 325
mission statement of, 286
popularity of, 287
talk radio and, 284–87, 289, 295,
319–20, 323–27
Nation's Business, The, 61, 69
NBC and WNBC, 6, 39, 53, 83, 94, 220,
295, 297–98, 303, 306, 349
audience research at, 130, 136, 139
-Blue, 128, 187, 193, 224
in censoring music, 92
and FM revolution, 261
founding of, 63
and ham radio, 337–38
news programs on, 166–68, 170,
176–77, 183, 185–87, 193, 196
-Red, 128, 168, 187, 224
sports broadcasting on, 206
NBC Symphony, 129, 143
"Nearer, My God, to Thee," 96
Nelson, Lindsey, 202, 210
Nelson, Ozzie and Harriet, 5, 220, 229
networks, 16–17, 220, 227, 344
in audience analysis, 125–26, 128–29,
134, 136, 156
broadcast journalism and, 161, 164,
166–68, 170, 172–98
consolidators and, 349
demise of, 224–25, 234

exploratory listening and, 56–57, 60,
62–64, 75–76, 79, 82
FM revolution and, 277–78, 283
ham radio and, 335–38
jazz listening and, 85, 92, 94, 98
and language usage on radio, 103
radio comedy and, 100, 104, 107
sports broadcasting and, 202–3,
210–11, 213–14, 218
talk radio and, 285, 289, 295–98,
300–301, 311–13, 316, 319
in Zen of listening, 24–25, 31, 38–39
see also specific networks
New Deal, 162, 164, 173, 181, 223–24
New Republic, The, 103, 154, 209
news, 12, 220, 225, 248, 252, 327,
354–55
in audience analysis, 124–25, 134,
142, 150
censorship of, 183, 185, 188–89,
195–97
DJs and, 228, 232
in exploratory listening, 75
FM revolution and, 273
ham radio and, 329–30, 336
NPR and, 319–25
in radio-listener relationship, 8
talk radio and, 285–86, 288, 290,
293–95, 298, 300–302, 305, 307–8,
310–13, 316, 319
in Zen of listening, 22, 25–27, 34
see also broadcast journalism
Newsedge, 349–50
News for Everyman (Culbert), 183
newsreels, 10, 162, 193, 338
Newsweek, 158, 209, 277, 301
New York City:
as cultural capital, 11
ham radio in, 334
jazz broadcasted in, 93–94
as radio capital, 79, 209
sports broadcasting in, 209
talk radio in, 284, 303, 306, 314
New York Evening Mail, The, 70–71
New York Giants, 211, 214–15
New York Symphony, 83, 125

New York Times, The, 18, 214, 323
  on broadcast journalism, 182
  on ethereal world, 42, 48, 52
  exploratory listening and, 59–60
  on FM radio, 269
  on ham radio, 328, 336–38
  talk radio and, 294, 316
New York Yankees, 213–14, 216
Niagra, Joe, 241
A. C. Nielsen Company, 125–26, 138,
  158–60, 226, 312, 353
nightclubs, 65, 86, 91, 93–95
Nixon, Richard, 281, 291
Noble, Edward, 224
Nobles, "Daddy" Gene, 239
Norris, John M., 299
"Nowhere to Run," 275

occult, 42–48, 52–53, 55
Office of Radio Research (ORR),
  130–31, 136, 139–44, 146, 148–50,
  153–54, 156, 168, 174–75
On the Air (Dunning), 199
"Open Letter on Race Hatred, An," 235
operas, 33–34, 85–90, 129, 143, 266
Outlook, 92, 95
Owens, Jesse, 207–8

Paley, William, 168, 181, 173, 214, 339
Panama Canal Treaty debate, 322
passive hearing, 27
Patterson, Thomas, 300
payola scandal, 223, 248, 250–52, 269
PBS, 320
Pearl Harbor, Japanese attack on,
  187–88, 192
Penner, Joe, 129, 197–98, 237
  linguistic slapstick of, 104, 110–13,
  116, 118
Perot, Ross, 300
Peyton, Dave, 93–94
Philco, 172–73, 225
Phillips, Dewey, 222–23, 236–38
phonographs, 46, 65, 78, 151, 228
  in music listening, 83–85, 88–91, 98
pianos and piano literacy, 84, 87, 96

Pigg, Tony, 229, 241, 245
  in FM revolution, 269–70, 272–73,
    279
pirate stations, 357
Pittsburgh Pirates, 213–14
Pointer Sisters, 305
politics, x, 13, 19, 100, 200–201, 206–7,
  212, 224
  in audience analysis, 125–27, 129–30,
    134–35, 137, 139, 142, 148, 155,
    158
  broadcast journalism on, 162–63,
    166–67, 170–73, 175, 180–87, 189,
    195–97
  DJs and, 222, 248–49
  in exploratory listening, 56, 62–65,
    71, 80–81
  FM revolution and, 258–59, 268,
    273–74, 276–77, 281, 283
  ham radio and, 329–30, 332–33, 335,
    342–43, 346
  impact of technological change on,
    20
  importance of radio in, 9
  in jazz listening, 88
  in language usage, 102
  NPR and, 319–20, 323–25, 327, 356
  radio comedy and, 107–9, 117, 123
  radio-listener relationship and, 4,
    6–7, 11
  and rock 'n' roll, 249
  sports and, 200, 206
  talk radio and, 284–305, 307–20, 327,
    356
  in Zen of listening, 23–26, 31, 33
  see also Congress, U.S.
pop music, 40, 212
  in audience analysis, 137–38, 149,
    151–53, 156
  DJs and, 228, 235
  FM revolution and, 259, 267, 269, 277
  see also jazz; rock 'n' roll
Pop Music Disc Jockey Convention,
  245, 248, 250
Poppa Stoppa, 240
Popular Mechanics, 60, 162, 265

"Popular Music Industry, The"
    (MacDougald), 151–53
Prairie Home Companion, A, 324–25
Presley, Elvis, 17, 227, 246, 249, 252
Pretenders, 286
Prince, Bob, 213
Private Parts, 302–3
Professor Quiz, 141, 145–48
program analyzers (Little Annies),
    137–39
programming, 19, 220, 347, 357
    in audience analysis, 128, 134, 136,
        138–39, 141–60
    black-oriented, 234–39
    consolidators and, 349–53
    debate about network vs. local, 16–17
    DJs and, 221, 227, 245–52
    in exploratory listening, 56–57, 63,
        72, 75–76, 78–79, 82
    FM revolution and, 257, 263, 267,
        269–73, 276–80, 282–83
    homogenization and standardization
        of, 79, 82
    and language usage on radio, 103
    in music listening, 84–87, 94
    niche, 354
    NPR and, 320, 326
    regulation of, 224
    talk radio and, 285, 288–89, 295–98,
        311–12, 315
    in Zen of listening, 33–34, 39
    see also specific types of programming
Project Oscar (Orbiting Satellite
    Carrying Amateur Radio), 343
Psychology of Radio, The (Cantril and
    Allport), 85, 130–36, 155–56,
    159–60
public affairs programming, 187,
    296–98
    audience analysis on, 142, 155–56
    talk radio and, 314
Public Broadcasting Act, 320
public service, 273–74
    ham radio and, 329–30, 332–33,
        335–38, 343
"Purple Haze," 33–34

Pyle, Ernie, 194
Pyne, Joe, 288

QST, 335–37, 341–42
Queen, 3
Quindlen, Anna, 307
Quiz Kids, The, 145
quiz shows, 250, 323
    in audience analysis, 141, 145–48, 155

Raaby, Torstein, 340
race and racism, 8, 18–19, 355
    in audience analysis, 128, 142, 147,
        150
    and DJs, 222–23, 228, 233–35, 238,
        240–44, 246, 248–49, 254
    in exploratory listening, 61, 66
    in jazz listening, 88, 92–99
    and language usage on radio, 103, 105
    in radio comedy, 106–9, 118
    radio in challenging, 18
    in radio-listener relationship, 5–6
    and rock 'n' roll, 249, 253–54
    and sports, 200, 202, 206–9, 216
    and talk radio, 302–5
    and teenagers, 249–50, 253, 255
    in Zen of listening, 23, 35
    see also African Americans
race records and music, 18–19, 87,
    90–91, 93, 228
Radio Act (1912), 60, 80
Radio Act (1927), 81, 91–92
radio and radios:
    anonymity afforded by, 311
    archival tapes of shows on, ix, 3, 9,
        161, 204
    in cars, 22, 27, 34, 40, 219–21,
        225–26, 229, 252–55, 267, 282, 311,
        347, 353
    consolidation in, 325–26
    deregulation of, 295–300, 343–44,
        349–50
    devolution of, 225
    dramatic displays of, 48–49
    fan letters generated by, 134
    flexibility of, 20

in future, 356–57
importance of, 9–10, 12
intimacy of, 311
invisibility of, 4
language usage on, 12, 102–5, 111
limitations of, 9–10
liveness conveyed by, 7, 16
as miracle, 28, 41–42, 44–48, 52–54, 73
nostalgia about, 3–4, 6–7, 11, 19, 25–26, 35–36, 47, 64, 324, 357
100th anniversary of, 21
origin of term, 48
out-of-body experiences provided by, 75
personal nature of, 17
proliferation of, 41, 52–53, 55–56, 61–62, 64–65, 68–70, 72–73, 77, 79, 128, 131, 133–34, 161–62, 205, 220–21, 225, 267, 280, 348
promise of, 20–21
as propaganda tool, 136
regulation of, 6, 38–39, 56, 58, 60–64, 71, 80–82, 91–94, 136, 167–69, 181–83, 187–89, 195–98, 223–25, 234, 259, 262–63, 267, 281, 294, 297–99, 305–6, 344, 357
relationships between listeners and, 3–8, 10–13, 17–19, 26, 28, 36, 40, 225
talking back to, 312
technology of, 15–17, 36–39, 41–42, 46–55, 57–59, 68–72, 77–79, 87, 89, 220–21, 225–26, 257–58, 264–66, 282, 289, 294–95, 297, 299–300, 303, 320, 328–31, 334, 341–43, 346, 348
at work, 353
Radio and the Printed Page (Lazarsfeld), 140–48, 174
Radio Broadcast, 69, 72, 74, 77–78, 102
on music listening, 83, 85–87
radio comedy, *see* comedy, radio
Radio Days, 6
Radio Digest, 57, 79–80, 200, 205
"Radio Ga-Ga," 3

Radio Ink, 351
Radio in the Television Age (Fornatale and Mills), 248
Radio Press Service, 69
Radio Research 1941, 140, 149–50, 153–56
Radio Research 1942–43, 140
"Radio Symphony, The" (Adorno), 143, 149, 153–55
Radio Voices (Hilmes), 18–19, 235
Radio Waves (Ladd), 271
Rambling with Gambling, 288
Random House, 195
rap music, 18, 33, 35, 90–91, 356
Rather, Dan, 292, 315
Raymond (Lodge), 44
RCA, 15–16, 46, 177, 187, 224
FM revolution and, 257, 260–63, 266
RCA Victor, 227–28
Reagan, Ronald, 100, 291, 294–96, 299, 303, 322, 327
Recording Angel, The (Eisenberg), 46
Red, Hot and Blue, 236
Red Lion decision, 298–99
Reed, B. Mitchell, 273
regionalism, ix, 156, 355
in exploratory listening, 57, 75–76, 79, 82
and language usage on radio, 102–3, 105
in sports broadcasting, 213, 216
talk radio and, 313–14
Reinartz, John, 80
religion, *see* spiritualism
Report on Chain Broadcasting, 187, 223–24
Repulse, 192–93, 195
Review of Reviews, 52, 61, 72
Rhythm Club, 93
Rice, Grantland, 203
Richbourg, "John R.," 239–41
Riesman, David, 241
Rimsky-Korsakov, Nikolai, 56, 151
rock 'n' roll, 8, 11–12, 16–19, 90–91, 347–52, 356
birth of, 246

rock 'n' roll (*cont'd*)
  censorship of, 228
  and consolidators, 350–52
  and DJs, 219–23, 225, 228–29,
    231–33, 236, 239–41, 245–49
  economics of, 250–51
  in ethereal world, 40
  and FM revolution, 256–58, 268–83,
    285
  and NPR, 325
  and payola scandals, 250–52
  and radio-listener relationship, 3–5,
    11
  remasculinization of, 274–76
  and teenagers, 219–23, 227–29,
    231–36, 239–40, 243, 246,
    249–55
  threats posed by, 249–50, 281
  types of, 348–49
  in Zen of listening, 33, 35
  see also Top 40 programs
Rock 'n' Roll Party Time, 233
"Rock Around the Clock," 250
Rock of Ages (Ward, Stokes, and Tucker),
  228–29
Rogers, J. A., 95
"Roll Over, Beethoven," 253
Roosevelt, Franklin D., 3, 129, 207–8,
  224
  broadcast journalism and, 163–64,
    166–67, 171–73, 181–82, 184,
    188–89
Roosevelt, Theodore, 14, 66
Rosko, 256, 272, 274, 279
Rotundo, E. Anthony, 15, 66–67
Rowswell, Rosey, 213
Royal Creolians, 93
"Runnin' Wild," 96
Russert, Tim, 308

Sahl, Mort, 319
St. Louis Blues, 178
St. Louis Cardinals, 213
Sander, Jerrold, 320
Sarnoff, David, 16, 219, 257, 259–62
satellite technology, 330

ham radio and, 342–43
talk radio and, 289, 294–95, 297,
  299–300, 303, 320
Saturday Review, The, 102–3, 265
"Says My Heart," 153
Schlessinger, "Dr. Laura," 300–301, 327,
  347, 349, 351
Schmeling, Max, 202, 206–8, 218
Schnell, Fred, 80
Schwartz, Jonathan, 279
Scopes trial, 41, 166
Scribner's, 49, 164, 187
Scully, Vin, 212
Sears, "Daddy," 240
Second Self, The (Turkle), 10–11
Section 315, 298–99
See It Now, 198
Seldes, Gilbert, 92, 96, 103–4, 106
"Semi-Charmed Life," 347
semiconductors, 225–26
Sevareid, Eric, 176, 180, 182–83, 189,
  194–95
sexuality, 154
  in jazz listening, 89, 91, 95–96
  radio comedy and, 114, 117
  talk radio and, 291, 294, 301, 304–7,
    319, 327
  teenagers and, 229, 242–43
Seymour, Robin, 241
Shadow, 4–5
Shankar, Ravi, 283
Sharkey, Jack, 206
Shaw, Artie, 152
Shepherd, Jean, 3, 33–34, 288
Shirer, Bill, 164, 176–84, 187, 189, 195,
  197
shock jocks, 14, 286–87, 303, 308, 318,
  351
"Shoo-Shoo Baby," 235
shortwaves, 38, 58, 60
  in broadcast journalism, 177–78, 185,
    192–93
  scientific research on, 80–81
  sports broadcasting via, 200, 205
  see also ham radio
Sidran, Ben, 20, 97–98, 243

Siegel, Mike, 287
Siemering, Bill, 286, 319
Sikes, Alfred, 305
Simon & Schuster, 307
Simpson, O. J., 19, 168, 310, 315
Sinatra, Frank, 228, 235, 250, 267
Sing Along with Mitch, 227
single-sideband suppressed carrier
    (ssbsc) transmission, 341–43
sky waves, 37–38
Smalls, Tommy "Dr. Jive," 241
Smith, A. Leonard, 48
Smith, Bessie, 85, 90–91, 93
Smith, Curt, 199, 202, 210, 213
Smith, Dinitia, 306
Smith, Kate, 235
Smith, Ken, 216
Smith, Mamie, 90
Smithsonian Institution, 239, 343
Smulyan, Susan, 56, 73
Snyder, Tom, 199
social classes, 11–12, 169–70, 242
    in audience analysis, 125–27, 131,
        133–34, 136–37, 141–44, 146–50,
        157
    in broadcast journalism, 164–65,
        170–72, 174–76, 179–80, 185,
        197–98
    DJs and, 228, 245
    in exploratory listening, 59, 62,
        65–68, 75–76, 82
    FM revolution and, 259–60, 268,
        277
    ham radio and, 332–34
    in language usage, 102–3, 105, 111
    in music listening, 85–86, 88, 90,
        95–96, 99
    NPR and, 320, 324, 327
    payola scandals and, 251
    radio comedy and, 106, 108, 114, 116,
        118–19
    sports broadcasting and, 200, 217
    talk radio and, 285, 289–90, 292–93,
        302, 305, 308, 311, 327
    teenagers and, 229, 241–42, 245
    in Zen of listening, 23

society, see culture and cultural
    differences
"Sparrows on the Roofs," 157
Spice Girls, 274–75
Spillane, Mickey, 345
spiritualism, 52–55
    in audience analysis, 149, 154, 158
    bridging gap between machines and,
        41, 45, 47
    broadcast journalism and, 178, 196
    in ethereal world, 40–48, 52–54
    in exploratory listening, 55–56, 61,
        64
    ham radio and, 333
    in music listening, 83, 88, 98
    and rock 'n' roll, 249
sports and sports broadcasting, 10–12,
    19, 112, 187–88, 193, 198–219, 232,
    347, 351, 354–55
    in addressing needs of men, 15
    and African Americans, 200, 202,
        206–9, 238
    in audience analysis, 127–29, 134
    of baseball, 8, 10, 64–65, 199–205,
        209–19, 232, 243
    blow-by-blow and play-by-play in,
        203, 212, 215
    of boxing, 10, 63–64, 77, 199–202,
        204–9, 217–18
    celebrity in, 201, 211
    and DJs, 221
    drama in, 203, 212, 216–17
    and exploratory listening, 56–57,
        62–66, 77
    objectivity in, 214–16
    and radio comedy, 122–23, 214, 218
    in radio-listener relationship, 5, 8, 10
    war metaphors in, 206
    in Zen of listening, 25, 28, 33
Sports Illustrated, 215–16
"Stairway to Heaven," 275
Stamberg, Susan, 320–21, 323
Stanton, Frank, 125–26, 130, 136–40,
    148–49, 160
static, 70–72
stations, 21, 70–71, 344, 356

stations (*cont'd*)
  assigning wavelengths to, 62–64, 71, 80, 82
  in audience analysis, 125, 128, 134, 136, 138, 149, 156–58, 353–54
  broadcast journalism and, 174–75, 181–89
  competition between, 233
  consolidation of, 349–53, 356–57
  on crystal sets, 70–71, 77
  DJs and, 220–21, 223, 227–34, 236–40, 247–48
  FM revolution and, 258, 260–63, 267–82
  in future, 356
  ham radio and, 334, 337–38, 340, 344
  interference between, 71–73, 77, 81
  in music listening, 85–87, 89, 93, 348–49
  newspaper ownership of, 181–82, 224
  NPR and, 320–21, 325–26
  payola scandals and, 251
  proliferation of, 77, 128, 220, 223–24, 233, 276, 278
  and rock 'n' roll, 250
  sports broadcasting on, 201, 203, 210–11, 213–14
  talk radio and, 287–88, 294–300, 302–3, 305–6, 313–14
  teenagers and, 245
  trade marks and slogans of, 75
  on tube sets, 77–78
  virtual, 350
  see also distance-signaling; *specific stations and types of stations*
Stearns, Marshall, 97
Steinberg, Martha Jean "the Queen," 237, 239, 242, 248, 254
Stern, Howard, 9, 12–13, 35, 351, 354
  talk radio of, 286–87, 289, 292, 294, 297–98, 302–8, 318–19, 324–25, 327
Stokes, Geoffrey, 228–29
Storr, Anthony, 23
story listening, 8, 81–82, 322, 324, 354
Storz, Todd, 247–48

Strawberry Alarm Clock, 34
Studlar, Gaylyn, 67
Suarez, Ray, 319
"Subterranean Homesick Blues," 256, 272
Suchman, Edward, 150–51
Suez to Singapore (Brown), 195
Sumner, David, 333–34
superheterodyne sets, 78, 86, 260
Supreme Court, U.S., 144, 187, 224, 299
Supremes, 18, 253, 272
Survey, 48, 95
Susman, Warren, 128
Swartz, Joshua, 337
Swing, Raymond Gram, 185
Swing and Sway, 238
Symphonic Hour, 154
Symphony No. 5 (Beethoven), 85, 155
syntonized telegraphy, 42

talk and talk radio, 9–10, 12–14, 19, 53, 166, 281, 283–320, 347, 351, 354, 356–57
  appeal of, 293–94
  audience of, 124–25, 141, 284–90, 292, 295, 301–3, 305, 307–19, 356
  and consolidators, 350–51
  credibility of, 313
  debate about pernicious influences of, 301–2
  in exploratory listening, 77
  of Imus, 286, 292, 302–3, 306–8, 318–19, 324, 327
  of Limbaugh, 286, 289, 292, 294, 297, 299–302, 308–19, 323, 327
  and NPR, 284–87, 289, 295, 319–20, 323–27
  popularity of, 287–88, 292
  proliferation of, 287, 300
  in radio-listener relationship, 6
  rise of, 283, 288
  sensationalism of, 289, 292
  of Stern, 286–87, 289, 292, 294, 297–98, 302–8, 318–19, 324–25, 327
  in Zen of listening, 26, 35

Talkers, 289, 301
Talk of the Nation, 319, 325
Talk Radio and the American Dream (Levin), 292–93, 302
Tamborru, Joe "Butterball," 254
Tan Town Jamboree, 237
Tarzan books, 14, 66
Tatum, Art, 235
teenagers, 17–18, 226–45, 348–49, 354
  consolidators and, 351
  delinquency among, 241–42, 250
  DJs and, 17–18, 219–22, 227–40, 242–46, 249, 252, 254–55
  FM revolution and, 256–57, 259, 268–69, 273–75, 277, 281
  in future, 356
  ham radio and, 334
  in jazz listening, 95–99
  musical tastes of, 32
  payola scandals and, 251–52
  radio comedy and, 113, 119
  and rock 'n' roll, 219–23, 227–29, 231–36, 239–40, 243, 246, 249–55
  talk radio and, 292, 303–4
  transistor sets owned by, 226–27
  in Zen of listening, 32, 35–36
Telecommunications Act, 297, 351, 353, 357
telegraph:
  ethereal world and, 41–42, 45
  ham radio and, 59–60, 330, 336, 338
  sports and, 207, 210–11
  technology of, 48–50
telephones, 21, 29, 131
  in audience analysis, 125–26, 136–37, 142, 158–59
  broadcast journalism and, 177
  in exploratory listening, 58–60, 63–64, 74
  ham radio and, 58–60, 329–31, 335–36, 338, 344
  in music listening, 86
  NPR and, 325–26
  talk radio and, 19, 287–90, 292–95, 302, 309–12, 316, 318

television, 8–9, 16–17, 250–51, 255, 281, 339, 353–55
  in audience analysis, 125–26, 160
  broadcast journalism and, 161–62
  and ethereal world of radio, 40
  FM revolution and, 259, 261–63, 266–69, 276
  ham radio and, 331–32, 341
  imagination in watching of, 19–20, 27, 29
  nostalgia about, 25
  NPR and, 320, 322–23, 325, 327
  radio comedy and, 114–15, 117
  radio-listener relationship and, 4–5
  rise of, 19, 219–20, 225
  sports broadcasting and, 204, 212, 215–16, 219
  talk radio and, 285–86, 289, 293–94, 296–97, 299–300, 304, 306–9, 311–13, 318, 327
  teenagers and, 219–23, 231–32, 234
  in Zen of listening, 22, 25–27, 29, 31
"Telstar," 294
Temple, Shirley, 105
tennis, 200–201
theaters, 65, 83, 107
Third Eye Blind, 347
Thomas, Clarence, 322
Thomas, Lowell, 15, 19, 167, 170, 174–75
Thomas, Rufus "Bear Cat," 234, 237–38
Thompson, Bobby, 211
Time, 195, 197, 264
  on NPR, 319, 324
  on sports, 207–8
  on talk radio, 289–90, 300–301
  on teenagers, 226–27
"Time Has Come Today," 258
Times Mirror Center for People and the Press, 309–11
Titanic disaster, 49, 60, 344
Today's Children, 143
Tonight Show, The, 299
Too Long, America, 235
Top 40 programs, 10, 286
  demise of, 254–55

Top 40 programs (*cont'd*)
    DJs and, 225, 228, 235, 245–52
    FM revolution and, 256, 269–71, 277
    payola scandals and, 250–51
    talk radio and, 306
    teenagers and, 221, 252–53
    see also rock 'n' roll
"Tossin' and Turnin'," 227
Town Hall Tonight, 118
Trammell, Niles, 220
Tramo, Mark, 28, 32
transistors and transistor radios, 17,
    220–21, 225–27, 229, 252, 258
Transradio Press, 168
Traugott, Michael, 309–10
Trout, Bob, 164, 177–79, 184, 190
tube sets (regenerative sets), 225–26
    problems associated with, 77–78
    vacuum tubes and, 51, 58–59, 69–70
Tucker, Ken, 228–29
Tunney, Gene, 77, 205
Turkle, Sherry, 10–11
Turner, Ike, 241
Tyson, Mike, 307

Understanding Media (McLuhan), 7, 25
University of Chicago Roundtable, 187

Vallee, Rudy, 40–41, 87–89, 125, 201
Vancheri, Joseph, 337–38
Variety, 94, 183, 190, 197
Vaughn, Les, 211
Vietnam war, 13, 216, 255, 317, 321
    FM revolution and, 273, 275, 282
    talk radio and, 290–91
Villard, Oswald G., Jr., 342
voice, 135
    in exploratory listening, 64–65, 70–71
    radio technology for transmission of,
    51, 53
Voice of Experience, The, 144
Voices of the Game (Smith), 199, 202

WABC, *see* ABC and WABC
Wade, Theo "Bless My Bones" (Brother
    Wade), 238

Wagner, Winfield G., 342
Walters, Barbara, 318
Ward, Ed, 228–29
Warner, Albert, 188
War of the Worlds, The, 31, 165
Wartime (Fussell), 162
Washington, Booker T., 209
Waters, Ethel, 93–94
Watkins, Mel, 18, 107, 118
Wayne, John, 13, 275, 345
WBCN, 270–71, 277–78
WDAI, 273–74
WDIA, ix, 39, 234, 237–40
We, the People, 235
WEAF, 39, 56, 167, 201, 338
Weber, Vin, 308–9
Welles, Orson, 165
Wertheimer, Linda, 12, 319, 322
West, Mae, 8, 120
Western Union, 207, 210, 295
Westinghouse, 52, 64, 263, 298
White, Paul, 182, 196–97
White Collar (Mills), 241–43
Whiteman, Paul, 90, 92
"White Negro, The" (Mailer), 18
"White Rabbit," 273, 281
whites, 18–19, 356
    DJs and, 221–23, 229, 234, 236–37,
    239–46, 248–49, 254
    in exploratory listening, 57, 59, 76
    FM revolution and, 259–60
    ham radio and, 332
    jazz listening and, 85, 87, 90–97, 99
    NPR and, 324
    payola scandals and, 251
    radio comedy and, 107–9, 111, 118
    and rock 'n' roll, 249–50, 253–54
    sports and, 206–9
    talk radio and, 290–93, 303–5, 308,
    311, 314
    teenagers and, 242–44, 249–50
Whitman, Ernie Q, 235
WHN, 93–94
"Who's on First?" (Abbott and
    Costello), 122
Wildmon, Donald, 305

Williams, Jerry, 287, 292–93
Williams, Mark, 287, 302, 310
Williams, Nat D., 237
Williams, Perry, 342
Willkie, Wendell, 235
"Will You Love Me Tomorrow?," 26, 275
Wilson, Don, 116–17, 121
Wilson, Jackie, 252, 255
Winchell, Walter, 24, 129, 137, 338
    broadcast journalism of, 164, 168–72,
    174–75, 180, 189, 197
WINS, 231–33
Winslow, Vernon (Doctor Daddy-O),
    240
WJAZ, 62–63
WJZ, 39, 64, 87, 338
WKBW, 232, 241
WLAC, 239–41
WMCA, 224, 230, 236, 245
WNBC, see NBC and WNBC
WNEW, 229, 236, 252–53
    in FM revolution, 256, 270, 272–74,
    276, 279
WNJR, 230–31, 236
WNYC, 150, 338
Wolff, Bob, 216
Wolfman Jack (Bobby Smith), 3, 5, 35,
    219, 222–23, 229, 236, 240–41,
    243–45, 254–55
women, 14, 19, 61, 242, 347, 351
    in audience analysis, 134–35, 142,
    148, 150
    in broadcast journalism, 164, 170,
    176, 191, 197–98
    DJs and, 220, 228, 236
    in exploratory listening, 66–70, 72,
    77–78
    FM revolution and, 265–66, 274–76,
    282
    ham radio and, 329, 336, 345
    in music listening, 84, 88–89, 95–96,
    99
    NPR and, 319–20

radio comedy and, 106–7, 109,
    111–20, 122
    sports and, 206, 211, 216–17
    talk radio and, 285, 289–93, 300–308,
    310, 312, 315, 317–19, 324, 327
    see also gender and gender differences
Woodruff, Louis F., 158
Woollcott, Alexander, 103–4
WOR, 34, 93, 166, 168, 270, 288
World News Roundup, 189
World Series, 62–63, 199–201, 203, 209,
    212, 214–15, 218
World War I, 53, 126, 169, 200
    ethereal world and, 42–44, 51
    ham radio and, 60
    music listening and, 89, 91, 98
World War II, 9–10, 17, 33, 192, 223,
    225, 234–35, 251, 297
    in audience analysis, 156
    broadcast journalism on, 161–63,
    165, 171–73, 175–80, 182–98, 286
    D day in, 193, 218
    FM revolution and, 257–58, 262,
    264–66, 282
    ham radio and, 333, 339, 341
    radio-listener relationship and, 3–5
    sports and, 207–8, 218
    Zen of listening during, 34–36
Wright, Jim, 287
Wrigley, William, 209
WSBC, 93–94, 229, 236, 238
Wynn, Ed, 164–65, 197–98, 201
    linguistic slapstick of, 104, 110–13,
    116, 118, 120–21

Yankee Network, 262
Yankelovich, Daniel, 293
Yevtushenko, Yevgeny, 256
Youngbloods, 274
Your Hit Parade, 246

Zenith, 62–63, 263